THE KANSAS
CONFLICT

THE KANSAS CONFLICT

BY

CHARLES ROBINSON

The Black Heritage Library Collection

BOOKS FOR LIBRARIES PRESS
FREEPORT, NEW YORK
1972

F685
R6

First Published 1892
Reprinted 1972

Reprinted from a copy in the
Fisk University Library Negro Collection

INTERNATIONAL STANDARD BOOK NUMBER:
0-8369-8975-9

LIBRARY OF CONGRESS CATALOG CARD NUMBER:
70-37599

PRINTED IN THE UNITED STATES OF AMERICA
BY
NEW WORLD BOOK MANUFACTURING CO., INC.
HALLANDALE, FLORIDA 33009

THE KANSAS CONFLICT

BY

CHARLES ROBINSON
LATE GOVERNOR OF KANSAS

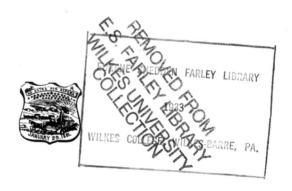

LAWRENCE, KANSAS
JOURNAL PUBLISHING COMPANY
1898

Dedicated

TO

ELI THAYER

WHO CONCEIVED AND EXECUTED THE PLAN OF ORGANIZED
EMIGRATION BY WHICH A FREE STATE IN KANSAS WAS MADE POSSIBLE
AND TO HIS CO-OPERATORS IN THE STATES; AND ALSO

TO

THE MEMBERS OF THE FREE STATE PARTY
BY WHOSE COURAGE, FIRMNESS, PRUDENCE, SAGACITY
AND SUFFERING WAS ACHIEVED A VICTORY AGAINST OPPRESSION
SECOND TO NONE IN THE ANNALS OF HISTORY

PREFACE.

AN apology may be due to the reading public for submitting to it the pages that follow. In an address before the Kansas State Historical Society, on retiring from the office of president, in the winter of 1881, I said:

"The time for writing the true history of Kansas has not yet arrived, and will not arrive till the historian shall be so far removed from the actors and passions of the hour as to be able to survey calmly the whole field, and to discern clearly, not only events, but causes and effects as well. Distance lends enchantment to a view, and clearness to the vision of the historian. A corporal might narrate with accuracy the exploits of his foraging squad, but he would be a poor historian even of his company. The part he played with his squad would be more important to him than all the other exploits of the larger body, however brilliant, and, in fact, would prevent him from seeing what his comrades were doing. The colonel of a regiment might relate with great fidelity the achievements of his regiment, but he in turn would be a poor historian of the brigade. A general of brigade or division might be well qualified to furnish facts connected with his immediate command, but the more strictly he attended to his own duties the less would he be competent to write the history of the army. So the General-in-chief could tell accurately, perhaps, of the movements which he had ordered and which had been made according to his direction, but before a true history of the war could be writ-

ten, the powers behind the General must be consulted. The
War Secretary, the Commander-in-chief of all the forces, the
Congress that directs the commander, the people who make
the Congress, with the influences and motives that control the people themselves—must all be taken into the account.

"The actors in any struggle are unfitted to be the historians of that struggle, and this unfitness extends to all their
sympathizers and partisans. Should an actor attempt to
write history, the attempt would necessarily result in magnify-
ing the part he had acted or witnessed, at the expense of all
others, while a sympathizer or partisan would be incapable
of treating all the actors with impartiality. The worst of
all historians is he who selects his own hero, and makes all
events revolve about him, as the planets around the sun.
Such a person may write tolerable romance or fiction founded
on fact, but history, never."

This being my belief, I make no pretense that this book,
while it gives the conflict in Kansas from my point of view,
is a complete history of that struggle. It is written for two
reasons: The first is the importunity of persons who were
actors or sympathizers in making a free State of Kansas;
and the second, that no writer thus far has taken the view
that seems to me the true one of the movements made by
the Free-State party, and of the causes and reasons for the
same. In May, 1868, Hon. D. W. Wilder, who has always
taken a deep interest in Kansas history, wrote asking for a
paper upon this subject, saying: "The point I aim at is to
give the man's own version of the scenes in which he has
been actor or witness—and that is what History will go back
to when she at last takes up her impartial pen to tell this
story."

Such, in the main, is this book. It is simply an account of
the struggle as witnessed by one of the actors. It was intended
to give details at length and the part taken by individuals in
different movements, but it was found that to do so would

extend the work beyond desirable limits, and much matter of this nature has been stricken out. There are many of the actors whose names deserve high honor, and whose deeds would fill a volume, who have been passed by with but a word, or perhaps not even mentioned. To have done complete justice to individuals would have obscured or abbreviated the outlines of the general conflict which I aimed to give.

While the contest between the Free-State and Slave-State men was most earnest, and casual observers would be induced to believe most bitter, the writer of this book can truthfully say that he never permitted his personal feelings to become enlisted from first to last. No uncivil word or act was heard or witnessed between myself and the most violent of the opposite party. Our personal intercourse was at all times most courteous. The same is true of factional differences among Free-State men. Not an uncivil word ever passed between myself and Lane, Brown, or any other partisan. The work in which all were engaged was too important for the workers who were actuated by principle to engage in personalities.

The conduct of the War of the Rebellion is perhaps treated with too little respect for great names, but there is not the least bitterness of feeling. Believing that there was the most inexcusable, unnecessary, and wanton destruction of life and property, I have characterized conduct as I think it merits, without other feeling than that of regret and a just indignation that such outrages should be permitted by those who had the power to prevent them.

It is very likely that the reader will find many shortcomings, many important matters omitted and some things said that might have been said better or, perhaps, should not have been said at all; but if anything has been written that shall aid the disinterested historian in getting at the truth of the most important conflict of this age and country, I shall feel abundantly rewarded for my labor.

That some readers will be disturbed and displeased is also very likely.   Oliver Wendell Holmes says:

"You never need think you can turn over any old falsehood, without a terrible squirming and scattering of the horrid little population that dwells under it.   Every real thought on every real subject knocks the wind out of somebody or other."

C. ROBINSON.

CONTENTS.

INTRODUCTION.

FOR years myself and others within and without the State have been urging Governor Robinson to write what he knows about the early history of Kansas. " Perseverance conquers all things," and at last the history is written. And, to my great surprise, I am complimented and honored with an invitation to write the introduction.

Any history of Kansas without Governor Robinson as the prominent figure would be like the "play of Hamlet with Hamlet left out." He has an array of facts and information that no other man has, without which any history of Kansas would be incomplete. I first met Governor Robinson (then Dr. Robinson) in Boston, March 5, 1855, on the eve of leaving for Kansas with the Manhattan Colony, and was especially indebted to him for valuable suggestions. I was peculiarly impressed with his qualifications for a great leader. He was tall, well-proportioned, commanding in appearance, yet winning in manner; with a clear, keen, blue eye; a countenance that denoted culture and intellect, and a will that few would care to run against. He would pass anywhere as a good-looking man, and in any crowd would command attention. With perfect control of himself, he could rule in the midst of a storm. His magnetism would inspire men to do and to dare in the cause of human Liberty, and the establishment of the great principles of Republican government.

In the history of the world, Providence has raised up men qualified for particular work. Where would British India have been to-day without Lord Clive, though at the com-

mencement of the great struggle he was a merchant's clerk?
What would the Pilgrims on Plymouth Rock have done
without the cool and brave Miles Standish? And in our
Revolution who could have led us to the victory except
George Washington? And still later on, who could have
conquered the Rebellion but the indomitable Grant? While
Eli Thayer, providentially the founder of the New England
Emigrant Aid Company, was flying over the North like a
flaming meteor, stirring up the people for money and recruits
in his grand crusade for the freedom of Kansas, Charles
Robinson, his trusty lieutenant, wonderfully prepared for it
by a like Providence by his California experience, was sternly
holding the helm amid the storms and breakers in Kansas.
Without Eli Thayer the emigrants would not have come, and
without Charles Robinson it would have been in vain that
they did come! Cool, clear-headed, and brave, he could see
the end from the beginning, and the sure way to reach it.
While others were all excitement, he was perfectly self-pos-
sessed, and knew the right thing to do, and did it. To his
mind two things were perfectly clear: First, there was to be
no resistance of the United States Government. Secondly,
the territorial laws made by a bogus Legislature were to be
ignored. To carry out these principles required clear heads
and many times a passive resistance worthy of the early
martyrs. His great idea was in every case so to manage
that the Pro-Slavery men should be in the wrong and the
Free-State men in the right. The first must be the aggressor,
and the second the passive sufferer, or act only in self-defense. In this way alone he could secure the united sympathy and support of the North.

The New England Emigrant Aid Company, without which
Kansas could not have been saved, was composed of a
remarkable body of men. Eli Thayer says: " No other corporation ever formed in this country can compare at all in
ability, character, influence, and wealth with the Directors of
the Emigrant Aid Company." And through his genius, skill,

and forethought it was created and made effectual in its great and glorious work. In his valuable book, "The Kansas Crusade," published in 1889, he has written a wonderful history of his grand and noble work which made it possible to save Kansas from slavery by outside work. And now we have Governor Robinson's history, which tells how Kansas was saved to freedom by inside work. They constitute two of the most important histories yet written, which tell how Kansas was made a free State. Let every· Kansan read them.

Governor Robinson has brought to the work honesty, conscientiousness, ability, and independence. Never did Dr. Robinson appear to greater advantage than in the Wakarusa war of December, 1855. Governor Shannon, inspired by Sheriff Jones and other pro-slavery leaders, issued a proclamation for volunteers to enforce the bogus laws, and in response some 1900 Missourians assembled at Franklin to wipe out Lawrence, the hotbed of rebellion against the supremacy of slavery. Dr. Robinson was the diplomatist who devised the policy adopted to thwart the enemy. Shannon's good sense and legal mind enabled him, on arriving at Lawrence, at once to grasp the situation. A treaty was made and the tables were turned. The army of Sheriff Jones was ordered to disperse, and a legal force found itself at once a mob, while Robinson and his force became law-abiding citizens, and were recognized by Governor Shannon to be so. By request of the Governor, who seemed to distrust his own power of persuasion, Dr. Robinson and General Lane accompanied him to Franklin to explain to the Missourians the true condition of affairs. Lane first spoke, but unfortunately provoked instead of conciliated, and the meeting was on the point of breaking up in confusion when Dr. Robinson was called out, and by an appeal to facts and their common sense, he conquered their prejudices and the victory was won. During this negotiation, as on other important occasions, came in the disturbing element of John Brown and a few followers who were as ready to fight the United States Government as they were the border ruffians. Brown himself wished to go out and open the fight with the enemy, and was only kept quiet by a threat from Robinson that he would place him under arrest.

It was while Dr. Robinson was a prisoner under a guard of United States soldiers at Lecompton, that General Lane proposed to release him and the other Free-State prisoners by force, when the General was very decidedly requested to keep quiet. Their liberation without force soon followed. It was while he was a prisoner that John Brown, with some half dozen men, in the night, on Pottawatomie Creek, called out and assassinated three men and two boys in a shocking manner. At a mass meeting called soon after by both parties, the act was denounced and disowned. Brown was condemned even by his own son Jason, with whom I rode a long distance on his way to California, in 1884. Nevertheless, that massacre was the commencement of those terrible atrocities that followed in south-eastern Kansas, and beyond the control of Dr. Robinson. Had his statesmanship prevailed everywhere, very little bloodshed would have attended the making of Kansas a free State. For Dr. Robinson the border ruffians had great respect, and when at Lawrence they had seized the polls and driven all other Free-State men away, on his approach they cried out, " Here comes the Doctor; let him vote," and the way was cleared. Even in that terrible massacre during the Lawrence raid, and when the Doctor slowly retired from his barn to the brow of Mt. Oread, near where several of Quantrell's men were on guard, they did not molest him. There was a certain something, a strange, commanding influence, a presence that neutralized for the time being any power to do him harm. In all of his Kansas experience, both when free and when for four months a prisoner, I never heard of his receiving a personal insult. The same was true of his California experience. He would meet hundreds of men single-handed and prevent the de-

struction of the squatters' property without a blow being
struck.

While I have always looked upon Governor Robinson as
raised up and specially qualified as the man, and the only
man, within the territory to lead on to certain victory, I have
never thought him a good politician. He is too honest and
outspoken; his sentiments, whether popular or unpopular,
are never concealed. With the highest appreciation of his
services in saving Kansas, and with a personal regard that
has few equals, it has so happened, fortunately or unfortunately, that ever since the war we have in most cases voted on
opposite sides, yet without disturbing our personal relations.
The world will never be quite right till we allow other people
the same freedom of thought and action that we claim for
ourselves.

Before closing I wish to quote from several contempo-
raries. G. Douglas Brewerton, correspondent *N. Y. Herald*,
who was in Kansas in December, 1855, and January, 1856,
thus speaks of Charles Robinson: " In Kansas politics General Robinson was a member of the State constitutional
convention, is chairman of the Free-State executive committee, and in addition to this holds the military rank of Major-
General and Commander-in-chief of the Kansas Volunteers,
as the Free-State army of Kansas style themselves. He
may be regarded as the real head—the thinking one, we
mean—and mainspring of the Free-State party, or, to speak
more correctly, of all that party who are worth anything.
We believe him to be a keen, shrewd, far-seeing man, who
would permit nothing to stand in the way of the end which
he desired to gain. He is, moreover, cool and determined,
and appears to be endowed with immense firmness; we
should call him a conservative man now, but conservative
rather from policy than from principle. He seems to have
strong common sense, and a good ordinary brain, but no
brilliancy of talent. In fact, to sum Governor Robinson up
in a single sentence, we consider him the most dangerous
B

enemy which the pro-slavery party have to encounter in
Kansas. In person he is tall and well-made, and more than
ordinarily handsome, gentlemanly, but by no means winning
in his manners, with one of those cold, keen blue eyes that
seem to look you through."

S. S. Prouty sums up the character of Governor Robinson
in an address January 27, 1881, before the Kansas State
Historical Society, as follows:

"One of the most conspicuous and influential leaders of
the Free-State party was Charles Robinson, the first Governor of the State of Kansas. He was noted for his sterling
common sense, firmness, coolness, and courage. Though an
uncompromising anti-slavery man, there was no sentiment
or gush in his composition. He was regarded as a conservative man and too business-like and practical by the ideal-
ists. He fancied fighting as well as any other man when it
was absolutely necessary, or when it would benefit the Free-
State cause. But he did not believe in sanguinary strife
simply for the love of it, or for ends but remotely associated
with the Kansas contest. Such men as Governor Robinson
were needed to hold in check the reckless and imprudent,
to bring order out of chaos, and secure the fruits of victory."

October 30, 1851, he married Miss Sara T. D. Lawrence,
daughter of Hon. Myron Lawrence, an eminent lawyer and
statesman of Massachusetts. Her mother was Clarissa
(Dwight) Lawrence. She was of the New England family
of Dwights, of western Massachusetts, of which President
Dwight, of Yale College, is a worthy scion. She is the
author of "Kansas; its Interior and Exterior Life," a book
which in its time was a not unworthy rival of "Uncle Tom's
Cabin," and did scarcely less in its sphere, to rouse the
Northern heart, in the early years of the Kansas struggle.
They have no children.

Eli Thayer, in his "Kansas Crusade,"* speaks of his first
meeting with Charles Robinson as follows:

* "Kansas Crusade," page 33.

" It was at one of the Chapman Hall meetings (in Boston)
that I first saw Charles Robinson (afterwards Governor of
Kansas), and engaged him to act as agent of the Emigrant
Aid Company. A wiser and more sagacious man for this
work could not have been found within the borders of the
nation. By nature and by training he was perfectly well
equipped for the arduous work before him. A true Democrat and a lover of the rights of man, he had risked his life
in California while defending the poor and weak against the
cruel oppression of the rich and powerful. He was willing
at any time, if there were need, to die for his principles. In
addition to such brave devotion to his duty, he had the
clearest foresight and the coolest, calmest judgment in deter-
mining the course of action best adapted to secure the rights
of the Free-State settlers. No one in Kansas was so much
as he the man for the place and time. He was a deeper
thinker than Atchison, and triumphed over the border ruffians
and the more annoying and more dangerous self-seekers of
his own party. The man who ' paints the lily and gilds
refined gold ' is just the one to tell us how Charles Robinson
might have been better qualified for his Kansas work. But
his character, so clearly defined in freedom's greatest struggle,
superior to the help or harm of criticism, reveals these salient
points of excellence—majesty of mind and humility of heart,
stern justice and tender sympathy, heroic will and sensitive
conscience, masculine strength and maidenly modesty, leonine
courage and womanly gentleness, with power to govern
based on self-restraint, and love of freedom deeper than love
of life. With such a man at the head of the Free-State
cause it is not strange that I felt no uneasiness about its
management. I never troubled him with letters of advice
about Kansas matters, which he was in a position to understand so well. In the three years' conflict very few letters
passed between us. He never knew where or when a letter
would reach me, as I was speaking all the way from the
Penobscot to the Schuylkill, and from the seaboard to the

lakes. It was my mission to raise men and money for the
security of freedom in the Territory, and to combine the
Northern States in this work. I did not doubt Robinson's
ability or fidelity in the use of means."

Colonel S. F. Tappan, a member of the pioneer party
from Massachusetts, in 1854; a Branson rescuer; newspaper
correspondent; Clerk of the State Legislature who was calling
the roll of the House when that body was dispersed by Colonel Sumner; descendant of the famous Tappan families of
New England and New York; Colonel of the First Colorado
Regiment during the war, and member of the Indian Peace
Commission afterwards, wrote to the Denver *Tribune* of
September 9, 1883, a communication in which he said:

"Having referred to the early history of Kansas, the long-
protracted struggle of its people to consecrate its soil to
freedom, efforts at last rewarded by the admission of Kansas
into the Federal Union as a free State, it seems appropriate
to make a brief reference to the man who more than any
other—in fact, more than all others—by being patient as
well as herioc—patient under the most adverse and trying
circumstances, patient when persecuted, patient when victorious, patient in council, patient in battle, and more than all,
patient in prison—so shaped and directed the policy of the
Free-State men as to bring about the most desired object,
the freedom of Kansas. When the first party of emigrants
to Kansas from New England—as early as July, 1854—
reached the city of St. Louis en route, they there met one
who had preceded them to Kansas and made a selection of a
location—now Lawrence—on the Kansas River, just west
of the limits of the Shawnee reservation, about forty-five
miles west of Kansas City, as a place for this party to make
a settlement. He then returned and met them at St. Louis,
further to aid them in their purchases for their new homes.
This man had been a pioneer in a new country, one of the
earliest of those who went to California, and while there was
shot through the body while endeavoring to vindicate the

rights of the settlers to the land, commanding and leading them against a monster monopoly which was seeking to obtain and control all of the public domain. After being shot, he was placed on board a prison-ship and there retained until the people had elected and called upon him to represent them in the Legislature. Upon the passage of the Kansas-Nebraska bill, he emigrated to Kansas, and ever since has been closely and prominently connected with its interests. Upon the commencement of hostilities between the Free-State men and the invaders, he was called upon to take command of the former. Had it simply been a question between the Free-State men and the Missourians, it would have soon been settled by a decisive action. But the question at issue was more than this; it was not local, but national. The Missourians were encouraged and sustained at the outset by the entire force of the Federal Government, by the slave power of the South, and their allies at the North. The Federal judiciary and the Federal army were also arrayed on their side and against the Free-State men. These were potent, because on the ground and ready to be applied in behalf of the invader. Under these adverse circumstances the cause of free Kansas seemed at first sight lost forever. To fully comprehend the situation and the best means of averting the storm required a man of the greatest patience, judgment, coolness, and courage; one able to consolidate and control the Free-State element in such a way as to prevent a direct conflict with the Federal authority, and at the same time to maintain a determined position of resistance to the invader of the Territory and oppressor of the settlers; one able to shape the policy of the people and direct it toward a final victory upon the appearance of every new movement of the enemy. Kansas had such a man, who proved himself equal to every emergency. When the invader had, by violence, obtained absolute control of the first Legislative Assembly, and had enacted an infamous slave code for the government of Kansas, this man then advised an open repudiation of the concern and the immediate formation of a constitution and the organization of a government under it of the people, by the people, and for the people, which was done. This movement proved a check upon the pro-slavery party. Then the Administration determined to destroy this new government, using the Federal judges and the Federal army for the purpose. This man was indicted, arrested, and imprisoned upon the charge of treason, held for months as a prisoner, restrained of his liberty by a company of United States troops. Colonel Sumner, with his regiment, dispersed the Legislature at the point of his sword. Free-State men were arrested, manacled, and in some instances driven for miles across the prairie by detachments of Federal troops. The army had become fully identified with the invaders and determined upon the enslavement of Kansas. It was a crisis in affairs. One false movement on the part of the people would jeopardize everything. But their leader, although a prisoner in a Federal camp, still directed affairs and controlled events. When the young men, smarting under the indignities heaped upon them—when they saw the army and flag of their country prostituted to the service of the slave party, imperilling the freedom of Kansas, felt impelled to rise up in armed resistance, attack the prison camp, and release their General, he said, ' No ; under no circumstances do you permit yourselves to fire upon the army or the flag of our common country.' Like the great discoverer Columbus, who had been arrested and put in irons by order of the tyrannic Governor of Hispaniola, Bobadilla, and sent to Spain, when importuned by the captain of his guard and the master of the ship to permit them to remove the manacles from his limbs, said, ' No ; they were placed upon me by order of my sovereigns, and there they must remain until removed by their command.' Our Kansas Columbus, in the same spirit, replied, ' These bonds were placed upon me by authority of the Government, and must remain until removed by the same power,' which was done, and this man became the first executive of free Kansas; its war Governor, the organizer of its heroic army that went forth to maintain the Federal Union and uphold its flag and authority against a colossal armed rebellion, in which 3420 Kansas men laid down their lives, that our Government might live."

The early settlers well understood Dr. Robinson and rallied to his support.

That he was appreciated is fully shown by his almost unanimous election to the highest office within the gift of the people, that of the first Governor of the State. And well did he earn his title of "the War Governor of Kansas."

ISAAC T. GOODNOW.

MANHATTAN, KANSAS, June 1. 1891.

CHAPTER I.

ON Kansas soil was gained the first decisive victory against the slave power of this nation. Had her pioneers failed to make Kansas a free State, slavery to-day would have been national and freedom sectional. From the year 1820 to 1854 the triumphal march of the slave power had been uninterrupted, and the time seemed at hand when the defiant threat of a Southern planter, that he would call the roll of his slaves under the shadow of Bunker Hill Monument, would be fulfilled. This may seem an extravagant claim, but it is susceptible of proof. Before this nation was born, while the Pilgrim Fathers were fleeing from the oppression of the Old World, and seeking liberty on the rock-bound coast of New England, a cargo of twenty African slaves was landed in Virginia, in the month of August, 1619. From this seed thus planted sprung the upas tree that overshadowed the land. At first no Mason and Dixon's line divided the country, but nearly all the Colonies had more or less slaves, not excepting New York and Massachusetts. The slave trade, carried on in Spanish, English, and Dutch ships, was very lucrative, and plied with energy till the question of holding slaves became one of public consideration. Good men from the first deplored the existence of slavery, and hoped for its early disappearance. Among them were Washington, Jefferson, Rush, Franklin, Jay, Hamilton, Hopkins, Wesley, Whitefield, Edwards, and others. As early as 1688

1

the Quakers of Pennsylvania protested against the "buying, selling, and holding men in slavery." In 1696 the yearly meeting advised that "the members should discourage the introduction of slavery, and be careful of the moral and intellectual training of such as they held in servitude." In 1780 they induced the Pennsylvania Legislature to begin the work of emancipation. Various anti-slavery societies were organized and conventions held against slavery during the Colonial period of the country. John Quincy Adams said, "The Fathers believed and meant slavery to be temporary; emancipation was the end in view, only the time and mode were uncertain." In 1784 Mr. Jefferson presented to the Continental Congress a deed of cession of all the lands claimed by Virginia northwest of the Ohio River. A committee, with Jefferson as chairman, was appointed, which reported a plan for the government of the land ceded or to be ceded. This plan contemplated its ultimate division into seventeen States. It was therein provided that, "after the year of the Christian era 1800, there shall be neither slavery nor involuntary servitude in any of these States, otherwise than in the punishment of crime, whereof the party shall have been duly convicted." This report covered not only the Northwest Territory, but also Kentucky, Tennessee, Alabama, and Mississippi. It was rejected for a report in July, 1787, by Nathan Dane, chairman, reporting an ordinance for the territory of the northwest of the Ohio, in which there should be neither slavery nor involuntary servitude. This ordinance was passed by the Continental Congress on the 13th of July, 1787. The provision excluding slavery was affirmed by Congress under the Constitution in 1789. Efforts were made by the Territory of Indiana to suspend this ordinance, but without avail.

Mr. Wilson in "Rise and Fall of the Slave Power," on page 38, 1st vol., says:

"By this legislation the character of all the territory of the United States was then fixed. Mr. Jefferson's proposition, made in 1784, would have prohibited slavery after 1800 in all that territory. It has ever been a source of profound regret to the friends of freedom that this prohibition failed. In the light of subsequent events, however, it is not at all clear that more would have been gained to freedom by its adoption than was secured by Mr. Dane's ordinance, which only applied to the territory northwest of the Ohio River. * * * While Mr. Jefferson's proviso might and probably would have failed to secure to freedom the territory south of the Ohio, it might have imperilled it in the territory northwest of that river. Mr. Dane's ordinance of 1787 probably won for freedom all that could have been securely held."

This was the first and last substantial concession to freedom by Congress.

In March, 1820, the Missouri Compromise was adopted admitting Missouri as a slave State and prohibiting slavery from all territory north of thirty-six degrees and thirty minutes. This Compromise was a victory for slavery, and caused great excitement in New England and the entire North. The Legislatures of New York, New Jersey, Pennsylvania, Delaware, Ohio, and Indiana passed resolutions affirming the power and duty of Congress to prohibit slavery in the States to be carved out of Western territory. The Legislature of Pennsylvania denounced the measure of admitting Missouri as a slave-holding State as one " to spread the crimes and cruelties of slavery from the banks of the Mississippi to the shores of the Pacific."

Next came the admission of Texas as a slave State, December 27, 1845. This was followed by the war with Mexico, resulting in the acquisition of California, New Mexico, and Utah. This triumph of the slave power served to keep alive the agitation throughout the North and embitter the two sections.

In 1850 came another compromise. California had adopted a Free-State constitution and applied for admission into the Union. As, according to the rules of popular or any other sovereignty, the State could not well be rejected, a compromise was effected by which Utah and New Mexico were made Territories with the right to become slave States, and the Northern States became hunting-grounds for fugitive

slaves by the enactment of the Fugitive Slave Law.   Here
was another triumph for slavery which again fired the North,
resulting in the passage of personal liberty bills in several
States.

Finally came the passage of the Kansas-Nebraska bill,
which ignored the compromise line of thirty-six degrees and
thirty minutes.   After giving the boundaries, these words
are used :

"The same is hereby erected into a temporary government by the name
of the Territory of Kansas, and when admitted as a state or states, the
said territory, or any portion of the same, shall be received into the
Union with or without slavery, as their constitution may prescribe at
the time of their admission.   *   *   *   That the constitution, and all
laws of the United States which are not locally inapplicable, shall have
the same force and effect within the said Territory of Kansas as elsewhere
within the United States, except the eighth section of the act preparatory to the admission of Missouri into the Union, approved March sixth,
1820, which, being inconsistent with the principles of non-intervention
by Congress with slavery in the States and Territories, as recognized by
the legislation of 1850, commonly called the compromise measure, is
hereby declared inoperative and void; it being the true intent and meaning of the act not to legislate slavery into any Territory or State, nor to
exclude it therefrom, but to leave the people thereof perfectly free to
form and regulate their domestic institutions in their own way, subject
only to the Constitution of the United States : provided that nothing
herein contained shall be construed to revive or put in force any law or
regulation which may have existed prior to the 6th of March, 1820,
either protecting, establishing, prohibiting, or abolishing slavery."

Here is the removal of all Congressional barriers to the
spread of slavery, not only north of thirty-six degrees and
thirty minutes, but northwest of the Ohio River ; between
the Atlantic and Pacific oceans, and the great lakes and the
Gulf of Mexico.   " It being the true intent and meaning of
the act not to legislate slavery into any Territory or State," etc.

This was the situation May 30, 1854.   So far as Congressional action could go, every foot of land in the United
States was open to slavery.   Was there any agency or power
anywhere that could prevent its extension to Kansas ?   There
were able champions of freedom in Congress—Sumner, Sew-

ard, Chase, Hale, Wilson, Giddings, and others—but their battle had been fought and hopelessly lost. They fought nobly and well, but their weapons were words, words, which were impotent in a contest of votes. Henceforth they were as powerless to resist the onward march of slavery as if they had already been sleeping their last sleep.

Senator W. H. Seward, on May 25, 1854, said:

" The sun has set for the last time upon the guaranteed and certain liberties of all unsettled and unorganized portions of the American continent that lie within the jurisdiction of the United States. To-morrow's sun will rise in dim eclipse over them. How long that obscuration shall last is known only to the power that directs and controls all human events. For myself, I know only this: that no human power can prevent its coming on, and that its passing off will be hastened and secured by others than those now here, and perhaps only by those belonging to future generations."

Senator B. F. Wade said:

" The humiliation of the North is complete and overwhelming. * * * I know full well that no words of mine can save the country from this impending dishonor, this meditated wrong, which is big with danger to the good neighborhood of the different sections of the country, if not to the stability of the Union itself. * * * An empire is to be transformed from freedom to slavery, and the people must not be consulted on such a question, so big with weal or woe to the millions who are to people these vast regions in all time to come."

The New York *Tribune* of May 24, 1854, said:

" The revolution is accomplished, and slavery is king. How long shall this monarch reign? This is now the question for the Northern people to answer. Their representatives have crowned the new potentate, and the people alone can depose him."

In June, 1854, it said:

" Not even by accident is any advantage left for liberty in their bill. It is all blackness without a single gleam of light—a desert without one spot of verdure—a crime that can show no redeeming point. * * * A Territory which one short year ago was unanimously considered by all, North and South, as sacredly secured by irrepealable law to FREEDOM FOREVER, has been foully betrayed by traitor hearts and traitor voices, and surrendered to slavery."

The field of battle was thus removed from the halls of Congress to the plains of Kansas. What other agency or power than Congress could be invoked?

There had been a Colonization Society that proposed to dispose of slavery by transporting the slaves to their former home, Africa. Appeals had been made for money to transport, and for slaves to be transported, but in vain. With all the efforts of the philanthropic, a few thousand colonists only could be sent, and the scheme was found to be wholly impracticable. It was repudiated in a public protest as early as 1833 by such Englishmen as Wilberforce, Macaulay, Stephen, O'Connel, and others, who declared the society to be "an obstacle to the destruction of slavery throughout the world," and pronounced its pretexts to be "delusion and its real effects dangerous." John Quincy Adams said of it: "The search of the philosopher's stone and the casting of nativities by the course of the stars were rational and sensible amusements in the comparison." Poor reliance this to prevent the spread of slavery to Kansas.

There was another organization, called the American Anti-Slavery Society, in full vigor, and also The New England Anti-Slavery Society. The American Society was organized in 1833, with this platform in part:

"We also maintain that there are at the present time, the highest obligations resting upon the people of the free States to remove slavery by moral and political action, as prescribed in the Constitution of the United States." The New England Society declared that "we will not operate on the exisiting relations of society by other than peaceful and lawful means, and that we will give no countenance to violence or insurrection. That the objects of the society shall be to endeavor, by all means sanctioned by law, humanity, and religion, to effect the abolition of slavery in the United States."

These were broad and practical platforms, and had they been adhered to, much assistance might have been rendered to the cause of free Kansas. Some sixteen hundred auxiliary societies were organized, with a membership of nearly a quarter of a million, before the year 1840. But when, in that year, in accordance with the principles of the original platform, William Goodell, Alvan Stewart, Myron Holley, James G. Birney, Joshua Leavitt, Gerrit Smith, and others called a convention at Albany to consider the question of nominating a candidate for President, to be voted for by the anti-slavery men, the Massachusetts Anti-Slavery Society said in an address: "For the honor and purity of our enterprise, we trust that the abolitionists of the several States will refuse to give any countenance to the proposed convention at Albany. Let their verdict be recorded against it as unauthorized and premature. Let the meeting be insignificant and local, and thus rendered harmless."

In 1843, the American Anti-Slavery Society resolved: "That the compact which exists between the North and the South is a covenant with death and an agreement with hell, involving both parties in atrocious criminalities, and that it should be immediately annulled."

Also, in May, 1844, the declaration was made that "henceforth, until slavery be abolished, the watchword, the rallying cry, the motto on the banner of the A. A. Society shall be, 'No union with slave-holders.'"

A resolution was adopted declaring that "secession from the Government was the duty of every abolitionist, and that to take office or to vote for another to hold office under the Constitution violated anti-slavery principles, and made such voter an abettor of the slave-holder in his sin."

In the "Writings of Garrison," the recognized leader of the A. A. Society, pages 118 and 119, are the following expressions:

"Know that its (the Union) subversion is essential to the triumph of justice, the deliverance of the oppressed, the vindication of the brotherhood of the race. It was conceived in sin and brought forth in iniquity. * * * To say that this covenant with death shall not be annulled—that this agreement with hell shall continue to stand—that this refuge of lies shall not be swept away—is to hurl defiance at the eternal throne, and to give the lie to Him who sits thereon.   *   *   * Accursed be the American Union, as a stupendous republican imposture. *   *   * Accursed be it, for its hypocrisy, its falsehood, its impudence, its lust, its cruelty, its oppression. *   *   * Accursed be it from the foundation to the roof, and may there soon not be left one stone upon another that shall not be thrown down."

In Parker Pillsbury's book, "Acts of the Anti-Slavery Apostles," page 20, he quotes from Garrison's writings as follows: "The members of this society (Non-resistance) agree in the opinion that no man, or body of men, however constituted, or by whatever name called, have a right to take the life of man as a penalty for transgression, that no one who professes to have the Spirit of Christ can consistently sue a man at law for redress of injuries, or thrust any evil-doer into prison; or hold any office in which he would come under obligation to execute any penal enactments, or take part in the military service; or acknowledge allegiance to any human government."

As slavery had to be excluded from Kansas, if at all, by votes according to law and the Constitution, no assistance could be looked for from the ranks of men who denounced the Constitution as a compact to be annulled, all law as a crime, and voting or holding office as a sin. Had the entire anti-slavery society been transferred to Kansas, as the members would not vote or hold office, one hundred pro-slavery men would have been sufficient to elect the Legislature, make the laws, and adopt a constitution establishing slavery, and all with the most profound peace and quiet in the Territory and nation.

Henry Wilson said of the influence of this society, Vol. I. p. 574:

"The parent society and its affiliated associations, having accepted this position, made it thereafter the distinctive feature of its organization, and the most prominent article of their creed. 'No Union with slave-holders' was the motto everewhere emblazoned on their banners.

Disunion was their recognized remedy. Other anti-slavery men, of whatever organization, were proclaimed to be wanting in an essential element of all true and effective opposition. However earnest and devoted, they were deemed inconsistent, and their labors were regarded as only partial, if not wholly inefficient. This general criticism embraced every class of anti-slavery men, and every form of anti-slavery effort. From the adoption of this policy of disunion in 1844, to the opening of the rebellion, so persistent were they in its promulgation, as the element of all effective effort, that the supporters of slavery seized upon the fact to identify all anti-slavery men with them, and to characterize all opposition to slavery as disorganizing, revolutionary, and unpatriotic. It was indeed a most potent weapon in the hands of the apologists, perpetualists, and propagandists of slavery. Nor did they cease its use until their voices were silenced by the patriotism of the nation, outraged as it was by their own treason or acknowledged complicity with it."

John G. Whittier, in a letter, said he was no blind worshipper of the Union, and as an abolitionist he was shut out from its benefits. " But I see nothing to be gained by an effort—necessarily limited, sectional, and futile—to dissolve it. The moral and political power requisite for doing it could far more easily abolish every vestige of slavery."

Emerson said of them :

" They withdraw themselves from the common labors and competitions of the market and the caucus. * * * They are striking work and calling out for something to do. * * * They are not good citizens, not good members of society; unwillingly they bear their part of the private and public burdens. They do not even like to vote. * * * They filled the world with long words and long beards. * * * They began in words and ended in words."

William Birney, in " Birney and his Times," says :

" Their strongest aspiration was to express in stinging epithets and vituperative language their infinite devotion to the cause of the slave; but they were serenely indifferent to its success or failure. They would not cast a ballot if the act would free three million of slaves."

Henry C. Wright, in his book entitled " Ballot-box and Battle-field," says :

" Suppose the abolition of slavery throughout the world depended on a presidential election, and that my vote would throw the scale for abolition. Shall I vote? * * * I may not vote for the war system that is founded in guilt and blood and utterly wrong in its origin, its principles and means, even to abolish slavery."

Eli Thayer, in "Kansas Crusade," says:

"The Northern people ardently desired to destroy the tree (slavery) itself, and were ready to adopt any legal and constitutional plan which might do this work. Garrison's method of casting out a devil by splitting the patient in two lengthwise they did not approve, for two reasons: 1st. Because the patient would die; 2d. Because the devil would live."

Schouler, in his last work, says:

"They were not actors in affairs, but agitators, critics, come-outers, coiners of cutting epithets, who scourged men in public station with as little mercy as the slave-driver did his victim, less pleased that their work was being done than displeased because it was not done faster. Their political blunders widened the breach between the North and the South, and their constant instigation was to throttle that law which was the breath of our being—to trample down the Union, rather than convert, constrain, or conquer slavery behind the shield of the Constitution. This was because of their fanaticism. Not one leader of this school ever took a responsible part in affairs, or co-operated in lawful and practical measures for promoting the reform they caressed in their preaching."

Samuel Bowles, in Boston *Evening Traveller*, May 29, 1857, says:

"The great majority of the Garrisonian party forfeit all claim to our esteem by being blasphemous, vituperative, coarse, and vile in their manners and language. We need not instance a man named Foss, who has the impudence to claim the title Reverend, and who began a sentence in a speech in New York week before last with the phrase, 'I hate the Union,' and ended it by saying, 'I hate Jesus Christ.' All the leaders of the Garrisonian party sat around, but no one of them rebuked the monstrous blasphemy. The speech was circulated through all the Southern papers, and Mr. Foss was denounced as 'a Republican.' If he had died in his cradle he would have done better by himself than to have lived to commit this sin. The same style of thought has been manifested at this gathering in the Melodeon. We listened yesterday to the comprehensive abuse uttered by Mr. Higginson, who also claimed to be a minister of the Gospel. If we had stayed five minutes longer than we did, and his effect had been equal to his effort, we should have been convinced that the population of the world consisted of one billion of depraved wretches and one perfect man named Higginson. It was just so with the whole of them, the same eternal whine, redeemed only in the case of Wendell Phillips by eloquence. All such stuff does harm. The few Garrisonians whom we believe honest in uttering it, we wish could be brought under different influences, for they are unconsciously injuring the anti-slavery cause. They are sustaining by their weight of character an organization four-fifths of whose members are selfish or indiscreet men and unsexed women ; an organization which has become fruitless, and will die in the next generation. * * * For the remainder of the Garrisonian party, the strong-minded women, and the professional humanitarians who earn their daily bread by injuring the noble cause they propose to serve, we have no feelings but of ridicule and contempt. It is useless to meet them in argument. They are not worth treating with pity. One of their peculiarities is a key to their whole character. The nearer a well-behaved man comes to their professed anti-slavery doctrines, the more vilely they abuse him."

Such opinions might be quoted indefinitely, but enough have been cited to show the estimation in which the advocates of no union, no voting, no government were held by the voting anti-slavery men of the time, and 'it requires no argument to prove that people entertaining such views of government could be of no use in arresting the progress of slavery by making a free State in Kansas. While this is true, among these men and women were some of the most eloquent and conscientious to be found in any country or age, and their antagonism to the Government and Church of the time had some excuse. They had seen the Government at Washington prostituted to the spread of slavery since 1820, with apparently no hope for the better within the Union. Having lost faith in Congressmen and President, they also lost faith in mankind. Being expert moral hair-splitters, they came to regard the Constitution as a shield for the protection of slavery, at least within the slave States, and authority for making every State in the Union hunting-ground for fugitive slaves. To justify this no-voting, non-action position they claimed that allegiance to a sinful government was sin, and as no human government on earth was perfect, they would

acknowledge no government except one in heaven, of which
"Border Ruffians" in Kansas had no conception. Being
non-resistants themselves, they believed they could dissolve
the Union without bloodshed or resistance on the part of
the Government, an error they recognized later when the
slave States attempted it.

As for the churches, they held every member accountable
for the resolutions and utterances of synods, conventions, and
prominent individuals of the different denominations. In
the early days of the agitation many of these were in defense
of slavery as a divine institution.

Geo. W. Julian, candidate for Vice-President on the Free-
Soil ticket in 1852, said, in his "Speeches on Political Questions," page 79 :

"What are our churches doing for the anti-slavery reform? Alas!
the popular religion of the country lies imbedded in the politics and
trade of the country. It has sunk to a dead level with the ruling secular
influences of the age. It has ceased to be a power, practically capable
of saving the world from its sins. * * * What are these religious
bodies doing for the slave? As I have already said, they are breaking
bread with his owner around the communion table. They are receiving
slave-holders into full fellowship. The preachers and members of our
Protestant denominations alone own over six hundred thousand slaves.
The Methodist, Baptist, and Presbyterian all have divided on the slavery
question, but both divisions tolerate slave-holding. * * * In all
the late publications of the American Tract Society, I am informed that
not a syllable can be found against slavery. Such sins as Sabbath-
breaking, dancing, fine dressing, etc., are abundantly noticed and condemned, but not even a whisper must go forth against the 'sum of all
villainies.'"

Two pamphlets were published, one entitled "The American Churches the Bulwarks of American Slavery," and the
other, "The Church as it is ; the Forlorn Hope of Slavery."
These pamphlets were wholly made up of testimony from
the churches and church members themselves, and afford
some excuse, at least, for the arraignment made by the no-
church abolitionists. As the leading preachers defended the
institution of slavery from the Bible, the abolitionists attacked

that book as of no more authority than any other work of ancient origin. As the churches claimed the Sabbath as too holy to be used for anti-slavery work, that too was assailed as a mere human device; and so on they went till not only the Constitution, but the Bible, churches, and the Sabbath were discarded and denounced. Much they said was merited and just, but the main mistake they made was in not improving every opportunity offered to help the slave as they found him. If, instead of fighting the Constitution, the Union, and the churches as such, they had joined with all anti-slavery men, church members and others, and filled Congress and the presidential chair with men who would go to the limit of the Constitution in abolishing slavery in the District of Columbia and the Territories, as well as the coastwise slave trade, the road might have opened before them for the final extinction of slavery, leaving the Constitution and the churches intact. Or, when beaten in Congress, they could have turned their attention to the settlement of Kansas, where the decisive battle of slavery was to be fought. Here was their irretrievable mistake. They were incapable of adapting their warfare to the changing conditions, and failed. While they were bombarding the Union and the churches, that they might reach the slave over their ruins, the door was thrown wide open, by way of Kansas, to the very citadel of the slave power, and that, too, under the sanction and protection of Constitution, Union, laws, and churches. Others saw this opening, entered it, and gained the victory, and to them must belong the credit. These men could see that the act organizing Kansas Territory opened every Territory and free State to slavery; but could not or did not see that the same act equally opened every Territory and slave State to freedom, if the people of these Commonwealths respectively would have it so. The language will bear repeating a second time: " It being the true intent and meaning of the act not to legislate slavery into any Territory or State, nor to exclude it therefrom; but to leave the people thereof perfectly free to form and regulate their domestic institutions in their own way, subject only to the Constitution of the United States." Here was a solemn pledge that Congress would not interfere to prevent the extension of freedom to every Territory and State of the Union. In this act the slave power overreached itself, and it was blunder number one in the " beginning of the end" of slavery. This the slave power did not see, neither did the no-union, no-voting abolitionists see it, but it was seen nevertheless, and turned to freedom's account, as will appear in the pages that follow. Charles Sumner said of the Kansas bill, that it was " at once the worst and the best bill on which Congress ever acted." It was the best bill, " for it annuls all past compromises with slavery, and makes all future compromises impossible. Thus it puts freedom and slavery face to face, and bids them grapple." Unfortunately, non-resistants would not use grappling-irons, and free States could not be made without votes.

One other organization existed which opposed the extension of slavery, called the Liberty or Free-soil party. The members of this organization were voters and fighters, if need were, but their party machinery was not adapted to making States. It had done good service in agitating the slavery question, and in securing the election to Congress of many able champions of freedom. Unlike the American Anti-slavery Society, this party was loyal to the Constitution and the Union. In the language of James G. Birney, their presidential candidate at two elections, they " regarded the Constitution with unabated affection. They hold in no common veneration the memory of those who made it. They would be the last to brand Franklin and King and Morris and Wilson and Sherman and Hamilton with the ineffaceable infamy of intending to engraft upon the Constitution, and therefore to perpetuate, a system of oppression in absolute antagonism to its high and professed objects. * * * In the political aspects of the question they have nothing to ask except what the Constitution authorizes—no change to desire but that the Constitution may be restored to its pristine republican purity."—" J. G. Birney and his Times," page 338.

This party cast in 1840, for President, 7100 votes; in 1844, 62,300; in 1848, 300,000; in 1852, 155,000. Besides members of this party, there were many belonging to the Whig and Democratic parties who were made indignant by the repeal of the Missouri Compromise, and who were ready to abandon their party organizations in the nefarious work of extending the institution of slavery to territory that had been consecrated to freedom by solemn compact. There was no lack of anti-slavery sentiment, or of desire to save Kansas to freedom, but the political parties could only act in their legitimate sphere—elect Presidents, Congressmen, and other officials—while the work in hand now was something that political parties, Congress, and the President could not do, and aid must be sought elsewhere, and other machinery invented. It is true, Hon. Geo. W. Julian had said:

" Does any one ask how we shall successfully wage war against this monster power? I answer that American politics and American religion are the bulwarks which support it, and that we must attack them. If we do this wisely and perseveringly we shall succeed. We need no new weapons, but only a faithful use of those we already possess, in more direct assaults upon these strongholds of the enemy." This was spoken in 1852, and the American Anti-slavery Society and the Free-Soil party had waged vigorous and persevering war with their religious and political " weapons " till 1854, when every foot of territory in the United States was open to slavery. Evidently some new weapons must be found or the victory of the slave power would remain final and complete.

CHAPTER II.

To understand what "weapons" and what machinery would be in demand in making a free State in Kansas, a survey of the field should be taken. The Organic Act left to the voters of the Territory the settlement of the question of slavery in the State. The first step in making a State was to elect a territorial Legislature, that might provide for a constitutional convention, which in turn could frame a constitution authorizing or forbidding slavery. The way was plain. But one road was open for making a free State, and that, and that only, must be travelled. Colonizing slaves in Africa, shouting "no union with slave-holders" in Boston, preaching the Wilmot Proviso in Congress, and political campaigns in the States, were of no avail in the pending struggle. Voters must be had, and as no person but a settler would have the right to vote, settlers were of the first importance. How could they be secured? Would they come from the free States in sufficient numbers to outvote those who should come from the slave States? The decree of the slave power had gone forth that Kansas should be a slave State, and that power in Church and State, in Synod and Congress, was omnipotent. Could it be successfully encountered in Kansas? If the eloquence of Phillips, Garrison, Sumner, and Seward was of no avail, what could be hoped from untitled, unheralded, and unknown settlers? Who would have the presumption to enter the lists? Slavery had every advantage. A slave State bordered Kansas on

the east containing a population sufficient in numbers and
daring to settle several new Territories. This population,
bold, blustering, and reckless like the people of most frontier settlements, was thoroughly aroused to the importance
of the conflict. Two billions of dollars worth of property
in slaves, besides the domestic relations of the people of the
Southern States, were involved. The life or death of slavery
was the issue, and was recognized to be the issue by both
North and South. The Charleston, S. C., *Mercury* presented
the question as follows :

" First. By consent of parties, the present contest in Kansas is made
the turning-point in the destinies of slavery and abolition. If the
South triumphs, abolitionism will be defeated and shorn of its power
for all time. If she is defeated, abolition will grow more insolent and
aggressive, until the utter ruin of the South is consummated.

" Second. If the South secures Kansas, she will extend slavery into
all the territory south of the fortieth parallel of north latitude, to the
Rio Grande, and this, of course, will secure for her pent-up institution
of slavery an ample outlet, and restore her power in Congress. If the
North secures Kansas, the power of the South in Congress will gradually be diminished, the States of Missouri, Kentucky, Tennessee, Arkansas, and Texas, together with the adjacent Territories, will gradually
become abolitionized, and the slave population confined to the States
east of the Mississippi will become valueless. All depends upon the
action of the present moment."

This issue was accepted by the people in the border counties of Missouri, and they were at first troubled with no fears
for the result. They were jubilant, bold, and defiant, threatening with death any anti-slavery man who should attempt
to settle in the Territory. In less than a month after the
passage of the Kansas-Nebraska bill, the writer started for
Kansas to arrange for its settlement. On passing Jefferson
City, the capital of Missouri, on the 4th of July, several
prominent politicians came on board the steamer, and among
them General Stringfellow. In the conversation it was assumed as a foregone conclusion that the fate of Kansas
was sealed. It was boldly asserted that "no damned abolitionist would be permitted to settle in Kansas, and every

2

man north of Mason and Dixon's line was an abolitionist."
On reaching Kansas City a reward was found offered for
"one Eli Thayer, a leading and ruling spirit among the
abolitionists of New York and New England. * * *
Representing all the abolitionists, he consequently bears all
their sins!"
General D. R. Atchison was the recognized leader of the
pro-slavery cause, and most of the leading politicians and
citizens of western Missouri were his co-workers. Such was
the condition of the border, while the administration at
Washington was wholly devoted to the establishment of
slavery in Kansas, Jefferson Davis being Secretary of War.
In the North and East the outlook was equally gloomy.
The American Anti-slavery Society never had any faith in
saving Kansas to freedom. Wendell Phillips said, as reported in the *Liberator :*

" Talk about stopping the progress of slavery and of saving Nebraska
and Kansas! Why, the fate of Nebraska and Kansas was sealed the
first hour Stephen Arnold Douglas consented to play his perfidious
part. * * * The moment you throw the struggle with slavery into
the half-barbarous West, where things are decided by the revolver and
bowie-knife, slavery triumphs."

Mr. Garrison said :

" While the Union continues, the slave power will have everything
its own way, in the last resort. * * * Slavery is certain to go into
Kansas, nay, slaves are now carried there daily, and offered for sale
with impunity. * * * Will Kansas be a free State? We answer,
no. Not while the existing Union stands. Its fate is settled.
* * * Eastern emigration will avail nothing to keep slavery out of
Kansas. We have never had any faith in it as a breakwater against the
inundations of the dark waters of oppression. * * * The omnipres-
ent power of the general Government will co-operate with the vandals
of Missouri to crush out what little anti-slavery sentiment may exist in
Kansas, and to sustain their lawless proceedings in that Territory. This
will prove decisive in the struggle."

Theodore Parker, in Music Hall, said :

" In the steady triumph of despotism, ten years more like the ten
years past and it will be all over with the liberties of America. Every-

thing must go down, and the heel of the tyrant will be on our necks. It will be all over with the rights of man in America, and you and I must go to Australia, to Italy, or to Siberia for our freedom, or perish with the liberty which our fathers fought for and secured to themselves, not to their faithless sons. Shall America thus miserably perish? Such is the aspect of things to-day."

Mr. Thayer, in his " Kansas Crusade," says:

" On May 30, 1854, the Kansas-Nebraska bill, containing the repeal of the Missouri Compromise, was signed by President Pierce, and became the law of the land. When this news reached the Northern States the bells were tolled for the death of freedom. The slave States, with thirty-five years of political supremacy and the prestige of this last great victory over the North, with perfect discipline and irresistible power, were confident of undisputed control in the Government for generations to come. They already had the Chief Executive, his Cabinet, the Supreme Court, both houses of Congress, and the army and navy to do their bidding. Great as was their present power, their prospective power was even more alarming. Kansas and Nebraska, with all the Territories west and south of them, were to become slave States. Five more were to be made of Texas. The purpose of acquiring Cuba and Central America for their further aggrandizement was developing into action. Why, then, should the South doubt for an instant the certainty of her perpetual power? In a few years her Senators in Congress would nearly double the number from the North. Their skill in diplomacy and politics, acquired by unremitting practice and study, much excelled that of the Northern people, whose minds were occupied by a manifold system of industries requiring constant attention, as well as by a great number of social, commercial, charitable, religious, and educational organizations. No wonder that we were hopeless and helpless. We had no political organization of any strength to oppose to slavery. * * * During all this period of the successful aggressive and increasing strength of slavery, there was in the North corresponding apprehension and alarm. On the repeal of the Missouri Compromise the apprehension became despondency, and the alarm became despair. * * * The speeches in Congress and the editorials of influential journalists prove that there was no hope of rescuing Kansas from the grasp of this resistless power, should the Kansas-Nebraska bill become a law."

While this is a faithful presentation of the effects of the repeal of the Missouri Compromise upon the North as a whole, there were many minds upon which that repeal pro-

duced other results. Conservative men, especially members
of the Whig party, were shocked at the bad faith shown by
their Southern colleagues in Congress—only one of whom
voted against the Kansas bill—and felt the necessity of seeking other party affiliations. For over thirty years all parties
had acquiesced in the settlement of the vexed question by
the compromise of 1820, although the North felt that it had
been overreached in the bargain, and now, after the South
had received its full consideration, to have the bargain repudiated was too much for even "hunker" Whigs of the
North to accept in silence.

Free-soil men also were aroused with fresh zeal, and determined to take the case to the people in all future elections and demand reparation for this bad faith. Congress-
man Meacham, of Vermont, said:

"I look on that compromise as a contract, as a thing done for a consideration, and that the parties to that contract are bound in honor to
execute it in good faith. The consideration on one side was paid and
received in advance."

This was the view generally taken at the North, although
combated by some members of Congress from the South.
Mr. Goodrich, of Massachusetts, said, "If the Kansas bill
should pass, the repeal of the Missouri Compromise would
wipe out as with a sponge all compromises"; and Mr.
Campbell, of Ohio, said he would wage "an unrelenting
war against slavery to the furthermost limits of the Constitution." Many Southern people disapproved of the repeal,
and warned slave-holders to beware of the agitation it would
create. Mr. Houston, of Texas, called upon the Southern
Senators, "to regard the contract once made to harmonize
and preserve the Union. Maintain the Missouri Compromise! Stir not up agitation! Give us peace! Union or
disunion depends upon the decision of this question."

Eli Thayer, in his "Crusade," says, "The South, stimu-
lated unreasonably by her former success, ventured foolishly
to overthrow a time-honored compact, and subject herself to

a charge of bad faith. In the repeal of the Missouri Compromise she illustrated the words of the sacred writer : ' Pride
goeth before destruction, and a haughty spirit before a fall.'
By this act she had made it possible to combine all political
parties in the North against the extension of slavery, should
the right method of doing this great work be well presented
and faithfully urged. All were ready now to rebuke the
arrogance of slavery, and also to end its existence, if that
could be done in accordance with the Constitution and the
Union."

But a combination of all political parties for mere political
action would not avail to save Kansas. It is true that, within
one year of the repeal of the compromise, eleven Senators
and 120 of the 142 Northern members of the House were
elected who repudiated the repeal, but even this number
could accomplish nothing in Congress. There was now but
one way of salvation for Kansas, and that was not through
the executive, legislative, or judicial departments of the
Government, through anti-slavery societies or political organizations, but the promised land, as of old, must be secured
by taking possession of it, or not at all. How could this be
done ? Here were bowie-knives, pistols, shot-guns, rifles,
and cannon in the hands of the Philistines on the border and
within the Territory, under direction of " Blue Lodges,"
" Sons of the South," and other secret organizations, and the
attempt to occupy the land by the ordinary methods of pioneer settlement would have been as futile as for the Israelites
thus to have taken possession of Canaan. Nothing short of
concerted action by the friends of freedom could avail, and
that could be secured only by organization. Where could
an organizer be found ? Garrison and Phillips were the great
anti-slavery agitators, but neither had faith in success. Like
the men who were sent to spy out the land of Canaan, they
predicted that the land would " eat up " the Free-State men :
" all the people we saw in it are men of great stature. And
there we saw the giants, the sons of Anak, which come of

the giants, and we were in our own sight as grasshoppers, and so we were in their sight." And all the anti-slavery society to which they belonged agreed with them, and would have nothing to do with taking possession of Kansas. But there were two of the spies, named Joshua and Caleb, that, when they heard this gloomy report, rent their clothes. "And they spake unto all the company of the children of Israel, saying, the land which we passed through to search it, is an exceeding good land. If the Lord delight in us, then he will bring us into this land, and give it to us ; a land which floweth with milk and honey. Only rebel ye not against the Lord, neither fear ye the people of the land ; for they are bread for us ; their defense is departed from them, and the Lord is with us ; fear them not." Some of the Joshuas and Calebs of the emigration to Kansas are named in Mr. Hale's " Kansas and Nebraska," published in 1854. On page 219 he says :

" Mr. Eli Thayer, a member of the Massachusetts House of Representatives, circulated a petition, in the month of March, 1854, for the incorporation, by the general Court of Massachusetts, of the Massachusetts Emigrant Aid Company. The petition was at once granted by the Legislature, and a charter given, of which the first section reads—

" ' Sec. 1. Benjamin C. Clark, Isaac Livermore, Charles Allen, Isaac Davis, William G. Bates, Steven C. Phillips, Charles C. Hazewell, Alexander H. Bullock, Henry Wilson, James S. Whitney, Samuel E. Sewall, Samuel G. Howe, James Holland, Moses Kimball, James D. Green, Francis W. Bird, Otis Clapp, Anson Burlingame, Eli Thayer, and Otis Rich, their associates, successors, and assigns, are hereby made a corporation, by the name of the Massachusetts Emigrant Aid Company, for the purpose of assisting emigrants to settle in the West ; and for this purpose they have all the powers and privileges, and be subject to all the duties, restrictions, and liabilities set forth in the thirty-eighth and forty-fourth chapters of the revised statutes.'

" The charter was signed by the Governor on the 26th day of April, and took effect immediately. The persons named in it, and others interested, met at the State House, in Boston, on the 4th of May, accepted the charter, and appointed a committee to report a plan of organization and system of operations. The committee consisted of Eli Thayer, Alexander H. Bullock, and E. E. Hale, of Worcester, Richard

Hildreth and Otis Clapp, of Boston, who submitted the following report at an adjourned meeting: ' * * * The inconveniences and dangers to health to which the pioneer is subject who goes out alone or with his family only, in making a new settlement, are familiar to every American. The Emigrant Aid Company has been incorporated to protect emigrants, as far as may be, from such inconveniences. Its duty is to organize emigration to the West and bring it into system. * * * With the advantages attained by such a system of effort, the territory selected as the scene of operations would, it is believed, at once fill up with free inhabitants. * * * It determines in the right way the institutions of the unsettled Territories, in less time than the discussion of them has required in Congress. * * * It is impossible that such a region should not fill up rapidly. The Massachusetts Emigrant Aid Company proposes to give confidence to settlers, by giving system to emigration. By dispelling the fears that Kansas will be a slave State, the company will remove the only bar which now hinders its occupation by free settlers. It is to be hoped that similar companies will be formed in other free States. The enterprise is of that character, that for those who first enter it, the more competition the better.' This report was signed by Eli Thayer for the committee."

By reason of objections to some of the provisions of the charter it was not made use of, and three trustees, Eli Thayer, Amos A. Lawrence, and J. M. S. Williams, conducted the business of emigration during the season of 1854. An organization was made in 1855, under another charter, called the New England Emigrant Aid Company, with the following officers: President, John Carter Brown, Providence; Vice-Presidents, Eli Thayer, Worcester, J. M. S. Williams, Cambridge; Treasurer, Amos A. Lawrence, Boston; Secretary, Thomas H. Webb, Boston.

Other emigration societies and leagues were formed in several Northern States, inspiring great faith in the ultimate success of freedom in Kansas. While these organizations furnished inspiration and moral support, their pecuniary means were limited, and of secondary importance. The report that the New England Society had a capital of $5,000,000 struck the South with terror, and inspired the North with hope, although in fact its capital was limited at first to a few thousand dollars advanced by its treasurer, Amos A. Law-

rence. History will give to Eli Thayer the credit of first
publicly accepting the challenge of the South with a plan for
organized emigration to contend with the Blue Lodges of
Missouri, and for his head was the first reward offered by
the exasperated slave power. But organized emigration was
not alone in the conflict. While Thayer began to preach
the crusade in the winter of 1854, a few settlers from the
Middle and Western States preceded his first colony which
settled at Lawrence. Most noted among these were S. N.
Wood, J. A. Wakefield, B. W. Miller, Rev. T. Ferril, and
others, who acted a most important part in the struggle that
followed. In truth, no line of demarkation can well be drawn
between settlers who came from different States, or under
different auspices, as on arrival they became a band of brothers
engaged in a common cause. It would be folly for the head
to say to the foot, I have no need of thee; and the eye to
the hand, I have no need of thee; and it would have been
equal folly for settlers from one State to say to the settlers of another State that the cause had no need of them.
No such feeling existed in the fifties, neither does it now
exist in the breast of any surviving actor. Colonel S. N.
Wood, whose settlement in Kansas preceded the settlement
of Lawrence, and whose services were indispensable, has
this to say of the pioneers, in his quarter-centennial speech
at Topeka :

"The pilgrims of the *Mayflower* sought the wild shores of America
that they might be free to worship God in their own way; free to believe
in religious matters whatever seemed right to their own conscience.
They sought freedom for themselves. But the pioneers of Kansas—
both Western and Eastern—heard the call which in every age has thrilled
the souls of men with heroic power. At this critical period, when the
hosts of slavery and freedom were marshalling for this great and decisive encounter, in their inmost souls they heard the Divine voice
calling for defenders of liberty ; and they obeyed the signal that pointed
to Kansas as the great battle-ground. The pioneers who became
trusted leaders among the Free-State hosts were men who could not
rest in their old comfortable homes when the demon of human slavery
was clutching at freedom's rightful heritage. Many of them were the

sons of the old anti-slavery agitators, and had learned from child-hood to hate slavery and to love freedom, and claim it as the right of all men, races, and conditions. These men, meeting upon our prairies for the first time, recognized each other as kindred spirits. They spoke the same language, and were working for the same good purpose."

CHAPTER III.

SOMETHING of the nature of the conflict in Kansas may be
learned from the characteristics of the contestants. Settlers
from the North and East came from communities where person and property were protected by law, and the carrying of
weapons for self-defense was unknown. Many had come to
look even upon war among nations as a relic of barbarism.
Not a few of the Kansas emigrants had imbibed something
of the views and spirit of the non-resistant agitators, and
were disposed to interpret the teachings of the Nazarene
literally, to return good for evil, when one cheek should be
smitten to turn the other to the smiter, and if compelled to
part with their coats, to give their cloaks also. As a rule, the
Free-State settlers were averse to a resort to physical force in
the settlement of any conflict, much less a conflict purely
moral and political. These were some of the characteristics
of the Northern settlers while at home, but they were found
unsuited to a Southern and Western climate. It was found
that the precepts of Christianity, including non-resistance,
might work admirably where all were Christians and non-resistants, but it was also discovered that the devil would flee
only when resisted, and that pearls were not suitable diet for
all animals and on all occasions.

The South and Southwest were in many respects most unlike the East and North. ˙ Where a large class was to be kept
in servitude, nothing but physical force would avail. Hence

deadly weapons and personal prowess were indispensable, and the man who would pass current as a gentleman must be prepared at all times to protect his person and his honor by force. Also in the new West, in the absence of the civil code, every man was a law unto himself and constituted in his own person judge, jury, and executioner. In such a community human life, instead of being sacred as in the North and East, was cheap, and could be sacrificed at any time to resent personal insult and to protect peculiar institutions, if not for sordid gain. At the same time the better class of the citizens of the South had a high sense of honor, and could not be excelled in any part of the country for civility, courtesy, hospitality, and business integrity.

Perhaps life in the newly settled West, and the mingling of the two civilizations as found in the law-abiding East and the go-as-you-please West, cannot better be illustrated than by giving an outline picture of the early days of California, from 1849 to 1851. As the Eastern emigration to that Territory largely passed through Missouri and Kansas Territory, drawing with it a large emigration from Missouri itself and the South, many things happened that had an important bearing upon the conflict in Kansas at a later date. This outline is the more important as it will serve to give the squatters' side of the most exciting conflict in the history of California, which has never been given by one of their number, although published and republished, iterated and reiterated indefinitely by their opponents. There is no better way to exhibit human nature unrestrained by law, and the mingling of the Eastern and Western civilizations, than by giving a brief narrative of that conflict.

On the discovery of gold in California, in 1848, the whole country was in a blaze of excitement, and men of all classes and conditions had symptoms of the gold fever, more or less well marked. Even staid New England did not escape the epidemic. In the winter of 1849 a party of some forty persons was organized in the vicinity of Boston for the purpose

of emigration to the land of gold. This party was composed of men of all classes and professions, including trades-
men, clerks, manufacturers, mechanics, farmers, and laborers.
It was organized in the form of a military company, with
a full list of officers from captain down. The privates and
non-commissioned officers wore gray uniforms, while the
commissioned officers wore navy-blue. An assessment was
made upon each member, and all property was purchased
and controlled by the officers. Among the number was a
physician, by the name of Robinson, who was to be exempt
from all duty except the care of the sick. The doctor, de-
siring rest from an extensive practice, was in pursuit of rec-
reation quite as much as of gold. He had been interested
in the peace and anti-slavery discussions of that day, and
was in theory a non-resistant and abolitionist. The party
left Boston in the winter of 1849, travelling by railroad and
canal to Pittsburg, and thence by steamboat to Kansas City,
or Westport Landing. The name of the boat was *Ne Plus
Ultra*, and it was engaged for the whole river journey. It
stopped long enough at Cincinnati for the doctor to purchase a beautiful cream-colored horse and a clarionet, and
at St. Louis for the purchase of supplies and to receive passengers, chiefly gold-seekers. Some members of the party
had seen much of the world, while many were unsophisticated and unsuspicious. These latter, when they paid their
assessments, paid tuition in a school of more varied knowledge and experience than can be found in any professed
place of education. There was a new lesson for each day,
and every lesson must be learned by heart. Drones and
truants were impossible, and at the end of the journey, on
the western coast, every member was a graduate, and had
witnessed or experienced more arts, devices, shifts and turns,
deeds of daring, honor, integrity, perfidy, rascality, and deviltry than all the educational institutions of the land could
have shown. On leaving St. Louis the boat was well filled
with passengers and their " plunder." The Boston party were

now in a decided minority of the passengers, and relatively
lost their importance, although still distinguished from other
passengers by their uniform.   It being generally known that
the Boston party had a physician with them, his services
were sought on all occasions of sickness and among all
classes of passengers.   The boat had not proceeded far on
its journey up the muddy Missouri River when the cholera
made its appearance on board.   Here was a new experience
for the doctor.   While he had read much of the disease, its
cause, symptoms, and treatment, he had never met with a
case in his practice.   Without a medical library, and with
but a limited variety and supply of medicines, he was thrown
upon his own resources, and accordingly made an object lesson of the first case.   It was found that all the fluids of the
body were leaving the surface and pouring into the alimen-
tary canal.   The features became pinched and anxious, the
skin pallid and bloodless, and the muscles of the extremities
were affected with painful cramps.   What was to be done?
Evidently the first thing to be done was to reverse the vascular and absorbent machinery, and send the fluids back to
the surface and other parts of the system, and relieve cramps.
What would accomplish this result, and did the medicine-
chest contain the required remedy?   On examination, the
doctor found tincture of opium (laudanum), tincture of cam-
phor, and compound tincture of capsicum (hot drops).   The
first two would have a tendency to send the fluids to the
brain and surface and relieve spasms, while the last would
excite action of the vascular and absorbent systems.   Accordingly, these tinctures were taken in a mixture of equal
parts, and administered in teaspoonful doses once in fifteen
minutes, more or less, according to symptoms, till the flow
of fluids should be reversed and the cramps cease.   Fortunately, this treatment proved successful in every case where
applied on first attack of the disease.

Another object lesson was given on this boat which has
not been forgotten.   As the steamer was about to leave St.

Louis, four men came on board in a somewhat free-and-easy
manner, occasioned by a free indulgence in the fashionable
beverage of the city.   One of these men proved to be a man
from Illinois, on his way to California, and the other three
were residents of St. Louis, and evidently blacklegs.   The
man from Illinois was said to have $1500, which he deposited
with the clerk of the boat.   As soon as the boat was well
under way, these four men engaged in card-playing, which
was diligently prosecuted early and late.   Large sums of
money were bet and nearly always won by one of the three
men from St. Louis, at the expense of the Illinoisan.   The
unsophisticated members of the Boston party had read of
gambling and desperate characters in the South and West,
particularly on board of river steamers, and some of them
became close observers of the game, especially the doctor,
whose state-room was near the gamblers' table.   It was observed that drinks were often ordered, and that the Illinois
man was kept in a jolly frame of mind, while the St. Louis
men were cool and sober.   On the evening of the first or
second day the playing became more earnest and the drinking more frequent, till the Illinois man became desperate,
and all left the table and went to the bar, where another drink
was called for, but declined at first by the victim.   But after
being bantered and coaxed, he emptied his glass, as did the
others.   At this stage the doctor retired to his state-room, but
not to sleep, for while conning this lesson in all its bearings,
he was called to prescribe for this man, who had been drugged
and was desperately ill.   Spasms and convulsions set in,
accompanied with groans and yells, till it became necessary
to remove him to the pilot-house that the passengers might
not be disturbed.   Before many hours had passed the poor
man died in terrible agony.   The boat soon after went ashore
and his body was left.   An inventory was had of his effects,
and no money except a small bill in his vest-pocket was
found.   A boat going down the river was hailed, and the
three gamblers went aboard; and thus ended this object

lesson, which was an eye-opener to the Doctor, and played havoc with his non-resistant theories. The Wyandotte Indian agent was on the boat, who was also a doctor, and well understood the case. When the Yankee Doctor proposed to have complaint made and these men punished, the Indian agent told him he was wild. He must remember that there was virtually no law that could or would reach the case; besides, if these men even had a suspicion that such a move was contemplated, the Doctor would be put where he could not be summoned as a witness. Also, should complaint be made, he would be retained as a witness, and would have to postpone his trip to California till after the trial, which might be delayed for a year. After fully digesting the case, with all its surroundings, it was concluded that one man could not remedy all the evils in the world at once.

At length the *Ne Plus Ultra* reached its destination, Westport Landing, or Kansas City, in the latter part of March or first of April. Here was a new experience. Like all joint-stock companies, made up of all classes and characters of independent, intelligent Yankees, no sooner was the journey commenced than the officers in control were subjects of suspicion, jealousies, innuendoes, reflections, and open charges of incapacity, inefficiency, crookedness, theft, and robbery. The farther removed from home and home influences, the louder the complaints, until on landing at Kansas City a general mutiny prevailed. No settlement of difficulties could be reached without a division of the party and a consequent division of the tons of supplies. Accordingly, two parties were organized, and a committee of three, of which the Doctor was one, was appointed to divide the "plunder." This quarrel and division, with the purchase of teams, consumed some four or five weeks of time, or till the first week in May. This delay afforded an excellent opportunity to study the peculiarities of the people, their habits and institutions. The doctor, with some other members of the party, procured board with a thrifty farmer several miles on the road to Independence, and there took lessons in Western farming and stock-raising. His time was fully occupied, for not only was a division of the supplies to be made between the two parties, and teams to be purchased, but calls for his professional services were frequent. During the first night after the party landed at Kansas City, nine of the citizens were attacked with cholera and died. The little hamlet was panic-stricken. Several physicians were in the place, but all had failed to save their patients. It became known in the morning that the Doctor of the Boston party had been successful in several cases on the boat while coming up the river, and his services were at once in demand. This demand did not cease till he started on his trip across the plains. The last case treated was that of a young physician who was a victim to the disease. The Doctor remained with him the entire night, until favorable symptoms appeared, when he joined the party ready to begin their long journey. Whether this physician died or recovered, the Doctor never learned till in the heat of the Kansas conflict, in 1856. There is reason to believe that this stay of some four or five weeks at Kansas City, in the spring of 1849, had an important influence on the struggle of 1854, 1855, and 1856, in Kansas Territory. The Yankees were thus enabled to learn some of the peculiarities of the border men, and they in turn of the Yankees. Each class bestowed and received favors, and parted with mutual good-will when the time came for the Yankees to pursue their journey. This good-will in some instances was uninterrupted, as will later appear, during all the border troubles in Kansas.

On the 10th of May, the two parties had completed their organizations, apportioned the property, procured their teams, and were ready to launch their "prairie schooners." One party had procured mules and the other oxen for motive power. Both mules and oxen were unbroken to the harness or yoke, with a few exceptions, as were most of the men in the parties unused to handling them. The experiences in hitching up, starting and driving these wild animals afforded much amusement as well as many hard knocks, mingled with the Western vernacular, which was learned and adopted by the drivers with remarkable alacrity. As the steers had had no Yankee schooling, and had not learned the definitions of the terms whoa, haw, and gee, the members of the party marched in irregular order on both sides of the teams, thus guiding them in the way they should go. At the short turns in the road, and the crossing of creeks and ravines, there was usually a revolt that sometimes lasted half a day. At night the steers would be unhitched from the wagons, but not unyoked, as to unyoke and yoke these teams on the open prairie at first would require twenty out of the twenty-four hours, leaving but four hours in which to eat and sleep, and no time for travel. On the first Saturday of the journey, darkness came on before reaching water, and the party camped on the high prairie. The next morning, on investigation, it was found that the Wakarusa Creek was some two or three miles away, and the teams must be hitched up and driven that distance, at least, although it was Sunday. So much was a work of necessity, and the strictest Puritan in the party acquiesced. But, after reaching the creek and watering the stock, the question arose, shall the party go further. Here was the first clash of Yankee theological steel. The discussion was, however, brief, and a vote of the party settled the question in favor of further travel. But the triumph of the Sunday travellers was brief, as in going through a depression, near the place where the town of Franklin was afterwards located, the chain between the cattle became slackened and twisted about a steer's leg. When the chain was straightened, it gave such a twist to the leg as to disable it. Here was a judgment of God for breaking the Sabbath. No further progress could be made that day, except in theological discussion. One party claimed that it was a direct interposition to punish Sabbath-breaking, while the other put the accident to the account of too long coupling-chains and bad

3

driving. One party appealed to the Decalogue, and the other called for its reading. When it was found that the seventh day, instead of the first, was enjoined to be observed, and that for a special reason which applied only to the Jews, an appeal was made to the New Testament, where it was claimed the command was made applicable to the first day of the week. The discussion was closed, on one side, by offering a dollar for every word in the New Testament enjoining the observance of any day as a Sabbath, and, on the other, by devoting the remainder of the day in searching the Testament. No claim was ever made for the prize money, and these sticklers for Sabbath observance were afterwards seen betting at monte in Sacramento, having evidently lost their Puritanic scruples. Persons who depend upon outside pressure for religion are apt to adopt the customs of their surroundings when that pressure is removed ; while the person who is governed by his own convictions of what is right and what is wrong, regardless of public opinion and public custom, will be but slightly influenced by externals.

As the Boston party travelled by river from Pittsburg to Kansas City, they saw nothing of prairie land till starting out across Kansas Territory. The second day, the 11th of May, was a revelation. No such landscape had ever blessed their vision. One of the party described the country and his sensations in his diary, as follows :

" May 11th, 1849.—Our course to-day has been over the rolling prairie, and we passed along without difficulty. The prairie seems to be an endless succession of rolls, with a smooth, green surface, dotted all over with most beautiful flowers. The soil is of the most rich and ertile character, with no waste land. The feelings that come over a person, as he first views this immense ocean of land, are indescribable. As far as the eye can reach, he sees nothing but a beautiful green carpet, save here and there perhaps a cluster of trees ; he hears nothing but the feathered songsters of the air, and *feels* nothing but a solemn awe in view of this infinite display of creative power.

" 13th.—Turned out this morning at four o'clock, to watch the cattle. Went up on a high roll of land, where I had an extensive and enchanting view of this seemingly boundless and ever-varying prairie. The sun is rising out of this sea of land in the east, a line of timber skirts Cedar Creek to the N.E., also Spoon Creek to the N.W., while still further on, in the same direction, is seen a thick fog, marking the course of the Kansas River. All is still save the grazing of the cattle, and the concert of birds, which is composed of a great variety of songsters. The cooing of the prairie hens, heard in every direction, constitutes the bass; the loud cawing of the crows, the tenor; the fine, sweet voices of the ground and small birds, the treble; and a noise as of distant wild geese, the alto.

"23d.—Passed a little creek of pure cold water, about twelve M., where we found a newly made grave. Ascended a high bluff near the creek, where I had a most delightful view of the country to a great distance. I was reminded of the view of the Connecticut River valley from Mt. Holyoke. There is this difference, however—while one is circumscribed by hills and forests, the other is illimitable in extent, and stretches from the rising to the setting sun; and while one is striped and checked with corn-fields and meadows like a carpet, the other is capable of being checked as numerously with States and nations."

The Boston party that left Kansas City in two divisions, before reaching California found itself in numerous subdivisions. In all his learning the Yankee had never learned the lesson of subordination. So long as dynamite cartridges will explode under favoring circumstances, so long will explosions occur in Yankee parties on a joint-stock basis while traversing a wilderness in pursuit of gold. The Israelites were not Yankees, and they had been long disciplined by the Egyptian task-master, but nevertheless they made the life of Moses a burden to him on their journey to the promised land. In consequence of these explosions of the Yankee party, but a few hundred miles had been travelled when the Doctor found himself one of a party of three persons, including himself, and all on horseback, with pack animals for their supplies. It seemed necessary that there should be at least two persons in every party, or this party of three would have been divided again. This journey was most favorable for developing traits, not only of human nature, but also of equine nature. The Doctor's horse, purchased at Cincinnati, proved to be as docile and affectionate as he was beautiful.

Whenever the Doctor appeared he would leave his grazing and place his head over the shoulder of his owner in an affectionate and caressing manner. Wherever the party camped, that was his home, and there was no danger of his taking voluntary leave. One incident that occurred, among many, will be given in honor of the race to which this horse, Charley by name, belonged. On reaching the north fork of the Platte River, it was found to be swollen and the current swift. Some place must be found, if possible, where it could be forded, as the pack animals could not well keep afloat with their luggage. Charley, as usual on such occasions, was in requisition for experiments. Several places were tried, but no fording discovered. At one place, when deep water was reached, in the struggle rider and horse became separated. The horse crossed the river, but on seeing the man struggling in the swift current, he neighed anxiously, and plunged into the stream again, reaching an island in the river at the same time with his owner, who was completely exhausted. The horse came and stood over him till he was sufficiently rested to ride to the main-land. It is unnecessary to say that the owner's attachment to his horse was stronger than that he had for his human companions, for the horse showed an affection which they did not, and when, at the squatter riot in Sacramento, Charley was killed in the fight, his death caused his owner a pang of regret greater than did the bullet that passed through his own body.

The incidents of this overland journey are not, for the most part, germane to the main subject of this book ; but the Land or Squatter Riots of Sacramento are worth describing here, both because the truth about them has never been publicly told, and because this conflict in California was a prototype of the later conflict in Kansas, having many points of resemblance, and having been prosecuted by similar, and some of the same, characters.

After a journey of some three months, fragments of the Boston party began to arrive in California, and a small detachment, including Dr. Robinson, stopped on Bear Creek for the purpose of washing out the precious metal. After some two weeks, Sacramento City was visited for supplies. Here, at the junction of the Sacramento and American rivers, seemed to be the head of navigation for shipping of all kinds, and a prosperous town was destined to grow up. Meals, consisting of meat and bread, were selling at from seventy-five cents to one dollar and a half each, and lodgings in proportion. It was apparent that more gold could be procured at Sacramento at such prices than on Bear Creek, and a partnership was soon formed and an eating-house opened. As mining at this time was confined to the bars in the creeks and rivers, as soon as the rainy season set in these bars were covered with water, and the miners sought the towns for winter quarters. During this season, in 1849, in the absence of vegetables and variety of food, many emigrants were on the sick list, and had to be cared for by the more fortunate or suffer and die alone in their tents or cabins. These tents, shanties, and cabins, were scattered over the unoccupied lands in and around Sacramento, and the proprietors of the Boston party eating-house furnished both food and medicine to many of these unfortunates. In the midst of this rainy season three men, including the Doctor, were passing along the levee between the Slough near I street and the river, when they met a pretended sheriff and posse well charged with whiskey. Curiosity caused the three men to stop and watch proceedings. The posse went directly to a structure of logs and canvas, where was a sick man who had been fed and nursed by the Doctor for several days. This man was ruthlessly hauled from his shelter, and the logs and canvas leveled with the ground. One of the three watchers exclaimed, "That is a damned outrage," and the others joined in the exclamation. It was then and there the movement commenced that culminated in the squatter riot of the next year. These three men, entire strangers to each other, resolved that such proceeding should be reported to the people. Accordingly, it was decided to advertise a meeting to be held on the levee in front of a ship's galley lying near I street. A cord of wood was procured to furnish light, and "dodgers" about six inches square were printed and posted all over the place, on wagons, mules, and things movable and immovable. It was decided that the oldest of the three men should preside at the meeting, and that the Doctor should prepare and present resolutions. The time for the meeting came, and with it apparently the entire population of the city. The cord of wood was set on fire and the older man mounted the galley as president of the meeting. He was small in stature and small in voice, and seemed incapable of preserving order. The speculators and their friends monopolized the speech-making till the Doctor, who was unaccustomed to public speaking, found that modesty must be ignored or the squatters' cause would be lost. After several speculators had spoken he made his way to the stand, and prefaced his resolution with an account of the situation and a statement of what he had witnessed. He then read the following preamble and resolution:

" Whereas, the land in California is presumed to be public land, therefore,
" *Resolved*, That we will protect any settler in the possession of land to the extent of one lot in the city, and one hundred and sixty acres in the country, till a valid title shall be shown for it."

This resolution was received with great enthusiasm. The crowd, which had listened to the speculators' harangues in silence, now went wild with excitement. No one could doubt the direction of the wind now, and men in abundance were found ready to endorse the resolution. This was the first move, and this the platform that remained the platform throughout the conflict. Before adjourning, steps were taken for a permanent organization, of which the Doctor was chosen president. Was there occasion or excuse for this movement? California had been acquired from Mexico by treaty, which respected all previous acts of the Mexican government relative to the occupying and ownership of the land. Under Mexican rule, governors of provinces, mayors of cities, and justices of the peace were authorized to issue grants of land subject to approval by the general government. In this way numerous grants had been made by the Governor of California, and one of eleven leagues to Captain Sutter. These grants were often loosely defined, and the boundaries could be made to cover many times the amount called for in the grant. At this time, when the squatters were organized, no grant to Captain Sutter had been seen by any one, and the boundaries were unknown, but title was claimed under it from the Three Peaks, some seventy miles north of Sacramento, to some unknown distance south of the town. It also extended from the "rivers to the ends of the earth," so far as known, east and west. No man could settle upon any part of this vast tract without being assailed by some pretended claimant under Sutter. Captain Sutter was a genial, generous old gentleman from Sweden, and, on account of his early settlement, was an important character, socially and otherwise. He was made much of, and of course must be treated to some drink by each new visitor. As it would be uncivil to decline one unless all were declined, and as he was not a teetotaler, he must drink with everybody. As he was unequal to the task of drinking everybody drunk in detail, everybody was sure to drink him drunk on every visit to the city. When in this condition he was very generous, and would sign almost any paper presented to him. In this way deeds were obtained at will by the unscrupulous speculators till the whole northern part of the State seemingly had been covered. Josiah Royce, in the *Overland Monthly* for September, 1885, on page 227, says:

"In 1848, when the gold-seekers began to come, Sutter began to lose his wits. One of the pioneer statements in Mr. Bancroft's collection says rather severely that the distinguished Captain thenceforth signed 'any paper that was brought to him.' At all events, he behaved in as unbusiness-like a fashion as could well be expected, and the result was that when his affairs came in later years to more complete settlement, it was found that he had deeded away, not merely more land than he actually owned, but, if I mistake not, more land than even he himself had supposed himself to own. All this led not only himself into embarrassments, but other people with him; and to arrange with justice the final survey of his Alvarado grant proved in later years one of the most perplexing problems of the United States District and Supreme Courts."

At this time California was not admitted into the Union, and there was no law except the old Mexican code that was recognized by the United States. The Mexican local law was ignored, as no officers existed to enforce it. A constitution had been adopted and so-called laws made under it, and it was such laws as these that were resorted to by the speculators to eject settlers from all northern California, claimed to be covered by Sutter's grant. At first no pretense of legal process was deemed necessary. The poor settler, who had erected his shanty or tent on some unoccupied land, would be visited by some person who would demand possession, purchase-money, or blackmail. Many who wanted no trouble would leave without further notice. But such as failed to heed the warning would soon be visited by the pretended sheriff and posse. He would make quick work and oust the intruder. The squatters' organization, when completed, played havoc with such ejectments. Either the president or some member of that association would happen at the place of ejectment and seriously interfere with the programme. The speculators, finding this game blocked, concluded to send for the Sutter title, in accordance with the demand of the squatters' platform. A certified copy was procured from the archives of Mexico and read to a large meeting called for the purpose of hearing it. But, unfortunately for the speculators, the boundaries of this pretended grant were fatally defective. The third and fourth sections of this grant read as follows:

" 3d. The land of which donation is made to him is of the extent of eleven *sitios da gauado major*, as exhibited in the sketch annexed to the proceedings, without including the lands overflowed by the swelling and current of the rivers. It is bounded on the north by *los Tres Picas* (three summits) and the 39° 41' 45" of north latitude; on the east by the borders of the *Rio de las Plumas* (Feather River); on the south by the parallel 38° 49' 32" of north latitude; and on the west by the river Sacramento.

" 4th. When this property shall be confirmed unto him, he shall petition the proper judge to give him possession of the land, in order that it may be measured, agreeably to ordinance, the surplus thereof remaining for the benefit of the nation, for convenient purposes. Therefore I order that this title being held as firm and valid, that the same be entered in the proper book, and that these proceedings be transmitted to the excellent Departmental Assembly."

Here are natural boundaries which would seem conclusive. On the north by the Three Peaks, about sixty or seventy miles north of Sacramento, on the east by the Feather River, on the west by the Sacramento River, and on the south by a parallel of latitude near the junction of those rivers, about twenty miles north of Sacramento. Besides, it expressly excludes land overflowed by the rivers, and Sacramento was under from two to six feet of water for four or six weeks. This document, of course, confirmed the squatters in their determination to stand by each other. But the fight was not abandoned by the speculators. Although they had no law or equity on their side, they proposed to rely upon a pretense of law, or the legal machine. They evidently supposed that squatters would know no difference between pretense and reality, and proceeded accordingly. As a posse with nothing behind it would work no longer, something else must be tried. The first agency appealed to was the City Council, in December, 1849. An ordinance was passed directing certain improvements to be removed from city lots occupied by squatters, says the Sacramento Directory of 1853, and a posse of several hundred men under the city marshal started out on their mission. The president of the squatters' association, however, met them at their first job, and informed them that

their authority to meddle with private' property was not
recognized by his association, and if they touched that
property they must kill at least one person then and have a
reckoning with the whole squatters' association afterwards.
This was more than had been expected, and, although the
little deputy marshal, who was charged to the muzzle with
whiskey, cried "Shoot the scoundrel," no shooting was done,
and the marshal with his posse retired to report to headquarters. Finding that this *form* of law wouldn't frighten
squatters and blood must be shed, some more impressive
form must be invented. This was easily done. The State
Legislature, so called, although no recognition of the State
had been made by Congress, passed an act concerning forcible entry and detainer, with the express purpose of meeting
the difficulty of settling possession without passing upon title
in a United States court. As the justice could have no
jurisdiction where the question of title was raised, the squatters repudiated this form of law, as in every case the squatter
was in peaceable possession, and no right to possession in
the claimant could be shown except by offsetting actual possession with title. This was accordingly done, notwithstanding the protests of the settlers. Sutter's title was pleaded in
every case, decided valid, and judgment rendered against
the squatter. He could appeal to the Probate Court by
giving bonds for the satisfaction of the judgment. Also the
bondsmen must be land-holders. No others would be taken.
In the spring the president was absent several weeks in the
mines, seeking a proper site for a sawmill, shipped around
the Horn by his brother. During his absence the speculators were very busy with suits, ordinances, and organizations. Mr. Royce, on page 238 of the *Overland Monthly*,
describes the situation as follows:

" To this act [Forcible Entry and Detainer] some of the land-owners
of Sacramento now appealed for help. Moreover, as they were in
control of the city council, they proceeded to pass, amid the furious
protests of the squatters, a municipal ordinance, forbidding any one to

erect tents, or shanties, or houses, or to heap lumber or other encumbrances, upon any vacant lot belonging to a private person, or upon any public street. The land-owners also formed a ' Law and Order Association,' and printed in the papers a notice of their intention to defend to the last their property under the Sutter title. They began to drill companies of militia. A few personal encounters took place in various vacant lots, where owners tried to prevent the erection of fences or shanties. Various processes were served upon squatters, and executed. The squatter association itself plainly suffered a good deal from the internal jealousies or from the mutual indifference of its members. Only the ardor of Dr. Robinson prevented an utter failure of its organization long before the crisis. In the latter part of June, and for some time in July, the movement fell into the background of public attention."

On his return, in July, the Doctor found great discouragement among the squatters. Suits were innumerable, and bondsmen were used up. The speculators would try no appealed case, that a legal decision might be reached in a United States court, but evidently intended to worry out the squatters in the justice courts. Under these circumstances bondsmen must be had or this line of defense abandoned. Noticing that the squatters who offered themselves as bail uniformly claimed that, although land-holders, their title was a squatter's title, a new move was made. The Doctor staked off several blocks of land in the outskirts of the city, put a large tent upon them and moved in. At the next trial he offered himself as bail. Being questioned as to his title, he simply said it was as good as there was in the city. After a long time spent in trying in vain to get from him that his title was a squatter's title, the prosecutor objected. But the justice said the bondsman claimed as good a title as there was in the city, and, as he could not try titles, he must accept the claim. On being questioned as to the value of the land, it was placed at $100,000. This put an end to justices' trials, as it was found bail could be given indefinitely. Next came a trial of an appealed case before Judge Willis, the Probate judge. This case, of course, was decided against the squatters, and an appeal asked to the District

Court, hoping to get from that court to a United States court. An appeal was denied, however, and the crisis forced. It was now evident, if the squatters acquiesced in this proceeding and allowed ejectment to be had under the circumstances, their fight was ended. But this issue was foreseen from the first, and some were ready to meet it, but not many. In the Sacramento Directory for 1853, this case is given as follows:

" The defendant appealed from this decision to the County Court, and on the 8th of August, 1850, the case came for hearing before Judge Willis, of the above tribunal. The defendant at this trial was assisted by McKune, Tweed, and Aldrich. Defendants moved for a nonsuit, on the ground that the Recorder's Court had no jurisdiction over the case. The plea was taken into consideration, but by the consent of the parties the case was submitted upon its merits. The claim of title from Sutter being offered by plaintiffs, defendant objected, and the objection was taken under advisement, which resulted in the court overruling the objection. The case was then argued, and the following day judgment was rendered, sustaining the decision of the inferior court.

" The defendant then asked to appeal to the Supreme Court, but there being no law at that time to sustain the appeal, the motion was overruled. During the proceedings of this trial both parties became excited to the utmost degree, and the squatters as a body declared against the restoration of the property pursuant to the judgment of the courts."

What occurred after the decision is thus described in the *Overland Monthly*, page 240:

" They rushed from the court to excited meetings outside, and spread abroad the news that Judge Willis had not only decided against them, but had decided that from him there was no appeal. Woe to such laws and to such judges! The law betrays us. We will appeal to the Higher Law. The processes of the courts shall not be served.

" Dr. Robinson was not unequal to the emergency. At once he sent out notices, calling a mass meeting of ' squatters and others interested,' to take place the same evening, August 10th. It was Saturday, and when night came a large crowd of squatters, of land-owners, and of idlers had gathered. The traditional leisure of Saturday night made a great part of the assembly as cheerful as it was eager for novelty and interested in this affair. Great numbers were there simply to see fair play; and this general public, in their characteristically American good humor, were quite unwilling to recognize any sort of seriousness in the occasion. These jolly on-lookers interrupted the squatter orators, called for E. J. C. Kewen and Sam Brannan as representatives of the land-owners, listened to them a while, interrupted them when the thing grew tedious, and enjoyed the utter confusion that for the time reigned on the platform. At length the crowd were ready for Dr. Robinson and his inevitable resolutions. He, for his part, was serious enough. He had been a moderate man, he said, but the time for moderation was past. He was ready to have his corpse left on his own bit of land, ere he would yield his rights. Then he read his resolutions, which suffi-ciently denounced Judge Willis and the laws; and thereafter he called for the sense of the meeting. Dissenting voices rang out, but the reso-lutions received a loud affirmative vote, and were declared carried. The regular business of the meeting was now done; but for a long time yet various ambitious speakers mounted the platform and sought to address the crowd, which amused itself by roaring at them, or by watching them pushed from their high place.

" Next day Dr. Robinson was early at work, drawing up in his own way a manifesto to express the sense of his party. It was a very able and reckless document. Robinson had found an unanswerable fashion of stating the ground for devotion to the Higher Law, as op-posed to State law."

The following is substantially the manifesto issued :

" TO THE PEOPLE OF SACRAMENTO CITY.

" It is well known that a few individuals have seized upon nearly all the arable public lands in this county, and the following are some of the means they have resorted to, in order to retain the property thus taken :

" First. They have used brute force and torn down the buildings of the settlers, and driven them from their homes by riotous mobs.

" Second. They have used threats of violence, even to the taking of life, if the occupant or settler persisted in defending his property, and thus extorted from the timid their rightful possessions.

" Third. They have passed or procured the passage of certain rules in the so-called Legislature of California, for the purpose, as their attor-neys affirm, of protecting themselves and removing the settlers from the land they may occupy whether right or wrong—thus settling the ques-tion of title in an *assumed legislative* body, which question can alone be settled by the Supreme Government of the United States.

" Fourth. Under said legislative regulations, by them called *laws*, they have continually harassed the settler with suits, and in many in-stances compelled him to abandon his home for want of the means to pay the costs of their courts. Many others have paid these costs with the hope of carrying their cause through these so-called courts to the proper tribunal for final decision, viz.: the Supreme Court of the United States.

" But these hopes were vain, for Judge Willis, so-called, has decided that from *his decision* there is *no appeal.*

" And now, inasmuch as the so-called Legislature is not recognized by Congress, and their rules and regulations not approved, and are therefore of no binding force upon the citizens of the United States, but simply *advisory*, and inasmuch as the so-called law of 'Forcible Entry and Detainer,' if passed for the purpose affirmed by their council, namely, to drive off settlers, with or without title, is unconstitutional, and would be in any State; the people in this community called settlers, and others who are friends of justice and humanity, in consideration of the above, have determined to disregard all decisions of our courts in land cases and all summonses or executions by the sheriff, constable, or other officer of the present county or city touching this matter. They will regard the said officers as private citizens, as in the eyes of the Constitution they are, and hold them accountable accordingly. And, moreover, if there is no other appeal from Judge Willis, the settlers and others, on the first show of violence to their persons or property, either by the sheriff or other person, under color of any execution or writ of restitution, based on any judgment or decree of any court in this county, in an action to recover possession of land, have *deliberately resolved to appeal to arms* and protect their sacred rights, if need be, with their lives.

" Should such be rendered necessary by the acts of the sheriff or others, the settlers will be governed by martial law. All property, and the persons of such as do not engage in the contest, will be sacredly regarded and protected by them, whether land-holders or otherwise, but the property and lives of those who take the field against them will share the fate of war."

As it was understood that the sheriff would take possession of the property in dispute on Monday morning, several squatters were on hand to protect it. The situation and spirit of the movement is described in a letter found in the Doctor's tent, and published in the papers of the day. It is as follows:

" August 12, 1850.—Although I have written one letter, yet, as I have been called upon by circumstances to remain in town, and as I have a little leisure, I will talk with you a little, *my dear* S. Since writing you, we have seen much and experienced much of a serious and important character, as well as much of excitement. The county judge, before whom our cases were brought, decided against us, and on Saturday morning declared that from his decision there should be *no appeal.* The squatters immediately collected on the ground in dispute, and posted, on large bills, the following: 'OUTRAGE !!! Shall Judge Willis be dictator ? Squatters, and all other republicans, are invited to meet on the Levee this evening, to hear the details.' It was responded to by both parties, and the speculators, as aforetime, attempted to talk against time, etc. On the passage of a series of resolutions presented by your humble servant, there were about three ayes to one nay, although the *Transcript* said they were about equal. Sunday morning I drew up a *manifesto*—carried it with me to the church—paid one dollar for preaching—helped them sing—showed it to a lawyer to see if my position was correct, *legally*, and procured the printing of it in handbills and in the paper, after presenting it to a private meeting of citizens for their approval, which I addressed at some length. After a long talk for the purpose of consoling a gentleman just in from the plains, and who the' day before had buried his wife, whom he loved most tenderly, and a few days previous to that had lost his son, I threw myself upon my blankets and ' anxiously thought of the morrow.'

" What will be the result ? Shall I be borne out in my position? On whom can I depend ? How many of those who are squatters will come out if there is a prospect of a fight ? Will the sheriff take possession, as he has promised, before 10 o'clock A.M.? How many speculators will fight ? Have I distinctly defined our position in the bill ? Will the world, the universe and God say it is just ?—etc., etc., etc. Will you call me rash if I tell you that I took these steps to this point when I could get but twenty-five men to pledge themselves on paper to sustain me, and many of them, I felt, were timid ? Such was the case.

" This morning I was early on my feet, silently and quietly visiting my friends, collecting arms, etc. Our manifesto appeared in the paper and in bills early, and the whole town is aroused. Nothing is thought or talked of but war. About two hundred men assembled on the disputed territory, and most of them sympathized with us. A few, however, were spies. We chose our commander, and enrolled such as were willing and ready to lay down their lives, if need be, in the cause. About fifty names could be obtained. I managed, by speeches, business, etc., to keep the spectators and fighters mingled in a mass, all unarmed, so as to let no one know but all were men of *valor*, and ready to fight. While thus engaged, the mayor appeared and addressed us from his saddle—not *ordering* us to disperse, but *advising* us to do so. I replied, most respectfully, that we were assembled to injure no one, and to assail no one who left us alone. We were on our own property, with no hostile intention while unmolested. After he left I, with others, was appointed a committee to wait upon him at his office, and state distinctly our positions, etc., so that there could be no possibility of mistake. He said he should use his influence as an individual to keep any one from destroying our property, and told us the sheriff had just told him that the executions from the court had been postponed. We returned, and after reporting, and making some further arrangement for another meeting if necessary, we adjourned. I told the mayor we should not remain together if no attempt was to be made to execute their warrants, but I told him if in the meantime a sheriff or any other person molested a squatter, we should hold him responsible, according to our proclamation. From this position we could not be driven, although we knew it was in violation of the regulations of the State. We were prepared to abide the result.

"It is said that a writ is made out for my arrest, as a rebel, etc. If so, it will not probably be served at present."

No sooner had the squatters left the property in dispute, than the sheriff, contrary to the assurances given by the mayor, appeared, removed the furniture and property of the owner, and placed a keeper in charge. Also he arrested some of the squatters and placed them on the prison ship. Thus another step had been taken. If the premises should be permitted to remain with the officers, the speculators would be victorious, as all other cases would take the same course. But, should the squatters retake this property in defiance of the so-called officer, nothing would be gained by the suit. It would have to be tried over again, *de novo*, as the lawyers say, or the squatters tried for contempt of court. As these courts, like the justice of the peace who fined a man in the street for contempt, were all and at all times objects of contempt, they would not be likely to resort to this remedy. But something must be done. It was now the squatters' turn to act. Leading squatters avoided arrest during the day, and a meeting was held at the Doctor's tent at night. Here the situation was fully discussed and a plan of procedure adopted. All were to meet early the next morning under an oak tree in the outskirts of the city and march to the disputed property and retake it. Maloney, a soldier in the Mexican war, was to be military leader. To avoid arrest, he and the Doctor went some six miles into the country and stopped over night at Maloney's claim. Early in the morning the two rode to the place of rendezvous, but found not a solitary squatter. They immediately started out to rally their forces. Evidently the courage that manifested itself so defiantly at squatter meetings, with no enemy in sight, had all oozed out of these brave men. Some of the loudest, and apparently the boldest, were found in bed trembling like aspen leaves. At length, after a search of some four or five hours, fifteen men, all told, were mustered. These were drilled for a short time by Captain Maloney before starting on their errand. The martial spirit took possession of Maloney and he wanted to ride the Doctor's cream-colored horse. A gentleman just in from crossing the plains, sympathized with the movement, and lent the Doctor his Colt's six-shooter rifle. The only swearing in was an oath to obey orders of the commander, or be shot as a penalty. Thus, after devoting the afternoon of one day and nearly the whole night, and the forenoon of the next day, an army of fifteen men, armed and equipped, was ready to carry into effect the resolution adopted soon after the sick man was dragged from his shelter and left exposed to the elements, eight months before. When the order was given, " Forward, march ! " it was high noon of a very hot day. The squatter army of fourteen men and one commander marched in a solid column, seven abreast, down N street, with all the circumstance of grim-visaged war. The house of A. M. Winn, former president of the City Council, was on the line of march, and, unfortunately, Captain Maloney had a bitter grudge against this ex-president. As the house was approached, Maloney turned upon his horse and said he would order this house destroyed. The Doctor at once denounced such a proceeding as fatal to the success of the squatter movement. The Captain apparently abandoned his purpose, but, when directly opposite the house, he turned again and

4

said, " We will never have a better time," and was about to
give his order. The Doctor sprang forward, rifle in hand,
and told him if he opened his mouth to order the destruction
of that property he would blow his brains out. This seemed
to stagger the Captain. Here was a private in the ranks
who, not fifteen minutes before, had taken an oath to obey
his orders or be shot, now, coming forward, rifle in hand,
and threatening to blow his brains out if he issued an order.
But he apparently made a merit of necessity and again
moved on, saying he would give the order when he came
back. At this exhibition of lack of comprehension of the
issue involved, and the work to be done, the Doctor was
greatly disturbed. To act on the defensive in protecting the
houses of peaceable settlers against the most arrogant usurpation and oppression was one thing, but to take the offensive,
destroy private property, where a school was in session, and
which was in no way connected with questions involved,
was quite another. In the first case the sympathies of all
good people would be enlisted, while in the second men and
women of all classes would unite to put down the vandals.
Evidently, this Maloney did not see, or, if he saw it, his
passions upset his judgment.

At length the house in controversy was reached, at the
corner of N and Second streets. The keeper placed in
charge by the sheriff was absent, and nothing remained to
do but take formal possession and replace the furniture and
property in the house where it belonged. Fearing Maloney
would be uncontrollable if he should return by the ex-president's house, the Doctor advised that a lot on I street should
be visited, where some lumber had been deposited from a
vessel without consulting the squatter claimant. This would
take the squatters out of town by another route. I street
was accordingly visited, but, as the owner of the lumber had
no designs upon the lot, nothing was to be done. Soon
after the march was commenced, the sheriff and mayor
could be seen on horseback galloping in every direction to

rally their friends to the rescue. As laboring people were released from work for dinner, many of them from curiosity joined the procession, which, by the time I street was reached was numbered by the thousand. Some were armed with rifles and shot-guns, and more with revolvers. The squatters marched and carried themselves like veterans, never breaking ranks or being disconcerted by the immense crowd at their heels.

As nothing was to be done at the lot on I street, Maloney was requested to march out of town on that street, as it was but thinly settled, and no disturbances would be likely to occur. He marched up I street to Third, when, to the amazement of the Doctor, he turned and passed to J street, the business street of the town. This was the home of the saloons, gambling-houses, and rabble, as well as the business places. Now the crowd of followers was increased immensely, and composed of the most desperate characters as well as of the curiosity-seekers. The march was up J street to Fourth, where a turn was made to the south. The squatters had but just turned the corner of J street and Fourth, when a shout was raised and the mayor, sheriff, and their adherents opened fire, doubtless contemplating a stampede of the army of fifteen. But on the instant Maloney gave the order to face about and fire. No one objected to this order, and it was promptly obeyed. No sooner was the fire of the mayor's crowd returned than all fled in hot haste. In less time than it takes to record it, the space was cleared in front of the squatters. As the mayor was on horseback, he was a shining mark, and was badly wounded, losing one arm. The city auditor, who had been very prominent and offensive, was killed. One squatter also was killed in the first encounter. After the crowd had fled, and while the squatters were still in line, one man, named Harper, passed up J street, and when opposite the Doctor, he suddenly stopped and fired his revolver, the ball passing through the Doctor's body two inches below the heart. The Doctor then raised his rifle and returned the fire, the ball striking the breast-bone of Harper and glancing off without entering the body. The next the Doctor knew, after firing at Harper, he found himself upon the ground. How he got there, or how long he had been there, he had no knowledge. On looking about, he could see no human being, either squatter, speculator, or spectator, and being thirsty, he crawled slowly into an eating-house opposite where he lay. The inmates were timid, and at first afraid to furnish the water craved. Soon, however, some physicians made their appearance, and he was placed upon a cot and well cared for. While in this position, rapid firing was heard in the street or alley near by, of short duration. It was soon reported that Captain Maloney and his horse were killed. It was afterwards learned that when all opponents had fled, the squatters quietly separated, each going his own way, and while Maloney was riding along the street the sheriff galloped up and denounced him in most ungallant terms. Maloney, although armed with no weapon except a saber, while the sheriff was loaded down with revolvers, turned and pursued his assailant, who led into a crowd of speculators well armed. They at once opened fire, killing the horse, and planting eighteen bullets in Maloney's body. Soon after the accomplishment of this heroic deed, this pretended sheriff, covered with sweat and glory, made his appearance at the eating-house to arrest the Doctor and take him to the prison ship. As at this time his wound was supposed to be mortal, and there being no pulsation at the wrist the end might be near, the physicians demurred and made the little dignitary wait. However, reaction came on, the pulse at the wrist returned, and in about three hours from the time of the encounter the Doctor was removed to the prison ship. As he was carried on the cot the whole city seemed to be on some of the streets through which he passed. Sidewalks, verandas, roofs, and everything that could hold a human being seemed to be in requisition. Not a word was uttered in the hearing of the prisoner, and there was an anxious silence that could be felt. On reaching the prison ship his brother, who had accompanied him thus far, was turned away, and the prisoner was placed in the forecastle. The only other occupant was a violently insane foreigner who muttered in an unknown language, beating the sides of the vessel with his head and otherwise most of the time. Here the prisoner was left until late the next morning, evidently with no expectation on the part of the officials of any other trouble than that of a burial.

The effect upon the town of this encounter is thus described by Mr. Royce, in *Overland Monthly*, page 243 :

" Like a lightning flash the battle came and was done. The array of the squatters melted away like a mist when the two leaders were seen to fall ; the confused mass of the citizens, shocked and awe-stricken when they were not terrified, waited no longer on the field than others, but scattered wildly. A few moments later, when Dr. Stillman returned with his shot-gun, which, on the first firing, he had gone but half a block to get, the street was quite empty of armed men. He waited for some time to see any one in authority. At length Lieutenant-Governor McDougal appeared, riding at full speed, ' his face very pale.'

" ' Get all the armed men you can,' he said, ' and rendezvous at Fowler's hotel.'

" ' I went to the place designated,' says Dr. Stillman, ' and there found a few men, who had got an old iron ship's gun, mounted on a wooden truck ; to its axles was fastened a long dray pole. The gun was loaded with a lot of scrap iron. I wanted to know where Mc-Dougal was ; we expected him to take the command and die with us. I inquired of Mrs. McDougal, who was stopping at the hotel, what had become of her husband. She said he had gone to San Francisco for assistance. Indeed, he was on his way to the steamer *Senator* when I saw him, and he left his horse on the bank of the river.'

" In such swift, dream-like transformations the experiences of the rest of the day passed by. Rumors were countless. The squatters had gone out of the city ; they would soon return. They were seven hundred strong. They meant vengeance. They would fire the city. Yes, they already had fired the city, although nobody knew where. No one could foresee the end of the struggle. The city had been declared under martial law. Everybody must come out. The whole force of the State would doubtless be needed. If the squatters failed now, they would go to the mines, and arouse the whole population there. One would have to fight all the miners as well. Such things flew from mouth to mouth; such reports the *Senator* carried to San Francisco, with the pale-faced Lieutenant-Governor."

When the speculators found that the squatters proposed to live up to their manifesto, and act only on the defensive, the panic began to subside. But some thought it a good opportunity to make an end of squatters and squatterism altogether. The military leader had been riddled with bullets, and the civil leader was mortally wounded in the hold of the prison ship. Who now would dare stand out against the Sutter grant? The daily papers were filled with glorification over the situation, and various officials and others were brevetted for wonderful deeds of valor. Especially was the little red-headed sheriff a marvel as a strategist and hero-general. These panegyrics were too much for so small a man, and he began to thirst for more blood and glory. The second day he rallied a posse and started into the country, some seven or eight miles, to arrest "old man Allen," as he was called. This man was a stalwart squatter, over six feet in height, from Missouri. He had a claim that somebody wanted, and he must go. It is true he was some seven or eight miles from the Sacramento River, and Sutter's grant was but one league wide, but that was immaterial; his grant was as valid in one place as another if a claim was made under it. On arriving at its destination, the sheriff's posse was divided into three squads, one for the front and one for each end of the house, while the rear was covered by the American River. The bold sheriff commanded the front squad, and marched up to the front door. When Allen, who was caring for his sick wife, who died in the *mêlée*, came to the door, his surrender was demanded. But he understood this game, and surrendered the contents of his shot-gun instead of himself. This quieted this brave officer effectually, and the posse took him back to town. Several shots were fired at Allen, but he escaped into the American River in the rear of his house. Two men in the house were

killed. When the posse left, Allen left his hiding-place and
went to the mines. On the return of this posse with the
dead body of its leader, the music was pitched in a new key.
The city, which, according to Mr. Royce, " was never safer,
as a whole, than a few hours after the fatal meeting at the
corner of Fourth and J streets," was again all excitement.
This same writer, on page 245, says:

" The city was not reassured by the news of the sheriff's death. In
the unlighted streets of the frightened place, the alarm was sounded by
the returning party about nine o'clock. Of course, invasion and fire
were expected. The militia companies turned out, detailed patrolling
parties, and then ordered the streets cleared. The danger was imminent that the defenders of the law would pass the night in shooting one
another by mistake in the darkness ; but this was happily avoided. The
families in the town were, of course, terribly excited. ' The ladies,'
says Dr. Stillman, ' were nearly frightened out of their wits ; but we
assured them that they had nothing to fear—that we were devoted
to their service, and were ready to die at their feet. Being thus assured, they all retired into their cozy little cottages, and securely bolted
the doors.' Morning came, bringing with it the steamer from San
Francisco. Lieutenant-Governor McDougal was on board. He felt
seriously the responsibilities of his position, and accordingly went to
bed, sick with the cares of office. In the city Sam Brannan and others
talked mightily of law, order, and blood. There were, however, no
more battles to fight. In a few days, quiet was restored ; people were
ashamed of their alarm. Squatters confined themselves to meeting in
the mining districts and in Marysville, to savage manifestoes, and to
wordy war from a distance, with sullen submission near home. The
real war was done. A tacit consent to drop the subject was soon noticeable in the community. Men said that the law must be enforced,
and meanwhile determined to speak no ill of the dead. There was a
decided sense, also, of common guilt. The community had sinned and
suffered. And soon the cholera, and then the winter, ' closed the
autumn scene.' "

The reader will notice a wonderful change in this extract
from the mighty talk of " law, order, and blood," by Brannan
and others, to the statement that immediately followed,
namely : " There were, however, no more battles to fight.
In a few days quiet was restored. * * * A tacit consent to drop the subject was soon noticeable in the com-

munity." But why was the subject dropped? This seems
to be a most lame and impotent conclusion of a great war
in which the speculators, according to this and other writers,
were victorious. The reasons for this sudden termination
of hostilities and apparent change of front, the speculators
and their defenders do not care to give, and they cannot be
censured for the omission. But they should be given for
the benefit of the historian. After the dead sheriff was
brought into town, the keeper of the prison ship visited his
squatter prisoner and reported what had happened. He
said the sheriff went out to arrest "old man Allen," and the
latter shot him dead. He seemed much excited and exasperated that any man should have the temerity to defend
himself in that way. The prisoner ventured to inquire after
the squatters. "Where were they and what were they doing?" "Squatters," said the keeper, "they are annihilated,
or will be as fast as found." This reply caused an invisible
and incredulous smile on the part of the prisoner, but nothing more was said.

About the second night after this transaction, the keeper
again visited his prisoner, still greatly excited, but in another
way. He now came to ask a favor. He said word had
come from the mines that the miners had resolved to visit
Sacramento, rescue the prisoners, and sack the town, if
another squatter was disturbed or the prisoners were ill-
treated. To prevent any further trouble, would the prisoner
be so kind as to authorize him to send word to the miners
that he, the prisoner, did not want to be rescued. This
would quiet the town, which was very much excited. The
prisoner said, while he had no desire for a rescue, he had no
word to send to the miners or other parties. They must act
as they thought best. Here was a new song, with a very
different tune from the one sung two nights before. It was
afterwards reported that old man Allen reached a mining
camp the next day, after killing the sheriff, while the miners
were at dinner. He was hatless and coatless, and covered

with mud and blood from head to foot. In this plight he told the story of the squatter riot and of his encounter with the sheriff. It is needless to say that here was the inspiration for the resolution to destroy the town if such proceedings did not cease. Two men were sent as spies from the speculators to see if Allen could be arrested. Naturally, their report was unfavorable.

Also, the visiting militia may have had something to do with the sudden change in the atmosphere at Sacramento. The company that came up from San Francisco called in a body upon the prisoner, in his forecastle, and after standing about the cot for a few moments, an officer whispered in the ear of the prisoner that he and his friends had nothing to fear from them, as they had investigated the matter and approved of the course the squatters had taken. Under all the circumstances, it is not surprising that "a tacit consent to drop the subject was soon noticeable in the community," and that there was also "a decided sense of common guilt" on the part of the speculators. Mr. Royce says, while there were meetings and manifestoes in the mines, "there was sullen submission near home." The platform of the squatters from first to last was protection to the occupant of land in possession of the same till title should be shown, and when all opposition to this possession ceased the war was over. As soon as all attempts ceased to get possession of land under forcible entry and detainer laws, and bogus acts of bogus city councils, there was nothing more to be done. The squatters had obtained all they ever demanded.

In order to make it appear that the speculators gained a great victory, and the squatters suffered a corresponding defeat, writers have deemed it necessary to misstate the issue. Instead of being the simple preamble and resolution adopted at the first squatters' meeting, namely, "Whereas the land in California is presumed to be public land, therefore, resolved, that we will protect any settler in the possession of land to the extent of one lot in the city and one hundred and sixty acres in the country, till a valid title shall be shown for it," the writers would make it appear that the squatters were agrarians, transcendentalists, higher-law men, and impracticable visionaries. A few quotations from Mr. Royce, in *Overland Monthly*, will illustrate the general method of treating the issue:

" Providence is known to be opposed to every form of oppression; and grabbing eleven leagues of land is a great oppression. And so the worthlessness of Mexican land titles is evident.

" Of course, the squatters would have disclaimed very generally so naked a statement as this of their position. But when we read in one squatter's card that ' surely Sutter's grant does not entitle to a monopoly of all the lands in California, which were purchased by the treasure of the whole nation, and by no small amount of the best blood that ever coursed or ran through American veins,' the same writer's formal assurance that Sutter ought to have his eleven leagues whenever they can be found and duly surveyed cannot blind us to the true spirit of the argument. What has this ' best blood ' to do with the Sutter grant ? The connection in the writer's mind is only too obvious. He means that the ' best blood ' won for us a right to harass great land-owners. In another of these expressions of squatter opinion I have found the assertion that the land speculators stand on a supposed old Mexican legal right of such as themselves to take up the whole territory of California, in sections of eleven leagues each, by some sort of Mexican preemption. If a squatter persists in understanding the land-owner's position in this way, his contempt for it is as natural as his wilful determination to make game of all native Californian claims is obvious. * * * A member, who has already been quoted, wrote to the *Placer Times* that, ' with the Sutter men there has been and is now money and power, and some of them are improving every opportunity to trouble and oppress the *peaceable, hard-working, order-loving*, and law-abiding settler, which, in the absence of the mass of the people in the mines they do with comparative impunity.' The italics are his own. The letter concluded with an assurance that the settlers were organized to maintain what ' country, nature, and God' had given to them. The mention of the ' absence of the people in the mines ' is very characteristic of the purposes of the squatters ; and the reference to ' country, nature, and God' illustrates once more the spirit of the movement. * * * The movement was plainly an agrarian and ultra-American movement, opposed to all great land-owners, and especially to all these Mexican grantees.

" The appeal quoted above, to ' nature, country, and God,' is also, as

I have said, characteristic of the spirit of the movement. The writer of the letter in question is very probably no other than the distinguished squatter leader, Dr. Charles Robinson himself, a man to whom the movement seems to have owed nearly all its ability. And when we speak of Dr. Robinson, we have to do with no insignificant demagogue or unprincipled advocate of wickedness, but with a high-minded and conscientious man, who chanced just then to be in the devil's service, but who served the devil honestly, thoughtfully, and, so far as he could, dutifully, believing him to be an angel of light. This future Free-Soil Governor of Kansas, this cautious, clear-headed, and vigorous anti-slavery champion of the troublous days before the war, who has since survived so many bitter quarrels with old foes and old friends, to enjoy, now at last, his peaceful age at his home in Lawrence, Kansas, is not a man of whom one may speak with contempt, however serious his error in Sacramento may seem. He was a proper hero for this tragic comedy, and ' nature, country, and God ' were his guiding ideals. Only you must understand the character that these slightly vague ideals seem to have assumed in his mind. He was a new-comer of '49, and hailed from Fitchburg, Massachusetts. He was a college graduate, had studied medicine, had afterwards rebelled against the technicalities of the code of his local association, and had become an independent practitioner. His friends and interests, as his whole subsequent career showed, were with the party of the cultivated New England Radicals of that day. And these cultivated Radicals of the anti-slavery generation, and especially of Massachusetts, were a type in which an impartial posterity will take a huge delight; for they combined so characteristically shrewdness, insight, devoutness, vanity, idealism, and self-worship. To speak of them, of course in the rough and as a mass, they were usually believers in quite abstract ideals : men who knew how to meet God ' in the bush ' whenever they wanted, and so avoided him in the mart and the crowded street; men who had ' dwelt cheek by jowl, since the day ' they were ' born, with the Infinite Soul,' and whose relations with him were like those of any man with his own private property. This Infinite that they worshipped was, however, in his relations to the rest of the world too often rather abstract, a *Deus absconditus*, who was as remote from the imperfections and absurdities of the individual laws and processes of human society as he was near to the heart of his chosen worshippers. From him they got a so-called Higher Law. As it was ideal, and, like its author, very abstract, it was far above the erring laws of men, and it therefore relieved its obedient servants from all entangling earthly allegiances. If the Constitution upon which our sinful national existence depended, and upon which our only hope of better things also depended, was contradicted by this Higher Law, then the Constitution was a ' league with hell,' and anybody could set up for himself, and he and the Infinite might carry on a government of their own.   *   *   *   Well, Dr. Robinson, also, had evidently learned much, in his own way, from teachers of this school.   The complex and wearisome details of Spanish law plainly do not interest him, since he is at home in the divine Higher Law.   Concrete rights of rapacious land speculators in Sacramento are unworthy of the attention of one who sees so clearly into the abstract right of man.   God is not in the Sutter grant, that is plain.   It is the mission of the squatters to introduce the divine justice into California; no absurd justice that depends upon erroneous lines of latitude, and establishments at New Helvetia, and other like blundering details of dark Spanish days, but the justice that can be expressed in grand abstract formulæ, and that will hear of no less arbiter than the United States Supreme Court at the very nearest, and is quite independent of local courts and processes.

" For the rest, Dr. Robinson added to his idealism the aforesaid Yankee shrewdness, and to his trust in God considerable ingenuity in raising funds to keep the squatter association at work.   He wrote well and spoke well.   He was thoroughly in earnest, and his motives seem to me above any suspicion of personal greed.   He made out of this squatter movement a thing of real power, and was, for the time, a very dangerous man.

" Thus led and moved, the squatter association might easily have become the centre of a general revolutionary movement of the sort above described."

The reader who has followed this narration thus far can estimate this wild, extravagant language at its true value, without further comment.   It is plain the only higher law the squatters were after was the law of the United States, and the decision of a legal tribunal.   This law and decision the speculators said should not be had, hence the conflict. Mr. Royce says the Supreme Court was a long way off, and to wait for its decision would work great hardship to the claimants under the grant.   But where would be the greater hardship?   This grant was sufficiently elastic to cover all northern California, and was used to enable a few men, with quit-claim or other deeds from Captain Sutter, to levy tribute upon every person of the many thousand who might want to settle in the country.   If the claimants could not wait for a legal adjustment, how could the hordes of destitute people wait that were pouring in from the Eastern States?   If the title should prove valid, the grantees would lose nothing. Even should the entire tract of eleven leagues be densely populated by thriving cities, it would only enhance the value of the grant a thousand-fold, while, should the land in question be not covered by the grant, the cormorants would have robbed every occupant of hard-earned money, never to be returned. Thus a valid claimant would lose nothing by waiting for the courts, even the highest court, while the squatter would lose all he might pay for a bogus title at the hands of a bogus claimant or speculator.

When the prisoner had partially recovered, he and his two companions were taken before a so-called magistrate and formally committed on a charge of murder and other crimes. The District Court, so-called, soon met at Sacramento, and the grand jury found true bills, one for murder, two for assault with intent to kill, and one for conspiracy. Soon after the finding of these bills the three prisoners were taken into court to plead to the indictment.

One of the attorneys employed to defend the squatters was Mr. Tweed, formerly of Florida. As the time approached for the election of members of the Legislature, he paid his client a visit on the prison ship, and engaged in a political discussion. He advocated the division of California into two States, one to be a slave State. This, he argued, would tend to allay the excitement in the country and prevent any attempt at a dissolution of the Union. He said there was a movement in this direction in California, though not as yet public. He desired the opinion of his client upon such a proposition. His client answered that he was opposed to slavery from conviction of its injustice, and could not favor its extension. Not many days after this, the attorney appeared again. This time he reported that he had learned that some parties proposed to support the prisoner for an election to the Legislature, and he advised that he should decline to be a candidate. This he did as attorney, for the good of his client. To allow his name to be used in that connection would prejudice his case in the courts. The prisoner at length informed his counsel that he had nothing to do with outside matters, and if the courts were disposed to hang him because some people chose to vote for him, they could do so. He was not inclined to interfere. The prisoner, by putting the two visits together, understood plainly that slavery extension to southern California was in issue, and that his attorney opposed his being a candidate solely because of his opposition to slavery.

After this, when the squatters called for a new manifesto for a campaign document, the prisoner furnished one which made a clear and brief statement of the situation, charging upon the speculators murder in the first degree, and placing the squatters in the position of defenders of their natural and constitutional rights. This manifesto was printed in the form of a poster and distributed throughout the county. Not a speech was made in this canvass, the manifesto told the whole story. The papers denounced the manifesto in the wildest and bitterest terms, saying that "these men who sleep nightly with halters about their necks have the audacity to charge the citizens of Sacramento with murder," etc., etc. Notwithstanding this bitter opposition of the press, pro-slavery men, and speculators, Mr. Royce, in the *Overland Monthly*, would make it appear that this election went by default and by general consent of all parties. On page 246, he says:

"As nowadays we elect a displaced university professor to the superintendency of public instruction just to give him a fair chance to do good to the university, so then it was felt by some good-natured folk reasonable to elect Dr. Robinson to the Legislature, not because people believed wholly in his ideas, but because his services merited attention. At all events, in a district of Sacramento County, Dr. Robinson's friends managed, with the connivance of certain optimists, to give him a seat in the Assembly, that late 'advisory' body, whose 'rules,' before the admission of the State, he had so ardently despised. The State was admitted now, and Dr. Robinson cheerfully undertook his share of legislation."

Soon after his election the prisoner was admitted to bail, and became one of the editors of a new paper called the *Settlers' and Miners' Tribune.* He was thus employed till the meeting of the Legislature, when he took his seat in that body. Here came to the front the slavery extension question. The Whigs had nominated for Senator, in place of Fremont, who drew the short term, T. Butler King, of Georgia, and the Democrats had nominated Judge Heydenfelt, of Alabama, both in favor of a division of California. Fremont alone of the candidates was opposed to this division, and, although the proprietor of a large land grant, the squatter supported him. Some twelve to fifteen others joined him, and holding the balance between the Whigs and Democrats, defeated the election for that session. The anti-slavery squatters approved of the course taken, while a few pro-slavery squatters were offended. At the next session the anti-slavery sentiment was so strong as to elect a Northern man, Mr. Weller from Ohio, and the question was effectually disposed of.

A law was passed at this session of the Legislature which quieted all illegal proceedings in land controversies, and all parties had to await the decision of the proper tribunals. A change of venue was had in the squatter cases to Benicia, but, after the session of the Legislature, the prisoners were discharged for want of prosecution. The prosecuting attorney would neither proceed with the trial nor enter a *nolle*, and the court turned the prisoners loose.

The *Overland Monthly*, pages 245 and 246 says:

" Dr. Robinson, indeed, was in little danger from his indictments when once the heat of battle had cooled. He was felt to be a man of mark; the popular ends had been gained in his defeat; the legal evidence against him was like the chips of drift-wood in a little eddy of this changing torrent of California life. With its little horde of drift, the eddy soon vanished in the immeasurable flood. After a change of venue to a bay county, and after a few months' postponement, the cloud of indictments melted away like the last cloud flake of our rainy season. *Nolle pros.* was entered and the hero was free."

From the squatters' standpoint, Dr. Robinson, though wounded, was not beaten. The squatters gained their cause. Neither was the failure to prosecute because of a lack of evidence. That was abundant, but, unfortunately for the speculators, it would convict them instead of Robinson. The manifesto before election distinctly indicted them for murder, and gave the evidence. The papers admitted the. indictment, and the election of Robinson was the verdict of Sacramento County of guilty as charged. The Legislature while in session volunteered, while the prisoner was sick and without his knowledge, to pass a joint resolution through both houses instructing the prosecuting attorney to *nolle* the case, to be vetoed, however, by the brave Lieutenant and Acting Governor McDougal, who fled down the river when the mayor was shot, and went to bed sick when the sheriff was killed. This joint resolution was a verdict by the whole State against the speculators of guilty of murder in the first degree. Of course, under such circumstances, they would be very glad if not only the evidence but the recollection of the squatter riots, would float "like drift-wood in a little eddy" to oblivion.

When the speculators found they could no longer settle a grant to eleven leagues of land in a justice's court, a case was brought in a court that had jurisdiction in such matters, which finally reached the Supreme Court, the "higher law" of the squatters. The disposition made of Sutter's grant by this court can be found in the Supreme Court reports. What reasoning was adopted in order to locate a grant of land bounded on the east by the Feather River so as to cover the town of Sacramento, it is not easy to understand. It is evident that there was some difficulty in the case, for Mr. Royce says, on page 227, "To arrange with justice the final survey of his Alvarado grant proved in later years one of the most perplexing problems of the United States District and Supreme Courts." It must have been difficult to locate a grant bounded on the north by the Three Peaks, on the east by Feather River, on the south by the 38° 49' 32'' parallel of latitude, and on the west by the Sacramento River, by boundaries given in Captain Sutter's quit-claim deeds for lands in and about Sacramento. A layman cannot understand what business the court had with any boundaries except such as were given by Alvarado. If the grant had boundaries, natural, plain, and unmistakable, Sutter's deeds could not change them; but if it had no such boundaries it was null and void. Many things in court decisions are too high for common people, and past finding out by them.

And poor old Captain Sutter, in whose name and for whose pretended benefit the suit was brought and carried to the Supreme Court, what became of his rights, his profits, and himself? Finding he was being defrauded by these claimants under his grant, he employed counsel to defeat them in despoiling him of his rightful possessions through the agency of the Supreme Court.

A fugitive newspaper clipping describes his condition, when the speculators had done with him, as follows:

" A sad story is that of General Sutter, a man noted for benevolence, but now reduced to poverty. The first gold found in California was discovered in the race of his mill, and soon thousands of squatters had ' prospected ' upon his possessions. With a hand open as the day to melting charity, he relieved the wants of all. We are told that the aged patriarch, guileless as a child, and totally wanting in commercial tact, unsuspectingly confided his secrets, his business, even his property, to any one who by an affectation of interest, or hypocritical show of assistance, offered himself to his friendship. One after another his broad acres slipped from his grasp; he placed his affairs in the hands of an agent who deceived, deluded, and robbed him of hard dollars; his property dwindled down to merely a tithe of what it had been, and the old man's sorrows were heavy upon him. In this condition he put a farm, his sole remaining support, into the hands of his son, who proved worse even than strangers, and robbed him of his last possession. He is now reduced to all but begging, but waiting the decision of some commissions in respect to a land claim."

5

CHAPTER IV.

SITUATION IN THE EAST.—ELI THAYER AND HIS ASSOCIATES.
SETTLEMENT OF LAWRENCE.—CLAIM CONTROVERSIES.

IN the winter and spring of 1854, while the Kansas-Ne-braska bill was pending in Congress, Massachusetts espe-cially was greatly moved. The agitation of the slavery question had disturbed the people, including churches and political parties, for several years, till the old order of things had been nearly broken up. Come-outers were distracting the churches, and Know-Nothings and Free-Soilers were playing havoc with political parties. Hunker Whigs and Bourbon Democrats seemed to be the only land-marks re-maining of the olden time, and now their peace was greatly endangered. If the sacred compromises were to go down before the advance of the slave power, by the votes of mem-bers of their own parties, what hope would there be for such parties in Massachusetts in the future? The no-Union abo-litionists were in high feather, as their claim of no hope for the slave within the Union seemed about to be vindicated. But, in the midst of all the excitement and confusion, a ray of hope appeared. One man had the temerity to prophesy that what was intended for evil should result in good; that the legislation which was intended to extend slavery indefi-nitely should be used to abolish that institution absolutely. He began to preach his new gospel, and all eyes were turned upon him. At first all seemed incredulous. Who was this man that hoped to stem the tide of slavery, to change the current of events, and to abolish that great iniquity by the very machinery that had been invented to make it perpetual and universal. The president of the first squatters' association in California was now returned to Massachusetts. He had traversed the goodly land about to be blighted, and earnestly hoped that it might be saved to freedom. He had talked and written about its good qualities, and was watching eagerly for information about this daring man—this David who seemed ready to challenge single-handed the Goliath of slavery. At length, to satisfy himself fully, to see of what material this man was made, whether he was a mere agitator, or a man who had convictions for which he would risk his life if necessary, the squatter attended one of his Boston meetings. Taking a back seat, the stranger paid the closest attention to the proceedings, and reached the conclusion that this was no counterfeit, but a true man who would meet any crisis without flinching. Evidently, here was a crusader who had thoroughly digested his plan, and had implicit confidence both in himself and in his scheme. No man could listen to him without partaking of his spirit, neither could any person, after listening, entertain any doubts of the feasibility of his plan, or of his ability to put it in successful operation. This man, of course, was Eli Thayer; for there was but one such in the nation. When, therefore, Mr. Thayer, with Amos A. Lawrence and J. M. S. Williams, trustees, in June, 1854, sent for the writer to meet them at Boston for the purpose of carrying this plan into execution, he could not refuse any duty that might be assigned him. No other evidence was needed of the inspiration of Mr. Thayer than the fact that he could impart his inspiration to other people of all classes and conditions. At one of his meetings J. M. S. Williams became inspired and subscribed $10,000 for the cause, and at another time Charles Francis Adams subscribed $25,000. Also W. M. Evarts was taken with the infection and subscribed one-fourth of all he was worth, or $1000. Mr. Thayer enlisted in his work the most conservative as well as the most radical, the richest and the poorest, the highest and lowest. Among those his inspiration infected was Amos A. Lawrence.   Mr. Lawrence was a conservative of the conservatives, a Hunker, as he chose to call himself, yet no man had greater enthusiasm or worked more persistently and earnestly than he from first to last.   His great wealth, and greater influence, were thrown into the cause without reserve.   No man in the nation stood higher financially, socially, or as a philanthropist, and with his name associated with the movement as treasurer, no man, however conservative, was afraid to endorse and aid the enterprise. Securing such men as Mr. Lawrence, Mr. Williams, Dr. Cabot, Rev. Mr. Hale, and others like them, Mr. Thayer could well afford to entrust the finances and details to them, while he preached the crusade among the people, and imbued the churches, the mechanics, the farmers, and laborers with his spirit, till men should be found to take possession of the land in conflict—men of conviction, and men who would die, if need be, in defense of their convictions.

Henry Wilson says of Mr. Thayer's work, in his "Rise and Fall of the Slave Power," Vol. II., page 465, as follows:

"To this work Mr. Thayer devoted himself with tireless energy and unceasing effort.   Fully impressed with the idea that the free States had the power to secure in this way freedom to the Territories, he travelled sixty thousand miles, and made hundreds of speeches enunciating these views, and calling upon the people to join in this grand crusade."

The effect of Mr. Thayer's speeches may be learned from a report of his speech at Cambridge, as found in the *Chronicle* of November 22, 1856, as follows:

" After Professor Hedrick's remarks, it was a relief when the broad, calm brow of Mr. Thayer loomed up before us.   We were requested not to report his speech, and shall therefore only speak of it in general terms.   It was more even than we had hoped for, and, whether considered as a speech or as an argument, was a powerful effort.   Such deep penetration into and entire grasp of his subject; such an aptness of expression, and illustration, we seldom find.   The views he took have not been presented by the press or public speakers—they are new to the people; but unquestionably sound, as they are hopeful to freedom;

and as he presented them we cannot doubt that they were convincing to his audience."

On arriving in Boston, in answer to the call of the trustees, Dr. Robinson found them in the office of the Emigrant Aid Company, with Dr. T. H. Webb, their very efficient secretary. Here the whole question of emigration to Kansas was discussed, ending with a *carte blanche* commission to the Doctor to visit the Territory and arrange for its settlement. Mr. Lawrence advanced the money for the expenses of the journey from his personal funds, and gave a letter of credit on a merchant of St. Louis for $200. It was arranged that a young lawyer of Holyoke, C. H. Branscomb, should join Dr. Robinson at Springfield and accompany him. Instead of following the route of the Boston party on their trip to California in 1849, by canal and steamboat, the route was taken through Chicago to St. Louis. Here a steamer was taken for Kansas City. As the boat passed Jefferson City, on the 4th of July, it took on board several men of note in political circles, as the Legislature had adjourned for the holiday. These men possessed many of the characteristics of the speculators of Sacramento in 1849 and 1850, and their threats and swagger about driving Northern men from Kansas had a familiar sound to one person, who was a listener rather than a talker. The Emigrant Aid Company received a large share of their attention, not excepting Eli Thayer, for whose head a liberal reward would be given. It was fully proclaimed that no anti-slavery man should be permitted to settle in the Territory, and all Northern men were anti-slavery, or abolitionists. On landing at Kansas City, it was found to be greatly improved since the spring of 1849. Some substantial buildings had been erected and the population greatly increased. Here were found, beside the noisy pro-slavery advocates, several quiet, civil, and accommodating business men. The Gillis House was a substantial brick structure, in charge of Gaius Jenkins, a most excellent man and obliging landlord. Also, here were Mr. Conant, a

merchant of the highest merit, and Mr. Riddlesbarger with
his commodious warehouse.   All these gentlemen welcomed
Free-State men with as much cordiality as pro-slavery, and
some of them with more.   One of the most genial and pub-
lic-spirited citizens to be found in any community was Dr.
Lykins, who was familiar with the situation, within and without the Territory, with the Indian tribes and reservations, as
well as with the lands opened to settlement by Indian treaties.
Mr. Gillis and Dr. Troost were also prominent figures in the
community, and most agreeable gentlemen.   Knowing that
Kansas City was likely to become the gateway to the vast
regions beyond, and that emigrants from the East must land
at this point, terms were procured for the purchase of the
Gillis House and of a tract of land where later was built the
Union Depot.   The hotel was purchased by the company,
but the land declined.   Mr. Thayer was favorable to this
purchase, as he would have the enterprise self-supporting,
but other members were in the movement purely from
motives of patriotism and philanthropy.   Had this land been
purchased, as recommended by the agent, its value would
now be beyond computation.   At this time treaties had been
made with the Delaware tribe of Indians for disposing of
some of their lands, but they were to be sold to the highest
bidder, and were not to be opened for pre-emption.   The
Shawnee treaty, not yet complete, would open to pre-emption their lands west of the diminished reservation, which
extended about thirty miles west of the Missouri State line,
though these had not yet been surveyed.   These lands, lying
along the Kansas River on the south side, were the most
eligible for settlement outside of Indian reservations.   To
learn the situation definitely, Branscomb and Robinson separated at Kansas City, the first going up the Kansas River
to Fort Riley, and the other up the Missouri to Fort Leavenworth.   Although the lands on the Missouri were not open
to pre-emption, some surveyors were found at work laying
off a town at the present site of Leavenworth City.   On re-

turning to Kansas City, Robinson found a letter informing
him that the first party of emigrants from Boston was about
to start for Kansas, and directing him to meet it at St. Louis,
which he did.   A letter was given to him directing him to
return to Boston as soon as this party should be taken to the
Territory.   As Mr. Branscomb would return to Kansas City
from his trip to Fort Riley before the party could reach that
point, a letter was forwarded to him to look after the emigrants, and Robinson started East to obey the summons.
When the party arrived at Kansas City it met not only Mr.
Branscomb, but Colonel Blood, of Wisconsin, who had been
employed by Mr. Lawrence to visit the Territory.   He had
much experience in new settlements and understood the pre-
emption laws.   His account of the arrival and settlement of
this party is given in the Lawrence *Journal* of January 12,
1891, as follows:

"In August of that year (1854), when the first party of
Eastern immigrants arrived at Kansas City, Mr. Branscomb
and I were both there.   We had considerable consultation
about where they should locate.   Mr. Branscomb appeared
very anxious that they should settle upon the Wyandotte
reservation.   In fact, he advocated that idea so earnestly
that he induced a committee, representing the party of settlers, to go the next day with us to see Abelard Guthrie, 'a
squaw man,' who offered his protection and assistance, and
proposed to allow us to lay out a town, and make a landing
on the Missouri River.   But as that country was then an
Indian reservation, no white men were allowed to settle or
reside there without permission of the United States Government; the committee concluded that the scheme was impracticable.   I think the committee that went with us over into
the Wyandotte country was composed of D. R. Anthony,
now of Leavenworth, Samuel F. Tappan, now residing at
Washington, and A. H. Mallory, now at Leadville, Colorado,
or Dr. Harrington.   As I had obtained information that
the Shawnee Indians had ceded their reservation south of

the Kansas River, except a tract extending thirty miles west
of the State of Missouri, and that the portion ceded was
suitable for settlement, and the most available, the party decided to come up here. Mr. Branscomb came with them.
I also came along on horseback, in company with a gentleman by the name of Cobb. The night before arriving here
the party went into camp at the Blue Jacket crossing of the
Wakarusa. Mr. Cobb and I stopped for the night at Dr.
Still's, a short distance east of the crossing. The next morning I rode to the top of Blue Mound, from there crossing
the Wakarusa at Blanton's Ford, arrived some time in the
forenoon on the hill where the University now stands, finding the party there pitching their tents and unloading their
wagons. I met Mr. Branscomb there that day. He informed me that he had bought a claim of a Mr. Stearns, and
had agreed to pay him $500 for it, and that Mr. Wade had
a claim some distance up the river that he offered to sell for
$1000, and he, Mr. Branscomb, advised and urged me to
buy it. I replied that I regarded the buying of claims at
that time as impolitic. Soon after, I think the next day, Mr.
Branscomb left here for the East, and did not return here
that year, nor for a long time after. * * * I was in
Kansas City when the second party arrived there in September, in charge of Charles Robinson and S. C. Pomeroy.
After consultation, they decided to come up here. On arriving here, we found a part of the first party still living in tents
on the hill. Most of them that remained here had taken
farm claims in the vicinity. We came down to the river,
and after viewing the location, they decided to locate and
lay out the town. Governor Robinson pitched his tent near
the bank of the river, near where the jail now stands. Soon
after a survey of the town was made, a town company or association was organized, and the town given a name, Lawrence. I believe the foregoing to be a correct statement of
events that occurred relating to the selection of the town
site. Governor Robinson and some one or two hundred

others who came with him remained here and engaged in the erection of buildings, founding the city."

With all the bluster and demonstrations from the South, and all the disadvantages under which the Free-State men would be placed, it required men of no little firmness to enlist as pioneers in the crusade. In a paper read by me before the "Old Settlers'" meeting at Emporia, September 18, 1889, this reference to them is made:

"Many looked upon Eli Thayer as mad, and his project as madness. Who could be found to go to Kansas with the certainty of meeting a hostile greeting of revolvers, bowie-knives, and all the desperadoes of the border? But the inspired prophet, who clearly saw the end from the beginning, had no doubts or misgivings, and obstacles which would have disheartened another man, were only incentives to greater efforts and more implicit faith in his plan. At length, after great labor, a party of twenty-nine men, who were willing to take their lives in their hands, went to Kansas in July, 1854. These men were regarded with as much interest as would be a like number of gladiators about to enter into deadly conflict with wild beasts, or with each other. Hundreds of people gathered to bid them a final farewell, and ovations greeted them at all principal points between Boston and Chicago. But their example was contagious, and, as they were not slaughtered on their arrival in Kansas, other parties soon followed, as well as men without parties, from all the Northern States."

The agitation relative to taking possession of Kansas was by no means confined to the East. It extended to every State in the Union with more or less violence. Neither were the members of the first Eastern party the first Free-State men to enter upon the field of battle. As before stated, such men as S. N. Wood, J. A. Wakefield, Rev. Mr. Ferril, and others were on the ground when this party reached its destination, but no men or party of men had attracted so much attention, either at the North or at the South, and they were

the focus of all eyes watching the struggle of the giants, freedom and slavery, about to commence on Kansas soil.   The
names of this party will go down the ages as the names of
men who dared begin a conflict against great odds.   To
single out individuals would seem invidious.   Few are still
living.   D. R. Anthony, brother of Susan B. Anthony, who
came with the party but returned East till 1857, is a fit
specimen of the material required to beat back the black
waves of slavery from Kansas.   He was and is and ever
will be irrepressible.   No cause espoused by him from conviction will be relinquished while his life remains.   The same
may be said of such men as S. F. Tappan, Ferdinand Fuller,
J. F. Morgan, G. W. Goss, and, in short, of the whole party.
S. N. Wood also, from Ohio, who preceded the party, was
a man without fear.   Colonel D. R. Anthony, in introducing
Colonel Wood at the quarter-centennial celebration, said:

"Thirty years ago I rode from Lawrence to Kansas City
with a gentleman who is now in this house.   At Westport
we stopped at what might now be called a saloon, and took
a drink—of water—and watered our horses.   On the wall
of this saloon was a poster, offering $1000 reward for Eli
Thayer, the founder of the New England Emigrant Aid Company, dead or alive.   We asked what they would do with
Eli Thayer if they had him; the reply was that he would be
hanged.   This gentleman who was with me stepped up and
said: 'I am Eli Thayer.   Proceed to hang.'   He was not
hanged, but I have the honor this evening of introducing him
to you.   He was one of the truest of the pioneers in the
great struggle.   His name is a household word; he is better
known as 'Sam Wood.'"

The second party sent out under the auspices of the
Emigrant Aid Company left Boston August 29, 1854, arriving at Kansas City September 6th, and was accompanied by
S. C. Pomeroy, financial agent, and Charles Robinson, resident agent, of the company.   This party went to Lawrence,
formed a union with the first party, and began the settlement

of the town, which was surveyed and platted by A. D. Searl, under the direction of a committee of which Robinson was chairman. No sooner had definite arrangements been made for a permanent settlement at Lawrence than the conflict began in earnest. The first act in the drama was to be the ejectment of all Free-State men on a pretense of prior claims to the land. The plot of this play was the same as of that at Sacramento, under Sutter's grant, with only a change of scenery. As several of the Free-State settlers at Lawrence had more or less prominent parts in that play, they were at home in this.

On or before the passage of the bill opening the Territory to settlement, pro-slavery men from Missouri rushed over the line, marked trees, and drove stakes in every direction. No claim could be taken by a Free-State man to which a pro-slavery man could not be found to assert a prior claim. It was the Sacramento game over again, with squatter's title instead of Sutter's deeds. Neither left an acre of unclaimed land for the *bona fide* settler. Colonel S. N. Wood, in his quarter-centennial speech at Topeka, said: "No sooner was Kansas opened to settlement than the minions of the slave power swarmed across the border, seemingly determined to occupy the whole Territory. Leavenworth, Atchison, Kickapoo, Iowa Point, Doniphan, and other places were occupied. These were the pioneers of the slave power."

Andreas, in his history, page 83, says: "The influx of Missourians into Kansas occurred immediately after the passage of the territorial act; indeed, prior to its final passage the best of the lands ceded by the tribes had been spotted and marked for pre-emption by residents of Missouri. This occupation was made with undue haste, and against the protests of the Indians whose time of occupancy under the treaties was yet unexpired. * * * The ubiquitous citizens, having homes in Missouri and squatter's claims in the adjoining territory, promptly organized defensively against

the possible encroachments of the expected and hated emigrants from the North."

Colonel Wood, in his speech at Topeka, said:

"The pro-slavery men from Missouri had met in Kansas and
adopted a code of squatter laws, and the whole Territory seemed staked
into claims. They had a register of claims, with an office at Westport,
Missouri. One law of this remarkable code provided that Nebraska
was for the North and Kansas for the South. One provision was,
that every white-livered abolitionist who dared to set foot in Kansas
should be hung; and, that there might be no mistake, they added,
'Every man north of Mason and Dixon's line is an abolitionist.'"

Andreas gives resolutions of squatter conventions and
newspaper extracts on page 83, some of which follow. At
a meeting at Salt Creek Valley it was resolved:

"That we recognize the institution of Slavery as *always existing in
this Territory*, and recommend slave-holders to introduce their property
as early as possible.

"That we will afford protection to no abolitionists as settlers of
Kansas Territory."

The *Democratic Platform*, Liberty, Missouri, June 8, 1854,
says:

"We learn from a gentleman lately from the Territory of Kansas
that a great many Missourians have already set their pegs in that
country, and are making arrangements to 'darken the atmosphere'
with their negroes. This is right. Let every man that owns a negro
go there and settle, and our Northern brethren will be compelled to
hunt further north for a location."

The Platte *Argus*, Missouri, has the following:

"Mormons—We are advised that the abolition societies of New
England are shipping their tools, at the public expense, *as* Mormons,
ostensibly for Salt Lake, but that it is the real *design* of these worthies
to stop in Kansas Territory for the purpose of voting to establish a
free State and an underground railroad. We say, let the Mormons go
their way in peace to Utah, but if they remain in Kansas to inflict the
blighting curse of their principles upon the future policy of the country
—let a Mormon war be declared forthwith.

"Citizens of the West, of the South, and Illinois! stake out your
claims, and woe be to the abolitionist or Mormon who shall intrude

upon it, or come within reach of your long and true rifles, or within *point-blank shot of your revolvers.* Keep a sharp lookout lest some dark night you shall see the flames curling from your houses or the midnight philanthropist hurrying off your faithful servant."

At a meeting held in Independence, Missouri, the sentiment of the people was expressed as follows:

"*Resolved,* That we, without distinction of party, desire to act in accordance with what is right and due, not only to interests of the South, but likewise to interests of the North, and though knowing that the North, through certain fanatics, has endeavored to *dictate* to the South, we yet wish to meet them as brothers and friends, and only ask our rights as compromise, viz.:

"That we, the South, be permitted peaceably to possess Kansas, while the North, on the same privilege, be permitted to possess Nebraska Territory."

In some instances the organization of Northern emigration was pleaded as an excuse for such action. But at no time had there been an attempt at the North to use other than legitimate means in assisting emigration. There was no employment of mercenaries, no defraying of expenses even, and no discrimination on account of political or other views the emigrant might entertain. A pro-slavery man had the same facilities as a Free-State man. The same was true of the settlements in the Territory. A pro-slavery man was entitled to all the rights, privileges, and immunities of the most favored Free-State man. The truth seems to be that the slave interest demanded Kansas, and it was to be secured at all hazards, legally or illegally, and the plea of organized Northern emigration was on a par with the plea of the speculators in California, that the squatters were "agrarians," "higher-law" men, bent on fighting all Mexican grants, right or wrong. In both cases an outrage was determined upon, and a false issue must be made to afford some excuse to the world.

Besides the organization at Salt Creek Valley, other associations were formed in different parts of the Territory, in the summer and fall of 1854, nearly all of which provided for the protection of all settlers except abolitionists. As Free-State settlers arrived in a neighborhood, these restrictions would be voted out and all but actual settlers disfranchised. Such a meeting was held at B. W. Miller's house, on the California road, southwest of Lawrence. When the pro-slavery non-residents failed to control the association, they reported at Westport, Missouri, where an organization could be perfected without opposition from the free-soil squatters of Kansas. The name of this association, which met at Miller's, was "The Mutual Settlers' Association of Kansas Territory," and it had for officers, a chief justice, register, marshal, and treasurer. While it was contemplated that all disputes would be settled by these courts, these were, in fact, but little used, as they were far too formal and dilatory to meet most cases. As a rule, squatters settled their disputes in person, appealing to no higher authority than physical force or bluster. One man, who had played the rôle of "Bombastes Furioso" in the squatter troubles in California, although not at the fight, was for a time quite useful in Kansas. When pro-slavery men would appear, if surrounded by his friends, he would become furiously excited, pulling off his coat and vest preparatory to a personal encounter. This would have the effect of inducing the pro-slavery men to pass on. At length, however, some men appeared who were not frightened by contortions or wind. Bombastes raved and writhed as usual, but produced no impression. The Missourians were rather amused than frightened. Even the shedding of coat and vest had no effect, and Bombastes had to call upon his friends to "hold me," and prevent a fatal encounter. This ended Furioso's career as bully, and he subsided.

The most serious and determined claim disputes were to be found at Lawrence, in the fall of 1854 and winter of 1855. At this time Lawrence was the only Free-State town of importance in the Territory, and, if possible, it must be obliterated. When the site was selected for a town, but one settler, Mr. Stearns, occupied it, and his improvement and claim were purchased by the agent of the Aid Company for $500, and the cabin converted into a store. Another settler, A. B. Wade, was near the site on the west, but he retained his claim, as it was not needed for the town. However, soon after taking possession, other claimants appeared, and insisted that the town should vacate for them. The most belligerent of these claimants was John Baldwin. He established himself within five or ten rods of the Stearns cabin bought for the town, and asserted his right to one hundred and sixty acres of land. He employed a young man named C. W. Babcock as his attorney. As the lands had not yet been surveyed, it was impossible to tell where section lines would run, and the town company were disposed to act strictly on the defensive. The managers were satisfied to leave the question of title to the Land Office or the courts, and it was immaterial how many persons set up claim to the town site. Not so, however, with Baldwin and Company. Although, if their claims were valid, the more occupants and improvements the better for them, they determined to remove all occupants and all improvements from their claims, which covered, or would cover if heeded, nearly the whole territory opened to settlement. While the motive that actuated pro-slavery men was to forestall the Free-State settlers and prevent them from getting a foothold in the Territory, some of the claimants at Lawrence cared nothing for the slavery question, but simply wanted to be bought off. They took advantage for this purpose of the pro-slavery sentiment. A town site was platted at Lawrence about two and one-half miles by one and one-half miles, although, under the pre-emption laws, but three hundred and twenty acres could be held for town purposes. This made it necessary to hold the excess by private entry, and men were assigned to different parts of the plat for the purpose. The pro-slavery men, or blackmail Free-State men, also laid claim to this land and would clear it of all comers.   The agent of the Aid Company advocated the same policy as was adopted by the squatters in California, namely, let each settler be protected in occupancy till a legal decision could be had, and this policy was adopted by the Lawrence town company.   But this would not answer the purposes of the contestants, for the pro-slavery men were determined to prevent the settlement of Free-State men, right or wrong, and the blackmailers knew they had no case, and must get blackmail then or lose all.

The first conflict threatened by this state of things is described in Andrea's history, on pages 314 and 315, as follows :

" In the meantime Baldwin associated with himself Messrs. Babcock, Stone, and Freeman, men of some means and influence, and put his business into the hands of a speculator named Starr, who immediately proceeded to lay out a rival city, which he named Excelsior, on the claim ; Mr. Baldwin and the Lawrence Association both occupying tents upon it, in proof of ownership.   The strife grew bitter, and although purely one of conflicting property rights—the parties being nearly all Free-State men—was represented, or misrepresented, to be a quarrel between the pro-slavery men and abolitionists.   Matters stood thus : Mr. Baldwin occupying his tent and the Yankees scowling defiantly at him across the ravine, until, on the 5th of October, notice was given that open war was declared, by the appearance of a wagon containing several armed men in the vicinity of the New England tent.   Hostilities were commenced by a woman, a sister of Mr. Baldwin, it was stated, who speedily packed the obnoxious tent with its contents into the wagon—the men with their rifles standing guard.   As soon as they were discovered by the Yankees, who were at work in the neighborhood, the city marshal, Joel Grover, rushed to the rescue unarmed, followed by Edwin Bond with a revolver.   The latter seized the horse by the bridle, ordering the surrender of the property, and others coming up, the intruders allowed the tent to be replaced, at the same time threatening to have two hundred Missourians on the spot in a short time, when their designs would be accomplished.   That night the Lawrence settlers organized what they called the ' Regulating Band,' to be ready for the next day's fray.   Soon after dinner on the 6th, 'the Missourians,' by which name all Southerners opposed to the aims of the Emigrant Aid Society were called, began to assemble in the neighborhood of Baldwin's tent, but open hostilities did not commence until four o'clock P.M. when the gage of battle was hurled at the Yankees in the shape of the following note :

" ' KANSAS TERRITORY, October 6th.

" ' DR. ROBINSON :—Yourself and friends are hereby notified that you will have one-half hour to move the tent which you have on my undisputed claim, and from this date desist from surveying on said claim. If the tent is not moved within one-half hour, we shall take the trouble to move the same. (Signed,)

" ' JOHN BALDWIN AND FRIENDS.'

" The following pithy reply was instantly returned:

" ' To John Baldwin and Friends.

" ' If you molest our property, you do it at your peril.

" ' C. ROBINSON AND FRIENDS.' "

E. D. Ladd, first acting postmaster of Lawrence, tells the remainder of the story in a letter dated October 23, 1854, and published in the Milwaukee *Sentinel*. He says:

" Prior to the notice, they had assembled to the number of eighteen, mounted and armed, at Baldwin's, the aggrieved man's tent, on the claim, and about twenty rods from our camp. Upon the notice being served, our men—those who were at work about and in the vicinity of the camp—to the number of about thirty, stationed themselves about ten rods from the contested tent, the enemy being about the same distance from it, the three occupying the angles of a right-angled triangle, the tent being at the right angle. Subsequent to the notice, a consultation was held at our position between Dr. Robinson and a delegate from the enemy's post, which ended on our part with the proposition of Dr. Robinson—which proposition he had previously made, both to Baldwin and his legal adviser, or rather speculator, who wished to make a ' heap of money,' as the Missourians say, out of him—to submit the question in dispute to the arbitration of disinterested and unbiased mén, to the adjudication of the squatter courts now existing here, or of the United States Courts, and on the part of the enemy by the assurance that, at the termination of the notice, they should proceed at all hazards to remove the tent, and if they fell in the attempt, our fate would be sealed, our extermination certain, for three thousand, and if necessary thirty thousand, men would immediately be raised in Missouri to sweep us and our enterprise from the face of the earth. It was all expressed, of course, in the Southwestern phrases, which I will not attempt to give. The hour passed on, or rather the half-hour, and in the meantime our military company, formed the evening before, went through a variety of—I don't want, out of respect for military science, to call them ' evolutions,' say we call them ' manifestations,' marching and counter-marching, in single file and by platoons, in a manner not to

6

be excelled in greenness by any greenhorns (in this business, I mean) on the face of the globe, our captain himself being as green as the greenest. General, I fear for your buttons could you have seen them. But there were strong arms and determined wills there. Had a man laid a finger on that tent, he would have been sacrificed instantly, and had another single offensive movement been made by one of them, there would not have been a man left to tell the tale. Our company of thirty men had about four hundred shots in hand, with their rifles and revolvers, and they would have used them to the last extremity. They had been annoyed by every means possible, and even tauntingly told to their faces, a dozen of them together, that no Yankee, except Cilley, ever dared to fire. Well, the half-hour passed, and another quarter, the enemy in full view in consultation, occasionally making a movement as if about to form in order for the execution of their threat, then seating themselves upon the ground for further consultation, perhaps occasioned by the ' manifestations ' of our military. While thus waiting, John Hutchinson asked Dr. Robinson what he would do if they should attempt to remove the tent? would he fire to hit them, or would he fire over them? Dr. Robinson replied that he ' would be ashamed to fire at a man and not hit him.' Immediately after this reply, a man who had been with the Free-State men, and till then supposed to be one of them, went over to the other party, which soon after dispersed. It was supposed at the time that the report of this spy brought the ' war ' to an end for that day. After the band had mounted and dispersed, the principals and principal instigators avoided our neighborhood. Some of the more honest dupes, however, seeing the absurdity of their position, and the reasonableness of our proposition, riding up to us had a social chat, cracking jokes, etc., and then rode off with the determination formed, and more than half expressed, of never being caught in so ridiculous a farce again."

Although no three thousand or thirty thousand men made their appearance after this bloodless war, the claimants were by no means satisfied, and dire vengeance was threatened. The report of the trouble was industriously circulated among pro-slavery settlers far and near, and at length the following call was issued:

" TERRITORIAL INDIGNATION MEETING.

" We, the Sovereign people of Kansas Territory, are requested to meet at Lawrence City, January 11, at 11 o'clock A.M., to adopt those measures that will protect us from all moneyed associations or influences, also the tyrannical encroachments daily made by the Lawrence

Association. On which occasion there will be speeches made to vindicate the squatters' rights of pre-emption, and the protection of his claim until entered.

" MANY CITIZENS."

The following, taken from " Incidents of Early Times," by Hon. John Speer, in the Kansas *Tribune*, will convey some idea of the quarrel and the character of the meeting to consider the claim dispute :

" We had several meetings, and had a good deal of bitterness at some of them. There were fights and fusses all around. In Lawrence the contest was a good deal between the ' outsiders ' and the ' insiders.' The latter were the Lawrence Association, and the former ' squatters ' who were in opposition to it. These associations related to claims to the town site, but as the town company was mostly Free-State men, it necessarily arrayed all the pro-slavery element against it, which with the property claimants in opposition made a strong force.

" Several persons from slave States professed to be against slavery in Kansas. They generally wanted a ' free white State.' Commotions and fights and rumors of fights were frequent. A few Yankees wanted to ' argue ' the matter, but the more they wanted to argue, the more their opponents were bound to fight.

" Among them came a man named Edward Chapman. He had a hare-lip and a tied tongue, and he made the most of these deformities by pretending that a bullet had passed through his mouth at the battle of Buena Vista. He boasted of his blood, but it was found that all his claim to superiority of blood was derived from having once been a groom to a race-horse. From his defective pronunciation, and to distinguish him from others of that name, he was called ' Hawhaw ' Chapman. A great man was Hawhaw. The mock-heroic of his composition was only excelled by his cowardice, but he was the bravest man where there was no enemy that we ever saw. They told a story of him that he was consulting with a Free-State man with the greatest profession of Free-Stateism, when suddenly a gang of armed pro-slavery ruffians rushed upon them. The Free-State man jumped into a thicket out of sight, but Hawhaw was headed off and he threw up his hands, exclaiming, ' I'm hro-hlavery, by 'od.' He cut down a cabin frame with an axe, and was arrested and taken before Judge Lecompte at the Shawnee Mission. His vandal spirit was a good deal broken, and we went his bail for appearance and to keep the peace. He understood the bond differently from ourselves, and wanted to keep a piece of the cabin he had mutilated—in other words, to steal the house. He killed a man with a club, but as it was a fight between two pro-slavery men, nobody ever took any other notice of it.   Hawhaw was elected as a pro-slavery man to the Legislature.   He was great as a statesman, for he could speak an hour without anybody knowing what he said.

"Fortunately, a specimen of his style is perpetuated in print.   A great squatter meeting was held to denounce the Lawrence Association, and Hawhaw presented his remarks and his resolutions in writing, and as nobody could tell what he said, his resolutions were passed unanimously amid great pro-slavery enthusiasm.   We quote from the Kansas *Tribune* of January 24, 1855:

"'Pursuant to the call, the squatters of Kansas Territory assembled in large numbers, on the 11th day of January, 1855, and long before the hour of meeting the streets were thronged with the multitude.   We had never before attended a meeting so boisterous and violent as this one.   There were five hundred persons present, all armed. —— Jones, still living here, undertook to speak against G. W. Clarke on a claim question.   The stand was a store box, and Clarke "went for him" in the rear, sending him at least a rod over the heads of the crowd around the stand.   Revolvers were quickly hauled, and Clarke undertook to shoot Governor Robinson.   Still there was no bloodshed.

"'When Hawhaw's printed proceedings came out, however, they were too ridiculous to excite anything but merriment.   When Robinson read them he merely remarked that he would rather be a "false Belshazzar" than a real one.'

"HAWHAW'S SPEECH.

"'FELLOW-CITIZENS: The assemblage of the sovereign people on this day, by a spontaneous impulse and for a common purpose, is a most glorious spectacle.   And we, too, friends and neighbors, are here together.   The toils and cares of our daily avocations are laid aside; the disquietudes and strifes that vex our poor humanity shall be lost in the mutual recognition of one grand sentiment.   And the turbulent, selfish interests here manifested for a period—under the overshadowing spell of sectional influences, which gloom pervades the hearts of men, whose actors upon the grand rostrum of the future, choose as their talisman the sovereign ear whose compunction some slight affectionate cares of every victim of the oppressor triumph as the idol of their vain madness, and of their midnight orgies, which forever crush the rights of this people.

"'We have been weak, now in justice we are strong—more imposing than of forty centuries from the old pyramids—the intellectual and progressive years of self-government of a free people.   The fraternal influences—what are they?   And why are we here this day?

"'A handful of men on the western bank of the remotest tributary, whose waters pay homage to the father of waters, and yet only in the centre of this immense confederacy, whose shade is a refuge for all nations of the earth, and the free breezes that unceasingly sweep through the branches, over the silent sepulchres of those who fought the good fight and proclaimed to the world to be a free, independent and sovereign people. The seed which they planted with tremulous apprehension are here this day, commingling their patriotic rebukes against that mercenary morbidness which characterizes the Lawrence Association as stock-jobbers and money-getters—men of exchanges and coteries and self-interest—covered from head to foot with the leprosy of materialism, until it shall submerge all opposition, by secret and unjust invasions which from their first advent in Kansas Territory up to the present is opulence, title, and despotism with civil feuds, dissevering all fraternal affections. We, the sovereign squatters, proclaim the manifesto of our absolute authority and an inexorable interdict to every despotic invader upon our rights, secured and sanctified by the Congress of the United States. "Thus far shalt thou go and no farther." We, the sovereign squatters, stand forth boldly upon our commanding eminence—the highest law of the land.

" ' Compromising the plighted faith of the Government that the land we now occupy shall be our future homes upon which eminence we this day invite for the last time the false Belshazzar who with restless gaze views the dauntless energy which guides us to this grand consummation. If wrong in statements here made this day of your unjust invasions, nerve the lost, mutilated, and tattered honor—dishonored and blackened with treason, incapable of sincere demonstration against our rights as sovereign squatters that these lands shall be our homes; on which occasion we proclaim to the world the wrongs which, by foreign intrigue and hypocrisy which you this day are called to deny the immutable facts whose design is imperishable tyranny; to take from the poor man his home; to enrich those that now in luxury dwell.'

"And this is what old Hawhaw proposed to do with the ' false Belshazzar ':

" '*Resolved*, That as on former occasions C. Robinson should again call to his aid the gallant hussars No. 1, supported by his shot-gun battalion, in forcing us from our rights; that we, the sovereign squatters of Kansas Territory, will take his honor and battalion and deal with them according to laws, rules, and regulations prescribed therein that we may adopt.'

"Ridiculous as these extracts are, they are literally just as they were passed and as Hawhaw wrote them out. They were mainly directed against Dr. (since Governor) Robinson, who was the ' false

Belshazzar' of the occasion, and although Robinson was present when
they were passed, as he couldn't understand a word that Hawhaw said,
how could he object?   But the other speeches by Clarke (the man who
afterwards murdered Barber), Wood, and others were very bitter on
Robinson and the whole association, and Robinson, Emery, Speer and
others did reply to them."

Andrea's history says of this meeting, page 318:

" Many who attended this meeting were diametrically opposed to the
proceedings, and to the resolutions adopted, and to make sure their
position should not be misunderstood, a meeting of the citizens not
members of the Lawrence Association was held at the ' church' on the
16th, which denounced the proceedings of that on the 11th as being
' held and conducted in a one-sided, indecent, mob-like manner, and
wholly in opposition to justice, right and honor,' and that as the
' endeavor was made to make us responsible for those proceedings, we
therefore disavow all complicity or assent thereto and denounce the origi-
nators as demagogues.'   The course pursued by the Lawrence Association was endorsed by the meeting of which S. J. Willis was president;
Dr. J. F. Merriam, secretary; Messrs. Stewart, Ladd, Pillsbury, Hart-
well, and Lowe, vice-presidents.   The resolutions presented by Messrs.
Ladd, Emery, Doy, Mailey, Hutchinson, Man, Searl, Simpson, and
Tappan were adopted.   The third and fourth resolutions follow:

" '*Resolved*, That the organization of the Emigrant Aid Society has
been of exceeding great benefit in the transmission of emigrants to the
Territory; and their establishing an agency in this city, and their investment of capital herein has been a decided advantage to the place, towards
its rapid growth, providing for the wants and alleviating the trials of
the settlers, and we believe that their efforts thus far have been entirely
disinterested; and we therefore most cordially invite them to remain
and continue their operations among us, at the same time assuring
them of our sincere approval of the past, and of our co-operation in the
future.

" '*Resolved*, That we, as citizens of Lawrence, *particularly* approve
of the course pursued by the Lawrence Association towards the Emigrant Aid Society in extending an invitation to that company to invest
their capital here, and the basis upon which they are allowed to operate;
and we shall duly respect their city rights, and support them in all lawful and liberal movements.'

" At the same meeting the committee of the Lawrence Association,
by their chairman, Mr. J. Hutchinson, reported the following resolutions, which were adopted:

" '*Resolved*, That while believing there is no legal redress for trespasses committed upon unsurveyed lands, we have never as an association approved of cutting timber upon individual claims, made in good
faith ; but we fully discountenance such acts, believing them to be contrary to equity and good order.

" '*Resolved*, That as the law holds a man's domicile no less sacred
and inviolate than his person, we regard all persons who shall molest
or destroy houses erected or in process of erection as men guilty of a
henious offense and regardless of the law of the land.

" '*Resolved*, That while we uphold only justice and good order, we
believe that neither the Lawrence Association nor their officers are
accountable for individual acts civilly or politically, and that the late
attempts to bring this association into bad repute and to cast upon us a
stigma as undeserved as it is unjust, will bring down threefold odium
upon the heads of the vile perpetrators.'

" Dr. Robinson, towards the close of the meeting, made a short and
sensible speech, refuting some of the charges made against him, coun-
selling his hearers of the danger of quarrels among themselves, and
impressing upon them the duty and necessity of union ; that they might,
' with voice and hand and means combined, defend these hills and valleys, these rivers and broad prairies from the curse of human bondage
and the chains of slavery.' "

But resolutions and counter resolutions availed nothing
except to place the respective parties on record. The Free-
State men were in no mood to be driven off, and the claimants were persistent for blackmail or the possession of the
land.   Hostilities were continued when occasion offered, to
the annoyance of all concerned, whether on or off the town
site.   One day, on the return of the agent of the Aid Company from a visit out of the settlement, he was informed that
his own house, erected on Oread Hill, was being cut down
by pro-slavery men. G. W. Deitzler, S. N. Wood, and S.
N. Simpson volunteered to go to the battle-field, but, as
soon as the house was reached, the cutting was discontinued and the vandals slunk away.   Such men never liked
Deitzler, Wood, and Simpson, and had no desire to associate
with them on such occasions.   They would sooner leave
their work in hand unfinished than remain in such company.

In the month of February, the resident agent of the Aid

Company went East, and returned with the first spring party in March, 1855. During his absence a compromise was effected with the claimants to the town site by limiting the area to six hundred and forty acres, and giving four or five men one hundred out of two hundred and twenty shares into which the site was divided, leaving one hundred and ten shares for the original town company, and eight shares for the Emigrant Aid Company, with two shares in trust for the endowment of a school. This compromise was made with the consent of the financial agent of the Aid Company, who resided at Kansas City, Missouri. Why it was made has never appeared. These town-site jumpers had no more legal or equitable title to this one hundred shares than Franklin Pierce or Jeff Davis.

The pre-emption law excepted from individual pre-emption all "sections or fractions of sections included within the limits of any incorporated town, every portion of the public land which has been selected for a site for a city or town, and every parcel or lot of land actually settled or occupied for the purposes of trade, and not agriculture."

Lawrence was selected as a town site on the last of July, 1854, and the commissioner of the Land Office said the Shawnee lands were not opened to settlement, by the extinguishment of the Indian title, till September 28th of that year, therefore no individual claimant could acquire any right whatever before that date. Neither could he after it, as the place had already been selected and occupied for a town and for "purposes of trade and not agriculture."

But the most unfortunate deal of all was the mutilation of South Park. That had been platted to extend to Quincy street on the north, Kentucky street on the west, Lee street on the south, and Rhode Island street on the east. To gratify the greed of the spoilsmen a strip of land, the width of one-half of a block on each side of the park was platted into lots, and divided among them, leaving the park as at present, bounded on all sides by alleys in the rear of the lots appropriated, where can be found outhouses, stables, coal and wood sheds, ash-heaps, garbage and offal of all descriptions common to back yards of a city. In the original arrangement, the members of the town association were to have every other lot, leaving the remainder to be divided equally between the Aid Company, and parties who would improve the lots. Under this arrangement the company had in contemplation not only mills and hotel, but the erection of an educational institution for advanced pupils. As soon as this surrender was learned in the East, there was virtually an end of stock subscriptions in the company as an investment, and an end of all college building at Lawrence. But few shares of stock were afterwards subscribed, and money had to be raised on the contribution plan. Mr. Thayer turned his attention in this direction, and in 1856 had the entire North organized on this basis.

Had this surrender quieted the title to Lawrence some equivalent might have been received, but it had no such effect. While the four town jumpers were quieted, a large number of other persons were dissatisfied, and set up protests and counter-claims, which were never put at rest till the title was finally adjusted by Government officials. The uncertainty of title was as great after the surrender as before, although the new claimants were content to await official action, while the jumpers were not. As late as August, 1855, over ninety occupants of the town made a protest against this settlement showing its injustice and illegality. Among other things they say :

" We beg leave respectfully to submit that they are deeply dissatisfied with the ' settlement ' entered into in March last between your association on the one part, and Messrs. C. W. Babcock, J. P. Wood, Wm. Lykins, Wm. and John Baldwin, on the other. We are dissatisfied with this so-called settlement, because it is extremely well calculated, in our opinion, to impair the interests and check the progress of this town. By its operations nearly one-half of all the land embraced in the town plot is monopolized by half a dozen persons, whose right thereto emanates from the association alone, while the number of actual inhabitants at the present time is not far from five hundred. At an early period the Lawrence Association adopted a policy with reference to those who desired to settle and acquire property in the town, well designed to stimulate its growth and · increase its prosperity. That association adopted a resolution, October 9, 1854, ' to set apart every fourth lot in the city to be given to those who would build upon them, or to those to whom the association might deem it proper to donate the same.' On the 16th December, 1854, it also enacted ' that every person who was then, or might become, a resident of the town, and should remain during the winter, should be entitled to three city lots of the standard size, on condition of making improvements respecting the rules of the association, etc.'

" These measures were just and judicious. They were just because they served to distribute the land upon which the town was located to all the inhabitants thereof upon terms graduated according to the amount of service respectively rendered in building up the town and making valuable the lands upon which it was located. And being just, they were also judicious, because they extended a fair chance and solid interest to all who thought proper to accept the same, and in this way secured the settlement of a large number of persons who otherwise would not have come, and whose exertions and improvements contribute greatly to the advancement of the town. By the adoption of this settlement their wise and beneficent policy was necessarily abandoned, and nearly half of all the land pertaining to the city site allowed to pass into the possession of five men, thus creating a monopoly which is already showing deleterious and injurious effects upon this community, by the rapid decrease in the value of real estate, and the uncertainty which rests upon all business transactions. In consequence of this, also, the association was compelled to disregard, in a number of instances, its engagements with those who had come into the town upon the conditions of its previous policy. So completely was it stript of its resources by this silly transaction that it was constrained to repudiate some of its most binding obligations. The impelling motive to the adoption by the association of this strange measure seems to have been the desire to get rid of a claim, by the gentlemen above named, to a portion of the city site, and the association seems to have assented to the arrangement under a gross misapprehension of the true grounds upon which that claim was based, but the claim, as can now be seen by the foregoing argument, was without the slightest foundation."

CHAPTER V.

SETTLEMENTS.—ELECTIONS.—PUBLIC SENTIMENT.

NOTWITHSTANDING the persistent effort of pro-slavery men
to harass and drive off Free-State men on a pretext of priority
of claims, not only at Lawrence but elsewhere, Free-State
settlers remained, defended their rights to lands settled upon,
and large accessions were constantly made to their numbers.
Before winter set in, people from all parts of the East, North,
and West, as well as the South, were moving to Kansas faster
than accommodations could be provided for their comfort.
The threats and bluster of the pro-slavery men and journals
had served to stimulate rather than prevent Northern emigration. The *Herald of Freedom* thus speaks of the emigration,
March 10, 1855:

" The first company, consisting of thirty-one persons, arrived in
Lawrence on the first day of August last; the second party arrived the
13th of September, and numbered one hundred and thirty; the third
party arrived the 8th of October, and numbered one hundred and sixty-
two; the fourth party arrived October 30th, and numbered two hundred
and thirty; the fifth party arrived November 20th, with one hundred
persons; the sixth and last regular party of the season arrived December 1st, and numbered fifty persons; amounting in the aggregate to six
hundred and seventy-three. But this does not begin to show the number who were induced to emigrate to Kansas in consequence of this
organization. Other portions of our confederacy, witnessing the great
movement westward set in motion by this company, were induced to
fall into line. The Pennsylvania company, numbering fully three hundred persons in all, were induced, to our certain knowledge, to come last
season in consequence of the advantage they expected to derive from
those connected with the Aid Company. Ohio sent forward her pioneers, who were also strengthened in their purpose to locate here from

the same cause. Hundreds on hundreds of individuals from all parts of the free North were wakened up on the subject, and induced to emigrate on account of the description of the country, and the advantages to the settlers first furnished to the public press, and afterwards extensively copied into nearly every anti-Nebraska journal, by the agents of this organization. Even the American Settlement Company, which claims to have done so much towards populating Kansas, was but an offshoot of the New England organization, and owed its existence to Mr. Thayer's great speech in the Tabernacle, New York; he having given birth to the New York Kansas League, and some of those connected with that League devised the Settlement Company. We have no doubt but, if all the instrumentalities which have operated to influence the public mind directly and indirectly, could be brought to light, it would appear that, instead of sending ' two or three hundred' into the Territory from the free States, it would be manifest that they had influenced the settling of thousands among us—not a fiftieth part, however, of the number they will eventually induce in the same direction, if need be, to make Kansas a free State."

On November 29th was held an election for territorial delegate to Congress. As this election had no direct agency in State-making, it attracted much less attention than the election for a territorial Legislature which was held in the spring of 1855. But it was deemed of sufficient importance by the pro-slavery men to make extensive preparations for an invasion from Missouri. The machinery for controlling elections had been well provided in advance, and was ready for operation. The Congressional committee, in the report of the majority, make this statement, based upon testimony taken by it :

" Before any election was or could be held in the Territory, a secret political society was formed in the State of Missouri. It was known by different names, such as ' Social Band,' ' Friends' Society,' ' Blue Lodge,' ' The Sons of the South.' Its members were bound together by secret oaths, and they had pass-words, signs, and grips, by which they were known to each other ; penalties were imposed for violating the rules and secrets of the order ; written minutes were kept of the proceedings of the lodges ; and the different lodges were connected together by an effective organization. It embraced great numbers of the citizens of Missouri, and was extended into other slave States and into the Territory. Its avowed purpose was to extend slavery not only into Kansas, but also into other Territories of the United States, and to form a union of all the friends of that institution. Its plan of operating was to organize and send men to vote at the elections in the Territory, to collect money to pay their expenses, and, if necessary, to protect them in voting. It also proposed to induce pro-slavery men to emigrate into the Territory, to aid and sustain them while there, and to elect none to office but those friendly to their views. This dangerous society was controlled by men who avowed their purpose to extend slavery into the Territory at all hazards, and was altogether the most effective instrument in organizing the subsequent armed invasions and forays. In its lodges in Missouri the affairs of Kansas were discussed. The force necessary to control the election was divided into bands and leaders selected. Means were collected, and signs and badges were agreed upon. While the great body of the actual settlers of the Territory were relying upon the rights secured to them by the organic law, and had formed no organization or combination whatever, even of a party character, this conspiracy against their rights was gathering strength in a neighboring State, and would have been sufficient at their first election to have overpowered them, even if they had been united to a man."

The great champion and leader of the slavery propagandists, General D. R. Atchison, is reported by the Platte *Argus* as explaining his position and that of his allies, at Weston, Missouri, as follows :

" He would now pass to the settlement of Kansas, its destiny, and the effect it was to have upon the State of Missouri.

" The organic law of the Territory vests in the people who reside in it the power to form all its municipal regulations. They can either admit or exclude slavery, and this is the only question that materially affects our interests.   *   *   *

" General Atchison said, that his mission here to-day was, if possible, to awaken the people of this country to the danger ahead, and to suggest the means to avoid it. The people of Kansas in their first election would decide the question whether or not the slave-holder was to be excluded, and it depended upon a majority of the votes cast at the polls. Now, if a set of fanatics and demagogues a thousand miles off could advance their money and exert every nerve to abolitionize the Territory and exclude the slave-holder when they have not the least personal interest in the matter, what is your duty ? When you reside within one day's journey of the Territory, and when your peace, your quiet, and your property depend upon your action, you can without an exertion send five hundred of your young men who will vote in favor of your institutions. Should each county in the State of Missouri only do its duty, the question will be decided quietly and peaceably at the ballot-box. If we are defeated, then Missouri and the other Southern States will have shown themselves recreant to their interests and will have deserved their fate. The abolitionists will have nothing to gain or lose. It is an abstraction with them. We have much to gain or much to lose. Said he: 'If you burn my barn, I sustain a great loss, but you gain nothing. So it is with the colonizationist societies and the dupes they send to abolitionize Kansas. If these abolitionists steal your negroes, they gain nothing. The negroes are injured; you are ruined. So much greater is the motive for activity on your part. Fellow-citizens, we should not be apathetic when so much is involved. We should be up and doing.' He was for meeting organization with organization. He was for meeting these philanthropic knaves peaceably at the ballot-box, and out-voting them. If we cannot do this it is an omen that the institution of slavery must fall in this and other Southern States, but it would fall after much strife, civil war, and bloodshed. If abolitionism, under its present auspices, is established in Kansas, there will be constant strife and bloodshed between Kansas and Missouri. Negro stealing will be a principle and a vocation. It will be the policy of philanthropic knaves, until they force the slave-holder to abandon Missouri; nor will it be long until it is done. You cannot watch your stables to prevent thieves from stealing your horses and mules; neither can you watch your negro quarters to prevent your neighbors from seducing away and stealing your negroes. If Kansas is abolitionized, all men who love peace and quiet will leave us, and all emigration to Missouri from the slave States will cease. We will go either to the North or to the South. For himself he could gather together his goods, and depart as soon as the most active among us. He had neither wife nor child to impede his flight. In a hybrid state we cannot live; we cannot be in a constant quarrel—in a constant state of suspicion of our own neighbors. This feeling is entertained by a large portion of mankind everywhere. Yet, he said, he was willing, notwithstanding his pacific views, to hang negro theives; he would not punish those who merely entertained abstract opinions; but negro thieves and persons who stirred up insubordination and insurrection among our slaves, he believed it right to punish, and they could not be punished too severely—he would not punish a man who believed that rape, murder, or larceny was abstractly right, yet he would punish the man who committed either. It was not sufficient for the South to talk, but to act; to go peaceably and inhabit the Territory, and peaceably to vote and settle the question according to the principles of the Douglas bill.''

Eli Thayer, in his "Kansas Crusade," gives his views of the issue on pages 31 and 32, as follows:

"The present crisis was to decide whether freedom or slavery should rule our country for centuries to come. That slavery was a great national curse; that it practically ruined one-half of the nation and greatly impeded the progress of the other half. That it was a curse to the negro, but a much greater curse to the white man. It made the slaveholders petty tyrants, who had no correct idea of themselves or of anybody else. It made the poor whites of the South more abject and degraded than the slaves themselves. That it was an insurmountable obstacle in the way of the nation's progress and prosperity. That it must be overcome and extirpated. That the way to do this was to go to the prairies of Kansas and show the superiority of free-labor civilization; to go with all our free-labor trophies: churches and schools, printing presses, steam-engines, and mills; and in a peaceful contest convince every poor man from the South of the superiority of free labor. That it was much better to *go* and *do* something for free labor than to stay at home and talk of manacles and auction-blocks and blood-hounds, while deploring the never-ending aggressions of slavery. That in this contest the South had not one element of success. We had much greater numbers, and much greater wealth, greater readiness of organization, and better facilities of migration. That we should put a cordon of free States from Minnesota to the Gulf of Mexico, and stop the forming of slave States. After that we should colonize the northern border slave States and exterminate slavery. That our work was not to make women and children cry in anti-slavery conventions, by sentimental appeals, BUT TO GO AND PUT AN END TO SLAVERY."

Amos A. Lawrence said, in his statement before the Massachusetts Historical Society:

"The enthusiasm increased; parties were formed all over the Northern States. The Emigrant Aid Company undertook to give character and direction to the whole. This society was to be loyal to the Government under all circumstances; it was to support the party of law and order, and it was to make Kansas a free State by *bona fide* settlement if at all."

G. W. Brown, in the first number of the *Herald of Freedom*, gives the position of the Free-State men as follows:

"Our great object is to make Kansas a free State; and to that end we shall labor by encouraging emigration. It is *not* our purpose to engage in a crusade against our Southern brethren, nor upon *their* institutions, so long as confined within their legitimate sphere. Our field is *Kansas*, and *here* we shall labor, and *here* shall erect anew the altar of LIBERTY. With the Declaration of American Independence in one hand and the Constitution of the Republic in the other, we engage in a defensive warfare for the Right. We firmly believe that victory will crown the efforts of the Sons of Freedom ; but the struggle will be long and arduous. We may be stricken down at first, but not defeated.''

While General Atchison's speech was comparatively conservative, not so the actions of his subordinates and the people of the border counties in Missouri. On the day of the election, and before, they invaded Kansas like an army of occupation for the purpose of voting, and voting only. They were residents of Missouri, and did not pretend to be *bona fide* residents of Kansas, or intend to become such. This army was recruited and paid as mercenaries to trample down the rights of the people of Kansas and pollute their ballot-boxes. On the other hand, no Free-State men were recruited except to become *bona fide* settlers, and they received no pay whatever.

The leading candidates for delegate at this election were Whitfield, Pro-slavery ; Fleniken, Democrat, and Wakefield, Free State. The character of the election can be seen from the testimony of H. Miles Moore, now one of the most respected citizens of Kansas. He testified before the Congressional committee as follows :

" I came into the Territory to reside in September, 1855, from western Missouri, where I had resided for about five years, practising as an attorney at law. I had resided in St. Louis a year previous to that. I came over to Leavenworth City on the 29th of November, 1854, to attend the election for delegate to Congress. Arrangements had been made throughout western Platte County, and western Missouri generally, as I have been informed, for the purpose of going over there and voting at that election. Messengers had been sent from one portion of western Missouri to another, to notify. Meetings had been held to make arrangements to come over here on that day to vote. For a day or two previous, large numbers had passed through Weston to the Territory, on horseback and in wagons, with their forage and provisions, from the counties lower down on the north side of the river—Clinton,

Platte, and Clay counties.   I saw parties from each of these counties at
the hotel ; among them, men whom I recognized.   The companies raised
about Weston and Platte County were generally sent to the back portions
of the Territory.   The lower counties sent men to the precincts near the
border.   I myself came over with a large party from Weston and Platte
County to Leavenworth ; a large crowd was present then on the ground.
The election was held at the Leavenworth hotel, kept by Keller & Kyle.
There was a great crowd around the polls all day.   There was a good
deal of excitement, and some quarrelling and fighting.   I remained there
all day till nearly night.   General Whitfield was the pro-slavery candidate ; Judge Fleniken was the Free-State candidate.   All our party from
Weston voted for Whitfield.   I believe I voted myself that day for
General Whitfield, but I do not see my name on the poll-books.   I
should think there must have been from one hundred and fifty to two
hundred Missourians who voted there that day.   The other Missourians
who came over said after they returned, that they went to the 14th and
15th districts, and other districts farther back."

The number of votes polled at this election was, for Whitfield, 2238 ; Wakefield, 248 ; Fleniken, 305 ; and scattering,
22 ; a total of 2833.   Of these votes it is estimated that
1114 were legal, and 1729 illegal.

The majority of the committee thus reports :

"Thus your committee finds that in this, the first election in the
Territory, a very large majority of the votes were cast by citizens of the
State of Missouri, in violation of the organic law of the Territory.   Of
the legal votes cast, General Whitfield received a plurality.   The settlers took but little interest in the election, not one-half of them voting.
This may be accounted for from the fact that the settlements were scattered over a great extent, that the term of the delegate to be elected
was short, and that the question of free or slave institutions was not
generally regarded by them as distinctly at issue.   Under these circumstances, a systematic invasion from an adjoining State, by which large
numbers of illegal votes were cast in remote and sparse settlements, for
the avowed purpose of extending slavery into the Territory, even
though it did not change the result of the election, was a crime of great
magnitude.   Its immediate effect was further to excite the people of
the Northern States, and to exasperate the actual settlers against their
neighbors in Missouri."

At this time every considerable settlement in the Territory,
except Lawrence and vicinity, was pro-slavery, and an in-

7

vasion was wholly unnecessary, as Whitfield could have been elected without. Being unnecessary, it was an inexcusable blunder, as it served to expose the game the pro-slavery men proposed to play, and increased the agitation and determination in the North. The conservatism, as well as the anti-slavery sentiment of the country, had received a serious shock in the repeal of the Missouri Compromise, and was in no mood for foul play in the game set by the slave interest. Had there been no invasion or illegal voting, all would have acquiesced in the election of Whitfield without a murmur. This is one of a series of blunders made by General Atchison's forces which was taken advantage of by Free-State men. The settlers contented themselves by making this protest to the governor:

"*To his Excellency, A. H. Reeder, Governor of Kansas Territory:*

"Believing that a large number of the citizens of the State of Missouri voted at the election of the 29th instant for delegate to Congress representing Kansas Territory, we respectfully petition your honor that the entire vote of the district receiving the votes of citizens of Missouri be set aside, or that the entire election be set aside."

SIGNED BY NUMEROUS CITIZENS.

Some of the pro-slavery editors and people professed to be greatly elated over the result of this election, and to regard it as a test of strength between the parties. The Kansas *Herald*, published at Leavenworth, had this to say:

"There is not a single doubt that Kansas will be a slave State. Our recent election shows a majority in its favor. General Whitfield, the pro-slavery candidate, had out of twenty-eight hundred votes polled twenty-two hundred. And notwithstanding the Aid Societies have poured in hordes of her paupers for the purpose of abolitionizing Kansas, they either become initiated in our institutions, or leave as fast as they arrive. Now, if the South does her duty, and especially Missouri, the Northern hope of abolitionizing Kansas will be a *phantom* hope.

*   *   *   *   *   *   *

"Where is Lawrence, the reservoir for the overflow of the Aid Societies? It is true she is still situated on the Kaw river, but is now one of the principal pro-slavery towns in Kansas."

Other papers were equally jubilant and earnest in their appeals to the South to take possession of the Territory at once with their slaves.   On the other hand, a few Northern papers were despondent and predicted the defeat of the Free-State cause.   Horace Greeley weakened, and said the chances that Kansas would be a slave State were as four to one, and he seemed to " hear the clanking chains of human bondage, and saw the hideous shambles for the sale of human flesh." However, the Missouri invasion was treated by most Northern papers as an outrage to be denounced and its repetition resisted to the bitter end.   Whatever the effect outside of Kansas, the *bona fide* citizens were unconcerned.   All parties knew that it was no test of strength and could have but little weight in settling the momentous question pending.   The Free-State men busied themselves with their work of cabin-building, and in preparing their claims for spring cultivation. They were men who had counted the cost and were not to be discouraged by claim conflicts, personal assaults, or invasions at elections.   This election afforded good grounds for encouragement.   The fact that the pro-slavery party deemed it necessary to import voters showed that it had no confidence in a majority of settlers of its own faith, and the invasion was conclusive evidence that law was to be disregarded whenever it was supposed to block the way to success.   The bullying and bluster from the first, and now this invasion, showed conclusively that the enemy, the Free-State men, were rated as inferiors and to be despised, trodden upon and crushed without ceremony.   All these things were carefully noted by the Free-State men, and gave great hope of success in the final result.   They would not have had it otherwise if they could, as, had the pro-slavery men treated all with civility and attended the elections under the forms of law, coming quietly into the Territory under pretense of being settlers, all elections could have been carried by them and no valid protest could have been made.   They had every advantage ; their forces resided on the border, and as all were recent settlers, no proof could have been easily furnished against them.

In the months of January and February, 1855, a census was ordered by the Governor, and an election was to be held March 30th for a territorial Legislature. This election was of the greatest moment, as, according to the organic act, the question of a free or slave State would most likely be settled by the first Legislature. The Free-State men, confident of their majority of voters, relied upon the promises of the Governor that a fair election should be held, and had no fears of the result. For the first time they held caucuses or conventions to agree upon candidates to be supported. This was no easy matter, as an effort had been made from the first to divide Free-State men into two hostile camps. Fortunately or unfortunately, three newspapers were started at Lawrence in the early winter, and all professed to be in favor of a free State. However, as is generally the case, a war sprung up between them, and what one paper advocated another must oppose. One paper, edited by men from the West and South, was hostile to men from the East, and especially made war upon everything and everybody connected with the Emigrant Aid Company.

The editors of this paper affiliated with the black law men, associated on friendly terms with the invaders of the polls and printed their tickets. They denounced the other editors, or one of them, as not sound on the slavery question, and he retaliated in kind. On April 26, 1855, he submitted this proposition:

"We propose that the pro-slavery journal of this city get a chapter of denunciations against the Emigrant Aid Company stereotyped, to be used on opportune occasions. It must be a matter of great inconvenience to reset its type so often with the same ideas, and all abounding with much vindictiveness. 'The good trees in the orchard are always the most stoned.' It is for this the Janus-faced press has been so violent against certain men and measures in this city."

This newspaper quarrel, while a question of the most vital importance was pending, disgusted all sincere Free-State men, till some person wrote the following, which was published in the *Herald of Freedom*, February 17, 1855:

"ADVICE TO THE THREE EDITORS.

"LAWRENCE, February 14, 1855.

"*Editor of Herald of Freedom:*

"As a subscriber to all three of the Lawrence papers, as one of the *earliest* pioneers to Kansas, as a well-wisher, and I trust co-worker in the Free-State army, and as a matter-of-fact man, I am surprised and annoyed and heartily sick at the course being pursued by *some* of the city papers. Under the most silly and child-like pretexts attacks are made, defamation of character attempted, influence and usefulness sought to be circumscribed, and the 'rule or ruin' principle endeavored to be carried into effect. * * *

"In your private jealousies, your petty feuds, family jars, contemptible bickerings, insolent calumniation, and harsh epithets, we have little or no interest, and they only beget disgust. We seek information, we desire respectability in our papers, and wish not to be ashamed to transmit them to our friends at a distance.

"While anxious inquiries are hourly being made about Kansas from abroad, her soil, her climate, her timber, her stone, her coal, water, commercial advantages, and the probable introduction of slavery therein, none are made as to the animosities, animadversion, or antipathy existing between Messrs. Brown, Miller, and Elliot, and the Brothers Speer, severally editors and proprietors of the *Herald of Freedom*, *Free State*, and *Tribune*. Gentlemen and brethren, if you cannot see alike, each see for yourself. If some of you desire to be more radical than your more conservative brother, it is your privilege. A generous and appreciating public will award to you that merit you deserve, whether you take either extreme, or a middle course between two. Were I not re-echoing the feelings of four-fifths of all your subscribers, a delicacy would prevent the plainness of this article. You all profess to be battling for the one common cause, 'Freedom for Kansas.' Do so honestly, peacefully, determinately, and successfully, and each in your own way. If wrong has been done you, seek redress elsewhere than through your own columns. If you have been insulted and *must* resent it, fight it out hand to hand, and not embroil your readers in the 'muss.' In the settling of your difficulties you must help yourselves. In making Kansas free, you will always have the help of

"A CONSERVATIVE."

At length the conflicting elements were sufficiently harmonized to present but one ticket to be voted for, instead of two, as at the election of delegate to Congress. While the Free-State elements were being conciliated and united, the pro-slavery men were earnestly at work. The border and territorial pro-slavery press sounded the alarm, beat their tom-toms and gongs, and rallied the faithful to the rescue. The *Frontier News*, of Westport, Missouri, as published in the *Herald of Freedom* of February 17, 1855, had the following:

"KANSAS—THE ELECTION CRISIS.

" The election which is ultimately to decide the destiny of Kansas is at hand: the census has been ordered, and the returns will be made on the 9th instant. Let the day of election come when it may, 'tis the result of that day's work which finally determines the institutions of the Territory, and the future State. It is therefore into this battle, heart and soul, that our Southern friends must throw themselves. The triumphant election of our delegate, though of no political importance as far as the great cause is concerned, yet acted as a powerful prestige, both to ourselves and to our abolition foes. Greeley was disheartened, declared that there were four chances to one in favor of Kansas being a slave State; and already heard 'the clanking chains of human bondage, and saw the hideous shambles for the sale of human flesh.' But this triumph was a mere skirmish, calculated to lull the energies of the South into a peaceful slumber. The real battle, the decisive conflict, has yet to be fought; and think you, Southerners, if we lose it, that the South can ever again obtain a foothold in the Territory? Vain thought! The code of Lawrence, digested by Messrs. Robinson, Thayer and Company, and enforced by abolition tyrants, will be the code of Kansas; and the chivalric South must bow beneath the yoke. How galling, how degrading to a sense of your manhood! Are you men? Then gird up your loins, be up and doing; remember, that which has been done once can be done again.

" It is now time for the South to rally; to wait no longer with folded arms for 'signs of the times,' but go to work boldly, fearlessly, and with a sustained buoyancy of spirit and fixedness of purpose to secure their great end.

" Southerners, you will baptize in a pond, and tar and feather a poor devil who believes he is doing God service when he persuades a slave to escape, and yet you will look on supinely when the whole institution is threatened with extermination—and stand by and see with composure a ' paradisiacal garden' marked and dedicated as an asylum for decoyed, stolen, and runaway slaves. Big-hearted but feeble-handed, you would look on, shedding tears of impotence and self-contempt.

" Freemen of the South, pioneers of the West, ' these are the times that try men's souls.' This is the twelfth hour of the night—birds of darkness are on the wing—the day will soon dawn—the battle will soon commence. Arouse and fight a good fight! Let the eagle of victory perch upon your banners. Steady, men! Forward!"

The Leavenworth *Herald* said :

" Remember that free-soilers and abolitionists have combined under the name of Free State, and boldly proclaim their hostility to the Douglas bill, and their defense of the Aid Societies! Such, ye Old Guard of the West, is the progress of the lying and dastardly crew you have to contend against. Saith the common law : When any number of persons band themselves together for a common object detrimental to the interest of any body, it is conspiracy! We say boldly that by law, all persons having connection with the Aid Societies are conspirators, and subject to indictment and conviction as such. They are criminals, and beside openly deny the powers of the Constitution of the United States, and consequently by their own acts have thrown themselves out of the protection of law."

Stringfellow, in a speech at St. Joseph, is reported as saying :

"I tell you to mark every scoundrel among you that is the least tainted with free-soilism or abolitionism, and exterminate him. Neither give nor take quarter from the d—d rascals. I propose to mark them in this house, and on the present occasion, so you may crush them out. To those who have qualms of conscience as to violating laws, State or national, the time has come when such impositions must be disregarded, as your rights and property are in danger ; and I advise you, one and all, to enter every election district in Kansas, in defiance of Reeder and his vile myrmidons, and vote at the point of the bowie-knife and revolver. Neither give nor take quarter, as our cause demands it. It is enough that the slave-holding interest wills it, from which there is no appeal. What right has Governor Reeder to rule Missourians in Kansas? His proclamation and prescribed oath must be repudiated. It is your interest to do so. Mind that slavery is established where it is not prohibited."

At length came election day, the 30th of March, and with it an invading horde from Missouri. They came with great

ostentation, with arms of every description, including cannon. They were detailed to every district in sufficient
numbers to secure every member of the Legislature should
their votes be counted. They paid little attention to formality, and less to legality. So open, unblushing, and overwhelming was the demonstration, that it defeated itself. It
required no search for testimony to prove its illegality in a
contest, as the invaders brought the proof with them and
proclaimed it to all the world. This was very satisfactory to
the Free-State men, and most of them looked on without
effort to prevent the illegal voting, except in a formal way
by entering protest before the judges of election. The affair
was thus described in the *Herald of Freedom* of the next
day :

"Of the disgraceful proceedings in this place on Friday last, by
which the ballot-box was converted into an engine of oppression, we
have hardly patience to write. To see hundreds of hired mercenaries
on horseback, on foot, and in wagons and carriages, coming into Kansas in a body from an adjoining State, and expressing a determination
to return so soon as they shall have polluted the freeman's safeguard
with their touch, and to see that purpose fulfilled without any action
whatever showing an intention to remain here for a single hour after
they shall have cast a ballot is, to say the least, enough to make a Republican ashamed of his national connections ; and were he not strongly
wedded to the Federal Constitution, in a moment of vexation he might
be led to exclaim that he desired ' no union with such base mercenaries.' "

The majority report of the Congressional Committee is
based upon the testimony of both parties, and is a revelation
new to republican government. A few extracts only are
given. It says :

"By an organized movement, which extended from Andrew County
in the north, to Jasper County in the south, and as far eastward as
Boone and Cole counties, Missouri, companies of men were arranged
in irregular parties, and sent into every council district in the Territory
and into every representative district but one. The members were so
distributed as to control the election in each district. They went to
vote, and with the avowed design to make Kansas a slave State. They

were generally armed and equipped, carried with them their own provisions and tents, and so marched into the Territory.   The details of this invasion form the mass of the testimony taken by your committee, and are so voluminous that we can here state but the leading facts elicited.

" First District.—Lawrence.

" The company of persons who marched into this district was collected in Ray, Howard, Carroll, Boone, Lafayette, Randolph, Macon, Clay, Jackson, Saline, and Cass counties, in the State of Missouri. Their expenses were paid; those who could not come contributing provisions, wagons, etc.   Provisions were deposited for those who were expected to come to Lawrence in the house of William Lykins, and were distributed among the Missourians after they arrived there.   The evening before, and the morning of the day of election, about one thousand men from the above counties arrived at Lawrence, and camped in a ravine a short distance from town, near the place of voting.   They came in wagons (of which there were over one hundred) and on horseback, under the command of Colonel Samuel Young, of Boone County, Missouri, and Claiborne F. Jackson, of Missouri.   They were armed with guns, rifles, pistols, and bowie-knives; and had tents, music, and flags with them.   They brought with them two pieces of artillery, loaded with musket-balls.   On their way to Lawrence some of them met Mr. N. B. Blanton, who had been appointed one of the judges of election by Governor Reeder, and after learning from him that he considered it his duty to demand an oath from them as to their place of residence, first attempted to bribe him, and then threatened him with hanging, in order to induce him to dispense with that oath.   In consequence of these threats he did not appear at the polls the next morning to act as judge.

" The evening before the election, while in camp, the Missourians were called together at the tent of Captain Claiborne F. Jackson, and speeches were made to them by Colonel Young and others, calling for volunteers to go to other districts where there were not Missourians enough to control the election, as there were more at Lawrence than were needed there.   Many volunteered to go, and on the morning of the election several companies, from one hundred and fifty to two hundred each, went off to Tecumseh, Hickory Point, Bloomington, and other places.   On the morning of the election the Missourians came over to the place of voting from their camp, in bodies of one hundred at a time.   Mr. Blanton not appearing, another judge was appointed in his place, Colonel Young claiming that, as the people of the Territory had two judges, it was nothing more than right that the Missourians should have the other one to look after their interests; and Robert A. Cummins was elected in Blanton's stead, because he considered that every man had a right to vote if he had been in the Territory but an hour.

" The Missourians brought their tickets with them; but not having enough, they had three hundred more printed in Lawrence on the evening before and on the day of election. They had white ribbons in their button-holes to distinguish them from the settlers.

" When the voting commenced, the question of the legality of the vote of a Mr. Page was raised. Before it was decided, Colonel Samuel Young stepped up to the window where the votes were received, and said he would settle the matter. The vote of Mr. Page was withdrawn, and Colonel Young offered to vote. He refused to take the oath prescribed by the Governor, but swore he was a resident of the Territory; upon which his vote was received. He told Mr. Abbott, one of the judges, when asked if he intended to make Kansas his future home, that it was none of his business; that if he were a resident then he should ask no more. After his vote was received Colonel Young got up on the window-sill, and announced to the crowd that he had been permitted to vote, and they could all come up and vote. He told the judges that there was no use in swearing the others, as they would all swear as he had done. After the other judges had concluded to receive Colonel Young's vote, Mr. Abbott resigned as judge of election, and Mr. Benjamin was elected in his place.

" The polls were so much crowded till late in the evening that for a time, when the men had voted, they were obliged to get out by being hoisted up on the roof of the building where the election was being held, and passing out over the house. Afterwards, a passage-way through the crowd was made by two lines of men being formed, through which the voters could get up to the polls. Colonel Young asked that the old men be allowed to go up first and vote, as they were tired with the traveling, and wanted to get back to camp. The Missourians sometimes came up to the polls in procession, two by two, and voted. During the day the Missourians drove off the ground some of the citizens—Mr. Stearns, Mr. Bond, and Mr. Willis. They threatened to shoot Mr. Bond, and a crowd rushed after him, threatening him; and as he ran after them some shots were fired at him as he jumped off the bank of the river and made his escape. The citizens of the town went over in a body late in the afternoon, when the polls had become comparatively clear, and voted.

" Before the voting had commenced, the Missourians said if the judges appointed by the Governor did not receive their votes they would choose other judges. Some of them voted several times, changing their hats or coats and coming up to the window again. They said they intended to vote first, and after they had got through the others could vote. Some of them claimed a right to vote under the organic act, from the fact that their mere presence in the Territory constituted them residents, though they were from Missouri and had homes in Missouri.

Others said they had a right to vote because Kansas belonged to Missouri, and people from the East had no right to settle in the Territory and vote there. They said they came to the Territory to elect a Legislature to suit themselves, as the people of the Territory and persons from the East and the North wanted to elect a Legislature that would not suit them. They said they had a right to make Kansas a slave State, because the people of the North had sent persons out to make it a free State. Some claimed that they had heard that the Emigrant Aid Society had sent men out to be at the election, and they came to offset their votes; but the most of them made no such claim. Colonel Young said he wanted the citizens to vote, in order to give the election some show of fairness. The Missourians said there would be no difficulty if the citizens did not interfere with their voting; but they were determined to vote peaceably, if they could, but vote any how. They said each one of them was prepared for eight rounds without loading, and would go to the ninth round with the butcher-knife. Some of them said that by voting in the Territory they would deprive themselves of the right to vote in Missouri for twelve months afterwards. The Missourians began to leave the afternoon of the day of election, though some did not go home until the next morning. In many cases, when a wagon-load voted they immediately started for home. On their way home they said if Governor Reeder did not sanction the election they would hang him.

"The citizens of the town of Lawrence, as a general thing, were not armed on the day of election, though some had revolvers, but not exposed as were the arms of the Missourians. They kept a guard about the town the night after the election, in consequence of the threats of the Missourians, in order to protect it. The pro-slavery men of the district attended the nominating conventions of the Free-State men, and voted for and secured the nominations of men they considered the most obnoxious to the Free-State party, in order to cause dissension in that party. Quite a number of settlers came into the district before the day of election, and after the census was taken. According to the census returns, there were then in the district 369 legal voters. Of those whose names are on the census returns, 117 are to be found on the poll-books of the 30th of March, 1855. Messrs. Ladd, Babcock, and Pratt testify to fifty-five names on the poll-books of persons they knew to have settled in the district after the census was taken, and before election. A number of persons came into the Territory in March before the election, from the Northern and Eastern States, intending to settle, who were in Lawrence on the day of election. At that time many of them had selected no claims, and had no fixed place of residence. Such were not entitled to vote. Many of them became dissatisfied with the country. Others were disappointed at its political condition, and in the price and demand for labor, and returned. Whether any such voted at the election is not clearly shown; but from the proof, it is probable that in the latter part of the day, after the great body of Missourians had voted, some did go to the polls. The number was not over fifty. These voted the Free-State ticket. The whole number of names appearing upon the poll-lists is 1034. After full examination, we are satisfied that not over 232 of these were legal voters, and 802 were non-residents and illegal voters. This district is strongly in favor of making Kansas a free State, and there is no doubt that the Free-State candidates for the Legislature would have been elected by large majorities if none but the actual settlers had voted. At the preceding election, in November, 1854, where none but legal votes were polled, General Whitfield, who received the full strength of the pro-slavery party, got but forty-six votes."

Here was a pretended election in open defiance of the organic act, the Constitution and all law, and what could or would be done about it? The Free-State men demanded that the whole farce should be ignored and a day set for another election. It was true, a provision had been made by the Governor for contests, in detail, but under the circumstances it was impracticable and unnecessary. The Governor resided at the Shawnee Mission, near the border of Missouri, and might have had ocular demonstration of the invasion if he had kept his eyes open. The *bona fide* settlers had a right to believe, from his previous pledges, that such an election would be ignored. In reply to a letter in the fall previous from citizens of Leavenworth, he used words of no ambiguous interpretation. In this reply, dated November 21, 1854, he said:

"The pledges of that law must be redeemed; and it were a poor and pitiless boon to have escaped from the domination of Congress, if we are only to pass under the hands of another set of self-constituted rulers, foreign to our soil, and sharing none of our burdens, no matter what may be their virtues or their worth as men and citizens at home. It may be very desirable for gentlemen to live among the comforts of the States, with all the accumulated conveniences and luxuries of an old home, and make an occasional expedition into our Territory to arrange our affairs—instruct our people and public officers, and control our government; but it does not suit *us,* and I much mistake the people of this Territory if they submit to it. One thing I am certain of, that having sworn to perform the duties of the office of Governor with fidelity, I shall denounce and resist it in friend or foe, and without regard to the locality, the party, the faction, or the ism from which it comes.

"Thus much the citizens of Kansas have a right to demand at my hands, and to fail in it would be the baldest dereliction of official duty. We believe that we are competent to govern ourselves; and as we must bear the consequences of our own errors, and reap the fruit of our own decisions, we must decline any gratuitous help in making them.

"We shall always be glad to see our neighbors across the river as friends and visitors among us, and will endeavor to treat them with kindness and hospitality. We shall be still more pleased if they will abandon their present homes and dot our beautiful country with their residences to contribute to our wealth and progress; but until they do the latter, we must respectfully, but determinedly, decline to allow them any participation in regulating our affairs.

"When that is to be done, we insist that they shall stand aside and permit us to do the work ourselves.

"This, gentlemen, with due respect for you personally, is the only reply I shall give to the suggestions in behalf of your meeting relative to the time and manner of taking our census and holding our election.

"Your obedient servant,

"A. H. REEDER.

"To F. Gwinner, D. A. N. Grover, C. Miller, Wm. F. Dyer, and Alfred Jones, Esqrs., *Committee.*"

Here was language worthy of a Jackson, and the people of the Territory supposed that a Jackson was behind it. When, therefore, Mr. Pomeroy sent word to Robinson that the Governor would like to have some friends near when he should declare the result of the election, a dozen men from Lawrence went immediately to his headquarters, ready to die with him if necessary while in the discharge of his official duty.

But what was their disappointment and chagrin when, after guarding him for about two days, he decided to issue certificates of election to a large majority of persons chosen by the invaders. Charity would plead ignorance as his excuse, but even that plea cannot be entertained, for out of his own mouth is he condemned. In a speech at Easton, on

the 30th of April, he did not plead lack of information. The
Boston *Atlas* thus comments on the speech and invasion, as
published in the *Herald of Freedom* of May 26, 1855:

" THE KANSAS OUTRAGES.

" In the address of Governor Reeder at Easton, on the 30th of April,
is the fullest official confirmation of the lawless violence with which the
legal rights of the free citizens of this Territory have been trampled in
the dust. Here we have a witness of the most unimpeachable veracity
—such an one as even the Boston *Post* or the Concord *Patriot* must
admit to be authority of the very highest and most indisputable character. An Administration Democrat of the straightest sect, appointed
by the President to the post of Governor of this Territory—a believer,
even now, in that hollow mockery miscalled ' popular sovereignty,' and
an advocate of this principle in the Nebraska bill. Against such a witness what whisper of doubt can these journals urge? None whatever.
They cannot but receive his testimony. And what is that testimony?
Is it that these outrages have been provoked by the eagerness of the
advocates of free territory, and therefore to some extent excusable, as
the *Post* would have its readers infer? Does he cast, even by imputation, the smallest blame upon the outraged citizens at Kansas? No!
He is open, explicit, dignified, and manly. He plainly and boldly puts
the whole wrong just where it belongs. He tells the citizens of Easton
that the people of the border counties of North Missouri have filled him
with amazement ' by their reckless disregard of all laws, compacts, and
constitutions,' that ' the Territory of Kansas has been invaded by an
organized army, armed to the teeth, who took possession of her ballot-
boxes and made a Legislature to suit themselves! '

" He testifies to the already established fact that on that occasion
' Kansas was subdued, subjugated, and conquered by armed men from
Missouri.' He told his hearers that the solemn duty devolved upon
the North ' to vindicate and sustain the rights of her sons who had
settled in Kansas on the faith of solemn contracts.' He also declared
' that the accounts of the fierce outrage and wild violence perpetrated at
the election, and published in the Northern papers, were in nowise
exaggerated.' He concluded by saying that Kansas was now a conquered country—conquered by force of arms, but that the citizens were
resolved never to yield their rights, and relied upon the North to aid
them by demonstrations of public sentiment, and all other legal means,
until they shall be fully and triumphantly vindicated."

Here Governor Reeder is reported as saying that the
" citizens were resolved never to yield their rights," and most

fortunate would it be for his memory if it could be truthfully said that he had not yielded them in their stead. But
the practical question was what could be done for a free
State in future? The Legislature, by the organic act, had
power to settle this question by special and explicit authority.
This body could enact a slave code, provide for all future
elections to be controlled by its own appointees, including
one for a constitutional convention, as in fact it proceeded
to do. No further invasion would be needed, as "returning
boards" would answer every purpose. It was evident that,
should this election be acquiesced in with its results, the
question at issue was finally disposed of. Should all hope
be abandoned, and if not, what policy should be adopted
and what action taken? If a stand was ever to be made for
a free State, should it be at the beginning or at the end of
the programme of the Slave-State party? If at the beginning, the battle must be fought in Kansas; if at the end, it
must be in Congress. But as Congress had uniformly failed
to accomplish anything for freedom for a generation, hope
in that direction was vain. Had it not just broken down
the barrier of the Missouri Compromise and told the people
of the world, including the State of Missouri, that it would
admit Kansas and Nebraska to the Union, with or without
slavery, as their constitutions might provide? Evidently, if
this battle was to be fought in Congress, the Free-State
settlers had made a mistake in coming to Kansas, and had
better go back East if they did not want to live in a slave
State. But if the conflict was to be settled in Kansas, what
steps were to be taken? The first was to be repudiation of
the fraud. Should this be attempted, a case must be made
out satisfactory to the civilized world, or the repudiators
would be repudiated and fail. As has already appeared, this
conflict involved the entire nation. The pro-slavery party
were dependent upon their friends in the South for sympathy,
material aid, and recruits, as was the Free-State party upon
the North. Fortunately this invasion, as proclaimed by the

pro-slavery press, both before and after the outrage, saved all trouble of procuring evidence or presentation of the case to the jury. Quotations of utterances before the so-called election have been already given, which show the intent, and a few are quoted that followed as a plea of guilty to the actual commission of the crime.

The following, from the St. Louis, Mo., *Republican*, of 31st March, the day after the election, tells how the irruptionists rejoiced over their mob triumph. It is a dispatch from Independence to the Eastern press:

"Several hundred returning emigrants from Kansas have just entered our city. They were preceded by the Westport and Independence brass bands. They came in at the west side of the public square and proceeded entirely around it, the bands cheering us with fine music, and the emigrants with good news. Immediately following the band were about two hundred horsemen, in regular order; following these were one hundred and fifty wagons, carriages, etc. They gave repeated cheers for Kansas and Missouri. They report that not an anti-slavery man will be in the Legislature of Kansas. We have made a clean sweep."

The following was issued in the shape of an extra from the Richfield, Mo., *Enterprise* office, of date April 2, 1885, and was headed in large capitals in display lines:

"O! K! on the Goose Question. All Hail! Pro-slavery Party Victorious!! The Smoke of the Battle is Over.

"Friday, the 30th ult., was a proud and glorious day—one long to be remembered; the triumph of the pro-slavery party is overwhelming and complete.

"Come on, Southern men; bring your slaves and fill up the Territory. Kansas is saved! Abolition is rebuked, her fortress stormed, her flag is dragging in the dust! The tri-colored platform has fallen with a crash; the rotten timbers of its structure were not sufficient to sustain the small fragments of the party.

"Kansas has proved herself to be S. Q. G.   *   *   *

"From the best information we have received, the pro-slavery party have carried their tickets in every district by a vote so decisive that the free-soil party will return to their masters, Thayer and Company.

"The election passed off quietly, without the slightest disturbance. There were on the ground from 1200 to 1500 persons. No man can

say that he was crowded from the polls.   Our opponents are chopfallen ;
they look most dolefully, they talk most hopelessly, and feel, no doubt,
awfully bad."

The Independence, Mo., *Messenger*, took up the same
strain :

"KANSAS ELECTION.

" On the 30th ult., the second political battle between slavery and
abolitionism was fought, and abolitionism driven to the bush.   The
victory of the pro-slavery party was complete, and it is to be hoped that
the question is now settled forever in that Territory.   The fanatical
propagandists of the North have only received a lesson in the Southern
political alphabet ; and it may be well for them if they do not push their
inquiries any further.   Yankee inquisitiveness is proverbial, but we
opine he has enough Southern and Western learning to do him for a
time.   The abolition vote in the Territory was extremely meagre, and
we do not suppose they will have a single member in either branch of
the Legislature.   What comes now of the Northern boast that they
were going to abolitionize Kansas, and make it a free State?   They
may yet do it, but their prospect is a little gloomy at present."

After this pretended election the pro-slavery papers professed great confidence in the final result.   The Kansas
Herald, published at Leavenworth, demonstrated the folly
of further Free-State efforts as follows :

"KANSAS SLAVE STATE.

" The brilliant and glorious triumph achieved by the noble and
unaided efforts of the gallant and chivalrous sons of the South over the
combined forces of the abolitionists, free-soilers and Emigrant Aid
societies in our late territorial election, furnishes a suitable occasion to
invite immigration from the South to our fair and fertile Territory.   It
is well known that the *seeming* uncertainty of Kansas becoming a slave
State, and the stupendous efforts of the so-called Emigrant Aid societies
to abolitionize our Territory by the importation of hordes of paupers,
hirelings, and convicts have served in a great measure to discourage
and impede emigration from the South.   We have been assured time
and again, nor do we doubt, that there are thousands of families in
many of the old Southern States who have been contemplating for
months past a removal to Kansas, but have been deterred from doing
so through fear of slavery not becoming one of her institutions.

" This obstruction is now obliterated, for the infernal machinations
of the Emigrant Aid societies have been defeated.   Abolitionism has

8

been rebuked and discomfited. Free-soilism has been crippled and overthrown. The Free White State Party has been annihilated, and Kansas has declared loudly and decisively in favor of slavery. That Kansas is to become a slave State will admit of no doubt. The question has been decided. Her fate is sealed, and what has long since been the hope of the pro-slavery party will soon be history.

" Everybody must admit that the popular vote at our late election is the most infallible exponent of the squatters' views in regard to the future introduction of slavery into Kansas. If this be so, we ask, does the *vox populi* oppose or favor the introduction of slavery? We pause for a reply.

" But let us for a moment recapitulate upon the returns of the late election, which speak for themselves. ' By reference to our issue, which contains the official returns of the election, we learn that the total number of votes polled in the Territory is no less than 5961, out of which 4893 were cast for the pro-slavery party, in favor of making Kansas a slave State, against 1068 for the free-soil party, in favor of making Kansas a free State. But why this great disparity, of what is it indicative? It shows conclusively that *seven-eighths* of our population are in favor of making Kansas a slave State."

The Free-State men had abundant evidence that the fraud was understood throughout the land both by friends and opponents. The New York *Tribune*, as quoted by the *Free State* of May 14, 1855, said:

" After such a gigantic and unmistakable outrage upon the rights of the real inhabitants of Kansas, we cannot conceive how Governor Reeder could have granted any certificates of election. It would seem that in doing so he must have yielded to intimidation. * * * It seems that the Governor did grant a number of these certificates, and then left for Washington. We shall be glad if some of our correspondents there can throw any light on Governor Reeder's mission thither. That no lives were taken by these brigands is very evident, because they were in every case so powerful in number as to render opposition useless.

" It is abundantly demonstrated, from what we have published on the Kansas election, that a more stupendous fraud was never perpetrated since the invention of the ballot-box. The crew who will assemble under the title of the Kansas Territorial Legislature, by virtue of this outrage, will be a body of men to whose acts no more respect will be due, and should be no more entitled to the weight of authority, than a Legislature chosen by a tribe of wandering Arabs, who should pitch their tents and extemporize an election on the prairies of that Territory."

The New Haven *Palladium* said :

" The recent outrages in Kansas by the border slave-holders of Missouri afford the free people of the North a foretaste of what they must *all come to, in due time,* if they permit this heartless despotism to make any further progress in this country. What is this Union worth with the preponderance of such influences within its limits? Who would not cry for dissolution more earnestly than did our fathers for a separation from the British Crown, if this overshadowing despotism is to encircle us with its brutalizing influences ; and its outrageous defiance of even the forms of law are to be continued? The last election in Kansas was more outrageously conducted than the first. Armed slaveholders from Missouri took entire possession of the polls, and votes were put into the boxes without any reference to the right, or even to a show of decency. All that we cherish in our Republican system as essential to domestic order and the safety of life and property was rudely trampled under foot. We would have the admission of that State to this Union resisted, though it costs rivers of blood and a hundred millions of treasure. We trust that when this crisis comes it will appear that there *is a North.*"

Again the New York *Tribune* says :

" We are not prepared either to say to what these proceedings are likely to lead. They seem, however, pregnant with the seeds of great good or evil. They sound in our ears like the distant roar of the coming tempest. Events of startling character and magnitude may stand in fearful proximity behind that dim and shadowy veil which divides the present from the future. There is Kansas. Her territory is free soil. It was never stained by the tread of a slave. Her plains never echoed to the lash of the slave-driver's whip, nor the groans of the enchained bondmen. The millions of the free States have thundered out the declaration that they never shall. On one side, the slave power has risen in its might and declared its purpose to subjugate that Territory, and plant slavery there in defiance of the North, in defiance of the pleadings of humanity, in defiance of the spirit of freedom. It has armed its myrmidons, marshalled and sent them forth to execute its purposes. The symbols of their errand were defiantly promenaded through the Territory in the late scandalous inroad, in the shape of negro fiddlers and negro attendants. As the conquerors of old carried their captives in their train, so did our modern brigands open their career by a similar demonstration. The appeal is now made to arms. By the sword they declare shall Kansas be gained to slavery. The vaunt is openly flung forth, and the challenge to all the world is, let him dispute us who dare. The first step taken has been to put beneath

their heel the real residents and occupants of the soil. The next is to
depose the Governor, and pronounce another in his place. A third is
to declare war against all who dare oppose their plans. The army of
slavery is thus encamped on the soil of Kansas, belligerent and fierce.
It pretends to hold the country by the conqueror's title.

"Such is the position of one side in the struggle for the possession
of Kansas. On the other stands a little band of the sons of freedom,
just now borne down by numbers, but resolute in purpose and ready to
do their part in repelling the barbarian invaders. The question is
whether they are to be seconded by the people of the North. Is there
a genuine spirit of freedom in the country, ready to do something
against the atrocious strides of the slave power to continental dominion?
Are there those who are willing to migrate to Kansas to aid in maintaining the freedom of Kansas at the cost of such perils as may arise?
Are the Northern people generally up to the demand of the civilization
and the humanity of the times? Do they mean Kansas shall be free?
If they do, that is enough. The force that shall drive out hordes of
land pirates who have made their descent upon Kansas will not be long
in forming. Swayed and inspired by the sentiments of freedom, they
will scatter its enemies like chaff. But we are not quite sure that the
people of the free States are in earnest in the resolve to maintain the
freedom of Kansas. We do not know whether the emigrants thither
from the free States will prove themselves to accept the responsibilities
of their position, and meet the issue raised by the slave-holders. If
they do, the time is here for the North to show that her people are
worthy of their sires. If it be otherwise, their degradation is unspeak-
able and they are fit only to live as the slaves of slaves."

The Worcester *Spy* said:

"Every account from Kansas concerning the occurrences which took
place there at the election on the 30th of March tends to establish the
fact of the perpetration by the Missourians of one of the grossest outrages that ever was committed upon American citizens. Alleged Aus-
trian and Cuban outrages upon the persons and liberties of our country-
men abroad dwindle down into utter insignificance in comparison with
the brigandism which was perpetrated upon the people of Kansas by
the ruffians of Missouri at the period named. Accustomed, as we have
been, to the almost boundless insolence and unrestrained aggressions
of the slave power, it still seems scarcely possible for us to believe that
men bearing the names of 'American freemen' could be guilty of such
cowardly assaults upon their fellow-citizens; such dastardly attacks
upon the very principle of 'squatter sovereignty,' which they profess
to cherish, and such unprovoked, unjustifiable assaults upon the freedom

and independence of a Territory with which they have no shadow of right to interfere, as have been committed by Atchison and Stringfellow, and the scoundrels with whom they have twice carried war into Kansas.

" It is shown that an army of Missourians, armed with rifles, revolvers, and knives, with a regular organized commissariat, and with cannon, invaded the Territory of Kansas on the 29th of March last; and on the 30th, prevented, by military outrage, the people of that Territory from voting for a territorial Legislature, at the same time dictating who shall be members of that Legislature.

" If Atchison and Stringfellow had organized their army of ruffians for the purpose of invading Mexico, the general Government would have seized those men and would have punished them severely for levying war. Why not do so in this case? It is the bounden duty of the general Government to protect our Territories from invasion and their inhabitants from foreign aggression. Why do they not do it in this case of Kansas? The old answer comes to us with the same everlasting response—the invaders of Kansas went there to establish slavery, and slavery, which is now the supreme power at Washington, strikes the Government blind and dumb with moral paralysis. It dare not act against the power that made it. It dare not complain of the outrages which it originally invited, by ignoring the Missouri Compromise, and which it has since encouraged by its drivelling policy.

" But this condition of things is not a permanent one. The next Congress will utterly condemn such proceedings. In the meantime let the freemen of the North and West pour into the Territory, and in a few months the freedom of Kansas will be established so that no ruffians will be able to browbeat and intimidate those who alone have the right to regulate its municipal affairs."

The New York *Evening Post* said:

" If there was any provocation either to force or fraud, it was simply a provocaton to retaliate by sending colonists friendly to the institution of slavery. The Territory was open to the inhabitants of slave States as well as free. All they had to do was to occupy it and frame its institutions after their own pattern, if they could.

" The emigration from the free States, say these apologists for the dishonest proceedings of the Missourians, was a challenge and defiance. Let it be a challenge to a race and not to a fight. It was boldly and openly made. 'Let us see,' they said, 'who, in a fair contest of speed, will get into the country first.' The Missourians, instead of abiding by the challenge and giving their antagonists a fair field, take arms in their hands and drive them out of it. It is precisely as if two men should bet on a horse race, and one of them seeing the other likely to win, should snatch the stakes out of the hands of the holder and run off with them. This is an illustration which we suppose will be understood in Missouri."

Some of the Southern papers did not seem as hopeful as the border editors. The Charleston *News* said:

"UNMITIGATED CURSE.

"There never was a completer or more disastrous miscarriage than the Nebraska bill. It has not only blasted every expectation that was originally formed of it, but it proved to its authors a positive and unmitigated curse. Instead of strengthening the harmony of the country, it has given rise to the intensest resentment and discord. Instead of giving effect and confirmation to the compromise of 1850, it has blasted that compromise into nothingness. Instead of securing two additional slave States to the Union, it has secured two additional free States. And instead of putting an end to free-soil doctrine, it has given that doctrine a power and a respectability which it never possessed before, and which, we believe, it could never have attained through any other medium than that opened by the bill."

The Louisville *Journal*, under the head of "The late Doings in Kansas and Missouri," said:

"It is painful to speak of the occurrences in Kansas and upon its borders within the last few weeks, but they are too important in their nature, and are likely to be by far too important in their consequences to be passed by in silence. We have waited to see statements from all sides in order that we might be able to speak upon the subject without danger of being mistaken. We have no feeling that could prompt us to speak as a partisan. We wanted the Missouri Compromise to be let alone, but, as it has been repealed, we wish to see Kansas admitted at the proper time into the Union as a State, either with or without slavery, as her own qualified voters shall decide.

"We have only slight means of judging whether a majority of the present population of Kansas Territory are for or against making it a slave State. But it certainly cannot be denied with a semblance of truth that the recent election, so called, of delegates to the territorial Legislature was the most open and scandalous mockery of an election ever heard of in the United States, the old Plaquemine election of 1844 scarcely excepted. An official census of the inhabitants of the Territory was carefully taken only four weeks before the election, and from this it appears that, in some precincts alone, the votes polled at the election considerably surpassed the whole number of voters in the entire Territory. The truth is, an army of Missourians, variously estimated at from three thousand to five thousand, armed with bowie-knives and pistlos and rifles, and even cannon, marched into Kansas on the day before election, distributed themselves wherever they were wanted, awed all opposition to silence, deposed and put up election judges to suit themselves, allowed the privilege of voting to whom they pleased, compelled by threats and the display of weapons the receiving of their own votes, offered personal violence to all who were obnoxious to them, carried everything before them, and, the next day, returned to Missouri under streaming banners, and to the music of fife and drum and trumpet. * * *

" The determination of the Missourians living near the borders of Kansas to make that Territory a slave Territory and a slave State at all hazards, and by whatever means, is abundantly evident from the late proceedings of the residents of Platte County, Missouri. In that case all the principal men of the county, to the number of two hundred, assembled as a mob, destroyed a newspaper press simply because it would not recognize the right of Missourians to vote in Kansas, attempted to take the lives of the editors and proprietors, and solemnly pledged their word and honor that, if those gentlemen should dare to settle in any portion of Kansas, they, the people of Platte County, Missouri, would follow them into the Territory and put them to death! Thus this Missouri mob, a portion of the army of pistol and bowie-knife voters who had crossed into Kansas and borne down everybody and everything at the election, now boldly and audaciously announced to the world that they claimed and would exercise the prerogative of deciding who should and who should not settle in the Territory of Kansas; that they would not permit the people of Kansas to decide this matter for themselves; that they would cross the line and cut the throats of any who should presume to become inhabitants of the new Territory against their wishes.

" If any man, whether editor or private citizen, chooses to brand us as free-soil in our propensities because we denounce the outrages of the Missourians upon the rights of the inhabitants of Kansas, and are in favor of permitting those inhabitants to fix their own institutions for themselves according to the provision of the Nebraska law and without obstruction or hindrance from any outside power, we have only to say that he is a calumniator. The late proceedings in Kansas and Missouri are infinitely more to be deplored by the South than by the North. We all know that a deep and terrible excitement was created throughout the North by the Missouri Compromise repeal, which gave to the people of Kansas the nominal power of deciding by their own votes whether they would have slavery or not, and we all know, too, that there has been, from the date of the repeal, a mighty array of strength in the North, resolved on never permitting Kansas to come into the Union as a slave-holding State, no matter with what kind of a constitution she might apply. By a course of fairness and moderation this perverse and wrong resolve on the part of the North might possibly, and even probably, be overcome, but we ask how it can fail to be vastly and boundlessly strengthened and increased when the people of a slave-holding State, in utter disregard of the rights guaranteed to Kansas, avowedly control her elections by physical force, decide in mob meetings who shall and shall not be tolerated within its borders, adopt measures for forcing a slave constitution upon her, whether her settlers are willing or not, and brandish the murderous blade before the eyes of the world as the instrument by which they mean, in the event of resistance, to execute their designs.''

CHAPTER VI.

REPUDIATION.—MEANS OF DEFENSE.—THE COUNTRY AGI-
TATED.—THE FIRST KANSAS CELEBRATION OF THE FOURTH
OF JULY.

IMMEDIATELY after the decision of Governor Reeder, the resident agent of the Emigrant Aid Company came to the conclusion that there was but one hope for a free State, and that was to repudiate not only the election, but Governor Reeder's action in giving certificates to the invaders. He had seen what law-making could effect in the control of oppressors as against the oppressed in California, and knew very well what might be expected from this Legis- lature that had just been legalized by the Governor's act, so far as illegality and fraud could be legalized. The Legislature could pass laws, as did the California Legis- lature regarding land titles, purposely to deprive one class of citizens of all legal protection. It was true, repudiation was a most desperate remedy, but the case was desperate. The fraudulent Legislature would be sustained by the Fed- eral Executive and territorial judiciary, backed by the ter- ritorial militia and Federal army. While the fraud was patent to all, had been published throughout the land and condemned by all Northern and many Southern men, it was no easy matter to draw the line and keep on the right side of it. While Northern papers would justify and uphold repudiation of the bogus Legislature and its enactments, scarcely a man north of Mason and Dixon's line would justify the lifting of a finger against Federal authority. It was therefore necessary in this conflict to draw the line at

that point.   But how could this be done ?   The laws would
be adjudicated by Federal judges and executed by a Federal governor and United States marshal.   All justices of
the peace, probate judges, sheriffs, and constables would be
creatures of the usurpation.   The Territory was without
other law, except common and Federal law, so far as this
was applicable to crimes, and the American people were
law-abiding.   What influence could keep the Free-State
settlers from giving in their adherence, and thus making
this usurpation a Government *de facto*, although not a Government *de jure ?*   No new election of both houses of the
Legislature would be held for two years.   Would it be possible to hold out that length of time without law, while
branded as repudiators and traitors by the Federal Executive
and one-half of the people of the country ?   Had the Free-
State settlers been high dignitaries, ex-members of Congress,
or ex-officers of any kind, such a course would have been
scouted as impracticable and utopian ; but, fortunately, all
the Free-State settlers at this time were actuated and governed by a conviction of right and natural justice, and did
not stop to count the cost.   And, even if they had stopped
to forecast the future, it would have been shrouded in thick
darkness.   There had been no precedents that could throw
light upon the situation, except on a small scale in California,
and they were obliged to make the venture in the dark,
trusting to prudent and wise conduct to bring them through.
Should this policy of repudiation be adopted, means of defense must be provided.   Even without taking this step, and
before the election, bullying, browbeating, and bluster had
become intolerable.   Four men with their pro-slavery allies
had frightened the whole town company of Lawrence into
giving up to them nearly one-half of the town site, to which
they had no legal or equitable right.   The result of the
election gave these blusterers and bullies new courage, and
they were and would be more unendurable than ever.   Accordingly, on returning from the Mission where the final act

in the drama had been played by the Governor, George W. Deitzler was sent with a letter to Eli Thayer for one hundred Sharp's rifles. These rifles were needed in self-defense against ruffians, and not for offensive war against the Federal Government, and were so used. General Deitzler, in his letter to the invitation committee of the Quarter Centennial Convention, at Lawrence, in September, 1879, gives this account of his mission :

"SAN FRANCISCO, September 8, 1879.

"*Judge J. S. Emery and others, Committee of Old Settlers, Lawrence, Kansas :*

"GENTLEMEN : I regret exceedingly that it will be impossible for me to accept your kind invitation to attend the meeting of Old Settlers of Kansas, at Lawrence, on the 15th inst.

"Time is making sad inroads upon our ranks. We are passing rapidly away. Soon the ' Old Guard ' will have none of their number left to call the roll. It is gratifying to observe that your State Historical Society is collecting the materials for a full and correct history of the stirring events of 1855 and 1856, and no doubt justice will be done to the people who perilled their all in securing freedom to Kansas, as well as to those generous and patriotic men and women who inaugurated and sustained the aid societies which proved such valuable instrumentalities in the furtherance of the cause. Among the latter stands the able and truly good man, Hon. Eli Thayer, whose letter of acceptance of your invitation, published in the Lawrence *Journal*, recalls an incident of 1855, to which I beg to refer briefly. Some six weeks after my arrival in the Territory, and only a few days after the territorial election of March 30th, at which time Kansas was invaded by an armed force from the Southern States, and the actual Free-State settlers were driven from the polls, Governor Charles Robinson, than whom no truer or braver man ever espoused the cause of free Kansas, requested me to visit Boston with a view of securing arms for our people, to which I assented. Preparations were quickly and quietly made, and no one knew the object of my mission except Governor Robinson and Hon. Joel Grover. At Worcester I presented my letter from Governor Robinson to Mr. Thayer, just as he was leaving Oread Home for the morning Boston train. Within an hour after our arrival in Boston, the executive committee of the Emigrant Aid Society held a meeting and delivered to me an order for one hundred Sharp's rifles, and I started at once for Hartford, arriving there on Saturday evening. The guns were packed on the following Sunday, and I started for home on

Monday morning.   The boxes were marked ' Books.'   I took the pre-
caution to have the (cap) cones removed from the guns and carried
them in my carpet sack, which sack would have been missing in the
event of the capture of the guns by the enemy.   On the Missouri River
I met Hon. John and Joseph L. Speer, for the first time.   They did
not know me, but may remember the exciting incidents at Booneville
and other points along the river.   I arrived at Lawrence with the
' Beecher Bibles' several days before the special election, in April,
called by Governor Reeder.   But no guns were needed upon that
occasion, as the ruffians ignored that election, and when the persons
elected upon that day presented their credentials to the Legislature at
Pawnee, they were kicked out without ceremony.

   " I have not referred to this transaction from any motives of personal
vanity, but simply to revive a feeling of gratitude towards Mr. Thayer
and his associates, for the kind and patriotic assistance rendered by
them to the Free-State people from the beginning to the end of the
great struggle which terminated, happily, in the overthrow of American
slavery, and to show how promptly they gave attention to the business
which took me to Boston.   Those rifles did good service in the ' border
war,' and their movements in the hands of the brave and fearless
Stubbs would furnish incidents for a very interesting chapter in the
history of the Old Settlers.   It was, perhaps, the first shipment of
arms for our side, and it incited a healthy feeling among the unarmed
Free-State settlers, which permeated and energized them until even the
Quakers were ready to fight.   The temptation exists to say more while
I am up, but I must forbear.   I beg to be remembered by all, and
trust the Old Settlers will have a jolly good time at this and at all
future meetings.

"Very respectfully,   Geo. W. Deitzler."

   These were the first weapons procured for the defense of
the settlers in their repudiation career, and were indispensable.   As soon as their arrival was known a change in the
atmosphere was perceptible, most agreeable to Free-State
men and most chilling to the ardor of Slave-State men.   So
salutary was their effect in the town that settlers wanted to
try them in the country, and the following letter was given
to Hon. J. B. Abbott:

" Lawrence, July 26, 1855.

   " Mr. Thayer—Dear Sir: The bearer, J. B. Abbott, is a resident of this district, on the Wakarusa, about four miles from Lawrence.
There is a military company formed in his neighborhood, and they are

anxious to procure arms. Mr. Abbott is a gentleman in whom you can place implicit confidence, and is true as steel to the cause of freedom in Kansas. In my judgment, the rifles in Lawrence have had a very good effect, and I think the same kind of instruments in other places would do more to save Kansas than almost anything else. Anything you can do for Mr. Abbott will be gratefully appreciated by the people of Kansas. We are in the midst of a revolution, as you will see by the papers. How we shall come out of the furnace, God only knows. That we have got to enter it, some of us, there is no doubt; but we are ready to be offered.

" In haste, very respectfully yours, for freedom for a world,
" C. ROBINSON."

(The above letter has the following endorsement:)

"OFFICE OF THE NEW ENGLAND EMIGRANT AID COMPANY,
" No. 3 Winter Street, Boston, August 10, 1855.

" Dr. Charles Robinson, within mentioned, is an agent of the Emigrant Aid Company, and is worthy of implicit confidence. We cheerfully recommend Mr. J. B. Abbott to the public.
" C. H. BRANSCOMB, *Secretary pro tem.*"

Major Abbott also procured a mountain howitzer with ammunition, as well as Sharp's rifles. During the spring and summer several invoices of arms were received for different parts of the Territory, nearly all furnished through the assistance of persons connected with the Aid Company. The following letters will show the interest taken by Amos A. Lawrence, one of the most earnest and efficient friends Kansas ever had:

" BOSTON, August 11, 1855.

" DEAR SIR: Request Mr. Palmer to have one hundred Sharp's rifles packed in casks, like hardware, and to retain them subject to my order. Also to send the bill to me by mail. I will pay it either with my note, according to the terms agreed on between him and Dr. Webb, or in cash, less interest at seven per cent. per annum.

" Yours truly, AMOS A. LAWRENCE.

" *Mr. J. B. Abbott, care of A. Rogers, Hartford, Conn.*"

" BOSTON, August 20, 1855.

" MY DEAR SIR: This installment of carbines is far from being enough, and I hope the measures you are taking will be followed up until every organized company of trusty men in the Territory shall be supplied. Dr. Cabot will give me the names of any gentlemen here who subscribe money, and the amount, of which I shall keep a memorandum, and promise them that it shall be repaid either in cash, or in rifles, whenever it is settled that Kansas shall not be a province of Missouri. Therefore keep them in capital order, and above all, take good care they do not fall into the hands of the Missourians after you once get them into use.

" You must dispose of these where they will do the most good, and for this purpose you should advise with Dr. Robinson and Mr. Pomeroy.

" Yours truly,   AMOS A. LAWRENCE.

"Mr. James B. Abbott, care of A. Rogers, Hartford."

" BOSTON, August 24, 1855.

" MY DEAR SIR: The rifles ought to be on the way. Have you forwarded them? How much money have you received? The Topeka people will require half of these.

" Yours truly,   AMOS A. LAWRENCE.

" *Mr. J. B. Abbott.*"

The howitzer was procured in New York through the agency of Horace Greeley, Olmstead, and others. It would seem that the statements of Deitzler and Abbott, with the letters of Lawrence, Olmstead, and others, on file at the rooms of the Historical Society, would be conclusive as to the date of furnishing arms to Kansas, and as to the instrumentality by which they were furnished, but at a reunion of abolitionists at Boston, in September, 1890, F. B. Sanborn said that " John Brown had carried for his sons' use a small stock of arms before the Sharp's rifles from Boston go there." On turning to " Appleton's Cyclopedia of Biography," page 405, it appears that John Brown's sons, when they went to Kansas, in 1855, " were so little prepared for an armed struggle that they had among them only two small shot-guns and a revolver," while John Brown himself did not go to Kansas till October of that year. This, however, is of no importance, except to show how romance differs from statements in cyclopedias and documents in historical societies. In this speech of Mr. Sanborn he belittles the work of the aid companies, and, while he concedes there may have been good accomplished in an indifferent manner by others, there were but two men indispensable and worthy to be named, and one of these was John Brown and the other James H. Lane. But, up to the 30th of March, at the election of a Legislature which was to decide the question of slavery or no slavery, neither of these indispensable men had put in an appearance, nor, in fact, did either appear till the policy of the Free-State men had been decided upon and arms had been ordered for putting it in force. According to a letter of John Brown, Jr., published in the Cleveland *Leader*, in the month of October, 1854, "five of the sons of John Brown, residents of the State of Ohio, made their arrangements to emigrate to Kansas." In the spring of 1855, three of them started from Illinois to drive through some cattle, while the two others went by rail, river, and land to a place eight miles west of Osawatomie. As he says, they had for the five brothers two squirrel guns and a revolver. Here, then, is the alacrity of the Brown sons, while the father did not arrive till October. How about Thayer and his Aid Company, and the settlers not worthy of a name in this conflict? Within one month of the passage of the Kansas-Nebraska bill, three agents of that company, Colonel James Blood, C. H. Branscomb, and Charles Robinson, were *en route* for Kansas to arrange for its settlement. Six parties had emigrated from the extreme East in the summer and fall of 1854, and several in the spring of 1855. Several parties not connected directly with this company also emigrated, besides a large number independently of all parties. Several Free-State newspapers had been published since the first of January, 1855—*The Herald of Freedom*, *Tribune*, and *Free State*—and several Free-State towns started, among them Lawrence, Topeka, Manhattan, Wabaunsee, and Osawatomie. All this had been done before the Browns got fairly waked up to what was going on in the United States of America. Suppose Thayer, Sam Wood, Wakefield, G. W. Brown, the Speers, Miller and

Elliot, Holliday, Sam Walker Deitzler, Abbott, Goodnow, Eldridges, Savages, Duncans, Smiths, Tappan, Fuller, Clarke, and others without number, had been as sleepy as the Brown family, where would free Kansas have been? Evidently the question would have been settled, and forever. There would have been no occasion for an invasion from Missouri and the South, as there would have been only pro-slavery settlers and voters in the Territory, and no persons would have ever afterwards migrated to Kansas unless they were willing to live in a slave state, which Kansas would have been without a struggle. Unquestionably the Free-State settlers who arrived in Kansas previous to the 30th of March, 1855, made the invasion necessary on the part of the Slave-State men, and the infamy and illegality of that invasion gave a fighting chance for success to the methods adopted by the Free-State party.

How did Lane, the other indispensable, welcome these Sharp's rifles? A letter from Lawrence to the Milwaukee *Sentinel*, supposed to be by E. D. Ladd, dated May 23, 1855, a short time after Lane's arrival in the Territory, gives this account of the reception of the rifles, just before the second election, called to fill vacancies in the Legislature:

"LAWRENCE, KANSAS, May 23d.

"An intense excitement was produced in the minds of a few of our citizens—I need not say who—preceding the election, by the arrival on the *Emma Harmon* of five boxes of *books*, which, on being opened, proved to be, instead of books, one hundred of Sharp's rifles, capable of discharging 1000 shots per minute. Threats and imprecations were loud and long. ' If not sent back immediately they would be thrown into the Kansas;' ' there would be an armed force from Missouri here to take them;' ' it was the work of the Emigrant Aid Society, for the purpose of overawing and holding in subjection the Western men;' ' it was opposed to the Constitution of the United States;'—Heaven save the Constitution if these men are its defenders!—' if there were two or three days before election, they would give us occasion to use them.' Such were the feelings and expressions. Even Colonel Lane, the distinguished ex-Congressman of Indiana, who is now one of our citizens, advised their being sent back. No, gentlemen, they never go back, and if they go into the Kansas, we go with them, and we don't go alone."

But to return from this digression to the condition of the Territory in the summer and fall of 1855. Notwithstanding the wholesome influence of the Sharp's rifles, petty annoyances were continued by the pro-slavery men whenever the advantage of an encounter was on their side. Two or more in company would pounce upon a Free-State man when unarmed and alone, and do more or less bodily harm. To put an end to this, a secret organization was effected of men pledged to stand by each other under all circumstances, and to see that these assailants were properly cared for. Also a California bully was engaged, and paid by the month to devote his time to the business in hand. This policy proved to be most successful. The name of this man was Dave Evans, and his only instructions were to act on the defensive with his fists and revolver, while with his tongue he might take the offensive according to the merits of each case. While from first to last it was the policy of the Free-State men to do no wrong, and commit no crime, self-defense was always in order. This the pro-slavery men could not understand. Because of the discreet conduct of Free-State men they were at first thought to be cowardly, but by degrees their opponents opened their eyes to the situation. The first man killed was in the fall of 1854, soon after the election of delegate to Congress. A pro-slavery man in an insulting manner assaulted a Free-State man, who shot him dead. A trial followed, but self-defense was pleaded successfully. After the second election another pro-slavery man was killed. Malcolm Clark, of Leavenworth, a pro-slavery man, assailed Cole McCrea, a Free-State man, with a piece of scantling, when McCrea shot him dead. This caused great excitement for a time, and McCrea was held a prisoner at the Fort, but as the facts became known the excitement subsided, no indictment was found by the grand jury, and the prisoner went free. A few lessons of this nature were eye-openers to many who had despised the Free-State men as hirelings and paupers. One of the most efficient men in this game was S. N.

9

Wood, of Quaker parentage, from Ohio.   He was ever ready
for a scrimmage.   One day, as he called for the mail for the
citizens of Lawrence, at the post-office at Westport, while
behind the boxes with the postmaster, some person in the
crowd in the store used insulting language about him, which
Wood overheard.   When he had procured his mail he
walked out from behind the screen and called for his insulter.   He was pointed out, when Wood suddenly placed
him upon the floor, and gave him the weight of a Free-State
fist in his face and left him among his friends.   Again, Wood
had a claim against a man for some money which he had refused to pay.   He said he had it in his pocket, but he defied
any one to get it.   Wood immediately proceeded to take
the amount due from the pockets of his debtor.   This was
all the law that was recognized at that time, and Wood, being a lawyer, knew how to enforce it.

Making life a burden and worrying out Free-State settlers
in Kansas by petty persecution was not the only occupation
of the Slave-State men.   There was a paper at Parkville,
Missouri, called the *Luminary*, that had dared to criticise the
raid into Kansas, and a pro-slavery paper gives this account
of its treatment, as published in the *Free State* of Lawrence,
May 7, 1855:

"PARKVILLE MOB RESOLUTIONS.

"*Resolved*, 1. That the Parkville *Industrial Luminary* is a nuisance
which has been endured too long, and should now be abated.

" 2. That the editors, to wit: G. S. Parks and W. J. Patterson, are
traitors to the State and country in which they live, and should be dealt
with as such.

" 3. That we meet here again this day three weeks, and if we find
G. S. Parks and W. J. Patterson in this town then, or at any subsequent time, we will throw them into the Missouri River, and if they go
to Kansas to reside, we pledge our honor as men to follow and hang
them wherever we can take them.

"4. That, at the suggestion of our Parkville friends, we will attend
to some other free-soilers not far off.

" 5. That we will suffer no person belonging to the Northern
Methodist Church to preach in Platte County after this date, under

penalty of tar and feathers for the first offense, and hemp rope for the second.

" 6. That we earnestly call upon our sister counties throughout the State to rise in their might and clean themselves of free-soilism.

" 7. That our peace, our property, and our safety require us at this time to do our duty.

" 8. That we request every pro-slavery paper in Missouri and Kansas to publish the above resolutions.

" The press was then shouldered, with a white cap drawn over its head and labelled ' Boston Aid '; the crowd followed in regular order. It was marched up through town nearly to the upper landing, and there, with three hearty cheers, it was deposited in the tomb of ' all the Capulets,' to wit, the Missouri River.

" A speech was then made to the crowd, and they dispersed peaceably, each taking the road to his own home.

" During the day frequent telegraphic dispatches were received from both ends of the line, of a most encouraging nature. *Sic transit gloria Saturdi.*"

All Free-State papers in Kansas were threatened with like destruction.

The Platte, Mo., *Argus*, published this under the caption " Quietus of the Press " :

" We further say, that *the people having determined that Kansas shall become a slave State,* will probably put a *quietus* upon abolition presses in Kansas Territory. The ' freedom of the press ' is not for traitors and incendiaries, but for those confining themselves within the bounds of the constitution and the laws ; and no bravado, no threats or challenges of any character whatever, will prevent the people of the South from driving from their midst men dangerous to their constitutional rights and liberties."

Although the Legislature had been secured by the invasion and the weakness of the Governor, those on the border and in Kansas knew very well that the Free-State men were not conquered, although temporarily beaten. While the pro-slavery men claimed everything, and declared that the question was forever settled, they were more active than ever in their efforts to arouse the South and intimidate the North. The *Herald of Freedom*, of June 16, 1855, quotes the St. Louis *Intelligencer* as follows :

"The light that is breaking upon the western horizon looks very much like the lurid flame of civil war. It is a solemn crisis that now impends over the country. We know that agents are out from western Missouri, striving to excite the people of the rest of the State to join them in the violent proceedings they have already started in Platte County.

"If they succeed, Missouri will soon be in a flame. It will spread to the South; the Union itself will perish like a burnt scroll!

"It is time for every patriot to be cool and firm. Our country must not perish thus. Our homes, our property, wives, and children must not be given up to civil war, mob law, and anarchy, to serve the purpose of a few desperate politicians. But there is great cause of alarm, and we warn our friends throughout the State that a volcano will speedily burst under their feet and destroy the State and the Union, unless they have virtue, prudence, and courage enough to resist approaches that will be made to them."

In the same issue the *Squatter Sovereign* is quoted as saying:

"From reports now received of Reeder, he never intends returning to our borders. *Should he do so, we, without hesitation, say that our people ought to hang him by the neck, like a traitor's dog, as he is, so soon as he puts his unhallowed feet upon our shores.*

"* * * Reeder is unworthy of the place he fills—wholly unfit to rule the independent sovereigns of Kansas. He cannot longer act as their Governor. They will not submit to it. We call upon our people to take the matter in hand. There is no other remedy. Vindicate your characters and the Territory, *and should the ungrateful dog dare to come amongst us again, hang him to the first rotten tree.* There is no other remedy, and the character of ourselves and our country requires us to act. A military force demanded—poor, contemptible puppy!—could an honorable, high-minded American citizen ever dream of such a demand? Nothing but the dark and muddy waters of abolitionism could have produced such an offspring as Reeder."

The St. Louis *News* had this to say:

"What has become of David R. Atchison, the former Vice-President, by courtesy, of the United States, the wagon orator, the man who contended with Stephen A. Douglas for the honor of having repealed the Missouri Compromise; the boozy backwoods speaker, who, in his maudlin speeches, blackguards better and greater men than himself, and speaks of John Bell as a 'miserable devil'—where is he? He left his seat and duties in the Senate, and came to Missouri, before the close of

Congress, to get himself elected to the Senate for a second term, but he didn't succeed.

" Rumors have reached us of tremendous threats made by him in relation to Missouri and Kansas, and we should like to know if he is going to carry them out. We understand and believe that David R. Atchison is at the bottom of all the troubles that have afflicted Kansas, and is the chief instigator of the meetings, mobs and cabals, threats and excitements which threaten to plunge the border into a wild fratricidal strife. Atchison is the prime mover, and Stringfellow is his man of all work. Atchison is safely and quietly ensconced in his Platte County farm, testing the glories of those five barrels of ' Derby,' while his myrmidons, to whom he gives his orders, are scouring the country and arousing the people by flaming appeals to strife and bloodshed.

" Does our boozy ' Old Bourbon ' think he is going to drift on the current of this fierce storm into the United States Senate? If so, he is mistaken. Missouri will not permit herself to be represented in the national councils by a political gambler, who would jeopardize his country's peace for his own selfish, sordid aggrandizement."

The Charleston, S. C., *Mercury* sent up this shout of victory :

" THE KANSAS HOWL.

" Never since the world began, among the demons in Milton's ' black abyss,' or the damned in Dante's Inferno, has there been heard such a howl as is now set up all over the North, by the dogs of fanaticism, upon their recent drubbing in Kansas. The abolition journals pour out daily diatribes against the hardy Missourians who drove away from their doors the horde of negro-stealers who threatened to overwhelm them. Now, really, the whole affair is decidedly ' the best joke of the season.' Bent upon ousting slavery from this fertile region by any and all means, not willing that civilization should flow on in its natural course, and determine by natural laws its institutions, but hastening to fill it up with hireling fanatics, seize the polls and control the Government. The abolitionists find themselves beaten, routed at their own game—*their own emissaries made to vote the slavery ticket*—while the triumphant Missourians march back to Independence with colors flying and bands of music, rejoicing that ' Kansas is safe!' No wonder they now howl and rend their garments, for fanaticism has for once met its master and been made to crouch. It is a signal and timely lesson. Had the South in its past contest exhibited half the courage and promptness of Atchison and his true men, abolitionism would have been long since a harmless thing. It is also a timely lesson to the North, yet which will scarcely be heeded in its present fierce and aggressive mood, that there is a point at which the South will rise and wipe out, with deeds worthy of her hope and destiny, the wrongs and shame of the past."

But, while the South was being thus cultivated for a new crop of invaders, the field in Kansas was not overlooked. Claim disputes were frequent, and persons singled out for mob violence. Near Lecompton two men, Hancock and Oakley, were removed from their claims, and one cabin burned. " Marauding expeditions," says the *Herald of Freedom* of June 2, 1855, " were frequently sent out for the purpose of annoying the settlers, or with the view of expelling them from their claims." Nothing could so influence the people of Missouri and the South as negro-stealing, as it was termed, and if a person was to be made specially obnoxious, this charge would be made. To mob a " nigger" thief would meet with the highest approval and reward. Among others the local agent of the Aid Company was set apart for consideration. The *Herald of Freedom* of June 16, 1855, has this clipping from the *Frontier News:*

" We every day see handbills offering rewards for runaway negroes from Jackson and neighboring counties. Where do they go? There is an underground railroad leading out of western Missouri, and we would respectfully refer owners of lost niggers to the conductors of these trains. Inquire of Dr. Robinson, sole agent for the transportation of fugitive niggers."

In the issue of the 23d of the same month is the following :

" Dr. Robinson is the sole agent for the underground railroad leading out of western Missouri, for the transportation of fugitive 'niggers.' His office is in Lawrence, K. T. Give him a call."— *Leavenworth Herald.*

To which the editor of the *Herald of Freedom* added :

" We will go bail for the Doctor that he will be happy to receive a visit from his friends at any time. Messrs. Eastin and Pollard, when shall we inform Dr. R. that you and party will call upon him? "

This defiant attitude was inspired by the one hundred Sharp's rifles, brought by Deitzler in April, which were put into the hands of a military company named "Stubbs."

The *Herald of Freedom* of June 16, 1855, presents this picture of the current gossip:

"A FALSE REPORT.

"A correspondent of the *Frontier News*, writing from Franklin, in this Territory, gives the following startling intelligence:

"'Three boats have passed up. One of them landed five hundred Sharp's rifles at Lawrence, as a present from the Know-Nothing Legislature of Connecticut to the Emigrant Aid Society. Now, what flourishes! Here guns have been fixed up in an armory, ready for use. Let another squad of Missourians go to Lawrence for their runaway negroes, and they will see sights. I understand that the Aid Society men are to be organized with a regiment of one thousand men, to be armed with these rifles—one gun to two men—one to hold while the other shoots. The valiant Dr. Robinson is to be commander. The Doctor has a military reputation—he killed his man in California by knocking out a sleeping man's brains with a bar of iron. The Doctor will do. This regiment is to march to Pawnee when the Legislature meets and compel that body to give seats to Wood, Wakefield, and other abolition candidates who were so badly defeated on the 30th of March.'

"Provided that report is true, when our border neighbors visit Lawrence again they will need to come strong-handed. If it required a thousand men and two cannon, with a heavy reserve who were sent to other districts beyond this, to reduce Lawrence to subjection on the 30th of March last, when we had less than two hundred resident voters in the city, and only partially armed with shot-guns at that, how many men, cannon, etc., will it require when we are prepared with five hundred Sharp's rifles, each capable of throwing ten balls per minute, with exact precision, a distance of one mile, and, it is said, will carry very accurately a distance of even three miles? We hope that the report of our neighbor's correspondent is true. We would suggest that the next paper which copies that statement add, as additional information, that one hundred thousand cartridges, ready for immediate service, accompanied the arms. The additional information will be in keeping with the other statement.

"And as to our commander: If Dr. Robinson killed his man in California after a ball had passed *through* his body only two inches below his heart, and had the ability to inspire a handful of men with so much bravery on that occasion, what will he not do when the eyes of the whole nation are upon him urging him to duty, and he is seconded in every action by the thousand brave men who are ready to die in preference to becoming slaves? Will our neighbor answer?"

While the partisans of the South were endeavoring to reap the fruits of the invasion, the effect in the North was very encouraging to Free-State settlers. They were firm believers in the law of retribution, and were only concerned that their own conduct should be such as to meet the requirements of this law. Action and reaction are equal, and the rebound from the election was most terrific. It shook to its foundations the most powerful party ever in authority. The leading organs of that party were as outspoken and denunciatory as the most radical press. Some extracts follow:

"RIFLES FOR KANSAS.

"It is stated that some hundreds of Sharp's rifles have been sent out from Massachusetts, at the request of the new immigrants, to assist in the election. With this, we understand, the aid associations have nothing to do; it is entirely an individual affair."—*Exchange.*

"Things are come to a pretty pass when 'rifles' are to 'assist in our American elections.' The violent and indefensible conduct of the Missourians residing on the border, in interfering in the affairs of Kansas in a forcible manner, is the cause of the 'material aid' now being sent out from Massachusetts in the shape of rifles. It is high time that the disgraceful scenes of turbulence and bloodshed, which have thus far characterized the organization of the Government in Kansas, were put an end to, for they are scandalizing the country. Upon Senator Atchison and his friends in Missouri rests the chief odium of this late highhanded proceeding."—*Cincinnati Enquirer.*

"SENATOR ATCHISON AND HIS OLD FRIENDS.

"No one could have felt more regret than ourselves at the course pursued by the armed bands of men who left Missouri, not with a view to settle in the Territory of Kansas, but to overawe the actual residents and control the elections there held. We saw clearly that public opinion, even among those who are willing to go all lengths to protect the South in her just rights, would not extenuate, much less sanction, so gross a violation of every principle of Republican Government.

"We have heard Southern men denounce the act as one of madness, which would, in the end, produce its bitter fruits, by alienating the patriotic men of the Middle States from the South, or render them lukewarm. Already the effect of Missouri violence begins to manifest itself, and Senator Atchison is denounced in a manner which will very much damage his reputation as a public man and a good citizen. Some of the papers not wedded to abolitionism describe him as a roving bandit, armed with a bowie-knife, revolver, and rifle, and marching at the head of an infuriated mob of misguided men.

" If this description be a truthful one, he is just the man that the Government should arrest, if it has the authority, or sustain Governor Reeder in doing the same thing, if the power is vested in him. Authority to punish such an offense lies somewhere, and in the absence of any statutory provision, the common law is adapted to just such an emergency.

" The story is current in Philadelphia that Senator Atchison remarked to a number of gentlemen in Washington City, ' that the duty of establishing slavery in Kansas had devolved on him.'

" ' He had pledged his word that should be done, and by all that was holy, he would do it at every hazard. His own salvation depended upon the successful execution of his pledge.' No fair-minded man can doubt the right of Senator Atchison to *legally* execute his purpose. We hold the Territory to be as much the property of the South as the North, and equally susceptible of receiving their peculiar institutions ; but their institutions can no more be established by violence than those of the most ultra abolitionists."—*Pennsylvanian.*

" When we characterize this as an infamous outrage, we use the mildest terms we can think of to convey our meaning. We supported the Nebraska-Kansas bill on principle, and we still believe the principle to be correct ; but in the name of justice and freedom, we solemnly protest against the conduct of the Missourian ruffians, and call upon the proper authorities of Kansas to repudiate the election as illegal and fraudulent. If the *actual residents* of Kansas, with all the blighting influences of slavery before their eyes, decide to plant that institution in their fair Territory, we shall submit, because the voice of the majority, fairly expressed, should and must govern in this country ; but God forbid that either the North or the South should stand by and see it planted there by force and fraud without raising their voice, and if needs be their arms, against the consummation of so gross and lawless an outrage."—*Harrisburg (Pa.) Union.*

"GOVERNOR REEDER, OF KANSAS.

" The Governor of Kansas, what is he? Who is he? Who made him? Why was he made? Does he stand for anything? Has he a function? A responsibility? An authority? A jurisdiction? Is he really a bearer of office? Is there a spark of gubernatorial life in or about him? Or is he a man of straw, a thing tricked out in official garb, but with a broom-stick for a back-bone and chalk for brains? It is high time for those whose handiwork he is to give an account of him, to tell us what manner of creature he is. If Governor Reeder is not a sham, so made and so kept up, he ought to know it. Either he himself is an imposition, or he is most outrageously imposed upon.

"One thing is certain, Governor Reeder practically counts as nothing in the administration of Kansas. The Territory is at the mercy of a most abandoned set of vagabonds, the most abandoned that ever polluted the free soil of a country. There is actually neither governor nor government. Brute force is the only rule. Men have talked of the Nebraska iniquity; but that iniquity is spotlessness itself in comparison with the abuse which has been made of it. The pledge-breaking was bad enough, but it was done in the name of a principle. It is now the principle itself that is set at defiance, and, in every conceivable way, outraged. The destroyers of the Compromise invoked the right of popular self-government as a justification of their bad faith, and therewith alone they carried their case. The Compromise disposed of, it is now the turn of the popular right itself, and its trustees, to suffer. The agreement of 1820 was superseded for the doctrine of squatter sovereignty. The doctrine of squatter sovereignty is superseded by invasion and violence. It is absolutely certain—as certain as full and uncontradicted testimony can make it—that the election in Kansas for delegates to Congress, and the recent election for members of the territorial Legislature, were both controlled by armed intruders from Missouri. The real settlers of the country were outnumbered by men who took possession of the polls with a strong hand, and voted without right. The Missourians themselves who engaged in this business not only admit it, but they boast of it. The journals of western Missouri not only furnish accounts of the departures and returns of the different detachments, but make grand flourishes over the success achieved. The only coloring they seek to put upon their baseness is a pretension that the errand of the invaders was to baffle like invasions from the Eastern States. It is a transparent mockery, which only adds insult to injury. * * *

"The wrong has been committed. The question now is, shall it stand? Is this usurped election to hold good? Governor Reeder is a witness against it; but what is Governor Reeder without the support of the Federal Government? He has not a man at his command. So far from being in a situation to extend protection to others, he has been covered with obloquy, been visited with deadliest threats; he has been obliged to repair to Washington to make his extremity better known, and upon his heels comes a proclamation that his power is at an end, and a demand is made upon the President of the United States that a Governor shall be designated in the same way as the Legislature was chosen;

in other words, that the original villainy shall be carried out with a fit instrument. The President has but one line of duty. He is bound to make the Federal law respected. He is bound to protect the territorial rights of the settlers of Kansas, and to uphold, in all the breadth of its application, the principle of squatter sovereignty. He is bound to invalidate the late election as a monstrous piece of illegality, and to provide Governor Reeder with an armed force sufficient to protect the polls. He is bound to install Governor Reeder, the judges, and the marshals, into not only nominal, but into real power, and to provide them with every means for completing the organization of the Territory in accordance with the law which gave it existence. If soldiers are necessary, soldiers must be sent. Bayonets would be a thousand times better turned against these depredators upon civil rights, these bandits of civilization, than against the wronged and suffering Indians of the wilderness. The President, who has the power, must either undo the wrong or share the guilt. He is to act neither as an anti-slavery man nor as a pro-slavery man, but as the Executive of the United States, sworn to see that the Federal laws are faithfully carried into effect.

" We have yet seen no evidence that the Southern people will sanction or countenance these trespasses. We cannot believe that they will; but whether they will or not, official duty remains the same.

" The settlers of Kansas must be protected in their rights. The principle of sovereignty which the law consecrates, under the guaranty and with a full understanding of which the settlers have moved their homes, must be fully sustained and vindicated."—*N. Y. Courier ana Enquirer.*

" This Congressional District, well known as ' the Old Tenth Legion,' gave General Pierce over five thousand majority, and sent Asa Packer to Congress by a still larger vote. No one will deny that he was a firm and consistent friend of the Kansas and Nebraska bill, and his course was approved by a larger majority than any member on the floor in the next House of Congress will be able to boast. The Democrats of this district are sound national men—neither nullifiers nor abolitionists. They despise the one as heartily as the other. They approve of the doctrine of ' popular sovereignty,' but they desire it to be fairly, legally, and honorably carried out. If it can be proven that men are sent from New England to Kansas for the mere purpose of voting, they should be expelled from the country. Such men have no business there. But we are inclined to doubt if this has ever been done. It is not very likely that men would travel two thousand miles with the single object to vote at a territorial election. Besides, we have ourselves seen hundreds of the men who went to Kansas under the auspices of the ' Emigrant Aid Company ' settled down on their claims, living in their cabins and ploughing up the land.   The Missourians do not do this ; they go one day and return home the next.   To this we have a right, as Democrats and American citizens, to object, and we do protest against it mòst solemnly.   It cannot be defended on any principle of right and justice, and if the doctrine of ' popular sovereignty ' is not enforced in its purity —if these invasions are not checked—if the state of things now existing in Kansas is not improved, we pledge our word and honor that it will be the *last* ' popular sovereignty ' bill the Democracy of Pennsylvania will ever aid in passing.   We look with equal contempt on the howlings of abolitionists and nullifiers, and profess to speak only for National Democrats, and the sensible and prudent of all parties."—*Easton (Pa.) Argus.*

Thus it will be seen that both the Free-soil and national Democratic press of the North afforded great aid and comfort to the picket guard of freemen on the frontier.   Only one party in the North gave no word of encouragement, and that was the Garrisonian party.   But one full-fledged Garrisonian, Charles Stearns, could be found in Kansas, and he quarrelled with the aid companies, their agents, and the policy adopted by the Free-State party.   So bitter were his denunciations of the resident agent of the Aid Company that the papers refused to print some of them.   He wrote to the *Liberator* of February 16, 1855, as follows:

" It is true we denounce the Emigrant Aid Company, because we believe it to be a hindrance to the cause of freedom, and a mighty curse to the Territory ; but we are the only ones who have taken a decided ground on the anti-slavery question.   I have never heard of the Lawrence Association ever passing any anti-slavery resolutions.

" Another point of importance is, that this association, with Robinson at its head, advocates brute force in opposing the Missourians. Said Mr. R. to the marshal, in reference to some Missourians arrested for threatening the Yankees : ' If they fire, do you make them bite the dust, and I will find coffins.' "

The *Liberator* of April 13, 1855, said : " Beyond a doubt the fate of Kansas is sealed."

In the same paper of June 1, 1855, it said :

" Will Kansas be a free State?   We answer no, not while the existing Union stands.   Its fate is settled.   We shall briefly state some of the reasons which force us to this sad conclusion.

" 1. The South is united in the determination to make Kansas a slave State—ultimately, by division, half a dozen slave States, if necessary. She has never yet been foiled in her purposes thus concentrated and expressed, and she has too much at stake to allow free speech, a free press, and free labor to hold the mastery in that Territory.

" 2. Eastern emigration will avail nothing to keep slavery out of Kansas. We have never had any faith in it as a breakwater against the inundation of the dark waters of oppression. Hardly an abolitionist can be found among all who have emigrated to that country. Undoubtedly the mass of emigrants are in favor of making Kansas a free State, as a matter of sound policy, and would do so if they were not under the dominion of Missouri ruffianism, or if they could rely upon sympathy of the general Government in this terrible crisis; but they have not gone to Kansas to be martyrs in the cause of the enslaved negro, nor to sacrifice their chances for a homestead upon the altar of principle, but to find a comfortable home for themselves and their children. Before they emigrated they gave little or no countenance to the anti-slavery cause at home. They partook of the general hostility or indifference to the labors of radical abolitionism; at least they could only dream of making ' freedom national and slavery sectional after the manner of the fathers,' and they were poisoned more or less with virus of colorphobia. If they had no pluck here, what could be rationally expected of them in the immediate presence of the demoniacal spirit of slavery? They represent the average sentiment of the North on this subject—nothing more—and that is still subservient to the will of the South. * * *

" 3. The omnipotent power of the general Government will co-operate with the vandals of Missouri to crush out what little anti-slavery sentiment may exist in Kansas, and to sustain their lawless proceedings in that Territory. This will prove decisive in the struggle.

" 4. On the subject of slavery, there is no principle in the Kansas papers ostensibly desirous of making it a free State. Here, for instance, is the *Herald of Freedom*, of May 12th, published in Lawrence, which claims to be, and we believe is, the most outspoken journal in Kansas in regard to the rights of *bona fide* settlers. What does its editor say? Listen: ' While publishing a paper in Kansas, we feel that it is not our province to discuss the subject of freedom or slavery in the States.' Is not this the most heartless inhumanity, the most arrant, moral cowardice, the clearest demonstration of unsoundness of mind?

" These are some of the reasons why we believe Kansas will inevitably be a slave State."

Rev. T. W. Higginson is reported in the *Liberator* of June 16, 1854, as follows:

" Here, for instance, is the Nebraska Emigration Society. It is, indeed, a noble enterprise, and I am proud that it owes its origin to a Worcester man ; but where is the good of emigrating to Nebraska, if Nebraska is to be only a transplanted Massachusetts, and the original Massachusetts has been tried and found wanting? Will the stream rise higher than its source? Settle your Nebraska ten years, and you will have your New England harvest of corn and grain more luxuriant in that virgin soil. Ah! But will not the other Massachusetts crop come also, of political demagogues and wire-pullers, and a sectarian religion which will insure the passage of the greatest hypocrite to heaven, if he will join the right church before he goes? And give the emigrants twenty years more of prosperity, and then ask them, if you dare, to break the law, and disturb order, and risk life, merely to save their State from the shame that has just blighted Massachusetts."

Wendell Phillips is reported in the *Liberator* of September 28 and August 10, 1855, as follows :

" Talk about stopping the progress of slavery and of saving Nebraska and Kansas! Why, the fate of Nebraska and Kansas was sealed the first hour Stephen Arnold Douglas consented to play his perfidious part.

" Why is Kansas a failure as a free State? I will tell you. You sent out there some thousand or two thousand men—for what? To make a living ; to cultivate a hundred and sixty acres ; to build houses ; to send for their wives and children ; to raise wheat ; to make money ; to build saw-mills ; to plant towns. You meant to take possession of the country, as the Yankee race always takes possession of a country— by industry, by civilization, by roads, by houses, by mills, by churches. But it will take a long time ; *it takes two centuries to do it.*

*   *   *   *   *   *   *

" The moment you throw the struggle with slavery into the half-barbarous West, where things are decided by the revolver and bowie-knife, slavery triumphs.

" What do I care for a squabble around the ballot-box in Kansas?"

The policy of repudiation of the election and Legislature gradually gained strength in Kansas, and was formally announced in resolutions. At a meeting held June 25, 1855, at Lawrence, these resolutions, among others, were adopted :

"*Resolved,* That we are in favor of making Kansas a free Territory, and as a consequence a free State.

"*Resolved,* That we look upon the conduct of a portion of the people of Missouri in the late Kansas election as a gross outrage upon the elect-

ive franchise and our rights as free men, and a violation of the principles of popular sovereignty; and, inasmuch as many of the members of
the present Legislature are men who owe their election to a combined
system of force and fraud, we do not feel bound to obey any law of their
enacting.

"*Resolved,* That the legally elected members of the present Legislature be requested, as good citizens of Kansas, to resign and repudiate
the fraud.

"*Resolved,* That in reply to the threats of war so frequently made in
our neighboring State, our answer is we are ready. (On account of
Sharp's rifles.)

"*Resolved,* That we urge upon the people of Kansas to throw away
all minor issues, and make the freedom of Kansas the only issue."

June 27, 1855, James H. Lane makes his first public appearance. He arrived in Kansas about the 20th of April,
but had not before appeared in public councils or conventions. Rumors said he came to Kansas in favor of slavery;
tried to purchase a female slave on credit in Missouri, but
could not get trusted; had quarrelled with and separated
from his wife, and jumped a Free-State man's claim, besides
voting in Congress to open Kansas to slavery. At this date
a National Democratic Convention was held, with James H.
Lane as chairman, and Dr. J. N. O. P. Wood as secretary.
A committee on resolutions was appointed, consisting of E.
Chapman, C. W. Babcock, Dr. James Garvin, J. S. Emery,
and Hugh Cameron. Resolutions were reported and adopted,
some of which follow:

"*Resolved,* That, in the opinion of this meeting, the best interests of
Kansas require an early organization of the Democratic party upon truly
national grounds; and that we pledge ourselves to use all honorable exertions to secure such a result.

"*Resolved,* That we fully endorse and re-affirm the Democratic platform as laid down at the National Democratic Convention held at Baltimore in 1852."

No repudiation here. Mr. Chapman, one of the committee on resolutions, had been elected councilman by the
invasion of the 30th of March, and Hugh Cameron, another

member, was judge of election and received the invaders'
votes.

The *Herald of Freedom*, of June 30th, thus comments upon
this convention :

"We regret to learn that measures were taken by a few persons on
Wednesday evening last to organize a Democratic party of this Territory. Such a movement can result in no good to any one, but may do
much damage. There is but one issue pending in Kansas, and that
issue must be settled before others are precipitated upon us. The
movement looks to us like an effort to suppress the public will, and we
hope it will not be successful."

The *Free State* and *Tribune* also took a similar position,
as the editors of both papers attended the Free-State meeting of the 25th, and endorsed the repudiation resolutions.

As the Fourth of July approached it was decided to celebrate that day in a fitting manner. The question of fitness
was not easily settled. Those who wanted a celebration to
glorify the Government and Union desired Colonel Lane for
orator, but such as wanted a celebration to correspond to the
condition of the people as subjects of Missouri desired Dr.
Robinson. As this was the more numerous class at Lawrence, he was selected. His speech was bitterly denounced
by National Democrats, but warmly endorsed by the repudiators. The gathering was very large, some walking sixteen
miles to attend it. The Shawnee and Delaware Indians
were present and participated in the proceedings. Being the
first Fourth of July celebration in Kansas, and Kansas being
virtually a conquered province, the like of it will never be seen
again. The two organized military companies, armed with
Sharp's rifles, besides many volunteers, appeared in uniform
and were presented with a beautiful silk banner by the ladies.
Mrs. Gates made the presentation speech, closing with these
words : " Let not threats of tyrants, foreign or domestic, intimidate you ; but move firmly and fearlessly in the path of truth
and right principle, and if you should fail to accomplish the
object of your mission, you shall at least have the sweet con-

sciousness of having stood steadfastly in a good cause. Never surrender that flag into the hands of your enemies, and save it from dishonor or perish in the attempt."

S. N. Wood, on behalf of the companies, responded with a patriotic speech, closing as follows: " And should a sanguinary conflict be forced upon us, I know I speak the character of every soldier who has or may rally under these talismanic stars and stripes, they will demean themselves like men. This flag and the sacred cause it represents will by them never be deserted or dishonored. Surrender this flag! No, never, while one of our men is able to bear it above the carnage of a battle-field, or falling, grasp its folds with his hand for a winding sheet! "

The condition of the people and spirit of the occasion may be learned by a few extracts from the address:

" This day, the 79th Anniversary of the Declaration of American Independence, finds us in a new and strange country, and surrounded by circumstances interesting and peculiar. While the echoes of the booming cannon are reverberating among our native hills, and the merry peals of the church-going bells are announcing to the world the rejoicings of a great and prosperous people, that their days of weakness, suffering, and thraldom are past, we are here in a remote wilderness, to found a new State, and to plant anew the institutions of our patriotic ancestors. It is a day to us of peculiar significance. While we would pay a tribute of respect to that period which, in the annals of this nation, will ever be regarded as most sacred; while, with one accord and one voice, we worship in the Temple of Liberty, uncontaminated by party distinctions or sectional animosities, and unite in the endeavor to raise some fitting memento of a nation's gratitude for the declarations of that day, the most glorious in the history of a mighty people, we should also gather lessons of instruction from the past by which to be guided in the erection of a new State in the heart of this great Republic. * * *

" The Colonies, both North and South, made common cause against the indignities and outrages heaped upon a part of the country, and united in a general convention of representatives from different Colonies, to devise ways and means for the common safety. The result of their deliberations was the Declaration of Independence, to the reading of which we have this day listened. The truths of that ever-memorable document were as old as the Christian religion, but their adoption as the rule of faith and practice by a vigorous and growing nation, marked

10

an era in the history of the world unprecedented. A belief in the
equality of man and the sacredness of life and liberty therein expressed,
can be cherished only by those who believe ' that all the nations who
dwell upon the face of the earth are made of one blood.' The establishment of these principles cost our ancestors a struggle with the
mother country of seven years' duration.   No sacrifice was counted too
dear to secure to the people of these United States the right to govern
themselves, to choose their own rulers, make their own laws, and worship God in their own way.   Peace at length was proclaimed throughout the land, and close in her footsteps came prosperity, which has
continued with but little interruption till the present time.   *   *   •

    " One lesson the history of our Government should teach us who
have chosen Kansas for our home, and that is especially applicable to
the instruction of this day, viz. : the more closely the principles of the
Declaration of Independence are followed as the basis of Government,
and the more universal they are made in their application, the more
prosperous the Government and people.

    " As the people of Kansas Territory are to-day the subjects of a
foreign State, as laws are now being imposed upon us by the citizens
of Missouri, for the sole purpose of forcing upon this Territory the
institution of slavery, I surely need make no apology for devoting the
few moments allotted me on this occasion to an examination of the
effects of that institution upon a State and people, whether politically,
morally, or socially.   I ask you not to-day to listen to arguments of
abolitionists, or for abolitionism.   I wish not now to wage war upon
slavery or slave-holders in any State of this Union, or to interfere in
any respect with our neighbors' affairs, but it is for ourselves, our
families, our own institutions and our prosperity—it is for Kansas I ask
your attention.   Is it politic, is it for our moral, intellectual or pecuniary
advancement to submit to the dictation of a foreign power in regard to
our laws and institutions?   This is the question that deeply interests us
all, and for the consideration of which this day is most appropriate.

        *   *   *   *   *   *

    " The foregoing are but a few paragraphs of the volumes that might
be quoted to prove the blessings of liberty and the evils of slavery.
Liberty, the goddess to whom this day is dedicated, showers upon her
votaries peace and prosperity, intelligence and enterprise, morality
and religion.   The inspirer and guide of Washington and the patriotic
fathers, may she become the presiding genius of our own beautiful
Kansas!   Slavery—the opposite and antagonist of Liberty, the ruin of
nations, the impoverisher of States, the demoralizer of communities, the
curse of the world, and child of hell—may she go to her own place.
On this day and this occasion we may speak freely, assured that no
offense can be given by the strongest expression in favor of freedom,

or in opposition to slavery, as no one who is in favor of the latter can join in the celebration of this day. No person who does not ' hold these truths to be self-evident: that all men are created equal; that they are endowed by their Creator with certain inalienable rights; that among these are life, *liberty*, and the pursuit of happiness,' can consistently participate in the festivities of this day. Nay, should we fail to speak in utter detestation of slavery, and to hurl defiance at the monster on this anniversary of freedom's natal day, especially when the tyrant has already placed his foot upon our own necks, why, the very stones would cry out.

" Fellow-citizens, let us for a moment inquire *who*, and *where*, and *what* are we?

"*Who* are we? Are we not free-born? Were not our mothers, as well as our fathers, of Anglo-Saxon blood? Was not the right to govern ourselves, to choose our own rulers, to make our own laws, guaranteed to us by the united voice of the United States?

"*Where* are we? Are we not in the most beautiful country that human eye ever beheld? Is it not, for surface, soil, and productions, worthy to be styled the garden of the world? A wilderness, yet already budding and blossoming like the rose? A new country, yet having the appearance in its diversity of meadow and woodland, hill and dale, of a land long inhabited, and most beautifully and tastefully laid out into parks and groves? With a mild and salubrious climate, a dry, pure atmosphere, must it not soon become the resort of the invalid from the consumptive East and the ends of the earth?

" Our situation, geographically, is in the centre of this Republic, at the half-way station between the Atlantic and Pacific, the Gulf of Mexico and the British possessions. The ' Father of Waters ' extends to us his great right arm, and proffers the commerce of the world and a market for all our productions; and the line of steam and telegraphic communication that is soon to encircle the globe will, of course, pass directly through this Territory, thus bringing to our very doors the commerce of China and the Indies.

"*What* are we? Subjects, slaves of Missouri. We come to the celebration of this anniversary, with our chains clanking about our limbs; we lift to Heaven our manacled arms in supplication; proscribed, outlawed, denounced, we cannot so much as speak the name of Liberty except with prison walls and halters looking us in the face. We must not only see black slavery, the blight and curse of any people, planted in our midst, and against our wishes, but we must become slaves ourselves. Hear our masters:

" ' Our Legislature should make the publishing or writing of abolitionism an offense of a high grade, both indictable and actionable, if loss is sustained.'—*Squatter Sovereign.*

" ' Only one Free-soiler will get a seat in the Legislative Assembly, and he will be expelled unless he mends his manners very much.'—*Squatter Sovereign.*

" ' It is to be admitted that they (the Missourians) have conquered Kansas. Our advice is, let them hold it, or die in the attempt.'—*Platte Argus.*

" At a meeting held at Leavenworth, our conquerors resolved as follows :

" '*Resolved,* That no man has a right to go into any community and disturb its peace and quiet by doing incendiary acts or circulating incendiary sentiments. We therefore advise such as are unwilling to submit to the institutions of this country, to leave for some climate more congenial to their feelings, as abolition sentiments cannot, nor will not, be tolerated here ; and while we do not say what may be the consequences, for the peace and quiet of the community we urge all entertaining and expressing such sentiments to leave immediately, claiming the right to expel all such as persist in such a course.

" '*Resolved,* That in the present state of public excitement, there is no such thing as controlling the ebullition of feeling, while material remains in the country on which to give it vent. To the peculiar friends of our Northern fanatics, we say, this is not your country. Go home and vent your treason where you may find sympathy.

" '*Resolved,* That the institution of slavery is known and recognized in this Territory, and that we repel the doctrines that it is a moral or political evil ; and we hurl back with scorn upon its slanderous authors the charge of inhumanity ; and we warn all persons not to come to our peaceful firesides to slander us and sow seeds of discord between the master and the servant, for much as we may be driven, we cannot be responsible for the consequences.

" '*Resolved,* That a vigilance committee, consisting of thirty members, shall now be appointed, who shall observe and report all such persons as shall openly act in violation of law and order, and by the expression of abolition sentiments produce disturbance to the quiet of the citizens, or danger to their domestic relations, and all such persons so offending shall be notified and made to leave the Territory.'

" ' Abolition editors in slave States will not dare to avow their opinions. It would be instant death to them.'—*Missouri Argus.*

" The Charleston *Courier* (11th August, 1835) declared that ' the *gallows and the stake*' awaited the abolitionist who should dare to ' appear in person among us.'

" ' The cry of the whole South should be death, instant death to the abolitionist, whenever he is caught.'—*Augusta (Ga.) Chronicle.*

" ' Let us declare through the public journals of our country, that the question of slavery is not and shall not be open to discussion ; that the system is too deep-rooted among us, and must remain forever; that the very moment any private individual attempts to lecture us upon its evils and morality, and the necessity of putting means in operation to secure us from them, in the same moment his tongue shall be cut out and cast upon the dunghill.'—*Columbia (S. C.) Telescope.*

" ' The true-hearted citizens of East Tennessee and property-holders ought to enter into leagues, and whip, black, and ride on a rail, irrespective of age, calling, family, association, every preacher, citizen, or traveller, who dares to utter one word in opposition to slavery, or who is found in possession of an abolition document. These are our sentiments, and we are willing and ready to help others to carry them out.' —*Parson Brownlow.*

" And who, or what is an abolitionist ? Why, everybody is an abolitionist, according to their dictionary, who dares to have an opinion of his own upon the subject of the rights of man in any respect differing from theirs. No distinction is made between the man who is opposed to the establishment of slavery in Kansas and him who is opposed to its existence in the States ; between the man who would return him who had escaped to his master and him who would direct the fugitive to the land of liberty. Said one of the chivalry, whose name is suggestive of hemp factories, ' Had I the power, I would hang every abolitionist in the country, and every man north of Mason and Dixon's line *is* an abolitionist.' This was said with the emphasis and accompaniments peculiar to the individual. These gentlemen and Christians ' repel the doctrine that it (slavery) is a moral or political evil,' and ' hurl back with scorn the charge of inhumanity,' and warn all persons of different views not to come to Kansas, for they shall be ' made to leave the Territory,' if they do. '*Made* to leave!' indeed. Well, a ' right smart good time of it,' may our neighbors have in making all leave Kansas who will not bow down and worship the calves they set up.

" Made to leave! Gentlemen, look at that beautiful banner, think from whence it came, and of the motives which prompted its presentation, and then think about being MADE TO LEAVE your country, for no crime! One thing appears evident : if we are made to leave, the ladies will be ashamed to follow, and will let us go alone.

" Persons may teach that the Declaration of Independence is a lie; that tyranny and oppression a thousand-fold more severe than that which our ancestors rose in rebellion against are right; that marriage is a mockery ; that the parent shall not have possession of his own child, nor the husband his wife; that education is a crime; that traffic in human beings, the bodies and souls of men, is a virtue. All this may be taught with impunity in this boasted land of ours, and those who teach such things must be recognized as gentlemen and Christians ; but to teach that all men are created equal; that they have an inalienable right to life and *liberty ;* that oppression is a crime, and that education, religion, and good morals are virtues—this is not to be tolerated for a moment. Tar and feathers, the gallows and stake, await all persons who dare express a belief in such dangerous doctrines, if we can believe our masters. *Masters*, did I say? Heaven forbid! Subjects? slaves? Oh, no! It is all a mistake. What! the whiskey-drinking, profane, blasphemous, degraded, foul-mouthed, and contemptible rabble that invaded our Territory at the late elections our masters? Never! never! I can say to Death, be thou my master; and to the grave, be thou my prison-house; but acknowledge such creatures my masters, never! No, thank God, we are yet free, and hurl defiance at those who would make us slaves.

" ' Look on who will in apathy, and stifle they who can,
    The sympathies, the hopes, the words, that make man truly man;
    Let those whose hearts are dungeoned up with interest or with ease,
    Consent to hear with quiet pulse of loathsome deeds like these!
    We first drew in New England's air, and from her hardy breast,
    Sucked in the tyrant-hating milk, that will not let us rest;
    And if our words seem treason to the dullard and the tame,
    'Tis but our native dialect,—our fathers spake the same.'

" With truth and justice on our side we have nothing to fear, for—

    " ' Thrice is he armed who has his quarrel just,
        And he but naked, though locked up in steel,
        Whose conscience with injustice is corrupted.'

" Whose conscience with injustice is corrupted, if not his who withholds from the laborer his due; who makes merchandise of men, women, and children; who sunders family ties, sending the husband perhaps to the cane-fields of Mississippi, the wife to a New Orleans brothel, and the children to the rice swamps of Alabama, never to see each other again, and all to spend their lives amid whips and chains? Is it not confirmation strong as holy writ,' that their conscience is corrupted, when such men ' repel the doctrine ' that such proceedings are wrong, either morally or politically? when they ' hurl back with scorn ' the charge that conduct like this can be inhuman? Perhaps it is not inhuman, if they are fair samples of humanity, but it is certainly unbeast-like.

" And who are the cowards in this contest, if not those who shun investigation, tremble at free discussion, or even the expression of an opinion; who cry out, ' Down with the press, down with the church, down with every man that disapproves of oppression? ' And what acts are cowardly, if it is brave and manly for scores of men, maddened with whiskey, to prowl about in the dark and destroy the defenseless, to seize peaceable and unarmed citizens, to tar and feather them, to throw printing presses into the river, and threaten to shoot governors and hang editors, and especially to march upon a weak and defenseless people by thousands, armed with deadly weapons of all kinds (the most deadly of which is whiskey), and trample under their feet the dearest rights of freemen, imposing upon a neighboring Territory a foreign government and laws not of their choice, at the point of the bayonet? If such acts are brave and heroic, what are cowardly and villainous?

" What reason is given for the cowardly invasion of our rights by our neighbors? No good reason is or can be given. They and their apologists say that if Kansas is allowed to be free, the institution of slavery in their own State will be in danger; that the contrast between a free and a slave State will be so great their own citizens will become abolitionists, or the under-ground railroad will relieve them of their slaves. But from the first cause there is no danger of alarm, if their doctrine is correct, that slavery is a blessing, and not a moral or political evil. If it is the humane institution they represent, who will want to see it abolished? As to the second cause, there is no ground to fear, provided the people of Missouri mind their own affairs and let ours alone, for it is not true that the settlers in Kansas have enticed away a single negro, or attempted to do so. On this point we speak by authority, for do not the Westport and other Missouri papers say that the general agency of this line of travel is under our charge, and did those papers ever tell an untruth? We say, then, *officially*, that up to the present time, not the first rail has been laid of this road in Kansas; but the workmen are in readiness, and will commence operations with a will, if our affairs are again interfered with by foreign intruders. If the people of Missouri make it necessary, by their unlawful course, for us to establish freedom in that State in order to enjoy the liberty of governing ourselves in Kansas, then let that be the issue. If Kansas and the whole North must be enslaved, or Missouri become free, then let her be made free. Aye, and if to be free ourselves, slavery must be abolished in the whole country, then let us accept that issue. If black slavery in a part of the States is incompatible with white freedom in any State, then let black slavery be banished from all. As men espousing the principles of the Declaration of the fathers, we can do nothing less than accept these issues. Not that we are unfriendly to the South—far from it. If there be any true friend of the South in this assembly, to him we say that our love of the South is no less than his. If, then, such friend demand why we are ready to accept this issue, this is our answer: Not that we love the South less, but we love our country more. ' Had you rather Cæsar were living, and die all slaves, than that Cæsar were dead, to live all freemen?' 'Who is here so base that would be a bondman? If any speak, for him have I offended.'

"Fellow-citizens, in conclusion, it is for us to choose for ourselves, and for those who shall come after us, what institution shall bless or curse our beautiful Kansas. Shall we have freedom for all her people, and consequent prosperity, or slavery for a part, with the blight and mildew inseparable from it?

"Choose ye this day which you will serve, slavery or freedom, and then be true to your choice. If slavery is best for Kansas, then choose it; but if liberty, then choose that.

"Let every man stand in his own place, and acquit himself like a man who knows his rights, and knowing, dares maintain them. Let us repudiate all laws enacted by foreign legislative bodies, or dictated by Judge Lynch over the way. Tyrants are tyrants, and tyranny is tyranny, whether under the garb of law or in opposition to it. So thought and so acted our ancestors, and so let *us* think and act. We are not alone in this contest. The entire nation is agitated upon the question of our rights. The spirit of '76 is breathing upon some; the handwriting upon the wall is being discerned by others, while the remainder the gods are evidently preparing for destruction.

"Every pulsation in Kansas vibrates to the remotest artery of the body politic, and I seem to hear the millions of freemen and the millions of bondmen in our own land, the patriots and philanthropists of all countries, the spirits of the Revolutionary heroes, and the voice of God, all saying to the people of Kansas, ' Do your duty.' "

CHAPTER VII.

THE TERRITORIAL LEGISLATURE.—THE TOPEKA CONSTITUTION.

ON the second day of July the so-called Territorial Legislature met at Pawnee, where it was called by proclamation of the Governor. Governor Reeder recognized this body as the Legislature of Kansas, and delivered an elaborate message in due form. The first action taken was to purge the body of the men chosen at the second election in place of such as had been refused certificates by the Governor, and to seat the latter in their stead. These men thus unceremoniously expelled had been importuned by the Free-State men, privately, and publicly by resolution, to repudiate the Legislature in advance, on the ground of invasion and fraud, but they decided otherwise. It is true they made a long and elaborate protest, but it had but little influence, as they had yielded the strongest objection, namely, the illegality of the body itself. M. F. Conway, on the other hand, who had been declared elected to the council by throwing out one precinct, stood up manfully and repudiated the whole performance. He had visited Robinson's house with Kersey Coates and Deitzler, and the whole matter was fully discussed. While Conway was at first inclined to follow Reeder in recognition of the legality of the Legislature, he yielded to the arguments of Coates, Deitzler, and Robinson, and, instead of presenting his credentials, sent his resignation to the Governor. As this resignation embodies the Free-State case, extracts are here given :

" It is a fact which has travelled the circuit of the whole civilized world, that this Legislature has been imposed upon the people of

Kansas by force of arms. Those who compose it, and those whom they represent, and for whom they act, are alien enemies, who have violently seized the legislative power of this Territory, and seek to disguise their tyranny under the form of constitutional enactments. Their Legislature is substantially a provincial council, instituted and ordained by a daring and unscrupulous league in the State of Missouri, and other parts of the South, to govern a people whose liberties they have ruthlessly stricken down. This fact has been placed beyond controversy by authentic details of concerted operations, looking to this end, and of overwhelming violence, at the recent elections, unparalleled in all our political history. Under these circumstances, it would be either fraudulent or pusillanimous in me to respect this as the Legislature of Kansas. I am not willing to do it. Whatever the timorous or the time-serving may suggest or advise, I shall do nothing of the kind. Instead of recognizing this as the Legislature of Kansas, and participating in its proceedings as such, I utterly repudiate and reprobate it, as derogatory to the respectability of popular government, and insulting to the virtue and intelligence of the age.

" As an individual citizen of Kansas, I am furthermore free to say to your Excellency, representing, as you do, the imperial authority of the Federal Government in this land, that, while I am entirely disposed to pay all respect to the lawfully constituted authorities, I am yet not willing, whatever power may command it, to bend my neck, like a satisfied and gentle slave, to the yoke of foreign tyrants. To do so, would prove me recreant to all the lessons of heroism or of duty I ever learned. I am so unfortunate as to have been trained to some crude notion of human rights—some such notions as those for which, in ages past, our foolish ancestry perilled their lives on Revolutionary fields. And, however widespread may be the disrepute into which the puerile fallacies have fallen in these sterling and enlightened times, I am still bold to withstand their violation, in my own person, to the last extremity of just resistance. Simply as a citizen and a man, I shall, therefore, yield no submission to this alien Legislature. On the contrary, I am ready to set its assumed authority at defiance, and shall be prompt to spurn and trample under my feet its insolent enactments whenever they conflict with my rights or inclination.

" Very respectfully yours,

" M. F. CONWAY.

"*Gov. A. H. Reeder, Pawnee, K. T., June 30, 1855.*"

After seating the members elected by the invasion, the Legislature adjourned from Pawnee, where the Governor had located the temporary capitol, to the Shawnee Mission,

near the border of Missouri. Governor Reeder vetoed this
action, but his veto was overridden with ease and Pawnee
was evacuated. Now the Governor joined the repudiators,
but, unfortunately, the ground of his repudiation was much
less firm than that occupied by the Free-State party, and he
never received the credit for heroic action that would have
been accorded had he placed his repudiation on the invasion
of the polls on the 30th of March. However, his course,
even at this late day, gave great strength and encouragement to the Free-State cause. From that time till the end
of the conflict he was a power second to none in the contest.
He was a lawyer of ability, a man of unimpeachable integrity, and universally recognized as a statesman and patriot.
No man stood higher in Kansas or out, and the Free-State
men were proud of counting him on their side.

S. D. Houston, the only Free-State member whose election was conceded by the Slave-State party, resigned his
seat, giving his reasons at length in a paper that was published and regarded as most able and conclusive, as to the
illegality of this pretended Legislature. As the Governor
refused to recognize the Legislature, an issue direct was
made that could not be ignored at Washington. The President must side either with the Governor or with the Legislature ; and if with the latter, the former would lose his official
head. Already steps had been taken to get rid of him. The
whole pro-slavery horde had demanded his removal, and
some charges or complaints had been made of land speculation and the like. The excitement over the territorial election had been so widespread that the Administration did not
dare meet the question fairly and give the true reason for
Reeder's removal. In the meantime two of the judges, with
unseemly haste, endorsed the validity of this Legislature and
the laws it might enact, foreshadowing the course of the Administration at Washington. The Legislature, although ignored by the Governor, whose prerogative it was to sign
their enactments, proceeded to business, and in sixty days

turned out a mass of statutes equal in volume, and almost identical in substance, with the statutes of the State of Missouri, providing that wherever the word " State " appeared in any law the word " Territory " should be substituted or understood.   At length, after various rumors, official information was received by the Legislature, August 16, 1855, that Governor Reeder was removed.

This removal, under the circumstances, reacted against the Slave-State party with scarcely less effect than did the invasion of the 30th of March.   Governor Reeder's answer to the charge of illegal speculation in land, a most tart and pungent reply to Commissioner Mannypenny, was published, and the most conservative Democratic papers denounced the removal and severely censured the Administration.   Thus far every step taken by the Slave-State party had helped the Free-State cause in accordance with the unwritten and universal law of retribution.   The Slave-State men having the Government in their possession, were arrogant, defiant, over-bearing, and despised their antagonists.   The Free-State men were ostensibly beaten, overwhelmed, and crushed, yet really self-reliant, hopeful, and exultant over the blunders of their opponents.

When the character of the enactments of this Legislature became known, another revulsion occurred most beneficial to the Free-State cause.   Not only was the worse than Draconian code enacted against Free-State men, but they were virtually disfranchised.   Instead of leaving the choice of county officers to the voters, the Legislature itself appointed them for a term of years, and gave them full control of all future elections, besides requiring a test oath of a challenged voter.   Many of the enactments were simply infamous, as some selected specimens will show :

" SECTION 1. If any person shall entice, decoy, or carry away out of this Territory, any slave belonging to another, with intent to deprive the owner thereof of the services of such slave, or with intent to effect or procure the freedom of such slave, he shall be adjudged guilty of grand larceny, and on conviction thereof, shall suffer death.

" SEC. 2. If any person shall aid or assist in enticing, decoying or persuading, or carrying away or sending out of this Territory, any slave belonging to another, with intent to procure or effect the freedom of such slave, or with intent to deprive the owner thereof of the services of such slave, he shall be adjudged guilty of grand larceny, and on conviction thereof, suffer death.

" SEC. 3. If any person shall entice, decoy, or carry away out of any State or other Territory of the United States, any slave belonging to another, with intent to procure or effect the freedom of such slave, or deprive the owner thereof of the services of such slave, and shall bring such slave into this Territory, he shall be adjudged guilty of grand larceny, in the same manner as if such slave had been enticed, decoyed, or carried away out of this Territory, and in such case the larceny may be charged to have been committed in any county of this Territory, into or through which such slave shall have been brought by such person, and on conviction thereof, the person offending shall suffer death.

" SEC. 11. If any person print, write, publish or circulate, or cause to be brought into, printed, written, published or circulated, or shall knowingly aid or assist in bringing into, printing, publishing or circulating within this Territory, any book, magazine, handbill or circular, containing any statements, arguments, opinions, sentiments, doctrine, advice or innuendo, calculated to promote a disorderly, dangerous, or rebellious disaffection among the slaves in this Territory, or to induce such slaves to escape from the service of their masters, or to resist their authority, he shall be guilty of a felony, and be punished by imprisonment and hard labor for a term not less than five years.

" SEC. 12. If any free person, by speaking or by writing, assert or maintain that persons have not the right to hold slaves in this Territory, or shall introduce into this Territory, print, publish, write, circulate, or cause to be introduced into this Territory, written, printed, published or circulated in this Territory, any book, paper, magazine, pamphlet or circular, containing any denial of the right of persons to hold slaves in this Territory, such person shall be deemed guilty of felony, and punished by imprisonment at hard labor for a term of not less than two years."

The organic act professed to leave the slavery question open for discussion and decision by the people, but this Legislature had closed the case and rendered the verdict, and proposed to send to the penitentiary every man who dared to ask for a hearing. This legislation, as soon as generally known, revived the interest in Kansas affairs in the North and East, where it had begun to flag. On account of the cholera, the political disturbances, the pretended election of a Slave-State Legislature, and for other reasons, the emigration had subsided during the summer, not only from the North, but from the South. While the question was undecided, men from the South did not care to remove where their slaves might be unsafe, and it required great courage on the part of men from the North to remove to a Territory where slavery so far had been triumphant. The St. Louis *Intelligencer*, as given in the *Free State* of October 10, 1855, says:

"Our news from western Missouri is of an ominous and most discouraging character. That region is suffering from mildew and blight. Its glory dimmed, its spirits abated, and its hope fading.

"The emigration to Kansas is almost entirely checked. Emigrants from the Northern and free States have ceased to go to Kansas, because they can find as good land elsewhere not cursed by mob law, nor ruled by non-resident bullies. Emigrants from the Southern States do not go to Kansas, because they will not put their slave property in peril, by taking it into a Territory where there is a free-soil element, threatening the security of slaves.

"Any man of sense might have foreseen this result. Alabama and Georgia may hold public meetings, and resolve to sustain the slaveholders in Missouri in making Kansas a slave State. But their resolutions comprise all their aid, which is not 'material' enough for the crisis. When slave-holders of Alabama and Georgia emigrate, they go to Louisiana, Arkansas, and Texas. They do not come with their slaves to Missouri or Kansas. Call they that, backing their friends?

"Thus the matter stands: The Northern emigrants shun Missouri and Kansas as plague spots of the nation. The Southern emigrants shun Missouri and Kansas, because here is the battle-ground between salvery and free-soil.

"The result is, Kansas, the fairest land under the sun, is neglected and idle; occupied by a few honest and earnest but disheartened pioneers, and lorded over by a dozen or two feudal tyrants of Missouri, who curse by their presence the land they have desolated.

*   *   *   *   *   *   *

"The most aggravating stories of insults and outrages committed by Missourians on the persons of emigrants from the Old World, or from the free States, who are found ascending the Missouri River, are circulated in the free States; and it is impossible to conceive of the hatred thus generated toward our whole State in the northern half of the Union.

"Between these fires Missouri is leading on her languid existence. St. Louis is retarded in a most woeful way. Our railroads creep at a snail's pace. We build ten miles while other Western States build one hundred. In every department of life we feel the paralysis. Instead of bounding forward, buoyant, strong, and rejoicing, we sit with dull eyes and heavy spirits, and listen to the tick of the death watch.

"These are the bitter fruits of the repeal of the Missouri Compromise—a base and wrongful deed—that will bring a hell of bitter self-reproaches to its authors. Missouri did not demand that repeal. The South never asked it. Atchison solicited it, and in a moment of political insanity the South consented to the wrong and made the wrong her own. This was the suicide of slavery.

*   *   *   *   *   *   *

"Atchison and Stringfellow, with their Missouri followers, overwhelmed the settlers in Kansas, browbeat and bullied them, and took the Government from their hands. Missouri voters elect the present body of men who insult public intelligence and popular rights by styling themselves 'the Legislature of Kansas.' This body of men are helping themselves to fat speculations by locating 'the seat of Government,' and getting town lots for their votes. They are passing laws disfranchising all citizens of Kansas who do not believe negro slavery to be a Christian institution and a national blessing. They are proposing to punish with imprisonment the utterance of views inconsistent with their own, and they are trying to perpetuate their preposterous and infernal tyranny by appointing for a term of years creatures of their own, as commissioners in every county, to lay and collect taxes, and see that the laws they are passing are faithfully executed. Has this age anything to compare with these acts in audacity?

*   *   *   *   *   *   *

"It has been a common opinion with thoughtless persons and thickheaded bullies of the West, that the Northern and Eastern men will not fight. Never was a greater mistake. The sons of New England and of the Middle States do not like to fight. They would rather work, plough, build towns, railroads, make money and raise families, than fight. But fight they will, if need be. Remember, the sons of New England shed the first blood in the American Revolution; and they were last to furl their flags in that terrible struggle. They have never disgraced their community by cowardice, and they will not. They are Americans, with spirit, courage, endurance, and deep love of liberty to animate them. The Free-State men in Kansas will fight before they will be disfranchised and trampled on. Mark the word.

"Here comes, then, the suicide of slavery. The outrages committed by Atchison and his followers in subjugating Kansas to non-resident rule, will bring on a collision, first in Congress and then in Kansas ; and who shall tell the end?

" Slavery will never sustain itself in a border State by the sword. It may conquer in some respects, but it can never ' conquer a peace.' Never! never! Once light the fires of internecine war in defense of slavery, and it will perish while you defend it. Slave-holders will not stay to meet the fight. Property is timid, and the slaves will be sent to Texas to be in a ' safe place ' while the fight lasts ; and as soon as the slaves are gone it will be found that Missouri has nothing to fight about, and the fight will end ' before it begins! '

" Thus the slavery propagandists who repealed the Missouri Compromise to make Kansas a slave State will make Missouri free; and in endeavoring to expel abolition from Kansas, they will fill both Kansas and Missouri with an entire free white population, worth more to the two States than all the negroes in America.

" Is not the Kansas outrage the suicide of slavery? Have not the people of Missouri, interested in the preservation of slavery in the State, brought themselves into a desperate predicament by following the insane counsels of Atchison and Stringfellow? "

So general was the condemnation of the conduct of the Slave-State party and of the Administration, that the indignation of the North was again aroused and emigration set in with renewed vigor.

In some respects the season of 1855 was the most disheartening of any in the history of the struggle. On the surface all was dark for freedom. The government, both local and national, was in possession of the enemy, and how it could be secured by the *bona fide* settlers was unknown. While there was no thought on the part of the leading Free-State men of abandoning the field, it was impossible to demonstrate to the isolated settlers an immediate way out. The situation, as viewed by one person, may be seen by a letter quoted by Professor Spring in his " Kansas," page 61. He says :

" November 1st, 1855, Dr. Robinson wrote A. A. Lawrence, reviewing somewhat in detail the progress of events up to that time. ' We must be as independent and self-reliant and confident,' he said, ' as the Missourians are, and never, in any instance, be cowed into silence or subserviency to their dictation. This course on the part of

prominent Free-State men is absolutely necessary to inspire the masses
with confidence, and keep them from going over to the enemy.   *   *   *
I have been censured for the defiant tone of my Fourth of July speech,
but I was fully convinced that such a course was demanded.   The
Legislature was about sitting, and Free-State men were about despairing.
*   *   *   A few of us dared to take a position in defiance of the Legislature, and meet the consequences.   We were convinced that our success
depended upon this measure, and the demonstration of the Fourth was
to set the ball in motion in connection with Conway's letter to Governor
Reeder, resigning his seat and repudiating the Legislature.   For a while
we had to contend with opposition from the faint-hearted, but by persevering in our course, by introducing resolutions into conventions and
canvassing the Territory, repudiation became universal with Free-State
men.   *   *   *   We conceived it important to disown the Legislature,
if at all, before we knew the character of its laws, believing they would
be such as to crush us out if recognized as valid, and believing we
should stand on stronger ground if we came out in advance.   *   *   *
The first of July forms an important epoch in our history.   It was
about that time that open defiance was shown our enemies.   *   *   *
Pro-slavery bullies were daily in the streets, and insulted all Free-
State men who they supposed would make no resistance.   This drove
our people into secret organization of self-defense, and it was not long
before they were glad to cry for quarter.   A Free-State Missourian, a
regular California bully, came among us and took them in their own
way, and frightened every pro-slavery man from the field.   His name
is David Evans; and if I had a Sharp's rifle at my disposal, I should
make him a present of it.   *   *   *   To divide into parties before our
admission into the Union would be ruinous, and give our enemies the
advantage."

The effect of the invasion and legislation upon the country
may be seen from the following extracts from leading journals of that time:

"THE BLACK LAW IN KANSAS.

"In another column will be found a transcript of a law recently
passed by the Lower House of the Kansas Legislature, in regard to the
'better protection of slave property.'   We invite the attention of Missourians especially, and in fact the whole people of the United States,
to its bloody provisions, whereby the life of a white man is made of
less consequence and value than the service of a negro slave.   Our
correspondent, writing from Kansas, speaking of its provisions, says
that, 'in utter disregard of the natural rights of free speech and thought,
11

it is only paralleled by one thing in all past history.' Many acts more severe in provisions, and more proscriptive as regards opinions, have been passed, and even the resolution *not to have the law printed* has been more than equalled in the past. A Roman emperor is said to have written his edicts so fine, and hung them so high, that people could not read them, and thereupon to have glutted his appetite for blood to the uttermost upon the unconscious violators. This, we think, fully parallels the decision of the Kansas Legislature not to print their Draconian code on the subject of slave property. To the twelfth section, however, it is our purpose at present to call more especial attention. It reads as follows:

" ' SEC. 12. If any free person, by speaking or by writing, assert or maintain *that persons have not the right to hold slaves in the Territory*, or shall introduce into Kansas, print, publish, write, circulate, or cause to be introduced into the Territory, any book, paper, magazine, pamphlet, or circular containing any denial of the rights of persons to hold slaves in this Territory, such person shall be deemed guilty of felony, and punished by imprisonment at hard labor for a term not less than two years.'

" This is neither more nor less than making a difference of opinion upon a constitutional question a penitentiary offense. It establishes the prison and the pillory as the arbiter of constitutional law in preference to the judiciary of the land, and makes the human mind square its convictions to the ideas of a few accidentally elected legislators. The ' procrustean bed' has been a myth heretofore; it promises soon to be a shamble and a slaughter-house in reality. Men are no longer to be permitted in the new Territory to express abstract opinions upon moral questions without suffering the ignominious penalties of a State penitentiary, and this is what is called opening the Territories to the people of a whole Union, and admitting all persons to the enjoyment of its fair lands. Squatter sovereignty was much lauded by General Cass and Mr. Douglas in the outset, and yet, under this phase of it, both Mr. Douglas and Cass would be sent to the State prison if they dared to utter in Kansas Territory what they have repeatedly said in glowing language in the Senate of the United States.

" In regard to this law, we have but few words to say, and they may be said very briefly. We are in favor of the protection of slave property and the rights of slave-holders, where slavery exists, by all laws and statutes that can be enforced, and that human intelligence does not revolt at. But this is none such. It could not be enforced, as was well said in the debate on its passage, even in South Carolina, much less in Kansas. It is foolish in operation, and will prove reactionary. Massachusetts assuredly destroyed the Know-Nothing party in the United States by the ultra course of her Legislature—by ignoring the

Fugitve Slave Law—and by enacting the Personal Liberty bill. The result, too, will prove that the Kansas Legislature has done more to destroy the prospect of making that Territory a slave State by its ill-tempered, senseless, school-boy legislation, and by the enactments of the present ' Black Laws,' than could have been effected by all the cohorts of the Emigrant Aid Society, or by all the zeal of Northern fanatical divines."—*Missouri Democrat.*

"THE GATHERING STORM.

" The clouds now rising upon the Western horizon are dark and portentous. Almost every mail from Kansas brings intelligence of the approaching struggle between slavery and the Constitution—a struggle which may be decided in blood. It would be useless to shut our eyes to the signs which seem to indicate an appeal to arms at no distant day. The crisis may be arrested, but only by exercise of a wisdom, moderation, and firmness by the Administration, which cannot reasonably be expected. The high-handed, unconstitutional, and aggressive acts already performed or proposed in the ruffian Legislature of Kansas conclusively show that despotism intends to wage uncompromising war upon the Constitution. Read the account in our paper to-day of the measures which have been introduced or proposed. The intended enactments of the mob Legislature of Kansas, we venture to say, can never be enforced. They are unwarranted by the Constitution of the United States, and therefore are not obligatory. Where does the Legislature of Kansas obtain the constitutional power to pass a law requiring a citizen emigrating from any State into that Territory to take an oath of allegiance to support the laws of the United States, and those which may be enacted by their own irresponsible body? Whence do they obtain the power to make the oath of allegiance a qualification for the rights of suffrage? What clause of the Constitution allows the authorities of Kansas to use the jails of Missouri for the punishment of offenders? Oh, the beauties of squatter sovereignty! Every day reveals more clearly the supreme ridiculousness of the miserable farce. There seems to be but one course to be pursued to prevent a civil war. The organization of the Territory should be begun at once, and the present miscalled Legislature to enact laws for Kansas must be chosen by the people of the Territory, not by an invading army from Missouri! This is the only course which will prevent collisions which may end in blood. The people of that Territory never will bow to the unconstitutional edicts of this mob-elected Legislature ; they never will recognize it as a legislative body ; and they will be acting right in the sight of God and of the country. Unless the general Government exercises authority in the matter to sustain the settlers in the assertion of their just rights, a few more weeks may see civil war raging in all its horrors upon the soil of Kansas."—*Boston Journal*.

" From this time it will be seen that the bill whereby the Kansas solons enacted that all officers in the Territory, for the term of six years ensuing, should be filled by the present Legislature, has become a law, and we are free to say that a more infamous invasion of the rights of any people, a more unwarranted assumption of power not delegated, was never perpetrated by any assembly that ever sat even in revolutionary France. Not content with legislating themselves into office in violation of the organic law of the Territory; not satisfied with denying to the inhabitants and citizens of Kansas the constitutional rights of free speech and a free press; but beyond and above all this, they now quietly inform the people that they, the Legislature, will now undertake to appoint, of their own free will and accord, the sheriffs, constables, attorneys, tax-assessors, and all local officers, not for the coming year, or until an election can be held by the citizens, but for six years from the present time."—*Missouri Democrat*.

" HELLISH.

" The above is harsh—almost an impious caption—but if the act does not deserve it, then we confess that we do not know how to head an article. If the freemen of the North submit to this without a murmur; if this does not arouse them to action against the slave power, then they deserve to be slaves. If this does not stir the freemen of Kansas up to civil war, then they deserve to wear the chains that the representatives of the Missouri mob have forged upon them. From the Federal Government we can expect nothing, while the cut-throat crew of Atchison and Stringfellow can command and the Government obeys with alacrity. The present Administration is the meanest despotism that ever disgraced the face of the earth, and its governors and judges will make law, as far as their sanction goes, of such damnable acts as this. The life of a free white man is thus made cheaper than the service of a negro slave! And to say that slavery is not right—to say that men have no right to hold slaves, is made a criminal offense, punishable with two years' imprisonment at hard labor!—it makes our blood boil to read such things. We shall rejoice when the first gun is fired in civil war in Kansas. Outraged, robbed, insulted, condemned to death for following the dictates of humanity; imprisonment for uttering manly words of truth, and all to please the slave power! Great God! Why is language so powerless! Why cannot we find words to express the thoughts and feelings that throng our heart and brain at such time as this? They pass the act, but they refuse to publish it; they condemn men to death and imprisonment for certain acts and words, but refuse to make known in a legal way what those acts and words are. The act elicited some debate, but passed almost unanimously."—*Galesburg (Ill.) Democrat.*

" THE CRISIS IN KANSAS.

" It is madness to suppose that any community of American citizens will submit to such tyranny as this. If the settlers in Kansas do not resist the enforcement of such laws to the last extremity—if they hesitate an instant to take up arms, if need be, against the dastardly tyrants who seek thus to trample their freedom under foot, and to spill the last drop of their blood rather than be thus degraded and conquered, they are unworthy of their name and descent. The provocation of our forefathers to Revolution was trifling compared with that which these Kansas settlers have experienced. And to this issue the matter must come, if the pro-slavery madmen persist in the measure by which they have thus far sought the accomplishment of their schemes. We are confident the people of Kansas will not submit to the domination of their invaders. They will resist the execution of the pretended laws. They will not permit their enforcement against a single inhabitant, and if their execution be attempted by force, it will be resisted by force, and then the issue will be one of simple strength.

" Under such a menacing state of affairs, it would seem natural to invoke the interposition of the Federal Executive. But the Administration at Washington seems to have been as thoroughly conquered by the Missouri invaders as the people of Kansas themselves. President Pierce seems to be as completely under the control of Atchison and Stringfellow as the myrmidons they marshal to the Kansas polls. It is idle, therefore, to hope for aid from this quarter. The people of Kansas must rely upon themselves for the defense of their liberties and the protection of their rights. And if they are compelled to encounter the weight of the Federal Government in their contest, they must appeal from that to the people. They can trust to the justice of their cause for final victory."—*New York Times.*

" KANSAS.

" When the affairs of Kansas were forcibly interfered with by intruders from Missouri, we could not, in the face of the evidence establishing the fact, deny its existence, or even justify it, because it had been provoked by an almost as criminal interference upon the part of the abolition Emigrant Aid Company of the East. We then expressed the opinion that the acts of the Missourians would be prejudicial to the South, placing it in a false position, and making it the violator of laws which it is specially interested in upholding for its own protection. The course pursued by the Kansas Legislature is already confirming what we then predicted. Its ultra radicalism upon all subjects that call into exercise its legislative functions, and the violence with which it proscribes opinions not squaring with the ideas of its leaders, have already made it a disgrace to the country, and thrown upon the cause which it pretends to uphold an enormous degree of responsibility. An instance of this is seen in a bill on the subject of slavery, which passed without opposition.

" Laws of this complexion, which undertake to punish as a penal offense differences of opinion, can but have one effect, and that is to provoke opposition, to keep alive excitement, and ultimately to secure their own repeal by the very strength of the objection they put in the mouths of their opponents."—*Baltimore American.*

" The free-soilers have determined to appoint a government of their own; have disowned all obedience to the territorial Government existing; have determined to elect a delegate to Congress through their own organization, and leave it to that abolitionized body to determine between it and the law of the land; and, finally, have determined to hold a convention for the purpose of framing a Constitution, and presenting themselves (a poor minority of the settlers of Kansas) for admission into the Union as a free-soil State.

" The plan is one of those astute contrivances that could not have originated on the frontiers. It bears the marks of Seward on every section of it, and the object is to transfer the power of the Territories over their domestic laws to the House of Representatives at Washington, where the revolutionary doings of a band of incendiaries, it is hoped, will be treated by their brother fanatics as the 'Higher Law.' "
—*Charleston (S. C.) Mercury.*

" CONDITION OF THINGS IN KANSAS.

" The enormous outrages that have been perpetrated in Kansas during the last six or eight months, are a disgrace to the country and the age in which we live. Furthermore, the excesses that have been committed there in violation of law, order, and decency, with the passive sanction of the Federal Government, will most assuredly be the means of defeating the object which the authors of the bill had exclusively in view—the organization of Kansas as a slave State. Messrs. Atchison, Stringfellow, and the Missouri borderers generally, have gone a little too far in their foray, and a time of retribution is soon to follow. We notice that a reaction has already commenced; however perverted and misdirected popular sentiment may become for a season, under the influence of violence, and the guidance and example of prominent but unscrupulous leaders, it is sure in the end to correct itself. The worst men, unless living entirely isolated, and beyond the soothing reach of civilization and association, cannot persist for any length of time in an uninterrupted course of violence and profligate disregard of all moral and civil obligation. The ruffians who are now committing these lawless excesses in Kansas must in time become satiated, and then mollified; and a resort to the refuge of the law will become a necessity to insure even an existence among themselves, for the existence of society is based upon the supremacy of the laws, and upon no other safe foundation.

"But in the meantime who can estimate the mischief, irreparable it may be, that these acts of lawless violence have already produced; the deep-seated hatred between contending factions on the spot, the sectional animosities, the bitter jealousies, the revilings and vituperation, criminations and recriminations, all of which are tending to sever social and fraternal ties, and ultimately, perhaps, to break asunder the bonds of Union!

"There is a grave responsibility resting upon the authors of the present state of disorganization in Kansas, and of the prospective trouble which is to ensue from this condition of things.

"No one can justify, or even extenuate, the outrages and violation, not merely of law, but of those conventional observances which exist in the most rude and primitive societies, which have been disgracing a Territory under United States Government for the past six months. But this negative condemnation is not enough; there should be direct and emphatic denunciation of this condition of affairs. The class of citizens who are friends of law and order, who deprecate the supremacy of mobs and lawless assemblages, and who desire to see the people exercise freely and peaceably the rights and privileges to which they are entitled, should set their faces against this domination of reckless and irresponsible power.

"We have seen, read, and heard enough of rows and mobs to hold them in special abhorrence. Of all domestic evils, they are the most to be deprecated; they disorganize society, injure reputation, private and public interests. The places where they prevail and are tolerated are plague-spots, which all peaceably disposed citizens and good men should avoid.

"The immediate consequences of the revolutionary condition of Kansas have been almost entirely to check emigration. The people of the free States do not choose to jeopardize their lives in a land cursed by mob law, and ruled by reckless bullies; the people of the slave States are averse to peril their title to their slaves in a Territory where the free-soil element so extensively prevails, and where there is no security of property. Another consequence of these violent proceedings, carried on under the sanction of the law, is, that they are having the effect of alienating the friends of the South in the Northern States.

We could quote the strictures of some of the most moderate and conservative journals in the free States upon outrageous legislation of the present hybrid Legislature of Kansas, which journals have been uniformly sustaining the cause of the South against the formidable combination of party which have arrayed against us and them. Some of the laws passed by the Kansas Legislature are so outrageously proscriptive and violent, and so disgraceful in character, that the most tolerant and forbearing of the Northern press cannot suppress their indignation, but are compelled to give it utterance."—*New Orleans Bulletin.*

"THE BATTLE GROUND.

" We can perceive no reason why we of the North should appropriate to ourselves the whole terror and dread of war. We cannot tell why the whole weight of its heaviest strokes will be for us; albeit our Southern friends evidently so regard it. We have more charcoal than they have; we have more saltpetre; we have more brimstone; we have more lead; we have more bone and blood, and nerve and muscle. Will they have a trial by these? Are they ready for it? Are they eager for the clinch of death? Let them beware! To insult and contumely long continued they have added monstrous and unthought-of perfidy, and now into the edge of that deep, slow-healing wound of our abused faith, they will drive the sting of open and outrageous violence. There is a time to stop. If at length force must end that struggle—by a swift and terrible blow will it then be ended.

" We hope not for this; we shall do all we can to avert it; but slavery will not get Kansas so. We are afraid that the ominous look of things is keeping away emigrants who ought to go there. If it were sure to become a slave State we would advise no freeman to seek his home there. No freeman could find one. But this is not certain, not in our view probable. A struggle there will be, and no man ought to go there who fears one. There will be a call for sacrifice and self-denial; but sacrifice and self-denial pay.

" The natural resources of Kansas, various and ample as they are, may not be superior to those of other sections of the West—but, while the great streams of emigration will doubtless take their direction mainly to the facilities offered for procuring a subsistence and for gaining wealth, we yet hope that among those now leaving us there will be found many with whom the wealth of the world is not all its worth, nor the ease of life its end; many who will not hold it a small thing that in a most important and critical time they are thus allowed to aid in rearing those institutions, civil, social, and religious, to whose benign working themselves owe so much. Such men, and none but such, are needed in Kansas. Far more is to depend on the thoroughness of character of the first free settlers, than on number. The danger of acquiescence is greater than the danger of overthrow. We say, then, to whoever is about deciding in this matter—if you are conscious of no higher motive than love of gain, don't go to Kansas—you may grow rich there, but you are likely enough to wish to do it by slave labor; if you desire only to live easily, don't go—sleepy men are not needed there now; if you want courage and moral firmness, don't go—proud, angry men will look you in the eyes there; if you believe liberty to be sweet only as *you* have it, and justice sacred only as it guards *your* rights, don't go—self-sufficient, self-seeking men sprout out of the ground anywhere; if you have a longing for office and favor, if you suppose yourself to possess the attributes of a postmaster, don't go— you may not be good for anything anywhere else, but then don't go to Kansas; if, on the contrary, you can take with you the mind and strength of a man, and the generous heart and life of a freeman, go— there is no better place in all the world for you."—*Springfield (Mass.) Republican.*

When it became evident that the Legislature would be en- dorsed by the territorial judiciary and the President, and that there would be no escape by election for at least two years, it was equally evident that some means must be de- vised to keep the settlers from abandoning the fight. While the majority of the Free-State party were anti-slavery from conviction, and would stand out against a slave State to the bitter end, a large minority were indifferent to the question of slavery, and had been driven to act with the Free-State party because of the invasion of their own civil and politi- cal rights. Under these circumstances it was deemed expe- dient to agitate the question of a State constitution. Such a movement would serve to occupy the minds of the people, attract the attention of ambitious politicians, become a rally- ing point for all opposed to the usurpation, and, in case of necessity, when all other means of self-preservation should fail, be used as a *de facto* government, even though not rec- ognized by Congress. This step was taken with caution. Influential Free-State men were consulted, especially Reeder, Coates, Deitzler, and the staunch anti-slavery men of con- viction. Lane, at that time, had not cast his lot fully with

the Free-State men, although the failure of his Democratic
convention had disgusted him with that venture. It was
known that he had recognized the legality of the Legislature,
and contemplated getting a divorce by its action. However, at an interview with several active Free-State men, he
said if those present would agree to support him for one of
the Senators under the constitution, he would enlist in the
movement. He was assured that if his labors should be
worthy of such a position he should have it. Accordingly, at
the convention of the 14th of August, 1855, this, among
other resolutions, was adopted:

" 5. That we consider the attempt to establish a territorial form of
government in this Territory as an utter failure; and that the people
of the Territory should, at some convenient period, assemble at their
several places of holding elections in the various districts of the Territory, and elect delegates to a convention to form a State constitution
for the State of Kansas, with the view to an immediate State organization, and application, at the next session of Congress, for admission
into the American Union, as one of the States of the American Confederacy."

While Colonel Lane opposed the resolution repudiating the
Legislature as a body, he favored this resolution and moved
its adoption. General Pomeroy thought the action premature, as he would prefer to know the wishes of the new
Governor appointed to fill Governor Reeder's place. When
the resolutions were first introduced by the committee, of
which Robinson was chairman, several politicians opposed
them, but after adjournment over night they had all received
new light, as they said, and the resolutions were adopted
without opposition. A mass meeting was called on the
15th, without distinction of party, and recommended a convention to be held at Topeka, September 19th, to take this
matter of a constitutional convention into consideration and
to provide for one if thought best.

Although several conventions had been held at Lawrence,
and resolutions adopted without number, it was concluded

to call a general convention of the Free-State party at Big Springs, September 5, 1855. The call was made by the convention of the 14th of August, held at Lawrence, and the notices were spread broadcast over the Territory. This convention was well attended, and nearly all the leading Free-State men were present in consultation, including the Free-State executive committee. Judge G. W. Smith was made president of the convention. Two important reports were made, one by Colonel Lane, as chairman of the committee on platform, and one by J. S. Emery, as chairman of the committee on the Legislature. The latter report was drawn by Governor Reeder.

The report on platform was substantially a repetition of reports at previous conventions held at Lawrence, except with reference to free negroes and abolitionists. It took strong ground against both, and proposed not to interfere with slave States or fugitive slaves. The report drawn by Governor Reeder was most emphatic in its denunciation of the Territorial Legislature. Among the resolutions are the following:

"*Resolved*, That we owe no allegiance or obedience to the tyrannical enactments of this spurious Legislature—that their laws have no validity or binding force upon the people of Kansas, and that every freeman among us is at full liberty, consistently with all his obligations as a citizen and a man, to defy and resist them, if he chooses so to do.

"*Resolved*, That we will resist them primarily by every peaceable and legal means within our power, until we can elect our own Representatives and sweep them from the statute book; and as the majority of our Supreme Court have so far forgotten their official duty—have so far cast off the honor of the lawyer and the dignity of the judge as to enter clothed with the judicial ermine into partisan contest, and by an extra-judicial decision giving opinions in violation of all propriety, have prejudged our case before we could be heard, and have pledged themselves to these outlaws in advance, to decide in their favor, we will therefore take measures to carry the question of the validity of these laws to a higher tribunal, where judges are unpledged and dispassionate—where the law will be administered in its purity, and where we can at least have the hearing before the decision.

"*Resolved*, That we will endure and submit to these laws no longer than the best interests of the Territory require, as the less of two evils, and will resist them to a bloody issue as soon as we ascertain that peaceable remedies shall fail, and forcible resistance shall furnish any reasonable prospect of success; and that in the meantime we recommend to our friends throughout the Territory the organization and discipline of volunteer companies and the procurement and preparation of arms.

"*Resolved,* That we cannot, and will not, quietly submit to surrender our great 'American birthright '—the elective franchise; which, first by violence, and then by chicanery, artifice, weak and wicked legislation, they have so effectually succeeded in depriving us of, and that with scorn we repudiate the ' Election Law' so-called—and will not meet with them on the day they have appointed for the election—but will ourselves fix upon a day, for the purpose of electing a delegate to Congress."

At this convention Governor Reeder was nominated for delegate to Congress, to be voted for on the second Tuesday of October, instead of the day fixed by the Legislature. He accepted the nomination and delivered a speech that set the convention wild with enthusiasm. Perhaps no convention was ever held of greater importance, or that so cemented the people of all shades of political views, except pro-slavery. One dissenting voice, and one only, was heard, and that was by Charles Stearns, the Garrisonian. As he was the only representative of that party in Kansas, and as that party now claims to have been instrumental in saving Kansas and abolishing slavery, his letter to the *Free State* of September 24th, is given:

"LAWRENCE, September 13, 1855.
" MESSRS. EDITORS: In your paper just issued, I notice the following remark:
" ' The platform is such as every Free-State man can stand upon, and, so far as we have learned, gives eminent satisfaction to all, except those who desire division in our ranks.'
" Of course, then, you will set me down as one who ' desires division in our ranks '—for rather than be satisfied with such a platform, I would submit to martyrdom. It fills me with grief and astonishment, and, if I am not mistaken, will render the party adopting it a by-word and reproach in the mouths of the nation.
" All sterling anti-slavery men, here and elsewhere, cannot keep from

spitting upon it; and all pro-slavery people must, in their hearts, perfectly despise the base sycophants who originated and adopted it.

" If such is the manliness of the ' Free-State ' party, commit me to the slave-drivers themselves, for, much as I abhor them, I do not so thoroughly despise them as I do a party that will ' make the welkin ring' about its anti-slavery principles, and then crawl, in the lowest dust, at the feet of the slave power. I can and do apologize for a pro-slavery man who has been educated under the influence of slavery, and sincerely believes that slavery is right; but for Northern men, who know better, to tell the South they are their most humble servants, and are willing to concede to them the right to buy and sell human beings, and to pursue with blood-hounds the panting fugitive, is perfectly infernal.

" If this is the platform the Free-State party are going to occupy, God forbid that I should ever stand upon its rotten planks.

" I do not wish to multiply words on this occasion, but merely ask, as a personal favor, that you will publish this renunciation of what I can no longer look upon but as a base pro-slavery party fully equal in depravity to either the Whig or Democratic parties.

" Yours, for genuine anti-slavery,

" CHAS. STEARNS."

Upon this the editor comments as follows:

" The author of the above communication is the only man in the Territory that is so thoroughly disgusted with the Free-State platform. It is due the author, however, to state that he is a Garrisonian abolitionist of the deepest dye—a class of men who imagine the Union conceived in sin and brought forth in iniquity, and therefore have no participation in its affairs. It is also due the public to state that the platform was not drafted for any such class of men, but for the Free-State party, and we would be just as much surprised to find them endorse it as we would be if Stringfellow and Atchison should endorse it."

Henry C. Wright, the non-resistant abolitionist, said he would not cast his vote for a President though he knew that vote would free all the slaves in the country, simply because the Government was based upon force; and so Mr. Stearns would not act with the Free-State party because in some particular it did not meet his views. He could not stoop in the least, even to conquer in one of the most important encounters of the age. Many of the Free-State men had no

sympathy with the black law or fugitive slave law, neither
were they afraid of abolition or abolitionists, but it was well
known that many Western and Southern Free-State men did
care for these things, and as these were not the issue then
before the people, they were willing to accept the platform
without opposition.   It would be time enough to attend to
such matters when the absorbing question of a free State
should be settled.   Eli Thayer, as he has often said, looked
upon the struggle in Kansas as the entering wedge in the
conflict for the overthrow of slavery in the nation.   Freedom once planted in Kansas would spread east and south
in accordance with the popular sovereignty of the Kansas-
Nebraska bill, till not a slave should be found in any State.
This was the view of the agents of the Aid Company and
many others who came to Kansas from the North and East.
If this view should prove to be right, it was immaterial
whether a resolution should be adopted in favor of a black
law or not, or against abolitionists ; for, when the struggle
should be ended, there would be no slavery, no fugitive
slaves to be returned, no prejudice against free colored men,
as all colored men would be free and abolitionists would dis-
appear when there was no slavery to abolish.   Hence, the
most radical Free-State men cared for but the one issue—
a free State.   If the emigrants from the West and South
wanted a resolution that the moon was made of cotton bales,
or coils of hemp rope, and Charles Stearns wanted one that
it was made of green cheese or Boston brown bread, they
would quarrel with neither, so they were right upon the question at issue.   John Brown, when he arrived a month later,
was also disgusted with the Free-State party.   Redpath, in
his " Life of Captain John Brown," page 103, says:

"The first time I heard of old Brown was in connection with a caucus at the town of Osawatomie.   It was shortly after his arrival in the
Territory.   The politicians of the neighborhood were carefully pruning
resolutions so as to suit every variety of anti-slavery extensionists ; and
more especially that class of persons whose opposition to slavery was

founded on expediency—the selfishness of race, and caste, and interest; men who were desirous that Kansas should be consecrated to free white labor only, not to freedom for all and above all. The resolution that aroused the old man's anger declared that Kansas should be a free *white* State, thereby favoring the exclusion of negroes and mulattoes, whether slave or free. He rose to speak, and soon alarmed and disgusted the politicians by asserting the manhood of the negro race, and expressing his earnest anti-slavery convictions with a force and vehemence little likely to suit the hybrids then known as Free-State Democrats. There were a number of emigrants from Indiana, I was told, whom his speech so shocked that they went over and remained in the pro-slavery party. This was John Brown's first and last appearance in a public meeting in Kansas."

The convention called at Topeka on the 19th of September met, decided to call a constitutional convention, and arranged for the election of members on the 9th of October to meet at Topeka on the fourth Tuesday of the same month to frame a constitution. The committee appointed to take charge of this work, called the Territorial Executive Committee, consisted of the following: J. H. Lane, chairman; C. K. Holliday, M. J. Parrott, P. C. Schuyler, G. W. Smith, G. W. Brown, and J. K. Goodin, secretary.

The Free-State Territorial Executive Committee, which superintended the affairs of that party, was: C. Robinson, chairman; J. K. Goodin, secretary; G. W. Smith, J. A. Wakefield, L. Macy, F. W. Giles, William Phillips, C. A. Foster, J. P. Fox, J. D. Stockton, W. R. Vail, John Brown, Jr., W. A. Ely, G. F. Warren, John Hamilton, H. Smith, L. Smith, M. F. Conway, S. D. Houston, Dr. L. R. Adams, Dr. L. B. Palmer, J. E. Gould, Abelard Guthrie.

Thus both committees had the same secretary, Joel K. Goodin. Mr. Goodin was perfectly fitted for secretary, and occupied that position on nearly all subsequent occasions of importance during the entire conflict. No man had a more sagacious or a cooler mind, and his counsel was invaluable. He had the courage of his convictions, and stood ready to thwart any wild scheme, as will hereafter appear.

The convention to frame the constitution met as provided, and the game of personal politics opened at once. The play was serio-comic from the first, often verging upon the tragic or ridiculous. The only officer of importance to be elected was president of the convention. To this position Colonel Lane, of course, aspired. As an evidence of his resources and political ingenuity, he based his claims to the highest office in the gift of the members on a damaging scandal. He asked for votes as an endorsement and vindication of his character. The *Free State* of October 29th makes this comment:

" It will be seen in another column that the constitutional convention has met and elected its officers. They, of course, put in the chair a certain individual, in order to counteract the effect of a true report that was abroad that might injure him, and as he declared that he would sink to hell rather than be defeated, we are rather afraid he will ' sink ' anyhow, notwithstanding his success."

The members of the convention were at once divided into two factions, so far as aspiring politicians could divide them. One was called the conservative and the other the radical wing of the party. The first had headquarters at the Garvey House, and the second at the Chase House. Slate-making was at once inaugurated at the Garvey House, while the radicals at the Chase House accepted the situation with good-nature, as they were willing to forego all honors and emoluments of office if they could only secure a free State. That a visible line might be drawn in the convention, a resolution was introduced endorsing squatter sovereignty and Democracy generally. This was discussed each evening for some time with considerable display of old campaign literature. Of course, no man who opposed this resolution could find a place on the Garvey House slate. A small segment of the members were thrown completely outside of all healthy political organization by voting for negro suffrage. Their names were R. H. Crosby, G. S. Hillyer, Amory Hunting, O. C. Brown, Richard Knight, Philip C. Schuyler, and C.

Robinson. Some of these, also, as if to make their political damnation sure, voted to strike out the word "male" as well as "white" from the constitution.

But Lane was not fully satisfied with his vindication by being elected president of the convention; he must put a gag in every man's mouth. For this purpose a resort was had to "the code." One night, after all had retired in the attic of the Chase House, G. P. Lowry, ex-private secretary of Governor Reeder, appeared, said he had a challenge from Lane to fight a duel, and wanted Dr. Robinson to act as his second. Robinson, of course, was indignant that the Free-State cause should be tarnished by such transactions, and said it must not be permitted. He utterly detested duelling, knew nothing of the code, and would have nothing to do with it. He, however, thinking he could shame Lane out of the business, went to the Garvey House attic to see Lane. There he found him trembling with fear, or shaking with the ague, so as visibly to move the cot on which he lay. On being reproved for bringing disgrace upon the party, he said Lowry had been repeating the scandal about himself and Mrs. Lindsay, and he had determined to put a stop to it at once and forever. Notwithstanding Lane had gone to Robinson's house early in the morning and begged of him to assist in preventing Lindsay from shooting him, and though Robinson had endorsed a note to effect a settlement, yet now Lane would try to make believe there was nothing to the matter, and he was bound to stop all such talk. After dwelling upon the folly of such a course, saying that if he should kill Lowry it would not stop the scandal nor vindicate him in public estimation, and if Lowry should kill him he would fare no better, Lane replied that he could do nothing about it, as Parrott was his second and the whole matter was in his hands. After saying that he had come to him not at the instance of Lowry, as he was anxious to fight, Robinson left the attic of Lane and returned to his own. It was concluded to accept the challenge in due form, and

12

Major Robert Klotz was engaged to superintend the duel. The fight was to come off at eight o'clock in the morning, and the challenged party had nothing more to do but to await developments. He did not wait long till a messenger appeared and desired to change the hour from eight o'clock to eleven o'clock. This evidently was the beginning of a back-down, as the convention would be in session at that hour, and most likely Lane would have some friend posted to stop the duel. Lowry, however, accepted the change of time and kept his peace. The convention opened as usual, and the planets retained their accustomed orbits. About half an hour before the fatal moment, Lane took the floor on some unimportant question and went off in one of his windy harangues. He talked up to the time set for the duel, when he, with great dignity and solemnity, closed, took his hat, and started to leave for the bloody battle-field. Instantly Judge Smith arose, in great apparent agitation, made the announcement that he had learned a hostile meeting was in contemplation, to which some members of the convention were parties, and he desired "to move the adoption of the following resolution," which had been previously prepared in due form. This resolution apparently created a great sensation, and proposed to expel any member of the convention who would be a party to such meeting, either as principal or second. Of course it was unanimously adopted, but the duel was not yet off. Robinson, as he was a member of the convention, and was disposed to conform to the resolution, deputized J. F. Legate to act as second in his stead. Legate was in his element, and demanded a fight or an ignominious back-down and apology on the part of Lane. It is needless to say the apology and back-down came to the full satisfaction of the challenged party. This was the first and last duel in Kansas, so far as known, although Lane had fought a similar duel in a similar bloodless manner when a member of Congress, and he had another afterwards with Senator Douglas, who charged him with forgery and lying when he presented the Topeka constitution to the Senate. Lane always had more or less solicitude about his reputation for valor. To vindicate his record in the Mexican war he had written a pamphlet, which he brought with him to Kansas. No one seemed to care about such matters except himself, but he evidently thought much ado about his honor and courage was necessary to secure the confidence of the people.

Notwithstanding the slate-making, political harangues and duel, the convention completed its labors in about two weeks, and the members departed to their respective homes. Bank law and black law provisions were attached, to be voted upon separately, and all factions were harmonized. On the whole, the convention was a grand success. The constitution itself was nothing remarkable, but answered all purposes for which it was made. Nothing could be more satisfactory than the interest it elicited among politicians. The Topeka State government in embryo had greater attractions for office-hunters than a full-fledged territorial government with officers appointed at Washington. Especially were the conservatives held as with hooks of steel, as they only would be eligible to office, the radicals having been already politically buried by common consent and with their own approval. They were safe to oppose the bogus Territorial Legislature and laws from principle, while the conservatives might need some other attraction than a mere free State. Hon. T. Dwight Thacher, who came to Kansas in 1857, in his address at the Quarter Centennial at Topeka, said: "If the question be asked what useful purpose the Topeka constitutional movement subserved, the obvious answer is that it served as a nucleus, the rallying point, the bond of union of the Free-State party during the most trying and dangerous period of our territorial history. Without it the Free-State forces must have drifted, been demoralized, and probably beaten. The prospects of success were sufficiently flattering to supplement the Free-State cause with the personal ambition of a large number of able men who would be called to official position under it."

This constitution was to be voted for or against on December 15, 1855, and, if adopted, State officers and a Legislature were to be elected January 15, 1856.

CHAPTER VIII.

THE MURDER OF DOW.—THE WAKARUSA WAR.—MURDER AND BURIAL OF BARBER.

THE unanimity with which the constitutional movement was endorsed by the Free-State men of all shades and factions gave good cause for alarm to the Slave-State party. " Hell hath no fury like a woman scorned," and the indifference shown to the Territorial Legislature and its laws was the most terrible punishment that could be inflicted upon the invaders. War would be infinitely preferable to such a peace. Here were all the men of character and influence in the Territory except Stringfellow and a corporal's guard of his satellites adhering to the State movement. The *Herald of Freedom, Tribune, Free State, Freeman*, and all other Free-State journals were harmonized and earnestly at work. Then there were the correspondents of the Eastern press. The battle-field was the nation, and no step in advance could be taken in Kansas that would not be sustained in the North and East ; and there was no way to reach the people except through the papers read by them. At this time, when the constitution was framed or soon after, a corps of correspondents was found in Kansas unexcelled if equalled elsewhere. There was William A. Phillips, who must be admitted to have been the leader of them, not only on account of his ability and activity, but because of the great influence and power of the paper for which he wrote, the New York *Tribune.* No paper at that time had such influence with the masses of the people, the industrial classes, as the *Tribune,*

and no man could speak with such authority as Horace
Greeley.   Equal in importance was the Missouri *Democrat*,
published in the enemy's country.   It is doubtful if Kansas
could have been saved from the grasp of the invaders but for
the hot shot poured into Atchison, Stringfellow and Company
by this paper.   James Redpath, the fearless, indomitable
friend of the oppressed of all colors and all climes, was its correspondent.   Neither he nor Phillips allowed any incident to
escape attention, and if every outrage by the invaders and
their accomplices was not so presented as to have the greatest possible effect upon readers, it was not for lack of will,
but of ability; and if any one had more ability in that line
than these young correspondents, he had not appeared in
Kansas.   Other papers, perhaps of less circulation, had
equally earnest, able, and efficient correspondents.   There
was Hutchinson, of the New York *Times*, S. C. Smith, S. F.
Tappan, Ladd, Hinton, and Realf, of several New England
and other papers, as well as many occasional correspondents.
Besides correspondents, educators went among the people
in person and preached the doctrine of salvation to Kansas
from outrage.   Thayer, of course, was always in the field,
and his equal as the preacher of a crusade has not been seen
since the time of Peter the Hermit.   Reeder, Pomeroy, and
Branscomb made raids in different parts of the country and
struck most effective blows.

Another agency must not be forgotten.   The churches
and clergy of the North and East enlisted with zeal in the
work of raising men and means for the cause of free Kansas.
As people would no longer take stock in the Aid Company
as a business venture, the churches and people subscribed
from considerations of patriotism or philanthropy.   Hundreds of ministers were made stockholders by contributions
from their churches, and a considerable amount of money
was thus raised.   Emigration revived in consequence of this
agitation, and means were sent forward.   Four aid companies' steam mills, of not less than twenty-five horse power

each, landed at Kansas City, in the month of August, 1855. In short, if public sentiment was any criterion, the bogus territorial government was in a most precarious condition, and something must be done. What should it be? If possible, this carcass must be galvanized into life, and, also, if possible, these hated and once despised, but now feared, Free-State men must be brought in conflict with Federal authority and officials. As the Free-State men would do no wrong nor break any law, it was difficult to make a case. The most that could be charged to them was refusal to use the territorial machine, and denunciation and repudiation of the fraud. Not only by word of mouth, but in print through every Free-State paper, the settlers in the most emphatic and pointed terms defied and disowned the enactments of the so-called Legislature. By the time of the adjournment of the constitutional convention, in October, the bogus government had become a by-word and reproach, a stench in the nostrils of almost all the people. It was under these circumstances that a case was made to order.

A pro-slavery man named Coleman killed a Free-State man named Dow at a place fifteen miles south of Lawrence, called Hickory Point, on Wednesday, November 21, 1855. The pretended reason for the killing of Dow by Coleman was a claim dispute, but the murder was evidently prearranged. Dow went to a blacksmith shop to have some work done, where he met some pro-slavery men. One of these had a wordy quarrel with Dow and threatened death with a musket, but did not fire. On his way home Coleman appeared, shot Dow with slugs, and left him to die alone in the middle of the road.

This murder caused intense excitement in the neighborhood, extending to Lawrence. A meeting of citizens was held at the place of the murder on the 26th, and resolutions adopted denouncing the outrage in fitting terms. In the night after this meeting, the bogus sheriff, Jones, appeared with a posse of fifteen men at the house of Mr. Branson, the landlord of Dow, and in a violent and insulting manner took him away. The news of this arrest spread rapidly, and a force of about fifteen men gathered and intercepted the sheriff and prisoner at the house of J. B. Abbott. Colonel S. N. Wood, one of the rescuing party, in a letter to A. Wattles, dated August 29, 1857, thus describes the rescue:

" DEAR SIR: You request me to give you a history of the Branson rescue. At this late date it would be impossible for me to give you an exact history of that affair, but with pleasure I proceed to give you some facts connected with the rescue.

" Charles Dow was from Ohio, from a Democratic family, his father, if not himself, having voted for Franklin Pierce for President. Dow was murdered on Wednesday, November 21, 1855. News of it came to Lawrence late Thursday evening. I felt much excited. Dow had come from an adjoining county in Ohio, had lived at my house in Kansas, and was a noble young man. Early Friday morning, in company with S. C. Smith, I drove to Hickory Point. We found that Coleman and others, charged with the murder of our friend, had fled to Missouri. Dow had just been buried, and a meeting agreed upon for Monday, the 26th. With the promise of attending said meeting we returned to Lawrence. Monday, the 26th, again went to Hickory Point. S. F. Tappan was also present. Found a meeting already organized. S. N. Wood was appointed a committee to question witnesses. Some pro-slavery men attended said meeting. The testimony clearly indicated that Dow had been murdered, not out of personal feelings, but on account of his principles, and that others were to meet the same fate, in hopes thus of harassing the Free-State men, and to frighten us all out of Kansas. All parties present deprecated the murder. One hundred men or more attended the meeting, and a unanimous determination was manifested to stop such murders. A committee on resolutions, of which S. N. Wood was chairman, presented a few resolutions regretting the outrages and resolving to do all in their power to search out the guilty parties and bring them to justice. The meeting lasted until almost sundown. Much feeling was manifested against Coleman, and a strong disposition exhibited to burn his house, which stood near. Three or four men broke down the door, rushed in, emptied a straw bed upon the floor, and fired it. S. C. Smith, S. N. Wood, and others rushed into the house, smothered the flames, clearing the house, and amid the greatest excitement, some crying, ' Burn the house,' and others interceding to save property. S. N. Wood jumped upon the fence and said murder, pillage, and arson were the peculiar avocations of our enemies, that houses were too scarce to be burned, and that this meeting must not be disgraced in this way. Wood moved as the sense of the meeting that the house be not burned, which was carried unanimously, and the meeting quietly separated.

"I set out with J. B. Abbott to return to Lawrence. It was very dark in the fore part of the evening. Losing our way we got belated, but finally, about ten or eleven o'clock, found our way to Blanton, where we were met and told that a large party of armed men had just passed towards Hickory Point. I immediately urged the necessity of following the party to ascertain if possible their business to Hickory Point. We finally adjourned to Abbott's for supper. After supper fresh horses were procured. One was sent up and down the Wakarusa to notify the settlers, two started upon foot to raise what Free-State settlers they could on the route and rendezvous near the old man Branson's, while Abbott and myself went to Hickory Point. Never shall I forget that seven miles' ride. Almost the whole distance was passed in silence. Just as we came to the timber I turned and inquired what we should do if we found the rascals at Branson's. Abbott replied, ' You are the leader; just what you say.' With tightened rein, revolvers in our hands, we galloped into the thicket, and in a moment were at the door of Branson's. Dismounting, I hastily inquired for Branson. His wife, an old lady, in choking accents replied, ' Twenty armed men have got him and gone.' ' Where?' I asked. ' Towards Lawrence,' she replied, and at the same moment said they would ' murder him,' which I believed true, and sprang into the saddle, and to the inquiry, ' Where are you going?' replied, ' To save your husband or die.'

"In a few moments we were again upon the open prairie, moon up and bright. Different paths were examined, but no signs of horses having passed. For two long hours we galloped over the prairie from house to house, inquiring for passing horsemen, but could get no tidings of the party.* At last, discouraged and dispirited, fearing they had escaped altogether, we separated, Abbott to go to our rendezvous near Hickory Point, I to see a few more settlers and to hasten to Abbott's house—to stop any parties of friends *en route* for Hickory Point. I got to Abbott's in time to stop a party of a dozen, when we were soon joined by Abbott, who did not wait for the men on foot. A consultation was called, and we were about sending messengers to the pro-slavery town of Franklin for information, when all at once some one announced, ' They are coming.' Pell-mell we rushed out of the house and got into the road ahead of them, they halting within two rods of us. A moment was passed in silence, when one of their party said, ' What's up?' Abbott asked, ' Is Mr. Branson there?' Branson replied, ' Yes,

* It turned out that the party left the road before getting out of the timber, and taking a circuitous route, went to a pro-slavery man's house a mile in an opposite direction and spent two hours in drinking and carousing.

I am here a prisoner.' Said S. N. Wood, ' If you want to be among your friends come over here.' Said some of the opposite party, ' If you move we will shoot you.' Said Huffs (a Hoosier), ' Shoot and be d—d.' Said Wood to Branson, ' Come on, let them shoot if they want to,' and, turning to them, said, ' Gentlemen, shoot, and not a man of you shall leave alive.' Said Branson to us, ' I will do just as you say.' All hands on our side said, ' Come on.' Branson attempted to ride to us; he was on a mule. Says some one, ' Whose mule is that?' ' Theirs,' says Branson. ' Get off of it,' said Wood, ' and let it go.' Branson dismounted. Wood left the ranks, kicked the old mule, and told it to go back among its friends. Guns were aimed and cocked upon both sides, but just as Branson left one of the opposite party lowered his gun with the remark, ' I ain't going to shoot.' Jones then advanced upon horseback, said his name was Jones, that he was Sheriff of Douglas County, Kansas, that he had a warrant to arrest the old man Branson, and he must serve it. He was told that we knew of no Sheriff Jones; that we knew of a postmaster at Westport, Missouri, by that name, but knew of no Sheriff Jones. We told him that we had no Douglas County in Kansas, and what was better, we never intended to have. But we told him if he must arrest Branson, to go at it. Jones still said he had a warrant to arrest him, and must do it. S. N. Wood said he was Branson's attorney; that if he had a warrant to arrest him he wanted to see it, and see if it was all right. Jones said he had it, but refused to show it. Wood asked him if it had been read or shown to Branson. Jones admitted it had not, when he was told that, until he produced the warrant, Branson could not go with him. An hour at least was spent in parleying, when Jones and Company bid our party good-night and left. Our party immediately organized. S. N. Wood was elected captain; S. C. Smith, lieutenant. The following persons were present at the time the rescue took place: S. N. Wood, J. B. Abbott, Daniel Jones, Philip Hupp, Miner Hupp, Philip Hutchinson, Harrison Nichols, Jonathan Kenneday, Elmore Allen, Carlos Halloway, Rev. Julius Elliot, John Smith, Edward Curlas, Wm. Mears, A. Rowley—just fifteen of us. We had eight guns and two revolvers. I shook hands with the most and counted the opposite party. There were fifteen of them, each with a rifle and revolver. I made a memorandum of the above names at the time. I was the only citizen of Lawrence engaged in the rescue. Just after the rescue took place S. C. Smith, S. F. Tappan, L. I. Eastabrook, and A. McCaw joined our party. A few moments afterwards Louis Farley, C. Kiser, Rev. J. E. Stewart, F. L. Loch, and Mr. Jeminson joined the party; S. N. Wood and S. F. Tappan still being the only two from Lawrence present. Our party being organized, we marched five miles to Lawrence, where we arrived about daylight."

That the matter was premeditated but few Free-State men at that time doubted. The killing of Dow was not of itself sufficient to bring on a conflict with a pretended legal officer, but the arrest of such a man as Branson when the people were enraged at the murder would most likely provoke a rescue, which was the excuse desired for calling out the militia, which meant the people of Missouri. To make the arrest the more exasperating, it was made on a warrant issued by the National Democrat and professed Free-State man who, as judge of election, received the votes of Missourians on the 30th of March, namely, Hugh Cameron. He was appointed justice of the peace by the county commissioners, who were appointed by the Territorial Legislature, which Legislature was elected by the invaders, aided and abetted by Cameron. On arriving at Lawrence, about four o'clock in the morning, the rescuing party went directly to the house of Dr. Robinson, on Oread Hill, and reported what had been done. Robinson said that probably this action would furnish the long-wished-for pretext for calling out a force against Lawrence, and advised that they report in town.

No one could doubt that the Governor would call out the militia, ostensibly to enforce the law, but really to humiliate the Free-State men and destroy Lawrence, or at least to compel the surrender of the Sharp's and other rifles at that place. Here, then, was the first skirmish, and what should be done? Undoubtedly the force would be called out by authority of the Governor, and to resist it would be to resist Federal authority, which could not be thought of for a moment. While the Free-State men might, under favorable circumstances, resist the bogus local authority, the moment a Federal officer appeared all were loyal citizens of the Republic. There was nothing left to be done but to thwart, baffle, and circumvent. If the President chose to persist in the enforcement of the fraud of the 30th of March, the *bona fide* settlers must so conduct themselves as to make it cost him more in popularity and ease than he would gain for the cause of slavery extension. In this case the policy should be to let the Governor call on his " dogs of war," the more the better, and after weeks of organization, pillage and outrage upon the inhabitants, thwart the whole movement by having no man in sight to arrest, leaving him nothing to do but swallow his rage and send home his minions. The spectacle would be one that would excite loathing, disgust, and ridicule from one end of the nation to the other, and the Administration would suffer more in reputation than by the loss of thousands of men in a pitched battle. If the Free-State men could succeed in compelling the Administration to raise an army of one or two thousand men every time a peace warrant was to be served, the people of the country at large would soon remind it that this kind of popular sovereignty was entirely too unpopular, and would insist that the people of the Territory should be left free to settle their own matters in their own way, according to the pledge of the organic act.

After the rescue the bogus Sheriff went to Franklin, a pro-slavery settlement four miles southeast of Lawrence, and from there sent off his dispatches. According to the testimony of L. A. Prather, before the congressional committee, the first dispatch was sent to Colonel Boone, of Westport, Missouri, and the second to the Governor.

Robinson met the rescuers in town about six o'clock in the morning and advised that, as Lawrence had no connection with the matter, any formal action or endorsement by its citizens would be impolitic. To this Colonel Wood and others readily assented, Wood saying that he would willingly be arrested in order to test in the Supreme Court the right of Missouri to make laws in Kansas. About nine o'clock Robinson made his second visit to the town, when he found a meeting of the citizens in progress. He was informed that a Committee of Safety had been appointed, of which he was a member. The committee was at once convened, and it decided that Lawrence had nothing to do with the affair, and should assume no responsibility for it as a town, although no person censured the rescuers for their action.

As the Free-State men had been accused by the Administration of insubordination and treason, it was important that their position should be clearly stated and published to the world. Accordingly, one of the first acts of the Committee of Safety was to make this statement:

" We, the citizens of Kansas Territory, find ourselves in a condition of confusion and defenselessness so great, that open outrage and midday murders are becoming the rule, and quiet and security the exception. And whereas the law, the only authoritative engine to correct and regulate the excesses and wrongs of society, has never yet been extended to our Territory—thus leaving us with no fixed or definite rules of action, or source of redress—we are reduced to the necessity of organizing ourselves together on the basis of first principles, and providing for the common defense and general security. And here we pledge ourselves to the resistance of lawlessness and outrage at all times, when required by the officers who may from time to time be chosen to superintend the movements of the organization."

After several days, a Leavenworth paper containing the Governor's proclamation was received, and the following answer was made: " That the allegations contained in the proclamation aforesaid are false in whole and in part; that no such state of facts exists in this community; that if such representations were ever made to Governor Shannon, the person or persons who made them have grossly deceived him; and no association of lawless men armed with deadly weapons has ever been formed in this community for the purpose of ' resisting the laws of the country, trampling upon the authority of its officers, destroying the property of peaceable citizens or molesting any person in this Territory, or elsewhere, in the enjoyment of their rights.' "

While the Free-State men were stating their position to the world, and acting strictly on the defensive, the other side was making, through the officials, the most extravagant and reckless assertions. The surveyor-general, J. Calhoun, sent

a letter to the St. Louis *Republican*, which is referred to by
the Kansas City *Enterprise* as follows:

" AUTHENTIC NEWS FROM KANSAS.

"Under this head the *Missouri Republican* publishes a letter from
Hon. John Calhoun, Surveyor-General of Kansas and Nebraska, detailing the events connected with the difficulties at Lawrence. From this
letter we make the following extracts; our want of room prevents the
publishing of the whole letter.

" After giving an account of the origin of the difficulty, the killing of
Dow by Coleman, his giving himself up to the sheriff, the arrest of
Branson, the leader of the band, who had been burning down houses
and driving women and children from their houses, either by force or
threats, he then gives the following extracts of a letter from Governor
Shannon :

" ' The excitement is up in Missouri. The appeals of flying women
and children, and the belief that the abolitionists have determined to
expel the pro-slavery men from Hickory Grove, has kindled a flame
that no human power can control.'

" The Governor further adds :

" ' The time has come when these armed men must be met, and
brought into subjection to law, or surrender the Government into their
hands. I have determined to have the laws executed, and to protect
the unoffending people of the Territory from lawless violence. If not,
there is no use in a Government ; and to let these armed bands triumph
now over law would be virtually surrendering the whole Government
to them. But I can do this by the force of our own citizens, and intend
to use no others. But who can control the storm? These abolitionists
are mad. They are bringing on themselves utter ruin, and all this is
the legitimate result of their lawless, secret military associations.'

" These are the facts as they have occurred up to this time. What
to-morrow will bring forth, amid the excitement which such outrages
have produced, none can tell. Of one thing rest assured, the laws of
this Territory will be executed. That Governor Shannon will do his
full duty in the present crisis no one need doubt. *   *   *

" It is estimated that some sixteen dwelling houses have been burnt, all
of them in the night time, with their contents, and their occupants, men,
women, and children, driven to the prairies without shelter or protection. The leading spirit of these lawless movements is C. Robinson,
the leading spirit also of the Topeka Convention. *   *   * It is said
that he has at least five hundred men, armed with Sharp's rifles and
revolvers, determined to offer a forcible resistance to the execution of
the laws. He has threatened to hang Sheriff Jones, Coleman, and

others, as soon as he can get hold of them. Men are coming to the aid of the Governor from all parts of the Territory. He is determined that the laws shall be executed, and that all these offenders shall be punished as the law directs. Yesterday he sent a dispatch to President Pierce, asking for authority to use the military force at Fort Leavenworth. To-day or to-morrow he will get a reply. If he should get permission to bring Sumner's regiment to his aid, the difficulty will be ended without bloodshed. If not, the most serious consequences may be apprehended.

"There is one view of Kansas difficulties which at this time deserves serious notice. While Robinson, the leading agent of the Massachusetts Aid Society, the head of the Reeder faction at Lawrence, is calling upon abolitionists and free-soilers to elect a Governor and other officers, in violation of all law, and is leading on five hundred fanatics openly to resist the execution of the law, and burning down dwellings and driving women and children from their homes, the Leavenworth wing of the Reeder faction, under the lead of Delahay and Shankland, and Parrott, the author of the Reeder proclamation, which says all sensible men ' scorn and repudiate ' the Territorial laws, are advertising a ' law and order ' convention, which is to take place on next Friday at Leavenworth. The violators of law, the associates of Robinson and his band of midnight desperadoes, are to have a law and order convention! This needs no comment. The object is too transparent not to be seen at a glance, and the ridiculous farce will fall as dead as their previous Topeka Convention.

"Respectfully, your obedient servant,

"J. CALHOUN."

When squads and companies of armed men began to arrive at Franklin and the Wakarusa, the Committee of Safety organized the men at Lawrence, some of whom had come from other localities, into a regiment in due form, with Lane as Colonel, under the general supervision of Robinson, who was given supreme control, subject only to the Committee of Safety or council. The town became a military camp, earthworks were thrown up and preparations for a defense made as complete as possible. Nothing could exceed the welcome given to the re-enforcements as they came with their Sharp's rifles from different settlements. Cheer upon cheer would go up till the whole town was enthusiastic. Especially was the arrival of one hundred men well armed, from Topeka,

hailed with great demonstrations of joy. The Free-State
men from Leavenworth, compelled from circumstances to be
conservative, came over to criticise the course of their more
radical Free-State brethren. But on meeting with the Committee of Safety, and learning the situation, they fully endorsed the course taken by the people and joined the army
of defense. Dr. James Davis, one of the Leavenworth men,
had been to Lecompton and learned that the pro-slavery
men were determined to demand a surrender of all Sharp's
rifles at Lawrence or elsewhere, and desired to know what
could be done about it. He was informed by Robinson
that another " Missouri Compromise " would be proposed in
such a case, namely, keep the rifles and surrender the contents. This would be the only surrender the people would
make, as was afterwards manifested at a public meeting.
The Free-State men were not over scrupulous in matters immaterial, and could shape their course relative to the bogus
laws and officers as policy might dictate, but when it became a question of the surrender of a constitutional right, like
the one to have arms for personal defense, no man or set of
men could influence them to yield that right. As soon as
the military organization was perfected, the Committee of
Safety was supplanted by a council consisting of all officers,
from captain up. By this council the position to be occupied was fully discussed, and all knew that it was impreg-
nable, and that no war would result unless by accident, or
in violation of orders. All could see that no Federal officer
would dare attack a city without cause, and Lawrence had
given no cause, and if all would obey orders no cause would
be given. Hence, having full faith in themselves, and in
the strength of their position, all went about their duties in
preparing for defense with cheerfulness, and general good
feeling. No demonstrations, no threats, no bullying was
seen or heard among Free-State men, and they witnessed
such conduct from Jones and other pro-slavery men with
amusement or disgust. The position of the men at Law-

rence may be seen from remarks made on the 2d of December, at a meeting of the citizens, as reported in Mrs. Robinson's " Kansas," page 122 :

" Dr. Robinson, having been called upon several times to speak, also having been called from the hall two or three times, at last said, in a plain way, and in brief, that ' It was a time, in his opinion, for acting rather than speaking; that Shannon had placed himself in a bad situation. At his bidding all these Missourians had come over to help him enforce the laws ; but when they come to Lawrence they will find that nobody has broken any laws ; for the people of Lawrence are a law-abiding people. Their real object was to destroy Lawrence; but it was a question whether they would attempt it without some pretext; and before the American people Shannon would be responsible for their conduct. Fearful of some atrocious act upon the part of his drunken rabble, he has been compelled to remove the most of them to the camps on the Wakarusa. They really were in a predicament. They were afraid, and with reason, to attack Lawrence without a pretext. He had learned, but would not vouch for its truth, that Shannon had telegraphed to President Pierce for the troops at the forts. It was also reported that Pierce had telegraphed back again that he might have them, and, of course, he would get them. Of course he would disarm the people when an invading force of drunken Missourians was almost at our doors, and we have no protection in the government of the country.' (Laughter, and cries of ' Of course.') ' Men of Lawrence, and Free-State men, we must have courage, but with it we must have prudence. These men have come from Missouri to subjugate the Free-State men, to crush the Free-State movement—their pretense, that outrages have been committed. They are sustained by all the United States authorities here; and while they do not think it essential that a good cause for fighting be given them, the authorities will wait at least for a plausible excuse before commencing to shed blood. This excuse must not be given them. Each man must be a committee of one to guard the reputation as well as the lives of the Free-State men. If the Missourians, partly from fear and partly from want of a sufficient pretext, have to go back without striking a blow, it will make them a laughing-stock and redound fearfully against Shannon. This is the last struggle between freedom and slavery, and we must not flatter ourselves that it will be trivial or short. The Free-State men must stand shoulder to shoulder, with an unbroken front, and stand or fall together in defense of their liberties and homes. These may be dark days, but the American people and the world will justify us, and the cause of right will eventually triumph.' The enthusiasm with which these remarks were received evinced the deep feeling and determined spirit of the meeting."

13

The forbearance of the Free-State men is shown on page 125 of the same book:

" A startling incident occurred last night.   One of our picket guards was fired upon.   Two of the guard were sitting together, when a party of Missourians approached and fired six shots at them.   Our men had strict orders not to fire, unless the emergency was desperate, and so bore the insult with remarkable prudence, and obeyed orders.

" Our people are acting strictly upon the defensive, and these provocations are continually offered us to provoke a collision.   They are endeavoring to draw them from the position which all the world will justify, that they may have a pretext for the destruction of Lawrence, which is really the whole cause of the invasion."

For the first week of preparation ·the pro-slavery men were bold and blustering, threatening the direst vengeance against the hated town of Lawrence and all abolitionists. Jones frequently passed through Lawrence undisturbed, as did other pro-slavery men, no person paying much attention to them.   On one occasion Jones was asked in presence of Robinson what he wanted? and he replied he would let the people know when he got ready.   Pro-slavery papers in Kansas and on the border of Missouri sounded the alarm and called loudly for volunteers to put down the terrible rebellion and wipe out once for all the hated abolitionists.   Such reports as follow were current:

" WESTPORT, November 27th.
" *Hon. E. A. McClarey, Jefferson City:*
" Governor Shannon has ordered out the militia against Lawrence. They are now in open rebellion against the laws.   Jones is in danger."

" (Private.)   DEAR GENERAL: The Governor has called out the militia, and you will hereby organize your division, and proceed forthwith to Lecompton.   As the Governor has no power, you may call out the Platte Rifle Company.   They are always ready to help us.   Whatever you do, do not implicate the Governor.
" DANIEL WOODSON."

" WESTON, Mo., November 30th.
" The greatest excitement continues to exist in Kansas.   The officers have been resisted by the mobocrats, and the interposition of the militia has been called for.   A secret letter from Secretary Woodson to General Eastin has been written, in which the writer requests General

Eastin to call for the rifle company, at Platte City, Missouri, so as not to compromise Governor Shannon. Four hundred men from Jackson County are now en route for Douglas County, K. T. St. Joseph and Weston are requested to furnish each the same number. The people of Kansas are to be subjugated at all hazards."

In addition to his proclamation declaring the Free-State men in rebellion, Governor Shannon sent this order to General Richardson:

" HEADQUARTERS, SHAWNEE MISSION, K. T.,
" November 27, 1855.

" *Major-General William P. Richardson :*

" SIR : Reliable information has reached me that an armed military force is now in Lawrence, and that vicinity, in open rebellion against the laws of this Territory, and that they have determined that no process in the hands of the Sheriff of that county shall be executed. I have received a letter from S. J. Jones, Sheriff of Douglas County, informing me that he had arrested a man under a warrant placed in his hands, and while conveying him to Lecompton he was met by an armed force of some forty men, and that the prisoner was taken out of his custody, and defiance bid to the laws. I am also duly advised that an armed band of men have burnt a number of houses, destroyed personal property, and turned whole families out of doors in Douglas County. Warrants will be issued against these men and placed in the hands of the Sheriff of Douglas County for execution. He has written to me demanding three thousand men to aid him in the execution of the process of law.

" You are, therefore, hereby ordered to collect together as large a force as you can in your division, and repair without delay to Lecompton and report yourself to S. J. Jones, Sheriff of Douglas County, together with the number of your forces, and render him all the aid and assistance in your power in the execution of any legal process in his hands. The forces under your command are to be used for the sole purpose of aiding the Sheriff in executing the law, and for no other purpose.

" I have the honor to be your obedient servant,

" WILSON SHANNON."

A similar order was sent to General Strickler.

General Eastin, editor of the Leavenworth *Herald*, both through his paper and otherwise, sought to arouse the Slave-State men. He sent out the following appeal:

"TO ARMS! TO ARMS!!

" It is expected that every lover of Law and Order will rally at Leavenworth on Saturday, December 1, 1855, prepared to march at once to the scene of the rebellion, to put down the outlaws of Douglas County, who are committing depredations upon persons and property, burning down houses and declaring open hostility to the laws, and have forcibly rescued a prisoner from the Sheriff. Come one, come all! The laws must be executed. The outlaws, it is said, are armed to the teeth, and number 1000 men. Every man should bring his rifle and ammunition, and it would be well to bring two or three days' provision. Every man to his post, and to his duty.

"MANY CITIZENS."

Governor Shannon, as has been seen, wrote John Calhoun, who published it in the St. Louis *Republican*, that " the time has come when these armed men must be met and brought into subjection to law. * * * If not there is no use in a government. * * * But I can do this by the force of our own citizens, and intend to use no other. Who can control the storm? These abolitionists are mad. They are bringing on themselves utter ruin, and all this is the legitimate result of their lawless secret military associations."

Surveyor-General Calhoun himself says: " Of one thing rest assured, the laws of this Territory will be executed."

So much for the first week of the invasion. Governor Shannon's proclamations and letters, and the bluster of others, intended to raise the wind for the purpose of serving a peace warrant, threatened to raise not only a whirlwind, but a cyclone, and they began to call upon the rocks and mountains to hide them from the impending wrath. L. J. Eastin, brigadier-general of militia, and editor of the Leavenworth *Herald*, who had been so bold and aggressive, sends this to Governor Shannon: " Information has been received here direct from Lawrence, which I consider reliable, that the outlaws are well fortified at Lawrence with cannon and Sharp's rifles, and number at least 1000 men. It will therefore be difficult to dispossess them. The militia in this portion of the State are entirely unorganized, and mostly without

arms.   I suggest the propriety of calling upon the military
at Fort Leavenworth.   If you have the power to call out
the Government troops, I think it would be best to do so at
once.   It might overawe these outlaws and prevent bloodshed."

Governor Shannon, who was so confident that he could
put down this rebellion with the "force of our own citizens,"
and who declared to Calhoun that he should "use no
others," now sent this dispatch to Colonel Sumner, dated
December 6th:

" WAKARUSA, December 6, 1855.
"*Colonel Sumner, First U. S. Cavalry:*

" SIR : I send you this special dispatch to ask you to come to Lawrence as soon as you possibly can.   My object is to secure the citizens
of that place, as well as others, from a warfare which, if once commenced, there is no telling where it will end.   I doubt not you have
received orders from Washington, but if you have not, the absolute
pressure of this crisis is such as to justify you with the President and
the world in moving to the scene of difficulty.   It is hard to restrain
the men here (they are beyond my power, or at least, soon will be)
from making an attack on Lawrence, which, if once made, there is no
telling where it will terminate.   The presence of a portion of the United
States troops at Lawrence would prevent an. attack, save bloodshed, and
enable us to get matters arranged in a satisfactory way, and at the same
time secure an execution of the laws.   It is peace, not war, that we
want, and you have the power to secure peace.   Time is precious—
fear not but that you will be sustained.
" With great respect,
" WILSON SHANNON."

He also sent to Jones :

" The known deficiency in arms and all the accoutrements of war,
which must necessarily characterize the law-abiding citizens who have
rushed to your assistance in the maintenance of order, will invite resistance from your opponents, who are well supplied with arms.   It
would be wrong, therefore, to place your men in a position where their
lives would be endangered when we shall, in all probability, have an
ample force from Leavenworth in a few days."

Sheriff Jones did not want to be hampered by Government troops, knowing very well that he had no case at Law-

rence that Sumner would recognize as authorizing his action, and he wrote the Góvernor as follows:

"CAMP AT WAKARUSA, December 3, 1855.

"*His Excellency Governor Wilson Shannon:*

"SIR: In reply to your communication of yesterday, I have to inform you that the volunteer forces now at this place and Lecompton are getting weary of inaction. They will, I presume, remain but a short time longer, unless a demand for the prisoner is made. I think I shall have a sufficient force to protect me by to-morrow morning. The force at Lawrence is not half so strong as reported. I have this from a reliable source. If I am to wait for Government troops, more than two-thirds of the men now here will go away very much dissatisfied. They are leaving hourly as it is. I do not by any means wish to violate your orders, but I really believe that if I have a sufficient force it would be better to make the demand. It is reported that the people of Lawrence ' have run off' those offenders from that town, and indeed it is said that they are now all out of the way. I have writs for sixteen persons who were with the party that rescued my prisoner. S. N. Wood, P. R. Brooks, and Samuel Tappan are of Lawrence, the balance from the country around. Warrants will be placed in my hands to-day for the arrest of G. W. Brown, and probably others in Lawrence. They say they are willing to obey the laws, but no confidence can be placed in any statements they may make.

"No evidence sufficient to cause a warrant to be issued has as yet been brought against these lawless men who fired the houses. I would give you the names of the defendants, but the writs are in my office at Lecompton.

"Most respectfully yours,

"SAMUEL J. JONES,

"Sheriff of Douglas County."

Anderson followed suit with this letter to General Richardson:

"*Major-General William P. Richardson:*

"SIR: I have reason to believe from rumors in camp, that before to-morrow morning the black flag will be hoisted, when nine out of ten will rally around it, and march without orders upon Lawrence. The forces of Lecompton camp fully understand the plot, and will fight under the same banner.

"If Governor Shannon will pledge himself not to allow any United States officer to interfere with the arms belonging to the United States now in their possession, and in case there is no battle, order the United

States forces off at once and retain the militia provided any force is retained, all will be well, and all will obey to the end, and commit no depredations upon private property in Lawrence.

"I fear a collision between the United States soldiers and the volunteers, which would be dreadful.

"Speedy measures should be taken. Let me know at once—to-night —and I fear it will then be too late to stay the rashness of our people.

"Respectfully your obedient servant,

"J. C. ANDERSON."

The council at Lawrence sent the following to the Governor, who was still at the Shawnee Mission:

"*To his Excellency, Wilson Shannon,*
"*Governor of Kansas Territory:*

"SIR: As citizens of Kansas Territory, we desire to call your attention to the fact that a large force of armed men from a foreign State have assembled in the vicinity of Lawrence, and are now committing depredations upon our citizens, stopping wagons, opening and appropriating their loads, arresting, detaining, and threatening travellers upon the public road, and that they claim to do this by your authority. We desire to know if they do appear by your authority, and if you will secure the peace and quiet of the community by ordering their instant removal, or compel us to resort to some other means and to higher authority."

(Signed by committee.)

This must have been a revelation to the Governor, as it was intended to be. Here was no appeal for mercy or pardon for crimes committed, no cry for help in time of distress, and no cringing of slaves to a master, but a stern demand of rights from citizens to an official servant. This message was taken to the Governor by two young men through the lines of the enemy camped at Franklin and on the Wakarusa. It was a most hazardous mission, as they had to encounter drunken men as well as sentinels nearly the whole distance. Their names are G. P. Lowry and C. W. Babcock, and well did they execute their trust. They reached the Governor in safety, and the interview is thus described by Lowry in his testimony before the congressional committee, as reported on page 1079:

"We got to Shawnee Mission a little after sunrise, and presented our letter to Governor Shannon, and he read it, as it was very short, and then we conversed upon the affairs here.

*   *   *   *   *   *

"Governor Shannon said he would answer the letter, and we went out while he was doing so. When we returned we had a long conversation concerning these affairs. He said there had been sixteen houses burned here by Free-State men, and women and children driven out of doors. We told him we were sorry that he had not taken pains to inquire into the truth of the matter before he had brought this large force into the country, which, perhaps, he could not get out again; and that his information was wholly and entirely false, as nothing of the kind had happened. We told him of what we knew, of our personal knowledge, of men from Missouri there; and he was not inclined to admit, at first, that there was anybody from Missouri there. He made a general argument against the Free-State men, and quoted their resolutions, passed at different meetings, in regard to the Territorial laws. We explained to him that the Territorial laws had nothing to do with this case; that we were getting ready at Lawrence to fight for our lives, and the only question was, whether he would be *particeps criminis* to our murder, or the murder of somebody else, should we be all slaughtered. We explained to him that the rescue upon which he based his proclamation took place a number of miles from Lawrence; that there were but three persons living in Lawrence who were alleged to have had anything to do with it, and that they had left the town, and were not there at all; that from what we could judge of the intentions of the force at Wakarusa, at Lecompton, and in the country about, from their own declarations, they intended to destroy the town for a thing in which they had had no part or parcel.

"We took our individual cases as instances that we had not been present at the rescue; that we did not undertake to have any sympathy with it, or talk about it at all; but that if we were to submit to the force which he had called in, all our throats would be cut together—the innocent and guilty, if there were any guilty. He then denied that these Missourians were here by his authority; that he had anything to do with them, or was responsible for them. He said he had communication with Colonel Sumner, of Fort Leavenworth, and had sent an express for him to meet him that night at Delaware Ferry, and go with him to the camp on the Wakarusa. He said he should go to Lawrence and insist upon the people agreeing to obey the laws, and delivering up their Sharp's rifles. We denied his right, or the right of anybody else, to make such a condition of a community, or make any such demand of them, until it had been shown that they had resisted the laws, which they had not done; that there had been as yet no proceedings in Lawrence under the Territorial laws, and he had no right to presume that there would be any resistance to them when they were instituted.   He gave up that point after some argument.   I asked him, then, why he insisted upon the giving up of Sharp's rifles, and if he meant to demand, too, Western rifles, shot-guns, and other arms.   He said he did not intend to demand other than Sharp's rifles, but should demand them because they were unlawful weapons.   After some time he then said they were dangerous weapons ; to which I agreed.   I then told him, if he had any such idea in his head as that, he had better stay away and let the fight go on, as I thought the thing was not feasible, as he would do no good by coming here if those were his terms.   I told him he might as well demand of me my pocket-book or my watch, and I would resent the one no more than the other.   I told him I did not consider myself safe, or that General Robinson or Colonel Lane would be safe, in going before our men with any such proposition.   He then gave us the letter he had written, and we started for Kansas City to change horses."

Although Governor Shannon, before the same committee, contradicted some of the testimony of Lowry, he got his eyes opened by the message and interview sufficiently, at least, to see "men as trees walking," and he hastened to the encampment of his army of invasion or occupation.   After conferring with the high officials in command, he sent to Lawrence, as previously arranged, for an escort to visit that town.   On arrival he and his friends were introduced to the council and others, after which a consultation was held with Robinson and Lane, who had been authorized to represent the citizens.   Governor Shannon needed no new facts or arguments, but at once confessed his mistake.   He had misunderstood the situation, admitted there was no cause to attack Lawrence, and that no crime or violation of law had been committed in the town.   His only solicitude was to get his army to their homes without bloodshed.   He did not claim that he had a right to disarm the people, although his army would demand the Sharp's rifles.   On being assured that no such demand would be listened to by the people of Lawrence, he did not press it.   He had sent a messenger to Colonel Sumner, and expected his arrival in a short time.   He

deemed it important to announce no conclusion of the conference till the next day, when Sumner would certainly be
present with United States troops.   An adjournment was
had accordingly.   In the meantime each party was to prepare a written statement that might assist the Governor in
reconciling his army to return without wiping out Lawrence,
as intended and promised by Jones and company.   The
next day the Governor returned, but there was no Colonel
Sumner or United States troops in sight.   The drafts for a
treaty or agreement were considered, and one finally approved
by both parties.   It reads as follows:

"WHEREAS, There is a misunderstanding between the people of
Kansas, or a portion of them, and the Governor thereof, arising out of
the rescue, near Hickory Point, of a citizen under arrest, and some
other matters; and whereas a strong apprehension exists that said misunderstanding may lead to civil strife and bloodshed; and whereas it is
desired, by both Governor Shannon and the people of Lawrence and
vicinity, to avert a calamity so disastrous to the interests of the Territory and the Union, and to place all parties in a correct position before
the world:

"Now, therefore, it is agreed by the said Governor Shannon, and
the undersigned people of Lawrence, that the matter in dispute be settled as follows, to wit:

"We, the said citizens of said Territory, protest that the said rescue
was made without our knowledge or consent, but, if any of our citizens
were engaged, we pledge ourselves to aid in the execution of any legal
process against them; that we have no knowledge of the previous, present, or prospective existence of any organization in the said Territory
for resistance against the laws, and that we have not designed, and do
not design, to resist the legal service of any criminal process therein,
but pledge ourselves to aid in the execution of the laws, when called on
by proper authority, in the town or vicinity of Lawrence, and that we
will use all our influence in preserving order therein; and we declare
that we are now, as we ever have been, ready at any time to aid the
Governor in securing a posse for the execution of such process: provided that any person thus arrested in Lawrence or vicinity, while a
foreign force shall reman in the Territory, shall be duly examined before
a United States District Judge of said Territory in said town, and admitted to bail; and provided, further, that Governor Shannon agrees to
use his influence to secure to the citizens of Kansas Territory remu-
neration for any damages sustained, or unlawful depredations, if any such

have been committed by the Sheriff's posse in Douglas County; and, further, that Governor Shannon states that he has not called upon persons resident of any other State to aid in the execution of the laws, and such as are here in this Territory are here of their own choice; and that he has not any authority or legal power to do so, nor will he exercise any such power, and that he will not call on any citizen of another State who may be here. That we wish it understood that we do not herein express any opinion as to the validity of the enactments of the Territorial Legislature.

(Signed),   "WILSON SHANNON,
                       "C. ROBINSON,
                       "J. H. LANE."

The people of Lawrence were willing to help the Governor out of his scrape as much as possible without compromising their attitude towards the territorial fraud, the Legislature. That there might be no quibbling as to the meaning of the terms of the agreement relative to territorial laws, Robinson added the last sentence to the document.

This was a most critical juncture. The Governor was terribly in earnest to effect a settlement, while the pro-slavery leaders, represented by Jones and the ultra men, were as determined that Lawrence should be attacked. The day before the arrival of the Governor at Lawrence, two men, G. W. Clark, Indian agent, and Mr. Burns, left their party, which was going from Lecompton to Franklin, and wantonly and without provocation killed Thomas Barber, a Free-State man, on his way from Lawrence to his home. Also the guard was frequently fired upon with a view to bring on a conflict. In one instance only was the fire returned, and that was when Coleman, the murderer of Dow, passed down the road on a mule and fired upon the guard. The return shot hit the mule, but not the rider. Governor Shannon was visibly affected when, on going up-stairs to the council-room, he saw the dead body of Barber stretched upon a bench, dressed as he had fallen from his horse, and with eyes apparently staring at the stairway, and the moans of the widow, as they were heard from another room, were not consoling to his feelings.

Probably the Administration at Washington was divided by the same influences that operated in Kansas. Governor Shannon telegraphed the President on the 3d of December for permission to use the troops at Fort Leavenworth. He was answered that he might use them. He sent this answer to Colonel Sumner, and he at first promised to respond, but on reconsideration of the matter he concluded to await an order from the War Department before moving. This order never came.

As Jeff Davis was the head of this department, and as he probably desired a conflict of the militia or posse with the citizens, and knew that the presence of United States troops would prevent it, he declined to send the order, as authorized by the President.

In his desire to reconcile his force to a back-down, Governor Shannon had arranged, before going to Lawrence on his second visit, to have a joint meeting of the opposing leaders. Accordingly he desired a delegation from Lawrence to accompany him to Franklin and meet with the captains of the militia. Lane and Robinson complied with his request. At the meeting in an unfinished building, Governor Shannon led off with an explanation of the settlement, giving the position occupied by the citizens of Lawrence. After him Colonel Lane attempted to speak, but his opening so offended the thirteen militia captains that they started to leave the room, saying they did not come there to be insulted. Governor Shannon begged of them to remain and hear Dr. Robinson. Lane did not proceed, and Robinson, in a few words, explained the action of the people of Lawrence, saying that no attempt had ever been made to serve any process in the town, legal or otherwise, by any officer, real or pretended. Jones was appealed to by a militia officer to know if Robinson told the truth. Jones replied that he did. Then, the response about the room was, "We have been damnably deceived." As to the Sharp's rifles, Robinson appealed to them to say if they would, as American citizens, submit to be deprived of the constitutional right to bear arms, or if they would respect any people who would thus submit? The leading men saw their predicament, and said, " Boys, it is no use, they have got us; we can do nothing this time," and the conference ended with a pressing invitation to remain to supper. This Lane and Robinson, as it was getting dark, and a strong north-west wind had risen, with heavy sleet, tried to decline. But they said that Governor Shannon and party had dined with Robinson, and no refusal would be accepted. When supper was over, it was so dark no object was visible, and the sound of the horses' hoofs upon the hard road was the only guide to the travellers. A solitary horseman started to escort the visitors through the lines, but he proceeded only about one hundred yards, when he said good-night and left his charge to get by the guards as best they could. At this Lane said to Robinson, " Hurry up, this means assassination; they mean to kill us," and started his horse upon the run. Franklin is situated on the old California road, and the first valley west of it is the place where the ox had its leg twisted on Sunday in 1849, and brought on the lively discussion of the Sabbath question. Deep gullies had been washed in the road at this point, causing travellers to turn sharply to the right to avoid them. As Robinson was on the left, his horse ran into one of these gullies, while Lane's escaped. The horse fell with great force, and for some minutes was unable to rise. No damage, however, was done, except the delay. This valley is undoubtedly an unfortunate place. In 1856 a Free-State man was killed near it, and Franklin has perished from off the face of the earth. The night after the ratification of the treaty of peace, and after all had retired at headquarters upon benches and on the floor, a guard reported that three men had driven some women out of a cabin east of town and taken possession, and he desired to know what should be done? All in the room heard the report, but all pretended to be in a sound sleep, including the officer of the day, whose duty it was to attend to the matter. After some minutes

Deitzler, who was adjutant-general, jumped up and said, "Damn a paper hero ; who will go with me and bring them in ? " In due time he brought in three heavily armed men, who claimed that in the darkness and sleet they had lost their way. In the morning, as the war was over, they were allowed to go. It is not doubted but these men were out for the purpose of killing the guests of the Governor and of the captains of militia. On the next day after peace was declared, Governor Shannon dismissed his militia and returned to Lawrence, where he expressed great satisfaction at the termination of the war. While being entertained by the citizens of both sexes, an alarm was raised that the disbanded forces were marching upon Lawrence, when the Governor gave this authority to Robinson and Lane :

"*To Charles Robinson and J. H. Lane:*

" You are hereby authorized and directed to take such measures, and use the enrolled forces under your command in such manner, for the preservation of the peace and the protection of the persons and property of the people of Lawrence and vicinity, as in your judgment shall best secure that end.

(Signed) " WILSON SHANNON.
" LAWRENCE, December 9, 1855."

However, on investigation, the rumor proved to be unfounded, the militia having left the Territory by the most direct route.

Such was the general rejoicing at Lawrence that a peace jubilee was held on the 10th, to which the Governor and other officials were invited, including Sheriff Jones. The Governor excused himself, but Jones attended. Several speeches were made, and all would have passed off pleasantly had it not been for an attempt to excite hostility to Jones to such a degree as to require the utmost exertion and care to prevent his assassination.

This is but a mere outline of the Wakarusa war, so-called, as conducted by the Free-State party. Governor Shannon, in his testimony, said that " the posse was over 1400, as reported to me by General Strickler, and I suppose there were about five hundred that had never organized themselves, or been placed under the Sheriff."

James F. Legate testified that Jones told him not over two hundred men in the posse were residents of the Territory, while the remainder were from Missouri. While some regard the result as the greatest victory, under all the circumstances, that could have been achieved, others call it a cowardly surrender and disastrous defeat. Such persons single out two men, Lane and Brown, and claim that their policy, if adopted, would have changed defeat to victory. They proposed to take the offensive against Federal authority instead of a defensive position. Colonel Lane one night was reported to headquarters as about starting to attack the militia, and doubtless would have done so had he not been threatened with arrest. John Brown, although he did not arrive till after the negotiations for peace had commenced, also proposed the same course. Lane also tried his best to procure the killing of Jones at the peace party, which, of course, had he been successful, would have opened the war in earnest, as the retiring disbanded posse or militia wanted no better excuse to attack the town. Mrs. Ropes, who was at the peace party, in her "Six Months in Kansas," page 143, referring to this matter, says :

"It seemed that some of the hotel crowd were not ready to give up the war spirit, and accept with grace the peace-offering of social intercourse offered * * * to those who had arrayed themselves so cruelly against us. And, although Sheriff Jones was nothing more nor less than an officer, acting under his oath of office, he became an apple of discord, because he was the only representative of Missouri. I have to confess to a feeling of mortification that everybody could not at once bridge over the rapid current sweeping between these two contending parties, and let ' by-gones be by-gones.' But perhaps this feeling came to the surface because I had not entered into the atmosphere of bloodshed, and had not made the creation of ' cartridges ' the occupation of my leisure hours. Colonel Lane's voice could be heard in different rooms, detailing to eager listeners the most painful circumstances of poor Barber's death, and, with wonderful ingeniousness, keeping up the wicked spirit of vengeance among those over whom he exercised any power. What on earth he was driving at by such a course, it seemed to my stupid self quite impossible to understand; while, at the same time, I knew very well that he aimed at something he could not otherwise attain so well. Any reader of human faces can never study his without a sensation very much like that with which one stands at the edge of a slimy, sedgy, uncertain morass. If there is any good in him, I never, with all my industry in culling something pleasant from the most unpropitious characters, have been able to make the discovery. And he has not, in lieu of anything better, that agreeable fascination of manner which so often gives currency in society to men as hollow-hearted as he. General Robinson stood like an aggrieved king. He not only stemmed the tide, but rolled back the surging emotions of the crowd; and the meeting closed much more like a gathering of peace than at one time seemed likely."

Mrs. Robinson, who was also present, in her " Kansas," page 155, says:

" Governor Shannon did not stay to the ' party.' When the morning came he found his business required his attention at the mission, and he went on his way. But ' Sheriff Jones ' was there, and there were some there beside who did not cherish that spirit of forgiveness and conciliation which makes man magnanimous in the treatment of an enemy; and the General's party at one time came near proving anything but a ' peace party.' There was a spirit there full of ambition, and a desire for office. And while the murder of young Barber was fresh in the minds of his friends; while the voice of poor, weak human nature would say revenge if the right cord was touched; and while ' Sheriff Jones,' an officer of the Territorial courts, was an invited guest of General Robinson, and political capital could be made; with what wonderful ingenuity it wrought to keep alive this spirit of revenge in their breasts! The object was evident to all, and the indignation of many was hardly kept within bounds. The event, however, proved but another instance of the evil, which was intended for another, recoiling upon one's own head."

With reference to John Brown's course, James Redpath, in his " Life of Captain John Brown," on page 92, quotes approvingly a correspondence in the New York *Herald*, as follows:

" After Governor Robinson had stated to the people who were gathered around the hotel the terms of the peace, Brown took the stand

aninvited, and opposed the terms of the treaty. He was in favor of
ignoring all treaties, and such leading men as Robinson, Lane, etc.,
and, proceeding at once against the border-ruffian invaders, drive them
from the soil, or hang them if taken. The Chairman of the Committee
of Safety ordered Brown under arrest."

Here is the position taken by the Free-State men, designated by F. B. Sanborn as "dastards," and the position
tried to be taken by the two "indispensable" heroes of that
gentleman, and the reader can take his choice. It is not
easy to conjecture what greater victory the Free-State men
could gain, or what greater defeat the pro-slavery men could
suffer, than to have 1900 men march from forty to one hundred and fifty miles to serve a warrant issued by a justice of
the peace and then return, after cursing, swearing, shivering
and freezing for two weeks, as they came, minus the whiskey,
without serving any process whatever, legal or otherwise. If
a more brilliant victory has ever been gained, it has not been
recorded. How many such defeats could the Administration afford in enforcing "popular sovereignty" where the
people were to be left perfectly free to settle their institutions
in their own way, subject only to the Constitution of the
United States ?

And what of the Free-State men called "dastards," who
obeyed orders and suffered wrong without doing wrong ? It
is safe to say an equal number of men, with a more unflinching courage, both moral and physical, has not been seen
since the days of the Revolution. A coward can give blow
for blow, eye for eye, and tooth for tooth, but it requires
true courage to suffer wrong without retaliation that a great
cause may be advanced. The Free-State men believed that
every outrage inflicted strengthened their cause and corre-
spondingly weakened that of their opponents ; that in their
sufferings lay their strength. In this respect the Wakarusa
war, while causing great annoyance and suffering, had enlisted the sympathies and support of the civilized world.

The conclusion of this campaign was the funeral of Bar-
14

ber, who was at first temporarily buried. This funeral was attended by all the military companies accessible, and was most solemn and impressive. As the remarks of Dr. Robinson present the issue of the war, placing the responsibility where it belonged, in his estimation, they are here given as published in the *Herald of Freedom* of December 22, 1855:

"THE BURIAL OF MR. BARBER.

" General Robinson read a eulogy upon Mr. B.'s life and character. We extract the following:

" ' The occasion which calls us together is one of deep interest and peculiar significance to every patriot and Republican.

" ' Our Territory has been repeatedly invaded, and our dearest rights trampled upon, by the citizens of a foreign State. They have taken possession of our ballot-boxes, and by force of arms have wrested from us the right to make our own laws and choose our own rulers, and imposed upon us a system of laws uncongenial to our natures and wants. Having accomplished all this by invasion and outrage, it was but natural to suppose that invasion and outrage would be necessary to enforce their enactments. " Misunderstanding " the facts and the temper of the people as well as their tactics, the Executive recently gave the signal for another invasion, and the armed hordes responded. Our citizens have been besieged, robbed, insulted, and murdered; and our town threatened with destruction for two whole weeks, by the authority of the Executive, and, as he now says, in consequence of a " misunderstanding." A misunderstanding on the part of an Executive is a most unfortunate affair.

" ' Our Governor having been told that the people of Kansas did not recognize the laws of Missouri, and were determined these laws should be a dead letter in the Territory, unwittingly fell into the error of supposing the people would array themselves against the Government of the United States, evidently not understanding how a code of enactments can be effectually resisted and no law violated. Had he carefully read the early history of his country, he might have understood the " Sons of Liberty " better than to suppose any United States law would be violated by the people, or, if violated, that the community would be guilty of violating it.

" ' By whose act do the remains of the lamented Thomas Barber now await interment at our hands? By whose hand is his wife made a widow? By whose instrumentality are we made to mourn the untimely fall of a brave comrade and worthy citizen? Report says Thomas Barber was murdered in cold blood by an officer or officers of the Government, who was a member of the Sheriff's posse, which was commanded by the Governor, who is backed by the President of the United States. Was Thomas Barber murdered? Then are the men who killed him, and the officials by whose authority they acted, his murderers. And if the laws are to be enforced, then will the Indian Agent, the Governor, and the President be convicted of, and punished for, murder. There is work enough for the " law and order " men to do, and let us hear no more about resistance to the laws till this work is done. If all Missouri must be aroused and the whole nation convulsed to serve a peace warrant on an unoffending citizen, may we not expect some slight effort will be made to bring these capital offenders to justice? Or are our laws made for the low, and not the high—for the poor, and not the rich?

" ' For the dead we need not mourn. He fell a martyr to principle; and his blood will nourish the tree of liberty. An honorable death is preferable to a dishonorable and inglorious life. Such was the death of our brother, and as such he will ever be cherished by his companions and fellow-citizens. It is glory enough for any man that a body of men like the Barber Guards should adopt his name to designate and distinguish their company.

" ' To his beloved and bereaved wife, to his brothers and relatives, to the members of his company, to all who have pledged property, honor, and life to the cause of freedom and humanity, I seem to hear the spirit of our departed brother say, " Be of good cheer; weep not for me; you are engaged in a good work, and your reward will be glorious. Death is no misfortune to the true; indeed, it is sweet to die in defense of liberty."

" ' But the shock produced by the murder of our friend is felt beyond the circle of his immediate relations and friends. It has shaken the entire fabric of our Government to its very base, and nothing but the unseen hand of the All-Wise Governor of the Universe could have saved this nation from civil war and political death.

" ' It is due to the bold stand taken by the freemen of Kansas during the late invasion that the sun of Liberty is still above the horizon; and cold indeed must be his heart, wherever found, that does not beat in unison with ours as we pay the last tribute of respect to the remains of our brother! Can the people of this nation approve the

" ' Costly mockery of piling stone on stone?
To those who won our liberty, the heroes dead and gone,
While we look coldly on, and see law-shielded ruffians slay
The men who fain would win their own, the heroes of to-day?

" ' No!
" ' Be callous as they will,
From soul to soul, o'er all the world,
Leaps one electric thrill.' "

CHAPTER IX.

As the "smoke of battle" cleared away, an opportunity
was offered to take a calm and unbiased survey of the field
and ascertain the gain or loss to the respective parties.

One item on the side of gain was the opening of the eyes
of the Governor to the character both of the Free-State and
of the pro-slavery men. He had heard nothing but evil of
the one, and nothing but good of the other. The Free-
State men in his estimation were a set of anarchists, made
up of the offscouring of the land, ready to overthrow any
and all government that might stand in their way, while their
antagonists were but little, if any, lower than the angels. He
undoubtedly modified both these opinions. Also he had
learned that the Free-State men were under complete control, and that no outrage, however aggravating, could discon-
cert them or drive them to take a false or untenable position.
On the contrary, the pro-slavery men were desperate and
ungovernable characters, determined to accomplish their purposes though the Government and the heavens should fall.

Another item of gain was that the Governer lost faith in
his militia as a *posse comitatus*. Before the "war" he was
self-confident and self-sufficient. On the 28th of November
he wrote the President:

"* * * Under these circumstances the Sheriff of the county has
called on me for three thousand men to aid him in the execution of the
warrants in his hands, and to protect him and his prisoner from the
violence of this armed force. The force required by the Sheriff is far
beyond what I believe to be necessary, and indeed far beyond what
could be raised in this Territory. From five to eight hundred men will

be amply sufficient, I have no doubt, to protect the Sheriff, and enable him to execute the legal process in his hands.   *   *   *

"The time has come when this armed band of men, who are seeking to subvert and render powerless the existing government, have to be met and the laws enforced against them, or submit to their lawless dominion.   If the lives and property of unoffending citizens of this Territory cannot be protected by law, there is an end to practical government, and it becomes a useless formality.

"The excitement along the border of Missouri is running wild, and nothing but the enforcement of the laws against these men will allay it. Since the disclosure of the existence and purpose of this secret military organization in this Territory, there has been much excitement along the borders of Missouri, but it has been held in check heretofore by assurances that the laws of the Territory would be enforced, and that protection would be given to the citizens against all unlawful acts of this association.   This feeling and intense excitement can still be held in subordination if the laws are faithfully executed; otherwise there is no power here that can control this border excitement, and civil war is inevitable.   This military organization is looked upon as hostile to all Southern men, or, rather, to the law and order party of the Territory, many of whom have relations and friends, and all have sympathizers in Missouri, and the moment it is believed that the laws will not furnish adequate protection to this class of citizens against the lawless acts of this armed association, a force will be precipitated across the line to redress real and supposed wrongs inflicted on friends that cannot be controlled, or for the moment resisted.   It is in vain to conceal the fact: we are standing on a volcano, the upheavings and agitations beneath we feel, and no one can tell the hour when an eruption may take place.   Under existing circumstances the importance of sustaining the Sheriff of Douglas County, and enabling him to execute his process, independent of other considerations connected with the peace and good order of society, will strike you at once; and to do this by the aid and assistance of the citizens of this Territory is the great object to be accomplished, to avoid the dreadful evils of civil war.   I believe this can be done; in this, however, I may be mistaken.   No efforts shall be wanting on my part to preserve good order in the Territory, and I will keep you constantly advised of the progress and state of things here.

"I have the honor to be, your obedient servant,

"WILSON SHANNON.
"*His Excellency, Franklin Pierce.*"

But after the "war" his tune was pitched in another key, and he wrote the President, December 11, 1855, as follows:

" Executive Office, Shawnee Mission,
        Kansas Territory, December 11, 1855.

" Sir: In my dispatch to you of the 28th ultimo, I advised you of
the threatened difficulties in relation to the execution of the laws of this
Territory in Douglas County.   The excitement which then existed continued to increase, owing to the aggravated reports from Lawrence and
that vicinity in relation to the military preparations that were being
made to attack the Sheriff and resist the execution of the law.   The
excitement increased and spread, not only throughout this whole Territory, but was worked up to the utmost point of intensity in the whole
of the upper portion of Missouri.   Armed men were seen rushing from
all quarters towards Lawrence, some to defend the place, and others to
demolish it.   The orders I had issued to Major-General Richardson
and General Strickler had brought to the Sheriff of Douglas County a
very inadequate force for his protection, when compared with the forces
in the town of Lawrence.   Indeed, the militia of the Territory being
wholly unorganized, no forces could be obtained except those who voluntarily tendered their aid to the Sheriff, or to Generals Richardson
and Strickler.   The whole force in the Territory thus obtained did not
amount to more than three or four hundred men, badly armed, and
wholly unprepared to resist the forces in Lawrence, which amounted
at that time to some six hundred men; all remarkably well armed with
Sharp's rifles and other weapons.   These facts becoming known across
the line, in the State of Missouri, large numbers of men from that State,
in irregular bodies, rushed to the County of Douglas, and many of them
enrolled themselves in the Sheriff's posse.   In this state of affairs, I
saw no way of avoiding a deadly conflict but to obtain the use of the
United States forces at Fort Leavenworth, and with that view I addressed you a telegraphic dispatch, and received on the 5th instant your
very prompt and satisfactory reply of the 4th instant, a copy of which
I immediately transmitted, by special dispatch, to Colonel Sumner, with
the request that he would accompany me with his command to the scene
of difficulty.   In reply, I was informed he would immediately do so,
having no doubt that in due time proper instructions would be received
from the War Department.   Information, however, which I received
from both parties convinced me that my presence was necessary to
avoid a conflict, and without waiting for Colonel Sumner, I repaired to
the seat of threatened hostilities, at the same time advising Colonel
Sumner, by special dispatch, of this movement.   On my way to Lawrence, I met a dispatch from Colonel Sumner, informing me that, upon
reflection, he had changed his determination, and that he would not
march with his command until he had received orders from the proper
department, but that he would be ready to move with his command the
moment such orders came to hand.   I proceeded as rapidly as possible

to the camp of General Strickler, on the Wakarusa, six miles east of Lawrence, and arrived in camp about three o'clock on the morning of the 6th instant. I found General Strickler, as well as General Richardson, had very judiciously adopted the policy of incorporating into their respective commands all the irregular forces that had arrived. This was done with the view of subjecting them to military orders and discipline, and to prevent any unlawful acts or outbreaks. The great danger to be apprehended was from an unauthorized attack on the town of Lawrence, which was being strongly fortified, and had about one thousand and fifty men well armed to defend it, with two pieces of artillery, while on the other side there was probably in all nearly two thousand men, many of them indifferently armed, but having a strong park of artillery. I found in the camp at Wakarusa a deep and settled feeling of hostility against the opposing forces in Lawrence, and apparently a fixed determination to attack that place and demolish it and the presses, and take possession of their arms. It seemed to be a universal opinion in the camp that there was no safety to the law and order party in the Territory while the other party were permitted to retain their Sharp's rifles, an instrument used only for war purposes. After mingling with all the leading men in the Wakarusa camp, and urging on them the importance of avoiding a conflict of arms, that such a step would light the torch of civil war and endanger the very Union itself, I still found that there was a strong desire with all, and a fixed determination with many, to compel the forces in Lawrence to give up their arms. Believing that such a demand would lead to a conflict which, if once commenced, no one could tell where it would end, and seeing no way to avoid it except by the aid of the United States forces, I again wrote another communication to Colonel Sumner, and sent it to him by special dispatch about three o'clock on the morning of the 7th instant, requesting his presence; a copy of which I send you herewith, marked E. I received no reply until my return to this place, after the difficulty had been arranged. I send you a copy of this reply, marked F. Early on the morning of the 7th instant I repaired to the camp at Lawrence, and found them busily engaged in their fortifications and in drilling their forces, and had a full and satisfactory interview with the committee appointed by the forces in Lawrence, in relation to the impending difficulties.   *   *   *

" Early on the morning of the 8th, through the influence of some leading men, I procured thirteen of the leading captains in the Wakarusa camp to be appointed a committee to confer with a committee from the Lawrence camp, to meet at Franklin, midway between the two hostile forces. I proceeded to the Lawrence camp, and returned to Franklin in the evening with the committee, where the proposed interview took place. This interview, which lasted for some time, resulted in producing a better state of feeling, and the committee from Wakarusa camp were satisfied to retire without doing anything more, and so reported to the army. This, with the active exertions of myself and others, produced a better feeling among the men, and by daylight on the morning of the 9th I felt I could with safety order the forces to disband, and accordingly did so. They retired in order, and refrained from any act of violence, but it was evident there was a silent dissatisfaction at the course I had taken. But I felt conscious I was right, and that my course would be sanctioned alike by the dictates of humanity and sound policy. I returned to Lawrence on the 9th, remained until the morning of the 10th, when, everything being quiet and safe, I returned to this place. Everything is quiet now; but it is my duty to say to you, frankly, that I have forebodings as to the future. The militia or volunteer corps cannot be relied on to preserve the peace in these civil party contests, or where partisans are concerned. A call on the militia will generally only bring in conflict the two parties. I am satisfied that the only forces that can be used in this Territory in enforcing the laws, or preserving the peace, are those of the ·United States, and with this view I would suggest that the Executive of this Territory be authorized to call on the forces of the United States when, in his judgment, the public peace and tranquillity, or the execution of the laws, may require their assistance. Should there be an outbreak, it will most probably be sudden, and before orders can be obtained from Washington the crisis will have passed. I send you herewith the copies of various affidavits, letters, etc., which will give you some information in detail touching the subject-matter of this dispatch.

" I have the honor to be, your obedient servant,

" WILSON SHANNON.

"*His Excellency, Franklin Pierce.*"

One item gained to the Free-State men was a knowledge of some of their own men. While the policy of the party was distinctly outlined by the Committee of Safety and Council, two men of influence proved disloyal to that policy. G. P. Lowry, in his testimony before the Congressional Committee, as reported on page 1081, said: "My impression is, that a conspiracy of one hundred men, to leave here (Lawrence) without orders and attack the camp on the Wakarusa, was found out shortly after Barber was killed, and put down by General Robinson."

It was thought best at the time, and even when the Congressional Committee visited the Territory, in 1856, to say but little about this movement or " conspiracy," and particularly of its prime mover, but Lowry, being on the general's staff, knew all about it, and that Colonel Lane was the instigator. Colonel Lane in this move was to the Kansas war what Captain Maloney was to the Sacramento riot when about to order an attack upon a private residence, with this difference, that Maloney was in supreme command while Lane was not. There has always been a question as to the motive that actuated Lane. It was well known to the leading Free-State men that at heart he preferred a slave State; tried to buy a slave; said in his first public speech at Lawrence he had as soon buy a " nigger " as a mule; recognized the Territorial Legislature as a legal body, and only consented to enlist in the Free-State constitutional movement when promised the support of the party for Senator. He was always on intimate terms with some of the pro-slavery leaders, and during the " war " had General Richardson and staff dine with him by invitation, when their forces were laying siege to the town and killed Barber. Whether he designed to change the position from one of defense to one of offense, and thus bring ruin upon the Free-State cause, or whether he wanted to court favor with inconsiderate and exasperated men to secure a little political prestige, may never be known. Fortunately for the Free-State cause he was so well understood, and his loyalty so questioned, that he was never implicitly trusted, and hence could not betray the cause if he should attempt it. John Brown proclaimed his position most emphatically as an enemy to both territorial and national government, but was able to mislead no party and but few individuals.

Nothing so disappointed the pro-slavery men as the fact that they could not get the Free-State men in collision with Federal authority. They had organized as an army with all the " circumstance of war," and one thing only was wanting to constitute treason, namely, that this war should be levied against the United States. Had the Slave-State men succeeded in their design, the indictments for treason found the next spring would not have been the burlesque they proved. Then convictions and executions would have followed with the same alacrity as against the Harper's Ferry raiders, and with the approval of the entire nation, with scarcely an exception. The Free-State cause would have been blotted out as easily and effectually as was the army of twenty-one young men who threw themselves against a United States arsenal in 1859, under the lead of John Brown, when he was generalissimo and commander-in-chief of his new Republic, with F. B. Sanborn, secretary of the Kansas Relief Committee, furnishing the sinews of war and out of the funds raised, ostensibly for the relief of Kansas.

Another item of gain or loss in this war was the knowledge the pro-slavery men gained of their antagonists. The despised New England paupers had all at once assumed in their estimation the proportions of men of courage and sagacity, who could not be annihilated by an oath or anathema. This was of great benefit to them and of no detriment to the Free-State men. But the greatest gain to the Free-State men, and corresponding loss to their antagonists, was the record made before the country. They had demonstrated their courage, sagacity, and loyalty to Federal authority. Both North and South recognized the fact that the men stigmatized by the border press as paupers and hirelings were not to be trifled with, and that the Administration, even with Jeff Davis at the head of the War Department, had its match in strategy and management generally. Also the marching of an army from the State of Missouri, with war equipments taken from a United States arsenal, to serve a peace warrant in a Territory which was to be left perfectly free to manage its own affairs, caused general indignation in the Northern States, in some of which resolutions were adopted announcing that if Kansas was to be thus interfered with by one State, all States would take a hand in the business, even though the Union should go up in smoke. Neither was the lesson entirely lost upon the President, as will later appear.

The Chicago *Tribune* said: "The Free-State men have acted well. We like their spirit. It is of the olden time —cool, yet resolved; deliberate, yet wisely courageous."

The year 1855 closed with a record less bloody than its successor. Two pro-slavery men had been killed since the opening of Kansas to settlement, namely, Henry Davis on November 29, 1854, and Malcolm Clark on April 30, 1855; and three Free-State men, C. W. Dow, November 21st, Samuel Collins in November at Doniphan, and Thomas Barber on the 6th of December, 1855. Several men had been brutally mobbed, all Free-State, among them William Phillips of Leavenworth, tarred and feathered, Pardee Butler of Atchison County sent down the Missouri on a raft, and J. W. B. Kelly, severely beaten at Atchison.

Two elections for delegate to Congress had been held, one on the 1st of October, when General Whitfield was voted for by the Slave-State men, and one on the 9th of the same month, when Governor Reeder was voted for by the Free-State men. Although there was no conflict, over 800 illegal votes were cast for Whitfield, as estimated by the Congressional Committee. These elections paved the way for a contest in Congress which resulted in the appointment of Howard, Sherman, and Oliver as a committee to visit Kansas in the spring of 1856 to procure testimony concerning the workings of "popular sovereignty."

On the 15th of December, a few days after the close of the Wakarusa war, the election on the adoption of the Topeka Constitution was held, resulting in 1731 votes for, and 46 votes against the Constitution; and 1287 against and 453 for free negroes. This vote on free negroes was to be construed as instructions to the Legislature to exclude them from Kansas by law. If not so excluded the constitutional provision would be inoperative. This little manœuvre was to catch both Eastern and Western congressional votes for admission into the Union. General Lane is entitled to full credit for setting the trap. Besides, as a large percentage of Free-State settlers at that time were from black law States, and many even from Missouri and the South, it seemed a very expedient provision, although vehemently denounced by the no-voting, no-policy abolitionists like Charles Stearns and John Brown.

On the 22d of December came the convention for the nomination of State officers to be voted for on the 15th of January. At this convention the Garvey House and all other "slates" were ignored, and a ticket selected of as many colors, politically, as Joseph's coat. Three candidates were prominent for governor—Judge Smith, W. Y. Roberts, and Colonel Lane. The first two claimed that each had the pledge of Lane for his support, when, to their great discomfort, Lane himself was a candidate with all the appliances of which he was master. As Lane distanced his other competitors on the first heat, they were virtually out of the race, and as those who were aware of Lane's career in Kansas, including his attempt to take the offensive at the late war, did not dare trust him at the head of the State movement, a new man was agreed upon, namely, Dr. Robinson. This name, of course, created some friction, as it always had and probably always will. He had voted in the convention not only for negro suffrage, but for woman suffrage also, and would be a bitter pill for many to swallow. No one knew this better than himself, and he would have declined the nomination, as he would have declined the conduct of the late war, if he could have been assured that Lane would not wreck the Free-State cause. The ticket was declared by a few men to be an abolition ticket, and a bolt was inaugurated, resulting in the nomination of an "anti-abolition" ticket, although five names were the same on each.

The *Free State*, then edited by Mr. Elliot, who never did like Robinson or the Aid Company, and who was nominated for State printer on the bolting ticket, opposed the ticket, and placed at its mast-head the bolters' ticket, because the first was "abolition" and the second "anti-abolition."

This was too ridiculous for even Charles Stearns, the Garrisonian, and he wrote the *Herald of Freedom*, closing as follows:

"'Anti-abolition ticket,' forsooth! Of course, then, Mr. Elliot, one of the principal supporters of the new ticket, must be a strong anti-abolitionist. Well, 'the times change' and men change with them, I suppose; but this same Mr. Elliot, together with myself and a few others, one year ago strongly condemned the leading nominee of what Mr. Elliot now terms the 'abolition ticket' because he was *not abolition enough*. The *Free State* denounced Dr. Robinson, as well as yourself, for taking 'conservative ground' on the anti-slavery question, and supported one of the nominees of the 'anti-abolition ticket' because he was *more* of an abolitionist, or anti-slavery man, than Dr. Robinson's favorite, Mr. Fleniken; but now Dr. Robinson is too much of an abolitionist for Mr. Elliot. Verily pro-slavery has had quite an effect upon our former redoubted champion of undiluted anti-slavery. For my part, I shall not support the first ticket for the reason that it is not an abolition ticket, and of course not the second, because it carries a lie on the face of it, as I have above explained.

"Yours respectfully,
"C. STEARNS."

Quite an effort was made for the bolting ticket, but the result showed for it 410 votes to 1296 for the other. This was the death and burial of "anti-abolition" or conservatism in Kansas. From that time nothing more was heard of "black law" or "anti-abolition"; and even Colonel Lane, who had been the champion of this cause, became the most radical of radicals, compelling the former radicals, like Brown, the Speers, Deitzler, Wood, Lowry, Robinson, and others to put on the brakes to prevent political wreck. At this time the correspondents of the Eastern press were distrustful of Lane, and no men were so active and influential in defeating his nomination for governor as they. Especially Phillips and Redpath were untiring in their devotion to the ticket as nominated.

The *Herald of Freedom* of January 19, 1856, reports a

meeting at which Colonel Lane presented a platform of principles diametrically opposed to his Nebraska resolution in the Constitutional Convention, and says that all the National Democrats endorsed it.   The editor adds :

"Kansas evidently is a healthy climate for the mind as well as body. The sophisms of the South cannot live here.   Lawrence is a pool of Bethesda, into which, if the life-long invalid step, he is straightway made whole.   Colonel Lane, for example, who came here with the squatter-phobia, of which he had been long and dangerously sick—having been bitten in Congress by Nebraska bill itself—and whose unfortunate constitution withstood every effort of Eastern political physicians to cure him—is now beginning to give evidences of speedy recovery—what he has hitherto denied—that he was deceived in imagining that squatter-phobia is a symptom of good health.   We have no doubt, if our people take good care of him, that in less than a year he may be pronounced politically convalescent.   If Colonel Lane adopts the Republican creed, he will make a valuable accession to the party.   As yet, he has not done so ; but he must do so ere long, if he wishes to preserve a character for consistency."

The winter of 1855–56 was one of preparation rather than of open demonstration.   It is true, R. P. Brown, of Leavenworth, was most brutally murdered, at an election held at Easton, by some drunken pro-slavery men.   Brown had been prominent in the defense of Lawrence, and was one of the noblest men ever in Kansas.   He was true as steel and brave as a lion, and hence was feared and hated by his opponents as were but few others.   His murder was most cowardly.   Its brutality was too much for Captain Martin, of the Kickapoo Rangers, who was at Easton and tried to save Brown from his fate, but the mob was too drunken and desperate to heed him or any one else.   Nothing would answer but his death, and he fell a hero and martyr in a noble cause.

Although on the surface there was general calm, mutterings of discontent, dissatisfaction, and preparation were occasionally heard, as of distant thunder before a storm, during the entire winter.   Jones and the ultra Slave-State men were never satisfied with the outcome of the Wakarusa war, and openly declared that next time they would wait till Secretary Woodson should be acting governor, when they would have their own way.

The *Squatter Sovereign* said:

" We would it were within the range of the most liberal indulgence for us to express satisfaction with the adjustment of the difficulties which called so large a number of the squatter sovereigns from their firesides to encounter the inclemency of bleak December winds. * * * Had the matter rested with Mr. Jones, the Sheriff, the result would have been different. The criminals would have been traced to their hiding-places, and safely secured against the audacity of a set of God-forsaken fanatics. This would have given satisfaction, answered the purpose of the requisition, and fulfilled the ends of justice. As it is, base, cowardly, sneaking scoundrels will go unpunished, and be left free to perpetrate their infamous outrages wherever they may find an unprotected pro-slavery family."

About the time of the murder of Brown, alarms of invasion from Missouri were frequent, causing some precautions to be taken by the Free-State men. Colonel Blood, in command of a squad of cavalry, visited Easton and vicinity to quiet the fears of the settlers in that neighborhood. Two dispatches were sent off to the President as follows:

" LAWRENCE, January 21, 1856.
" *To Franklin Pierce, President of U. S. A.*

" SIR : We have authentic information that an overwhelming force of the citizens of Missouri are organizing on our borders, amply supplied with artillery, for the avowed purpose of invading this Territory, demolishing our towns, and butchering our unoffending Free-State citizens.

" We respectfully demand on behalf of the citizens of Kansas, that the commandant of the United States troops be immediately instructed to interfere to prevent such an inhuman outrage."

(Signed by Lane, Deitzler, Goodin, and Robinson.)

" LAWRENCE CITY, January 23, 1856.
" *To the President of the United States.*

" SIR : We notified you that an overwhelming force, supplied with artillery, were organizing on our border for the avowed purpose of in-

vading Kansas, demolishing the towns, and butchering the unoffending
Free-State citizens, and they constituting fourteen-twentieths of the entire population.   We earnestly request you to issue your proclamation
immediately, forbidding the invasion.   We trust there may be no delay
in taking so important a step to prevent an outrage which, if carried out
as planned, will stand forth without a parallel in the world's history.

"Yours respectfully."

(Signed by Lane and Robinson.)

It was well known that a movement was contemplated
against Kansas, but the time could not be ascertained when
the forces were to march.   Meetings were being held in all the
border counties, some of them delegate conventions embrac-
ing all western Missouri.   One such meeting was held at
Lexington.   Such was the threatening aspect that many
Free-State men became anxious for the future, and there
was danger that so many would leave in despair as to discourage such as might remain to meet the anticipated shock.
At the time when the clouds were the most threatening a letter
was received from Eli Thayer describing a new gun he was
making of about an inch and a half calibre, which would
carry several miles as accurately as the best rifle at a shorter
range.   This was to be breech-loading and with it every
officer of the enemy's forces could be picked off before the
battle should begin by the rank and file.   This letter was
read and re-read to squads and individuals, and it inspired
great confidence in the drooping spirits of the despondent.
Not only would such a weapon be of great importance, but
the fact that the friends of Kansas were active in its behalf also gave great encouragement.   A report at this time
reached Kansas of a meeting held at Worcester, at which it
appeared that General Pomeroy spoke, and many leading
citizens of Worcester, among them Mr. Thayer, who offered
to give ten Sharp's rifles in advance of the guns being made
at his foundry, on condition the number should be made up
to one hundred by the other citizens.   A large sum was reported as pledged at the meeting.   Also other cheering news

was received from different Northern States showing the deep interest felt for the pioneers.

As spring approached, various rumors reached Kansas from Washington. Governor Shannon, after the "war," repaired to the Capitol, where the situation might be discussed without the formality of official correspondence. Washington letter-writers to the New York papers, such as the *Herald* and *Times*, sent contradictory dispatches—one day that Governor Shannon on his return to Kansas would be instructed to arrest all the members of the State Government should it attempt to organize on the 4th of March, as contemplated, and the next day this report would be denied by one stating that the President would recognize the right of the Legislature to meet undisturbed. Such was the agitation throughout the country both North and South, in some States appropriations being proposed or made to defray the expenses of men to be sent to Kansas, that the President issued his proclamation as follows :

"*Whereas*, Indications exist that public tranquillity and the supremacy of the law in the Territory of Kansas are endangered by the reprehensible acts or purposes of persons both within and without the same, who propose to control and direct its political organizations by force; it appearing that combinations have been formed therein to resist the execution of the territorial laws and thus, in effect, subvert by violence all present constitutional and legal authority ; it also appearing that persons residing without this Territory, but near its borders, *contemplate armed intervention* in the affairs thereof ; it also appearing that other persons, inhabitants of remote States, are collecting money and providing arms for the same purpose ; and it further appearing that combinations in the Territory are endeavoring by the agencies of emissaries and otherwise to induce individual States of the Union to interfere in the affairs thereof in violation of the Constitution of the United States ; and *whereas*, all such plans for the determination of the future institutions of the Territory, if carried into execution from or within the same, will constitute the fact of *insurrection*, and from without that of *invasive aggression*, and will in either case justify and require the forcible interposition of the whole power of the general Government, as well to maintain the laws of the Territory as those of the Union :

"Now, therefore, I, Franklin Pierce, President of the United States,

15

do issue this my proclamation, to command all persons engaged in unlawful combinations *against the constituted authority of the Territory of
Kansas*, or of the United States, to disperse and retire peaceably to
their respective abodes, and to warn all such persons that an attempted
insurrection in said Territory, or aggressive intrusion into the same,
will be resisted, not only by the employment of the *local militia*, but
also by that of any available force of the United States; to the end of
assuring immunity from violence and full protection to the persons,
property, and civil rights of all peaceful and law-abiding inhabitants of
the Territory. If in any part of the Union the fury of faction or fanaticism, inflamed into disregard of the great principles of popular sovereignty, which, under the Constitution, are fundamental in the whole
structure of our institutions, is to bring on the country the dire calamity
of an arbitrament of arms in that Territory, it shall be between lawless
violence on one side and conservative force on the other, wielded by legal
authority of the general Government.

" I call on the citizens, both of adjoining and of distant States, to ab-
stain from unauthorized intermeddling in the local concerns of the Territory, admonishing them that its organic law is to be executed with
impartial justice; that all individual acts of illegal interference will incur
condign punishment, and that any endeavor to interfere by organized
force, will be firmly withstood.

" I invoke all good citizens to promote order *by rendering obedience
to the law;* to seek remedy for temporary evils by peaceful means; to
discountenance and repulse the counsels and the instigations of agitators
and disorganizers, and to testify their attachment to their pride in its
greatness, their appreciation of the blessings they enjoy, and their determination that republican institutions shall not fail in their hands by
co-operating to uphold the majesty of the laws and to vindicate the
sanctity of the Constitution.

" In testimony whereof I have hereunto set my hand and caused the
seal of the United States to be affixed to these presents.

" Done at the City of Washington, eleventh day of February, one
thousand eight hundred and fifty-six, and of the Independence of the
United States, the eightieth.

" By the President.   " FRANKLIN PIERCE.

" W. L. MARCY, Secretary of State."

Governor Shannon also was clothed with authority to call
on the officers at Fort Leavenworth whenever he might think
best.

Most frantic appeals were made to the South to furnish

men and money for the conflict, and widely circulated, both North and South. The Springfield, Ill., *Journal,* makes this reference to them:

" In the *National Intelligencer* of a recent date, we find published a circular from the Kansas Emigration Society of Missouri, addressed to the people of the Southern States, some of the statements of which are well worthy the consideration of the people of the North. After directing ' the attention of the people of the slave-holding States to the absolute necessity of immediate action on their part,' and the adoption of prompt and decisive measures in relation to the settlement of Kansas Territory, the circular makes the following acknowledgment:

" ' The western counties of Missouri have for the last two years been heavily taxed, both in money and time, in fighting the battles of the South. Lafayette County alone has expended more than $100,000 in money, and as much more in time. Up to this time the border counties of Missouri have upheld and maintained the rights and interests of the South in this struggle unassisted, and not unsuccessfully. But the abolitionists, staking their all upon the Kansas issue, and hesitating at no means, fair or foul, are moving heaven and earth to render that beautiful Territory a " Free State."

" ' Missouri, we feel confident, has done her duty, and will still be found ready and willing to do all she can, fairly and honorably, for the maintenance of the integrity of the South. But the time has come when she can no longer stand up single-handed, the lone champion of the South, against the myrmidons of the entire North. It requires no foresight to perceive that if the " higher law " men succeed in this crusade, it will be but the commencement of a war upon the institutions of the South, which will continue until slavery shall cease to exist in any of the States, or the Union is dissolved.

" ' The great struggle will come off at the next election, in October, 1856, and unless the South can at that time maintain her ground, all will be lost. We repeat it, the crisis has arrived. The time has come for action—bold, determined action. Words will no longer do any good; we must have men in Kansas, and that by tens of thousands. A few will not answer. If we should need ten thousand and lack one of that number, all will count nothing. Let all, then, who can come do so at once. Those who cannot come must give their money to help others to come. There are hundreds of thousands of broad acres of rich lands, worth from $5 to $20 per acre, and open to settlement and pre-emption at $1.25 per acre. Shall we allow these rich lands and this beautiful country to be overrun by our abolition enemies? We tell you now, and tell you frankly, that unless you come quickly, and come by thousands, we are gone. The elections once lost are lost forever.' "

The State Legislature assembled on the 4th of March, 1856, according to the provision of the Constitution, without interruption.   Both Houses were organized, a message was delivered, and Reeder and Lane elected United States Senators.   A codifying committee was appointed to prepare bills for future action, when the Legislature adjourned to the 4th of July, 1856, after adopting a memorial to Congress asking for admission into the Union as a State.

The constitution and memorial were taken to Washington by Senator elect Lane and delivered to General Cass of the Senate and Daniel Mace of the House.   Galusha A. Grow prepared a bill for the admission of Kansas into the Union which passed the House July 3, 1856, by a vote of 99 to 97, but it failed to pass the Senate.

The committee to visit Kansas in the interest of the contest for the seat of territorial delegate was appointed March 19, 1856, consisting, as before stated, of Messrs. Howard and Sherman, Republicans, and Oliver of Missouri, Democrat.   They arrived in Kansas on the 18th of April and proceeded to take testimony relative to the troubles in the Territory previous to their appointment.   The committee, after taking a large volume of testimony, reported as follows:

"MAJORITY REPORT.

" Your committee report the following facts and conclusions as established by the testimony:

"*First.* That each election in the Territory, held under the organic or alleged territorial law, has been carried by organized invasion from the State of Missouri, by which the people of the Territory have been prevented from exercising the rights secured to them by the organic law.

"*Second.* That the alleged Territorial Legislature was an illegally constituted body, and had no power to pass valid laws, and their enactments are therefore null and void.

"*Third.* That these alleged laws have not, as a general thing, been used to protect persons and property, and to punish wrong, but for unlawful purposes.

"*Fourth.* That the election under which the sitting delegate, John W. Whitfield, holds his seat, was not held in pursuance of any valid law, and that it should only be regarded as the expression of the choice of these residents who voted for him.

"*Fifth.* That the election under which the contesting delegate, Andrew H. Reeder, claims his seat, was not held in pursuance of law, and that it should be regarded only as the expression of the resident citizens who voted for him.

"*Sixth.* That Andrew H. Reeder received a greater number of votes of resident citizens than John W. Whitfield for delegate.

"*Seventh.* That in the present condition of the Territory a fair election cannot be held without a new census, a stringent and well-guarded election law, the selection of impartial judges and the presence of United States troops at every place of election.

"*Eighth.* That the various elections held by the people of the Territory preliminary to the formation of the State Government have been as regular as the disturbed condition of the Territory would allow; and that the constitution passed by the convention held in pursuance of said elections embodies the will of a majority of the people.

" As it is not the province of your committee to suggest remedies for the existing troubles in the Territory of Kansas, they content themselves with the foregoing statement of facts.

" All of which is respectfully submitted.
" W. A. HOWARD,
" JOHN SHERMAN."

" MINORITY REPORT.

" In conclusion, the undersigned begs to report the following facts and conclusions, as he believes established by the testimony and sanctioned by law :

"*First.* That the first election held in the Territory under the organic act, for delegate to Congress, General John W. Whitfield received a plurality of the legal votes cast, and was duly elected as such delegate, as stated in the majority report.

"*Second.* That the Territorial Legislature was a legally constituted body, and had power to pass valid laws, and their enactments were therefore valid.

" *Third.* That these laws when appealed to have been used for the protection of life, liberty, and property, and for the maintenance of law and order in the Territory.

"*Fourth.* That the election under which the sitting delegate, John W. Whitfield, was held was in pursuance of valid law, and should be regarded as a valid election.

"*Fifth.* That as said Whitfield, at said election, received a large number of legal votes without opposition, he was duly elected as a delegate in this body, and is entitled to a seat on this floor as such.

"*Sixth*. That the election under which the contesting delegate, Andrew H. Reeder, claims his seat, was not held under any law, but in contemptuous disregard of all law, and that it should only be regarded as the expression of a band of malcontents and revolutionists by the House.

"*Seventh*. As to whether or not Andrew H. Reeder received a greater number of votes of resident citizens on the 9th than J. W. Whitfield did on the 1st of October, 1855, no testimony was taken by the committee, so far as the undersigned knows, nor is it material to the issue.

" All of which is respectfully submitted.

" M. OLIVER."

The House voted to declare the seat vacant by 110 yeas to 92 nays, neither admitting Whitfield nor Reeder.

CHAPTER X.

ANOTHER scene in the tragedy called "popular sovereignty" was to be enacted in the spring of 1856. This was
to be a second edition of the Wakarusa war, with only a
change of scene and characters. The Free-State men had
no new moves to make, as their policy had already been
adopted, and they had only to hold their ground and fill
the Territory with Free-State voters and have them in readiness for the election of a Territorial Legislature to be held
in 1857. In the meantime they had only to "thwart,
baffle, and circumvent" the Slave-State party in establishing
slavery in Kansas by means of the legislation resulting from
the invasion of the 30th of March, 1855. As in the fall of
1855, so now, the game on the Slave-State side was to get
the Free-State men pitted against Federal authority. General Whitfield wrote to his friend Clark, who shot Barber,
as follows:

"WASHINGTON, 1st March, 1856.

"MY DEAR CLARK: I assure you I have not forgotten our mutual
friend, Dr. Rodrique. I have sent him seeds, documents, etc. One
thing you perhaps are not aware of, that two-thirds of the seeds are
stolen, and having to pass through that *Hell Hole* (Lawrence) it is reasonable to suppose that nearly all are stolen there. Say to the Doctor
that his name is on my special list. Clark, you have no idea of the work
I have to do in addition to my labors as delegate. I must confess that
Reeder and his army of abolitionists give me some trouble. I have
thrown him twice, and I think I will give him another tip. I feel certain they have despaired of his getting a seat, and only hope to send the
election back. The last move is to send for persons and papers; one
object is to pay his army of abolitionists that he has here. I think,

though, he will be defeated, and a commissioner will be sent out. If
so, I will get S. F. Woodson and others to take depositions. I have
labored hard every day since I left Kansas to induce Southern men to
go to Kansas, and I have strong hopes that we shall have a large emigration. Our friends should meet and appoint committees in every town
to attend to them on their arrival.

"Shannon is with you, I hope, before this, with full and ample
power to put down the abolitionists in the Territory. We think here
that Mr. Pierce comes up to the scratch nobly. Your humble servant
is charged with figuring in getting up the message. One thing certain,
Clark, if they attempt to fight Uncle Sam's boys, the ball is open, and
civil war is inevitable. If so, you will see me in Kansas. You can
command me here at any and all times.

                                          " Yours truly,
                                                  " J. W. WHITFIELD."

"One thing certain, Clark, if they attempt to fight Uncle
Sam's boys, the ball is open, and civil war is inevitable."

Yes, yes! But fortunately the Free-State men were as
well aware of this fact as Whitfield, and there was more
prospect of getting the Slave-State men in collision with
Uncle Sam's boys than the Free-State men, unless by accident or disregard of orders.

The preliminary skirmish was by "Sheriff" Jones, who
appeared at Lawrence, April 19th, to arrest S. N. Wood, who
had returned from the East where he had been lecturing on
Kansas affairs. Wood was to be arrested as one of the
Branson rescuers. Although at first submitting to an arrest,
the bystanders good-naturedly jostled him away from Jones,
leaving the Sheriff to return to Lecompton without his prisoner. The next day, Sunday, he returned with additional
writs, and called for a posse to enable him to serve them.
But the citizens were desirous of attending church, or were
otherwise inclined, and proved very inefficient as a posse.
However, Jones seeing S. F. Tappan, another Branson rescuer, somewhat roughly attempted to arrest him, when Tappan struck him in the face. This answered every purpose,
and Jones called upon Governor Shannon as aforetime for
assistance. Shannon promptly furnished a lieutenant and

six United States soldiers. With these Jones again visited Lawrence, but not to meet with resistance. The soldier's uniform was a safe passport in any Free-State community. However, such as did not desire arrest were invisible and no one seemed to know where they were, or if so, would not tell. Wood, especially, was not found, and Jones concluded to spend the night at Lawrence in the officer's tent. Some person, in violation of the policy and wishes of the Free-State party, shot Jones in his tent, the ball striking him between the shoulders. This was a very impolitic act, and was just what was wanted to arouse the Slave-State party to the highest pitch of enthusiasm for their cause. Their papers announced that Jones had been killed in the hated town of Lawrence, and war had already commenced. The people held a meeting and denounced the outrage in severe terms, and offered a reward of $500 for the arrest and punishment of the criminal. The following correspondence will show how the matter was viewed by Colonel Sumner and the public:

" HEADQUARTERS FIRST CAVALRY,
" CAMP NEAR LAWRENCE, April 27, 1856.

" SIR: As there are no municipal officers in the town of Lawrence, I think proper to address you before returning to my post. The recent attempt made upon the life of Sheriff Jones will produce great excitement throughout the Territory and on the Missouri frontier, and I consider it of the utmost importance that every effort should be made by your people to ferret out and bring to justice the cowardly assassin. It is not too much to say that the peace of the country may depend on it, for, if he is not arrested, the act will be charged by the opposite party upon your whole community. This affair has been reported to Washington, and whatever orders may be received will be instantly carried into effect. The proclamation which requires obedience to the laws of the Territory as they now stand until legally abrogated, will certainly be maintained, and it is very unsafe to give heed to people at a distance who counsel resistance. If they were here to participate in the danger, they would probably take a different view of this matter.

" I am, sir, very respectfully, your obedient servant,
" E. V. SUMNER,
" Colonel First Cavalry Commanding.
" *To Mr. Charles Robinson.*"

" REPLY.

" LAWRENCE, K. T., April 27, 1856.

" SIR : Your note of this morning is received, and in answer permit me to say that the cowardly attack upon Mr. Jones receives no countenance whatever from the citizens of Lawrence, but, on the contrary, meets with universal condemnation, and if the guilty party can be found, he will most certainly be given over to justice. It is and has been the policy of the people of Lawrence to yield prompt obedience to the laws and officers of the Federal Government, and as Mr. Jones was acting with the authority of that Government on the day of the assault, the guilty party was an enemy to the citizens of Lawrence no less than a violator of the laws. The people of Lawrence are without any organized municipal government, and consequently no person or persons can speak or act officially for them, but from what I know of their feelings and disposition, I have no hesitation in saying that they will ever be found loyal citizens of the Government, and ready to do all in their power to maintain the laws of their country. As an evidence of the public sentiment of this community, I enclose a copy of the proceedings of a public meeting held on the morning after the unfortunate affair occurred. Very respectfully, your obedient servant,

" CHARLES ROBINSON.

"*Colonel E. V. Sumner.*"

Although Jones was not fatally injured he was disabled for a time, and his duties devolved upon Deputy Sheriff Salter.

After this, preparations on a more elaborate scale were made to subdue the hated rebels. The District Court was held the second week in May, and Chief Justice Lecompte foreshadowed the plan in his charge to the jury. Among other things he said :

" This Territory was organized by an act of Congress, and so far its authority is from the United States. It has a Legislature elected in pursuance of that organic act. This Legislature, being an instrument of Congress by which it governs the Territory, has passed laws. These laws, therefore, are of United States authority and making, and all who resist these laws resist the power and authority of the United States, and are therefore guilty of *high treason*. Now, gentlemen, if you find that any person has resisted these laws, then you must, under your oaths, find bills against them for *high treason*. If you find that no such resistance has been made, but that combinations have been formed for the purpose of resisting them, and individuals of notoriety have been aiding and abetting in such combinations, then must you find bills for *constructive treason*."

As Lane and Brown had failed to use the force at Lawrence against the Federal, or any other authority, no *treason*
could be discovered; and as the force at Lawrence was
organized for purely defensive purposes, not even constructive treason could be successfully charged. This charge to
the jury was conclusive evidence of the programme, and the
trap was ingeniously set, but it was in full view of the bird
to be caught and proved to be in vain. The plan was well
laid. As treason was supposed not to be a bailable offense,
an indictment would enable them to place in confinement
all such persons as were not wanted to run at large. Accordingly, Reeder, Deitzler, G. W. Brown, G. W. Smith,
Gaius Jenkins, and Robinson were indicted, and all but
Reeder, who escaped in disguise, shut up or confined on the
prairie. Lane and S. N. Wood were also indicted, but not
arrested. As the plan was to bring the Free-State men in
conflict with " Uncle Sam's boys," and as Wood had led the
rescue of Branson, and Lane and John Brown tried to lead
an attack upon the Governor's militia, they were supposed
to be of more use running at large than in confinement.
All the men arrested, except, perhaps, Robinson, were cool,
sagacious, and conservative, and could not be driven to take
a false position. The same is true of S. N. Wood, though
the Slave-State men did not know that fact. But before
any indictments were found, the Free-State men were put in
possession of the purposes of their opponents and hence
were not taken unawares. James F. Legate, one of the
Grand Jury, met Howard and Sherman of the Congressional Committee, and Reeder and Robinson, at or near
Tecumseh, and divulged the plan as foreshadowed in the
Grand Jury room. This plan contemplated the indictment
not only of those active in the defense of Lawrence for
treason, but of all persons connected with the State Government, whether State officers or members of the Legislature. Such as resided in Douglas County were to be indicted by the jury then in session, and the others would be

indicted when the court should convene in Shawnee County, where the Legislature had met and organized. The night after receiving this information Howard, Sherman, Reeder, Roberts, Mrs. Sherman, Mrs. Robinson, and Robinson held a " council of war " in the Garvey House, which continued till nearly daylight. A full and free discussion of the situation was had and this conclusion reached, namely, that in the execution of the plan of the Slave-State men there was a possibility of a geneal conflict of arms; that should it be impossible to avoid such conflict without a surrender of the Free-State cause, it must be met, and if met the Free-State men should take issue rather in defense of the State organization than offensively against the territorial. In view of such a contingency it would be necessary to have the sympathy and aid of the people of the Northern States, and they must be informed of what might occur. It was decided at this council that Robinson was the proper person to send East to visit the governors and other sympathizers; and, as there had been no law passed by the State Legislature that could be used in such contingency, it was decided that if it were thought necessary to use the State Government, Lieutenant-Governor Roberts should convene the Legislature before the court should sit in Shawnee County, that militia, *habeas corpus* and such other laws as might be needed should be passed. Robinson would complete his mission and return at the convening of the Legislature. He was desired also to carry with him the testimony already taken by the Congressional Committee as there was great danger that it might be seized and destroyed. As no indictments had yet been found by the Grand Jury, no interference was anticipated with Robinson, at least before his return. Accordingly, he started on his mission the 9th day of May, with Mrs. Robinson, without concealment or disguise. But a general pro-slavery convention had been held at Lexington not long before, where doubtless the plan of campaign had been matured, and it was there known that Robinson was to be indicted,

if he had not already been, and he was arrested on pretense
of being a fugitive from justice.   It happened in this wise.
Having spent one night in consultation at Topeka with the
Congressional Committee; another at Lawrence in consultation with leading Free-State men, and a third at Kansas
City with Kersey Coates, as soon as Robinson could get to
his state-room on the steamboat, anticipating no interference
of any kind, he improved the occasion for a sound sleep.
He was thus occupied when on arriving at Lexington he
was aroused by loud raps at the door of his room.   On
opening it he was confronted by some gentlemen, who informed him they were appointed a committee to notify him
that he must leave the boat at that place.   On inquiring of
them the name of the place and why he must stop there, he
was told that the place was Lexington, and the people had
understood he was a fugitive from justice.   Robinson said
he had heard of no indictment as yet found, that he had
been openly in the Territory and was going to the States on
business and not as a fugitive.   On being told that a large
number of people were on the boat and drinking freely at
the bar, Robinson desired to address them, as he was sure
he could satisfy them they had no business to interfere with
him.   To this the committee decidedly objected, as the mob
would not listen to reason from any one, much less from
him.   It appearing that force would be used if necessary,
Robinson referred the matter to Mrs. Robinson, whether to
use such means of defense as he had—one revolver—or go
with the committee, when she promptly replied, "They will
kill you if you go, and you may as well make a stand
here."   But the committee assured her that no harm should
come to her husband, they would pledge their honor and
lives if need be for his protection, if he would go with them;
when Mrs. R. withdrew her objection, and both left the boat,
avoiding the crowd at the bar.   The landing was covered
with people, but there was no disturbance, and the prisoners
with their baggage were taken to Judge Sawyer's, who was

afterwards a member of Congress. He had resided in Fitchburg, Massachusetts, where he had studied law, and treated
his prisoner more like a prince than a fugitive from justice.
At night a boat came down the river and remained till morning. A gentleman on board, learning that a man by the
name of Robinson was held as prisoner in Lexington, called
at Judge Sawyer's place to see him. On being admitted he
proved to be Dr. R. H. McDonald, the "Vinegar Bitters"
man, now a millionaire, who was the physician of Sacramento County in 1850, and extracted the ball from Robinson's body when he was shot in the squatter riot of that
year. His first salutation was, "Well, it is you, sure
enough! When I heard a man with your name was a prisoner I thought it must be you, as you are always in some
scrape."

As Mrs. R. was not regarded as a fugitive from justice,
or labor, she was permitted to go on her journey, taking
with her the testimony of the committee.

Judge Sawyer informed his prisoner that two men from
the country tried one day to get up a mob to lynch him,
but when it was proposed to turn Robinson into the street
against these two men with the same kind of weapons they
should have, they subsided and nothing more was heard of
lynching.

As no indictment had been found against Robinson, he
was held in Lexington about a week while messengers could
go to Lecompton for an indictment, and to the Governor of
Missouri with a requisition from Governor Shannon after it
should be found by the Grand Jury, which could furnish any
indictment to order on short notice. In this case it was for
usurpation of office on account of having been elected Governor under the State constitution. The treason indictment
came later.

At length, the Deputy United States Marshal Preston
appeared at Lexington, armed and equipped with requisition, posse, revolvers, and conveyance. The route by land

instead of river was taken, and soon Westport was reached, where a halt was made. Soon after entering the hotel, the prisoner was called upon by W. H. Russell, a lawyer who was employed in California by the squatters in their land conflicts. He was now a resident of Missouri, had heard of the arrest of a man by the name of Robinson, and called to see if it was his old client indicted for murder, etc., in Sacramento. He was ready to be employed again if desired, and engaged in the case. One question he wished to ask. He said there was a man by the name of Hayes now at Westport who had some slaves taken from him in California on a writ of *habeas corpus* by a man named Robinson. He was very bitter, and swore that if the prisoner was that Robinson he would shoot him on sight. Russell desired to know the facts, and if the prisoner had nothing to do with the matter he would like to know it. Robinson informed him that while in California he had nothing to do with such a case, but had heard of a man of the same name with a family who was connected with the freeing of some slaves. However, Hayes proposed to investigate the matter for himself, and took his position at the foot of the stairs as the prisoner descended for his dinner. No demonstration, however, was made except a mutual *stare* as the dining-room was entered. At Westport, Robinson sent for Colonel Kersey Coates, and retained him as attorney. From him Robinson learned the situation at Lawrence, which had not yet been entered by the Marshal's posse of eight hundred men. On his way East Colonel Coates had given Robinson the result of an interview with a man connected with the Blue Lodges, and at Robinson's request had imparted that information to the people at Lawrence, with the advice that under no circumstances should Federal authority be resisted. Here, with proper caution, was an opportunity for gaining a grand victory. If the United States Marshal, or any other officer under sanction of the Federal authority, would enter Lawrence unresisted and execute such writs as were in contemplation, it would be a victory against the bogus laws and officials, including the President of the United States, that could not be achieved by a hundred battles and the killing of thousands of men. The infamy would be unparalleled, and the more wanton and extensive the outrage, the greater the victory to the Free-State cause. Colonel Coates agreed fully with this view.

Governor Shannon, in a letter to the Secretary of State, gave his view of the rebels and the rebellion in part as follows:

" I herewith transmit a certified copy, marked No. 8, of evidence that was elicited by the Grand Jury of Jefferson County, at their last term, in relation to a secret, oath-bound military organization, which exists in this Territory. It will be perceived that it is different and much more dangerous than the one which was exposed some time since. I have satisfactory information that this secret organization exists in the East, and that by means of the signs and grips the new emigrants from the East are enabled to recognize their fellow-members in this Territory to whom personally they are unknown. I am now able to state, upon reliable information, the whole plan of resistance to the territorial laws and their execution, which has been adopted by those who pretend to deny their validity. This plan is well understood and supported by a dangerous, secret, oath-bound organization of men who, it is believed, from the manifestations and threats already made, will be unscrupulous as to the use of means to accomplish their objects. The plan is this : whenever an officer, whether United States marshal, sheriff, or constable, shall attempt to execute a writ or process issued under any territorial law, aided and assisted by a posse of United States troops, he is to be evaded, but not openly resisted. Should an attempt be made by any officer to execute any writ or process issued under the laws of this Territory, unaided by a posse of United States troops, he is to be resisted by force at all hazards. There is a determined purpose to carry out this programme, regardless of all consequences, and the country is filled with armed men, the greater portion of whom have recently arrived in the Territory, ready to carry out this plan by force of arms. It will be obvious to the President that, if every officer of the Government charged with the execution of legal process, issued under, and to enforce the territorial laws, is compelled to call on a military posse of United States troops to aid in executing the law, that the territorial Government will be practically nullified. It will be impossible to collect the taxes assessed for county or territorial purposes if this plan of resistance should be successful.

" Indeed, the people of the Territory will not submit to it without an attempt at least to enforce the laws against all.   There is now in the town of Lawrence an arsenal well supplied with all the munitions of war, which have been purchased in the East and secretly introduced into that place.   They have ten pieces of artillery, at least one thousand stand of Sharp's rifles, and a large supply of revolvers.   There are said to be about five hundred men in the town of Lawrence at this time who refuse to submit to the territorial laws, and who openly declare that no officer shall execute any process issued under these laws without being resisted by force.   A large portion of the country people who took an active part with the citizens of Lawrence in the difficulty last fall seem to hold themselves entirely aloof from the difficulties with which we are now threatened, and are now open in their denunciations of C. Robinson and his party.   But the recent emigrants from the East (with some exceptions, of course) seem determined to provoke a civil conflict.   The law-and-order party of the Territory so far seem determined, on the other hand, to avoid this calamity.   But it is in vain to conceal the fact that we are threatened on all sides with most serious difficulties, and that a dangerous crisis is rapidly approaching.   Sheriff Jones had a very extensive acquaintance not only in this Territory, but also in the border counties in Missouri, where he formerly resided, and was universally respected and esteemed as a high-minded, honorable, and brave man. The dastardly attempt to assassinate him while in the discharge and for the performance of his official duties, connected with the threats openly made of assassination against others, and the firm conviction in the public mind that this is a part of a settled policy, to be carried out through the agency of a secret order or organization, have already produced strong feeling of excitement throughout the whole country, which is rapidly on the increase, and it is difficult to see at this time where it will end.   Large parties, both from the North and South, are daily arriving with pre-existing prejudices and hostile feelings, which will greatly increase the difficulty of preserving the peace of this Territory.

" I have the honor to be your obedient servant,

" *Hon. W. L. Marcy.*"   " WILSON SHANNON.

While the statements relative to secret organizations and arms and men at Lawrence are greatly exaggerated, the purpose on the part of the Free-State men to thwart and baffle territorial officials unaided by Federal authority, so as to make the bogus enactments a dead letter, is correctly stated. The object was not only to prevent any advantage to slavery from being gained by the usurpation, but, by compelling

16

a resort to United States troops, or United States militia or marshal's posse to serve every warrant, however trifling, to hold the fraudulent government up to the contempt of all people, and so to harass the Administration that it would be glad to get out of the difficulty by insuring or permitting a fair election for the next Legislature, to be chosen in the fall of 1857. It was thus immaterial how many printing presses, hotels, and bridges were indicted and destroyed, or how many men should be killed in the operation, so that the responsibility could be placed upon the Federal authority. Of course, the destruction of life and property under any circumstances, would be a misfortune to such as might suffer, but every such outrage would react against the usurpation with more force than a pitched battle. In fact, could the Administration plead the least armed resistance to Federal authority, the justification of the officers would be complete, and the reaction would be against the Free-State men. This was, in one sense, a state of war, but unlike any other war known to history, inasmuch as the more outrages the people could get the Government to perpetrate upon them, the more victories they would gain, and this simply because the field of battle embraced the entire country, and the chief victories at this stage were to be moral, political, and national.

To show what desperate efforts were made by the officials to exasperate the Free-State men, and drive them to take position against Federal authority, the following memorial is given, as sent to the President, setting forth the whole case from the settlers' point of view. But two things were done which might as well have been omitted ; one was the expression, "we make no resistance to the execution of the laws, national or *territorial*." Had they stopped at the word "*laws*," leaving every person at liberty to reject as laws the bogus enactments, the expression would have been generally endorsed. Also, the voluntary delivery of the howitzer to Jones was uncalled for and did no good. With these exceptions the memorial is a representative document:

"MEMORIAL TO THE PRESIDENT FROM INHABITANTS OF KANSAS.

"*To his Excellency Franklin Pierce, President of the United States.*

"SIR: The undersigned residents of Kansas Territory, and a committee of the citizens of the town of Lawrence and vicinity, appointed to represent to your Excellency the insufferable wrongs which they are called upon to endure at the hands of territorial officials, and to petition for redress and prevention of the same.

"The statements made in this communication are of facts mostly within our personal knowledge, and all of them we are prepared at any time to substantiate by testimony conclusive and unimpeachable.

"The first of the recent great outrages on the town of Lawrence of which we complain is the following proclamation of the United States Marshal of Kansas Territory:

"' PROCLAMATION.

"' *To the People of Kansas Territory:*

"' Whereas, certain judicial writs of arrest have been directed to me by the First District Court of the United States, etc., to be executed within the County of Douglas; and, whereas, an attempt to execute them by the United States Deputy Marshal was violently resisted by a large number of citizens of Lawrence; and as there is every reason to believe that any attempt to execute these writs will be resisted by a large body of armed men:

"' Now, therefore, the law-abiding citizens of the Territory are commanded to be and appear at Lecompton as soon as practicable, and in numbers sufficient for the proper execution of the law.

"' Given under my hand, this 11th day of May, 1856.

"' I. B. DONELSON,
"' United States Marshal for Kansas Territory.'

"The allegations contained in this proclamation are untrue in fact, as well as grossly unjust in effect to the people of Lawrence.

"A demonstration has been made by the Deputy Marshal towards the arrest of ex-Governor Reeder, while here in attendance on the Congressional Committee; but as the latter demurred to the legality of the process, and denied the jurisdiction, the attempt was not made. This was a circumstance involving no violence on the part of the citizens of Lawrence; as no posse was called for by the official, it is clear that they can in no way be held accountable for any of its results. No actual effort to arrest any person in Lawrence had been made by the Marshal previous to this proclamation.

"At this time there were in the Territory many hundreds of men who had entered it in organized companies from Southern States, actuated by an avowed political purpose, and proclaiming a deadly hostility to the town of Lawrence. These men were immediately enrolled in the Marshal's posse, and supplied by the Governor with arms belonging to the United States, and intended for the use of the territorial militia. All the facts warrant the belief that it was the intention of the Marshal, by this proclamation, to justify this misuse of these national arms, and to give, as far as possible, to the outrages being perpetrated by these companies, the sacred sanction of the law. Without this sanction it was known that these outrages would be resisted by any and all means of defense in the power of an indignant, and not yet enslaved people. This posse of the Marshal was further increased by accessions from the neighboring State of Missouri, and supplied from the same source with several pieces of artillery. Camps were formed at different points along the highways and on the Kansas River, and peaceful travellers subjected to detention, robbery, and insult. Men were stopped in the streets and on the open prairie, and bidden to stand and deliver their purses at the peril of their lives. Cattle, provisions, arms, and other property were taken wherever found, without consent of the owners. Men were choked from their horses, which were seized by the marauders, and houses were broken open and pillaged of their contents.

"Resistance to these outrages was followed by further violence, and in some cases by the most wanton and brutal sacrifice of life. The passage of the United States mail was frequently interrupted, and examinations made in defiance of law. In the border counties of Missouri, citizens of Lawrence were seized without warrant, conveyed to the various camps, and there subjected to detention and unlawful trial, accompanied by threats of immediate death.

"In the meantime these alarming demonstrations have excited apprehension in the community, and a letter was sent to the Governor as follows:

"'LAWRENCE CITY, May 11, 1856.

"'DEAR SIR: The undersigned are charged with the duty of communicating to your Excellency the following preamble and resolution, adopted at a public meeting of the citizens of this place at seven o'clock last evening, viz.:

"'*Whereas*, We have the most reliable information from various parts of the Territory, and the adjoining State of Missouri, of the organization of guerilla bands, who threaten the destruction of our town and its citizens: therefore,

"'*Resolved*, That Messrs. Topliff, Hutchinson, and Roberts constitute a committee to inform his Excellency, Governor Shannon, of these facts, and to call upon him, in the name of the people of Lawrence, for protection against such bands by the United States troops at his disposal.

" ' All of which is respectfully submitted,

" ' Very truly, etc.,

" ' C. W. TOPLIFF,

" ' W. Y. ROBERTS,

" ' JOHN HUTCHINSON.

" ' *His Excellency Wilson Shannon, Governor of Kansas Territory.*'

" This letter drew forth the following reply:

" ' EXECUTIVE OFFICE, LECOMPTON, K. T., May 12, 1856.

" ' GENTLEMEN : Your note of the 11th instant is received, and in reply I have to state that there is no force around or approaching Lawrence except the legally constituted posse of the United States Marshal and Sheriff of Douglas County, each of whom, I am informed, has a number of writs in his hands for execution against persons now in Lawrence. I shall in no way interfere with either of these officers in the discharge of their official duties.

" ' If the citizens of Lawrence submit themselves to the territorial laws, and aid and assist the Marshal and Sheriff in the execution of process in their hands, as all good citizens are bound to do when called on, they, or all such, will entitle themselves to the protection of the law. But so long as they keep up a military or armed organization to resist the territorial laws, and the officers charged with their execution, I shall not interpose to save them from legitimate consequences of their illegal acts.

" ' I have the honor to be, yours, with great respect,

" ' WILSON SHANNON.

" ' *Messrs. C. W. Topliff, John Hutchinson, W. Y. Roberts.*'

" In commenting upon this letter, we have only to say that the implied charge upon the citizens of Lawrence of keeping up 'a military or armed organization to resist the territorial laws, and the officers charged with their executions,' is utterly untrue ; and that Governor Shannon must have been fully aware of its falsity, or ignorant to a degree of criminality.

" The proclamation of the Marshal was not made public by him in Lawrence ; but a copy having by chance reached the town, another meeting of citizens was called on the 13th of May, and the following preamble and resolution adopted :

" ' *Whereas*, By a proclamation to the people of Kansas Territory, by I. B. Donelson, United States Marshal for said Territory, issued the 11th day of May, 1856, it is alleged that certain " judicial writs of arrest have been directed to him by the First District Court of the United States, etc., to be executed within the County of Douglas, and that an attempt to execute them by the United States Deputy Marshal was violently resisted by a large number of the citizens of Lawrence, and that there is every reason to believe that any attempt to execute these writs will be resisted by a large body of armed men " ; therefore,

" ' *Resolved*, By this public meeting of the citizens of Lawrence, held this 13th day of May, 1856, that the allegations and charges against us contained in the aforesaid proclamation are wholly untrue in fact, and the conclusion entirely false which is drawn therefrom. The aforesaid Deputy Marshal was resisted in no manner whatsoever, nor by any person whatever, in the execution of said writs, except by him whose arrest the said Deputy Marshal was seeking to make. And that we now, as we have done heretofore, declare our willingness and determination, without resistance, to acquiesce in the service upon us of any judicial writs against us by the United States Marshal for Kansas Territory, and will furnish him a posse for that purpose, if so requested ; but that we are ready to resist, if need be unto death, the ravages and desolation of an invading mob.

" ' J. A. WAKEFIELD, President.

" ' JOHN HUTCHINSON, Secretary.'

" The indications of an intended attack upon the town continuing to increase, on the 14th instant another meeting of citizens was called, of which G. W. Deitzler was president and J. H. Green secretary, and the following letter prepared and sent to the United States Marshal:

" ' LAWRENCE, May 14, 1856.

" ' DEAR SIR: We have seen a proclamation issued by yourself, dated 11th May, instant, and also have reliable information this morning that large bodies of armed men, in pursuance of your proclamation, have assembled in the vicinity of Lawrence.

" ' That there may be no misunderstanding, we beg leave to ask respectfully (that we may be reliably informed) what are the demands against us? We desire to state most truthfully and earnestly that no opposition whatever will now, or at any future time, be offered to the execution of any legal process by yourself, or any person acting for you. We also pledge ourselves to assist you, if called upon, in the execution of any legal process.

" ' We declare ourselves to be order-loving and law-abiding citizens, and only await an opportunity to testify our fidelity to the laws of the country, the Constitution, and the Union.

" ' We are informed, also, that those men collecting about Lawrence openly declare that their intention is to destroy the town and drive off the citizens. Of course we do not believe that you give any countenance to such threats; but, in view of the excited state of the public mind, we ask protection of the constituted authorities of the Government, declaring ourselves in readiness to co-operate with them, for the maintenance of the peace, order, and quiet of the community in which we live. Very respectfully,

" ' ROBERT MORROW,
" ' LYMAN ALLEN,
" ' JOHN HUTCHINSON.

" ' *I. B. Donelson, United States Marshal for Kansas Territory.*'

" The following reply was received to this communication:

" ' OFFICE OF THE UNITED STATES MARSHAL,
LECOMPTON, K. T., May 15, 1856.

" ' On yesterday I received a communication addressed to me, signed by one of you as president and the other as secretary, purporting to have been adopted by a meeting of the citizens of Lawrence, held on yesterday morning. After speaking of a proclamation issued by myself, you state "that there may be no misunderstanding, we beg leave to ask respectfully (that we may be reliably informed) what are the demands against us? We desire most truthfully and earnestly to declare, that no opposition whatever will now, or at any future time, be offered to the execution of any legal process by yourself, or any person acting for you. We also pledge ourselves to assist you, if called upon, in the execution of any legal process," etc.

" ' From your professed ignorance of the demands against you I must conclude that you are strangers, and not citizens of Lawrence, or of recent date, or have been absent for some time; more particularly when an attempt was made by my deputy to execute the process of the First District Court of the United States for Kansas Territory against ex-Governor Reeder, when he made a speech in the room and presence of the Congressional Committee, and denied the authority and power of said court, and threatened the life of said deputy if he attempted to execute said process; which speech and defiant threats were loudly applauded by some one or two hundred of the citizens of Lawrence, who had assembled at the room on learning the business of the Marshal, and made such hostile demonstrations that the deputy thought he and his small posse would endanger their lives in executing said process.

" ' Your declaration that you " will truthfully and earnestly offer no opposition now, nor at any future time, to the execution of any legal process," etc., is, indeed, difficult to understand. May I ask, gentle-

men, what has produced this wonderful change in the minds of the
people of Lawrence? Have their eyes been suddenly opened, so that
they are now able to see that there are laws in force in Kansas Territory which should be obeyed? Or is it that just now those for whom I
have writs have sought refuge elsewhere? Or it may possibly be, that
you now, as heretofore, expect to screen yourselves behind the word
"legal," so significantly used by you. How am I to rely on your
pledges, when I am well aware that the whole population of Lawrence
is armed and drilled, and the town fortified—when I recollect the meetings and resolutions adopted in Lawrence, and elsewhere in the Territory, openly defying the laws and officers thereof, and threatening to
resist the same to a bloody issue, and recently verified in the attempted
assassination of Sheriff Jones while in the discharge of his official
duties in Lawrence? Are you strangers to all these things? Surely
you must be strangers at Lawrence! If no outrages have been committed by the citizens of Lawrence against the laws of the land, they
need not fear any posse of mine. But I must take the liberty of executing all processes in my hands, as the United States Marshal, in my own
time and manner, and shall only use such power as is authorized by law.
You say you call upon the constituted authority of the Government for
protection. This, indeed, sounds strange coming from a large body of
men armed with Sharp's rifles and other implements of war, bound together by oaths and pledges to resist the laws of the Government they
call on for protection. All persons in Kansas Territory, without regard
to location, who honestly submit to the constituted authorities will ever
find me ready to aid in protecting them; and all who seek to resist the
laws of the land and turn traitors to their country will find me aiding
and enforcing the laws, if not as an officer, as a citizen.

" ' Respectfully yours,
" ' I. B. DONELSON,
" ' United States Marshal of Kansas Territory.

" ' *Messrs. Deitzler and J. H. Green, Lawrence, K. T.'*

" We should consider this letter entirely unworthy of criticism were
it not official. Its chief misstatements, however, must be corrected,
and of these we shall notice the following :

" 1. That ex-Governor Reeder threatened the life of the Marshal,
and was applauded therefor by the people of Lawrence; the fact being
that the words used by the former can only by forced construction be
made to imply a threat against the person of the officer; and that the
Deputy Marshal had no personal fear of the citizens is proven by the
fact that he frequently, during these difficulties, entered the town, and
remained during his pleasure, without molestation or insult.

" 2. His reiteration of the falsehoods that the whole population is armed and drilled, and the town fortified, while he possessed evidence through his deputies that such was not the case. That the so-called fortifications as there existing were not considered formidable for defense is proven by his subsequent neglect to demolish them while the town was in the hands of his posse.

" 3. His wanton misapplication of certain resolutions passed at some other point in the Territory, and having no relation to the officers of the United States.

" 4. His effort to fasten the attempt on the life of Samuel J. Jones on the citizens of Lawrence, when it is a known fact that said citizens denounced that attempt in a most emphatic manner, and made all practicable effort to detect its author.

" 5. The compound falsehood that the citizens of Lawrence are a large body of men armed with Sharp's rifles, bound together by oaths and pledges to resist the laws of the Government they call on for protection, it being undoubtedly well known to himself that no such oaths or pledges exist, and that the citizens of Lawrence have never been combined to resist the laws of the United States.

" From a reply thus disingenuous and partisan in character, the threatened town could derive no hope. Nevertheless, as the movements of the marauding forces grew daily more menacing in their character, the following letter was sent to the Marshal on the 17th instant:

" ' DEAR SIR : We desire to call your attention, as citizens of Kansas, to the fact that a large force of armed men have collected in the vicinity of Lawrence, and are engaged in committing depredations upon our citizens, stopping wagons, arresting, threatening, and robbing unoffending travellers upon the highway—breaking open boxes of merchandise and appropriating their contents—have slaughtered cattle, and terrified many of the women and children.

" ' We have also learned from Governor Shannon that there are no armed forces in the vicinity of this place but the regularly constituted militia of the Territory. This is to ask you if you recognize them as your posse, and feel responsible for their acts. If you do not, we hope and trust you will prevent a repetition of such acts, and give peace to the settlers. On behalf of the citizens,

" ' C. W. BABCOCK,
" ' LYMAN ALLEN,
" ' J. A. PERRY.'

" To this letter no reply was vouchsafed. The same day a communication was sent to the Governor by Messrs. S. W. and T. B. Eldridge, proprietors of the Eldridge House, asking for it protection against destruction threatened by the mob in the Marshal's posse. The building itself was the property of the Emigrant Aid Company, but it had been furnished by the Messrs. Eldridge at heavy expense, and was not yet opened as a public house. A verbal reply was returned by the Governor to this appeal, expressing regret that the proprietors had taken possession, and giving some encouragement for protection. On the 18th he was visited by the Messrs. Eldridge in person, and a full and truthful representation made of all the facts in the case. At this interview, the Governor, as well as the Marshal, seemed disposed to accord the protection needful. In addition to their own personal appeal, the Messrs. Eldridge presented a communication from the citizens of Lawrence, as follows:

" ' LAWRENCE, K. T., May 17, 1856.

" ' GENTLEMEN : Having learned that your reason for assembling so large a force in the vicinity of our town, to act as a posse in the enforcement of the laws, rests on the supposition that we are armed against the laws and the officers in the exercise of their duties, we would say, that we hold our arms only for our own individual defense against violence, and not against the laws or officers in the execution of the same; therefore, having no further use for them when our protection is otherwise secured, we propose to deliver our arms to Colonel Sumner so soon as he shall quarter in our town a body of troops sufficient for our protection, to be retained by him as long as such force shall remain among us.   Very truly, etc.,

" ' MANY CITIZENS.

" ' *His Excellency Wilson Shannon, Governor, and I. B. Donelson, Esq., United States Marshal for Kansas Territory.*'

" Both the Governor and the Marshal expressed satisfaction with this proposition, and agreed to its terms in case a demand should be enforced for the surrender of the arms. If no resistance was offered his force, the Marshal gave a positive promise of protection to the property of the citizens. But it was said that a portion of the posse was clamorous for the destruction of the hotel and the printing offices; and the Messrs. Eldridge were invited to return again on the following day, after time had been afforded for consultation with the captains of the companies.

" It is worthy of remark, that all messengers to the Executive and Marshal were under guard during the whole time of their being within the lines of the besieging camp and on the road to Lecompton, and that the following pass was given to the Messrs. Eldridge on their departure this day:

" ' LECOMPTON, May 18, 1856.

" ' The bearers of this, S. W. and T. B. Eldridge, desire to return to Lawrence this evening and return in the morning.

" ' Now, therefore, all persons will permit these gentlemen to go and return without molestation or delay.

" ' WILSON SHANNON,
" ' Governor of Kansas Territory.
" ' *J. B. Donelson, United States Marshal, Kansas Territory.*'

" On the 19th Messrs. Eldridge renewed their visit according to agreement, but found a great change in the tone of the officials. It would appear that the companies composing the posse would be satisfied with nothing short of some destruction of private property, and this feeling was so strong as to defy the power of the Marshal. The Messrs. Eldridge, on behalf of the citizens of Lawrence, offered the Marshal their services, and proposed, if he would supply them with weapons, to make all necessary pledges to sustain him in the protection of property and the execution of the laws. This offer the Marshal did not see fit to accept, alleging only the excuse of a deficiency of arms. It was evident that a course of violence was resolved upon. One of the captains —a Colonel Titus, of Florida, a member of the late expedition against Cuba—declared boldly that the printing presses must be destroyed to satisfy the boys from South Carolina. But promises of protection to the hotel were renewed, and the Marshal pledged his word that if no resistance was made, he would enter the town with a small posse of unarmed men, and that the remainder should not be admitted. He also further promised not to dismiss them in the vicinity of the town. The incongruities of these various statements it is not for us to reconcile.

" Feeling from all these circumstances the necessity to the town of efficient protection, the Messrs. Eldridge made a last effort to secure aid from the Governor. He disclaimed all authority over the force of the Marshal, and stated that he should not interfere with the officer's operations. He was implored to summon to his aid the force of Colonel Sumner for the protection of the property of the citizens, but peremptorily refused. It was represented to him that the Marshal's posse had resolved on perpetrating unlawful outrages in Lawrence, and he said the people of Lawrence must take such consequences as should ensue ; that he could protect them with the United States troops if he chose, but that he should not do so. When apprehensions were expressed to him that these outrages would finally madden the people to the point of resistance, and precipitate all the horrors of civil war, he turned angrily away and left the room with the expression, ' War then it is, by God ! '

" These were the last words spoken to persons representing the people of Lawrence by the highest officer of the Territory.

" During the following day the Deputy Marshal, W. P. Fain, a resident of Calhoun, Georgia, visited the town, and in conversation with a citizen expressed the belief that the printing presses would be destroyed, but that the Eldridge House would be spared.

" On the morning of the 21st instant a cavalry force was seen stationed on a hill commanding the town. It was soon increased by a company of artillery and another of infantry. A white flag was first displayed, which soon gave place to a red one. This emblem would have incited the citizens to resistance but for the known fact that the force was commanded by a United States officer (whose pledge of protection had been given) and armed with national weapons. Beside the red flag, whose motto was ' Southern rights,' soon floated that of the Union.

" The Deputy Marshal entered the town with less than ten men, and proceeding to the Eldridge House, summoned both the proprietors to act on his posse, together with Dr. Garvey (Garvin?), John A. Perry, C. W. Topliff, and Wm. Jones, all citizens of the town. This summons was promptly obeyed, and all required assistance cheerfully given. Only two arrests were made during the morning, and with these, after dinner, the whole posse repaired to the camp. Colonel Topliff was charged with the delivery to the Marshal of the following communication:

" ' LAWRENCE, K. T., May 21, 1856.

" ' We, the committee of public safety for the citizens of Lawrence, make this statement and declaration to you as Marshal of Kansas Territory:

" ' That we represent citizens of the United States and of Kansas who acknowledge the constituted authorities of the Government; that we make no resistance to the execution of the laws, national or territorial; and that we ask protection of the Government, and claim it as law-abiding American citizens.

" ' For the private property already taken by your posse we ask indemnification, and what remains to us and our citizens we throw upon you for protection, trusting that under the flag of our Union and within the folds of the Constitution we may obtain safety.

" ' SAMUEL C. POMEROY,
" ' W. Y. ROBERTS,
" ' LYMAN ALLEN,
" ' JOHN A. PERRY,
" ' C. W. BABCOCK,
" ' S. B. PRENTISS,
" ' A. H. MALLORY,
" ' JOEL GROVER.
" ' *I. B. Donelson, United States Marshal, Kansas Territory.*'

" It was now hoped that the crisis had passed. On summoning on his posse the proprietors of the Eldridge House, Deputy Marshal Fain had renewed his promise to protect their property. The officials had been treated with every courtesy, and even generous hospitality. But by three o'clock the streets were filled by a company of armed horsemen, headed by Samuel J. Jones, Sheriff of Douglas County, who drew up his force in front of the Eldridge House and demanded of the citizens, in the name of the law, the surrender of their rifles and cannon. He gave five minutes for a reply. He was answered by General Pomeroy that the cannon, and all rifles not individual property (if any such there were), would be given up on his giving an official receipt for the same. General Pomeroy and General Roberts proceeded with him to assist in their delivery. This done, it was announced that the printing offices and the Eldridge House must be destroyed. Remonstrance was in vain.

"In the meantime, the remainder of the force, comprising several hundred men, with United States muskets and fixed bayonets, were taking position in the town. Men endeavored by argument, and women by tears, to alter the determination of Jones, but in vain. At 3:15 o'clock he announced to Messrs. Eldridge that he would give them till five to remove their families and furniture from the house. The work of pillage had already commenced; the contents of the printing offices were scattered in the streets, and the red flag planted on the roof, first of the office of the *Herald of Freedom*, and afterwards of the Eldridge House. The family of Mr. G. W. Brown were driven from their home, and the immediate pillage of the hotel prevented only by the resolute interference of a few citizens, aided by some individuals of the mob, who kept a strict guard at the doors, and insisted that the families of the proprietors should have the time promised by Jones in which to collect their most necessary effects and leave. At last the cannon were placed and ready, and it was announced to Colonel S. W. Eldridge that the bombardment would commence in five minutes. His wife and children, and such personal effects as they had been enabled to collect, were placed in carriages and driven off between files of United States bayonets, and amidst the yells of the impatient mob. As they left the town the first boom of a cannon told that the work of destruction had begun. Soon (as the impression made by the cannon was not great) the building was fired, and with the aid of gunpowder reduced, with its furniture and stores, to a pile of ruins.

"The work of pillage spread through the whole town, and continued until after dark. Every house and store which could be entered was ransacked, trunks broken open, and money and property taken at will. Where women had not fled, they were in some cases insulted, and even robbed of their clothing. From one house over two thousand dollars in money were carried away. The house of Charles Robinson was pillaged and burned to the ground. The same evening, forces were drawn off to their camp, and the sack of Lawrence was concluded.

" Some incidents of this authorized outrage here demand mention. While Messrs. Topliff and Perry were aiding the Marshal in making the arrests, both their houses were broken open and pillaged. Some of the flags which floated beside that of the Union had for mottoes, ' Superiority of the white race,' ' Kansas the outpost,' ' South Carolina'; while one had the national stripes, with a tiger in place of the Union; another had alternate stripes of black and white. While the cannon were being placed for the destruction of the Eldridge House, David R. Atchison, late Vice-President of the United States, was conspicuous among the mob. When the final doom of the hotel and printing offices was pronounced, it was said by the officials to be by order of the Government, as the Grand Jury of Douglas County had ordered them abated as nuisances. The only charge against the Eldridge House was its ownership by the Emigrant Aid Company.

" To evade the pledge given by the Marshal that he would not allow his posse to enter Lawrence, they were disbanded by him, after the arrests were made, and enrolled as a sheriff's posse by Samuel J. Jones; the Marshal thus keeping one pledge at the expense of another. On the next day they were again enrolled as the posse of the Marshal.

" There are also some facts of another character which we wish to record. We believe that many of the captains of the invading companies exerted themselves to the utmost for the protection of life and property. Some of them protested against these enormous outrages, and endeavored to dissuade Samuel J. Jones from their perpetration. Many used personal effort to remove such property as was possible from the Eldridge House before its destruction. Among these stood prominently Colonel Zadock Jackson, of Georgia, who did not scruple either in Lawrence or his own camp to denounce the outrages in terms such as they deserved. Colonel Buford, of Alabama, also disclaimed having come to Kansas to destroy property, and condemned the course which had been taken. The prosecuting attorney of Douglas County, the legal adviser of the Sheriff, used his influence in vain to prevent the destruction of property.

" We have thus given an outline of the events which have concluded an unparalleled chapter in the history of our country. That we have dealt mildly with the facts, and fallen short of the real atrocity of the case, will be proven by the testimony which, in time, public opinion will not fail to gather. So gigantic is that official villainy of which we are being made the victims that the understanding almost refuses to believe the evidence, however strong. That any set of men in a representative Government like ours can be so reckless, and so defiant of right, as to attempt the administration of law on principles of perjury and brigandage is a combination of fatuity and corruption almost passing belief. Yet the facts spring out with startling boldness on the picture of events, and we see the spectacle of rulers utterly ignoring the oaths they have taken, and perverting the beneficent power of government to the base uses of a ruthless despotism—at will despoiling men of their property and lives—endeavoring to bind fast the hands of the loyal citizens who look to them for protection, and to deliver them over as bondmen to an invading force. We cannot but feel that you will be slow to believe facts such as we have stated here, and for the credit of humanity we cannot otherwise hope; yet we cherish the trust that you will heed the voice, however feeble, that pours its complaint into your ear, and exert the influence of your office to prevent the *possible* occurrence of abuses of power on the parts of those officials who are directly responsible to you for the faithful discharge of their duties; and to institute such a scrutiny into their past conduct as will reveal its true character and inspire a salutary caution in future. In making such a scrutiny it seems to us inevitable that the communications of the territorial officers of Kansas, as given in this memorial, coupled with the undisputed facts resulting from their action, will show at least a criminal disregard of good faith sufficient of itself to prove their unfitness for the responsibilities they have assumed. And in the meantime we have been driven to the appointment of a committee of protection, whose duty it will be to organize and use all means for the defense of our liberties and property, during such time as we are unable to procure protection from the Government under which we live.

" As regards the pecuniary damage sustained by this community at the hand of the Government as administered by these officials, we cannot doubt but you will see the justice of our claim, and employ the influence of your position to procure for us an adequate compensation. The readiest way to do this would seem to be by an appropriation by Congress, which it is within your province to recommend. It is at present impossible to estimate this damage, as new depredations are continually being made. How long these will be permitted to continue will depend to a great extent upon the pleasure of our rulers. But it is certain that the amount is, even at present, for a community like ours very great. The loss to the proprietor of the Eldridge House alone is to nearly the full extent of their investments, time being denied them to remove any material portion of the costly furniture and abundant stores provided for its use. The destruction of the printing offices, like that of the hotel, involves not only the cost of the property, but the complete ruin of the business in which it was employed. And then there is scarcely a freeholder in Lawrence, or for many miles around, but has had costly experience of that depredatory action which the Marshal in his proclamation has called ' the proper execution of the law.'

" Were the destruction of property, however, the gravest result of this mal-administration, it would be shorn of its chief importance. But it must not be forgotten that among ts consequences has been loss of life, and it is due to the community that justice be administered upon those who caused it.   And surely when we say to your Excellency that our country is still being overrun, and that this very day has brought to our ears the fresh complaints of property taken, and women ravished in their homes, it will not be considered either disrespectful or ill-timed in us to urge, with all the earnestness of men who know the truth of the things whereof they speak, that the facts herein set forth, and the petitions preferred, receive the earliest attention in the power of your Excellency to bestow.

> " O. E. LEARNARD,
> " S. W. ELDRIDGE,
> " C. W. BABCOCK,
> " J. M. WINCHELL,
> " LYMAN ALLEN,
> " S. B. PRENTISS,
> " L. G. HINE,
> " JOSEPH CRACKLIN,
> " JOHN PERRY.

" LAWRENCE, K. T., May 22, 1856."

Here is an arraignment of the Government more terrible than an "army with banners." The indictment of the Slave-State party had been made on paper and sent broadcast over the land—the invasions at elections, the despotic code enacted, the Wakarusa war and general lawlessness— but here is the *conviction* of official crime before the American people as a jury, and the verdict was unanimous. The Wakarusa war was a great victory, but this was much greater ; as the first simply resulted in compelling nearly two thousand men to march to Kansas and then march back again, accomplishing nothing, not even serving a peace warrant issued by a bogus justice of the peace, while this demonstrated the nature of the Government imposed upon American citizens in Kansas. Here were the law-abiding citizens, having committed no crime, ready to act as a posse to ferret out and arrest criminals, if any there were, almost on their knees as suppliants for protection from outrage by an official mob, without avail. The picture cannot be duplicated in the most despotic government on earth. Did the people do right in permitting this official infamy without resistance ? F. B. Sanborn says no. His two heroes, Brown and Lane, might have said no, had they been present and not timid, judging them by their designs at the Wakarusa war. But when it is remembered that this struggle was national and not local merely, that the Federal authority was desirous of abetting the Slave-State party, and of crushing out the Free-State men, that this Government had to be held up before the country in its true light, the answer must be in the affirmative. Had this mob been unofficial, could it have been attacked without attacking Federal authority, as was the case at Osawatomie, Franklin, Fort Saunders, and Titus, it would have been utterly wiped out by the men who were at Lawrence, who much preferred to fight rather than submit passively to insults from this official mob. In the estimation of the world, these men showed more true courage and heroism than even when Titus' fort was afterwards taken within sight of the Federal army. Suppose, for a moment, Sanborn's policy had been adopted—this hero who, although an accomplice with Brown in Harper's Ferry raid, was at a safe distance from harm in Massachusetts when the fight came off, and at a safer distance in Canada when the accomplices were being picked up—suppose an excuse had been given by armed resistance to enter Lawrence, the Administration would have been vindicated in its assumptions that the Free-State men were rebels to Federal authority. And even the burning and pillage of the entire town would have been regarded as the merited punishment of a nest of traitors. That success, if possible for the moment, would have lasted only till Colonel Sumner could have reached Lawrence with his soldiers, all men of ordinary intelligence must know. In such a case, instead of the approbation and sympathy of all good people everywhere, the Free-State men and cause would have been abandoned by all its friends at home and abroad, and from that moment, hanging of traitors—real traitors—and the expulsion of all

17

remnants of anti-slavery would have been the congenial
work of the Atchisons, Stringfellows, and their allies of the
Slave-State party.   Besides, in no other way could the
infamy of the territorial usurpation be so conclusively demonstrated as by the official destruction of printing presses
and hotels as nuisances, without trial or hearing of any kind.

As in the Wakarusa war, so in this case, the pro-slavery
men were divided in counsel.   Some were conservative and
some ultra.   Governor Shannon and the President were
opposed to the Marshal's employment of civilians, but the
Marshal was controlled by the fire-eaters.   Governor Reeder,
in hiding at Kansas City during this invasion, in his diary
under date of May 15th, six days before the serving of the
writs, refers to this division of sentiment as follows:

" He [Colonel Coates] says, also, that Donelson, the Marshal, has issued a proclamation calling for a force, and reciting generally that he
has writs against sundry citizens of Lawrence.   He says also, on the
authority of Colonel Sumner, that Shannon had become alarmed, but
was powerless, and no better than a prisoner in the hands of those around
him; that he had essayed to take into his own hands the collection of a
posse, but the Marshal would not allow it; that he had insisted that
Donelson should not accept the service of any Missourians, to which a
reluctant assent was given, but that this was a mere evasion, and that
there were camps of Missourians now in the Territory who called themselves Georgians, as was learned from a man by the name of Wise, who
was in the camp.   There have come to the Territory this spring some
three or four hundred young men, including Buford's party, who evidently came here to fight, and whose leaders probably understood the
whole programme before they left home.

" Under cover of these men and assuming their name and character,
the citizens of Missouri will doubtless come over.   Mr. Coates also
says, on authority of Colonel Sumner, that Shannon has actually fled
the country, under pretense of business, to avoid the storm which he
cannot control and dare not face.   Also, that our friends at Lawrence
sent a messenger (Captain Walker) to Shannon, with a letter requesting him to order out the troops for the defense of the town; that Walker
had difficulty to get into town, and was compelled to conceal himself,
and send in another person; that he was recognized and fired at, but
not hit.   Shannon's reply was written while surrounded by the ultra
men about him, and was evasive and unsatisfactory.   Also, that the at-

tack was fixed for to-morrow evening.   This is most alarming news, and I tremble for our people."

Governor Shannon, in his letter to the President, under date of June 17th, said: "I have already stated my opinion as to the utter impossibility of preserving order or preventing civil war by means of the militia of the Territory.   Their use would lead to a contrary result."

The position and solicitude of the President may be seen by reference to his dispatches to Governor Shannon as follows:

"EXECUTIVE OFFICE, May 23, 1856.

"Has the United States Marshal proceeded to Lawrence to execute civil process?   Has military force been found necessary to maintain civil government in Kansas?   If so, have you relied solely upon troops under the command of Colonels Sumner and Cooke?   If otherwise, state the reasons.   The laws must be executed; but military force should not be employed until after the Marshal has met with actual resistance in the fulfillment of his duty.

"FRANKLIN PIERCE.

"*Wilson Shannon, Governor of Kansas, Lecompton, Kansas Territory.*"

"EXECUTIVE OFFICE, May 23, 1856.

"Since my telegraph of this morning was sent, the Secretary of War has laid before me Colonel Sumner's letter to you of the 12th instant. His suggestion strikes me as wise and prudent.   I hope that before this reaches you decisive measures will have been taken to have the process in the hands of the Marshal quietly executed.   My knowledge of facts is imperfect; but with the force of Colonel Sumner at hand, I perceive no occasion for the posse, armed or unarmed, which the Marshal is said to have assembled at Lecompton.   The instructions issued to yourself and Colonel Sumner during your last visit to this city must be efficiently executed.   Sufficient power was committed to you, and you must use it.

"Obedience to the laws and consequent security to the citizens of Kansas are the primary objects.

"You must repress lawless violence in whatever form it may manifest itself.   "FRANKLIN PIERCE."

"EXECUTIVE OFFICE, June 6, 1856.

"Were my dispatches of May 23d received by yourself or Colonel Sumner?   If they were, why have they not been acknowledged?   Confused and contradictory accounts continue to reach me of scenes of dis-

order and violence in Kansas.   If the civil authorities, sustained by the
military force under the command of Colonels Sumner and Cooke placed
at your disposal, are not sufficient to maintain order and afford protection to peaceable and law-abiding citizens, you should have advised me at
once.   I hardly need repeat the instructions so often given.   Maintain
the laws firmly and impartially, and take care that no good citizen has
just ground to complain of the want of protection.

                                                    "FRANKLIN PIERCE.
"*Hon. Wilson Shannon (care of Colonel Sumner), Fort Leavenworth*
    Kansas Territory."

Governor Shannon, in his letter to the President, May
31st, says: "Had the Marshal called on me for a posse, I
should have felt myself bound to furnish him with one composed entirely of United States troops.   Knowing this to be
the case, and feeling satisfied that, with a posse composed of
such troops, the parties to be arrested would evade the
service of process, he determined, by virtue of the legal
powers vested in him as Marshal, to summon his own posse
from the citizens of the Territory."

It will be seen that Governor Shannon has more than
once unwittingly conceded that the Free-State policy was more
than a match for the Government.   As before quoted, in his
letter to Secretary of State Marcy, dated April 27, 1856, he
says: "It will be obvious to the President that, if every
officer of the Government charged with the execution of
legal process, issued under, and to enforce the territorial
laws, is compelled to call on a military posse of United
States troops to aid in executing the law, the territorial
government will be practically nullified."

Take this in connection with this statement to the President on June 17, 1856: "I have already stated my opinion
as to the utter impossibility of preserving order or preventing civil war by means of the militia of the Territory.   Their
use would lead to a contrary result."   And this from his
letter to the President dated December 11, 1855, immediately after the Wakarusa war: "The militia or volunteer
corps cannot be relied on to preserve the peace in these civil

party contests, or where partisans are concerned.   A call on the militia will generally bring in conflict the two parties. I am satisfied that the only forces that can be used in this Territory in enforcing the laws, or preserving the peace, are those of the United States "; and yet, should this course be adopted, according to his letter of April 27, 1856, " the territorial Government will be practically nullified."

Now, the Free-State men had been able to study this all out in advance, and before they sent for the first installment of Sharp's rifles.   Several of them had been through the same process in California, and knew what "thwarting, baffling, and circumventing " could accomplish.   But it took the Administration more than a year, till September, 1856, to learn by bitter experience what the Free-State men studied out soon after the 30th of March, 1855.

About the time that Robinson started East, steps were taken to arrest Governor Reeder, who was in attendance upon the Congressional Committee.   He plead his privilege from arrest as Member of Congress, but it was ineffectual. He then refused to be arrested, and told the Deputy Marshal that if he attempted it, he would do so at his peril. But Governor Reeder's friends, seeing that his presence would precipitate a conflict with Federal authority, or result in his being held a prisoner, advised that he should visit the States and Washington.   He reached Kansas City, where he remained concealed for about two weeks, when he escaped, and arrived in Illinois.

Mrs. Robinson, after the arrest at Lexington, was permitted to go on her journey.   She met Governor Chase, of Columbus ; Amos A. Lawrence, of Boston ; H. B. Claflin, of New York, and such men as Lovejoy, Arnold, Browning, Medill, Ray, Lincoln, and Brown, of Illinois.   To these people she explained the situation in Kansas.   Mr. Lawrence at once set about procuring petitions, for calling together Northern Legislatures, and drew up a remonstrance to the President, to be signed by Northern governors.   Mrs.

R. attended the State convention at Bloomington, Illinois, at which Governor Reeder appeared, fresh from his concealment at Kansas City. J. S. Emery was also at this convention. The appearance of Reeder created the wildest enthusiasm. In a word, the invasion of Lawrence on the 21st of May by Federal authority, with the official destruction of the best hotel west of St. Louis and two printing offices, fired the whole North. It did more to arouse the people than Robinson, had he been permitted to go on his mission, could have done in a year. It was seized upon by the Republican party as its special campaign thunder, and it reverberated all along the political skies from Maine to California. A convention was held at Buffalo, which organized a National Relief Committee, with headquarters at Chicago, and Thaddeus Hyatt, of New York, was made President. This convention appointed Eli Thayer a committee of one to organize the entire North in the interest of free Kansas. Also, other large organizations, besides the National, were effected, among them the Massachusetts, of which George L. Stearns was chairman, and F. B. Sanborn became secretary. Many of the Kansas settlers took the field in the States, among others Lane, Emery, Conway, Schuyler, Holliday, Roberts, Smith, Wood, and others. Thus the Slave-State party did immeasurably more for their opponents than their opponents could have done for themselves. Men and money from this time were raised with the greatest ease for the purpose of rebuking this tyranny, and making sure a free State in Kansas. Even the Slave-State men were far from jubilant over their conduct. The memorial to the President, as above quoted, makes this honorable mention:

"There are also some facts of another character which we wish to record. We believe that many of the captains of the invading companies exerted themselves to the utmost for the protection of life and property. Some of them protested against these enormous outrages, and endeavored to dissuade Samuel J. Jones from their perpetration. Many used personal effort to remove such property as was possible from the Eldridge House before its destruction. Among these stood prominently Colonel Zadock Jackson, of Georgia, who did not scruple, either in Lawrence or his own camp, to denounce the outrages in terms such as they deserved. Colonel Buford, of Alabama, also disclaimed having come to Kansas to destroy property, and condemned the course which had been taken. The prosecuting attorney of Douglas County, the legal advisor of the Sheriff, used his influence in vain to prevent the destruction of property."

Thus, not only was their pretended victory a most disastrous defeat before the country, but it served to alienate many of their allies, men who were supposed to be unscrupulous in the work of establishing slavery in Kansas.

It was under such circumstances that the Marshal's posse, after the execution of pretended writs by the destruction of innocent property departed, singly or in squads, to their homes in Missouri. So far, the record of the Free-State men was without a blot or blemish of any kind, and was universally applauded. Up to this point no Federal official had been resisted or threatened, and no crime had been committed. Their friends on the stump, in the press, or elsewhere, had no mistakes to explain, and no apologies to make. Even the pro-slavery party, including the Administration, could point to no crimes except the crime of entertaining opinions and expressing them. The battle, to all appearances, was fought to the finish, and won by the Free-State party. Governor Shannon was satisfied, in the fall before, that no militia could ever be used in Kansas, and he never would use it. Also, he had admitted that the policy of the Free-State men, of compelling the use of the army to enforce peace warrants, "practically nullified" the territorial Government; and now the Marshal had had an experience he would not forget, or, if he should forget it, the President would most surely remind him of it. What more could be done by the Slave State men? Nothing whatever that could seriously annoy their antagonists. They could not enter upon a course of lawlessness, for the Administration was responsible for the peace of the Territory, and could

not afford to have its own adherents bring discredit upon
the Government.   Fortunately for the Slave-State party,
there was one man among the Free-State men as sorely disappointed at the result as they were.   This was John Brown.
He had come to Kansas " not to settle " or " speculate "—or
from idle curiosity ; but for one stern, solitary purpose—to
have a shot at the South."   (Redpath, in " Roving Editor.")
But that "shot at the South " was not the making of a free
State in Kansas, according to the plan of the Free-State
party, but the engaging the country in a civil war.   This is
abundantly shown by his biographer, James Redpath.
When he arrived at Lawrence, near the close of the Wakarusa war, he was given the command of a company, and
Redpath, on page 86 of his " Life of Captain John Brown,"
quotes an eye-witness as saying : " From that moment he
commenced fomenting difficulties in camp, disregarding the
command of superior officers, and trying to induce the men
to go down to Franklin, and make an attack upon the pro-
slavery forces encamped there.   The Committee of Public
Safety were called upon several times to head off his wild
adventure, as the people of Lawrence had planted themselves on the law, claiming that they had not been guilty
of its infraction, and that no armed body of men should
enter the town for any purpose whatever, and that they
would not go out of town to attack any such body.   Peace
was established, and Old Brown retired in disgust."

CHAPTER XI.

THIS decisive victory over the Slave-State party was achieved May 21, 1856, and to all appearance it was final, as neither the Governor's militia nor Marshal's posse would ever be called upon again, and the United States soldiers were perfectly harmless in their attempts to foist upon the people the territorial usurpation. Nothing remained but to fill up the Territory with *bona fide* settlers, and to take possession of the Government at the election of the Legislature, when the day should arrive.

But now came a new conflict, inaugurated by John Brown. As his friends and foes alike have conceded that the testimony of James Townsley is trustworthy, extracts from it are here given, in order to show the nature of the war to be waged henceforth. This testimony was taken by John Hutchings, an able lawyer of Lawrence, and some of it is as follows:

"I joined the Potawatomie rifle company at its re-organization in May, 1856, at which time John Brown, Jr., was elected captain. On the 21st of the same month information was received that the Georgians were marching on Lawrence, threatening its destruction. The company was immediately called together, and about four o'clock P.M. we started on a forced march to aid in its defense. About two miles south of Middle Creek we were joined by the Osawatomie company under Captain Dayton, and proceeded to Mount Vernon, where we waited about two hours, until the moon rose. We then marched all night, camping the next morning, the 22d, for breakfast, near Ottawa Jones's. Before we arrived at this point news had been received that Lawrence had been destroyed, and a question was raised whether we should return or go on. During the forenoon, however, we proceeded up Ottawa Creek to within about five miles of Palmyra, and went into camp near the residence of Captain Shore. Here we remained undecided over night. About noon the next day, the 23d, Old John Brown came to me and said he had just received information that trouble was expected on the Potawatomie, and wanted to know if I would take my team and take him and his boys back, so they could keep watch of what was going on. I told him I would do so. The party, consisting of Old John Brown, Watson Brown, Oliver Brown, Henry Thompson (John Brown's son-in-law), and Mr. Winer, were soon ready for the trip, and we started, as near as I can rememreber, about two o'clock P.M. All of the party except Winer, who rode a pony, rode with me in my wagon. When within two or three miles of the Potawatomie Creek, we turned off the main road to the right, drove down to the edge of the timber between two deep ravines, and camped about one mile above Dutch Henry's crossing.

"After my team was fed and the party had taken supper, John Brown told me for the first time what he proposed to do. He said he wanted me to pilot the company up to the forks of the creek, some five or six miles above, into the neighborhood where I lived, and show them where all the pro-slavery men resided; that he proposed to sweep the creek as he came down of all the pro-slavery men living on it. I positively refused to do it. He insisted upon it, but when he found that I would not go, he decided to postpone the expedition until the following night. I then wanted to take my team and go home, but he would not let me do so, and said I should remain with them. We remained in camp that night and all the next day. Some time after dark we were ordered to march.

"We started, the whole company, in a northerly direction, crossing Mosquito Creek above the residence of the Doyles. Soon after crossing the creek some one of the party knocked at the door of a cabin, but received no reply—I have forgotten whose cabin it was, if I knew at the time. The next place we came to was the residence of the Doyles. John Brown, three of his sons, and son-in-law went to the door, leaving Frederick Brown, Winer, and myself a short distance from the house. About this time a large dog attacked us. Frederick Brown struck the dog a blow with his short two-edged sword, after which I dealt him a blow with my sabre, and heard no more of him. The old man Doyle and two sons were called out and marched some distance from the house towards Dutch Henry's, in the road, where a halt was made. Old John Brown drew his revolver and shot the old man Doyle in the forehead, and Brown's two youngest sons immediately fell upon the younger Doyles with their short two-edged swords.

" One of the young Doyles was stricken down in an instant, but the other attempted to escape, and was pursued a short distance by his assailant and cut down. The company then proceeded down Mosquito Creek to the house of Allen Wilkinson. Here the old man Brown, three of his sons, and son-in-law, as at the Doyle residence, went to the door and ordered Wilkinson to come out, leaving Frederick Brown, Winer, and myself standing in the road east of the house. Wilkinson was taken and marched some distance south of his house and slain in the road, with a short sword, by one of the younger Browns. After he was killed his body was dragged out to one side and left.

" We then crossed the Potawatomie and came to the house of Henry Sherman, generally known as Dutch Henry. Here John Brown and the party, excepting Frederick Brown, Winer, and myself, who were left outside a short distance from the door, went into the house and brought out one or two persons, talked with them some, and then took them in again. They afterwards brought out William Sherman, Dutch Henry's brother, marched him down into the Potawatomie Creek, where he was slain with swords by Brown's two youngest sons, and left lying in the creek.

" It was the expressed intention of Brown to execute Dutch Henry also, but he was not found at home. He also hoped to find George Wilson, Probate Judge of Anderson County, there, and intended, if he did, to kill him too. Wilson had been notifying Free-State men to leave the Territory. I had received such a notice from him myself.

  *   *   *   *   *   *   *

" Brown wanted me to pilot the party into the neighborhood where I lived, and point out all the pro-slavery men in it, whom he proposed to put to death. I positively refused to do it, and on account of my refusal I remained in camp all of the night upon which the first attack was to be made, and the next day. I told him I was willing to go with him to Lecompton and attack the leaders, or fight the enemy in open field anywhere, but I did not want to engage in killing these men. That night and the acts then perpetrated are vividly fixed in my memory, and I have thought of them many times since.

  *   *   *   *   *   *   *

" I make this statement at the urgent request of my friends and neighbors, Judge James Hanway and Hon. Johnson Clarke, who have been present during all the time occupied in writing it out, and in whose hearing it has been several times read before signing.

"JAMES TOWNSLEY.

" LANE, KAN., December 6, 1879."

This massacre occurred on the 24th of May, 1856. On the 28th this mode of warfare was continued by the robbery of Morton Bourn of his money, guns, horses, saddles, and store. Mr. Bourn testified, as found in the report of the Congressional Committee, on page 108, as follows:

" I own slaves, and have a crop of corn and wheat growing. Have never taken any active part with the pro-slavery party, only voted the pro-slavery ticket, and was for sustaining the laws. *   *   *   These men said I must leave in a day or two, or they would kill me, or hinted as much—said I would not fare well, or words to that effect. I left for fear of my life and the lives of my family. They said that the war was commenced,that they were going to fight it out, and drive the pro-slavery people out of the Territory, or words to that amount. The men that robbed my house and drove me away from my property were abolitionists, or free-soilers. *   *   *   I believe they hated me so because I am a pro-slavery man, and in favor of the territorial laws, and because I served on the last Grand Jury at Lecompton."

The store of J. M. Bernard was robbed on the 27th of May. Of this robbery, John Miller testifies:

" I was in the store with Mr. Davis. Whilst there a party of thirteen men came to the store on horseback, armed with Sharp's rifles, revolvers, and bowie-knives. They inquired for Mr. Bernard. I told them that he had gone to Westport. One of them said to me, ' You are telling a God damned lie,' and drew up his gun at me. Some of them came into the store, and the rest remained outside. They called for such goods as they wanted, and made Mr. Davis and myself hand them out, and said if we ' didn't hurry' they would shoot us. They had their guns ready. After they had got the goods—they wanted principally blankets and clothing—they packed them upon their horses and went away. Mr. Joab Bernard is a pro-slavery man. [Mr. Miller recognized one of the party as an active Free-State man.] They on the next day came back with a wagon, and took the remainder of the goods in the store, except about one hundred and fifty dollars' worth—including flour, sugar, coffee, bacon, and all kinds of provisions, as well as two fine horses, three saddles, two bridles, and all the money there was in the store."

In the conclusion of his affidavit, Mr. Miller says:

" When they first came, they looked up at the sign, and said they would like to shoot at the name."

•James Redpath, in his " Life of Captain John Brown," page 101, says that Charley Lenhart and John E. Cook,

after the 21st of May, left Lawrence, "to commence reprisals." Also, he says on page 117:

"On the 23d of May, John Brown left the camp of his son, at Osawatomie, with seven or eight men, and from that moment began his
guerrilla warfare in southern Kansas."

The same author fully justifies this midnight assassination
and robbery, and from that time this kind of warfare continued in full force till the 14th of September.

Andreas, in his history, page 131, says:

"The aggressive warfare thus begun was not in accordance with
the plans or purposes of the leaders of the Free-State movement; on
the contrary, it was in direct opposition to their counsel, and had been
persistently decried and successfully restrained up to this time. For
the disorders that ensued, the Free-State organization was in no manner responsible."

Two attempts at justification are made for this mode of
warfare:

First, it was a means of self-defense against like outrages.

Second, it quieted the disturbances in the Territory. The
first and principal witness for the defense theory is James
Redpath. Up to this time he and the other newspaper
correspondents were loyal to the policy of the Free-State
party, but now they, some of them, defended its enemies.
Redpath, in his "Life of Captain John Brown," beginning at page 115, gives this account and defense of this
tragedy:

"I have spoken of the rumors of midnight murder in the Potawatomie region, and stated that Captain Brown was accused by the invaders
of having done the deed. The charge is false. It was first made by
his enemies, who feared him, and desired to drive him out of the district, and subsequently repeated by a recreant Free-State journalist,
who sold himself to the Federal Administration for the paltry bribe of
the public printing.

"The killing of the ruffians of Potawatomie was one of those stern
acts of summary justice with which the history of the West and of

every civil war abounds. Lynch law is one of the early necessities of far-western communities; and the terrors of it form the *only* efficient guarantee of the peaceful citizen from the ruffianism which distinguishes and curses every new Territory. The true story of Potawatomie is briefly told.

" In all that region, ever since the opening of the Territory for settlement, the pro-slavery party had been brutally tyrannical, Free-State men were daily robbed, beaten, and killed; their property was stolen, openly, before their eyes; and yet they did not dare to resist the outrages. One or two families alone were occasionally exempted, by their character for desperate courage, from these daring and unwarrantable assaults. Among them were the sons and son-in-law of Old John Brown; and even they had repeatedly suffered from the conduct of the ruffians, until the arrival of their father in the autumn, with arms. Then, until the months of April and May, a season of peace was allowed them. But when, in fulfilment of the plan of the Missouri secret lodges, the Territory was to be conquered for slavery, it at once became a question of life, death, or immediate banishment to the settlers in southern Kansas how they should act against the invading pro-slavery party and their allies among the squatters. Men who have passed their lives in the quiet of New England's valleys, or in Eastern cities, can never know what it is to be in earnest on what is seemingly a mere question of political right or constitutional interpretation. Hence this chapter may shock them; but it is my duty, nevertheless, to write it.

" The pro-slavery party, in all the region around Potawatomie, renewed their system of aggressions on the Free-State men. John Brown began to stir himself and prepare for the defense of his neighborhood. With his two sons or friends he went out into the prairies where a number of invaders were encamped, and, pretending to survey the country, drove his imaginary lines through the middle of their camp. All the Government officers in Kansas, from the Governor down to the humblest workmen, were at this time, and for long afterwards, ultra pro-slavery men; many of them professed secessionists, who publicly cursed the Union as a burden to the South. John Brown frequently adopted this plan of entering the camp of the invading forces, and not only never was suspected, but was never asked what his political opinions were. Never doubting that he was a Government surveyor, the Southrons never doubted his political orthodoxy.

" The men in this camp freely told him their plans. There was an old man of the name Brown, they said, who had several sons here whom it was necessary to get out of the way, as, if they were driven out or killed, the other settlers would be afraid to offer any further resistance. They told him how Wilkinson, the Doyles, and a Dutchman named Sherman, had recently been in Missouri, and succeeded in securing forces to drive out the Browns, and that it was determined to kill them in the latter part of May. They mentioned several other prominent Free-State men who were to share this fate.

" John Brown left their camp, and at once notified the settlers who had been marked out· for destruction, of the murderous designs of the Missourians. A meeting of the intended victims was held; and it was determined that on the first indication of the massacre, the Doyles—a father and two sons—Wilkinson, and Sherman should be seized, tried by Lynch law, and summarily killed.

" On the 23d of May, John Brown left the camp of his son, at Osawatomie, with seven or eight men, and from that moment began his guerrilla warfare in southern Kansas. He ordered them to the vicinity of his home, to be ready for the Missourians when they came. He himself went in a different direction, for the purpose of obtaining further aid.

" On the night of the 25th of May, the Doyles, Wilkinson, and Sherman were seized, tried, and slain. This act was precipitated by a brutal assault committed during the forenoon on a Free-State man at the store of Sherman, in which the Doyles were the principal and most ruffianly participators. These wretches, on the same day, called at the houses of the Browns; and, both in words and by acts, offered the grossest indignities to a daughter and daughter-in-law of the old man. As they went away, they said, ' Tell your men that if they don't leave right off, we'll come back to-morrow and kill them.' They added, in language too gross for publication, that the women would then suffer still worse indignities.

" What redress could the husbands of these women have received had they asked the protection of the law? They would have been obliged to seek it from Wilkinson, one of these ruffians, who was the magistrate of the Potawatomie District! This instance had hundreds of parallels.

" I do not know whether New England people will be able to vindicate the summary punishment inflicted on these wretches; but I do know that nearly every Free-State man then in Kansas, when he came to know the cause, privately endorsed it as a righteous act, although many of them, ' to save the party,' publicly repudiated and condemned it.

" These facts I derived from two squatters who aided in the execution, and who were not ashamed of the part they took in it. Neither of them was a son of John Brown. They were settlers in the neighborhood.

" John Brown himself subsequently corroborated their statements, without knowing that they had made them, by his account of the affair and denial of any participation in it. ' But, remember,' he added, ' I do not say this to exculpate myself; for, although I took no hand in it,

I would have advised it had I known the circumstances; and I endorsed it as it was.'

"'Time and the honest verdict of posterity,' he said, in his Virginia cell, 'will approve of every act of mine.' I think it will also endorse all the acts that he endorsed; and among them this righteous slaughter of the ruffians at Potawatomie. John Brown did not know that these men were killed until the following day; for, with one of his sons, he was twenty-five miles distant at the time. He was at Middle Creek. This fact can be proved by living witnesses. It is false, also, that the ruffians were cruelly killed. They were tried, made confession, allowed time to pray, and then slain in a second."

R. J. Hinton has said: " Doyle was engaged with others in a fiendish attempt to outrage the persons of Captain Brown's daughter and daughter-in-law, the wife of one of Brown's sons."

A brother of John Brown, in the Cleveland *Plaindealer*, November 29, 1859, says:

" My brother John and his two sons were living in the same neighborhood, and a committee of five from the border ruffian camp called upon him, and said they were instructed to warn him that if the Free-State men were found there the next Thursday night, they would kill every one of them."

Dr. G. W. Brown, in his " Reminiscences of Old John Brown," gives other current reasons or excuses for this massacre. Among them are these: " A band of pro-slavery men went to the house of John, Jr., insulted his wife, burned his cabin, and drove off his cattle."

" John Brown's cabin was burned, his blooded stock were driven off, and the women of his family were grossly insulted. Wilkinson, Sherman, and the Doyles were caught in the act of hanging a Free-State man, and were shot by friends of the injured party."

John Brown is reported as saying, in a speech before the Legislature, at Boston, on the 18th of February, 1857:

" He saw a great deal of Buford's men in Kansas; that they spoke without hesitation before him, because he employed himself as a surveyor; and as nearly all the surveyors were pro-slavery men, they probably thought he was ' sound on the goose.' They told him all their plans; what they intended to do; how they were determined to drive off the Free-State men, and possess themselves of the Territory, and make it a slave State at all hazards, cost what it might.   *   *   *   They did not hesitate to threaten that they would burn, kill, scalp, and drive out the entire Free-State population of the Territory, if it was necessary to do so to accomplish their object."

This is a partial report of the case, as made up by letter-writers and others, and it was the only case for many years, and until disinterested historians gathered their materials. Supposing the statements of Redpath, the correspondent of the *Missouri Democrat*, and others, had given substantially the facts, the writer of this excused the massacre as best he could, as an act of retributive justice for similar outrages already committed against Free-State men. But, unfortunately for the vindication of such an outrage, it was the first of its kind in Kansas, and a professed Free-State man commenced this war of midnight assassination. It is now evident, since the testimony of Townsley, admitted by the friends of Brown to be substantially correct, that this blow was not struck to punish criminals, or protect Free-State men, or to aid the cause of a free State in Kansas, but to involve the sections, North and South, in war, in accordance with Redpath's purpose, as given in his " Roving Editor," page 300, as follows:

" I believed that a civil war between the North and South would ultimate in insurrection, and that the Kansas troubles would probably create a military conflict of the sections. Hence I left the South, and went to Kansas; and endeavored, personally and by my pen, to precipitate a revolution. That we failed—for I was not alone in this desire—was owing to the influence of prominent Republican statesmen, whose unfortunately conservative character of counsel—which it was impossible openly to resist—effectually baffled all our hopes: hopes which Democratic action was auspiciously promoting."

The testimony of Townsley would seem to be conclusive on this point. He says, as already quoted:

18

"He [Brown] said he wanted me to pilot the company up to the forks of the creek, some five or six miles above, into the neighborhood where I lived, and show them where all the pro-slavery men resided; that he proposed to sweep the creek as he came down of all the pro-slavery men living on it."

Again he says:

"Brown wanted me to pilot the party into the neighborhood where I lived, and point out all the pro-slavery men in it, whom he proposed to put to death. I positively refused to do it, and on account of my refusal I remained in camp all of the night when the first attack was to be made, and the next day."

From this testimony it appears that John Brown was not hunting for criminals who had insulted his family, driven off his stock, killed his son or any one else, but simply for pro-slavery men, innocent or guilty, it mattered not which. It has been seen that Brown could tell the Massachusetts Legislature only that the pro-slavery men had used "threats" of driving off Free-State men. He didn't pretend that any one had been driven off or molested in any manner. When it is known that such threats were as plenty as blue-berries in June, on both sides, all over the Territory, and were regarded as of no more importance than the idle wind, this indictment will hardly justify midnight assassination of all pro-slavery men, whether making threats or not. Governor George A. Crawford, in a letter to Eli Thayer dated August 4, 1879, says that Brown "gave as a reason" (for the slaughter) that the men were carriers of news to the Missourians, that they kept a "grape-vine telegraph" with Missourians, and were endangering the settlements by bringing in invaders.

And John Brown, Jr., in the Cleveland *Plaindealer*, says: "The Doyles, Wilkinson, and Sherman were furnishing places of rendezvous and active aid to armed men who had sworn to kill us and others." Here are more threats. Had all men been killed in Kansas who indulged in such threats, there would have been none left to bury the dead.

John Brown, Jr., and H. H. Williams, both prominent men at or near Osawatomie, were brought to the camp of the treason prisoners soon after this massacre, and neither gave information of any wrong-doing on the part of the men killed. And Mrs. Brown, wife of John, Jr., associated intimately with Mrs. Robinson, Mrs. Jenkins, and others in camp, but never referred to any outrage or threatened violence upon her person. But a report of a meeting of men of both parties has been discovered and published, which ought to be conclusive. It is referred to in Andrea's history, on page 132, as follows:

"At a meeting of the citizens of Potawatomie Creek, without distinction of parties, held at the branch between Messrs. Potter and Partridges, on the 27th day of May, 1856 (three days after the killing), C. H. Rice was chosen chairman and H. H. Williams secretary. The chairman then stated the object of the meeting, and a committee was appointed to take the subject under consideration. The committee consisted of R. Golding, R. Gilpatrick, N. C. Dow, S. V. Vanderman, A. Castele, and John Blunt. After consultation, the committee reported the following preamble and resolutions, which were unanimously adopted, and a copy of them ordered to be printed.

"'Whereas, an outrage of the darkest and foulest nature has been committed in our midst by some midnight assassins unknown, who have taken five of our citizens at the hour of midnight from their homes and families, and murdered and mangled them in an awful manner; to prevent a repetition of these deeds, we deem it necessary to adopt some measures for our mutual protection and to aid and assist in bringing these desperadoes to justice. Under these circumstances, we propose to act up to the following resolutions:

"'*Resolved*, That we will from this time lay aside all sectional and political feelings and act together as men of reason and common sense, determined to oppose all men who are so ultra in their views as to denounce men of opposite opinions.

"'*Resolved*, That we will repudiate and discountenance all organized bands of men who leave their homes for the avowed purpose of exciting others to acts of violence, believing it to be the duty of all good-disposed citizens to stay at home during these exciting times and protect, and, if possible, restore the peace and harmony of the neighborhood; furthermore, we will discountenance all armed bodies of men who may come amongst us from any other part of the Territory or from the States, unless said parties shall come under the authority of the United States.

" ' *Resolved*, That we pledge ourselves, individually and collectively, to prevent a recurrence of a similar tragedy, and to ferret out and hand over to the criminal authorities the perpetrators for punishment.

" ' H. H. WILLIAMS, Secretary,
" ' C. H. PRICE, President,
" ' R. GOLDING, Chairman,
" ' R. GILPATRICK,
" ' N. C. DOW,   } Committee.' "
" ' S. V. VANDERMAN,
" ' A. CASTELE,
" ' JOHN BLUNT,

Among the active men of this meeting are some of the most radical Free-State men of the Territory, and most certainly had there been any palliation or excuse for this killing, it would have been given.*

Did this slaughter of five men and boys quiet the disturbance in the Territory? As has been seen, the official disturbances had run their course, and the members of the last Marshal's posse had retired to their homes in Missouri or elsewhere, with but few exceptions. Up to this time no Free-State men had been killed south of Douglas County, notwithstanding the statement to the contrary of Redpath and others, and no such massacre as that on the Potawatomie had ever occurred anywhere within the Territory or without. Its equal in atrocity must be sought for in the dark ages, as it cannot be found in modern times. No violence had been offered in southern Kansas of a serious character except at Stanton, in Miami County. This is thus recorded in Andrea's history, page 895:

"At the meeting of April 16, 1856, at which resolutions were adopted against the payment of taxes, and at which John Brown made an abolition speech, the Rev. Mr. White several times offensively interrupted the speaker. As the reverend gentleman was generally exceedingly obnoxious to the Free-State men, a few nights after the above-mentioned meeting occurred, a party of twelve of them attacked his house, opening fire upon it. The firing was vigorously replied to by those inside. The attacking party soon retired, taking White's horses with them. On

* See Appendix A.

the next day White moved to Missouri, settling permanently in Bates County."

As will be seen, this same Rev. Martin White, after this massacre, had the satisfaction of killing Frederick Brown, just before the battle of Osawatomie.

Here is the only serious disturbance with deadly weapons in southern Kansas so far as known, and that happened to be on the wrong side to be pleaded as an excuse for the midnight slaughter by John Brown, May 24th, of the same year. If no unusual troubles can be found existing before May 24th in southern Kansas, did any occur after that date, and if so, were they "quieted" or caused and aggravated by John Brown's new warfare? It is claimed by Redpath and others that Brown's family were disturbed by pro-slavery men before this massacre. Although this claim is not supported by evidence, how much better was their condition afterwards? G. W. Brown, in his "Reminiscences of Old John Brown," page 30, gives this account of the effect of the massacre on John Brown, Jr.:

"John Brown, Jr., and H. H. Williams were brought into the camp, near Lecompton, about the 16th of June, 1856, and were held as prisoners with us. They were indicted on the 27th of May, at Paola, then Lykins County, charged with 'conspiracy to resist the collection of taxes.' John was also suspected of responsibility for the Potawatomie murders, but I am glad to say there was no truth whatever in this allegation. He became an occupant of my tent, and remained with me some time after he was brought into camp. He was partly insane: his mind seemed continually running on the Potawatomie massacre, and he appeared to suppose he was under arrest for that offense. During the entire period he was with us—nearly three months—whenever that event was mentioned in his hearing his eyes would flash and sparkle like a mad man's. He would exhibit the wildest excitement, and express himself in the severest terms at the enormity of the outrage. On several occasions I attempted to allay his irritation by offering an apology for it. He replied invariably: 'There can be no apology for such a transaction. Every feature of it was too barbarous to admit of an apology.' And then I would divert his mind as speedily as possible, engage his thoughts on some other subject, when he would gradually regain his composure.

" In his ravings about these murders on the Potawatomie, John, Jr., told me of the incidents lying between his disbanding his command when the news reached him, on the morning after its committal, until his arrest. He said his best friends in Osawatomie turned the ' cold shoulder ' on him when he arrived in the town; a public meeting of Free-State men was soon held, which repudiated it, and denounced the actors; he called on his wife and child, and made his way to the bottom lands, where he secreted himself behind logs and trees. He forded the river several times to avoid exposure. A severe storm of rain and lightning came on, and he thought, in the flashes, he could see his pursuers. He said he suffered for food; but his wife occasionally found and relieved him. Finally, at the suggestion of his friends, he voluntarily surrendered himself to the civil authorities, and was taken in charge by Federal troops. He was removed to Paola; thence to Tecumseh, where he had a hearing before United States Commissioner Hoagland, and was sent to camp for safe-keeping. He represented that he was bound with ropes and chains, and was compelled to ' trot along,' thus bound, between two horsemen, for forty miles, in a hot June sun."

The effect upon old Brown himself may be learned from the Springfield, Mass., *Republican*. It says:

" In a letter written to his wife and children at North Elba in June, 1856, Brown gave the only written account of the expedition which has been received from him. Portions of this letter have been published, but not the whole. In it he says: ' On the second day and evening after we left John's men—which was Saturday, May 22, 1856—we encountered quite a number of pro-slavery men, and took quite a number prisoners. Our prisoners we let go, but we kept some four or five horses. We were immediately after this accused of murdering five men at Potawatomie, and great efforts have since been made by the Missourians and ruffian allies to capture us. John's company soon afterward disbanded, and also the Osawatomie men.'

" In the original letter, which was written in pencil, something has been erased after this, and a note on the margin, in Brown's handwriting, adds: ' There are but very few who wish real facts about these matters to go out.' Apparently Brown himself is willing that the real facts should be known, but, for the sake of others, does not state them. Towards the end of the letter, after describing the fight at Black Jack, the burning of his son's house at Brown's Station, on Middle Creek, ten miles west of Osawatomie, and other ' trying events,' Brown says:

" ' Since then we have, like David of old, had our dwellings with the serpents of the rocks and wild beasts of the wilderness, being obliged to hide away from our enemies. We are not disheartened, though nearly destitute of food, clothing, and money. God, who has not given us over to the will of our enemies, but has, moreóver, delivered them into our hands, will, we humbly trust, still keep and deliver us. We feel assured that He who sees not as men see does not lay the guilt of innocent blood to our charge.' "

It is very remarkable that this man, who, according to F. B. Sanborn and others, put an end forever to all difficulties in Kansas by this " one stroke," should himself become an outlaw, and have to dwell " with the serpents of the rocks and wild beasts of the wilderness."   If the pro-slavery men had been all driven from the Territory, and profound peace reigned, as some of his eulogists claim, who was there to trouble either him, the " Liberator," or his son ?

As has been stated, Deitzler, G. W. Brown, Jenkins, and Smith were arrested for treason on or about the 21st of May, and taken to Lecompton by the Marshal.   G. W. Brown, in his " Reminiscences," page 12, gives the effect of the news of this massacre, as follows :

" On Sunday, late in the afternoon of the 25th of May, '56, information was given to the treason prisoners, at Lecompton, of whom the writer had the honor of being one, that a terrible massacre of pro-slavery men had been perpetrated on Potawatomie Creek ; that the news had reached the Kickapoo Rangers, Atchison Tigers, and such other pro-slavery organizations as were still about Lecompton after their successful raid of the 21st on Lawrence. The excitement was reported very high among them.

" On the evening of the 25th, Marshal Donelson entered the building in person, and said that a party were organizing among the Rangers, Tigers, etc., to take the prisoners and hang them in retaliation for these murders. He said he had learned that we were all Odd Fellows or Masons ; that he had so reported ; and besides enlisting all the territorial officers, including the Governor, Judges, etc., and such members of the Order as he could find in Lecompton, he had found some in the several companies, and with these he hoped to be able to save us ; that they should stand guard through the night, and if an attack was made he should place arms in our hands, that we might aid in our own defense.

" The guard was kept up for the night. The next day the Marshal's ' posse ' were again discharged, and left Lecompton ; but Donelson himself remained with us in the room for the night, for our protection against contingencies, as he asserted."

Robinson arrived at Westport, Missouri, as has been stated, on the 20th of May, and there remained until the service of the writs at Lawrence on the 21st, when he was taken to Lecompton by way of Leavenworth. He was at Leavenworth when the news of the killing was received.

A Westport paper had published an account of the killing of "eight pro-slavery men" on the Potawatomie, whose bodies were brutally mutilated, and this was republished in the Leavenworth *Herald*. The excitement in the town was intense. A public meeting was held, and steps taken to drive all Free-State men and women from Leavenworth. G. W. Brown, in his book, says, on page 23, as follows:

"Governor Robinson was taken by a mob at Lexington, Missouri, while descending the Missouri in company with his wife. He was detained there for a few days ; thence taken by way of Westport, to Franklin, within four miles of Lawrence; thence back to Kansas City, and up the Missouri to Leavenworth, where he arrived on the eve of these murders on the Potawatomie. The news of the massacre caused the most intense excitement. It was all that active pro-slavery men, who were warm personal friends of the Governor, some of whom were under lasting obligations to him for favors rendered in California and on his way thither, could do to save him from violent death. Indeed, the people were wrought up to such a furious frenzy that his death was expected at any moment. An eye-witness of the scene told me that the cooler and better class of the citizens, thinking they were powerless to save him, wept like children as one by one they took him by the hand and bade him farewell.

"The Congressional Investigating Committee were in session at Leavenworth. They could not proceed with business because of the excitement, hence removed to Kansas City, where they also found it impossible, with personal safety, to continue their investigations, and left for Washington, one of the members remaining long enough to obtain affidavits detailing the incidents of this awful tragedy, portions of which I have copied. In his minority report to Congress, he said of these murders: 'In savage barbarity and demoniac cruelty they have scarcely an equal in the history of civilized man.' The majority of the Committee were compelled to stultify themselves, and throw out important evidence they had already taken, in order to suppress the loathsome details of the butchery.

" A lady resident of Leavenworth, at the time the news of the tragedy reached the city, told me, on her way up the Missouri in the following spring, returning for the first time after the occurrence to Kansas, of its effects on the Free-State population there. She said a public meeting of pro-slavery men was immediately called, when the account of the Potawatomie massacre was narrated to the already crazed pro-slavery mob. The most violent denunciatory and threatening speeches were made. Resolutions were passed of a fiery character, setting forth that the first blood had been shed by the Free-State men ; that the midnight assassins were not satisfied with simply murdering their victims, but that they had mutilated them in a shameful manner. They declared that it was impossible for the abolitionists and the pro-slavery settlers to live together in Kansas, and that the former must leave. She said a body of armed men marched through the streets, visiting each dwelling, and ordered every Free-State man, woman, and child to go at once to the levee. They would not allow her even to close her house ; but with her chidren she was marched to the river, where she found hundreds of others. All were forced upon a steamer lying at the levee, including her husband, whom she found there. The Captain was ordered to take these involuntary passengers to Alton, and there leave them. She re mained in that city until the spring of 1857, when she returned with her husband, and again settled in the Territory."

Phillips, in his " Conquest of Kansas," page 318, says :

" On the morning of the 28th of May [four days after the murders, as the reader will observe], the office of the Leavenworth *Herald* issued a reprint of a violent ' war ' extra of the Westport paper, the design of which was to excite the border men to acts of violence against the Free-State settlers of Kansas. In the forenoon of that day a pro-slavery meeting was held, at which Stringfellow and General Richardson were prominent actors. At this meeting it was decreed that all persons who had taken an active part as Free-State men must leave the Territory."

When Robinson arrived at Leavenworth, he was placed in charge of Captain William Martin, of the Kickapoo Rangers, and three assistants. On the day of the excitement, Captain Martin was called to attend private meetings of the pro-slavery men, reporting occasionally to his prisoner the determination relative to himself. He said the pro-slavery men wanted him to surrender his prisoner that night, and when he declined, they wanted him to lock him in a room and leave him without a guard. He said he got mad and told them that when a prisoner was placed in his charge by the United States Government, he would protect that prisoner while his own life should last. Martin had served one or more enlistments in the United States army, and had a sense of honor which all civilians did not possess. Being Captain of the Kickapoo Rangers, he had acquired a bad reputation, but it was not wholly deserved. According to testimony before the Congressional Committee, he did what he could to save the life of R. P. Brown, killed at Easton, and surely no man could have acted more honorably than he did while he held the writer as prisoner. It is doubtful if there was another pro-slavery man who would or could have saved him from the wrath of the excited mob.

In the afternoon, the keeper announced a caller, who was shown into the parlor of the Shawnee House, where the prisoner was guarded. This caller seemed much affected, and immediately left the room without speaking. He, however, soon returned, and asked the prisoner if he remembered him? On being answered in the negative, he said, "Do you remember attending a young physician attacked with cholera at Kansas City the night before you started overland for California in 1849?" On being answered in the affirmative, he said, "Well, I am that physician, and you saved my life, and I have been trying all day to save yours, but have so far failed. They have determined to kill you to-night, and I can't prevent it." In saying this, he shed tears like a child. Robinson tried to console him in his distress, saying it might result better than he feared; at any rate, all had to die once, and it was not very material as to the time. This physician's name is Dr. Ridge, of Kansas City, now a millionaire and influential citizen. Although then pro-slavery, he is and was a gentleman with a large and generous heart.

However, the officials did not agree to the programme of the meeting, and Judge Lecompte and Marshal Donelson slept by the door of the prisoner's room, while General Richardson occupied his bed. Early the next morning, before the excited people were on the street, a company of United States dragoons from Fort Leavenworth appeared with an empty saddle, which was soon filled by the prisoner, when he was taken to Lecompton to join the other "traitors" on the prairie, under charge of United States troops.

As another evidence of the "quieting" effect of John Brown's warfare, inaugurated on the Potawatomie, a few extracts are given from Mrs. Robinson's "Kansas." On returning from the East, about the first of June, she was compelled to remain several days at Kansas City on account of the disturbances in the Territory. She reports as follows, beginning on page 273:

"I arrived at Kansas City on the night of June 3d, at twelve o'clock, after my Eastern flying trip, and in hopes soon to join my husband. * * * The last day or two of the trip on the Missouri River rumors of war became more frequent. Inflammatory extras were thrown upon the boats at different landings. People at Lexington, and other points along the river, were much excited and preparing for a new invasion. The extras stated the murder of eight pro-slavery men, by the abolitionists, and the cruel mutilation of their bodies; the death of the United States Marshal, of H. C. Pate, and J. McGee. Deeds of blood and violence, of which they were hourly guilty, were charged upon the Free-State men. The following is a sample of the incendiary extras which flew through the border counties: 'Murder is the watchword and midnight deed of a scattered and scouting band of abolitionists, who had courage only to fly from the face of the wronged and insulted people, when met at their own solicitation. Men, peaceable and quiet, cannot travel on the public roads of Kansas, without being caught, searched, imprisoned, and their lives, perhaps, taken. No Southerner dare venture alone and unarmed on her roads!' Such were the false statements made to arouse the passions of the border men.

*   *   *   *   *   *   *

"The threats of destroying this hotel were still frequent, and nightly the danger of attack was imminent. The Mayor of the city had kept out a guard one or two nights. But he had declined doing this longer, and, a meeting of the citizens being called, it was decided to ask the 'Eldridges' to sell the hotel, to save it from the fury of the South Carolinians and border men; they expressed to them at the same time their regret that such was the excitement against it.

"Again and again the mob had assembled, and with groans, whose hideousness no one can appreciate who was not forced to listen, and with yells, declared the house should come down. The 'Eldridges' proposed their terms, which were accepted, and, on the morning of the tenth, the hotel passed into the keeping of two pro-slavery men. * * * Robberies and murders were repeated every day in the early part of June. Every evening's intelligence was of some fresh outrage. * * *

"A Mr. Cantrell, then recently from Missouri, but a Free-State man, was taken prisoner on the evening of the 5th of June by one of General Whitfield's scouting parties. On the next day he was carried down the Santa Fé road. At Cedar Creek he was taken out into a ravine by two men. Then there was a shot;—then a cry, 'O, God, I am shot!—I am murdered!' Then another shot, and a long piercing scream;—another shot, and all was still!

"A Mr. Bailey narrowly escaped a violent death, and through many sufferings at last reached his friends. He had started from his home to get a load of provisions for himself and his neighbors. When near Bull Creek, Coleman, who had twenty men encamped close by, came and ordered him to stop over night. Among these twenty men were Buckley and Hargous, his accomplices in the murder of Dow. In the morning his horses were missing, their halters having been cut. The men expressed sympathy for his loss, and told him the horses could be found in the camp at Cedar Creek, and they proposed to go with him to find them. Before reaching Cedar Creek they met a company of two hundred men. A consultation was held with them, and Coleman said, 'There may be treachery used.'

"Soon after the company passed on, three men took Mr. Bailey into the prairie about one hundred yards from the road, and demanded his money; without hesitation or one word of objection he gave them forty-five dollars, all he had. One of the men raised his gun as though he would fire. Mr. Bailey said, 'If you mean to kill me, you will kill a better man than yourself;' to which the ruffian, lowering his gun, replied, 'I wish you to take off those pantaloons; perhaps they will get bloody.' But Mr. Bailey said, 'They are mine as long as I live.'

"This tool of the Administration, armed with a United States musket, again raised his gun and fired. The ball struck Mr. Bailey in the side, glancing along the ribs, and lodged in the back. Mr. Bailey fell, and was struck at again and again with the musket. Then two of the men disappeared, and left this more than demon to finish the work of killing a peaceable man. He jumped on the body of the prostrate man, stamping on his face and head. But as Mr. Bailey caught hold of the musket, and was able to hold on upon it, the murderer ran after the others, calling upon them to return. They, however, were too far away. After lying in the grass three hours, Mr. Bailey attempted to find his way home. In doing so, he passed near their camp the next morning at daybreak, and for a while lay hid in the grass, to learn their movements. While there, he heard a cry, ' Are you going to hang me? ' and no reply, save the ringing of a bell. In about five minutes, he heard a shot, then a whistle, and six other shots at intervals of five minutes. He lay in the woods all day, and at night crawled along about two miles ; was hid near the Wakarusa all the next day ; saw a wagon stopped by five men ; heard angry words, and a shot fired. In the night, worn down by his sufferings from the wound and bruises, having had nothing to drink but stagnant water, he reached the house of Dr. Still, at Blue Mound.

"A young man, by the name of Hill, was going to Missouri, also for provisions, and as night came, he asked two men on the road where he could find water for his horses. They said they would show him, if he would go with them. When he had gone with them to the ravine, where they said he would find water, they searched him, took whatever he had of money, and threatened to kill him. He told them he had a mother, and young brothers and sister dependent on him ; that day after day, as she looked out for his coming, and night only brought a renewal of the sad suspense as to his fate, in sorrow she would go to the grave ; but there was no pity in their hearts, no mercy. They tied the young man's arms behind him, and, bending his feet backwards, tied them also to his arms ; then put a stick an inch and a half wide in his mouth, prying it open, and tied the string back of his head. Then, more barbarous than the New Zealanders, they cut places in his hat, and tied that also over his face, and laid him face downwards on the stones. They went away, leaving him to die.

"After a time they came back ; and, as one placed his pistol directly over his eye, he feeling its pressure through the hat, the other said, ' Don't shoot him ; he will not go any further on his journey to-night.' They left again to report at the camp, probably, another victim to the vile tools of slavery propagandism.

" When this young man found himself again alone, and thought they would not return, he commenced making an effort to extricate himself from his painful position. By working his boot upon the sharp stones, he found the rope loose enough for him to draw his foot out. His feet were thus left at liberty, while one boot was swinging on his back. By working his hat between his knees, he was able to pull it off his face. Then with the strip of board still lacerating his mouth, and hands fastened with strong cords behind him, he set out to find some house in the darkness of the night.

" He had come from Iowa in the spring, and was but little acquainted with the country.   After travelling eleven miles, he knew, by the barking of the dogs, he was near a house, but was unable to get over the fence.   The strange cries he made at last attracted the attention of the family, but, supposing him to be a drunken Indian, they did not at first come to his aid.   He was, however, cared for by them.   Elliot, who with Titus pledged five hundred dollars for the head of Captain Walker, when the United States Marshal offered, with his usual servility, to send a posse for him, was one of the actors in this savage transaction. Other men were continually shot and robbed.

" A man who had a pass from United States Marshal Donelson, with a load of freight, was returning to his home in the Territory.   On the evening of the day he left he returned, robbed of his money, wagon, and oxen, and saved his life only by a promise to leave the Territory. The men who attacked him were encamped about two miles from Westport, armed, as all their men were, with United States rifles and side arms.

" The questions asked of him were, ' Where do you live ?   Where are you from ?   What are your politics ?   How much money did that d—d Emigrant Aid Society give you to come out here?   What the h—l did you come out here for ?   Did you come to make Kansas a free State ?   Why didn't you go to Nebraska ?   That's a good country, and you d—d Yankees may have it ; but Kansas you'll have to fight for, and we'll whip h—l out of you, but we'll get it, Union or no Union! That's a game that must win, I am thinking.'   The question was finally asked, ' If we will let you go, will you take a gun and march with the pro-slavery party ? '

" ' *Never!* ' was tne invariable rꞓply.   In an instant, the cry resounded through the camp, ' The rope, boys, the rope!'

" It was thrown over his head, and he was dragged to the nearest tree, exclaiming, ' You do not intend to kill me in this manner, do you ? '

" The reply was, ' Yes, G—d d—n your abolition heart, and all like you ! '

" He asked, if he was thus to be sacrificed, for time to collect his thoughts, and arrange his worldly affairs.   The fiends told him he could have ten minutes to make any disposal of his property, and his peace with God.   He then gave a list of his effects to one of the captains, asking him to send it East to his friends ; and, at the expiration of the ten minutes, the rope was thrown over a limb and they jerked him from the ground. After being let down, he was asked, ' Will you leave the Territory, if we'll spare your life ? '

" The prisoner objected, stating he had broken no law, infringed upon no man's rights. The leader, who had ordered him let down when hanging, again interposed, saying he must make this promise, or lose his life. He told the men that this gentleman had a ' right to be a Free-State man, though no right to hold such views in Kansas ; that he was guilty of no crime.' With a guard he was sent back to Kansas City.

" Others, going out with loaded teams, soon returned, having gone through the same operation of questioning and hanging. In one instance, as one was released, and left the camp, he heard the screams of another man in the camp across the road. * * *

" A young man and his wife, formerly from Iowa, came to Kansas City. They were fearful, and dared not stay longer in the Territory. Nine yoke of cattle, which he was going to take into Iowa to sell, were taken from him by a ruffianly band just as he approached Kansas City. Some gentlemen stopping at Kansas, who had lost teams on their way down, were anxious to get back into the Territory. They started one day, but returned ere its close. They thought, by going on foot, and keeping off of the travelled roads, they should be able to get through without molestation ; but, when about twelve miles out, they fell into the enemy's hands. They were released after a time, and advised to return to Kansas City, 'as they would meet other bands, where they might fare worse.' "

Phillips, in his " Conquest of Kansas," relates as follows :

" While near Osawatomie, he contrived to seize two of the old man's sons—Captain John Brown, Jr., and Mr. Jason Brown. These were taken while quietly engaged in their avocations. Captain Brown, Jr., had been up with his company at Lawrence, immediately after the sacking of the place, and at the time the men at Potawatomie were killed. He had returned home when he saw he could not aid Lawrence, and quietly went to work. He and his brother Jason were taken by Pate, charged with murder, kept in irons in their camp, and treated with the greatest indignity and inhumanity. While Pate was thus taking people prisoners without legal authority or writs, he was joined by Captain Wood's company of dragoons, who, so far from putting a stop to his violent career, aided him in it, and took from him, at his desire, two prisoners, keeping them under guard in their camp, heavily ironed and harshly treated. While these companies were thus travelling close to each other, Captain Pate's company burned the store of a man named Winer, a German ; the home of John Brown, Jr., in which, among a variety of household articles, a valuable library was consumed; and also the house of another of the Browns—for the old man had six grown sons; and also searched houses, men, and Free-State settlers, and acted in a violent and lawless manner generally.   Not being able to find Captain Brown, Sr., at Osawatomie, Pate's company and the troops started back for the Santa Fé road."

James Redpath, in the " Life of Brown," on pages 136 and 137, says:

" When the news of the defeat of Clay Pate reached Missouri, a force of twenty-one hundred mounted men, not one of them citizens of Kansas, set out from the border village of Westport, under the lead of the territorial delegate to Congress, with the triple purpose of rescuing their brother-highwaymen, seizing Old Brown, and completing the conquest of the disputed land.   *   *   *   But the Federal troops hastened down, and induced the Missourians to retire; which, knowing our readiness to fight, they willingly consented to do; but not until, in cold blood, they had murdered seven Free-State men, not one of whom was armed, when they were taken prisoners by the invading forces.   Mr. Cantrell was murdered by a ruffian named Forman, one of Captain Pate's men, who was wounded at Black Jack, carefully nursed at Prairie City, and dismissed by his captors uninjured.   Of such were the Southern companies."

Other testimony of the " quieting " effect of the Potawatomie massacre is given by Andreas on page 133 of his history:

" As soon as the news of the Ossawatomie murders reached the Missouri border towns, the soldiers just returned from Lawrence were rallied for a new invasion, not as before, under the call of the United States Marshal, but, as the pro-slavery papers put it, to protect the pro-slavery settlers who were being driven from their homes or slaughtered without mercy by their abolition neighbors."

Holloway, in his history, on page 351, says that this occurrence, the Potawatomie massacre, " was used as a pretext for new outrages by Southerners and Missourians. The usual 'war extras' were issued," etc.

Andreas, on page 132, says of Henry Clay Pate:

" On hearing of the murders, he set out for Osawatomie with his company, with the design of 'capturing or killing old Brown,' who was assumed to be the leader of the murderous gang. The old man was in hiding on his arrival. Failing to find him, he took prisoners two of his sons, John Brown, Jr., and Jason, whom he found at work upon their claims, on suspicion of being accessories to the crime. They were charged with murder and put in irons. Other arrests of Free-State men were made and a few cabins burned. A company of United States dragoons, under Captain Wood, joined Pate soon after the arrests were made, and to them he turned over his prisoners. On the 31st the two companies moved together as far as Middle Ottawa Creek. There they separated. * * * Six of Henry Clay Pate's men had that day (June 1st) made a raid on Palmyra, in retaliation for the Potawatomie massacre, and had taken several prisoners, among them two of the Barricklows and Dr. Graham. They then concluded they would go over to Prairie City and take that village also."

Page 133:

"In addition to the command of Captain Pate, whose career was temporarily checked at Black Jack, a considerable force was raised at Westport, Independence, and other Missouri towns for a new invasion. The commander-in-chief was General Whitfield, the pro-slavery delegate to Congress, who had left the Investigating Committee, then in session at Leavenworth, to engage in the more congenial work of organizing and leading a force from Missouri into the Territory, to 'whale' into submission the abolition part of the constituency he claimed to represent. The force with which he left Westport for the seat of war numbered something over two hundred and fifty men, well armed and accounted for a short campaign. He entered the Territory on June 2d."

How "quieting"! These hostile demonstrations from Missouri once more called together the Free-State forces, which attacked and captured Pate on the 2d of June, and attacked, but did not capture, Franklin on June 4th. Seeing a civil war being waged with all the earnestness of bitter partisans, Governor Shannon issued another proclamation, and called upon Colonel Sumner to enforce it. This proclamation begins with a "Whereas, information has been received by us that armed bodies of men exist in different parts of the Territory, who have committed and threaten to commit acts of lawless violence on peaceable and unoffending citizens—taking them prisoners, despoiling them of their

19

property, and threatening great personal violence." He proceeds to say that all illegal bodies of armed men must be dispersed, and all persons of whatever party must be protected in their persons and property.

Here is some official testimony as to the "quieting" effect of John Brown's war. In his letter to the President, dated May 31, 1856, Governor Shannon has this:

"I send you herewith three communications which I have received —one from General Heiskell, one from General Barbee, and the third from Judge Cato (Nos. 3, 4, and 5), detailing the circumstances attending the murder of six men in the County of Franklin, which is the county immediately south of this. Comment is unnecessary. The respectability of the parties and the cruelties attending these murders have produced an extraordinary state of excitement in that portion of the Territory, which has heretofore remained comparatively quiet. As soon as I was advised of these horrid murders, I sent an express to Captain Wood, at Lawrence, to move out into that section of country with his whole command, and to protect the people as far as possible from these midnight assassins. He moved with his whole command immediately, but I have received no intelligence from him yet. I hope. the offenders may be brought to justice; if so, it may allay to a great extent the excitement; otherwise, I fear the consequences.

*   *   *   *   *   *   *

"At this time affairs seem to wear a favorable aspect, except in the Wakarusa valley, and south of Lawrence, in the region of country where the recent murders were perpetrated."

Judge Cato testifies:

"PAOLA, LYKINS COUNTY, May 27, 1856.

"DEAR SIR: You will have learned, perhaps, before this reaches you, that Mr. Allen Wilkinson, Mr. Doyle and two sons, and Mr. Sherman, all of Franklin County, were on Saturday night last most foully and barbarously murdered. There can be no doubt of the fact that such murders have been perpetrated, and that the community, as I understand, generally suspect that the Browns and Partridges are the guilty parties. I shall do everything in my power to have the matter investigated, and there seems to be a disposition on the part of the Free-State men in Franklin to aid in having the laws enforced. As soon as the proper evidence can be procured, warrants will be issued for the arrest of the parties suspected, and I have promised the officers to whom these warrants will be intrusted all the aid necessary to execute the law. These murders were most foully committed in the night time by a gang of some twelve or fifteen persons, calling on, and dragging from their houses, defenseless and unsuspecting citizens, and, after murdering, mutilating their bodies in a very shocking manner.

" As the murders were committed in the night, it has been difficult, so far, to identify the perpetrators. I hope, however, that sufficient evidence may be procured.

" Most respectfully, your obedient servant,
" S. G. CATO.

" *General William Barbee.*"

" CAMP HEADQUARTERS, SECOND BRIGADE,
" SOUTHERN DIVISION, KANSAS MILITIA,
" PAOLA, Monday morning, May 25, 1856.

" DEAR SIR : We were all surprised this morning by the sad intelligence that Allen Wilkinson (late member of the Legislature) was, together with a Mr. Sherman and three Messrs. Doyle, on Saturday night taken from their beds by the abolitionists, and, in the hearing of their families, ruthlessly murdered and hacked to pieces ; also, a man found dead at the Potawatomie. There were some twenty in the gang. All is excitement here ; court cannot go on.

" I have just had an interview with the bereaved wife and family, that they spared, also a McMinn ; all of whom I am acquainted with, so that there can be no doubt as to the correctness of the report. Families are leaving for Missouri. Yankees concentrating at Osawatomie and upon the Potawatomie, also at Hickory Point, where they have driven off the inhabitants without even provisions or clothing, save what they had on.

" We can, perhaps, muster to-day, including the Alabamians, who are now encamped on Bull Creek, about a hundred and fifty men, but will need a force here. I have dispatched to Fort Scott for one hundred men. The men will come from Fort Scott under Major Hill. There will be more men in readiness, if needed, at Fort Scott. We are destitute of arms ; send wagons for both my brigade and General Heiskell's, we are together ; we have scarcely any arms. I wait further orders.

" Your obedient servant,
" WILLIAM BARBEE,
" Commanding Second Brigade, S. D. K. M."

General William A. Heiskell writes :

" PAOLA, May 26, 1856.

" DEAR SIR : All here is excitement and confusion. We have just heard of the murder on Saturday night of Allen Wilkinson, Doyle and his two brothers, and William Sherman ; all living in Franklin County, near Potawatomie Creek. The body of another man has been found at the ford of Potawatomie. These murders, it is supposed, were committed by the abolitionists of Osawatomie and Potawatomie creeks, on their return from Lawrence.

"How long shall these things continue? How long shall our citizens, unarmed and defenseless, be exposed to this worse than savage cruelty? Wilkinson, it is said, was taken from his bed, leaving a sick wife and children, and butchered in their sight. The two young Doyles were unarmed, and shot down on the prairie like dogs.

"We have here but few men, and they wholly unarmed. We shall gather together for our own defense as many men as we can; we hope you will send us as many arms as possible, and if, under the circumstances, you can do so, send as many men as you may think necessary. General Barbee is here. He has sent to Fort Scott for aid. We must organize such forces as we can, but for God's sake send arms. General Coffey is in the neighborhood; I have not yet had an opportunity to see him; he will be here to-day.

"We hope to be able to identify some of the murderers, as Mr. Harris, who was in their hands, was released, and will probably know some of them.   Yours truly,

"WILLIAM A. HEISKELL.
"*Governor Wilson Shannon.*"

Colonel Sumner, in his letter to the Adjutant-General of the army, dated May 28, 1856, says: "From present appearances, it looks very much like running into a guerrilla warfare. * * * As the affair now stands, there is great danger of our being compelled to use force."

Governor Shannon writes:

"EXECUTIVE OFFICE, LECOMPTON, K. T., May 27, 1856.

"SIR: I received last night, about twelve o'clock, reliable information by a special dispatch from Osawatomie, in the County of Franklin, that on last Saturday night five persons had been taken out of their houses and cruelly murdered; that it seemed to be a regular system of private assassination which the Free-State party had adopted towards their opponents. Under these circumstances, I am compelled to send into that country Captain Woods with his whole command, who is stationed at Lawrence, leaving that place without any force. I have to ask you, therefore, to send me two more companies, with directions for them to camp at or near Lawrence until they receive further orders.

"Yours, with great respect,

"WILSON SHANNON.
"*Colonel Sumner.*"

Major John Sedgwick writes to Colonel Sumner, June

1, 1856: "There are, undoubtedly, many outrages committed daily; some of them of the most atrocious character."

Colonel P. St. George Cooke, in a letter to the Adjutant-General, dated June, 1856, said: "The disorders of the Territory have, in fact, changed their character, and consist now of robberies and assassinations, by a set of bandits whom the excitement of the times has attracted hither."

Colonel Sumner writes:

" HEADQUARTERS FIRST CAVALRY,
" FORT LEAVENWORTH, June 23, 1856.

" SIR: I returned to this post last night. I have been busily engaged in dispersing armed bodies of both parties, and have been so fortunate as to do it without meeting resistance.

" I have stationed five companies in two camps near Westport, to prevent any further inroads from that part of Missouri.

" I do not think there is an armed party in the Territory, with the exception of a few freebooters, who may be together in small numbers.

" Very respectfully, your obedient servant,
" E. V. SUMNER,
" Colonel First Cavalry, Commanding.
"*Assistant Adjutant-General, Department of the West, St. Louis, Mo.*"

" HEADQUARTERS FIRST CAVALRY,
" FORT LEAVENWORTH, June 23, 1856.

" COLONEL: I returned to this post last night. On the 14th instant I concentrated several companies at Palmyra, on the Santa Fé road, and moved down that road towards the Missouri line. I met two armed parties on their way into the Territory—one from Missouri and one from Alabama—but they both returned into Missouri.

" I do not think there is an armed body of either party now in the Territory, with the exception, perhaps, of a few freebooters, who may be together in small numbers. These fellows belong to both parties, and are taking advantage of the political excitement to commit their own rascally acts. I have stationed five companies near the Missouri line, to indicate plainly to all that the orders of the President and the proclamation of the Governor will be maintained.

" I am, Colonel, very respectfully, your obedient servant,
" E. V. SUMNER,
" Colonel First Cavalry, Commanding.
"*Colonel S. Cooper, Adjutant-General.*"

" EXECUTIVE OFFICE, June 14, 1856.

" SIR: I send you two copies of the proclamation—all I can find.

"The complaints of robberies on the roads near Westport are distressing.

"I hope you will clear those roads and drive those people back at once. Yours, etc.,

"W. SHANNON.

"*Colonel Sumner.*"

While the war of murder and pillage thus inaugurated was being prosecuted by the revolutionists in a private manner, the larger bodies were becoming formidable. Pate's company was encountered at Black Jack on the 2d of June by about thirty Free-State men, and, after exchanging shots several hours from the ravines and tall grass, Pate, seeing Captain Abbott with his company approaching to reinforce the Free-State men, surrendered. No serious harm was done. A skirmish was had at Franklin on the 4th of June, and Osawatomie was sacked by the pro-slavery forces. Of this attack, Gihon says:

"On the 7th, Reid, with one hundred and seventy men, marched into Osawatomie, and, without resistance, entered each house, robbing it of everything of value. There were but few men in town, and the women and children were treated with the utmost brutality. Stores and dwellings were alike entered and pillaged. Trunks, boxes, and desks were broken open, and their contents appropriated or destroyed. Even rings were rudely pulled from the ears and fingers of the women, and some of the apparel from their persons. The liquor found was freely drunk, and served to incite the plunderers to increased violence in the prosecution of their mischievous work. Having completely stripped the town, they set fire to several houses, and then beat a rapid retreat, carrying off a number of horses, and loudly urging each other to greater haste, as 'the d—d abolitionists were coming!' There are hundreds of well-authenticated accounts of the cruelties practised by this horde of ruffians; some of them too shocking and disgusting to relate, or to be accredited if told. The tears and shrieks of terrified women folded in their foul embrace failed to touch a chord of mercy in their brutal hearts; and the mutilated bodies of murdered men hanging upon the trees, or left to rot upon the prairies or in the deep ravines, or furnish food for vultures and wild beasts, told frightful stories of brutal ferocity, from which the wildest savages might have shrunk with horror."

All these movements resulted from the massacre. Colonel Sumner, in accordance with the Governor's proclamation, took the field, and soon sent home the Missourians as well as the Free-State forces. John Brown subsided or left the country, and comparative quiet was restored.

Colonel Sumner thus refers to his action in a letter to the Adjutant-General, U. S. A., under date of June 8, 1856:

"HEADQUARTERS FIRST CAVALRY,
"FORT LEAVENWORTH, June 8, 1856.

"COLONEL: I have just returned to this post to prepare the last two companies of my regiment to take the field. On the 5th instant, as soon as I received the inclosed proclamation, I moved from Lecompton with about fifty men to disperse a band of free-soilers who were en-camped near Prairie City; this band had a fight with the pro-slavery party, and had taken twenty-six prisoners. As I approached them, they sent out to request me to halt, which of course was not done, and the leaders then came out to meet me as I was advancing. They yielded at once, and I ordered them to release all prisoners and to disperse immediately, which was complied with. While engaged in this camp in seeing my orders carried into effect, I received intelligence that two or three hundred of the pro-slavery party, from Missouri and elsewhere, were approaching, and I immediately turned my attention to them. I found them halted at two miles' distance (about two hundred and fifty strong), and, to my great surprise, I found Colonel Whitfield, the member of Congress, and General Coffey, of the militia, at their head. I said to these gentlemen that I was there by order of the President and the proclamation of the Governor to disperse all armed bodies assembled without authority; and further, that my duty was perfectly plain, and would certainly be done. I then requested General Coffey to assemble his people, and I read to them the President's dispatch and the Governor's proclamation.

"The General then said that he should not resist the authority of the general Government, and that his party would disperse, and shortly afterwards they moved off. Whether this is a final dispersion of these lawless armed bodies is very doubtful."

Colonel Sumner's efforts so far succeeded as to enable General Smith, who succeeded him in command, to write on July 26, 1856, as follows: "Colonel: Everything has been tranquil in the department since I assumed command. In the Territory of Kansas there have been no disturbances, but

emigrants are coming in armed, as though they were prepared to begin again when an opportunity offers."

Also, August 1st he wrote: "Things remain apparently
quiet in Kansas Territory, and I hear of no threatened hostilities from Indians."

Governor Shannon and Colonel Sumner construed their
instructions from headquarters to require the dispersion of
the State Legislature, which was to meet on the 4th of July.
This was done by Colonel Sumner in a manner to entitle
him as a man and officer to the respect of the Free-State
men, believing he was simply obeying orders from his superi-
ors.   But such was the detestation in which the act was held
throughout the country, that the President and Secretary of
War denied all responsibility for it, and left Sumner under a
cloud of implied censure, which he resented in his correspondence.

As this was to be an inexcusable interference with the
rights of the people, even though by Federal authority, the
Legislature would be justified before the world in making at
least a show of resistance.   Accordingly, the treason prisoners sent this letter to the members of the Legislature :

CAMP NEAR LECOMPTON, KANSAS, July 1, 1856.
"To the Friends of ' Law and Order,' convened at Topeka :

" The undersigned desire to say a word to their friends in regard to
the present aspect of affairs in Kansas.

" It is highly important at this time that the oppressed people of
Kansas should occupy a tenable position, one which the country and
the world will sustain.   There is, it seems to us, a position which we
can occupy and be triumphant, whether overcome by numbers or not ;
while there is another position, which, if taken, would prejudice our
cause and might lead to defeat, and weaken the confidence and support
of our friends in the country.

" The first and true position is, defense of the State organization.
You have a constitutional right to meet as a Legislature, complete the
State organization, and pass all laws necessary to the successful administration of justice, and the Federal Government has no authority to
interfere with you in the exercise of this right ; should it do so, resistance becomes justifiable self-defense.

" The second and untenable position is resistance to a Federal officer in the service of a legal process, when the defense of the State organization is not involved.   Should a collision occur under such circumstances, it would be most unfortunate, and should be avoided if possible.   If an attempt, however, is made to arrest the members of the State organization merely because they are such, with a view to disable it, then resistance becomes defense of the State organization, and is manifestly justifiable.

"Accordingly, all persons against whom indictments are known to be pending, for any other charge than that of being a member of the State organization, should not be found at the capital, as that might involve the people in their cases.   We feel that our hope of success in this important crisis depends, first, upon a right position, and second, upon calm and unflinching firmness.

" You have met for the purpose of doing what other new States have done, and what you have a constitutional right to do, and no man or class of men have a right to interfere, not excepting even the President of the United States.

" Our desire to be with you in this crowning emergency is almost irresistible, and nothing but the fear that your position might be changed from a defense of the State organization to a resistance to our re-arrest, can reconcile us to this absence.   As it is, you have our earnest solicitude and fervent prayers that all may go on well with you, and that you may earn, as you will if every step is judiciously and firmly taken, the gratitude of millions of your fellow-men and the approbation of the God of Justice and Humanity.

> " GEORGE W. SMITH,
> " CHARLES ROBINSON,
> " GAIUS JENKINS,
> " G. W. DEITZLER,
> " HENRY H. WILLIAMS,
> " JOHN BROWN, JR."

Colonel Sumner reported his action on that occasion to Washington, and the following endorsement was made upon his report:

" The President's proclamation having been sent from this department to Colonel Sumner, as a part of his instructions, a general reference to that paper is no compliance with the requirements of the letter addressed to him, dated July 21, 1856.   If any portion of that proclamation was understood as directing military officers to use the force under their command for the dispersion of an illegal legislative body, that part of the proclamation should have been specially cited.

" If the ' serious consequences ' anticipated by the Colonel commanding First Cavalry from the convention of the Free-State Legislature of
Kansas had been realized, it might have been necessary for him to use
the military force under his command to suppress resistance to the execution of the laws, and he would have no difficulty in finding his authority, both in the President's proclamation and in the letter of instructions
which accompanied it.   But if the exigency was only anticipated, it is
not perceived how authority is to be drawn from either, or both, to
employ a military force to disperse men because they were 'elected and
organized without law.'

" The reference to the dissatisfaction of the Missourians seems to be
wholly inappropriate to the subject under consideration, and the department is at a loss to understand why that reference is made; the more
so because, in answer to an inquiry from Colonel Sumner, he was distinctly informed by letter of March, 1856, that the department expected
him, in the discharge of his duty, to make no discrimination, founded
on the section of the country from which persons might or had come.

" JEFFERSON DAVIS, Secretary of War.
" WAR DEPARTMENT, August 27, 1856."

Thus it appears that, had there been a conflict, the action
of Sumner would not have been sustained, and the victory
would have been with the Free-State party.

Colonel Sumner visited the prisoner's camp after this
transaction, and complained that the Legislature compelled
him to make a show of force, when Robinson told him the
movement was violating a constitutional right of the people,
and had he been at Topeka, he would have made it necessary for him to kill some one in doing so.   Colonel Sumner
replied that he would not have killed any one, but would
have arrested them.   Yet he had no writs for such arrest.

As, after the shipment of the Free-State people from
Leavenworth down the river, after the Potawatomie massacre, it became unsafe for immigrants from the North and East
to travel that route, a way was opened through Iowa and
Nebraska.   During the summer large parties were raised all
through the Northern States, more or less well armed and
equipped for their own protection.   With some of these
parties Lane and Brown appeared on the line of Nebraska.

But those in charge of the parties were unwilling to enter the Territory under their auspices, and went by themeslves.

Professor Spring, in his " Kansas," page 169, says:

" July 29th, Dr. S. G. Howe and Thaddeus Hyatt, representatives of the National Kansas Committee sent out to investigate matters, reached the Nebraska camp. They found many of the immigrants in forlorn condition—ragged, almost penniless, poorly supplied with even the scanty furniture of a camper's outfit. Leadership had fallen into Lane's hands, and the whole expedition became accredited to him, though he was neither directly nor indirectly concerned in raising more than a fourth part of it. The committee demanded that his connection with it should be completely severed on penalty of withholding further supplies. Considerations which led to this summary step were the fact that papers had been made out for Lane's arrest—a circumstance which might lead to complications ; that in an emergency his discretion and self-command could not be trusted. These considerations, the committee reported, 'conspired to create a well-grounded apprehension in our minds that, by some hasty and ill-timed splurge, he would defeat the object of the expedition if suffered to remain even in otherwise desirable proximity.' Lane took the decision much to heart. * * * But he sullenly yielded, set off towards the Territory with old John Brown, Captain Samuel Walker, and three or four others."

Both of these men appeared at Topeka, August 10, 1856, and commenced operations. Lane had been absent since early in March, and, as Brown was usually in hiding, it was not definitely known when he left the Territory. As has been seen by the dispatches of General Smith, quiet had been partially restored since the Potawatomie killing, and this, of all things, was what Brown, and perhaps Lane, would most dislike. But if they had had their way this quiet would soon have been exchanged for general war against the Federal Government. John Brown sent word from his hiding-place, near Topeka, to his son, John, Jr., with the treason prisoners, proposing a rescue from the soldiers who had him in charge.

Redpath, in his " Life of Brown," page 142, says : " Slowly coming to the Territory, with a little army, but a mightier influence of inspiring rude men with furious passions, was

General 'Jim Lane'; while in the woods, near the town
[Topeka], lay John Brown encamped, who did not despair,
but was ready to release the prisoners at Lecompton, or
attack the dragoons, if the party would advise it.   They did
not; and he left the town."

Lane sent this letter, written with his own hand, to the
treason prisoners:

"TOPEKA, August 10, 1856.

"DEAR FRIENDS: I am here at last with a sufficient force and
ready to rescue you.

"It were better if you can escape to do so, and let me meet you with
my defending force just outside of your prison-house.

"It is necessary for me to remind you that time is all-important—
my whereabouts cannot long be concealed from the bloodhounds who
are seeking my blood.   Act promptly; if you cannot escape, I can and
will attack your guard, although it were better policy, if blood is to flow,
that it be shed in your defense rather than in your rescue; decide, and
that quickly.   Time is everything.

"Yours, etc.,

"J. H. LANE.

"*To His Excellency C. Robinson, Governor State of Kansas ; George
W. Smith, Councillor ; General George W. Deitzler, George W.
Brown, Esq., Hon. John Brown, and others, Free-State prisoners
at Lecompton.*"

The Attorney-General of Ohio wrote to Eli Thayer, from
Columbus, May 30, 1856, and said:

"I have had a long personal interview with him [Lane].   *   *   *
I might add that the great inducement for Lane's immediate return, and
which has induced him to do so, is to save Governor Robinson.   He
thinks he has only one hope—a rescue."

"Truly your obedient servant,

"F. D. KIMBALL,

"Attorney-General of Ohio."

Lane came into the Territory disguised as "Captain Joe
Cook."   He always magnified his importance in the estimation of the pro-slavery men, and always would make it
appear that they were after his "heart's blood."   It is true,
some Administration men regarded Lane as a disturber and

mischievous character, yet the ultra men did not want him arrested or disturbed in his career. His disguise, of course, was the merest sham, as his identity was always known, and he could have been arrested at any time by a single orderly of Colonel Sumner or any other United States officer. The same also was true with reference to John Brown, although Redpath, and perhaps others, claim that no man dared arrest him. These men depended upon the Free-State party for their protection, if in danger, and that party could not be brought in conflict with Federal authority on account of a regiment of Browns, Lanes, or any other such characters. In fact, it is notorious, that a large number of the leading Free-State men, those who devised the policy of the party, regarded the cause as much safer in their absence than when they were present.

CHAPTER XII.

FREE-STATE AND PRO-SLAVERY FORCES.— ARRIVAL OF GOV-
ERNOR GEARY.— END OF THE WAR.—THE PARTS PLAYED
BY BROWN AND LANE.

SEVERAL questions will arise for the future historian regarding the motives that led Brown and Lane to propose a
rescue of the treason prisoners from the custody of the officers of the United States army.   The arrest of Deitzler,
Brown, Smith, Jenkins, and Robinson, on a charge of
treason, and their confinement with the officers in whose
hands was placed largely the responsibility for the peace of
the Territory, was the best investment for the Free-State
cause, and the worst for its opponents, that was made during that season, excepting only the destruction of the hotel
and printing offices by bogus officers.   During most of the
season, the prisoners were in immediate charge of Captain
Sackett, under Major Sedgwick and Colonel Sumner, all
Free-State men and in full sympathy with the prisoners and
their cause.   The prisoners were in daily, and sometimes in
hourly, communication with the Free-State men outside, and
with the Captain in charge at all hours.   Thus the United
States officers knew with absolute certainty how far the
Free-State men would go, and were in no fear of being compromised by them.   They were also kept informed in regard
to every movement of the two parties, including the territorial officers, bogus or otherwise.   The Governor and his
party became aware of all this, and tried hard to cut off
communication between the prisoners and their friends out-

side.   Failing in this, word was sent to General Smith to have them removed to Fort Leavenworth.   Even this was declined.   In Mrs. Robinson's " Kansas," page 319, these efforts are referred to as follows :

" On the 20th [of July] Cramer, the deputy marshal, came to camp, and ordered Captain Sackett not to allow any person to converse with the prisoners privately.   ' His responsibility, since the sacking of Lawrence, in regard to the prisoners, had weighed upon him much.'   But Captain Sackett at once informed him, ' he need give himself no further trouble on the subject, as the responsibility of their safe-keeping rested upon him.'   The little fellow appeared pleased; but his wrath was only pent up.   He met a man soon after leaving camp, and poured it forth in execrations upon the Captain, declaring that ' Robinson was more the Governor of the Territory than Shannon ' ; that ' the prisoners should be taken from Captain Sackett's charge, and that their lives would not be safe an hour.'   On the 21st the little deputy came again, with a letter from Governor Shannon, in which he advised that ' persons and letters be not allowed to go into camp ; that the Territory had never been in so bad a condition ; that he believed the prisoners were implicated in these disturbances, and in great measure the occasion of them.'   Cramer, at the Captain's tent, also said, ' The Governor don't know what to do.'   He talked so loudly it was quite impossible not to hear what was said.   It will be remembered that only two days had passed since the Governor had been informed that, if such outrages as that of Titus continued, the people would try to suppress them.   Word was returned to the Governor from Captain Sackett, that ' he had his orders from Colonel Sumner to give up the prisoners to the civil authorities if unnecessary restrictions were placed upon them.'   Governor Shannon upon immediately sent to Captain Sackett that ' he did not know he had orders from Colonel Sumner, but, if he had, of course he must obey them.'   He swore, however, ' he would see if he could not make Captain Sackett obey orders,' and sent an express to General Smith at the fort.   General Smith proposed not to interfere in matters in the Territory, and, no change being made in the treatment of the prisoners, the Governor was disappointed, and unable to carry out his threats.   On the 19th he was heard to say, as at many other times, ' that Governor Robinson would be hung.' "

Not only did the confinement of these men help the cause in Kansas, but it had a most beneficial effect throughout the country.   Here were five men charged with a " constructive " crime, held in confinement on the prairie, pouring " hot shot " in the shape of letters to the press of the country, dated at " Treason Camp," which did more to damage the Administration politically than these men could have done at liberty in any capacity.

Then why did Lane and Brown propose the rescue ?

In Brown's case the answer is easy, as Redpath's biography, his own confessions, and his later course in Virginia show that a desire for revolution and civil war actuated him. Did it also actuate Lane ? Brown and Lane agreed in a policy that would have produced this result at the Wakarusa war the fall before ; and were they acting in concert and by previous agreement now ? Or, did Lane believe such a course would be the overthrow of the Free-State cause and the establishment of a slave State in Kansas, which he had preferred ? According to official report of army officers, he was seen in friendly communion with General Richardson, of the territorial militia, when the bogus officials were pretending to want him arrested. Was he in collusion with the enemy to betray and ruin the Free-State cause ? He was well aware that the treason prisoners believed him to be totally without convictions or principles of any kind, cowardly and treacherous. Did he desire their destruction by the army, which certainly would have shot them down like dogs had a rescue been attempted ? Jenkins, one of these prisoners, whose claim he had jumped, he afterward killed with his own hands in a most cold-blooded and cowardly manner. These questions will not be answered by the writer, for it is too early. The future historian, however, will consider them.

Notwithstanding armed bodies of men had disappeared under the active operations of Colonel Sumner, to such an extent that General Smith could say all was peace and quiet on the surface, there was no time during the summer that Brown's disciples, such as Whipple, or Stevens and Cook, both of whom lost their lives at Harper's Ferry, Leonhardt and others, were not more or less active in the " reprisal " business. Professor Spring, in his "Kansas," says: "So great was the enterprise and success in what one of the victims called 'the roguing business,' that few pro-slavery men of the neighborhood [Topeka] escaped. Free-State depredators, in larger or smaller gangs, scoured the region, filling the air with profanity, intimidating pro-slavery settlers, shooting at those who were not sufficiently docile, and plundering right and left." While the Free-State men were thus active, the pro-slavery men were by no means idle. Their thefts and robberies, if they did not equal those of the Free-State men, were not far behind. As no forces were permitted by the vigilance of Colonel Sumner to take the field, both parties established places of rendezvous, from which they could emerge, accomplish their work, and return. The bases of operations for the Free-State men were the larger settlements, like Topeka, Lawrence, and Osawatomie, while the pro-slavery men, having but few towns of importance, resorted to log cabins and camps on creeks and other favorable places. Several of these camps were established during the summer. One was in southern Kansas, near Osawatomie, one at Franklin, one at Fort Saunders, and one at Titus's house, near Lecompton.

When the depredations from these nests of thieves and plunderers became intolerable, it was decided to break them up. As John Brown had left southern Kansas for Nebraska, Captain Cracklin, with a company from Lawrence, went for the fort near Osawatomie and frightened the occupants away. This was about the 8th of August. Fort Saunders, on Washington Creek, had become quite troublesome to the neighbors, and after repeated appeals to the authorities for protection, the people took the matter in hand. A staunch Free-State man, Major Hoyt, visited the camp, and was riddled with bullets. Before attacking them, however, it was decided to break up the nest at Franklin, where the enemy had a cannon, as well as other war supplies. Accordingly, on the night of the 13th of August, after a

20

fight in the dark for several hours, a load of hay was set on fire and started for the fort or block-house. This brought a cry for quarter and the desertion of the place by its defenders. The cannon and other stores were captured. As no ammunition was found for the cannon, one day was occupied by Captain Bickerton in making moulds and casting balls from what was left of the type of the *Herald of Freedom* office. On the 15th, the attack was made upon Fort Saunders, on Washington Creek, where Hoyt had been murdered. As this was Lane's first appearance as commander in a battle, some particulars of it are given, as furnished by his friend John Speer, in the Lawrence *Tribune*, July 20, 1876:

" He [Lane] ordered out all his forces of cavalry. Then he gathered in all the farmers' wagons ; and placing boards across them like seats, made holes in these boards, into which he stuck pegs, and around these pegs he tied bundles of straw so as to make them at a distance look like men. Thus prepared, the whole force of live and straw men made their appearance upon the heights in sight of Fort Saunders. As the view of them was an oblique one from the Fort, the teams were spread out a good distance apart, but still looked as if they were close together. As they emerged from the woods, they seemed to keep coming as if there was no end to them. The ruse had its effect, and before a gun was fired the men were seen fleeing in all directions."

After this battle, Lane left the army with a body-guard of half a dozen men, going by way of Topeka. He crossed the Kansas River in the night, for Nebraska, where his friends say he at once commenced throwing up breastworks on or near the territorial line. These details of the work of Brown and Lane are only important because Higginson, the historian, and Sanborn, the biographical writer, say that it was their military prowess that saved Kansas to freedom, and all readers will be interested in their exploits. After the commander, Lane, had started for Nebraska, the army at first disbanded. However, learning that Colonel Titus was active in his expeditions of plunder, and that his wife and family had just left for Missouri, the men were rallied again, and under Colonel Walker started for Fort Titus, within sight and hearing of the United States camp, where were guarded the treason prisoners. This was a most daring enterprise, and most skillfully managed. Lane's "straw" men were left behind, and solid men and solid shot soon told the story. The men did not escape as at Fort Saunders, but were taken prisoners to Lawrence. Captain Shombre, a brave Free-State man from Indiana, was killed, and two pro-slavery men. As soon as the firing commenced, one ball whizzing past the United States camp, boots and saddles was sounded, but the soldiers leisurely took their position between Titus's house and Lecompton, apparently well pleased to witness the little battle that was being fought. The next day Governor Shannon, Major Sedgwick, and Dr. Rodrigue went to Lawrence, met with Colonel James Blood and William Hutchinson, committee, and made a treaty and exchanged prisoners. Also the howitzer, taken by Jones from Lawrence on May 21st, was returned. Here ended another chapter in the guerrilla warfare inaugurated by John Brown on the 24th of May. Thus far the Free-State men, in this brief campaign, had triumphed, but their victory was to be short-lived. Governor Shannon, who would under no provocation call out the territorial militia, resigned and abandoned the Territory, leaving Secretary Woodson acting Governor. This was glory enough for the Slave-State men. Now the machinery for invasion, devastation, and annihilation was put in order. Even Jeff Davis was ready to come to the rescue of his friends.

At this point it may be appropriate to give a specimen of the way in which the history of Kansas has been written, which will serve to show how heroes are made—and unmade. General James Blood, who came to Kansas in July, 1854, has been a prominent character ever since, and has filled various positions of responsibility. His attention being called to some historical writing by Mr. Sanborn and Owen Brown, he made this answer:

"WAS JOHN BROWN A FRAUD?

" *To the Editor of the Transcript:*

"My attention has been called to a letter signed F. B. Sanborn, dated Concord, July 12, 1884, and published in the Boston *Evening Transcript* of July, 1884.

"Some of the statements in Mr. Sanborn's letter in regard to what transpired here in Kansas in the summer of 1856 are so new to me that they are really quite interesting.   To illustrate, I quote as follows :

"That Brown's brave fighting record in Kansas, during the summer of 1856, was the glory of the friends of freedom all over the North, and that when difficult or dangerous work in Kansas was proposed, Brown was called for by the Kansas people to take part in it.   Thus, on the 12th of August, 1856, General Lane, who had returned to Kansas from the North with several hundred armed Free-State men, but was passing under the name of ' Joe Cook,' sent this message through his aid, Mr. Stratton, to John Brown :

"'TOPEKA, 7 p.m., August 12, 1856.

"' General Joe Cook wants you to come to Lawrence this night, for we expect to have a fight on Washington Creek.   Come to Topeka as soon as possible, and I will pilot you to the place.

"' Yours in haste,   H. STRATTON.'

"This fight actually took place August 15th, and Brown had the credit of the victory with the Georgians and Missourians who were beaten.   The next day Captain Samuel Walker, a friend of Brown's, * * * made an attack on ' Fort Titus,' a pro-slavery block-house, not far from Lecompton, and was also successful ; so that on the 17th of August, Shannon, the pro-slavery Governor of Kansas, went to Lawrence and made a ' treaty of peace ' very favorable to the Free-State men. These matters and some others, throwing light on the condition of Kansas then, are thus related in a letter from Owen Brown (a son of John), who was then recovering from illness in Iowa, to the wife of John Brown, among the Adirondack Mountains.

"'OWEN BROWN'S COMMENTARIES ON THE KANSAS WAR.

"'TABOR, FREMONT COUNTY, IOWA, August 27. 1856.

"'DEAR MOTHER : The last news we had from Kansas, father was at Lawrence, and had charge of a company of the bravest men the Territory could afford.   Those who come through here from the Territory say that father is one of the most daring, courageous men in Kansas.   You have, no doubt, heard that the Free-State men have taken two forts or block-houses, with a fine lot of arms, several prisoners, and two cannon. Shannon was obliged to flee for his life; afterwards came to Lane to negotiate for peace. He proposed that the Free-State men should give up the prisoners and arms they had taken; at the same time they (the enemy) should still hold our men as prisoners and keep all the arms they had taken from the Free-State men. But Lane would not consent to that; he required Shannon to deliver up the howitzer they had taken at Lawrence, release some prisoners, disarm the pro-slavery men in the Territory, and do all in his power to remove the enemy from the Territory. With fear and trembling Shannon consented to all of Lane's demands. * * * And now the news comes from reliable sources that Lane is about to enter Leavenworth with two thousand men; that he has sent word to the citizens of Leavenworth requiring them to deliver up a few prisoners they had taken, with some wagons and other property, or he will destroy the town forthwith. Colonel Smith, of Leavenworth, commander of the Government troops, refuses to protect the pro-slavery men of the Territory, replying that Lane is able to dress them all out, troops and all. Shannon made a speech to them, urging them to cease hostilities, that he could not defend them (*i.e.*, our enemies). At present our enemies and the Missourians are trembling in their boots, if reports are true. * * * For the want of time I leave out many particulars in connection with the taking of those forts which would be quite interesting, and show Yankee skill and strategy at least.'

"This letter of Owen Brown to his mother in the Adirondack Mountains is truly romantic. Then follows a letter from John Brown to his wife, dated 'Lawrence, K. T., 7th September, 1856,' giving a fictitious account of what took place at Osawatomie on the 30th of August. Following these letters the truth-seeking Sanborn indulges in a little flowery rhetoric and gushing sentiment. I will make no more quotations from Mr. Sanborn's article at this time. But believing it to be a duty, I have reluctantly concluded to call attention to some of the errors contained in the above quotations. A large convention of the settlers in Kansas was held at Topeka on the 4th of July, 1856, at which a large territorial committee was elected, to look after and take charge of the interests of the settlers, as Governor Robinson was a prisoner under guard of United States soldiers, and the Legislature was that day broken up and dispersed by Federal troops. The committee immediately organized, and appointed a sub-committee of five, who were charged with the duty of looking after and taking immediate charge of all public affairs and interests of the people of the Territory, and to provide for their protection from armed bands of guerrillas and ruffians. Mr. William Hutchinson and myself, then residing in Lawrence, were appointed members of the sub-committee. Lawrence was made head-quarters, and the business of the committee was transacted here. As

Mr. Hutchinson and myself were the only members of the territorial committee residing here, most of the work devolved upon us; consequently it became our duty to be informed in regard to what was taking place. I make the above statement that you may judge of my opportunities for obtaining or possessing correct information or knowledge of what transpired here at the time, as well as of the principal actors and their part in affairs. In regard to the first statement quoted from Mr. Sanborn's article, I wish to say that Mr. Sanborn is mistaken. John Brown had no such record here. The second statement is utterly without foundation in truth. John Brown was never called upon by the Kansas people to take part in any difficult or dangerous work. Perhaps the best way to correct or refute the statements contained in the quotations from Mr. Sanborn's article would be to make a correct statement of what did take place here at the time. In August, 1856, we found that armed bands of ruffians were stationed at Franklin, a few miles east of Lawrence, on the road to Kansas City, and that they engaged in robbing travellers and freighters, and pillaging settlers in the neighborhood. Another band was at what was called Fort Saunders, on Washington Creek, near the old Santa Fé road, and about fifteen miles southwest of here. At this place a number of robberies and murders had been committed. Major Hoyt had been murdered here. Another band was about twelve miles northwest of here, and near Lecompton, called Fort Titus. As the United States authorities were doing nothing for our protection, we determined to protect ourselves. We had been for some time preparing to attack them, and try to drive them out of the country or stop their depredations, and had decided to attack the camp at Franklin on Wednesday, the 13th of August. The attack was not made till evening, when considerable of a fight took place. On the morning of that day I was informed by Mr. Hutchinson that Lane had just come in from Iowa, and was in concealment over his store, and had assumed the name of Captain Joe Cook. At his request I went up and saw Lane. I said to him that, in my opinion, there was no necessity for his hiding, that he was in no more danger than the rest of us. In the evening, when the 'Stubbs' Company and others had started for Franklin, Lane came down from his hiding-place and mounted a horse, and in company with several gentlemen rode down to a point between Lawrence and Franklin, where they remained upon their horses, taking no part until the fight was over. After killing one of our men and seriously wounding several others, the band of ruffians in the block-house surrendered. They were disarmed and ordered or allowed to leave the country on their promise never to return. Among other arms captured was a brass cannon. Immediately after the affair at Franklin was over, our men started for Fort Saunders, and went into camp on Rock Creek, a short distance east of Bloomington. The cannon taken at Franklin was brought to Lawrence, as there was no ammunition for it. The next morning (the 14th) I went with Captain Bickerton and a few others to the *Herald of Freedom* office, and took a quantity of type to a blacksmith shop, where Captain Bickerton spent the day in casting balls from the type, while another force was occupied in making cartridges. By night we had quite a supply of ammunition prepared for the cannon, which we loaded into a wagon with the gun, and loading one or two more wagons with provisions and ammunition for the men in camp on Rock Creek, we started with a small guard that we were able to collect, arriving at the camp some time in the night, when a consultation was held with the officers, at which General Lane was present, and it was decided to march upon Fort Saunders the next morning. John Brown was not present—at least I did not see or hear of him. The next day (the 15th) our men went over to Fort Saunders, but upon their arrival there they found the place deserted, not a man, woman, or child to be found. Dinner had been cooked, but was left upon the table untouched. Yet Sanborn states positively ' that a fight actually took place at Fort Sáunders, August 15th, and that Brown had the credit of the victory with the Georgians and Missourians, who were beaten.' However, it is certain that there was no fight that day, and that John Brown was not there. Our men returned that night to the camp on Rock Creek. Lane, with H. Stratton and a few others as aids or body-guard, left for Nebraska, crossing the ferry at Topeka about midnight. The next heard of them here was about a week afterwards, when they were found to be engaged in the ludicrous employment of throwing up breastworks near the Nebraska line. Saturday morning (the 16th) the attack was made upon Fort Titus under command of Colonel Walker. Captain Bickerton placed the cannon taken at Franklin in range of the block-house and opened fire, sending the balls made from the *Herald of Freedom* type into it. At this fight Captain Shombre, who had recently arrived from Indiana and was in command of a company, was killed. After Titus had been seriously wounded, as well as some of his men, he surrendered. The buildings were burned, and the prisoners were brought here and placed under a strong guard. Sunday morning, the 17th, Governor Shannon, accompanied by Major Sedgwick, came down from Lecompton and sent for the committee. As Mr. Hutchinson and myself were the only members of the committee here, we went to the Cincinnati House, where they were stopping. The Governor commenced negotiations for the release of Titus and his men. The most of the day was spent in discussing various propositions for a settlement. The terms finally agreed upon were about as follows, to wit : That we should keep the arms taken at Titus and at Franklin, including the cannon ; that the howitzer taken from here at the sacking of Lawrence by the United States Marshal's posse in May should be delivered to us here in good condition; that some five to eight prisoners arrested a day or two before by the United States Marshal, charged with being concerned in the attack upon Franklin, with robbing the post-office at Franklin, and other crimes against the United States Government, should be unconditionally released and delivered to us here unharmed, and that he should issue a proclamation disbanding the so-called territorial militia, and order all bands of armed men to disperse, and for all such bands of non-residents to leave the Territory, and do all in his power as Governor to protect the settlers and restore peace. That then we would release Titus and his men. After we had agreed upon the terms of settlement with Governor Shannon and Major Sedgwick, we sent for Colonel Walker and stated to him the terms of the agreement, and as we were obliged to keep a strong guard over the prisoners to prevent their being mobbed by some of our own men, we were glad to get rid of them. Colonel Walker approved of what we had done, and only asked to go up with his company and get the howitzer and bring it into town. Monday morning (the 18th) the howitzer was brought down here, and the prisoners were brought in a Government ambulance. The ambulances were then driven to the guard-house, and Titus and his gang were put into them and escorted out of town. The terms of the agreement were carried out by Governor Shannon, as far as it was in his power to do. But he was very soon compelled to leave the Territory, and was at once removed, and Geary appointed in his place.

" In the foregoing I have endeavored to truthfully narrate what occurred here during those few eventful days in August, 1856. Important occurrences may not have come to my knowledge, or may have escaped my memory. I am sure that I have not been actuated by malice or ill-will towards any one, living or dead. I have submitted this to Colonel Walker, who says that, as far as he knows, or can recollect, it is correct. He says he does not remember seeing John Brown during that time until Sunday, the 17th, when he saw him here denouncing the leaders of the Free-State party and their policy, and denouncing the committee for making terms with Governor Shannon, and trying to incite a mob to overpower the guards and kill the prisoners. Brown was not in charge of any company here.

" But, according to Mr. Sanborn's story, John Brown was here making a record that was the glory of the friends of freedom all over the North, to the end that General Lane was able to make a treaty of peace very favorable to the Free-State men, while in fact Lane was not in the Territory at the time, having left two days previous for Nebraska, as before stated.

" In regard to the letter of Owen Brown to the wife of John Brown, among the Adirondack Mountains, regard for the truth requires me to say it is pure fiction from beginning to end, entirely destitute of any shadow of truth. I deny each and every allegation contained therein. Mr. Owen Brown drew upon his imagination, or was badly informed. John Brown never had the confidence of the Free-State party here in Kansas, and never was intrusted with any command. They feared that his want of discretion would involve the Free-State people in trouble, embarrassment, and disgrace, and endanger the cause. I have written the above, believing the time has come when it is best to ' tell the truth.'

" Respectfully,   J. BLOOD.

" LAWRENCE, KANSAS, December 18, 1884."

" I have examined the accompanying statement made by J. Blood, in regard to what occurred here in August, 1856, from the 13th to the 18th, and believe it to be correct as far as I know or can now remember.   " SAMUEL WALKER.

" LAWRENCE, KANSAS, December 19, 1884."

After the capture of Titus all pro-slavery parties took fright. Governor Shannon, on the 17th of August, sent this dispatch to General Smith :

" EXECUTIVE OFFICE, LECOMPTON, K. T.,
" August 17, 1856.

" SIR : This place is in a most dangerous and critical situation at this moment. We are threatened with utter extermination by a large body of Free-State men.

" The report of Major Sedgwick, which will accompany this, will give you the particulars of the various outrages which this body of armed men have perpetrated within the last few days. I have just returned from Lawrence, where I have been this day, with the view of procuring the release of nineteen prisoners that were taken. I saw in that place at least eight hundred men, who manifested a fixed purpose to demolish this town. I know that they intend an attack, and that, too, in a very short time. I have correct information that they have five hundred men over in the Osawatomie country, some forty miles south ; about three hundred in the valley of the Wakarusa, and a large body above this place, variously estimated at from three to six hundred. There can concentrate at this place, in a very short time, some fifteen hundred or two thousand men, well armed, with several pieces of artillery. It would seem that the business of ' wiping out,' as it is called, of the pro-slavery party has been commenced. This heavy force has most unexpectedly sprung into existence, and made its appearance within a few days past. The women and children have been mostly sent across the river, and there is a general panic among the people. The force here

is small—say eighty or a hundred dragoons, and some hundred and
twenty citizens poorly armed, and badly supplied with ammunition.
Under these circumstances, I have to request you to send from the fort
all disposable force. A few companies of infantry would be very desirable, and some light artillery. Permit me to express the hope that
whatever force you can dispatch to the relief of this place will be sent
as soon as possible. Delay may be ruinous.

        " Yours, with great respect,   WILSON SHANNON.
"General P. F. Smith."

The next day, the 18th, General Richardson, in command
of the northern division of the territorial militia, wrote
General Smith as follows:

    " HEADQUARTERS FIRST DIVISION KANSAS MILITIA,
        " DONIPHAN COUNTY, KANSAS, August 18th.

  " SIR: In addition to the extra herewith inclosed, I have received
reliable information that a state of actual war exists in Douglas County,
and that in other parts of the Territory within this division, robberies
and other flagrant violations of law are daily occurring by armed bodies
of men from the Northern States. In the absence of all information
from the Governor of the Territory, I have taken the liberty of exercising the authority in me vested in cases of invasion, by ordering out the
entire strength of my division, to rendezvous at various points of the
division to receive further orders.

  " The object of this is to ask of you, as commandant of this district,
how far your orders require interference with the militia of the Territory, and whether or not their being thus assembled to repel such invasions is in violation of your instructions.

        " I am, sir, your most obedient servant,
             " WILLIAM P. RICHARDSON,
           " Major-General First Division Kansas Militia.
*"Brigadier-General Persifer F. Smith, Commanding, Leavenworth,
   K. T."*

On the 25th of August, Acting Governor Woodson issued
this proclamation:

  " Whereas, satisfactory evidence exists that the Territory of Kansas
is infested with large bodies of armed men, many of whom have just
arrived from the States, combined and confederated together, and amply
supplied with all the munitions of war, under the direction of a common
head, with a thorough military organization; who have been and are
still engaged in murdering the law-abiding citizens of the Territory,

driving others from their homes and compelling them to flee to the
States for protection, capturing and holding others as prisoners of war,
plundering them of their property, and in some instances burning down
their houses, and robbing United States post-offices and the local militia
of the arms furnished them by the Government, in open defiance and
contempt of the laws of the Territory and of the Constitution and laws
of the United States, and of the civil and military authority thereof; all
for the purpose of subverting by force and violence the government
established by law of Congress in the Territory:

" Now, therefore, I, Daniel Woodson, Acting Governor of the Territory of Kansas, do hereby issue my proclamation, declaring the said
Territory to be in a state of open insurrection and rebellion; and I do
hereby call upon all law-abiding citizens of the Territory to rally to the
support of their country and its laws, and require and command all officers, civil and military, and all other citizens of the Territory, to aid and
assist by all means in their power in putting down the insurrectionists,
and bringing to condign punishment all persons engaged with them, to
the end of assuring immunity from violence and full protection to the
persons, property, and civil rights to all peaceable and law-abiding inhabitants of the Territory.

" In testimony whereof, I have hereunto set my hand and caused to
be attached the seal of the Territory of Kansas.   Done at the city of
Lecompton, this 25th day of August, in the year of our Lord eighteen
hundred and fifty-six, and of the independence of the United States,
the eightieth.

[L. S.]   " DANIEL WOODSON,
                              " Acting Governor Kansas Territory."

On the 18th of August the *Argus*, of Platte City, Missouri,
issued an extra with these head-lines:

" IMPORTANT FROM KANSAS.—CIVIL WAR AND REBEL-
LION.—WOMEN AND CHILDREN FLYING FROM THEIR
HOMES FOR THEIR LIVES ! "

After a greatly exaggerated description of disturbances in
Kansas, it closes as follows:

" Above, fellow-citizens, we have given you the facts, as far as we
have learned them, of this recent unprovoked, inhuman, and unparalleled attack upon the peaceable citizens of Kansas Territory by a band
of as arrant traitors as ever cursed the soil of any country; an attack
premeditated and planned in the North to destroy your rights, or to
dissolve the Union.   Even now, while we write, our beloved Union,

purchased by the blood of our ancestors, may be no more. Missourians! the war rages upon your borders—at your very thresholds! Your
brethren and friends in Kansas are this day being butchered and driven
from their homes, and they now call upon you for succor and protection.
The Constitution of your country, and the laws under which you have
so long lived, as well as your own rights, menaced by as reckless and
abandoned a foe as ever erected its bloody crest to disturb the repose of
society, demand that you should rise up as one man and put an instant
and effectual quietus to the hired tools of abolition, disunion, and aggression, now roaming rampant over the plains of Kansas with firebrand
and sabre.

" Citizens of Platte County! the war is upon you, at your very
doors. Arouse yourselves to speedy vengeance, and rub out the bloody
traitors.   Recollect that, although this unholy and unnatural war is carried on in Kansas, it is against you and your institutions.   By a prompt
and vigorous action you may put it down and save the Union; but if
you lay supinely on your backs and allow the black treason to get a firm
hold in Kansas, you will find, when it is too late, that you have allowed
the golden moments to pass, and a long and bloody war, involving all
the States of the Union, will be inaugurated; and then you will have
to fight, not for your rights, but for your very existence; not for the
Union and Constitution—for they will have been destroyed in the onset
—but for some sort of an existence among the nations, either as slaves
or abject dependents of some power, perhaps, of Europe.   While you
are inert, the powers of the Union, North and South, will be slowly
mustering for the mighty conflict that is to follow; and all Europe will
look on with satisfaction at the termination of this Republic and the end
of Liberty.   Rouse up, then, and strangle the demon of disunion and
destruction.   Patriotism and the love of country, law, and liberty, demand it at your hands.

"*Still later.*—A dispatch, extra, just received this morning from Independence, signed A. G. Boone and others, corroborates the above
statements.

" Lecompton is burned down."

General Smith responded to Governor Shannon's request,
and prepared to send all his available force into the field,
but he wanted to be rid of his treason prisoners as badly as
Lane and Brown wanted to relieve him of their custody.
He wrote Shannon, on the 18th of August: "It will be
necessary that you should make some arrangement for the
custody of the prisoners that will take them out of the hands

of the troops. A small guard cannot be left with them safely; a large one cannot be spared, and they cannot be marched with the troops, whose movements they will retard and embarrass."

To this Acting Governor Woodson replied, August 26th, as follows:

" LECOMPTON, KANSAS TERRITORY,
" EXECUTIVE OFFICE, August 26th.

" SIR: In reply to your letter to Governor Shannon, requesting him to make some provision for keeping the prisoners now in charge of the army near this place, I have to say that those prisoners are in the custody of the United States Marshal for the Territory, Colonel I. B. Donelson, and that the Executive has no power to interfere with his duties.

" Colonel Donelson is, I understand, at Leavenworth City at this time.

" Very respectfully yours,
" DANIEL WOODSON,
"Acting Governor Kansas Territory.
"*Brigadier-General Smith, Commanding Army of the West.*"

Jefferson Davis, September 3d, made requisition upon the Governors of Kentucky and Illinois for two regiments of infantry from each State to put down rebellion in Kansas, and also authorized General Smith to use the territorial militia.

General Smith, instead of driving out armed bodies of men from Missouri, as did Colonel Sumner under Shannon's proclamation, instructed that " it will not be within the province of the troops to interfere with persons who may have come from a distance to give protection to their friends or others, and who may be behaving themselves in a peaceable and lawful manner."

He also gave directions that no action by the troops must be allowed against the territorial militia; and all armed pro-slavery men from Kansas or Missouri could be classed under that head.

Thus the decks were cleared for another and final engagement in this war. Guerrilla parties of pro-slavery men infested the whole Territory as by magic. Intercourse with Leavenworth and Kansas City was cut off, and the beleaguered town of Lawrence was nearly destitute of provisions as well as ammunition. Men unarmed and defenseless were shot down like dogs, and in one instance, at least, scalped. All appeals to Woodson for protection were in vain, and the end seemed fast approaching. The grand rally was to be from the eastern border. All the great generals, from Atchison, Reid, and others from Missouri, down to the smaller fry of the Territory, were on hand. The first demonstration was to be upon the reputed home of John Brown. Professor Spring truthfully says, in his " Kansas," page 190: "To Dutch Henry's Crossing must be charged much of the havoc and anarchy in which the Kansas of 1856 weltered. That affair was a festering, rankling, envenomed memory among pro-slavery men. It set afoot retaliatory violences, which for a while were successfully matched, and more than matched, by their opponents, but finally issued in a total military collapse of the Free-State cause."

On the 30th of August, General Reid, with a detachment from the main army, visited the hated town of Osawatomie. On approaching it, Rev. Martin White, who had personal reasons for remembering the Brown family, who attacked his cabin and took his horses in April of that year, met Frederick Brown, and exclaiming, " Why, I know you," shot him dead. The town had about forty Free-State defenders, and fell an easy prey to the enemy. A few shots were exchanged by the parties, W. W. Updegraff, John Brown, and Captain Cline, in command of the citizens, who soon fled across the creek out of harm's way. Six Free-State men lost their lives, either at the fight or before and after the encounter, and two pro-slavery men, according to Reid's report. The town was laid in ashes, excepting only four houses.

These bold movements of Atchison, which were counte-

nanced by Woodson, once more aroused the Free-State men.
Lane had now returned from a two weeks' absence in "forti-
fying the Nebraska line," and with about three hundred and
fifty men marched towards the invading forces. On coming
within sight of the enemy, near Bull Creek, he ordered a
retreat eight miles, where he camped for the night, returning the next morning to Lawrence without the loss of a man.
In the meantime the Governor's militia had not been idle
about Lecompton. Seven Free-State men had been burned
out of house and home, besides other outrages daily perpetrated in the vicinity. As some Free-State prisoners were
held at Lecompton by the militia, the men at Lawrence
concluded to visit the territorial capital in force. Colonel
P. St. George Cooke, September 5th, thus reports the affair:

"About a mile from town I joined the dismounted command, and,
rising the hill prairie above the town, came upon the flank of about
sixty mounted men in line, who remained motionless. Ordering the
dragoons to halt nearly in open column, I rode in front of the Lawrence
men, and accosted Captain Walker, who was in command, asking what
he came after. He answered, that they came to release prisoners and
have their rights. He said they had sent into town to treat with the
Governor. I asked him if that was all their men. He said, Oh, no,
there were seven hundred more close by. I told him it was a very unfortunate move on their part, that the prisoners had been ordered to be
released; and, among other things, said if they attacked the town, I
should attack them. He asked me if I would go with him to the main
body. I consented, and sent an order to Colonel Johnston, then arriving on the hill, to remain there in command of the troops until I returned; and taking Lieutenant Riddick, acting Assistant Quartermaster, an orderly, and bugler, rode with him towards the woods, near the
town.   *   *   *

"I asked Mr. Walker to collect the officers in front of the line, and
some twenty or thirty approached me, mounted. At the moment there
was an altercation with Mr. Cramer, treasurer of the Territory, whom
they had just made prisoner, who appealed to me, stating that he was a
United States officer, and that he had been sent to me. I addressed
these principal men. I said: 'You have made a most unfortunate
move for yourselves; the Missourians, you know, have gone, and the
militia here are nearly gone, having commenced crossing the river yesterday morning, to my knowledge. As to the prisoners, whilst I will

make no *terms* with you, I can *inform* you that they were promised to be released yesterday morning; and the Governor this morning told me he would order the release of all of them, and was to send me word at what hour I should send a guard to escort them to camp; that, therefore, I could assure their prompt return to their homes; that everything was going in their favor, and that it apparently would be so if they would refrain entirely from reprisals or any outrages, return to their occupations, and show moderation.' I required the release of the prisoner, Mr. Cramer, and their return to Lawrence.

"I was asked if I could promise that affairs would be set right at Leavenworth, and they have power to go and come? Mentioning several cases of murders or killing, even this morning, I answered, 'I could only answer for this vicinity; that things could not be settled in a moment; that General Smith was close to Leavenworth, and that his powers and views, I believed, were the same as mine.' I was then asked the ever-recurring question, if I should attack them if they attempted there to redress themselves or defend themselves? I replied, 'I give no pledge; that my mission was to preserve the peace.'

"Great regret was expressed by them that they had not been informed before of these events; they said they had waited long; that their messengers were killed or made prisoners, and mentioned that a regiment was then over the river, and apprehended it would lead to bad results, and I was asked to send to them to go back to Lawrence. I suggested that a written order should be sent, and one was afterwards handed me; they then released three prisoners, and marched off to return, whilst I rode over to the town with the released prisoners. I found one or two hundred militia, whom I had previously seen opposite, among the walls of the new capitol, under General Marshall.

"I found the Governor, and informed him of my action and its results. He said the prisoners had been released, but, in fact, the order had not yet been executed."

Colonel Cooke said the Governor and others pretended to desire the arrest of Lane, who did not make his appearance in the consultation. In his letter dated September 7th, Colonel Cooke says:

"I sent down yesterday Mr. Hutchinson and friends. He promised me that all prisoners should be released, and that the people would return to their occupations.

"In town *nine* other prisoners, released by order of General Richardson, were delivered to me. Some had been taken, as teamsters, I believe, near Leavenworth, ten or twelve days ago. I sent them with a small escort to Lawrence. General Richardson went with them; he had intended to go without escort. The sergeant of escort reports that, soon after his arrival, he rode out on the Franklin Road with General Lane and Captain Walker, perhaps to insure his safety.

" A large number of militia went off undischarged for their homes ; others, with some organization, pretending that they would resupply themselves and *return*. A large company remains in town, which I object to. General Marshall says they are a company from the Blue."

From this second letter it would seem that a deception was being practised upon the army officers and the people. While prisoners about Lecompton were discharged and militia companies were leaving ostensibly for their homes, these companies were not mustered out, but some of them claimed they would resupply themselves and return. Evidently they simply went *towards* Missouri, but brought up in Atchison's camp on the border. Also, the fact that General Richardson, on his way to join Atchison, could ride on friendly terms with Lane, when only the day before they claimed to want him arrested, is at least significant, and Lane's conduct soon after adds to its significance.

Mrs. Robinson, in her " Kansas," page 337, says:

" The prisoners came over to the camp at evening (September 5th) and, under military escort, went to Lawrence the next day. General Richardson, of the ' Kansas militia,' made a visit in Lawrence. He was received kindly by General Lane, who escorted him on his way to Franklin. He stated ' he was on his way to disperse the Missourians, who were coming into the Territory.' "

If he so stated, he made a false statement, as he did nothing of the kind.

While war manifestations were lessening on the west of Lawrence, they were assuming gigantic proportions east of it. All the border counties of western Missouri were aroused and apparently moving Kansas-ward. Steamboats coming up the Missouri River were loaded with armed men and munitions of war. Even the boat which brought the new Governor, Geary, was no exception to the rule.

At Lecompton all prisoners, including the treason pris-

21

oners, were turned loose, the latter on the 10th of September, just four months from the arrest of Robinson at Lexington. These prisoners were met by a long procession from Lawrence, and, as other prisoners arrived in the town on the same day, a general jubilee was held. But the rejoicing came to a sudden close. Lane, while he met the prisoners on arrival, left soon after, with a body-guard of about thirty men, in the direction of Nebraska. As this army from Missouri, said to be the most formidable ever seen in Kansas, was moving towards Lawrence, and Lane was moving towards Nebraska, an investigation of the situation was at once made. While army officers had estimated the force at Lawrence, at different times, from five hundred to eight hundred strong, and Captain Walker told Colonel Cooke he had seven hundred men with him on the south side of the river, at Lecompton, and Colonel Harvey had one hundred and fifty men on the north side, there could not be found in Lawrence, when Lane left, over three hundred men with arms of any kind, and of this number Lane sent a dispatch for all the best arms and the cannon to go to him at Hickory Point, in Jefferson County, where he had met some men who had organized for mutual protection. Official and other testimony is to the effect that these men were of both parties, united for protection against the thieves and marauders of all kinds. Colonel Harvey took one hundred men, with Sharp's rifles and the cannon, and went to help Lane out of the Territory, leaving only about fifty Sharp's rifles in town, and two hundred men and no cannon.

Mrs. Robinson, in her "Kansas," page 330, says, under date 24th of August: "It was estimated that in twelve hours' time from fifteen hundred to two thousand men could be rallied to defend Lawrence." This force was placed under the command of Lane, and now, when an army of two thousand eight hundred men was marching upon the Free-State settlements—had already destroyed Osawatomie —the towns were left utterly defenseless.

The future historian will have several questions to solve relative to the motive and purpose of Lane in this wonderful generalship. Among the queries to be answered will be these: Was he moved by fear, as when he left Kansas between the great battle with "live and straw" men at Fort Saunders, and the battle at Fort Titus? Did he think, as the treason prisoners would be the first to "go up" should the pro-slavery army enter Lawrence, he might thus get rid of a claim dispute without having to kill his contestant—Gaius Jenkins, a late treason prisoner—with his own hand? or did he think it a good time to give a final *coup de grace* to the Free-State cause?

Governor Geary arrived at Fort Leavenworth September 9th, and at Lawrence on the 12th. As he had known Robinson by reputation in California, when the entire militia of that embryo State was called out to put down fifteen men, of whom he was one; and as Robinson had known Geary by reputation as Mayor of San Francisco in trying times, they met and became at once frank and somewhat confidential in their interview. Governor Geary assured Robinson that he was in earnest in putting an end to the troubles in Kansas, as it was a political necessity for the Democratic party. The whole North was a seething caldron of excitement over Kansas affairs, and Buchanan's election was in danger. He had issued a proclamation ordering all armed bodies of men to disperse, which he brought to Lawrence.

Robinson questioned the propriety of enforcing this order while the Missourians, under pretense of militia, were marching upon the town. Governor Geary said they would be under his control, and he would guarantee protection. Upon being told by Robinson that he did not know his militia, that they might or might not obey his orders, he consented that the people of Lawrence might retain their military organizations till he should send the Missourians home. He went again to Lecompton, promising to return in time to meet the Missourians before they should reach Lawrence.

On the 14th of September, the enemy arrived at Franklin.
A messenger was dispatched with the information to Governor Geary.   In the afternoon a large party of horsemen
approached the town from the direction of Franklin.   Immediately all who were armed with Sharp's rifles started
upon the double-quick to intercept and repulse them. About
fifty men thus went out, formed a skirmish line, and drove
them back.   As soon as this body of horsemen made its
appearance, other dispatches were sent to Geary at Lecompton, one by G. W. Brown, who had been introduced to him
by a letter of a mutual friend, and one by Robinson.   Governor Geary immediately applied to Colonel Cooke, who
started the troops at once for Lawrence, they arriving in the
night, their artillery on Oread Hill, and the dragoons in the
valley between Lawrence and Franklin.   When this force
arrived Robinson became insane, and procured some wine
and carried to the officers who but recently had him in
charge as a treason prisoner, and treated them.   This was
the first and last time in his life he was guilty of such an in-
discretion.   Governor Geary and Colonel Cooke arrived
early in the morning, and met the Missourians as they were
moving towards Lawrence.   He immediately held a consultation with their officers, and the war, inaugurated May
24th on the Potawatomie by John Brown, ended then and
there.

As it is claimed by Mr. Sanborn, Redpath, and others
that John Brown saved Lawrence at this time, it may be
important to refer to the matter.   While Robinson was present and endeavored to watch the situation from first to last,
his testimony will not be given, as he may be thought to be
an interested witness by some.   Major J. B. Abbott was
officer of the day, according to Colonel Walker, and wore
his sash as such, while Joseph Cracklin was ranking officer,
being appointed Lieutenant-Colonel by Lane a short time before.   Colonel Cracklin was a member of the Boston party
that went to California in 1849, was an intimate associate

with Robinson, had been a sailor, and was well versed in all matters of peace and war. He was a most valuable factor from first to last, and was captain of the famous " Stubbs " until promoted. From his account of the preparations and proceedings of that time, as published in the Lawrence *Tribune*, the following extracts are made :

" Editor Tribune :

" SIR : It was with much pleasure I read the very interesting article of Governor Robinson, in your issue of the 16th instant. The perversion of history referred to by the Governor, and the desire on the part of the friends and worshippers of John Brown, intentionally or otherwise, to give him credit where it was not due, is sincerely to be regretted. As the Governor truly says : 'John Brown never had anything whatever to do with erecting or commanding any fortification about Lawrence, and never saved the town from attack, or did any more towards it than the most obscure person in the town.' The Governor is right. I was here and took an active part in all the troubles, as Captain of the ' Stubbs,' and certainly ought to know. * * * John Brown had nothing to do with either building or commanding any fort or breastwork about Lawrence, or with the defense of Lawrence against any attack whatever. A day or two before the arrival of the ruffian two thousand seven hundred, I met General Lane on the street. He took me by the arm and requested me to accompany him to his office ; arriving there, he presented me with a lieutenant-colonel's commission. At first I was disposed to reject it, not wishing to sever my connection with the Stubbs ; but he urged me so strongly to accept that I finally yielded, and sent my resignation as captain to Lieutenant Cutler. The company immediately called a meeting and proceeded to fill the vacancy by electing Cutler. Soon after, Lyman Allen informed me that Governor Robinson wanted to see me at his office. I called on the Governor, who congratulated me on my promotion, and said he had reliable information that a large force were on their way to attack and destroy Lawrence ; that our force in town was small, and would still be more reduced by the absence of Colonel Harvey, who intended to start that night on a private expedition. But the Stubbs were not to leave under any consideration, without orders from headquarters. He also said he wanted me to make the best disposition of the force we had, for the defense of the town, in doing which I was to use my best judgment. Accordingly, in compliance with his instructions, I had a strong guard posted around the town that night, and the next morning proceeded to station our men to the best advantage. One body of men was stationed in the circular fort at the junction of Massachusetts and Henry streets, one at the foundation of my house on Rhode Island street, under the command of Jeff. Conway. I went for the Stubbs, but, to my sorrow, I found they had disobeyed orders, and left town with Colonel Harvey. I had notified Captain Cutler personally of the Governor's orders on the evening before. I regretted their absence very much. I then hunted up the Wabaunsee Rifles. I could find but ten; these I posted under Captain Lynde at the point where Roberts' box mill now stands, with instructions to remain there until the enemy came within gunshot, when they were to open fire, and if obliged to retreat, to fall back gradually and orderly under cover of the buildings, keeping up a running fire. I then left them to make further disposition. As I was returning, I heard some one cry out, ' There they come.' I stopped, turned my eyes in the direction of Franklin, and I saw a large force of horsemen going towards Mr. Haskell's. I immediately started on a run for the Wabaunsee boys, and told them to follow me, and started on a dog trot towards the cabin of John Speer, and halted a short distance from it on the top of a ridge. At the time I halted, the enemy had passed into the timber beyond Haskell's. Supposing it was their intention to pass into the bottom and approach the town in that direction, I concluded to wait where I was until they showed themselves, feeling that, with them in the bottom, I would have the advantage of position and could attack them with a plunging fire. I was disappointed, however. In a few minutes they made their appearance, coming out of the timber and heading towards us. As soon as they got in range I ordered the boys to open fire. We had not fired more than a dozen shots, when, looking towards town, I saw quite a number of men on the run to our assistance. In the meantime the enemy had disappeared in a hollow or ravine.

"As fast as my friends arrived I placed them in line, deployed as skirmishers at six paces intervals, until my force amounted to fifty-eight. Not seeing anything of the enemy, I sent Ed. Bond, who was mounted, to see what they were doing. We watched him until he arrived at the entrance of the ravine, where the enemy were concealed, when he stopped, levelled his rifle, and fired; he then put spurs to his pony and galloped back. He reported them in the ravine at a halt, and some dismounted. I then ordered a forward movement, with my line extended as skirmishers. We had a space of half or three-quarters of a mile to cross before we would reach the ridge that separated us from the enemy. On reaching it, we discovered them just going out of the upper end of the ravine in the direction of Hanscom's farm. I ordered the boys to open fire, to load and fire at will; our whole line immediately commenced blazing away. They fired several shots in return, but they fell short. One of their men was seen to fall near Hanscom's fence. They put spurs to their horses and galloped away towards Franklin. * * *

" The only fighting done on that day was done by the gallant little force I had the honor to command, and John Brown had nothing to do with it, either directly or indirectly, Redpath and other worshippers to the contrary notwithstanding.

" J. CRACKLIN."

Captain Cutler, who succeeded Cracklin as Captain of the Stubbs, gives as his reason for leaving Lawrence against Cracklin's orders, that he was ordered to do so by Colonel Harvey, who ranked ,Cracklin. Harvey received his orders from Lane, and hence the desertion of the town by its best men and arms in the face of an advancing enemy.

As much other work performed by the Stubbs and other companies under command of Captains Cracklin, Walker, Abbott, and others has been credited to John Brown, extracts are given from a letter of Captain Cracklin, published in the Lawrence *Tribune* of April 19, 1881 :

" They had four camps at different points in the Territory, from which they sallied for murder and robbery, viz. : Doniphan, Franklin, Washington Creek, and one near Osawatomie had become such an unendurable pest in the neighborhood they infested that no traveller could pass the roads in safety. Appeal was made to the United States for protection, but in vain, when, at the instance of the Free-State settlers in the immediate vicinity of this Georgia camp, an expedition was planned at Lawrence and given in my charge. I selected the Stubbs, Coal Creek, and Franklin companies, in all ninety-one men, and left Lawrence in the early part of August, 1856, and on the second day after, arrived at Osawatomie, where, after learning the position of the camp and the strength of the enemy, I made preparation for an immediate attack. Dividing my force in two divisions, about dark in the evening we ascended the hill, upon which the enemy had erected a large block-house, which served a double purpose, as a fort and residence. Advancing in open order on two points, we were surprised on arriving to find the fort abandoned. I immediately gave orders to remove everything of value and set fire to the building. I would here state, that at that time, John Brown was in Iowa, consequently he could have taken no part in the expedition. Yet, notwithstanding, Redpath gives him the credit of commanding the force that broke up this Georgia pest, that had so long harassed the settlers in that neighborhood.

" This little affair was followed up by a series of attacks on all their camps. Next was Franklin, where I led the attacking party, composed

of Stubbs, and a portion of the Coal Creek and Franklin companies,
with a few others, and after a sharp little fight of three hours, we routed
the enemy, took their camp, and captured one cannon and a large
quantity of small arms. (The cannon is now in our city, and known
as ' Old Sacramento.') In this engagement I had one man killed, and
four wounded—Arthur Gunther, wounded severely in the breast and
chin; George Henry, slightly wounded in the breast; John Crocker,
slightly wounded in the head; George W. Smith, Jr., slightly wounded
in the head and leg. George Sackett, a very estimable young man, was
killed, shot through the head.

"This was followed by the attacks on Washington Creek, Titus
Fort, and Hickory Point, in all of which the Stubbs took an active
part, until they were unfortunately captured, without resistance, by the
United States troops, disarmed, and kept several months in a loathsome prison at Lecompton.
                                                   " JOSEPH CRACKLIN.

This capture of the Stubbs was occasioned by their
answering the call of Lane when he fled to Nebraska as the
2800 Missourians were marching upon Lawrence.

When Colonel Harvey with his men reached Hickory
Point, Lane had passed on with his body-guard in safety to
his destination, the States. Harvey opened fire upon the
cabin where the citizens and others had gathered for mutual
protection, and after a skirmish in which shots were given
and returned, a settlement was effected, all parties joining in
a treat. But as Governor Geary's proclamation had been
issued, the United States troops went for Harvey's men and
arrested them. Some escaped, but 101 were brought to
Lecompton, and were kept prisoners several months, all on
account of the generalship of Sanborn's "indispensable"
hero, Lane.

This is a very brief outline of the conflict of 1856. As it
has been claimed that two men, and not the policy and
members of the Free-State party, saved the cause of free
Kansas, care has been taken to give their course in full. As
has been seen, this policy of the Free-State men and party
had been to do no wrong, commit no crime, but to prevent
the establishment of slavery by the so-called territorial laws

by making them a dead letter—by the baffling process which Governor Shannon conceded would nullify them. As Andreas says, the policy of assassination, plunder, theft, robbery, arson, and murder was inaugurated by John Brown, and his followers practiced such outrages through the entire season. This, of course, gave excuse for retaliation in kind, which was most successfully practiced by the Slave-State party until the Free-State men were virtually subdued and driven from the field. Had there been no outside influences to interfere, three days more would have sufficed to lay waste every Free-State settlement in the Territory, including Lawrence, Topeka, and Manhattan. Their fate would have been that of Osawatomie. The territory outside of these settlements was already a conquered province. Lawrence was in a state of siege and nearly destitute of provisions, under the exclusive generalship of Lane and Brown, while the atmosphere was blackened with the smoke of burning shanties and cabins of Free-State men.

Governor Geary gives a striking picture of the situation as seen on his arrival, as follows:

"I reached Kansas and entered upon the discharge of my official duties in the most gloomy hour of her history. Desolation and ruin reigned on every hand; homes and firesides were deserted; the smoke of burning dwellings darkened the atmosphere; women and children, driven from their habitations, wandered over the prairies and among the woodlands, or sought refuge and protection even among the Indian tribes. The highways were infested with numerous predatory bands, and the towns were fortified and garrisoned by armies of conflicting partisans, each excited almost to frenzy, and determined upon mutual extermination. Such was, without exaggeration, the condition of the Territory at the period of my arrival."

Redpath says that nearly all Free-State settlers had been driven from Linn and Miami counties, the neighborhood of Brown's Dutch Henry's massacre, and all north of the Kansas River was completely subjugated; so much so that Lane, the commanding General of the Free-State forces, did not dare attempt his escape through this region without a body-

guard of nearly or quite thirty men.   But, it will be asked,
did not these men, Brown and Lane, show remarkable traits
of generalship?   The only battles in which Brown was engaged were at Black Jack and Osawatomie.   At the first
Captain Shore had nineteen men and Brown nine.   Shore
with his men attacked Pate from the open prairie and drove
him into the ravine, while Brown took to the ravine at once,
and was not in sight of the foe at all.   Shore also went into
the ravine, and shots were exchanged for several hours, till
Captain J. B. Abbott appeared in sight of the enemy with
his company, when Pate surrendered.   This is substantially
the part played in this battle by Brown.

At the other battle, the second raid upon Osawatomie, all
the Free-State men, under command of Captains Updegraff,
Brown, and Cline, immediately went to the timber of the
Marais des Cygnes, where a few shots were exchanged.
When pressed by the enemy, there was no orderly retreat,
as is usual on such occasions, but a general "skedaddle,"
every man for himself.   John Brown disappeared with the
rest, and was not again seen till near night, when Captain J.
M. Anthony, brother of Susan B. Anthony, saw him.   Captain Anthony, after caring for Dr. Updegraff and others,
says: " I went back to the Crane house, and began to think
about getting something to eat, as we had gone out without
breakfast, and had had nothing to eat all day.   I went down
to the barn-yard to milk the cow, and while doing that saw
John Brown advancing up the ravine.   When he got to
within about twenty feet of me, or just across the fence, he
stopped, and said, ' Hello, is that you?'   I replied that it
was undoubtedly, and we talked for several minutes, he asking me all about the result of the day's engagement.   He
seemed to be entirely ignorant of the result, and, like Dr.
Updegraff, and indeed everybody else, thought the whole
community had been killed."   These are the only battles in
1856 where Brown had any men or exercised any authority,
notwithstanding, according to Redpath and company, it

would be inferred he was a prodigy of valor and generalship. Lane's encounters have already been given. He marched his "live and straw men," according to his special friend and eulogizer, John Speer, to Washington Creek, and then fled between two days to Nebraska, where he threw up breastworks to fortify the line, whether to prevent ingress or egress does not appear. He also, as Andreas says, "made a faint feint" against Reid's forces near Bull Creek, after the destruction of Osawatomie, at which "he was an adept," and his march with the command to Lecompton, led by Colonel Samuel Walker. These are all of his exploits, except stripping Lawrence of its arms and men to help him escape from the 2800 Missourians in September. These particulars are given simply because, on account of the scribblings of hero-worshippers, these men have been made to appear as the saviors of Kansas, when from the standpoint of the Free-State policy, Kansas would have been saved with much less suffering and bloodshed without than with them. Also it is a great injustice to the really brave and fighting men, whose courage, prudence, and firmness did save the cause, in spite of the reckless course of Brown and the reckless advice of Lane.

The men relied upon for fighting purposes were those connected with the different military organizations, and others; while the policy was adopted by the rank and file of the Free-State party, except the two heroes who would have brought the party in conflict with Federal authority on more than one occasion, had they not been prevented.

CHAPTER XIII.

THE CONDUCT OF THE ARMY IN KANSAS.—AGITATION IN
THE EAST.—THE PRESIDENTIAL ELECTION.—GOVERNOR
GEARY'S FAILURE.

THE question will be asked, if Kansas was powerless to
save itself, what agency or agencies did save it? The immediate and direct agency was Governor Geary with the
United States troops; and President Pierce sent the Governor to do the work; but what induced the President to
take this action? The answer is rather intricate. It will be
remembered that a messenger was sent East after the consultation of Howard and Sherman, of the Congressional
Committee, with Reeder, Roberts, Mrs. Sherman, Mrs.
Robinson, and Robinson. This messenger visited, among
others, Amos A. Lawrence of Boston. Mr. Lawrence was
familiar with every movement that had been made in Kansas affairs, and comprehended the situation at once. He
immediately set his machinery in motion. He caused petitions to be circulated for assembling the Legislatures in the
Northern States, that steps might be taken to protect their
citizens in Kansas from Federal and border ruffian outrage.
Also a strong protest to the President against this oppression
was drawn up, to be signed by Northern governors, all to
induce him to call a halt if he would prevent civil war in
the country.

The Congressional Committee made a report which
shocked the nation from centre to circumference. All reports of outrages sent from Kansas were more than confirmed by the sworn testimony taken by this committee.

Abolitionists, Free-soilers, Whigs, and Democrats stood aghast at this revelation of infamy.

The blockade of the Missouri River by the land pirates along its banks added fuel to the flames of indignation, and armies began to collect and march through Iowa and Nebraska to engage in the civil strife.

The arrest and confinement of men guilty of no crime but that of defending their homes from outrage, and the destruction of a hotel and printing presses by pretended law, capped the climax.

A Presidential election was pending, and should the outrages and disturbances continue, no power on earth could save the Democratic party from utter defeat.

Add to all this, the personal appeal of Mrs. Lawrence, mother of Amos A., whose good opinion the President said he preferred to that of all the politicians, and it is not difficult to discern some of the reasons why Geary was sent out and Kansas relieved.

The appeal of Mrs. Lawrence to the President is thus referred to in Professor Spring's " Kansas," on page 196 :

" It is said that a letter was received from a lady—the wife of one of the prisoners, and probably Mrs. Robinson—which put the case in a favorable light, and being read aloud by Mrs. Pierce to her husband, it took hold of the feelings of both. These expectations were not disappointed. 'I have given such orders concerning Dr. Robinson as will please you,' President Pierce informed the Boston friends, and the ' Bastile-on-the-prairies ' was broken up. Mr. Lawrence's knowledge of the letter, a not inconsiderable factor in effecting the modification of Federal policy towards Kansas, which now took place, and in hastening the arrival of Woodson's successor in the Territory, was not so slender as his language might seem to imply. He drafted the letter himself, and sent it to Mrs. Robinson, who copied and forwarded it to Mrs. Pierce."

A word about the officers and men of the United States Army. It has been customary for letter-writers and stump orators to denounce the army as the ally of the Slave-State party, and as the enemy of freedom. This is a great mistake. The army was entirely independent of both parties, and was always on the side of law, Federal law, and the Constitution, with the one exception of dispersing the Topeka Legislature, on the 4th of July, 1856. It is safe to say that, had it not been for the officers of the United States Army, the Free-State struggle would have ended in disaster on more than one occasion. After the massacre on the Potawatomie, all western Missouri was moving upon Kansas to avenge this outrage upon unoffending pro-slavery men. It is true, with the assistance of the Sharp's rifles in the possession of Shore's and Abbott's companies, Pate had been captured and was held prisoner by Brown, but two armies were marching to rescue him, one under General Whitfield and one under General Coffin.

Either of these forces would have annihilated Brown as soon as found, and the appearance of Colonel Sumner, in obedience to the proclamation of Governor Shannon, alone saved him. Colonel Sumner sent all the Missouri invaders home, as well as the Free-State military companies.

During the summer of 1856, had the troops been hostile to the Free-State cause and acted as partisans, there were several occasions when the Free-State men would have suffered. One of these was when Titus's house was destroyed and he taken prisoner; another was when Lecompton was visited by a force of seven or eight hundred Free-State men to procure the release of persons held as prisoners.

At another time Governor Woodson directed Colonel P. St. George Cooke to visit Topeka, make a general attack upon it, as in rebellion, and destroy its defenses. Colonel Cooke promptly and emphatically refused to comply with this order or demand. Here is the correspondence:

" EXECUTIVE OFFICE, LECOMPTON, K. T.,
" September 1, 1856.

" SIR : The Marshal of the Territory having officially reported to me that ' the ordinary course of judicial proceedings and the powers invested in him as United States Marshal are wholly inadequate for the suppression of the insurrectionary combinations known to exist through-

out the whole extent of the Territory,' it becomes my duty, as the Acting Executive, to make a requisition upon you for your entire command,
or such portion of it as may, in your judgment, be consistently detached
from their ordinary duty, to aid me in suppressing these insurrectionary
combinations and invasive aggressions against the organized government
of the Territory of Kansas.

"Your command, or such part of it as may be deemed necessary,
will therefore proceed at the earliest practicable moment to invest the
town of Topeka, and disarm all the insurrectionists or aggressive invaders against the organized government of the Territory to be found
at or near that point, retaining them as prisoners, subject to the order
of the Marshal of the Territory.

"All their breastworks, forts, or fortifications should be levelled to
the ground.

"It is very desirable to intercept all aggressive invaders against the
Government on the road known as ' Lane's trail,' leading from the Nebraska line to Topeka. If, therefore, your command is sufficiently
large to admit of it, a detachment should be stationed on the road with
orders to intercept all such ' aggressive invaders ' as they may make
their appearance.

                "Very respectfully, your obedient servant,
                            "DANIEL WOODSON,
                    "Acting Governor of Kansas Territory.
" *Lieutenant-Colonel P. St. George Cooke, Commanding United States
    Dragoons, near Lecompton.*"

                "HEADQUARTERS, CAMP NEAR LECOMPTON, K. T.,
                            "September 2, 1856—6 A.M.

"SIR: I received last night your letter of September 1st, informing
me that the Marshal of the Territory had officially reported to you that
' the ordinary course of judicial proceedings and the powers vested in
him as United States Marshal are wholly inadequate for the suppression
of insurrectionary combinations known to exist throughout the whole
extent of the Territory,' and you therefore make requisition to aid you
' in suppressing these insurrectionary combinations and invasive aggressions ' by marching to invest the town of Topeka, ' disarming all the insurrectionists or aggressive invaders, retaining them as prisoners, subject to the order of the Marshal,' and to level to the ground all breastworks, etc.

"Since my instructions from the Secretary of War (February 15th),
I am instructed by a letter from the Adjutant-General to Colonel Sumner,
dated March 26, 1856, in relation to the course to be pursued towards
armed bodies coming into the Territory, that ' it is only when an armed
resistance is offered to the laws and against the peace and quiet of the

Territory, and when under such circumstances a requisition for a military force is made upon the commanding officer by the authority specified in his instructions, that he is empowered to act.'

" I am further instructed by General Smith (August 28, 1856), that if it should come to my knowledge ' that either side is moving upon the other with a view of attack, it will become my duty to observe their movements and prevent such hostile collision.' But it will not be within the province of the troops to interfere with persons who may have come from a distance to give protection to their friends, or others who may be behaving themselves in a peaceable or lawful manner. And, further, ' to make every exertion in my power with the force under my orders to preserve the peace and prevent bloodshed.'

" It is evident, both under the laws and my instructions, that the last resort—the effusion of the blood of the citizens by the military power—must be induced by a special act of resistance to the civil officer in the execution of his legal duty when assisted by that power. In no case yet has the Marshal of the Territory, thus aided, been resisted. No specification of resistance by the people of Topeka is made in your requisition, nor is my aid asked to assist the Marshal in the execution there of any law or the process of any court. It is simply a call upon me to make war upon the town of Topeka, to ' invest ' it, ' make prisoners,' level defenses.

" Your request that I should station troops on ' Lane's trail ' to 'intercept aggressive invaders,' would be clearly inconsistent with my last instructions ' not to interfere with persons who have come from a distance,' etc., as well as those of March 26th.

" In my best judgment, I cannot comply with your call. If the army be useless in the present unhappy crisis, it is because in our constitution and law civil war was not foreseen, nor the contingency of a systematic resistance by the people to governments of their own creation, and which, at short intervals, they may either correct or change.

" Your letter will be forwarded by express to Major-General Smith, for his consideration and action.

" With great respect, your obedient servant,
" P. St. GEORGE COOKE,
" Lieutenant-Colonel Second Dragoons.
" *His Excellency Acting Governor Daniel Woodson, Lecompton, K. T.*"

In this Colonel Cooke was sustained by General Smith, then in command at Fort Leavenworth. While the instructions of General Smith not to interfere with persons who had come from a distance to protect their friends in Kansas, so long as they behaved themselves and violated no law, seemed at first sight to be intended to aid the pro-slavery party in protecting the people from Missouri when they should come to protect their partisan friends from mid-night assassinations, it is but just to say that he was impar-tial in the application of such instructions, and Free-State men from the North through Iowa and Nebraska were treated with the same leniency as were the pro-slavery men from Missouri and the South. The Free-State prisoners in charge of the troops, as soon as Colonel Sumner visited their camp, were treated with all the courtesy and kindness they could claim under the circumstances, and without exception the prisoners became ardent friends of their keepers.

At the close of the conflict of arms, on the arrival of Governor Geary, the United States troops were indispen-sable in bringing hostilities to an end. Had it not been for the command of Colonel Cooke before Lawrence, the 15th of September, 1856, there is but little question that Lawrence and Topeka would have shared the fate of Osawatómie. Without the troops at his back, Governor Geary would have been ignored till this had been accom-plished.

Take it all in all, the conduct of the army during the Kan-sas conflict, even though under the direction of Jefferson Davis, Secretary of War, is worthy of all praise, with the single exception of the dispersion of the Legislature, and this was afterwards disapproved even by Secretary Davis and the President. Army officers, as a rule, are above all partisan bias, and are governed strictly by the Constitution, law, and army regulations. No branch of the Government is so free from partisan or personal influence, and no offi-cials are governed by a sense of honor as are army officers. The experience in the Kansas conflict has shown the value of the regular army in all conflicts among the people. This is the only force that can be relied upon to hold the scales of justice even when "madness rules the hour."

Governor Geary having brought the olive branch to Kan-
22

sas, there was a general stampede of such leading Free-State
men as had remained through the season to the States where
the Presidential campaign was raging with great fury.
General Fremont was the nominee of the Republicans and
James Buchanan of the Democrats. Fremont had warmly
espoused the cause of the Kansas settlers, and had many
elements of popularity. Had the unbiased sentiment of the
voters prevailed, he would have been elected, but money
was used to carry Pennsylvania in the October election for
the Democrats, and from that time there was no such thing
as stemming the tide that set Buchanan-ward. The October
vote of Pennsylvania was offered to the Republican National Executive Committee for a consideration, but the
money was not forthcoming, and the transfer was made to
the other party. Here was the first object-lesson on a large
scale of machine politics the writer had ever witnessed.
From that time to the present he has had but little faith in
the triumph of principle, pure and simple, in national politics. The oppressed people may agitate, educate, and organize for relief, but when election-day arrives, the demagogues who seize the reins of their party will sell out to the
highest bidder for cash or spoils. Such has been uniformly
the case in the past, and such it will probably continue to
be in all powerful governments, whatever the form.

The election of James Buchanan was notice to all Kansans that their struggle was not ended. While the conflict
of arms might not be renewed, there was to be one of politics which would require all the skill of veterans to manage
successfully.

The agitation of the Presidential campaign and the cessation of hostilities started the Free-State emigrants to Kansas
in great numbers, and there was to be no question as to majorities. No political action would be called for until 1857, and
the respective parties had plenty of time to lay their plans.
While there was an election in 1856 for one branch of the
Legislature, the Free-State men ignored it, as it would give

them but one House, even if successful. Besides, the Slave-State party had the "returning boards," and there must be some assurance that they would make honest counts and honest returns. In the meantime Governor Geary was taking his first lesson with his own party. He had come to Kansas with a purpose, namely, to quiet disturbances that the election of Buchanan might be secured. This had been accomplished, and he vainly imagined that he was a character of great importance, and that he could rule the destiny of Kansas. But he was not long in discovering his error. When he sent to their homes the 2800 men menacing Lawrence, one party passed up the California road to Lecompton. A man of this party named Hays wantonly shot a peaceable settler, a cripple, named Buffum, almost in the presence of Geary, who took the poor man's hand in his own as he was dying and pledged him that his murderer should be brought to just punishment. At great expense the Governor caused the arrest of Hays, when Judge Lecompte issued his writ of habeas corpus, and discharged him on bail. Then Governor Geary became indignant, and demanded of the President the removal of Lecompte. But he soon discovered that Lecompte was the favorite at Washington, and not Geary, and that the effort to fasten slavery upon Kansas had been by no means abandoned. Geary eventually learned that he was mere surplusage, and only nominally Governor of the Territory. Before this fact dawned upon him, however, he conceived a plan of settling forever the conflict in the Territory by securing admission to the Union as a State under the Topeka Constitution. He sent for Robinson, the Governor elect, for an interview at his office. Governor Geary was confident that Buchanan would be glad to be rid of the controversy in any feasible way, and was quite sure, if the office of governor could be made vacant that some Democrat might fill the position, there would be no question of the approval of the Administration at Washington. It was evident that Governor Geary would expect to be the successful candidate for State governor. Robinson, who had staked his all upon the single issue of a Free-State for Kansas, and would be glad of success at whatever cost to himself, short of dishonor, at once agreed to make a vacancy in the office of governor, and visit Washington to advise with the Republicans in Congress; while Geary was to reconcile the Administration, which he had no doubt could be easily accomplished. Accordingly, Robinson gave his resignation to Lieutenant-Governor Roberts, and went to Washington. He was not long in learning, however, that the Democrats had regard neither for this plan nor for Governor Geary. It was evident that Geary's plans and recommendations were at a great discount at Washington. While Geary supposed his mission to Kansas for quieting the Territory that Buchanan might be elected meant also the abandonment of the Slave-State contest, the party manipulators meant no such thing. They gladly used Geary, and suspended hostilities to tide over the election, but the endeavor to subjugate Kansas to slavery was by no means to be abandoned.

As soon as it became generally known that the State Governor elect had left his resignation with Lieutenant-Governor Roberts and gone to Washington, a howl went up from his enemies, of which he always had an ample supply, accusing him of desertion of the Free-State cause, and of all the political crimes known to the calendar. Even the *Herald of Freedom* joined the chorus. The Legislature was to meet in January, but neither Robinson nor Roberts was present. Instead of presenting the resignation of Robinson to the Legislature as expected, Roberts was himself absent. The indignation manifested was legitimate and the censure merited. However, at the convention held on March 10, 1857, Robinson had returned and explained his course to the convention, when a resolution was adopted expressing satisfaction with the explanation and requesting a withdrawal of the resignation. The resignation, which had never been presented to the Legislature, was revoked and peace once more prevailed.

Instead of paving the way for admission to the Union by his scheme, Governor Geary found he had merely involved himself in trouble. The Territorial Legislature held a session, and soon war raged with the Executive. Bills would be vetoed only to be passed by a two-thirds vote as soon as returned; and had the Governor and Legislature belonged to opposite political parties, the hostility could not have been more bitter. At length matters reached a crisis, when the Governor refused to appoint a Mr. Sherard to an office he desired. Sherard grossly insulted the Governor, whose friends called a mass meeting to denounce the insult. But the insulter appeared, drew his revolver, and commenced shooting at random, when Mr. Jones, a friend of the Governor, shot him dead. From this time henceforth there was no rest in Kansas for Governor Geary, and he took advantage of the darkness and the services of Colonel Walker to make his exit. His resignation took effect on the 4th of March, the day the man he had been instrumental in electing President entered upon his office.

No Governor had a more difficult rôle to play than Geary. If his course should please one party, it was sure to offend the other. His first move of pacification, however, was accepted by both parties—by the Free-State party because their constitutional rights were restored to them, and by the pro-slavery party because of the political necessity. Had Geary after the election ignored his pledges to the people and joined in the effort to fasten slavery upon Kansas by means of the Lecompton Constitution provided by his Legislature, he might have retained his office, but at the expense of his plighted word. He chose to remain true to his pledges, and retain his honor and self-respect, and was discarded by his party.

His plan for putting down the thieves and outlaws of both parties was excellent. He had mustered into the service two companies of the citizens, one under Colonel Titus and one under Captain Walker. This worked to a charm. The pro-slavery company would see that no depredations were committed upon their friends, and the Free-State company would attend to the others. At this time a large number of "reprisal" men, professedly Free-State, were subsisting on the people by robbery, and they had no idea of giving up their occupation. Dr. Brown, in his "Reminiscences," page 41, refers to some of them as follows:

"AN EXCITING INCIDENT.

"To illustrate the times and disturbed state of Kansas during this interesting period in the history of the Territory, I give the following facts:

"After our release from imprisonment; the arrival of Governor Geary; the return of Generals Heiskell and Reid, with their invading army of twenty-seven hundred to Missouri; the disappearance of Old John Brown, his sons, and their families towards Iowa; the arrest and imprisonment of Colonel Harvey and his command of one hundred, who had unwisely responded to an 'order' of General Lane's, after Governor Geary's proclamation of peace; and while Governor Geary and his escort were making a tour of southern Kansas to tranquillize the agitation in that quarter, probably some time during the last days of October, I was sitting at my table, in the sanctum of the *Herald of Freedom* office building, preparing copy for the paper. A rap at the inner door. I arose, opened it, and saw three men standing before me, armed with revolvers and bowies, and I think Sharp's rifles. Speaking to them, one introduced himself as Captain H. Shaking hands with him, he then introduced the others, one as 'my First Lieutenant,' giving his name, which has escaped me; the other as 'Second Lieutenant,' whose name is also forgotten. I passed them chairs, and took a seat myself at the table where I had been writing.

"Captain H. opened the conversation; inquired how soon the *Herald of Freedom* would again appear; congratulated me on my restoration to liberty, and then said, with a hearty laugh, in which the whole trio joined: 'Governor Geary is tranquillizing the Territory.' I replied that he seemed to be doing much in that direction, and from the character of letters to me from personal friends in Pennsylvania, who knew Governor Geary well, I had no doubt of his success, provided the authorities at Washington would not interfere with his work.

"'He can never do it,' replied Captain H. 'It is too late. The ruffians have overrun Kansas, have had their day until the Free-State men are thoroughly organized for revenge, and now they want to *tranquillize* us. Ha, ha, ha, they can't do it. Let me tell you, Mr. Brown, my lieutenants here and myself have been following in the rear of Governor Geary's pacific tour, and we have been trying to show that the thing won't tranquillize.' He then proceeded to narrate various crimes they had committed, entering into details, telling of murders, arsons, rapes, horse-stealing, and other offenses of an aggravated character. * * *

" ' I think you mistake the true policy. Our ambition is to make Kansas a free State. Our success is contingent upon the number of actual settlers we have from the free North, who will co-operate with us. To get these settlers it is our interest, as well as duty, to quiet down the excitement, show up the beauty of the country, the healthful climate, productive soil, and satisfy them that we have the ability to make it free, and we will see such an emigration Kansas-ward next spring as the world has never seen before. You must remember, Captain, that the great mass of us are here with our families, our property, with all we have in the world. We came here to build up homes and free institutions, and to be successful we must have peace and quiet.'

" ' You can't do it. You can't do it. It is too late. We have got stirred up in the matter, and by G— we shall keep it stirred up. I have told you what we have done. We shall continue in the rear of Governor Geary's movements, and we shall continue to agitate,' replied the Captain, the lieutenants with oaths endorsing his threats.

" ' Gentlemen, if this is the case, I shall feel in honor bound to repeat this conversation to Governor Geary, and, much as I despise the bogus authorities, I shall hope to see you arrested and convicted for your crimes.' * * *

" They retreated down-stairs; and twenty-two years have passed since then. Whether any of them are now living, I don't know, but the facts are in every essential particular as I have narrated."

But Walker and Titus were too much for the thieves, and some of them left the Territory and joined John Brown in the States, and others went into southern Kansas, to appear again later.

CHAPTER XIV.

THE year 1857 was as noteworthy for its political conflicts as was 1856 for its warlike demonstrations. The Legislature of 1856 had provided for a State Constitution, the members of the convention for which were to be elected June 15, 1857; the Topeka State government required an election of State officers and a Legislature; and the election of a Territorial Legislature was to be held on the 5th and 6th of October.

The first question to be met was, Shall the Free-State party participate in the election of members of the Lecompton Constitutional Convention? On examining the regulations for the election as provided by the Territorial Legislature, it was found that no honest election was intended or would be permitted. The *Missouri Democrat*, of March 13th, thus speaks:

" If ever means were taken to pack a convention, they have been taken in this case. Nothing has been omitted—nothing left to chance. The plan of packing is as elaborate and as perfect as the wit of man can make it. The time, the mode, and the machinery have been selected with Satanic skill. Every contingency is provided for in this compact and complicated scheme. From the taking of the census by the county sheriff to the organization of the convention, through the graded surveillance of election judges, probate judges, etc., the felon Legislature has provided as effectively for securing the desired result as Louis Napoleon did for getting himself elected emperor.

" The irresponsibility of the convention and the integrity of its production from the subsequent action of the people, are also carefully provided for. The ratifying voice of the people, contrary to usage, is ignored. No freedom of election and no official fidelity can be expected.

Afraid of the spring immigration, the felon Legislatùre disfranchised every one who should not be a resident on the 15th instant; and to prevent the rejection of the constitution (adopted long since in the caucuses of the Blue Lodge), no provisions were made for submitting that radiant scroll to the people. The convention will be packed from the foundation-stone to its eave-stone, and every honest man in Kansas will therefore see the propriety of shunning it as he would Pandemonium itself."

President Buchanan appointed Hon. Robert J. Walker Governor, and Hon. F. P. Stanton Secretary of the Territory, to take the places of Governor Geary, resigned, and of Secretary Woodson.

Secretary Stanton arrived in April, one month in advance of Governor Walker, and on the 24th of that month visited Lawrence, where he addressed the citizens. Like all other officials, he promised to enforce the territorial laws even to the extent of causing "war to the knife and knife to the hilt." In all other respects his conduct was such as favorably to impress the citizens. Mr. Stanton, his companion McLean, and Horace White, of the Chicago *Tribune*, were entertained by Robinson at tea, when a full and frank discussion of the questions at issue was had, particularly with reference to voting for delegates to the Constitutional Convention. A part of this interview, as reported by Horace White for his paper, is given as follows:

"When the penumbra of the new Administration appeared in Lawrence, accompanied by a border ruffian in steeple boots, the citizens greeted him pleasantly and called him 'Governor.' They received a pleasant greeting in return; Governor Robinson made up a tea-party for 'Governor' Stanton and his travelling companion, and it was announced that Mr. Stanton would address the citizens in the evening.

"My impression of Mr. Stanton, derived from some little intercourse previous to his speech, was not unpleasant. The impression derived from the speech itself was far from gratifying. I happened to be present at the tea-party mentioned above, and as nothing confidential transpired, and nothing but courtesy and good feeling manifested itself, I shall take occasion to report some parts of the conversation to which I was a listener. I do this more especially because it presents a brief summing up of the positions of two parties in Kansas, and hints con-

cerning a third.   It will be seen that the discussion was mainly conducted by Governor Robinson and Mr. Stanton's friend from Lecompton, one General McLean, who casually informed us that he led the
advance guard of the two thousand eight hundred braves who marched
towards Lawrence some time last summer:

" McLean—Whenever the Free-State party in Kansas convince me
that they have an actual majority of the residents of the Territory over
the National Democracy, I and my friends will be found making preparations to depart.   If the National Democracy—

" Robinson—We won't dispute about titles, General, unless they
have an especial significance, but I would like to hear your definition
of a National Democrat.

" McLean—A National Democrat is any man from the North or
South, from the East or West, whose faith is clearly enunciated in the
Cincinnati platform.

" Robinson—But I happen to know several men in Kansas answering just that description, who declare themselves utterly hostile to
slavery.   These men are mostly new-comers.   They say they voted for
Buchanan for the purpose of making Kansas free, and now they are on
the ground to contribute still further to that enterprise.   What is the
distinction between these and the Free-State party?

" Stanton—If you call one party Free-State, General, you must cer-
tainly call the other pro-slavery.   I have found men claiming to be
Democrats, myself, who intend to vote for Free-State delegates to the
Constitutional Convention.

" McLean—That is all very well; but I prefer a name which ap-
plies equally to all sections of the country—something National!   By
the National Democracy of Kansas, I understand that party which proposes no interference with the rights of the South.

" Robinson—But, my dear sir, I propose no interference with the
rights of the South, and yet I shall object to anybody fastening me to
the Cincinnati platform.

" McLean—I think the distinction is plain enough.   The National
Democracy have invited the Free-State men to come to the polls on a
certain day and determine by vote which party has a majority of the
actual residents of Kansas.   You Free-State men hold a convention and
resolve that you have four-fifths of the population, and that you *won't*
vote.   Now, what sort of consistency is there in this?

" Robinson—The action of the Topeka Convention was predicated on
certain facts which have been well known to the ' National Democracy '
from the beginning.   Firstly, the Free-State men of Kansas have never
recognized the ' Territorial Legislature,' as some people call it.   Whoever else may recognize it or fail to recognize it, the Free-State men
deny its legal existence.   They claim that it is not even a government

de facto. They do not appeal to its laws nor have dealings with its officers. No one pretends to execute these laws, and they exist merely for
the benefit of the public printer. Consequently, the Free-State men
see nothing in the proposed election but the old farce with new decora-
tions and scenery. No law requires them to vote. They will not interfere with your voting. They have no objection to your doing all the
voting. In this way you will secure unanimity, and I see no reason
why the plan should give the ' National Democracy' a moment's uneasiness. Secondly, the law providing for this election takes all power
out of the hands of the people, after the delegates are elected. It
thrusts the Constitution into Congress as the work of the people, without giving the people an opportunity to pronounce upon that work.
These delegates may frame a constitution infringing the liberty of speech
and the press. They may decree test oaths as a qualification for voting.
They may make murder a bailable offense. They may infringe the
right of the people to assemble together in a peaceable manner to consult for their common good. They may establish negro slavery, or any
other kind of slavery, as a permanent institution of Kansas. They may
take away the right of amending this Constitution from the latest posterity. We have had specimens of all these things in Kansas legislation, and we have no business to infer that the creatures of any legislative body will be better than the Legislature itself. The Free-State
men regard it as indispensable that the entire work of the Constitutional
Convention be submitted for the approval or disapproval of those whose
welfare it affects. Thirdly, the Free-State men consider that the whole
machinery of this election is thrown into the hands of their bitter enemies, and that no safeguards are interposed for their protection, either
in the vote itself or the subsequent counting of votes. I need not
enumerate for this company the provisions of that law in this regard.
The experience of the Free-State men on former occasions has not been
such as to impress them favorably with the elective franchise as operated by the bogus Legislature. Men who have lived two years in Kansas understand that the Free-State party have no rights on election day
which Missourians are bound to respect, and none which the United
States Government takes the trouble to ' recognize.' The provision of
your law concerning the registration of votes does not prevent the
registration of all the unemployed residents of western Missouri, nor
does it require that the actual residents of Kansas shall be registered.
Your registry being perfected, the result of the election is ascertained
before the voting commences. After the voting is finished, we have no
guarantee that the returns will correspond either with the ballots deposited or the printed list of qualified voters. I am free to confess that I
doubt the integrity of three-fourths of the officers who will conduct this
election. We are solicited, in the face of a two years' experience,

which requires no comment from me, to confide everything we hold dear as American citizens to the keeping of our worst enemies, and go away trusting to their honor, presuming that they have sufficient virtue to register none but actual citizens of Kansas, to register all the citizens of Kansas, to receive the votes of all the citizens who choose to vote, to make the returns according to the votes, even in case such returns ruin the business which has afforded them occupation for two years. The Free-State men of Kansas are not such idiots. The evidence is overwhelming that this election was not intended to ascertain the relative strength of parties in Kansas, but to entrap our party, defraud them of all their rights, and make a slave State of Kansas. So much for the Topeka Convention. How have subsequent events shown the propriety of their action? Here are two thousand Missourians registered as voters in Douglas County—men whom no citizen of Kansas ever heard of except as he met them on some foraging excursion. We look over this list for the names of the oldest citizens of Lawrence, and they are not to be found. In Quindaro, where I live, public opinion is divided on the question whether the census-taker has been there or not. Two or three men pretend to have seen him. I haven't, and I doubt whether he has been there at all. If he has ever visited that place, it was not for the purpose of completing the registry of Leavenworth County. The list was published some weeks ago, and our town left entirely out of the reckoning. Some of the neglected ones in the town of Wyandotte have sent their names to the proper officer, with evidence of their citizenship, and he has either refused or neglected to place them on the list.

" At Osawatomie, I am informed, three-fourths of the list is made up of citizens of the adjoining county in Missouri. At a place thirty or forty miles southwest of here the citizens do not know, except by hearsay, that there is to be any election. They have never known, from the beginning, whether they were enjoying the blessing of a sheriff and county judge or not. They don't know whether they have a census-taker among them or not, and I should judge they didn't care. These are specimens of our territorial job work. To my mind they demonstrate that the action of the Topeka Convention was entirely proper, and if that Convention was to be held over again, my part in it would simply be a repetition of my part in the other.

" Stanton—But you have an ample remedy for all this alleged fraud, in the law creating these officers. Bring me one man who has taken the proper steps to have his name registered and been refused, and then see what becomes of the officer. Establish that the list of Douglas County contains the name of one resident of Missouri, and see how rapidly that list is expurgated of the falsehood. The trouble is, you Free-State men are not willing to take any steps looking to the correction of the evils you complain of. The Executive of this Territory is here for the purpose of administering impartial justice, and when you have been denied redress in that quarter, I will acknowledge for one that there is something radically wrong in the government of Kansas.

" Robinson—Having determined to take no part in the election, we are naturally not solicitous about the purity of the voting lists, or of the voters themselves; but you now offer us a practical impossibility. In the first place, the citizens of Quindaro, Lawrence, and Osawatomie are men of business. Their time is valuable to them and indispensable to their families. They cannot leave their business and go hunting a sheriff or a census-taker, particularly if he spends most of his time in another State. The gentleman with the census roll was appointed to visit them, not they the officer.

" I have no time to waste in that way, and I presume my neighbors will say the same thing. The other proposition, that we show the lists to be fraudulent in respect of the names of Missourians, is an utter impossibility. It is an attempt to establish a negative. Mr. Jones Jenkins may be a resident of Westport, Missouri. I may know it, and a dozen others may know the same thing. We may establish that Mr. Jones Jenkins does live in Westport, Missouri. We then visit twenty of the oldest residents of Douglas County, and inquire whether Mr. Jenkins has ever resided there. They have never heard of any such man in that vicinity. Here we have established that one person bearing this name lives in Missouri, and have shown that twenty citizens of Douglas County never heard of him in Kansas. Is this legal demonstration? We have not shown that some man bearing this name positively does not live somewhere in the county. We have not shown that he may not have lived here, and gone East for his family. We have not and never can show that he was not here on the day prescribed by the law, and that he did not answer every requirement of that law. When we multiply this case by two thousand, we appreciate somewhat the nature of the job we have undertaken.

" Stanton—I think, Doctor, you magnify all the difficulties which stand in the way of·a fair election. Concerning the submission of the Constitution to a subsequent vote of the people, I would say that it is proposed to make a provision of this sort, and, so far as my influence extends, it shall be exerted to bring about a full expression of the popular will on the subject of the domestic institutions of the Territory, after the work of the convention is complete.

" Robinson—We do not doubt your good intentions, Governor, in this, as in other matters; but we very gravely doubt the extent of your power. Several governors of Kansas have been greatly surprised to find how short a distance their influence extends. I believe that the right of calling out the militia has been placed in the hands of county sheriffs. You will doubtless regard this a very great infringement on the privileges of the Executive.

" Stanton—Oh, you must be mistaken. No Legislature, no sheriff, will undertake to call out the militia while I hold the office of Governor. Ridiculous!

" McLean—But they will when the occasion comes. It was found necessary on the part of the Legislature to reserve this right.

" Stanton—Reserve ! No such right ever belonged to any Legislature under the sun. Nonsense!

" McLean—Nonsense or not, we have the right of calling out militia, and intend to exercise it whenever we find it necessary; that's all!

" Stanton—Oh, you are altogether mistaken, etc.

" I need not follow this pleasant little expression of views any further. Our party adjourned to the Cincinnati House and listened to Mr. Stanton's speech. I have already made this letter longer than I had intended. The conversation above reported is eminently suggestive, and I think speaks for itself. If it should meet the eyes of any of the participants, they will recognize its correctness in all essential particulars; and if I have set down aught in malice, I trust the *Tribune* will be open for the amplest correction to the injured party. Messrs. Stanton and McLean having expressed their views publicly and without reserve in the streets of Lawrence, both before and after this dialogue, it will not be deemed any breach of confidence that some portion of those views should take on the illumination of the types.

" OCCIDENT."

The next morning after Secretary Stanton's speech at Lawrence, several citizens presented him with a written proposition, providing,. first, " that two persons shall be selected in each township or district to correct the registry list, one by the pro-slavery and one by the Free-State party, who shall proceed in company to take the census and register all legal voters, and the probate judges shall correct the first lists, and the apportionment of delegates shall be made according to the returns thus made.

" Second, four judges shall be selected for each voting precinct, two of the pro-slavery and two of the Free-State party, and the names of three of said judges shall be required for a valid certificate of election to a seat in the convention." To this proposition Mr. Stanton made a lengthy reply, disclaiming any power over the probate judges and judges of election. He, however, said, if left to him, he would appoint one Free-State National Democrat, one pro-slavery National Democrat, and one Republican. This was fair enough so far as judges were concerned, but even this power he could not exercise, and hence the Free-State men wholly ignored the election.

Governor Walker reached Kansas in May, stopping at Leavenworth, where, instead of a speech, he had $250 worth of liquors distributed among the people in the street. He visited Lawrence on the 26th, and attended a meeting in company with Senator Henry Wilson, Rev. John Pierpont and Dr. Samuel Howe of Massachusetts. He pledged the enforcement of the territorial laws, but said the Lecompton Constitution when framed should be submitted to a fair vote of the people for adoption or rejection. The meeting was held in the Unitarian church, and continued till a late hour, Judge Conway presiding. Besides the Governor, Henry Wilson, Dr. Pierpont, Daniel Foster, Conway, Phillips, and Robinson were called out. The provisions for the election for the delegates to the Lecompton Constitutional Convention were dwelt upon at length, and Governor Walker had an opportunity to learn something of that matter, as well as of the spirit of the people.

Governor Walker issued a lengthy address to the people, which, as usual with such documents in Kansas, gave satisfaction to neither party. The Free-State men were disgusted with his threats to enforce the territorial usurpation, and he gave too many promises of fairness to the "rebels" to suit the Slave-State party. The Richmond *South* is a sample of Southern criticism. It says:

"We intend no imputation upon the Democracy when we affirm that, with individual exceptions, all parties in the North desire the admission of Kansas as a free State. It is morally impossible to hope for any other result.

"But we do reproach and denounce the Hon. Robert J. Walker, for that, being the chief Executive Magistrate in the Territory, and bound by every consideration of honor and duty to observe a strict

neutrality between the contending interests, he openly allies himself
with the anti-slavery faction, and employs all the influence of his position to deliver Kansas into the power of the Free-State party.

" Do we accuse him unjustly? Not unless it be impossible to convict him of the charge on the evidence of his own official declarations.
No candid person can read his inaugural address and resist the conclusion that he goes out to Kansas with the deliberate design of wresting
the Territory from the power of the South. It is idle to answer that
his policy is opposed by the Black Republican party. The struggle
between Walker and Robinson is not upon the issue of slavery or no
slavery; it is a competition for the glory of converting Kansas into a
free State. Of course the Black Republicans will fight any plan which
threatens to rob them of the conquest.

" Under any circumstances, the loss of Kansas would be a grievous
calamity for the South ; but to have it snatched from our grasp by the
stealthy manipulation of a politician who affects a frank and honest purpose is an insult and a wrong which we cannot bear with patience."

The State Legislature met on the 9th of June, in accordance with the adjournment from its regular session in January, and with the Legislature came a mass meeting of the
citizens. As the Government would expire with this Legislature unless an election law should be enacted and an election held for State officers and members of a new Legislature, unusual efforts were made to induce the members to
attend the session. A circular letter, signed by many leading citizens, was sent to all the members of the Senate and
House, urging them to be present. But when the day arrived no quorum appeared. It required much skill to get a
quorum, and no legal quorum could be secured by any device know. . to parliamentary proceedings. Members were
sent for in hot haste, but still no quorum. As Governor
Walker was watching with eagle eye, and ardently praying
for the Topeka Government to fail, it was deemed important
that the real condition should be kept from his knowledge.
It was thought that if Governor Walker could be made to
believe that the Topeka Government was in a condition to
become a live Government, should he fail to give the people
a fair election, either for or against the Lecompton Consti-

tution, or for a Territorial Legislature, he would be more
likely to do his duty regarding those elections.   Enough had
been learned of the Governor to know that he feared nothing
so much as this Topeka State Government.   Hence he must
be kept in ignorance of the strait to which it was reduced.
Among the devices resorted to in order to procure a quorum,
was providing impromptu elections.   William A. Phillips
was thus elected to the House to fill a vacancy.   William
Hutchinson was sent to Douglas County to secure the attendance of Senator B. W. Miller.   When he found the
senator had just died, he called an election immediately,
returned to Topeka the next day, and was duly sworn in as
senator.   In this way, and by declaring several vacancies,
a nominal quorum was secured.   Steps were taken to complete the organization of the Government, by providing for
taking the census, making an apportionment, and for an
election of State officers and a Legislature, to be held on
the first Monday in August.

The promises of Walker and Stanton that the territorial
ballot-boxes should be restored to the people had produced
a marked effect upon the Free-State men; and being tired
of living without law, and having but little hope of relief
through admission to the Union under the Topeka Constitution, many were ready to make an effort to get possession
of the Territorial Legislature at the election to be held in
October, and were accordingly indifferent to the fate of the
State Government.   Senator Douglas had exposed the ma-
nipulations of Lane to such an extent, convicting him of
lying and forgery with reference to the Topeka Constitution,
that even Republican senators would have nothing to do
with that document; and Free-State men well posted had
no hope of admission to the Union under it, although it had
passed the House of Representatives.   Notwithstanding all
this, some men were loud in their demands that this Government should be set in motion at all hazards.   Perhaps the
most bitter enemies Robinson ever had he made by de-
23

claring such a move to be, under the circumstances, insane.

The taking of the census had a double purpose: one was to answer the demand of the Constitution that an apportionment for members of the Legislature might be made, and another that proof might be furnished of illegal voting at the territorial election, which was to be held without an accurate census. Senator Wilson appreciated the importance of this census, and promised Robinson that he would send a man with sufficient funds to defray the expenses. Accordingly Hon. T. J. Marsh, ex-Treasurer of the State of Massachusetts, appeared in due time and paid all the census bills, as audited and approved by the State Governor.

At the mass convention, held at the time of the meeting of the Legislature, resolutions were adopted repeating the former denunciations of the territorial usurpation and strongly adhering to the Topeka Constitution.

Judge Conway dissented from the report of the committee on resolutions, and offered as a substitute one proposing, while professedly not intending to resort to force, that the people should "universally accept the State Government as their only rightful government." That they "should look to it exclusively to extend protection to individual rights and regulate the relations of society * * * to the end that the aforesaid government shall become the living government of the community." Also, his resolutions contemplated the enactment of laws sufficient to meet the wants of the people in every department of life. This substitute was supported by Conway, W. A. Phillips, C. F. W. Leonhardt, and W. F. M. Arney.

It was not adopted by the convention. The people had adopted the Topeka Constitution because they had been deprived of the territorial law-making power by invasion and fraud, not because it was intrinsically better for them than that form of government; and now, as there was a prospect of recovering what had been stolen, they were disposed to await the result of the territorial election so soon to be held. In fact, there was no alternative, as it was impossible to procure a legal quorum of the Legislature or pass a legal enactment of any kind. All did not know this, but the State Governor knew it, and his aim was to impress upon the territorial Governor the importance of securing to the people an honest election. If he should do that he would have nothing to fear from the State Government, otherwise there might be serious trouble. Robinson had satisfied himself, by frequent interviews and otherwise, that Walker and Stanton intended to act in good faith towards the people, and he was disposed to throw no obstacle in their way, but, on the contrary, give them what aid he could in carrying out their pledges.

Another convention was held at Topeka, July 15th and 16th, of which General Lane was chairman. This convention adopted substantially the same resolutions as the previous one, except the following:

" Whereas, Governor Walker, in his speech at Topeka, as reported in the *Kansas Statesman* of June 9th, holds the following language: ' In October next, not under the act of the late Territorial Legislature, but under the laws of Congress, you, the whole people of Kansas, have a right to elect a delegate to Congress, and to elect a Territorial Legislature; ' and

" Whereas, Governor Walker has, on various occasions, used similar language; and

" Whereas, Under the above decision ' the whole people of Kansas ' may participate in an election for delegate for Congress and for members of the Territorial Legislature, without recognizing the validity of a bogus Legislature, imposed upon them by fraud and by force; therefore,

" *Resolved*, That we recommend to the people of Kansas that they assemble in mass convention at Grasshopper Falls on the last Wednesday in August, to take such action as may be necessary with regard to that election."

At this convention M. J. Parrott was nominated for representative to Congress.

Judge Conway offered this resolution, which was adopted:

" Whereas, we have reliable information that preparations are being made in some parts of the State of Missouri to control the result of the coming elections in Kansas ; therefore be it

" *Resolved*, That General James H. Lane be appointed by this convention, and authorized to organize the people in the several districts, to protect the ballot-boxes at the approaching elections in Kansas."

Of course there was no "reliable" information of proposed interference with any election favored by Judge Conway or Lane, as both these gentlemen opposed taking part in the territorial election of a Legislature, and no Missourian would interfere with the election under the State auspices. But it served to give employment to Lane and furnish an excuse to send East for money, which was promptly done, two messengers being sent for that purpose. Had both Conway and Lane favored the territorial election, they well knew that no Kansas troops outside of regular militia would be needed, as Governor Walker had taken upon himself the responsibility for that election, and had plenty of United States troops to protect the polls. These he did station at some places, although unnecessary, as no invasion was longer needed. The pro-slavery men had the "returning boards," and voters from Missouri or elsewhere were unnecessary, as was proven when the returns were sent in to the Governor.

The time intervening between this convention of the 15th of July and the Grasshopper Falls Convention, the last Wednesday in August, was improved by Lane and Conway in opposing the territorial election, but without avail. When that convention met it was nearly a unit for voting, although Conway made a speech against it. Lane, seeing the sentiment, changed front and favored the election, although opposing it in committee.

W. A. Phillips offered the following resolution, which was referred to the committee, but never acted upon by the convention :

" *Resolved*, That should any power, legislative or otherwise, be obtained by any force of Free-State men, or Free-State votes, at the proceeding called an election in October next, this convention resolves that such power shall be used only for the destruction of usurpation, that a territorial Government shall not be perpetuated, but that the Government under the Topeka Constitution is the only legitimate Government."

Andreas, in his "History," page 126, says:

"Colonel Lane, who at the Topeka Convention held in May had declared his radical opposition to any participation in the election, had gradually grown reticent and considerate, and now came fully over to the other side."

He did not come over, however, till he reached the convention, as, on his way there, he predicted that all who favored voting, referring to Smith, Robinson, and others, would be buried so deep the resurrection would fail to reach them.

Andreas further says, same page:

"Governor Robinson defined his position, which had doubtless come to be that of a large majority of the Free-State party. In his speech favoring the resolutions, he said: ' We started out on the Topeka Constitution, and I shall work under it; but here is a battery all the time at Lecompton playing upon us. Let us take the battery and use it for our own benefit, without defining the use we shall put it to, and thus avoid side issues in every county in the Territory. If we get the battery and spike it so it cannot be used against us, we shall have accomplished a purpose. I do not feel that there will be any backing down in doing so. I am more hopeful than some, and not quite so hopeful as others; but I have no doubt we shall be triumphant. From the census returns I am satisfied there is not a district in the Territory in which we have not a large majority of voters. If we are defeated by fraud, we shall be in a position to show up the fraud. It has been said that I was always opposed to this movement. Such is not the case. I have always been in favor of voting with the least show of success in our favor."

Parrott was nominated for territorial delegate to Congress, and comparative harmony in the ranks was secured.

Lane's military exploits during the summer were only eclipsed by Governor-Walker's when he came against Lawrence with his United States troops. He made a great flourish of trumpets and assumed airs of as much importance as he would if the destiny of nations depended upon his action. As this was to be a war without an enemy, there would be no danger to life or limb, neither would "breast-works" have to be erected on the Nebraska line to cause frequent visits from the General-in-Chief. E. B. Whitman and J. B. Abbott went East for the sinews of war, but from all accounts had poor success. Unfortunately for the success of this begging expedition, Senator Wilson, Horace White, and others had recently visited Kansas, and knew very well that there was no more occasion for this military demonstration than there would be at an election in Massachusetts.

In Redpath's " Life of Brown," he quotes one of Brown's sons as saying, September 30, 1857, that " efforts were made to raise a fund to send cannon and arms to Lane ; " and adds that they "proved a failure." Mr. Whitman reported poor success in his efforts. But the most farcical of all is the great apparent effort to get John Brown with his two hundred Sharp's carbines from Tabor, Iowa, into Kansas. As is now well known, John Brown was already preparing for his Virginia raid ; had ordered his pikes, sent for his men, and had a drill-master already at work.   In A. Wattles' testimony before the Senate Harper's Ferry Investigating Committee, on page 221, is a letter from Brown to Wattles, dated June 3, 1857, in which he says:

" There are some half dozen men I want a visit from at Tabor, Iowa, to come off in the most *quiet way*, viz. : Daniel Foster, late of Boston, Massachusetts ; Holmes, Frazer, a Mr. Hill, and William David, on Little Ottawa Creek ; a Mr. Cochran, on Potawatomie Creek ; or I would like equally well to see Dr. Updegraff and S. H. Wright of Osawatomie ; or William Phillips, or Conway, or your honor. I have some very important matters to confer with some of you about. Let there be *no words* about it."

Colonel Hugh Forbes was engaged by Brown in March or April, 1857, to drill men for the work in hand, and, according to Redpath's " Life of Brown," this work was to be in Virginia or Maryland.   Besides, in a letter to Wattles, dated April 8, 1857, Brown writes, " I bless God that He has not left the Free-State men of Kansas to pollute themselves by the foul and loathsome embrace of the old rotten ———."   This old monster was the territorial Government. Was it likely a man with such sentiments would aid in an election under such a Government?   In a letter to E. B. Whitman, dated October 5, 1857, he calls this election, that Lane was proposing to protect, "bogus."   How much sincerity was there in this war movement?

Richard Realf, the Secretary of State of John Brown's new Republic, set up in Canada, and moved over to Harper's Ferry, wrote January 30, 1860, as follows about Brown's position :

" Nor was Brown himself, nor any of his coadjutors, committed to the Republican creed.   Henry Wilson, in 1857, advised that party to secure the Legislature by voting under the laws of the Territorial Legislature.   Not one of Brown's original party voted.   Some of us were at the time correspondents of the Eastern press, and in the interim between the Grasshopper Falls convention, at which it was decided to vote, and the day of election, we opposed the action of the party in every possible way, by letters, speeches, and in every available manner, for which we were denounced as abolitionists by the leading Republican journal of the Territory."

It is evident from the correspondence between these great " Generals," Lane and Brown, that Lane wanted to get the arms in Brown's possession at Tabor, Iowa; and Brown wanted to get all the money he could out of Whitman and others for his work in Virginia.   It will be seen by the letters which follow that the territorial election was a mere pretext, as Lane was as desirous of getting the munitions of war after that election as before.   The pretense that Brown wanted very much to get to Kansas is in keeping with his whole career while preparing for his Virginia raid.   He always begged for money and supplies on a pretense of wanting them for Kansas, while he intended to use them elsewhere.   The following letters were exchanged by the parties.

From J. H. Lane, Lawrence, September 7, 1857, as follows:

"SIR: We are earnestly engaged in perfecting an organization for the protection of the ballot-box at the October election (first Monday). Whitman and Abbott have been East after money and arms for a month past. They write encouragingly, and will be back in a few days. We want all the materials you have. I see no objection to your coming to Kansas publicly. I can furnish you just such a force as you may deem necessary for your protection here, and after your arrival. I went up to see you, but failed.

"Now what is wanted is this—write me concisely what transportation you require, how much money, and the number of men to escort you into the Territory safely, and if you desire it I would come up with them.

"Yours respectfully,
"J. H. LANE.
"*To Captain John Brown, Tabor, Iowa.*"

"TABOR, FREMONT COUNTY, IOWA, September 16, 1857.
"*General J. H. Lane:*
"MY DEAR SIR: Your favor of the 7th instant is received. I had previously written to you expressive of my strong desire to see you. I suppose you have my letter before this. As to the job of work you inquire about, I suppose that three good teams, with well-covered wagons, and ten *really ingenious, industrious* men (*not gassy*), with about $150 in cash, could bring it about in the course of eight or ten days.

"Very respectfully, your friend,
"JOHN BROWN."

"FALLS CITY, NEBRASKA, September 29, 1857.
"DEAR GENERAL: I send you Mr. Jamison, Quartermaster-General, Second Division, to assist you in getting your articles into Kansas in time. Mr. Whitman wrote us he would be at Wyandotte yesterday, one week ago—that he was supplied with the things—but he had not arrived when I left. It is *all important* to Kansas that your things should be in at the *earliest possible moment*—that you should be much nearer at hand than you are. I send you all the money I have, $50, and General Jamison has some more. We want every gun, and all the ammunition. I do not know that we will have to use them, but I do

know we should be prepared.   I send you ten true men.   You can rely upon General ——.   What he tells you comes from me.

"Yours ever,

"J. H. LANE.

"*To General John Brown, Tabor, Iowa.*"

"TABOR, FREMONT COUNTY, IOWA, September 30, 1857.
"*General James H. Lane :*

"MY DEAR SIR: Your favor from Falls City by Mr. Jamison is just received, also $50 sent by him, which I also return by same hand, as I find it will be next to impossible in my poor state of health to go through on such short notice, four days only remaining to get ready, load up, and go through.   I think, considering all the uncertainties of the case, want of teams, etc., that I should do wrong to set out.   I am disappointed in the extreme.

"Very respectfully, your friend,

"JOHN BROWN."

"TABOR, IOWA, October 5, 1857.

"MY DEAR SIR: Please send me, by Mr. Charles. P. Tidd, what money you have for me, not paper.   He is the second man I have sent in order to get the means of taking me through.   General Lane sent a man who got here without any team, with but fifty dollars of Lane's money, as he said, which I returned to him, and wanted me to start right off, with only four days' time to load up and drive through before this bogus election day, which my state of health and the very wet weather rendered it impossible to do in time, and I did not think it right to start from here under such circumstances.   Do try to make me up the money all in good shape before Mr. Tidd returns, and also write me everything you know about the aspect of things in Kansas.   Please furnish Mr. Tidd with a horse to take him to Osawatomie, and greatly oblige me.   The fifty dollars Lane sent was only about enough to pay up my board bill here, with all I had on hand.   I need not say my disappointments have been extreme.   Your friend,

"JOHN BROWN.

"*To E. B. Whitman.*"

"P.S.—Before any teams are now sent I want to hear further from Kansas.   Yours respectfully,

"JOHN BROWN."

From E. B. Whitman, dated Lawrence, October 24, 1857, and indorsed as having been received at Tabor, November 1st, as follows:

"MY DEAR FRIEND: Your two first messengers are sick at Tecumseh. I helped them to start back, with the information that you should soon hear from me, but they were taken sick on their way. Mr. Tidd has been waiting some time for me to receive remittances from the East, but as the crisis approaches I feel in a hurry to get him off. You are wanted here a week from Tuesday. I will wait no longer, but have raised on my personal responsibility $150. General Lane will send teams from Falls City, so that you may get your guns all in. Leave none behind if you can help it. Come direct to this place. See me before you make any disposition of your plunder, except to keep it safe. Make the Tabor people wait for what you owe them. They must. Make the money I send answer to get here, and I hope by that time to have more for you. Mr. Tidd will explain all.

"Very truly yours,
"E. B. WHITMAN."

From J. H. Lane, Falls City, October 30, 1857, as follows:

"DEAR SIR: By great sacrifice we have raised and send you by Dr. Tidd $150. I trust this money will be used to get the guns to Kansas, or as near as possible. If you will get them to this point, we will try to get them on in some way. The probability is Kansas will never need the guns. One thing is certain, if they are to do her any good, it will be in the next few days. Let nothing interfere in bringing them on.   Yours,
"J. H. LANE."

The last letters of Lane and Whitman were after the election, and yet they are as urgent for the arms as any before that event.

It will be seen that Lane was at Falls City, Nebraska, on September 29th, six days before the election, and must have taken a deep interest in that event. Also he was in Nebraska October 30th. Whether the fortifications he threw up along the territorial line in 1856 needed repairing, or new ones had to be made, does not appear.

While this correspondence was in progress between "General" Lane and "General" Brown, the election of the Territorial Legislature came off. There was no invasion or illegal voting of consequence, but illegal returns were made. The small village of Kickapoo sent in 500 votes; McGee County, where there were no legal voters, returned over 1200 votes; and Oxford, a hamlet of six houses on the east line of the Territory, sent up 1628 votes. These fictitious returns would, if counted, give the Legislature to the pro-slavery party. What would be done? All parties had accepted the pledge of Governor Walker that no fraud should be tolerated, and now all parties demanded the fulfilment of his pledges. That he would be inclined to favor his own party and recover the confidence of the South which his inaugural had lost him seemed likely. Besides, he had become exceedingly bitter on account of the opposition and ridicule of Free-State orators and papers. There was apparent hesitation as to his course, and he was waited upon by all parties with demands for prompt and decisive action. The conservatives, especially, would brook no shortcoming. G W. Brown, editor of the *Herald of Freedom*, had defended the Governor in his paper till now, and he waited upon Governor Walker in his office and warned him that if he faltered in his duty now his paper would henceforth join the cry against him.

The Governor of the State organization, who had relied upon personal as well as public pledges, and had discouraged radical measures on account of these pledges, gave notice that should the territorial Governor fail to do his whole duty there would henceforth be no conservative party in Kansas, and the machinery of the State Government might be put in order at once. Governor Walker was so afraid this would be done during the summer that he had brought the United States troops to Lawrence because that town had organized for mutual assistance in preserving order, abating nuisances, and the like. His excuse was, that should all the towns of the Territory thus organize independently of the territorial Government, it would become supplanted entirely, and the State Government would be established instead. All this had been argued at the convention in June at Topeka by Conway, Phillips, Arney, and others. In fact it was a most simple process, that all could understand, and it was held in abeyance solely for the purpose of avoiding friction, and be- cause Governor Walker had assured the people they should have their rights through this territorial election.

Governor Walker and Secretary Stanton—although they found sufficient cause for rejecting the returns from Oxford on their face, as there was no evidence the judges of elec- tion took the prescribed oath, or that the paper was one of the two poll-lists required by law—chose to visit Oxford that they might learn from personal inspection the number of actual voters in the neighborhood or county. They be- came satisfied the returns were simulated and fictitious, and like honorable men refused to count the Oxford vote. This was one of the most important acts in the whole struggle. Had this Oxford vote been counted, the Legislature would have been given to the Slave-State men, and no power on earth could have quieted the people. They had submitted to the invasion of the 30th of March, 1855, simply because they were few in number, unarmed and unorganized. Be- sides, the Free-State majority at that time was small; but now that majority was as twenty to one, as estimated by the *Herald of Freedom*, after taking the State census, and the people were comparatively well armed. While the Federal Government might, and probably would, have broken down a formal State Government, the people could and would have made it impossible for any usurpation to occupy the soil of Kansas. The result might have been no active gov- ernment from any source, but the Free-State men could afford to occupy that position as long as the Federal Ad- ministration could afford to have them.

Should a President of the United States be elected by the people and have but one majority, every member of his party would claim that the election was due to his vote, and the spoils would be demanded accordingly. So in this case, every Free-State man in Kansas was loud in his de- mands for an honest count, and there were dire threatenings from every quarter; and many are the persons who claim to have influenced the Governor to do his duty. The friends of Lane claim that, while he did not go near the Governor, it was his pawing the earth, beating the air and bellowing, as usual, like a bull of Bashan, that frightened the Governor. Prominent men like Colonel Eldridge, Deitzler, Allen, Duncans, and other conservative men, were active and influential; G. W. Brown, also, was in a position to bring a stronger influence than any other single man; and the radicals who were clamorous for setting the State Government in operation regardless of consequences had their influence. But, giving full credit to all parties, individually and collectively, the "old blood-stained banner," the Topeka Government, was indispensable. As has been said, the Administration hated this movement with a perfect hatred, as any settlement of the difficulties through this instrumentality would be a political defeat and humiliation of the Democratic party. Any other way out might be tolerated, but this never. Governor Walker saw clearly that there were men enough, and brains enough, in the State movement to "thwart, baffle, and circumvent" till the Democratic party should be utterly ruined, if he did not redeem his pledges relative to this territorial election. That it was the State movement he feared is evident from his proclamation throwing out the Oxford votes. After giving his argument against the votes he says:

" In view of the condition of affairs in Kansas for several years past, of the efforts so long made to put in operation here a revolutionary government, and of the facts that this effort was suspended under the belief that the political difficulties of this Territory might at length be fairly adjusted at the polls; if that adjustment should now be defeated and the people deprived of their rightful power under the laws of Congress by fictitious returns of votes never given, it is our solemn conviction that the pacification of Kansas through the exercise of the elective franchise would become impracticable, and that civil war would immediately be recommenced in this Territory, extending, we fear, to adjacent States and subjecting the Government of the Union to imminent peril."

At an Old Settler's meeting at Bismarck Grove, Septem ber 2, 1884, Hon. F. P. Stanton in his speech said :

" Very soon after he came to the Territory, Governor Walker went out among the people and made addresses in several places, in which he urged the abandonment of the Topeka movement, and earnestly solic- ited them to go to the polls in the October elections and assert their supremacy in the State Constitution. President Buchanan was pledged to the policy of submitting the Constitution to the vote of the people for ratification or rejection. Governor Walker did not hesitate to promise all his influence in favor of the same policy, and solemnly pledged him- self to oppose any constitution not so submitted. At the Free-State Convention at Topeka, on the 9th of June, 1857, being called out by the people at his lodgings there, he gave these assurances in the most solemn and explicit manner, at the same time repeating his declaration that the territorial Government, with the aid of the army of the United States, if necessary, would maintain peace at the polls, secure a full op- portunity for every citizen to vote, and prevent and repudiate every fraud or wrong which it was possible to resist or remedy by the executive authority.

" I was not in the counsels of the Free-State party, and knew their designs only through their public avowals. It was well understood, I believe, that they were divided in opinion. One party in the conven- tion, under the lead of General J. H. Lane, was in favor of extreme and violent measures, and proposed to put the Topeka Government into im- mediate operation ; the other was understood to be headed by Governor Charles Robinson, and to advise a more moderate and rational line of policy, being willing so far to confide in our pledges as to try their strength at the polls in the October elections. There was a bitter con- test between these two sections of the Free-State party, and, according to our information, there was imminent danger that the Lane party would prevail. Such at least were the intimations given out to the public, and I had no doubt at the time that they were substantially true; but if they were not, then it remains for those who were inside the Free-State movement to show that these public outgivings were not sincere, and to explain the real intentions of the parties concerned.

" But, at any rate, eventually the counsels of the moderate men pre- vailed. The extremists were withheld from the execution of their dan- gerous designs, and the masses of the Free-State party were induced to participate in the October elections, and thus to get legal control of the territorial Government, instead of embarking in a rebellion against the United States. What was the result of this policy of wisdom and mod- eration, I have already shown. By the rejection of the Oxford frauds the majority of the people were installed in their rightful supremacy in the Territory.   By the election of the 4th of January, authorized by the law passed at the extra session of the Legislature, you demonstrated that the Lecompton Constitution was not the creation of the people. You passed laws to punish frauds and false returns at the elections, and thereby drove from the Territory John Calhoun and his dishonest coadjutors, who had sought to pollute the sources of political power and to maintain the usurpations of a corrupt minority.   You placed Mr. Buchanan and his Administration, and all those Democrats who supported them, in the wrong.   And thus placing them in the wrong before the eyes of the whole world, you were enabled to defeat them and break them up.   And finally, you had the great triumph of establishing your own Topeka Constitution, substantially, according to your own will.

"Now, suppose that different counsels had prevailed at Topeka in the summer of 1857—suppose the extreme men had succeeded in persuading the majority to set up the Topeka State Government in rebellion against the Government of the United States.   Instead of placing Mr. Buchanan in the wrong, you would have been in the wrong yourselves. Instead of dividing the Democratic party on the Lecompton question and finally breaking them to pieces, you would have consolidated them on the question of sustaining the Federal Government, in support of the laws, against its rebellious citizens.   In the midst of conflict and civil war, there would probably have been no frauds at Oxford and no exposure of the methods adopted by your opponents, because violence would have taken the place of fraud, and that violence justified by your own fatal example.   It is impossible to conjecture exactly what would have been the course of events.   But the whole history of the Territory would have been altered and its destiny materially modified.   The Lecompton Constitution would probably have been adopted, and Mr. Buchanan succeeded by another Democratic President.   In the course of time you would, no doubt, have moulded the Constitution to the will of the majority; but the obstacles would have been great and your progress would have been slow and with feeble paces compared to those rapid strides by which you have reached your present magnificent position.   I do not for a moment suppose that slavery could have been very long continued under any circumstances; but the process of destroying it might have been much more prolonged and difficult, and your implication in it might have been much more disastrous and destructive to all your interests.

"Allow me to say here, that, in my judgment, Governor Walker has never received the full measure of applause which he deserved for his efforts to conciliate the people, and his success in bringing them to a trial of their strength in the territorial elections.   This was the true exodus out of the wilderness of your troubles.   It was the policy of true wisdom and exalted patriotism.   You met him half way, and notwithstanding his forced resignation as Governor, this policy which he had inaugurated was carried out successfully, and triumphed in the end.

"Mr. Blaine, in his recent history of 'Twenty Years in Congress,' sums up the result of Governor Walker's administration in Kansas with the simple but emphatic declaration that he 'failed.' But, I must insist, it was no failure. Mr. Buchanan deserted him, and left him the alternative of coming back here to be dismissed, as I was, or of resigning the position which he could no longer hold with honor. But, in spite of all this, by your co-operation and the wise course of moderation which you pursued, he had prepared the way for that result which brought merited rebuke to Mr. Buchanan and defeat to the bad schemes he sought to promote. The failure was Buchanan's, and not Walker's. The triumph was yours; but you will not fail to do liberal justice to the memory of the man who was the author of the policy which finally prevailed, but who was not permitted to enjoy the fruits of his patriotic exertions. It was his fortune, as it was mine, to stand on the eminence of truth and right from which he could see the promised land; but that was all.

"You alone, ye men of iron, worthy fathers of this great State, pioneers and heroes in the times that tried men's souls, you alone had the privilege of crossing the Jordan that intervened, and entering this goodly land of liberty. May it continue forever to blossom like the rose, and may it never cease to flow with milk and honey."

CHAPTER XV.

WHEN the Territorial Legislature was secured, the principal battery of the enemy had been captured and they had but one hope left, namely, to get admitted to the Union under the Lecompton Constitution. How should that hope be frustrated? The convention for drafting their constitution had adjourned from September 7th till October 19th. One party, the voting party, said, let the convention meet, as it had a right to do, and adopt a constitution, and then vote the constitution down. If, as was feared, no fair opportunity were given for such vote by the convention, then let the Legislature provide the opportunity, which it would have the power and disposition to do, either at a called session by the acting governor or at the regular session on the 4th of January, 1858. Another party, headed by Lane, said make war upon the convention and prevent the making of the constitution. Possibly this was in contemplation by Conway when he presented his resolution to the convention in July. And this may also explain the urgent request to "General" John Brown at Tabor before and after the territorial election. Be this as it may, as the time approached for the meeting of the convention, Lane took the war-path and gathered his forces. This was done under cover, and probably in the main through the secret order of Danites, as but few, if any, knew of his movements outside of the order till he was ready to strike his blow. As Robinson was absent from Lawrence when this blow was to be struck, a state-

24

ment made by Dr. G. W. Brown, who was then editor of the *Herald of Freedom*, the first Free-State paper published in Kansas, is quoted from his " Reminiscences of Governor Walker," as follows :

" It is remembered that, on the 16th of July, General Lane was instructed to organize the military forces in Kansas ' for the protection of the ballot-box.' But this was not the source of his authority. A secret order was instituted by Lane, ostensibly to oppose the aggressions of the slave power in Kansas. This organization was under the management of those who opposed the voting policy. They were always talking about fighting the Government if it stood in their way. Their leaders fled the Territory on the first approach of danger, to return when all was over, and renew the agitation which cooler heads had allayed during their absence.

" William A. Phillips, the special Kansas correspondent of the New York *Tribune*, wrote his journal, dated June 17th, 1857 :

" ' Mark my words ! Nothing but a sufficient force of the United States army will be able to keep that Constitutional Convention in Kansas.'

" At Osawkee, in July, while the Delaware Trust Lands were being sold, speaking of his military organization, General Lane said : ' They will assemble at Lecompton on the day the Constitutional Convention assembles, for review.'

" I think it was near noon of Saturday, the 17th of October, 1857, Augustus Wattles, at that time our associate editor, entered the sanctum of the *Herald of Freedom* office in an excited manner, very unusual to him, and said hurriedly :

" ' Why, Brown, we are on the eve of a revolution ! General Lane has ordered the organized Free-State forces of the Territory to assemble on Monday next, with arms and three days' supply of provisions, the purpose of which is to march on Lecompton and kill every member of the Constitutional Convention. It is also his purpose to wipe out the Territorial Government, and set up the Topeka Government. The United States troops are *en route* for Utah, and now is thought a good time to strike. Unless headed off in his insane movement, notwithstanding our recent success at the polls, all is lost ; for the country will never endorse this scheme of wholesale murder ! '

" I questioned him sufficiently to know that he was making a statement on positive knowledge. Catching my hat, I rushed to the different business houses, and made them acquainted with the information Mr. Wattles had imparted. G. W. Collamore, G. W. Smith, Wesley and Charles Duncan (both now living at Lawrence), George Ford,

Columbus Hornsby, and, indeed, all the substantial men whom I met, were invited to assemble immediately in a vacant room over the store of Messrs. Duncan for consultation. In a very short time they were in session, probably from fifty to one hundred. We organized, with Judge Smith as chairman. The object of the meeting was briefly stated, when, on motion of Mr. Collamore, a committee of three was appointed to invite General Lane to attend the meeting.

"The committee soon returned, accompanied by the General. The chairman stated to him what the people had casually learned in regard to his proposed descent on Lecompton, and the assassination of the members of the Constitutional Convention, and inquired of him if they were correctly informed.

"The General at first seemed to evade a direct answer. He entered into a disquisition on the wrongs the people of Kansas had sustained from the pro-slavery party, and was really eloquent, in his way, as he recounted our grievances. While he was speaking in this strain, avoiding an answer to Judge Smith's interrogatory, a crowd of young men, ' boys,' as Lane always called them, came pouring in at the lower end of the room, and, as was their habit, when Lane pointed his long, bony finger and said 'Great God!' in his peculiar way, they cheered heartily. Seeing that his backers were with him, he became more bold and defiant. I was without writing material, but with pencil, old envelopes, backs of letters, and on finger-nails, wrote down the substance of Lane's wildest utterances. * * *

"It was apparent by the vociferous cheering, long before he concluded, that then and there was not the time or place to vote on the question, so an adjournment was had until evening, in front of the Morrow House.

"During the afternoon the whole town was advised of the character of the evening meeting, and the attendance was very large. Judge Smith called the meeting to order. General Lane desired a further hearing, and was given the temporary stand. He came prepared for the occasion, and his backers were with him. They cheered him to the echo. Mr. Collamore and myself moved among the crowd, and both despaired of the result.

"Some other person followed Lane. I think it was Judge Schuyler, who, in a mild and pacificatory speech, deprecated such a condition of the country, and expressed his opinion that the occasion did not demand such extreme measures as were proposed.

"As the second speaker retired, Joel K. Goodin mounted the rostrum. Mr. Collamore and myself expressed surprise to see him take the stand. He commenced by saying he had received an order from his superior officer to report at Lawrence, armed and equipped for efficient military duty, and to bring provisions and camp-equipage for three

days' service; that, ' In obedience to that order, I am here to-night with
my command, having made the journey all the way from Centropolis
especially to obey it. (Cheers.) I feel that the occasion is one which
demands great sacrifices. (Cheers.) We have worked all summer in
a quiet way to regain the rights wrested from us by the invasion of the
30th of March, '55, and in spite of fraud and artifice we have triumphed!
We have seen this Territory torn and disturbed by hostile parties; men
murdered in cold blood; our homes burned, and our families scattered;
and we, at times, compelled to seek personal safety in flight. Governor
Geary came here and restored order; and Governor Walker has bent
all his energies in the same direction. Under his wise administration,
we saw in imagination a brilliant future before us. But here is that
Lecompton Constitutional Convention threatening us with new danger,
when we supposed our dangers were all passed. General Lane tells us
that further peaceful measures are out of the question; that our only
remedy for this new trouble is by shedding blood. I fully agree with
him! (Boisterous cheers.) Nothing but blood will quiet this agitation,
and restore tranquillity to Kansas. Nothing but blood will make Kansas a free State. (Cheers.) I came here expressly to spill blood, and
I propose to do it before I return home. (Protracted cheering.) It is
not just that the whole country shall be convulsed; that disorder and
violence shall be continued; that the perpetuity of the Government shall
be endangered by a revolution, when a little waste of worthless blood
will restore order and tranquillity again! (Cheers on cheers.) But I
may differ with some of you as to the proper place to begin this blood-
spilling business. (Hear! hear!) No person has occasioned more
strife, or been the more fruitful cause of our disturbances than—James
H. Lane! He demands blood! We all want it; but it is his blood
that is demanded at this time; and if he presses on his assassination
project, I propose he shall be the first person to contribute in that
direction.' (The wildest cheering possible, greatly prolonged, followed.)

"General Lane seemed perfectly confounded. The whole throng
were taken by surprise, and the business portion of it were delighted
beyond expression that some person had the ability and sufficient force
of character to meet a bold, bad man, and throttle his murderous plans
at their inception."

As to the truthfulness of this report, Dr. Brown has kindly
permitted the use of the following letters of endorsement.
It is unnecessary to say to such as know the gentlemen
writing these letters that no persons stand higher for integrity and veracity than they:

" LAWRENCE, KANSAS, May 8, 1881.

" DOCTOR BROWN: With regard to your ' Reminiscences of General Walker,' I am glad to say, after a careful perusal of the work, it embodies the exact facts in every essential particular as they came under my personal observation.   In reading I could not but feel grateful that one of the 'old guard' remained who could so truthfully and minutely record every important event occurring during the period of which you write.   I assure you, friend Brown, that your work is highly prized, and shall be carefully preserved.

" Yours respectfully,
" C. S. DUNCAN."

" OTTAWA, KANSAS, November 30, 1881.

" MY OLD FRIEND: I received yesterday the galley proof of your ' Blood and Thunder' article, Chapter 16, in your ' Reminiscences of Governor Walker,' and have carefully read it.   It freshly brought to mind many past scenes and incidents.   My little ' blood speech' is correctly reported as near as I can remember it—at least you have given its import.   We were being called from our homes every few days to satisfy the ambition and caprice of the uneasy and tireless Lane, and were becoming not only disgusted but *mad*, and proposed to have it ' dried up.' A most fearful and wanton system of ravaging and assassination was being planned by Lane, which the Free-State party were intended to be held responsible for, not only to our own Government, but to the world.   For one, I was unwilling to take any such responsibility. Those I had with me felt the same way, and urged that I give public expression to their views.   This I did fearlessly and plainly, and was most happy then, as I am now, that I contributed something towards turning the tide of proposed outlawry and bloodshed into channels of peace.

" In the early days we always had a bad element at Lawrence.   I refer to the young, undisciplined bloods, who were without reputable means of support, always ready and anxious to take part in any hellish scheme set on foot to stir up strife.   This element was largely controlled by, or rather was ready to effervesce at, the dictum of Lane. Their time was nothing, while we in the country had to undergo many severe privations in running after Lane's orders, messages, and commands as self-imposed military dictator.   No wonder we tired and felt in a degree revengeful.   For years I could not agree with him, and was constantly in his way in the ' Executive Committee,' thwarting his ridiculously impracticable, reckless, extravagant, and sometimes atrocious plans and suggestions.   Usually I had Judge Smith, yourself, and Holliday, when present, with me, which gave us the majority.   He would curse and fume, but we were firm and inflexible, so he would

soon drop his crazy project, to immediately concoct another equally ob-
jectionable.   I feel that we did our duty well, and am content to abide
the decision of the future historian who shall review our actions.

"Truly yours,

"J. K. GOODIN."

On motion of Dr. Brown the meeting voted to hold a
mass convention at Lecompton when the Constitutional Convention should meet, and fire off some resolutions and
speeches instead of Sharp's rifles.   General Lane was present at that convention and relieved himself by making a
characteristic speech, and the war cloud passed off.

When the convention completed its labors, it submitted a
slavery provision only to be voted upon, and this was ambiguous.   The votes were to be "for the constitution with
slavery" or "for the constitution with no slavery."   The
constitution with no slavery made that institution perpetual
as to slaves then in the Territory and their offspring.

The constitution declared that slaves were property and
that

"The right of property in slaves now in the Territory shall
in no manner be interfered with.

"No alteration shall be made to affect the right of property in the ownership of slaves."

This election was ignored by the Free-State men.   It was
held on the 21st of December, and 6266 votes were cast for
the constitution with slavery, and 569 votes for the constitution with no slavery.   A large part of these votes, as estimated, were fraudulent.

The Free-State men petitioned Governor Stanton—Governor Walker having gone to Washington never to return—
to convene the Legislature, now Free-State, that provision
might be made for submitting the constitution as a whole to
a vote of the people.   Accordingly, the Legislature was
convened on the 7th day of December, and the constitution
was submitted as desired.   At this election the vote for the
constitution with slavery was 138; for the constitution with

no slavery, 23; while against the constitution the vote was 10,226.

This was a severe blow and should have been fatal in any "well-regulated community," but political parties sometimes become desperate and slavery propagandists were always so. It was feared the Administration had votes enough in Congress to admit the fraud even against this overwhelming vote of the people, and the President recommended that it should be done, hence one more "job" remained for the Free-State men, namely, to elect the State officers and Legislature under this constitution, that it might be speedily changed if admitted. Upon this question they were divided. A convention was held at Lawrence, lasting two days, to consider the matter. Those in favor of voting regarded the question as most vital and were intensely interested, while some who were opposed to voting pleaded inconsistency and a backing down from the high position previously occupied; and another class preferred anarchy to law, confusion to peace; and these two classes when united out-voted the conservatives by getting their friends recognized as delegates in different parts of the Territory not fully represented, and by voting by districts. A majority of the members present were in favor of voting, but when the vote was taken by districts the proposition failed. As this was the rule of the convention the conservatives were beaten. Lane was not in the convention, but was a party to a characteristic trick thus described in G. W. Brown's "Reminiscences of Governor Walker:"

"And this result was reached by an artful ruse of General Lane and his backers, which is worthy of note in this connection: Just as the vote was being taken, General E. B. Whitman appeared on the scene and asked to be heard. He represented that he had left the camp of General Lane, near Sugar Mound, in south-eastern Kansas, on Tuesday night at nine o'clock; that he had ridden continually, changing horses four times, having been twenty hours in the saddle; that he had travelled one hundred miles, stopping to eat only one meal on the whole route, to bring the convention the intelligence. He said General Lane had about two hundred men under his command; that he held a strong position; was well supplied with provisions, and was expecting an attack the next day from a company of one hundred United States troops and a large force of Missourians. He further stated that General Lane had issued a proclamation stating that war had been made upon the peaceful, unoffending inhabitants, and that he had consented to take command of the people, at their urgent solicitation, to resist aggression; that all persons taken in arms from Missouri who were arrayed against the people of Kansas would be put to death; that he is only acting on the defensive, and when the attempt at subjugation shall be abandoned, his command will return to their ordinary avocations.

"General Whitman went on to say that persons were marching forward from all parts of the Territory to the scene of excitement, to stand or fall with General Lane and his brave command. He represented the danger as imminent, and the probability is that the contest will become general. After this statement he proceeded to harangue the convention, charging them with wasting their time over a question of no importance whatever, while the real battle was being fought between freedom and slavery in southern Kansas. 'This is no time for hair-splitting questions,' he said, 'but it is the moment for brave and vigorous action.'

"Whitman's wild manner and excitement was extended to the audience. Hinton, falsely representing Breckenridge County, being a resident of Lawrence, sprang upon a seat and called for three cheers for General Lane. The vote was taken immediately following this episode, with the results stated.

"After packing the convention on Wednesday, it was very apparent the result reached would be attained. On that evening about thirty members of the convention held a meeting at the *Herald of Freedom* office, where the situation was discussed, and the fact was shown that the convention was controlled by a secret organization, at the head of which was General Lane, Whitman being understood as second in rank. This fact was demonstrated a day or two after Whitman's crazy speech, by the redoubtable General, who was 'on the eve of fighting the United States troops,' appearing on the streets of Lawrence congratulating his friends on the result of the convention."

But the feeling was so intense on the part of the conservatives that a mass meeting was immediately held in the basement of the *Herald of Freedom* office and a ticket nominated, headed by G. W. Smith for Governor.

The men most active and efficient in this bolt were G. W. Brown, Thomas Ewing, Jr., and S. N. Wood. To these men is due a large share of the credit for the vigorous campaign that followed. Ewing furnished the sinews of war, probably not less than one thousand dollars.

When Lane appeared in Lawrence after his ruse, he was very smiling and complaisant, thinking he had obtained a great victory ; but he soon found that the bolters' ticket was being endorsed by all the influential citizens and that it would be elected, even with his opposition, and he joined the procession. As he had no use for a minority party, whenever he found his malcontents and " Danites " were to be beaten he would join the conservatives. Being destitute of principles or convictions of any kind, and of moral or physical courage, and being consumed by an inordinate ambition, he was an unsatisfactory and untrustworthy leader of his faction.

The election came off on the 4th of January, 1858, and the Free-State ticket was successful. It was true General Calhoun, the president of the convention, with the president of the council and speaker of the house, was to count the votes, and he withheld certificates and hid the returns under a wood pile in a candle box at Lecompton ; but Colonel Walker found the box, the Legislature passed a stringent law against frauds in elections, and Calhoun left Kansas. Now there was but slight motive on the part of the Democrats to admit Lecompton, and the famous English Bill was passed permitting another vote on the fraud.

This vote was taken August 2, 1858, with 1788 for and 11,300 against Lecompton in its new garb. This ended the struggle so far as a Slave-State constitution was concerned. Governor Stanton is entitled to great credit for his course throughout in the matter, and especially for convening the Legislature for the purpose of submitting Lecompton to a fair vote of the people. By this act he lost his official head, but he gained the lasting gratitude of the people, and a most enviable place in history as a patriot who held country higher than party, and personal honor higher than political preferment.

General J. W. Denver, Commissioner of Indian Affairs, was on a visit to the Indian tribes in Kansas when the action of Stanton in convening the Legislature was reported to Washington, and he was immediately appointed Secretary and acting Governor in Stanton's place. The first information of this action that reached Kansas was in the St. Louis *Democrat*. As Robinson was on his way to Lecompton, he called upon Governor Stanton at the old "Clark cabin" with this paper, and there found General Denver as his guest. It was evident that Stanton had been removed because of his action towards Lecompton, and Robinson declared that if Stanton's work was to be undone and the people subjected to further outrage, all conservative counsels would end at once. General Denver, who had remained silent for some time, at length said the matter was new to him and entirely unexpected, but of one thing all might rest assured: if he should act in place of Stanton, he should finish the work already begun and should do everything in his power to preserve the peace of the Territory under the control of the majority of the citizens. On this assurance Robinson pledged earnest support, and never had occasion to withdraw or regret his pledge.

The Territorial Legislature met January 4, 1858, in regular session, and enacted a large volume of new statutes. Among others a law of the called session was perfected, at the instance of Lane, creating a "Military Board," consisting of several generals, with Lane general-in-chief. As this was an attempt to override the authority of the Governor as commander-in-chief of the militia, it was most impolitic, as it was not only in violation of the Organic Act and would necessarily arouse antagonism where there should be co-operation and harmony, but, worst of all, it gave the semblance of authority to the leader of the lawless bands that infested the Territory, whose only business was plunder and pillage, and whose only aspirations were for disorder and revolution. Not long after the Military Board was organized Lane became thirsty for blood and proposed a general massacre of pro-slavery men.

Robinson was in Lawrence at this time, and he was invited to join a secret order, which invitation was accepted. After the initiation ceremonies Lane arose with great dignity and said he had ordered General —— to strike at Leavenworth, General —— to strike at Atchison, General —— to strike at Kickapoo, and other places were to be struck by other generals, closing his solemn announcement by saying, "It now remains for Lawrence to say what shall be done with Lecompton." After this revelation silence reigned for the space of several minutes, when from different parts of the room Robinson was called for. He responded to the call, and said he had heard a very remarkable statement and he would like to know by whose authority this general massacre was to be made. Lane replied, "By the authority of the Military Board." Robinson said that neither the Military nor any other board had any such authority, and he gave notice that whoever attempted to execute any such orders would have him to fight.

One of these remarkable orders has been preserved, which reads as follows:

"DONIPHAN, KANSAS TERRITORY.

"*Brigadier-General J. G. Losee:*

"GENERAL: The bearers of this, Colonel Leinhart and his friend Dickinson, have some idea of colonizing Kickapoo. If you could furnish them forty or fifty hardy pioneers who could bear the exposure of such a settlement, I am clear that it would be attended with good results to Kansas and the cause of freedom. Leinhart and Dickinson are the men to put through without flinching anything they may undertake. I trust you will give this matter your earnest and immediate attention, as Kickapoo should be colonized at an early day.

"Yours truly, J. H. LANE."

It is unnecessary to say that as soon as Lane's insane projects came to the surface they were squelched by the people, but how much private assassination and infamy was practised the Judgment Day alone can reveal.

That both Lane and Brown were monomaniacs there is but little question—one, like all timid men with arbitrary power, cruel and bloodthirsty; and the other believed he was commissioned by God to free the slave and exterminate the slave-holders. But the friends of these men will not permit the plea of insanity, and hence the other alternative must be accepted—if not monomaniacs, they were demoniacs.

Whether the secret order in which Robinson was initiated was the "Danite" order, so called, or some other, he does not know, as he was never notified of another meeting; but that it could be used to aid unprincipled men in a career of crime was self-evident. The only revelation of the "Danites" that was published by one of its own members was by James Redpath, in his paper called the *Crusader of Freedom*. He called its name "Danite," and as it engaged in the same work proposed by Lane in the order at Lawrence, it was probably the same association. That its character and the character of its leader may be understood, Redpath is quoted as follows:

"We are ready to swear in any court of justice, or to make solemn affidavit of the fact, that General Lane intimated to us that if Governor Denver challenged him, he would have him put out of the way by the ' secret order known as the Danites.'

"We thought he could not be in earnest, but circumstances subsequently ascertained convinced us of our error. It was the corroboration of this intention that determined us, at whatever cost, to throw the human viper off. It will cost us everything we possess in Kansas—press, landed property, and business prospects; but we prefer to be free and poor, rather than remain in the power of an assassin.

"As, a few weeks before, he had tried to make me the agent for assassinating Robert S. Kelly; as he was pursuing Mr. Shepherd, with whom he quarrelled when he could not make him a tool—with a malignity it would be euphony to characterize as infernal. I peremptorily refused.

"Lane organized a club of Danites in Doniphan County. I became a member of it. Although *he* could have attended it, and was expected to attend it, he attempted, on the second night of its meeting, to make me the agent to induce the club to kill Bob Kelly. * * * I never hated Lane till he asked me to do this deed. I did indeed despise him from the bottom of my soul, but did not believe him capable of a scheme as diabolical as to involve a young man, without any cause, in a criminal act of private revenge. It was so cowardly, contemptible, and hellish that I left him without saying a word.

" I am not the only young man whom he has tried to use for his cowardly schemes of secret and criminal revenge, and he may find, too, that he has reckoned without his host in more cases than in mine.

" But beware, Lane, beware! for I have not told all that I know."

From the time of the election of State officers and Legislature under the Lecompton Constitution, on the 4th of January, till the submission under the English Bill in August, 1858, there was a state of suspense and uncertainty. No one could predict the fate of Lecompton in Congress, and much discussion was had by the Free-State men. Some advocated another constitutional convention to be called by the Legislature that it might have the same authority in this respect as Lecompton. This method was at length adopted, all parties acquiescing. A bill was passed by the Legislature just before adjournment, and sent to the Governor, but as he thought Kansas had constitutions enough already, and as it did not reach him till within three days of the expiration of the session, he pocketed it. Here was a dilemma. If he would veto the bill and return it, there would be no difficulty in passing it over his veto; but how could it be reached under the circumstances?

Governor Denver, at the Old Settlers' meeting in Bismarck Grove, September, 1884, had this to say of this constitution:

" Well, I concluded that I would not approve that bill for calling a convention to frame a new constitution. Several committees were appointed by the Legislature to call upon me, begging me, if I would not approve it, to return it to them that they might act upon it. I told them no, that I had made up my mind, and that I was not to be moved; that I thought we had constitutions enough, and that I had an absolute veto in that case, and I proposed to exercise it, which I did.

" The next night, after twelve o'clock, a bill was brought to me purporting to be a bill calling a convention for a new constitution, and endorsed on it that it had been returned by the Governor and passed by a two-thirds vote, notwithstanding these objections. That was signed by the four officers—the presiding officer of each house, the Secretary of the Council, and the Clerk of the Assembly. I immediately sent for them, and told them that while that act of theirs, if I was disposed to act upon it, gave me power to do something much to their disadvantage, I did not desire to do it, because I did not want any trouble or disturbance in the Territory; that that act was all wrong on their part; that they certified to that which was not true; that that paper had never been before the Governor; that the bill sent to him never had been out of his possession, and he had not returned it to the Legislature with his objections, and consequently the whole statement was false.

"Mr. Currier had the bill in his hands. He asked me what I wanted them to do. I told them I wished them to do one of two things: to give me a certificate of the fact that that had never been acted upon by the Legislature at all, or else to destroy it there, in my presence. They said that that would be pretty rough. Currier said that he would not put his name to any such paper as that, and said he: 'What shall we do with it?' Deitzler said: 'Destroy it.' He said: 'All right,' and tore it up and stuck it in the stove. That was the last of that bill.

"Now, a resolution was passed after the term had closed, after twelve o'clock at night, and the legal term of the Legislature had absolutely closed—a resolution was passed, declaring that that bill had been properly passed by the Legislature, and they resolved that they would go on and hold the convention. Notwithstanding all that had occurred, and the failure of the bill to become a law, they decided to hold the convention."

This failure to give legality to the convention left it on a par with the Topeka Constitution, and it failed to receive the endorsement or support of many Free-State men. However, such men as Conway, Phillips, Ritchey, Lane, and others, who wanted some person at the head of the State Government who could be used to set the Government in motion against the territorial authority, besides many conservative men, attended the election for members of the convention and the convention itself. The members first met at Minneola, the new capital of the Territory, but after organizing adjourned to Leavenworth; hence this constitution bears the name of that town. The location of the capital at Minneola, on an open prairie, with plenty of shares of stock in and around the Legislature, shows that the Free-State men were human, as much so in some respects as the border ruffians. Of course Governor Denver paid no attention to the new seat of government, and the archives remained at Lecompton. Attorney-General Black gave his opinion that the bill calling the Leavenworth constitutional convention did not become a law, and so indifferent did the people become to this instrument that it received only about 3000 votes in a voting population of about 14,000 or 15,000 in the Territory.

Notwithstanding the want of faith in the constitution, all parties rallied to the nominating convention for state officers, April 28-29, to see that proper men should be selected. The ticket, headed by H. J. Adams for Governor, was satisfactory to the conservatives, as it had upon it the names of some of the safest men in the Territory.

Lane and the extreme radicals were disappointed, as they failed to get what they had labored for. Some of these men favored setting the Government in operation even against the territorial Government, whether Lecompton should be admitted or not, but they could not control the convention nor get such men nominated for State officers. Even Lane, who went to the convention declaring he would have a nomination for United States senator, utterly failed to get an endorsement for that position.

As in 1856 there were men desirous of coming in conflict with Federal authority without rhyme or reason, so now, in 1857-58, the most ultra and wild schemes were advanced. The Free-State men, thanks to the men of political sagacity like Thomas Ewing, G. W. Smith, W. Y. Roberts, G. W. Brown, S. N. Wood, and those who secured the election of State officers and Legislature under the Lecompton constitution, now had possession of every Government in the Territory—the Territorial Legislature, the Topeka State Government, the Lecompton State Government, and would have the Leavenworth State government—and yet some of the "ultra-radical" men were almost dying for some scheme that would result in a conflict. They were very bellicose because when the Territorial and State Legislatures met in January, both at Lawrence, the State Governor and Legislature did not at once proceed to make war upon the Territorial Legislature, although both were equally Free-State, and one had not a dollar in money and could not get a dollar except by taxing an impoverished people, while all the expenses of the other would be paid by the Federal Government. The Free-State men of both governments reviewed the situation in a most amicable manner, and decided upon the course adopted without bitterness or friction of any kind ; yet some men had grown very wise, in their own estimation, and belabored the stupid and cowardly office-holders with a political cat-and-nine-tails. Most officious in this work was Mr. E. B. Whitman, formerly of Massachusetts. He never seemed pleased that the ruse which he played in the convention in December, when he made a sensational speech about Lane's great exploits in the southern part of the Territory, should come to naught. The election of the State officers and Legislature, after such an effort to defeat it, was more than a common Christian could bear, especially a Unitarian Christian. Hence he and Conway wrote most remarkable letters to George L. Stearns, of Massachusetts, for money to enable them to procure the election of the right kind of men for the State officers under the Leavenworth constitution. As Mr. Whitman's letter gives the "ultra-radical" view, and as it, with Conway's, was published in circular form and distributed broadcast in the East, it is here given :

"LAWRENCE, April 13, 1858.
" *George L. Stearns, Esq.*

" MY DEAR SIR : Yours of March 18th and 30th are both before me. Politically, I can answer both in the same terms. A brief review of the course which events have taken here for the last six months will enable you to understand our position and appreciate our necessities.

While Kansas is blessed with many of the truest men of the age, men who are fully up to the emergency, she is also cursed with some of the most unprincipled demagogues that ever afflicted any country. Principles are of use to them only to subserve personal or party ends; and what makes the matter worse is, that some of them are among those who have heretofore been looked up to as leaders.

"In January last a large number of the people were induced, by the grossest deception, to go into an election for State officers under the Lecompton Constitution. The distinct declaration was made that the aim, in this move, was to fill the offices to the exclusion of others, slavery men, and then to refrain from touching the unclean thing, and allow the people to set up their own government, either the Topeka or some other, to be inaugurated by the Legislature about to assemble. No sooner were they elected than some of the more bold and incautious began to avow their intention to *put the Government* in operation, and make *it* the parent of the future government. In January the two Legislatures met—the Territorial Legislature of Free-State men, and the Topeka State Government Legislature. It very soon became evident to the most casual observer that there was very little unity of purpose, and in fact a real antagonism of principle. Long before the Territorial Legislature adjourned, it was pretty well understood that designing men were making tools and fools of the Topeka Legislature, to subserve unworthy ends; to keep the people quiet while they matured their plans for its overthrow. Nothing, however, was said openly, but everybody was suspicious of his neighbor. The bill for a new Constitutional Convention was evidently postponed with a design to defeat it, and yet it was held up as the compromise ground on which both extremes were to meet. On Saturday the Territorial Legislature adjourned, and in the afternoon a mass meeting was held to consider of the public welfare. The Topeka Legislature had not adjourned, but was anxiously inquiring what to do. In order, if possible, to draw out an open declaration of secretly cherished purposes, and to compel men to show their real colors, I introduced a resolution to the effect 'that in case the Lecompton Constitution should be adopted by Congress, and a government inaugurated under it, before the Constitutional Convention just created should have time to complete its work, then it would be the duty of every Free-State man to fall back upon the so-called Topeka Government, and rally under it to the last.' This called forth one of the warmest and the ablest debates that has ever taken place in Kansas, which was continued until one o'clock Sunday morning. It compelled a full declaration of opinion and of purpose. Governor Robinson declared 'that the Topeka Government was dead, and had been since last June.' Other prominent men declared—*some*, that the Free-State officers and Legislature under the Lecompton Constitution, if recognized,

25

would assemble, organize, and take the *oath of allegiance, choose two United States senators,* provide for a new Constitutional Convention, and then adjourn.   Others, that ' they would organize, and call the Convention, but *not* choose senators;' and still *others* that 'they should hold together, and pass such laws as *the occasion required,* be they more or less.   How the vote upon the resolution would have stood, I know not; but having accomplished my purpose of drawing out an open declaration of purpose, I withdrew the resolution, and the meeting adjourned.   On Monday the Topeka Government formally broke up, killed by its professed friends, deserted by those who had created it. But the *members went home,* and the people went to work in their own way, with a full knowledge of the issue, as made up, to choose delegates to the Constitutional Convention.   This Convention met, and when I say they elected M. F. Conway president, it indicates their complexion. The instrument you have, ere this, seen, and it will speak for itself.   In the test votes on *citizenship,* etc., the Lecompton faction showed steadily nineteen votes only, out of a convention of eighty, and many of those had succeeded by political manœuvering in obtaining seats.

" In the course of the debates, which took somewhat of a wide range, a severe blow was given to the purpose of those who had proposed to make any use whatever of the Lecompton Constitution, if accepted. The Lecompton Free-State men, mortified and discomfited, have returned home, determined, if possible, to secure the offices also under *this Constitution,* and then *let this one die.*   The doctrine of the *people* is for the Free-State officers under the Lecompton Constitution to take *no oath,* to *refrain* from all action under it, but letting it quietly fall and die, *to give place to the people's government just now formed.*   It held that under such circumstances the Federal Government could have no show of right to interfere, and all would end well.   If the Lecompton Constitution is adopted, and pro-slavery men receive their certificates, or enough of them to secure their ends, the boys —— —— ——.   If the Free-State men get their certificates, or if the Constitution is rejected, then everything will depend upon the character of the men elected under the new Constitution.   If the *right men are put in power* under it, then *they will make it the living Government* of the State, and no power on earth can withstand it.   *They made it to stand by it, and for no boys' game.*   But the Lecomptonists, or, in other words, the *Hunker Conservative Democratic Free-State men,* if they can possess its offices, will quietly let it die.   They are strict legitimists, and have all at once a holy horror of anything not having the forms of law, though it be ever so bogus—and a moral dread of the Federal displeasure. They are seeking, *if possible,* to save a corrupt Administration from the just retribution for its sins.

" You will easily understand, from this brief exposé, how important *we ultra-radical men* deem it to have true men to fill the offices. The people are right, but the leaders, or the would-bes, are wrong; but *you know how much tact, money, and wire-pulling can do to outwit and defeat the will of the people.*

"The Administration, with Denver as its agent, will spare no efforts to defeat this movement, and to clear the track of this people's measure, as they did of the former one. They have means at command, and will lose no time in working their cards. Our people are generally poor, except in principles, and are illy prepared to go into the canvass. If we had only the money which I solicited at Worcester, for a purpose for which it *never was used,* to aid now in the election, it might change the result entirely.

"If anything can be done for us in that way, no time is to be lost. The State Convention meets on the 28th to nominate State officers, and on the third Tuesday of May they are to be voted for. If wrong men should secure the nomination, *the field should be contested at the polls, by volunteer candidates, and they would need money.* As the tragedy draws to a close, we all find our feelings more deeply enlisted. We feel grateful for your sympathy; for *force,* we shall have no occasion, I hope, and if so, *a small domestic one* will do the work *effectually.* But if you can furnish some funds, it will be a God-send to us in the present crisis. Send none to those *but whom you know* to be politically sound. If anything is done, telegraph to Simmons & Leadbeater, or to S. C. Davis & Co., to draw upon Boston for it, and forward by express without delay.

"If the people's government is put in operation, and the Federal power attempts to interfere, there will be a desperate struggle. We shall do our best to maintain our honor and the right. The free States must call their Legislatures at once together, remonstrate with the general Government, raise money, raise troops, and *by a loud demonstration cause the President to pause in his career.* But will they do that? I fear not. I do, however, believe that many a Spartan 'three hundred' can be found here to fill the pass, and who would infinitely prefer to fall, with arms in hand, to a shameful and ignominious existence, after having betrayed the interests of humanity so basely here in Kansas. Pardon the haste and imperfections of this; you can doubtless decipher it; the midnight hour must be the excuse.

"Very truly your friend, E. B. WHITMAN."

The effect of such a letter may be seen by the following, sent to Robinson from one of the most devoted friends of Kansas. Although marked private, as it refers only to matters of public interest it may not be improper to insert it:

"BOSTON, May 6, '58.

"DEAR SIR: The inclosed paper (Whitman and Conway's circular) was handed me by Mr. Stearns yesterday, and has enlightened me as to the use of the fund which has been raised here. This fund was to be placed in the hands of Mr. Conway and Mr. Whitman to defeat the adoption of the Lecompton Constitution under the English Bill. * * * On reading the Kansas newspapers and this circular, I see how matters are going, and have written a note to Dr. Howe requesting that my small portion of the money shall not be used for advancing the interest of the Lane, Phillips, and Conway party.

"The world is made up of all sorts of men, but Kansas seems to have more than its share of the weaker brethren and rogues.

"Yours truly,

"AMOS A. LAWRENCE."

The nominating convention was held before the fate of Lecompton in Congress had been decided, and it resolved that, should Lecompton be admitted without a provision for voting upon its adoption by the people, the Leavenworth Government should become the *de facto* Government of Kansas. But this resolution was chiefly to operate upon Congress. Had Lecompton been admitted, as the Government under it was Free-State there would have been no more friction than between the Topeka State Government and the Territorial Legislature, unless the Leavenworth Government should be officered by the "ultra-radicals," like Lane, Whitman, and company.

The State officers under the Lecompton Constitution were G. W. Smith, Governor; W. Y. Roberts, Lieutenant Governor; P. C. Schuyler, Secretary of State; A. J. Mead, Treasurer; Joel K. Goodin, Auditor.

The State officers under Leavenworth were: Governor, Henry J. Adams; Lieutenant Governor, Cyrus K. Holliday; Secretary of State, E. P. Bancroft; Treasurer, J. B. Wheeler; Auditor, George S. Hillyer.

These officers were all conservative and reasonable men, not one of whom could be induced by Lane or any one else to jeopardize the peace of the Territory over a technicality, abstraction, or mere matter of form. It is safe to say that, with such men representing the respective organizations, there would have been no occasion for Whitman's contemplated war, whatever action Congress might take. As has been stated, the English Bill was overwhelmingly voted down when submitted, and the political war came to an end with victory on the side of the conservative Free-State men. What the result would have been had the policy of the "ultra-radicals" prevailed is mere conjecture, as in no case was it adopted, but it certainly was most hazardous. Here was a great national party in full control of the Federal and territorial Governments, and the policy adopted from the Organic Act down was the policy of this party, backed by the entire slave interest of the country, which had controlled the Government for many years. For a handful of men to act offensively against this power would have been as suicidal as the assault upon Harper's Ferry proved. But to have acquiesced in the result of the invasion of the 30th of March, 1855, would have yielded the question at issue, as, had the laws been recognized and acquiesced in till the next general election, in 1857, slavery would have been as firmly established as in South Carolina, and the power of the usurpation through "returning boards" or otherwise would have been perpetual. There remained but one way of escape, and that was the method adopted by the Free-State party, namely, to act strictly on the defensive as to the Federal authority, but to thwart and baffle the usurpation till the Federal authority itself should be compelled by the popular outcry to yield a fair election to the *bona fide* settlers. This was the course recommended and adopted by the conservative Free-State men, although opposed at every step by Lane, Brown, and other "ultra-radicals."

Had the policy of Whitman's letter to Stearns been adopted, and had it resulted, as he contemplated, in a war, the free States could not have been relied upon in such an issue. Instead of defending constitutional rights, such as the possession of arms or meeting for consultation, as on the 4th of July at Topeka, the issue would have been forcible resistance to Federal officers in maintaining the authority of the Federal Government, which all parties would recognize as legitimate, Republican and Democratic alike—Sumner and Seward equally with Davis and Pierce or Buchanan.

In such a war Thayer, Lawrence, Stearns, Howe, and all Massachusetts would have enlisted on the side of Pierce, Davis, Atchison, and South Carolina, leaving the "ultra-radicals" alone in their glory, hiding their diminished heads behind Lane's "breastworks" on the Nebraska line, which he so often visited during the defensive operations of the Free-State party in 1856.

CHAPTER XVI.

AFTER the defeat of the English Bill the political crises were well-nigh passed, and no danger was to be feared from radicals or conservatives, as neither could prevent the admission of Kansas into the Union as a free State by the adoption of any policy however reckless, the enemy having abandoned the field. In fact, after the arrival of Geary the struggle was between factions of Free-State men rather than with Slave-State men. It was well known that the latter could win only by fraud and sharp practice, rather than by votes; and their only hope was to take advantage of any political mistake the Free-State men might make.

Politics subsiding, attention was called to disturbances in southern Kansas. This part of the Territory had been more or less disturbed since the Potawatomie massacre, but politics and State-making after the arrival of Geary had so absorbed the interest of the people that but little attention had been given to it. George W. Clark, the former Indian agent, who killed Barber at the time of the Wakarusa war, had changed his residence from Douglas to Bourbon County, where he was connected with the Land Office.

This man Clark was as extreme and reckless against abolitionists, or Free-State men, as Brown and Montgomery were against Slave-State men. Land claims were often the pretext for the disturbances, but undoubtedly the slavery question had much influence with the respective parties;

while the hordes of thieves and plunderers cared for nothing but deviltry and spoils. The policy of Brown and Montgomery was not always in harmony. Montgomery professed to desire to protect the Free-State settlers in their claims, from which some of them had been driven, while Brown wanted war and revolution pure and simple. As early as the fall of 1856 Clark marched some men, said to be from Missouri, into Kansas, and Montgomery returned the compliment by visiting Missouri for reprisals. From that time there was no settled peace till after the Marais des Cygnes massacre, by Captain C. A. Hamilton, on the 19th of May, 1858. This massacre had but one parallel, the Potawatomie, on May 24, 1856, and shocked the nation with its atrocity. Patrick Ross, B. L. Reed, William A. Stillwell, Asa and William Hairgrove, Austin and Amos Hall, William Colpetzer, M. Robinson, Asa Snyder, and John F. Campbell, peaceable and most worthy citizens, were arrested while about their business, marched into a ravine, drawn up in line, and deliberately shot down like so many criminals. Five of them were killed, five wounded, and one unharmed, although falling with the others and feigning death. The killed were John F. Campbell, William Colpetzer, Patrick Ross, William A. Stillwell, and M. Robinson.

It had been reported that Hamilton had made out a list of Free-State men intended for slaughter, and Montgomery, says Andreas, "had determined to kill Hamilton at the first opportunity. To this end, about the 1st of May, he approached Hamilton's house, a log one, with a party of men, for the purpose of capturing him; but finding he could effect nothing in the way of an attack with rifles alone, he sent a squad of men to bring the howitzer. But before it arrived a body of United States troops, on their way to Leavenworth, were called to Hamilton's relief, and Montgomery was obliged to disperse his men. Montgomery then went to the sheriff of Linn County, acquainted him with Hamilton's designs, showed him the list of the proscribed Free-

State men, and received assurances from that official that the men so proscribed should be protected from all harm. The descent when made was made unexpectedly. Montgomery was away in Johnson County. He returned the evening of the day of the massacre." A company of about two hundred men was immediately organized and went in pursuit, but Hamilton was never disturbed. One of his men, William Griffith, was afterwards arrested, tried, convicted, and hanged, Asa Hairgrove, one of the wounded men, acting as hangman.

This massacre was made the text for "John Brown's Parallels," dated at the Trading Post, January 3, 1859. He had made his raid into Missouri; one old man was killed by one of his parties, and eleven slaves, with horses and other personal property, carried or driven away. His parallel is as follows:

"TRADING POST, KANSAS, January, 1859.

"GENTLEMEN: You will greatly oblige a humble friend by allowing the use of your columns while I briefly state two parallels, in my poor way.

"Not one year ago, eleven quiet citizens of this neighborhood, viz., William Robertson, William Colpetzer, Amos Hall, Austin Hall, John Campbell, Asa Snyder, William A. Stillwell, William Hairgrove, Asa Hairgrove, Patrick Ross, and B. L. Reed, were gathered up from their work and their homes by an armed force under one Hamilton, and without trial or opportunity to speak in their own defense, were formed into line, and all but one shot—five killed and five wounded. One fell unharmed, pretending to be dead. All were left for dead. The only crime charged against them was that of being Free-State men. Now, I' inquire, what action has ever, since the occurrence in May last, been taken by either the President of the United States, the Governor of Missouri, the Governor of Kansas, or any of their tools, or by any proslavery or Administration man, to ferret out and punish the perpetrators of this crime?

"Now for the other parallel. On Sunday, December 19, a negro man called Jim came over to the Osage settlement from Missouri, and stated that he, together with his wife, two children, and another negro man, was to be sold within a day or two, and begged for help to get away. On Monday (the following) night, two small companies were made up to go to Missouri and forcibly liberate the five slaves, together with other slaves. One of these companies I assumed to direct. We proceeded to the place, surrounded the buildings, liberated the slaves, and also took certain property supposed to belong to the estate.

" We, however, learned before leaving that a portion of the articles we had taken belonged to a man living on the plantation as a tenant, and who was supposed to have no interest in the estate. We promptly returned to him all we had taken. We then went to another plantation, where we found five more slaves, took some property and two white men. We moved all slowly away into the Territory for some distance, and then sent the white men back, telling them to follow us as soon as they chose to do so. The other company freed one female slave, took some property, and, as I am informed, killed one white man (the master), who fought against the liberation.

" Now for a comparison. Eleven persons are forcibly restored to their natural and inalienable rights, with but one man killed, and all ' hell is stirred from beneath.' It is currently reported that the Governor of Missouri has made requisition upon the Governor of Kansas for the delivery of all such as were concerned in the last-named ' dreadful outrage.' The Marshal of Kansas is said to be collecting a posse of Missouri (not Kansas) men at West Point in Missouri, a little town about ten miles distant, to ' enforce the laws.' All pro-slavery, conservative Free-State, and doughface men, and Administration tools, are filled with holy horror.

" Consider the two cases, and the action of the Administration party.

" Respectfully yours,

" JOHN BROWN."

Had John Brown compared the Potawatomie and Marais des Cygnes massacres, the parallel would have been more perfect. In the latter, as has been stated, men were taken without previous warning, simply because they were Free-State men, drawn up in line and shot down like dogs. In the first, the Potawatomie, men were also taken without warning, because they were pro-slavery men, and cut to pieces with cleavers or short swords.

The Hamilton massacre is thus described by Andreas:

" Returning to the main body, Hamilton ordered a forward march, and the prisoners were led down to a cañon or gulch by a by-path between rocks, single file, when the commands were given, ' Halt,' ' Front face,' ' Close up,' to the prisoners; and his own men were formed in line in front of them on a shelf or rock about as wide as a good wagon road, and somewhat higher than the prisoners' heads. Deliberately the orders were given by Captain Hamilton, ' Make ready,' ' Take aim,' but before the order ' Fire ' could be uttered, one of the worst of the border ruffians, Brockett by name, turned his horse away, whereupon Hamilton said to him, ' Brockett, G——d d——n you, why don't you wheel into line?' Brockett said, ' I'll be d——d if I will have anything to do with such a G——d d——d piece of business as this. If it was in a fight I would fire.' At this, Hamilton took out his revolver and fired at the prisoners, giving the order to his men to fire at the same time. Alvin Hamilton's gun, which was aimed at B. L. Reed, missed fire the first time; Reed not being hit, turned partly round to see his companions fall, and, Hamilton's gun being immediately re-cocked and fired, received the ball on one of his ribs and fell. Thus all these innocent, brave men were brought down. On their part there was no flinching or begging for quarter. Mr. Hairgrove, just before the order to fire was given, said, ' Gentlemen, if you are going to shoot us, take good aim.' After waiting a few minutes, Hamilton gave the order to his men to go down and see who were dead, and to shoot those who were not. Two of the ruffians went down among the fallen and fired three shots at different ones who gave signs of life. Amos Hall was shot through the mouth. One said, ' Old Reed ain't dead.' ' Which is him?' was asked. ' Why, there the old devil is looking at you.' But Pat Ross got the balls and he was killed. Another ruffian said, ' See that man humped up, he ain't dead.' The man ' humped up ' was Austin Hall, and his body was perfectly rigid. One of those finishing the butchery kicked Mr. Hall, rolled him over, and remarked, ' He's as dead as the devil,' and so let him alone. Mr. Hall was the only man not hit."

Here is Hamilton's massacre. Can it be paralleled? It would seem impossible, yet Brown's massacre of May 24, 1856, was the object lesson which Hamilton was imitating. Some testimony concerning that massacre reads as follows :

" On Saturday night about eleven o'clock on the 24th day of May last (1856), a party of men came to our house; we had all retired; they roused us up, and told us that if we would surrender they would not hurt us. They said they were from the army; they were armed with pistols and knives; they took off my father and two of my brothers, William and Drury. We were all alarmed. They made inquiries about Mr. Wilkinson, and about his horses. The next morning was Sunday, the 25th of May, 1856. I went in search of my father and two brothers. I found my father and one brother, William, lying dead in the road, about two hundred yards from the house; I saw my other brother lying dead on the ground, about one hundred and fifty yards from the house, in the grass, near a ravine; his fingers were cut off; his head was cut open; there was a hole in his breast. William's head was cut open, and a hole was also in his side. ` My father was shot in the forehead and stabbed in the breast. * * *

' JOHN DOYLE."

"That on Saturday, the 24th day of May, A.D. 1856, about eleven o'clock at night, after we had all retired, my husband, James P. Doyle, myself, and five children, four boys and one girl, * * * we heard some persons come into the yard and rap at the door and call for Mr. Doyle, my husband. This was about eleven o'clock on Saturday night of the 24th of May last. My husband got up and went to the door. Those outside inquired for Mr. Wilkinson and where he lived. My husband told them that he would tell them. Mr. Doyle, my husband, opened the door, and several came into the house, and said they were from the army. My husband was a pro-slavery man. They told my husband that he and the boys must surrender, they were their prisoners. These men were armed with pistols and large knives. They first took my husband out of the house, then they took two of my sons—the two oldest ones, William and Drury—out, and then took my husband and these two boys, William and Drury, away. My son John was spared, because I asked them in tears to spare him. In a short time afterwards I heard the report of pistols. I heard two reports, after which I heard moaning, as if a person was dying; then I heard a wild whoop. They had asked before they went away for our horses. We told them that the horses were out on the prairie. My husband and two boys, my sons, did not come back any more. I went out next morning in search of them, and found my husband and William, my son, lying dead in the road near together, about two hundred yards from the house. My other son I did not see any more until the day he was buried. I was so much overcome that I went to the house. They were buried the next day. On the day of the burying I saw the dead body of Drury. Fear of myself and the remaining children induced me to leave the home where we had been living. We had improved our claim a little. I left all and went to the State of Missouri.

her
" MAHALA   X   DOYLE."
mark.

"On the 25th of May last, somewhere between the hours of midnight and daybreak, cannot say exactly at what hour, after all had retired to bed, we were disturbed by barking of the dog. I was sick with the measles, and woke up Mr. Wilkinson, and asked if he 'heard the noise, and what it meant?' He said it was only some one passing about, and soon after was again asleep. It was not long before the dog raged and barked furiously, awakening me once more; pretty soon I heard footsteps as of men approaching; saw one pass by the window, and some one knocked at the door. I asked, 'Who is that?' No one answered. I woke my husband, who asked, 'Who is that?' Some one replied, ' I want you to tell me the way to Dutch Henry's.' He commenced to tell them, and they said to him, ' Come out and show us.' He wanted to go, but I would not let him; he then told them it was difficult to find his clothes, and could tell them as well without going out of doors. The men out of doors, after that, stepped back, and I thought I could hear them whispering; but they immediately returned, and, as they approached, one of them asked my husband, 'Are you a Northern armist?' He said, 'I am.' I understood the answer to mean that my husband was opposed to the Northern or free-soil party. I cannot say that I understood the question. My husband was a pro-slavery man, and was a member of the Territorial Legislature held at Shawnee Mission.

" When my husband said, ' I am,' one of them said, ' You are our prisoner. Do you surrender?' He said, ' Gentlemen, I do.' They said, ' Open the door.' Mr. Wilkinson told them to wait till he made a light; and they replied, ' If you don't open it, we will open it for you.' He opened the door against my wishes, and four men came in, and my husband was told to put on his clothes, and they asked him if there was not more men about; they searched for arms, and took a gun and powder-flask, all the weapon that was about the house.

" I begged them to let Mr. Wilkinson stay with me, saying that I was sick and helpless, and could not stay by myself. My husband also asked them to let him stay with me until he could get some one to wait on me; told them that he would not run off, but would be there the next day, or whenever called for. The old man, who seemed to be in command, looked at me and then around at the children, and replied, ' You have neighbors.' I said, ' So I have, but they are not here, and I cannot go for them.' The old man replied, ' It matters not,' and told him to get ready. My husband wanted to put on his boots and get ready, so as to be protected from the damp and night air, but they wouldn't let him. They then took my husband away. One of them came back and took two saddles; I asked him what they were going to do with him, and he said, ' Take him a prisoner to the camp.' I wanted one of them to stay with me. He said he would, but ' they would not let him.' After they were gone, I thought I heard my husband's voice, in complaint, but do not know; went to the door, and all was still. Next morning Mr. Wilkinson was found about one hundred and fifty

yards from the house, in some dead brush. A lady who saw my husband's body said there was a gash in his head and in his side; others
said that he was cut in the throat twice. * * *

" My husband was a poor man. I am now on my way to Tennessee
to see my father, William Ball, who lives in Haywood County. I am
enabled to go by the kindness of friends in this part of Missouri.

" Some of the men who took my husband away that night were
armed with pistols and knives. I do not recollect whether all I saw
were armed. They asked Mr. W. if McMinn did not live near. My
husband was a quiet man, and was not engaged in arresting or disturbing anybody. He took no active part in the pro-slavery cause so as to
aggravate the abolitionists; but he was a pro-slavery man. Mr. Mc-
Minn mentioned above is a pro-slavery man; so also is the said Dutch
Henry.　　　　　　　　　　　　　　" LOUISE JANE WILKINSON."

" Old John Brown drew his revolver and shot the old man Doyle in
the forehead, and Brown's two youngest sons immediately fell upon the
younger Doyles with their two-edged swords.

" One of the young Doyles was stricken down in an instant, but the
other attempted to escape, and was pursued a short distance by his assailant and cut down. The company then proceeded down Mosquito
Creek to the house of Allen Wilkinson. Here the old man Brown,
three of his sons, and son-in-law, as at the Doyle residence, went to
the door and ordered Wilkinson to come out, leaving Frederick Brown,
Winer, and myself standing in the road, east of the house. Wilkinson
was taken and marched some distance south of his house and slain in
the road, with a short sword, by one of the younger Browns. After he
was killed his body was dragged out to one side and left.

" We then crossed the Potawatomie and came to the house of Henry
Sherman, generally known as Dutch Henry. Here John Brown and
the party, excepting Frederick Brown, Winer, and myself, who were
left outside a short distance from the door, went into the house and
brought out one or two persons, talked with them some, and then took
them in again. They afterwards brought out William Sherman, Dutch
Henry's brother, marched him down into the Potawatomie Creek, where
he was slain with swords by Brown's two youngest sons, and left lying
in the creek. * * *　　　　　　　　　　　" JAMES TOWNSLEY."

The number killed in each case was the same, five; and
in neither case was the leader arrested or punished, while in
one case one of the perpetrators was hanged, William
Griffith; and in the other, one was shot, Frederick Brown.
Griffith had the rope placed about his neck by Hairgrove,

one of his victims; while Frederick Brown was shot, August, 1856, by Martin White, whose house was fired into and whose horses were stolen by the Browns in April of the same year. The atrocity of these massacres was such that it was but human for Mrs. Doyle, when John Brown was to be hanged for removing his Republic, formed in Canada, to Harper's Ferry, without first obtaining leave from Federal authority, to write this man as follows:

"CHATTANOOGA, TENNESSEE, November 20, 1859.
"*John Brown :*
"SIR: Although vengeance is not mine, I confess that I do feel gratified to hear that you were stopped in your fiendish career at Harper's Ferry, with the loss of your two sons. You can now appreciate my distress in Kansas, when you then and there entered my house at midnight and arrested my husband and two boys, and took them out in the yard, and in cold blood shot them dead in my hearing. You can't say you did it to free our slaves; we had none, and never expected to own one; but it only made me a poor disconsolate widow, with helpless children. While I feel for your folly, I do hope and trust you will meet with your just reward. Oh, how it pained my heart to hear the dying groans of my husband and children. If this scrawl gives you any satisfaction, you are welcome to it.   "MAHALA DOYLE."

"N.B.—My son, John Doyle, whose life I begged of you, is now grown up, and is very desirous to be at Charlestown on the day of your execution; would certainly be there if his means would permit it, that he might adjust the rope around your neck, if Governor Wise would permit.   "M. D."

It was not easy to form a correct view of the responsibility for the outrages of the spring of 1858. Persons and newspapers took sides, and apparently could see nothing but good in one party and nothing but evil in the other. While Hamilton was killing Free-State men in Linn County, May 19, 1858, the *Herald of Freedom* of May 22d gives the following account of Montgomery and his followers:

"ROBBERS.

"On the 11th inst., about four o'clock P.M., a party of twenty men, all on horseback, and well armed, commanded by Captain Montgomery, from Sugar Mound, rode up to the store of James M. Wells, at Willow Springs, in this county, dismounted, hitched their horses, and entered the store. A lady, apprehensive of the character of the movement, attempted to cut the horses loose. While doing so, one of the party came out with a revolver, and guarded the door. The nineteen persons in the inside proceeded to rifle the drawers of their contents, divested themselves of their worn-out or soiled clothing, and put on such as they could find to supply their place; robbed Mr. Wells of his pocket-book, and searched him for his arms; then calicoes and all sorts of fabrics were tied up in buffalo robes, handkerchiefs, etc.; and packages thus made up, with boots, shoes, and numberless other articles, to the amount of between three and four hundred dollars, were added to the plunder, and thus loaded they rode away.

"The same party visited Mr. McKinney that night, plundered the house of all the money they could find, set it on fire, stole a mule and horse, and then rode off. The fire was extinguished, hence the house was not destroyed.

"On Sunday, the same party were seen prowling about Minneola, and a descent was contemplated upon some pro-slavery men in that neighborhood. The policy seems to be to rob, pillage, and drive out every pro-slavery man in Kansas, and Montgomery and his banditti are the instrumentalities employed for that purpose.

"They have visited Olathe, robbing a store there. From thence they proceeded to Gardner and McCammish, committing depredations at each of those places.

"These same men have been prowling about the Territory for months, committing all sorts of depredations, and keeping the country in a constant ferment. They are, to a great extent, responsible for the troubles around Fort Scott. We have heard of them repeatedly, and been told of their visiting private residences, compelling families to rise at midnight and cook meals for them, and then renewing their journey and visiting some new place, where the same excesses are repeated. Horses, guns, revolvers, etc., are almost invariably taken wherever found; and in some instances drafts have been drawn upon Government officials to pay for articles thus taken. Several stores have been pillaged, and the money or proceeds have gone to enrich these freebooters.

"In the letter of Mr. Whitman, which we publish this week, this band of land pirates are thus undoubtedly alluded to:

"'We feel grateful for your sympathy; and for force we shall have no occasion, I hope; but if so, a small domestic one will do the work effectually!'

"We have said, time and time again, that the policy of Lane, Conway and company was to embroil this Territory in civil strife. Here is the proof. Here are the overt acts of a set of scoundrels who are plundering stores and dwellings in open day, and committing violence upon the inhabitants. An individual is marked by them for destruction, the fiat goes forth, and he disappears—where, no one can tell. His property is confiscated, and thus one after another of our population is wiped out.

" We are frank to confess that we have no love for these things. They must be stopped, and immediately, else civil war must follow. Life nor property is safe! The horrors of 1856 are being inaugurated. A guerrilla party, in the time of profound peace—their object, plunder —is among us. What shall be done? Should not the people meet for advisement, and pledge themselves to each other to stop this high-handed procedure at once, and declare all persons outlaws who are known to be engaged with such parties? * * *

" Can't something be done to stop this robbing of men in various parts of the Territory? If there is no other way, a company of reliable men should be organized, whose province it should be to ferret them out and shoot them down like dogs. These men constitute a regular banditti, organized to rob and plunder, and they deserve any punishment which an outraged public are disposed to bestow upon them. The people of the various towns should hold meetings, and band together to put an end to this."

By comparing dates it will be seen that it was while Montgomery was thus engaged in Johnson and Douglas Counties the Hamilton massacre occurred.

To show the partisan spirit of the times, the following quotations are made from the *Herald of Freedom* and Lawrence *Republican*. The editors of these papers were among the ablest ever in Kansas, and were doubtless sincere and meant to be truthful, but viewed matters from different standpoints and received their information from opposing factions:

" But those men who desired revolution, who had been sojourning for a whole year in Kansas, *and living upon funds sent here by the benevolent in the East to relieve the wants of the destitute*—they suddenly appeared upon the southern border, and upon the most flimsy pretext plunged the country again in blood. The fiery eloquence of some of the leaders of that warlike expedition has been previously detailed, when the convention of the 22d and 23d of December, 1857, was in session! Our readers too well remember the destruction of the ballot-box by Montgomery at Sugar Mound, and the drawing of knives and revolvers

26

at Clinton on those who wished to vote for officers under the Lecompton Constitution to defeat its action, and all the various expedients then resorted to to kindle a flame in southern Kansas; how party after party left Lawrence, taking with them our brass howitzer, and subsisting by pillage, and returning in due time with *stolen* horses. These expeditions were all sustained by Redpath and his associates, and the Lawrence *Republican*, Leavenworth *Times* and *Crusader of Freedom* were the organs of those forays. * * *

"But it is denied that the objects of Redpath, Lane, Thacher, Vaughan, Conway, *et omne genus*, were revolutionary, and when we make these charges against them they only resist by pronouncing them false. We assert before Heaven, that the plan of a servile negro insurrection on the border of Missouri was divulged to us by a leading Free-State man while a prisoner near Lecompton, in the summer of 1856; and that it was designed to be participated in by Free-State men in Kansas, who were to furnish arms and counsel; and that it was designed to extend until the whole Union should become involved in it, and a dissolution should follow, and American slavery be wiped out in blood. We assert, further, that we resolved to stem this tide, though it should cost us our life; and when the *Herald of Freedom* was revived in the fall of that year, we several times showed what our position would be in a contest of this character. The whole movement on our southern border has been a carrying out of the programme of the revolutionists, and our hostility to it is but in furtherance of the position taken in '56. The evidence is indubitable that Captain Brown came on from the East, endorsed by prominent disunionists, to head a revolutionary movement, and he only left the Territory, as Redpath had done before him, when all hopes of success had failed.

"We are conscious that our positions are bold and startling to many, and perhaps will be believed by but few; yet we have evidence which will be satisfactory to any one, and would establish the fact before any intelligent jury.

"It is well established that Thacher, Vaughan, Conway, Phillips, Hinton, Redpath, old Brown, Montgomery, Lane, etc., all co-operated in their views, and all worked together in advocacy of the various positions which have come before the country since 1856; and all have been opposing a peaceful solution of the Kansas problem. * * *

"It is but the work of a moment to connect the persons whose names are given above in a common enterprise, and that to prolong our Kansas troubles to the latest possible period. True, Lane and Redpath fell out, still it was not because they did not agree in ' the great crusade for freedom,' as they called it, but, as Redpath claimed, because he could not enter, heart and soul, into Lane's plans of private assassination.

" Redpath has just published a book entitled ' The Roving Editor, or Talks with Slaves in the Southern States,' published by A. B. Burdick, New York. The work is dedicated to ' Old John Brown.' Turning to page 300, we find the following paragraph, which we copy verbatim and entire :

" ' I believed that a civil war between the North and South would ultimate in insurrection, and that the Kansas troubles would probably create a military conflict of the sections. Hence, I left the South, and went to Kansas ; and endeavored, personally and by my pen, to precipitate a revolution. That we failed, for I was not alone in this desire, was owing to the influence of prominent Republican statesmen, whose unfortunate conservative character of counsel, which it was impossible openly to resist, effectually baffled all our hopes—hopes which Democratic action was auspiciously promoting.' "—*Herald of Freedom.*

" HOW STANDS THE RECORD?

" After an excited and heated contest, with the clearing away of the smoke and the cessation of the din of strife, men naturally wish to know whether they have made a drawn battle or proved triumphant. With no feeling of exultation or overbearing triumph, we desire to review the position which the Republican took with regard to the Southern troubles, and know whether we were justly subjected to the railing and offensive accusations of the Lecompton *Democrat* and kindred journals, both in this place and elsewhere in the Territory.

" After Denver had visited southern Kansas, we understood from a hundred different sources that the basis of the settlement of the troubles there was the blotting out of the past, the opening of new books, and a clean page to start anew with. The people there, we *know*, understood the settlement that way. In the popular language of Linn and Bourbon counties, we believed ' by-gones were to be by-gones.' We honestly understood the settlement in this way ; and when hostilities broke out there, we frankly stated it to be the result of the infringement of the Denver treaty. At this statement a great howl was raised by the pro-slavery organs, charging us with being supporters of ' jay-hawkers,' ' murderers,' ' outlaws,' and Heaven knows what all. Well, we patiently endured abuses, and, though traduced, answered not.

" A copy of the treaty was flung in our face, and we were told, ' Read that and be abashed!' Well, it was a staggering document, and we could only reply, ' The people in Linn and Bourbon counties understood the treaty as we have given it.'

" At last, Truth, slower of foot by one-half than Error, makes her appearance. It seems there was a treaty, the treaty, which distinctly gave the people there to understand that the past should be buried—

that all things should be made new. This was what the people understood. Then there was the written treaty, which we published some
weeks ago. It, of course, contained no clause blotting out the past,
since Governor Denver would hardly dare to go so far as that; for although the only way to secure peace, yet to the uninitiated, to the outsiders, it would have borne a bad look. But that he assured the people
that they should not be harassed by the past, we are assured by the
most undoubted testimony.

" When this agreement was violated, we protested against it. For
the sake of peace, we insisted upon the religious observance of the
Denver compact. Our voice was not heeded. The past was harrowed
up; old offenders and outlaws were invited to come back; peaceful
settlers were harassed with the fear of indictments and prosecutions.
The country was alive with excitement. Our readers know what followed. Troops marched and remarched; Missourians enlisted into
posses; men were hunted down like wolves or rabid dogs, and houses
were rifled in the name of peace. And now comes the close.

" The Legislature step in and authoritatively declare, as Denver and
the people had declared nine months before, ' By-gones shall be by-
gones.' They who had clamored loudest for vengeance upon Montgomery and the people were the most earnest in procuring the passage
of the 'Amnesty Act.'

" With this review we close, sincerely hoping this is the last article
we shall ever be called upon to pen respecting troubles in southern
Kansas."—*Lawrence Republican.*

After the massacre by Hamilton both parties were struck
with terror, and the people, irrespective of party, cried for a
cessation of this mode of warfare. Governor Denver, early
in June, visited southern Kansas, arriving at Fort Scott on
the 13th. He had invited Judge J. W. Wright and Robinson to accompany him. A mass meeting was held on the
14th, which was attended by both parties. After speeches
by Governor Denver, Wright, Ransom, and Robinson, a
settlement was effected. The old county officers were asked
to resign and new ones were selected by a vote of the people
present, and Governor Denver appointed them. It was
recommended that old scores should be forgotten, although
the written agreement left all criminal matters to the grand
jury. Montgomery did not meet Governor Denver, although
he talked with Wright and Robinson and expressed himself

as much pleased with the settlement. A military company, commanded by Captain Weaver, was furnished to keep the peace, and for several months quiet reigned. At length some men procured the indictment of a Free-State man named Rice for an old offense and had him arrested. Montgomery claimed that this was in violation of the understanding, and gathered his forces again. By this time John Brown had returned to southern Kansas, because of an exposure to Senator Wilson and others of his plans to attack Virginia, by his drill-master, Hugh Forbes.

In Cook's confession another reason is given for Brown's visit to Kansas in 1858. Cook says:

" In his [Brown's] trip East he did not realize the amount of money that he expected. The money had been promised *bona fide*, but owing to the tightness of the money market they failed to comply with his demands. The funds were necessary to the accomplishment of his plans. I afterwards learned that there was a lack of confidence in his scheme. It was therefore necessary that a movement should be made in another direction, to demonstrate the practicability of his plan. This he made about a year ago, by his invasion of Missouri, and the taking of about a dozen slaves, together with horses, cattle, etc., into Kansas, in defiance of the United States marshal and his posse. From Kansas he took them to Canada *via* Iowa City and Cleveland. At the latter place he remained some days, and, I think, disposed of his horses there. It seems that the United States marshal was afraid to arrest him, and this was all that was wanting to give confidence to the wavering in the practicability of his plan and its ultimate success."

His men were on hand, including Kagi, his secretary of war. Montgomery kept Brown in the background, as, he said, if he should have command there would not be left one stone upon another of Fort Scott. The town was entered, Rice rescued, and Mr. Little killed, and his store robbed of $7000 worth of goods. From this time until the passage of the amnesty law by the Legislature anarchy reigned supreme, and thieves, robbers, and murderers plied their calling with great success. John Brown and his party were in their glory. In December he made his trip to Mis-

souri and brought back with him eleven slaves, some horses,
oxen, and other property, one man being killed.

George A. Crawford, a Free-State Democrat of Fort Scott,
had an interview with Brown about this raid, and wrote the
following to Eli Thayer:

"As to the raid into Missouri, it was made on the 20th December,
1858, four days after the raid into Fort Scott. It was led by Captain
Brown in person. Captain Montgomery refused to go along—protested, as I have understood, against it—but came to the aid of the
Kansas settlers when retaliatory raids were afterwards expected. The
Captain's company marched down the Little Osage River, in the north
part of this county, and about twelve miles from here, and proceeded
into Vernon County, Missouri, a distance of three or four miles.

"The Missouri *Democrat* of December 30, 1858, gave the Missouri
statement of the losses. I presume it is correct. Files of other papers
of the period would show. It states that they 'murdered' David Crews
(or Cruise), 'kidnapped a negro woman,' took wagon, horses, etc.,
and robbed Mr. Martin and family of a fine mule; took from the estate
of James Lawrence, in possession of his son-in-law, Henry Hicklin,
five negroes, two horses, one yoke of cattle, an ox-wagon, a double-
barrel shot-gun, saddle, and clothing. From Isaac B. LaRue, five
negroes, six horses, one yoke of cattle, clothing, and took prisoners
whom they released.

"In the conversation to which I have alluded, Captain Brown said
he had sent the slaves on to their freedom; that they had earned the
property of their masters; and that his young men were entitled to forage to the extent of their subsistence. He denied the current rumor
that the slaves had been taken away by violence and against their will.

"As to the killing of Cruise, he said that he had given strict orders
for the careful use of the guns; and that there should be no firing unless resistance was offered. He had divided his men into two squads,
one on each side of the stream. In the house of Cruise one of his
quick-blooded young men, supposing that Cruise was about to draw a
weapon, had fired, killing him instantly. I inferred that the Captain
was not present. He claimed to have reprimanded the young man for
his haste.

"Cruise was a good citizen—a plain, unoffending farmer. It was
reported that he had no weapons on his person. The killing of him
was an unjustifiable outrage, and it subjected our settlements to great
danger from retaliatory measures.

"I protested to the Captain against this violence. We were settlers,
he was not. He could strike a blow and leave. The retaliatory blow

would fall on us. Being a Free-State man, I myself was held personally responsible by pro-slavery ruffians in Fort Scott for the acts of
Captain Brown.

" One of these ruffians, Brockett, when they gave me notice to leave
the town, said: ' When a snake bites me, I don't go hunting for that
particular snake. I kill the first snake I come to.'

" I called Captain Brown's attention to the facts that we were at
peace with Missouri; that our Legislature was then in the hands of
Free-State men to make the laws; that even in our disturbed counties
of Bourbon and Linn we were in a majority, and had elected the officers both to make and execute the laws; that without peace we could
have no immigration; that no Southern immigration was coming; that
agitation such as his was only keeping our Northern friends away,
etc.

" The old man replied that it was no pleasure to him, an old man,
to be living in the saddle, away from home and family, and exposing
his life; and if the Free-State men of Kansas felt they no longer needed
him, he would be glad to go.

" He seemed very erratic—at war with all our accustomed ideas on
the slavery question—but very earnest.

" I think the conversation made an impression on him, for he soon
after went to his self-sacrifice at Harper's Ferry.

" Yours,
" GEORGE A. CRAWFORD."

The nature of the difficulties in southern Kansas is thus
set forth by two correspondents in the *Herald of Freedom* of
January 8, 1859:

"THE DIFFICULTIES SOUTH.

" A friend writes us from Mound City, Linn County, on the 26th
ult., in which he says:

" ' I regret to observe that there are newspapers in Kansas, whose
editors profess to be governed by principle, which continue to uphold
the crimes daily perpetrated, by sustaining highway robbery, murder,
and the expulsion of our population from Kansas, because of a mere
difference of opinion. These journals have done more to prolong our
troubles than all other causes. If such editors have no sense of moral
justice, and cannot be influenced otherwise, the indignation of the whole
country should be roused against them.

" ' I have lived in Linn County since October, 1855, and have seen
enough of crimes of every grade, perpetrated both by night and day, to
satisfy any man not steeped in crime. Little did I think, in '56, that

professedly Free-State men would be guilty of the same crimes for which we denounced the pro-slavery men of that year, and which raised such a storm throughout the nation.

"'Men of sense ought to know that the daily repetition of crime will never restore peace. They ought to know that outrage begets outrage, and the longer it is continued the farther we are from an honorable and peaceful adjustment of our difficulties.

"'Your comments on the late Convention here were very just. Though it was agreed that the troubles should cease, and all parties should lay down their arms, yet the Montgomery faction, in the face of that compromise, raised a body of men, marched to Fòrt Scott, liberated a prisoner there under indictment by a Free-State grand jury for murder, robbed a store of some five thousand dollars' worth of goods, rifled trunks of their contents, and shot down one of the citizens of the town, and held others prisoners as long as it suited their caprice. I confess I cannot see the difference between those crimes committed by these Free-State men, and the burning of hotels and dwellings, the destroying of printing-offices, and the outrages in Lawrence in May of '56. It only proves that human nature, under the influence of a bad heart, is about the same everywhere.

"'The ordering off of citizens, the stealing of horses, mules, and cattle, the plundering of houses, and the stealing of negroes still goes on, and will, until the strong arm of the law is made effective against crime and violence.'

"Another gentleman, a clergyman, writing us from the vicinity of Moneka, says:

"'I have watched the progress of these troubles here until I am sick, heart-sick with humanity. Here are men claiming to be Christians, and even ministers of the Gospel, who profess to be guided in their actions by the teaching of the Prince of Peace, who have organized a body of murderers, robbers, gamblers, and horse-thieves, and subsisting by plunder, they are riding over the country and committing the basest of crimes. If this is Christianity, anything would be preferable to it; but it is not! Christ taught no such sentiments, but the reverse!

"'The strangest of all is to see peace men, those in the States who were members of peace societies, and who were sending delegates to peace congresses, laboring to inaugurate civil war, with the expressed object of working a revolution throughout the nation, ultimating in a dissolution of the Union; and all to procure the emancipation of the slave. Simple men! They should learn that revolutions involving such grave consequences are not usually set on foot by murderers and thieves. Though Brutus triumphed over the dead corpse of Cæsar, yet it is not believed that in this age of enlightenment a few ignoramuses and desperadoes of the character of those in this county can succeed in crushing out slavery, and with it American freedom.

"'We thank you most heartily for the manly and independent course of the *Herald of Freedom* throughout this protracted contest. It has been a terror to those wretches who have been involved in those crimes, and has been the only restraint which has been exerted over them. Had other journalists showed the same spirit and devotion to the right, our troubles would have ended a year ago; but while Montgomery and his followers are backed up by the hireling press, so long will he continue to ride rough-shod over the country, setting the laws at defiance, and stamping his iron heel into the breasts of his victims; so long will all right be disregarded, and our beautiful country, the loveliest heaven has ever smiled upon, will be the home of an organized banditti as desolating in its consequences as were those of Spain or Italy in the darkest period of the world's history.'"

The *Herald of Freedom* of January 1, 1859, makes this comment upon Colonel Samuel Walker's report of his trip:

"FROM THE SOUTH.

" Captain Samuel Walker, the present sheriff of Douglas County, a gentleman whose word was never contradicted by any party, has just returned from a visit to Linn and Bourbon counties, where he has been on a commission from the Governor, inquiring into the truth of the difficulties in that quarter. His recital of outrages practiced by the Montgomery faction upon persons there is enough to draw tears from the eyes of any one not hardened in crime. Outrages, he states, have been committed by those desperadoes equalling in atrocity those of the vilest border ruffians in the campaign of 1856. Captain Walker states that there has been a great revulsion in public sentiment there within the last few weeks. Everywhere he met men who had sustained Montgomery in the past, who now say they can do it no longer. He has gathered about him all the desperadoes of the Free-State party, and they live by plunder and crime. No man is safe among them. At Fort Scott the Captain found the whole country gathering in there with their property, to protect themselves from these freebooters. The professed object of this banditti is to inaugurate a civil war and bring on a dissolution of the Union, and to that end all their exertions are directed.

" We hear from other sources that Captain Brown is a compeer of Montgomery, and that only a few days ago he made a marauding expedition into Missouri, and after committing various 'excesses,' armed a party of slaves, mounted them on horses, and marched them over into Kansas. Thus outrage after outrage is committed, and newspapers

professing respectability endorse them, and urge on their perpetrators to
the commission of greater crimes."

January 15, 1859, the *Herald of Freedom* gives what it
calls "a review" of the troubles, as follows :

" A REVIEW.

"The fire-eating portion of the Territorial Legislature, and the extreme radicals in general, who are sustaining Montgomery in his murderous movements in the southern part of the Territory, are now rejoicing over the fact that the quasi-general Lane has written a letter to
Governor Medary, informing that gentleman that if the Governor will
invest him with authority for that purpose, he will go South, take
Montgomery and Brown, or any of their command, and bring them to
Lawrence, or wherever the Governor may direct, and that without the
aid of a *posse*, or any assistance whatever.   How this may appear to
others, we cannot say, but to us it is conclusive evidence of the complicity of Lane in those disturbances.   He commissioned Montgomery
upwards of a year ago, and set him to work in southern Kansas to fight
pro-slavery men.   Lane visited that quarter in person, and pretended
to be the ' commander-in-chief of the military forces of Kansas.'   There
is not a doubt but that he directed the original movements in that quarter.   Many of our readers will remember his celebrated *coup d' état* on
the evening of the 22d of December, 1857, at the territorial convention
then in session in Lawrence, when an express from Lane's army entered that convention, and announced, almost breathless, that ' war has
actually begun.'   ' Why will you stand here,' he said, ' and talk about
voting for officers under the Lecompton Constitution, thinking thereby
to defeat it, when your brethren in the southern part of the Territory
are already in arms?   It is the duty of every man here to rush at once
to the scene of the contest, and shoulder to shoulder with General Lane
and his able associates, Captain Montgomery and others, drive back the
invaders of our Territory to the State from which they came.'   And
with a peroration worthy of Patrick Henry in the most trying hour of
our revolutionary history, his arm extended to heaven, his voice gently
raised, and every gesture adapted to the sublime occasion, he declared,
' I would sooner cut off my right arm than cast a vote for any officer
under that constitution.'

"It was then, when the excitement was at its height, and 'Inton
stood on tiptoe, swinging his hat, and hallooing with all his might, and
the lesser lights, such as Thacher, Phillips and Company, were echoing
the shout, that S. N. Wood stepped forward, his patriotism apparently swelled to the sticking-point, and called for volunteers to start the

next morning towards Fort Scott, to stand by General Lane and his brave comrades, in their extremity.   The messenger reported the men suffering for the necessaries of life!   They needed guns, and munitions of war of all descriptions, and at that hour mostly provisions.   Said he: 'I divided my last biscuit with some of these men this morning, and have ridden eighty miles without hardly getting out of my saddle, to bring you this startling intelligence.'   Mr. Wood was more enthusiastic in calling for volunteers than usual.   He recapitulated what the messenger had said.   That whole convention, consisting of what purported to be delegates from every part of the Territory, called together at an inclement season to consult upon the destinies of the Territory, with freedom or slavery before it, was suspended in its action while these war incidents were being enacted, but Mr. Wood could get 'nary' volunteer. Dr. Robinson, who was chairman of the convention, for merely suggesting that the whole thing was a ruse gotten up to affect the action of the convention, became seriously involved with some of the '*Inton* faction, and for a time it seemed probable we might have a fight in the Kansas valley.

"The convention finally decided not to participate in the election, and the next day after, Lane appeared in our streets, and his friends laughed at the successful stratagem employed to bring about the result.

"From that day the excitement South has gone on.   In February or March, Lane issued his memorable letter to Montgomery ordering him to disband; but Montgomery has stated, to gentlemen whose veracity cannot be questioned, that while he was in receipt of these letters for the public eye, he was in receipt of private letters from that same General Lane, applauding him for his acts and advising him to push matters to even greater extremes than he felt justified in doing.   We have not the most remote doubt that every important movement of Montgomery's, from the destruction of the ballot-box at Mound City on the 4th of January, a year ago, down to the release of Rice at Fort Scott, who was indicted for murder by a Free-State grand jury, was advised and directed by Lane; and his letter to Governor Medary is all the proof needed to establish that he is a *particeps criminis* in all that has been done thus far!

"The rebuke which Governor Medary has given Lane was well merited.   Had the Governor added that he did not feel justified in employing those whose hands were yet wet with innocent blood to arrest other men guilty of similar crimes, the reproof would have been none too severe."

Some of the turbulent men in southern Kansas were very reluctant to abandon their unlawful career.   As late as the fall of 1860 they were on the war-path. Notwithstanding the Free-State men were in full control of the machinery for punishing criminals, excepting only the district judges, in November of that year, Samuel Scott, a well-to-do pro-slavery man, and Russell Hinds were hung by Jennison's men, one of them on a charge of returning a fugitive slave to his master. The law for this hanging was found in Exodus, 21st chapter and 16th verse: "And he that stealeth a man, and selleth him, or if he be found in his hand, he shall surely be put to death." Montgomery endorsed this hanging in a note to Judge Hanway as follows:

"Russ. Hinds, hung on the 12th day of November, 1860, for man-stealing. He was a drunken border ruffian, worth a great deal to hang, but good for nothing else. He had caught a fugitive slave, and carried him back to Missouri for the sake of a reward. He was condemned by a jury of twelve men, the law being found in the 16th verse of Exodus xxi."

Had it not been for the revulsion of feeling such proceedings caused in the Territory, these men would indefinitely have prosecuted their nefarious business in the name of God. No man is so unreasonable, arbitrary, and cruel as he who imagines he is commissioned by God, as was Joshua, to inflict punishment upon His enemies. The laws of mind and matter are ignored for the simple "Thus saith the Lord," which comes to his inner consciousness; and that command will invariably be in harmony with his wishes, or righteous (?) indignation or depraved nature or instincts. Whether such kill a President, as did Guiteau; a daughter, as did Freeman; pro-slavery men, as did Brown, Montgomery, and Jennison; or a Free-State or any other man who might cross his path, as did Lane—such men are more dangerous than ten times their number who acknowledge accountability to the immutable laws of cause and effect, and the rights of their fellow-men.

By this time Free-State men were becoming sick of such performances, and were outspoken in their condemnation. A. Wattles, with whom Brown often made his home, in his testimony before the Senate Harper's Ferry Committee, on page 223 of the report, says:

" He called in to see me * * * in going out of the Territory, and I censured him for going into Missouri contrary to our agreement, and getting those slaves. He said, ' I considered the matter well; you will have no more attacks from Missouri; I shall now leave Kansas; probably you will never see me again; I consider it my duty to draw the scene of the excitement to some other part of the country.' "

Here is more evidence that his mission was to cause disturbance and not quiet; war and not peace.

He told the writer substantially the same. He said, " From the standpoint of a free State the party have acted wisely and have succeeded; but from my standpoint they have failed. Nothing but war can extinguish slavery, and the sooner war is inaugurated the better." Had he lived through the Rebellion, he would have learned that the North had all it could do to save the nation and abolish slavery when it had possession of the Government; and had the war commenced while the Government was in the possession of the South, it would have ended, as it commenced, with slavery intact. At least, so reasoned some of the Free-State men. Their policy was to have all the Territories enter the Union as free States and abolish slavery in them by the votes of the inhabitants. After Kansas was secure, Thayer commenced the colonization of Virginia and Tennessee, and had not the South rebelled, slavery would have been peaceably voted out of existence in a few years, without the killing of one million of men and the expending and destruction of billions of wealth. The men and treasure sacrificed were of tenfold more value than all the slaves in the nation, if not in the world. All this would have been saved had not the Southern States repeated Brown's mistake of making war upon the Federal Government.

The amnesty bill was passed by the Legislature in February, 1859, with the concurrence of all parties, and the war was at an end; and as Brown "drew the scene of the excitement" to Harper's Ferry, peace was permanent.

The historian of the future will note these facts, among others, relative to the disturbances in Kansas during 1857 and 1858:

First, after the arrival of Geary there was no longer need of solicitude for the peace of the Territory as there had been before that time, as the Federal Government had abandoned the attempt to establish slavery in Kansas by force. This became still more evident on the arrival of Stanton and Walker. As early as July, 1857, all indications pointed to the taking possession of the Territorial Legislature in October by the Free-State men, and after the Grasshopper Falls convention there was no doubt of it. At length the Territorial Legislature was secured, under Walker and Stanton as executive officers, who were as favorable to an honorable administration of the Government as would have been Seward, Chase, or Sumner.

Second, notwithstanding this condition of affairs, a certain class of men, notably Lane, Brown, and Montgomery, and their followers, were more active in warlike demonstrations than ever before. Messengers were sent East for the sinews of war; "Generals" Lane and Brown were in vigorous correspondence on war movements during the summer and fall of 1857—as earnestly after securing the Legislature as before; a scheme was concocted by Lane to assassinate the members of the Lecompton Constitutional Convention, which, had it been carried out, could have but resulted in open war; an illegal enactment was procured creating a "Military Board," with Lane at its head; as general-in-chief of this "Board" he proposed a general massacre of proslavery men in the various towns of the Territory; and when all these movements were defeated by their own party in central and northern Kansas, the whole crowd, under Lane, Brown, and Montgomery, set up business in southern Kansas, and did everything in their power to inaugurate civil war ; and but for the interference of conservative Free-State men they would have succeeded. When the Free-State men secured the Territorial Legislature, the local officers and juries, they were responsible for the peace of the Territory, and had ample remedy through the courts for all grievances ; but it was just at that juncture when these men became the most belligerent, and murder, robbery, and outrage were most rampant in southern Kansas. It is not easy to decide which the Free-State cause had more to fear, the pro-slavery party, sustained by the Administration, Congress, and the South, or these thieves, marauders, and revolutionists. It was almost a miracle that the first were " thwarted, baffled, and circumvented," and it is a double miracle that the second did not wreck the cause and involve the nation in civil war. Had these men been permitted to have their way, Brown would have been hanged in Kansas instead of Virginia, and two of his companions would have been Lane and Montgomery. There is little doubt that such will be the verdict of history.

Thus far attention has been chiefly directed to civil and political conflicts in the early days, but these were not all of Kansas. It is true that the pioneers kept their armor in readiness, whether for war or politics, but all except professional politicians engaged in the various industries which thrive in times of peace. Agriculture, manufactures, house and town building, engaged the attention of most of the settlers, while speculation in town lots and shares was by no means overlooked. The towns most prominent during the political and civil strife of 1854–58 were Leavenworth, the home of wealth and conservatism ; Atchison, the home of the Stringfellows and the Squatter Sovereign ; Fort Scott, the seat of the Land Office ; Topeka, the State capital city, founded in December, 1854, by Eastern men, with the best town builder in the West, Colonel C. K. Holliday, as general manager ; Manhattan, founded by such men as I. T. Goodnow, Dr. Dennison, Mead, and Hunting ; Osawatomie, under the chief management' of O. C. Brown; Lecompton, the territorial capital; Burlington, Burlingame, Council Grove, Emporia, Wabaunsee, and Lawrence. All these towns still have a name to live, while many others might be named which promised great things, but have lost their importance, such as Kickapoo, Douglas, Tecumseh, Calhoun, Pawnee, Oxford, Council City, Delaware Crossing, Hampden, Franklin, and others.

While most of the interior towns were Free-State, the Missouri River towns, until after the arrival of Governor Geary, were more or less under the control of Slave-State men. At Kansas City, Missouri, Governor Reeder was in danger of assassination, and remained concealed nearly two weeks before escaping in disguise; at Leavenworth Free-State men and women were driven out by the hundred; while at Atchison, Pardee Butler, and Kelly could be mobbed with impunity.

After the return of the campaigners for Fremont, it was considered important to have a town on the Missouri River where Free-State men could be secure from insult or molestation of any kind. Accordingly, the site, for a time known as Quindaro, was purchased and platted by some Free-State men in the fall of 1856. This place was advertised as the only landing on the river where Free-State men had control, and in the spring of 1857 nearly all the immigrants from the North seemed bound for Kansas by way of Quindaro. The effect upon other localities was miraculous. Wyandotte was organized under Free-State auspices, with Lieutenant Governor W. Y. Roberts as figure-head; Leavenworth elected Free-State officers; Atchison reorganized with General S. C. Pomeroy in the lead; Doniphan sent for Lane for an advertising card, while Sumner could boast an Ingalls; Delaware had a town company hailing from Lawrence; Elwood could show more Free-State young men of promise than all the others combined; while White Cloud had Sol. Miller, and the *White Cloud Chief*, the premium newspaper of Kansas. The effect of this revolution in the old towns, and the starting of so many new ones, was to distribute the transportation and other business where the best accommodations could be furnished, and many of the mushroom towns collapsed, among them the one that had started the Free-State town boom. As Kansas City, Missouri, was the natural gateway to all the country west of it, and as Colonel Kersey Coates, the brainiest man and shrewdest manager in Kansas, settled there, this place soon took the lead of all others, and has retained it ever since. Even the overflow from this city has made the metropolis of the State of Kansas, called Kansas City, Kansas.

But something more was needed than a landing on the Missouri River. Kansas was being rapidly settled throughout its eastern portion for more than one hundred miles from water transportation, and some means must be devised for transporting farm products, or they would be worthless except for home consumption. As Robinson had resigned his agency of the Aid Company while a prisoner, and was free to enlist in any business that might need his services, when the slavery conflict subsided he gave his attention to the transportation question. He abandoned politics, as by nature he was unfitted to run with a political machine. He could agitate, but could not wear a muzzle, and hence would be an unavailable candidate and an unsuitable officer for any party. He always preferred the unwritten laws of the universe to State statutes, Church creeds, or Madam Grundy's edicts, and so was necessarily a poor politician. Being solicited to engage in party politics, he wrote a letter to the *Herald of Freedom* of May 7, 1859. As it gives his views of the situation at that time, extracts are here given:

"LAWRENCE, April 30, 1859.

"*Editor Herald of Freedom :*

"DEAR SIR: * * * As you have called me out, I will give a few reasons why I shall attend no political convention, either mass, dele-

27

gate, or constitutional. As these reasons apply to no one else, they
will be personal, and perhaps egotistical.

" In the first place, I am not a politician, never was, and so long as
I have my reason never mean to be. It is true I voted for Harrison
for President, because I thought the Whigs honest and the Democrats
corrupt. Since that time I could see but little difference between them,
and have voted for no presidential candidate, but have occasionally
joined in popular movements against both Whigs and Democrats.

" In California I joined a popular movement to secure the legal
rights of the citizens against unscrupulous speculators and sharpers, and
was thrown into prison by one party and into the Legislature by the
other, but it was not a political contest.

" In Kansas, not only the political, but the civil, legal, and natural
rights of the people were being struck down, and I did what I could to
protect them. At the urgent solicitation of friends I was induced to
occupy a somewhat prominent position in the contest. Until the defeat
of the Lecompton Constitution I regarded it as a duty to labor with my
fellow-citizens to free them from the tyranny that threatened to overwhelm and crush out all their constitutional rights. Up to the vote on
the English Bill, during the whole struggle it was my good fortune to
approve cordially of the policy of the people of Kansas. It is true, I
did not agree with the policy adopted at an adjourned delegate convention, neither did the people, as was demonstrated at the polls. The defeat of the English Bill was regarded as a complete victory over all outside enemies; was, accordingly, the signal for the politicians to enter
the ring, and for all others to retire. From that time I have avoided
all political gatherings, and turned my attention more particularly to the
development of the material interests of the Territory. Kansas, although more beautiful and desirable on some accounts, has probably
less commercial advantages than any State in the Union. Her lands,
so rich and beautiful, must lie unimproved and comparatively valueless
without the means of getting their products to market. Owing to the
emigration to the gold mines, corn sells at Leavenworth and Kansas
City for sixty cents per bushel, but it costs fifty cents per hundred, or
thirty cents a bushel, to carry it from Lawrence to the Missouri River,
making it worth at this place about thirty cents per bushel, and thirty
miles southwest of here it is worth nothing for export. In ordinary
seasons, when corn is worth but twenty-five cents per bushel on the
river, it will not sell for enough to pay for hauling to market. Should
things remain as they are, and no railroads be built, the land in Missouri River counties will increase in value, while the lands of the interior cannot rise above the price of grazing lands, or from one to five
dollars an acre. So with the towns. The river towns will increase in
importance, as all articles of export must be carried to them by the

farmer, while the interior towns will lose even their present trade. Believing that without the early construction of a system of railroads Kansas would experience a stagnation of business that would be ruinous alike to all departments of industry, I felt it to be of the highest importance to seize the first opportunity to procure grants of lands from Congress for railroad purposes.

"Having been placed in a position by the people of Kansas during our early struggle that was likely to carry with it some influence, I felt it a duty to use that influence for their benefit. Accordingly, I declined to be a member of the Leavenworth Constitutional Convention, and avoided political controversies, with a view to secure a grant of lands while there was land to grant, and when it could be of service to the people. I visited three successive sessions of Congress, chiefly for this object. Last winter a large and respectable delegation from Kansas agreed upon a system of roads, and a grant would probably have been made had not the political demagogues interfered. That system would have given five, if not six, roads to Lawrence, and would have increased the value of every lot in town tenfold, every farm in the county fourfold, and every acre of land east of Fort Riley, on an average, twofold. The grant was to have been made to the Legislature, and no man at Washington would have had the least advantage over any other citizen of the Territory. * * *

"C. ROBINSON."

Failing to get action by Congress, R. S. Stevens, S. N. Simpson, and Robinson procured the assent of the leading men of the Delaware tribe of Indians to make a treaty by which their land should be sold in the interest of a railroad up the Kansas valley. But when the council was held, the agent, being a pro-slavery man, and not liking such men as had worked up the treaty, inserted the name of a road running from Leavenworth instead of the mouth of the Kansas River. When this action became known the Indians signed a protest which resulted in a compromise, and the two roads were provided for, one from Leavenworth and one from Wyandotte. Stevens, Simpson, and Robinson became directors and stockholders, and all went smoothly till Lane was elected to the United States Senate, when, as he was hostile to Stevens and Robinson, the latter sold out his interest and Lane was conciliated. The road was, after long delays, constructed, and became the Union Pacific, with a large endowment in lands and bonds. This was the beginning of roads in Kansas, but not the end, as the State is gridironed with them from end to end, no State of the same age equalling it in railroad mileage.

CHAPTER XVII.

THE KILLING OF JENKINS.—THE SERVICES OF LANE AND
BROWN.—ADMISSION OF KANSAS TO THE UNION.—SECES-
SION.—THE GOVERNOR'S FIRST MESSAGE.

THE year 1858 was noteworthy as completing the conflict
against Lecompton and territorial usurpation. It was noteworthy, also, for the murder of Gaius Jenkins by Colonel
Lane, over a pretended claim quarrel. As Jenkins was one
of the treason prisoners confined during the summer of 1856
with the United States troops, and as this claim question
may have been one reason why Lane proposed their rescue
by force, and why he left Lawrence defenseless when the
two thousand eight hundred Missourians were marching
against it, a brief statement is made of the character of the
claim dispute and the killing.

General James Blood, one of the first and most trust-
·worthy settlers of Kansas, made a statement in 1884, in
which occurs the following:

"The claim was located by Gaius Jenkins in the fall of 1854, in my
presence. The first log-house was built by Jenkins, he furnishing all
the means and material, and paying Chapman in full for all the work
done on it by him. Stillman Andrews, with others, dug the well at the
first log-house built as above stated, and was paid for it by Jenkins.
The frame house was put up on the claim by Jenkins in September or
October of 1855. Jenkins had a well dug by the frame house in the
fall of 1855, sixty odd feet deep, and found no water. Aaron Perry
and Samuel Fry dug this well. The double log-house was bought by
Jenkins of Lane, about the last of December, 1855, according to the
statement of both Jenkins and Lane to me at that time."

S. C. Russell, Esq., who had charge of the Jenkins estate, including the claim contest, says:

"In 1857 Lane had a pre-emption claim in Doniphan County, which I proved by the most reputable citizens in Doniphan and Troy, in the summer of 1860, Lane in person acting for himself; and I can go there now and make the same proof. * * * Lane either built a saw-mill on or contracted for one to be built on this Doniphan claim, and afterwards sold it out to other parties. * * *

"Jenkins's hired men had for some time prior to the shooting complained to Jenkins that Lane had nailed up the gate leading to the well, and had threatened to shoot them. Jenkins said he would have to go and see if he could get some water. The day he went over there were with him his hired man, Ray Green, and two nephews—young boys. Jenkins had a pail and an axe, the axe to open the gate, which had been spiked and securely fastened up with additional plank and the well locked up. * * * The only shots fired were the first one by Lane, that killed Jenkins instantly, and the second one by Ray Green, with a four-inch Colt's revolver; he was quite a distance in the rear of Jenkins, and must have made a good shot if he hit Lane, which has been doubted —the truth of which I know nothing, only by report. * * *

"Lane said to Judge G. W. Smith, in Smith's office, more than a month before he shot Jenkins, that he would shoot him. He said to Charles H. Branscomb, 'I will have the blood out of his G——d d——d black heart.'"

Henry W. Petriken wrote, February 19, 1884:

"MONTOURSVILLE, PA., February 19, 1884.
"S. C. Russell, Esq.:

"DEAR SIR: I remember you very well as the attorney of Jenkins —the victim of Lane's murderous villainy—in the case of Jenkins vs. Lane before the Local Land Office at Lecompton.

"I acted as clerk for the greater part of the time, and perhaps the whole of it, after the case was reopened in the taking the testimony in the case. I do not know what became of the book of testimony in this case, unless General Brindle knows something of it. It was probably destroyed as waste lumber, or perhaps turned over to General Brindle's successor.

"Soon after the taking of the testimony was finished, Lane seems to have thought his case a hopeless, or at least a very doubtful one, as he requested me to be at my office on a certain evening *alone* and to have the book of testimony with me, as he wished to look over it. Lane came to my office after I had waited until near midnight, and was disappointed and disgusted when he found I had not the book with me.

The case was decided most unequivocally in favor of Jenkins by the Local Office. Soon after the Local Office acted on the case Lane requested another interview, which I granted, and though this talk lasted nearly all night, I can sum it all up by saying that the whole object of it was to *induce* me to show General Brindle good and sufficient reasons for changing his decision in this case before it was sent to the General Land Office. Lane's first *inducement* was an offer to guarantee to Brindle and myself twenty, and afterwards forty, acres of the disputed land. After finally convincing Lane that it would be a dangerous experiment to intimate anything of the kind to General Brindle, he left. I did not mention the matter to Brindle then, and indeed I am not sure that I ever have since. There are two prominent gentlemen now living in Kansas—one a prominent ex-county office-holder at Topeka, and the other in the banking business at Emporia—who, I have no doubt, will remember this last interview, as at my request they were *within calling distance*, they being at the time in the place of business of the former gentleman, one or two doors above my office.

" Heartily sympathizing in your every effort to protect the memory of the murdered Jenkins, I remain,

" Your well wisher and friend,

" HENRY W. PETRIKEN."

Extract from General William Brindle's letter of February 7, 1884 :

" We had decided that Jenkins was entitled to his claim before he was killed ; at the time of his death we were hearing the case again (it had been sent back to enable Lane to put in additional testimony, which we received, but which did not show him to have been the prior settler).

" WILLIAM BRINDLE.'

Eli Moore, son of the register of the Land Office at Lecompton, writes this letter to Robinson :

" *Hon. Charles Robinson :*

" MY DEAR SIR : In answer to your question as to whether or not the Land Office at Lecompton had decided in the land case between Jenkins and Lane at the time of Jenkins's death, and as to my knowledge as to the case itself, will state : That the case had been decided by the register and receiver of the Pawnee Land District, then located at Lecompton, in favor of Gaius Jenkins and adverse to James H. Lane. This decision had been given several weeks before the shooting of Jenkins. Lane was apprised of this decision by the register and receiver, and by his attorney in the case, Wilson Shannon. I took all the evidence in the case, was and am familiar with the facts in the litigation. The Secretary of the Interior had also confirmed the decision of the Land Office at Lecompton. All of these facts were in the possession of Lane at the time of and before the killing of Jenkins.

"After Lane was elected United States senator he had the case re-opened, and the Secretary of the Interior reversed the decision of the Land Office and of the former Secretary of the Interior.

"Respectfully,

"January 8, 1884."   'ELI MOORE.

Governor J. W. Denver, who accepted the office of Secretary of the Territory December 21, 1857, and of Governor May 12, 1858, resigned his office October 10, 1858, and was succeeded by Samuel Medary. It is due to Governor Denver to say that he was a man of the highest honor, integrity, and patriotism. His position was no sinecure, but he discharged the duties of his office with impartiality and great ability. He had lived in the West, knew Western people, and they knew him. He was not a man to be trifled with—even Lane knew this, as, according to Redpath, he proposed to have him assassinated by the Danites, should he notice his gross insults—and all parties respected him. As he was about to leave the Territory, a banquet was given him at Leavenworth by men of all parties and factions, where the utmost good feeling was manifested.

As soon as he learned the situation in Kansas relative to the Lecompton Constitution, he sent Judge Elmore to President Buchanan to urge him to recommend its rejection by Congress.

But the President had already committed himself, and was unwilling to change his position. Governor Denver thus refers to this action in his Bismarck speech, September, 1884:

"I sent for him [Judge Elmore] to come down and see me at Lawrence. He did so. We talked the matter over, and I presented to him my views in reference to the Lecompton Constitution. He agreed with me.

"'Then,' says I, 'Judge, I want you to go to Washington city and see the President on this subject.'

" He says, ' When?'

" I said, ' To-morrow morning.'

" ' Why,' says he, ' I have got nothing—I have no clothing with me.' Says I, ' You don't need anything; all you will want will be a shirt, and that you can buy anywhere as you go along; start in the morning.' That night I wrote a long letter to the President, in which I summed up the condition of affairs here in the Territory, as I then understood them, and I urged him not to present the Lecompton Constitution to Congress at all, but to ask Congress to pass an enabling act to let the people of the Territory hold a convention and adopt a constitution, and to wipe out all of those unauthorized constitutions that were presented.

" Judge Elmore went on to Washington city and presented my letter to the President, and had a long conversation with him, and also with his own brother-in-law, Senator Fitzpatrick, and other Southern gentlemen whom he knew there ; and they all agreed to my advice.

" Mr. Buchanan said he was very strongly impressed with it, and that he was very sorry he had not had the information earlier, because he had prepared his message in relation to the Lecompton Constitution, and he had shown it to several senators, and could not withdraw it. It went in. You know the result."

All constitutional rubbish having been virtually cleared away, the Topeka and Leavenworth Constitutions being without legal recognition, and Lecompton having been defeated under the form of the English Bill, a move was made in the winter of 1859 for a fourth Constitution.

In his address at the Quarter Centennial, at Topeka, January 29, 1886, Hon. B. F. Simpson thus alludes to the movement :

" Time aided the persistence and patience of the Free-State settlers ; immigration was coming in from the North; the Legislature and local offices were now controlled by the *bona fide* residents, and the friends of Kansas were about to control the lower House of Congress, and were gaining in the Senate. Encouraged by these good indications, the Legislature of 1859, on the 11th day of February, passed an act authorizing a vote of the people to be taken on the question of the formation of a Constitution and State Government. The vote was taken on the 28th day of March, and resulted four to one in its favor. An election for delegates was then ordered on the 4th day of June. At that election there were more than fourteen thousand votes cast. The convention met on the 5th day of July. * * *

" On the 4th day of October the work of the convention was ratified
by the people. There were about sixteen thousand votes polled at the
election, and more than two-thirds of them were for the Constitution.
On the 6th day of December an election for State officers, a member of
Congress, and members of the Legislature was held. On the 14th day
of February, 1860, it was presented to the Senate of the United States.
* * * On the 21st day of January, 1861, the bill for the admission of
Kansas passed the Senate by a vote of thirty-six for and sixteen against.
On the 29th President Buchanan signed the bill, Kansas became a State,
the struggle was over, the battle won ; and the good people of Kansas
are to-day enjoying the fruits of the victory."

Judge Simpson, in his address, gives this account of the
reception of the news of the admission to the Union during
the session of the Territorial Legislature at Lawrence :

" I remember the earlier part of the night of the 29th day of January,
1861, very distinctly. I was at the Eldridge House, in Lawrence, a
member of the last Territorial Legislature, that was then holding its
session in that dearly beloved Free-State city. There were from three
to four inches of snow on the ground (an unusual sight in Kansas in
those days), and the night was windy and cold. It must have been as
late as nine o'clock when D. R. Anthony, the same Anthony who is
now president of our Historical Society, came into the hotel with sturdy
stride and flashing eyes, and told us that the President of the United
States had that day signed and approved the bill admitting Kansas into
the Union. He brought with him and scattered around extras issued
by a newspaper published at Leavenworth, called the *Conservative*, announcing the joyful tidings in flaring headlines. * * * There was a
' sound of revelry' that night in Lawrence, for the news ran through
the town like wildfire. Houses were lighted, doors were thrown open
(and some were broken open), the people gathered in public places.
' Old Sacramento ' was taken from his resting-place, and emphasized
with hoarse throat the good tidings ; toasts were drunk ; songs were
sung ; speeches were made, and—well, the truth is, that my recollection
is not good after midnight. You must recollect that the main question
then was admission, not prohibition."

The New York *Tribune* of January 29, 1861, thus refers
to this event :

" The House yesterday passed the Senate bill for the admission of
Kansas, which thus becomes the thirty-fourth State of the Union, and
the nineteenth free State. This act not only opportunely adds to the

Confederation a sound and loyal member, untainted by the pestiferous blight of slavery, but does rightful though tardy justice to a State which has suffered for five years greater wrongs and outrages from Federal authority than all the slave States together have endured since the beginning of the Government, even if their own clamor about imaginary oppression be admitted as well founded.

" The present generation is too near to these events to see them in their true proportions, but in the future, in impartial history, the attempt to force slavery upon Kansas, and the violations of law, of order, and of personal and political rights, that were perpetrated in that attempt, will rank among the most outrageous and flagrant acts of tyranny in the annals of mankind."

The admission of Kansas into the Union was the end of the conflict against slavery in Kansas; and the "beginning of the end" of the conflict against slavery in the nation. The importance of the Kansas struggle cannot be overestimated. It settled the destiny of slavery, not only in Kansas and the nation, but, eventually, in the world. When Robinson gave J. B. Abbott a letter to Eli Thayer for more Sharp's rifles, subscribing it, " In haste, yours for freedom for a world," he truthfully represented the extent of the battle-field. Such being the importance of the struggle, the men who were victorious are entitled to great credit. Who were they ? The writer believes they belong to the rank and file of the Free-State party ; that it was the policy adopted by that party that saved Kansas to freedom. Others claim that two or three men whose policy was diametrically opposed to that adopted by the party saved the cause. F. B. Sanborn calls John Brown the "Liberator" of Kansas, and T. W. Higginson, in the Boston *Advertiser* of September 15, 1879, says, "The leaderships of Brown, Lane, and Montgomery were what finally saved Kansas to freedom." To say the least, if their leadership saved Kansas, it is remarkable that their policy was never adopted, but uniformly opposed and defeated. But it is not the purpose to settle such questions by argument or discussion of the merits or demerits of individuals or parties. It is sufficient to furnish what are believed to be facts, and all can draw their own conclusions. It is evident a most important and difficult work was accomplished, and if a movement with results as beneficial, and with as little bloodshed and violence—barring the massacres, robberies, and outrages by individuals—has been recorded in ancient or modern history, it has escaped observation.

As a few individuals have seen fit to publish their views of the conflict in Kansas, and singled out their heroes, and made all movements revolve about them, a few opinions of some of the actors in the tragedy are here given by way of contrast.

S. N. Wood,* one of the Branson rescuers, and a man who has no superior in a mental or physical encounter, thus writes, in 1884, of John Brown:

"I now give it as my deliberate judgment that John Brown never did any good in Kansas, that we would have been better off if he had never come to the State. His object was war, not peace. It was his constant aim to produce a collision between the Free-State men and the Government, which would have wiped us out in Kansas as effectually as he and his little band were wiped out in Virginia. The truth is, Brown never had the confidence of the Free-State men of Kansas, and no sensible man dared follow his lead. * * *

"By this wanton murder on the Potawatomie the Free-State men of Kansas suffered terribly.

"There cannot be any question to a man who knew Brown as I did that he was crazy, or, rather, had that religious delusion that he was another Gideon, or rather a chosen instrument in the hands of God to accomplish a great work. 'He died as the fool dieth,' and for one I was willing to let his 'soul go marching on.' But to have him thrust down this generation as ever being of any benefit to Kansas is an insult to the men who made Kansas free.

"Yours truly,
"S. N. WOOD."

Another Branson rescuer, the secretary of the Leavenworth Constitutional Convention, and correspondent of the

* S. N. Wood has been brutally assassinated, in the presence of his wife, since the above was written.

Eastern press, S. C. Smith, has this to say in a letter dated April 18, 1880:

"I believe Kansas was saved to freedom through the influence of those who so conducted themselves within it as to merit the approval and support of the friends of freedom throughout the North. * * * It seems to me that all the Free-State party could do, in the early struggle, from 1854 to 1857, was, if possible, to 'hold the fort,' and wait for the triumph of the Republican party to secure their own complete victory. This in fact was what they did do.

"Brown, Lane, and Montgomery would have plunged us into all sorts of excesses, put our friends in the East on the defensive, rallied the Democratic party under the banner of the 'Constitution and the Union,' as against civil war and incendiary abolitionists, and Kansas would have been lost by the folly and insanity of its leaders in doing those acts which the sentiment of the North could in no wise sustain."

Solomon Miller, of the *Kansas Chief*, thus refers to Mr. Rastall:

"John E. Rastall, of the Burlingame *Chronicle*, protests against the publication of letters by the State Historical Society, in which General Lane is criticised unfavorably. He thinks Lane's services to Kansas should at least secure silence. That may be just as one looks at it. History is history, and let the truth be told, hit where it may. Lane did Kansas some service, but his services were greatly overestimated. He also did a great deal of bad. He was the originator of the corruption in politics that Kansas is credited with. His forte was bulldozing and deceit. Many good men and tried friends of Kansas were kept under through his influence, and many scoundrels placed on top. He killed himself, because he undertook to sell Kansas out, but found he couldn't deliver the goods. Let the truth be published, whether it be for or against him."

The State was admitted into the Union on the 29th of January, 1861, and the first Legislature convened the last of March. At that date seven States had already seceded from the Union, and eight others were threatening to follow should coercion be resorted to by the Federal Government. Although without secession Kansas might not have entered the sisterhood of States, at least at the date named, she was loyal to the Federal Government, as she had been in her territorial days, and her first message gave no uncertain sound. Her people were ready to join issue at once on the slavery question, which was the real and only issue. Had Kansas controlled the Federal Executive, the announcement would have been made immediately after the attack upon Fort Sumter, that, unless rebellious States should return to their allegiance by a day named in the proclamation, slavery would be abolished. Such a proclamation might have been premature and a mistake, but, if left to Kansas, it would have been made. A few sentences from the first State message are given, as follows:

"When Kansas applied for admission into the Union, it was supposed there was a Federal Government that would endure until the present generation, at least, should pass away. Recent developments, however, have given rise to serious doubts as to its existence. Theoretically, such a government is extended over thirty-four States, but practically it does not exist in some. In seven States the laws are openly repudiated, the forts are seized, the revenue stolen, the Federal officers defied, and the flag of the nation insulted with impunity; and eight others threaten to do likewise if the Government attempts to assert its authority by force in any rebellious State. Such is the condition of affairs as bequeathed by the late Administration to the present.

"The future none can predict. Should matters progress as for a few months past, and coercion be decried as at present, not a prominent seaboard State will remain in the Union, and not a law of the United States will be enforced anywhere. Our Government, once regarded as a power on earth, will become a hissing and a byword among the nations—a stench in the nostrils of all men. This nation occupies a very remarkable position before the civilized world. It has heretofore been prompt and efficient in putting down treason and rebellion, and the whole force of the army and navy has been called into requisition at once whenever danger threatened. The whiskey insurrection, South Carolina nullification, and the John Brown raid were all summarily disposed of with no cry of 'coercion.' Now, when certain persons in the South have seized upon the revenues, forts, ships, post-offices, mints, arms, and army and navy stores, waged war upon the United States troops, set up an independent government, and bid defiance to all law, the position of the authorities has been simply that of non-resistance. Two independent and hostile governments cannot long exist at the same time over the same territory without conflict, and either the Confederated States of the South or the Federal Government must succumb, or civil war is inevitable.

"A demand is made by certain States that new concessions and guarantees be given to slavery, or the Union must be destroyed. The present Constitution, however faithfully adhered to, is declared to be incompatible with the existence of slavery; its change is demanded, or the government under it must be overthrown. If it is true that the continued existence of slavery requires the destruction of the Union, it is time to ask if the existence of the Union does not require the destruction of slavery. If such an issue be forced upon the nation, it must be met, and met promptly. The people of Kansas, while they are willing to fulfil their constitutional obligations towards their brethren in the sister States to the letter, even to the yielding of the 'pound of flesh,' cannot look upon the destruction of the fairest and most prosperous government on earth with indifference. If the issue is presented to them, the overthrow of the Union or the destruction of slavery, they will not long hesitate as to their choice. But it is to be hoped that this issue will be withdrawn, and the nation advance in its career of prosperity and power, the just pride of every citizen and the envy of the world.

"The position of the Federal Executive is a trying one. The Government, when assumed by him, was rent in twain; the cry against coercion was heard in every quarter; his hands were tied, and he had neither men nor money, nor the authority to use either. While it is the duty of each loyal State to see that equal and exact justice is done to the citizens of every other State, it is equally its duty to sustain the Chief Executive of the nation in defending the Government from foes, whether from within or without—and Kansas, though last and least of the States in the Union, will ever be ready to answer the call of her country.

"C. ROBINSON."

At the first session of the Legislature two United States senators were elected. The principal candidates were S. C. Pomeroy, J. H. Lane, M. J. Parrott, and F. P. Stanton. Neither had a majority of friends in the Legislature, and some sharp practice was resorted to. Lane was equal to the occasion. Although his supporters were largely in the minority, they were, as a rule, so positive and firm in their attachment that they would trade with any other candidate to secure votes for their favorite. But no other candidate had trading friends enough to elect Lane, and hence he must get the trading votes of at least two. Both Pomeroy and Parrott were ready to give Lane votes for an equivalent, while

Stanton's friends could not be traded to Lane for any consideration.   The same was true of some of the supporters of
Pomeroy and Parrott.   Both Pomeroy and Parrott knew
that Lane was promising the same men to each in exchange
for votes for himself, and did not dare trust his election
alone and first, and Lane would not trust them.   Accordingly both senators were to be elected at one roll-call.   As
the roll was called, some of the men promised by Lane to
Parrott voted for Pomeroy, and *vice versâ*.   Then began
changes of votes which continued for hours, until all persons
who kept the tallies were completely confused.   Finally
voting ceased, and the clerks agreed to announce Pomeroy
and Lane as elected, although many believed they were not.
At this election every appliance was used ever brought into
requisition in the older States, such as bribery with money
and bribery with promise of office, flattery, threats, and every
weapon that promised to procure a vote.

Before the close of the session of the Legislature, Sumter
was fired upon by the Rebels, and war was inevitable.   A
militia law was passed, also authority was given to the Governor, Secretary of State, and Auditor, or a majority of
them, to issue $150,000 of seven per cent. bonds, to be sold
at a minimum of seventy per cent.; and the treasurer was
authorized to sell ten per cent. war bonds for $20,000, to be
sold by him price unlimited.

The sum of $12,000 was realized from the latter in the
market, but the other bonds had no market value.   The
Governor wrote and telegraphed to Eastern brokers, but
could get no offers.   The claim was that Kansas might be
compelled to go with Missouri into the Confederacy, and
nobody wanted her bonds.   Even Minnesota, Wisconsin,
and Iowa could realize but little for their bonds, some of
them selling as low as forty per cent.   While the Governor abandoned all efforts to sell Kansas bonds in the
market, the Secretary and Auditor went to Washington, and
with the assistance of Pomeroy, Lane, and Conway, sold

some of them to the Secretary of the Interior for Indian money, realizing to the State sixty per cent. Colonel R. S. Stevens was employed by the Secretary and Auditor, who made the negotiations. The Department paid eighty-five per cent., but the State officers could get but sixty per cent. Where the difference between the price paid and received went, except $500 to Lane's private secretary, never appeared, but at the trial for impeachment it was shown that neither of the State officers who were parties to the transaction received any of it. It was well understood at the time that the negotiations could be made on no other terms, and it was also understood that the agent for the Secretary and Auditor received no more than the usual rate for his services. Perhaps persons familiar with such matters at the Departments in war times can understand it. That the Secretary and Auditor tried hard to get all the money paid for the bonds, except a reasonable fee to their agent, and that they for a time refused to take less than seventy per cent., was evident. The question for them to decide was whether to take sixty per cent. for the State or nothing, and as the State had no money, they took what they could get, believing they were thus doing the State a great favor. Although at the instigation of Lane they were afterwards impeached, no taint of corruption or dishonor attached to either. They were proceeded against simply because Lane wanted the Governor out of his way, and supposed he could either connect him with the sale of bonds, or at least put him under a cloud until the State Senate should try the impeachment. But he failed to do more than connect his name with the others in the House finding, while he procured the conviction of two of his political friends, and caused them to die of broken hearts.

28

CHAPTER XVIII.

No sooner were laws passed by the new State Legislature than there was occasion for their use. The first call of the President for troops to put down the rebellion was issued April 15, 1861, for seventy-five thousand men, and although none were allotted to Kansas, she furnished six hundred and fifty. The Governor, from his knowledge of the enemy and his experience, believed that the war would be a long and bitter one, and at once organized the State militia, hoping to have every able-bodied man enlisted. J. C. Stone of Leavenworth was appointed Major-General of the Northern Division, and James Blood of the Southern. In a short time over two hundred companies were duly organized. But soon came calls for volunteers for three years or during the war, and every one of these calls was responded to by twice as many men as called for. During the term of the first Governor calls were made upon Kansas for 5006 men, and 10,639 were furnished. The people of no State in the Union understood this war better than those of Kansas, and no people could have been more ready to enlist. But while the State was thus patriotic and loyal, the tocsin of war was the signal for the resurrection of all the thieves, plunderers, and murderers of the territorial days. Montgomery and Jennison, it is true, called upon the Governor after admission to the Union, and pledged loyalty to the State Government; and the first was appointed colonel, and the second given a letter to General Fremont. It was believed that if they were in the United States service their warlike propensities would be gratified in a legitimate manner. No complaints were made of Montgomery on the score of irregular warfare, but Jennison acquired a bad name before the war was ended. Montgomery later went South and took command of a negro regiment. T. W. Higginson, who also had command of a like regiment in the same locality, is reported as saying in a speech at Topeka that Montgomery had the "egotism of a fanatic, a superficial fanaticism in which self came uppermost. * * * While he was pronounced utterly incapable of any large command, hating all drill and all fixed routine, he would shoot his own soldiers without trial, and claim that he had the direct command of God."

Montgomery and Brown were alike in capacity. Neither could command successfully more than a score of men, and each was adapted for such exploits as killing, plundering, and bushwhacking on the borders of Kansas and Missouri. But the thieves and plunderers did not lack leaders, even though Montgomery, Jennison, and Brown were otherwise occupied. They organized in bands and conducted their operations with as much order as the regular army. At first they claimed to be Free-State and hailed from Kansas, and pretended to plunder and kill only pro-slavery men; but this left some good horses and other desirable property beyond their reach, as it belonged to men of their own party. However, they were equal to the occasion, and soon, like bodies of thieves, were in the field, claiming to be pro-slavery, and these hailed from Missouri, and plundered Free-State men. Thus the people of the border counties were menaced by these outlaws, whatever their political views. The authorities in both States were desirous of protecting their citizens from spoliation, and for a time partially succeeded, the Governor of Kansas returning the spoils taken from Missouri, and authorities in Missouri reciprocating the favor to citizens of Kansas.

But now James H. Lane reappears upon the stage. Although before his election to the Senate he was always in a minority, after that election he became omnipotent. Kansas had just passed through a severe drought, and all the people were poor and needy and desirous of securing the means of subsistence for themselves and families. As nothing promised to relieve them so satisfactorily as Government pap, and as Lane was chief dispenser of Federal patronage, he at once became a political autocrat. He evidently formed a compact with the President and Secretary of War, and was not only to be senator with Federal patronage, but to be assisted to get control of the State of Kansas so far as military affairs were concerned. Accordingly, although the Governor had doubled the quota of all calls upon Kansas, Lane was given authority to raise and officer two regiments, the 4th and 5th, and to have command of a brigade. Under such auspices there was an end to discipline and order, and the whole border was despoiled.

A faint picture of the situation may be had by reference to official correspondence of the officers of the United States army.

The condition of Lane's brigade on the arrival of General Hunter to take command at Fort Leavenworth is thus described by Hunter's Adjutant-General, Charles G. Halpine, March 14, 1862, on page 615, eighth volume of the "War of the Rebellion," as follows:

" Nothing could exceed the demoralized condition in which General Hunter found the Third and Fourth Kansas Infantry and Fifth and Sixth Kansas Cavalry, formerly known as "Lane's Brigade," on his arrival in this department. The regimental and company commanders knew nothing of their duties, and apparently had never made returns or reports of any kind. The regiments appeared in worse condition than they could possibly have been in during the first week of their enlistment, their camps being little better than vast pig-pens, officers and men sleeping and messing together; furloughs in immense numbers being granted, or, where not granted, taken; drill having been abandoned almost wholly; and the men constituting a mere ragged, half-armed, diseased, and mutinous rabble, taking votes as to whether any troublesome or distasteful order should be obeyed or defied.

" Vast amounts of public property had been taken from the depot at Fort Scott and Fort Lincoln without requisition or any form of responsibility, and horses in great quantities and at extravagant prices had been purchased under irregular orders and paid for by the United States ; these horses being then turned over to men and officers who were then drawing forty cents extra per day for them as private property.

" Without troops from other States or of a better kind to hold the mutinous in subjection, General Hunter had a difficult and most laborious task in the administration of the department. The few officers willing to do right, if they knew how, had to be instructed in nearly every branch of their duties, and this was the more difficult, as for the first two months the department was almost entirely destitute of blanks, and has never had a proper supply.

" To remedy these things, mustering officers were sent to remuster the regiments of Lane's Brigade and consolidate the companies to the minimum standing, mustering out the surplus officers and all who could prove they had been enlisted as Home Guards under General Lyon's call. These mustering officers found that the companies ranged from twenty-five to sixty men each, but the average about fifty, each having a captain and two lieutenants, and in some instances more ; and had the department, as previously, been without troops from other States, there is every probability that a general mutiny of the regiments named would have taken place, instead of the partial mutinies which have been suppressed."

The conduct and influence of Lane and his brigade is thus referred to by General Halleck in a letter to General McClellan, dated December 19, 1861 :

" The conduct of the forces under Lane and Jennison has done more for the enemy in this State than could have been accomplished by twenty thousand of his own army. I receive almost daily complaints of outrages committed by these men in the name of the United States, and the evidence is so conclusive as to leave no doubt of their correctness. It is rumored that Lane has been made a brigadier-general. I cannot conceive of a more injudicious appointment. It will take twenty thousand men to counteract its effect in this State, and, moreover, it is offering a premium for rascality and robbing generally."

General McClellan writes to the Secretary of War, February 11, 1862, as follows:

"HEADQUARTERS OF THE ARMY,
"WASHINGTON, February 11, 1862.
"*Hon. E. M. Stanton, Secretary of War:*

"SIR: I would respectfully submit to you the following extracts taken from the report of Major A. Baird, Assistant Inspector-General, United States Army, on the inspection of the Kansas troops, viz. :

"If the practice of seizing and confiscating the private property of rebels, which is now extensively carried on by the troops known as Lane's Brigade, is to be continued, how may it be managed so as to prevent the troops being demoralized and the Government defrauded?

"The practice has become so fixed and general that I am convinced that orders arresting it would not be obeyed, and that the only way of putting a stop to it would be to remove the Kansas troops to some other field of action.

"The fact that the property of citizens has been seized and confiscated by the troops engaged in the service of the United States is substantiated by both official and reliable private evidence, and from the frequent repetition of these acts the commanding officers in Kansas appear to have assumed its legality. The authority under which it is done is unknown to me, further than such destruction of private property as is unavoidable from a state of war conducted according to the established usages of civilized nations. I would therefore request the policy of the Government for my guidance in dealing with questions of this nature.

"To what extent can the right of confiscation legally be carried, and by what tribunal, civil or military, are the questions that will naturally arise to be decided that the innocent will not suffer while punishing the guilty, and that the dignity and justice of the Government may not be at the mercy of individuals governed by cupidity or revenge? This question has assumed such proportions that it will require vigorous means and well-defined authority to suppress or direct its application.

"I am, sir, very respectfully, your obedient servant,
"GEO. B. McCLELLAN,
"Major-General Commanding."

General Halleck writes to Secretary Stanton, March 25, 1862:

"SIR: Your letter of the 19th instant in relation to military outrages in Jackson County, Missouri, is just received. I have had two regiments stationed or moving in Jackson County for some time past, in order to put a stop to these depredations. This is as much as I can do, for many other counties in this State are equally urgent in their calls for protection, and to gratify them all would require an army of fifty thousand men to be distributed through Missouri in addition to the militia.

" That many and in some cases horrible outrages have been committed in this State, I do not doubt. They have been committed by three classes of persons :

" 1st. The enemy's guerrilla bands. Since the expulsion of Price they are rapidly diminishing. Nevertheless it will require some severe examples to be made in order to suppress them.

" 2d. The Kansas jay-hawkers, or robbers, who were organized under the auspices of Senator Lane. They wear the uniform of, and it is believed receive pay from, the United States. Their principal occupation for the last six months seems to have been the stealing of negroes, the robbing of houses, and the burning of barns, grain, and forage. The evidence of their crimes is unquestionable. They have not heretofore been under my orders. I will now keep them out of Missouri or have them shot."

Confederate General Benjamin McCullough writes to the Confederate Secretary of War, J. P. Benjamin, November 19, 1861, as follows:

" Sir : I shall return to Arkansas, put my troops in winter quarters soon, and ask permission to come immediately to Richmond, so as to give to the Administration correct information regarding affairs in this region before it acts on matters here. The Federals left eight days since with their thousand (?) men, quarreling among themselves, and greatly injured their cause by taking negroes belonging to Union men. General Lane went to Kansas, General Hunter to Sedalia, and General Sigel to Rolla."

General Halleck to General McClellan, December 10, 1861, writes:

" I am satisfied that the authorities at Washington do not understand the present condition of affairs in Missouri. The conduct of our troops during Fremont's campaign, and especially the course pursued by those under Lane and Jennison, has turned against us many thousands who were formerly Union men. A few more such raids, in connection with the ultra speeches made by leading men in Congress, will make this State as unanimous against us as is Eastern Virginia.

" It may be supposed by some that the number of organized Missouri regiments in this department indicates a different feeling. It should, however, be remembered that nearly all of these so-called Missouri regiments are composed of foreigners or men from other States.

From a dispassionate examination of this matter in all its bearings, and after conversing with leading men from all parts of this country, I am satisfied that the mass of the people here are against us, and that a single false step or defeat will ruin our cause. " Can't we get some arms soon? I cannot move without them. Winter is already upon us, and I fear much longer delay will render it exceedingly difficult to operate, and yet a winter campaign seems absolutely necessary to restore our lost ascendancy and the quiet of the State.
        " Very respectfully, your obedient servant,
                " H. W. HALLECK, Major-General."

Notwithstanding this and more official evidence of the demoralization and crime that occurred under Lane's verbal commission to roam at will with a brigade at his heels, he was not satisfied, and wanted the President to give him a written commission for a campaign into New Mexico with an army under his control. The correspondence of the President, Secretary of War, and others concerning this movement reveals conduct scarcely worthy of a petty province of Mexico, or of the Sandwich Islands. After this expedition was well under way—on paper—General Hunter wrote the following letter:

        " HEADQUARTERS DEPARTMENT OF KANSAS,
            " FORT LEAVENWORTH, KANSAS, February 8, 1862.
    " Major-General H. W. Halleck, Commanding Department of Missouri,
        St. Louis, Mo. :
    " GENERAL: Believing that the public interests may be promoted by an interchange of views between us, and a knowledge with each (in some general sort) of what the other intends, I venture on intruding some outlines of the condition of affairs in this department on your attention.
    " It seems, from all the evidence before me, that Senator J. H. Lane has been trading at Washington on a capital made up partly of his own senatorial position and partly of such scraps of influence as I may have possessed in the confidence or esteem of the President, said scraps having been ' jay-hawked ' by the Kansas senator without due consent of the proper owner.
    " In other words, I find that ' Lane's great Southern expedition ' was entertained and sanctioned by the President under misrepresentations made by somebody to the effect that said ' expedition ' was the joint design and wish of Senator Lane and myself. Mr. Lincoln doubtless

thought he was obliging me, and aimed to oblige me in the matter, but so little was I personally consulted, that to this hour I am in ignorance of what were the terms or striking points of Senator Lane's programme. Never, to this hour, has Senator Lane consulted me on the subject, directly or indirectly, while the authorities at Washington have preserved a similar indiscreet reticence, thinking, no doubt (as General Thomas intimates in a recent letter), that as the plan was of my own concoction in joint committee of two with Senator Lane, there could be no use, but rather an impertinence, in any third parties trying to explain the general drift and details to one of the original patentees.

" Thus I am left in ignorance, but it is more than probable that you have been more favored.

" Your co-operation certainly would be necessary to make effective any such expedition as that talked of, and as you have never been suspected of enjoying Senator Lane's confidence and sharing his counsels, I think it more than probable that the veil of mystery must have been lifted in your particular case. If so, let me know, for otherwise I must lower myself in the estimation of the authorities at Washington by confessing that I have never at any time, directly or indirectly, consulted with or been consulted by the Kansas senator in reference to this or any other military operation whatever, and that as to any brotherly confidence between us, there is just about as much now as there ever was.

" You can hardly conceive to what an extent the authorities at Washington have carried their faith in the representations of Mr. Lane and their belief in a sort of Damon and Pythias affection between that gentleman and myself. Regiments have been sent here with orders to ' report for duty with the forces under General J. H. Lane ; ' blanks telegraphed for by me have been shipped to ' Brigadier-General Lane, Fort Leavenworth,' and have never reached these headquarters. In fact, I may say that, so far as Washington was concerned, the Kansas senator would seem to have effectually ' jay-hawked ' out of the minds of the War Department any knowledge or remembrance of the general commanding this department.

" And now we have reached an aspect of the case which would be intensely ridiculous, if it were not so fraught with humiliation to officials and detriment to the public service. I am daily receiving letters from majors, colonels, and lieutenant-colonels, announcing that they have been appointed additional aides-de-camp on the staff of General McClellan, with orders to report to me in person, that I may again order them to report on the staff of ' Brigadier-General J. H. Lane.'

" The trouble is, that I know of no such brigadier-general, Senator Lane having told me expressly and in terms, at the only interview we have had since his return to Kansas, that he had not accepted his commission, and was only my visitor ' as senator and member of the Military Committee of the Senate of the United States.' I may add that in the opinion of those who know him best it is not his intention to accept the brigadiership, his hue and cry for that position having only been raised at a time when he thought it probable that Stanton (or whosoever was Governor Robinson's nominee) might oust him from the Senate. They say that he will never resign his seat in the Senate unless he can have supreme control of this department, with liberty to appoint his personal adherents and the legion of army contractors who follow in his wake in charge of the quartermaster's and subsistence departments of the public service in Kansas. This statement I believe.

"As to the vote obtained by him in the Kansas Legislature, asking that he be appointed major-general, etc., I have heard from men thoroughly informed that it was also 'jay-hawked' from the reluctant lips of an overwhelming opposition majority by Lane's positive promise to resign his senatorship forthwith in case it was passed. This made all Lane's legislative enemies his most active friends, on the principle of 'anything to get rid of him,' and all the aspirants for his seat at once impressed their friends into voting anything that would create a vacancy.

"Now what is to be done with this erractic senator, or how are the authorities at Washington to be convinced that it is neither wise nor quite decorous to act in matters vitally affecting a department without the knowledge or sanction of the department commander? On these points I have to ask light from you, my 'confidential' relations being apparently confined to Senator Lane, while you, and very deservedly, I confess, are believed to receive beams from the light of 'the inner sanctuary.'

"Disappointed himself, Lane is now bent on making trouble and obstructing the expedition which he finds he cannot control. He is bestirring himself in a thousand little irritating processes, trying to make a quarrel or 'disagreement' with me his pretext for backing out of an employment which he never intended to accept. As a specimen of the work he is at, and the friends he is working with, I send you this copy of a telegram sent to him a few days since, a copy having been sent to me by a friend at Washington:

" 'General Lane, Fort Leavenworth :   " 'WASHINGTON.

" 'I have been with the man you name. Hunter will not get the money or men he requires. His command cannot go forward. Hold on. Don't resign your seat.
                                                " 'JOHN COVODE.'

"And now, having given you a pretty thorough insight of the shape of matters here, and reserving a statement of my own plans and the military condition of the department for another letter, I am, General, very truly and obediently yours,   " D. HUNTER."

This was answered as follows:

"St. Louis, February 13, 1862.

"*Major-General D. Hunter, Commanding Department of Kansas, Fort Leavenworth, Kansas;*

"General: Your very kind letter of the 8th is this moment received. I must write you a very hasty answer to-day. You are entirely mistaken about my having received any information, official or unofficial, from Washington about the ' great jay-hawking expedition.' Not a word or hint has been communicated to me. Orders were sent by General Thomas direct to various regiments in this department to immediately repair to Fort Leavenworth and report to General Hunter as a part of General Lane's expedition. No notice of such orders was given to me. To put a stop to these irregularities I issued General Orders, No. 8, and protested both to General Thomas and General McClellan against such an irregular and unmilitary proceeding. No reply. I stopped some of the troops on their way, and reported that they could not move till some order was sent to me. No reply.

" I am satisfied that there have been many of such orders issued directly by the President and Secretary Cameron without consulting General McClellan, and for that reason no reply could be given without exposing the plans of the great jay-hawker and the imposition of himself and Cameron on the President. Perhaps this is the key to the silence of the authorities at Washington. I know nothing on the subject except what I see in the newspapers.

" In regard to my own plans, they are very simple. I have sent some sixteen thousand or seventeen thousand men, under General Curtis, against Price at Springfield. He has been reinforced by McIntosh, and it is said that Van Dorn and Frost are also marching to his relief. If it would be possible for you to move a cavalry force rapidly by Fort Scott to threaten Price's right flank, it would have a most excellent effect. This possibly was the original intention of Lane's expedition, but I protested to Washington against any of his jay-hawkers coming into this department, saying positively that I would arrest and disarm every one I could catch.

" The remainder of all my available force will be sent to the lines of the Cumberland and Tennessee. Who will take the immediate command there is not yet determined.

" Yours in haste,

" H. W. Halleck."

When the Governor of Kansas had learned from what appeared to be reliable authority that the President had appointed Senator Lane brigadier-general he gave Frederick

P. Stanton a commission as United States senator for Lane's seat. About this time Lane skulked back to his seat in the Senate, and the President and Secretary of War said no general's appointment had ever been made.

Although Hunter had been given a hint that if he desired a leave of absence for about twenty days he could probably have it, while Lane should take his army to New Mexico, he concluded to continue in the field and go in person to attend to the foraging and other matters. He accordingly issued an order as follows:

"HEADQUARTERS DEPARTMENT OF KANSAS,
"FORT LEAVENWORTH, KANSAS, January 27, 1862.

"1. In the expedition about to go South from this department, called in the newspapers General Lane's expedition, it is the intention of the major-general commanding the department to command in person, unless otherwise expressly ordered by the Government.

"2. Transportation not having been supplied, we must go without it. All tents, trunks, chests, chairs, tables, campstools, etc., must be at once stored or abandoned. The general commanding takes in his valise one shirt, one pair of drawers, one pair of socks, and one handkerchief, and no officer or soldier will carry more. The surplus room in the knapsack must be reserved for ammunition and provisions. Every officer and soldier will carry his own clothing and bedding.

"3. The general commanding has applied to the Government for six brigadier-generals, that his command may be properly organized. Until their arrival, it is necessary that he should appoint acting brigadier-generals from the senior colonels. To enable him to do this, in accordance with the order on the subject, each colonel will immediately report the day on which he was mustered into the service of the United States.

"D. HUNTER,
"Major-General Commanding."

This order, with the commission to Stanton as senator, "broke the camel's back," and Senator-General-Governor Lane wrote to his friend, John Covode, January 27, 1862, as follows:

"See the President, Secretary of War, and General McClellan — answer what I shall do.

"J. H. LANE."

It is unnecessary to say that here ended the great Lane

expedition, and the following order, declaring martial law, ended the jay-hawkers while Hunter remained in command.

"GENERAL ORDERS, No. 17,
    "HEADQUARTERS DEPARTMENT OF KANSAS,
        "FORT LEAVENWORTH, KANSAS, February 8, 1862.

"I. The civil authorities of Kansas being manifestly unable to preserve the peace and give due security to life and property, and having in various instances notified the general commanding of their inability to uphold the laws unassisted by the military arm, and the crime of armed depredations or jay-hawking having reached a height dangerous to the peace and property of the whole State and seriously compromising the Union cause in the border counties of Missouri: Now, therefore, martial law is declared throughout the State of Kansas, and will be enforced with vigor.

"II. It is not intended by this declaration to interfere with or supersede the action of the civil authorities in cases of the ordinary nature with which said civil authorities may be competent to deal, but it is the resolve of the general commanding that the crime of jay-hawking shall be put down with a strong hand and by summary process, and for this purpose the trial of all prisoners charged with armed depredations against property or assaults upon life will be conducted before the military commissions provided for in General Orders, No. 12, of this department, current series, and the interference of the civil authorities in such cases is prohibited.

"III. A suitable provost-marshal, with the necessary officers and force, will immediately be appointed to carry out the terms of this order.

    "By order of Major-General Hunter.
                "CHAS. G. HALPINE,
            "Major and Assistant Adjutant-General."

General Hunter was succeeded by General Denver, in spite of the strong objections of Lane. Denver had been Governor in Kansas, and Lane could not use or frighten him. It would seem that Secretary Stanton at this time for some reason could not be used by Lane as aforetime. E. A. Hitchcock, aid-de-camp to the Secretary, writes to General Halleck from Washington, March 22, 1862, in part as follows:

"General H. W. Halleck, etc., St. Louis:

"MY DEAR GENERAL: I have just left the Secretary (late in the evening). When about to bid him good-evening he conversationally told me that Jim Lane had been to him to-day with an order from the President for you not to put Denver in command in Kansas, but that Davies (a recent appointment from New York) was to be assigned to that command.

" He told me that his answer to Lane was a positive refusal to attend to any such order, and if its enforcement should be attempted he would leave the office. "

Probably this man Davies was the same man that report said President Johnson afterwards promised to appoint Collector of New York if Lane would defeat the Civil-tenure-of-office Bill. He was said to be a relative of Lane.

When January, 1863, arrived, the first State Governor gladly delivered up the executive chair to his successor, Governor Thomas Carney. Enough had been seen and experienced of the management of the war in the West, permitting the most brutal and inhuman outrages, all to gratify personal greed, malice, or ambition, to disgust any person not entirely given over to subsisting upon human misery. Governor Carney, being a friend of Lane, issued commissions at first to Lane's appointees in the army whom Robinson refused to commission, but he soon tired of the business of being simply an automaton, and proposed to be Governor in fact as well as in name. This, of course, made trouble, and the President was visited and finally concluded to recognize Kansas as a loyal State entitled to some consideration by the Federal Government.

Under Governor Carney's administration the retaliatory raids, which Robinson had feared and guarded against as best he could, occurred, including the massacre of one hundred and eighty-three of the people of Lawrence by Quantrell, August 21, 1863. The border was now under control of volunteer generals and other officers, with Lane as master of ceremonies, although without a commission. It was no secret that an expedition in the border counties of Missouri was preparing to enter Kansas in retaliation for the outrages of Lane and his thieves, yet it was permitted by a Union force of one hundred men to march forty miles to Lawrence, kill nearly two hundred people and burn the town, spending three or four hours at the work of destruction before Federal officers could straighten out their red tape and join in pursuit. However, after leaving what was left of Lawrence, about three hundred citizens and Federal troops were rallied under Lane and Colonel Plumb, who did escort duty to the one hundred and seventy-five men under Quantrell. They escorted them over the line into Missouri with due consideration, not a gun being fired or a man injured. It should not be inferred, however, that Lane was afraid of blood or opposed to killing people, as afterwards, when Quantrell was not near, he marched through some of the counties of Missouri and made a clean sweep of all men found, whether Union or dis-Union. Quantrell was more considerate than Lane had been, as he told one of his prisoners, taken at the Eldridge House, that he should spare the women from outrage, which Lane in his raids in Missouri did not do. He also said, as Robinson, while Governor, did what he could to preserve peace on the border, he should not molest him or his property. Of this intention Robinson had no knowledge, but both his person and property were spared, although the raiders were within a short distance of him, and in full view, and could have destroyed him and his property without trouble. Had the raid not been for retaliation for similar raids in Missouri, there is no reason why Robinson's property should not have shared the fate of Lane's, nor why he should not have been killed as were others when completely in the power of the raiders.

So great was the shock to the country of this Quantrell retribution that it was necessary something should be done to obscure the delinquencies of the officials, and " General Order No. 11 " was issued, depopulating some of the border counties of Missouri. Loyal and disloyal citizens alike had to vacate and leave their homes to the tender mercies of the thieves and despoilers, who left nothing but chimney-stacks as monuments of the desolation in their wake. This order was a most humiliating confession of the utter failure of the war of rapine permitted, if not encouraged, by the officials at Washington under Lane and his red-leg thieves, whether within or without the ranks of the army. Had the President favored the policy of protecting non-combatants, as the officials of the State of Missouri and Kansas desired, "Order No. 11" would have never been needed, and Quantrell's raid at Lawrence would never have occurred.

It must be borne in mind that the Kansas troops referred to by the general officers and by the writer comprise only a small portion under the control or influence of Lane and his partisans. The large majority of Kansas troops were under control of honorable officers, who despised such conduct and would have no share in it. The bulk of Kansas troops made an honorable record, and no State could excel Kansas in the proportion furnished to the army, or show a greater percentage lost in battle. Kansas may be justly proud of her war record, with these exceptions, and will not fail to confer the highest honors upon her brave warriors.

One other raid, called the "Price raid," menaced Kansas, but General Pleasanton was close in Price's rear, while General Deitzler, in command of about ten thousand of the State militia, Curtis, Blair, Moonlight, and others met him on the State line. He beat a hasty retreat towards Arkansas, and the war clouds on the border were dissipated. It has been unfashionable and unpopular to breathe the least criticism of the conduct of the late war, and of its officers, from the President down, but the time has passed when it will be deemed honorable warfare to kill and outrage women and children, flocks, herds, and "all that breathe," of the enemy. Non-combatants, whether friends or foes, are entitled to be recognized as human beings; and that officer, whatever his rank, who will use his soldiers to persecute and despoil innocent people is a cowardly brute, and should be held up to the scorn and contempt of civilized people. It is remarkable that the two men who were conspicuous for permitting or practicing inhuman atrocities are said to have committed suicide to be rid of their own society. As time goes on, the facts of the late war will come to the surface, men will dare to publish them, and then will be a "revaluation" of Stanton and Lane as there has been of John Brown. While the latter lived, he and all his friends denied some of his most important acts, and manufactured a condition of affairs that had no foundation in fact that they might have a consistent hero; but some men have dared to look beneath the surface and have discovered that the beautiful structure of which is made a hero rests upon "falsework" only and as soon as this shall be removed down comes the hero. So in regard to Stanton and Lane, some are already daring to speak out gently and tell some truths, and it is to be hoped it will not be long before the whole truth can be told. Hon. Sol. Miller, a most determined Republican, and the most popular as well as the best-informed editor in Kansas, referring to the writer's address before the Loyal Legion, has this to say of Lincoln and Stanton:

"All the statements made by the Governor were facts. The treatment of the loyal Governor of Kansas by President Lincoln and Secretary Stanton, at the instance of Lane, was most shameful. The Governor of no other loyal State was so treated. It was and still is unaccountable how a man like Lincoln could do such a thing. It has left a stain upon his Administration that even his martyrdom cannot efface. It may have been through the malign influence of Stanton, who is known in history as the 'Great War Secretary,' but who did many things that would not do honor to his memory if daylight were let in upon them. There is no doubt that his arbitrary and even tyrannical rule caused many disasters to the Union armies, and sent many a general into disgrace, who, if let alone, might have won honorable fame. The stipulation demanded by General Grant before he would consent to take command of the Army of the Potomac, that his command must be absolute, without any interference whatever from the Secretary of War, shows that Stanton was known and dreaded by the officers; and Grant's success where all others had failed leaves a dark suspicion of the calamities that Stanton's influence brought about. We do not doubt that his influence was responsible for much of the trouble in Kansas."

29

Mr. Miller refers to the situation in Kansas during the war in his paper of February, 1891, in answer to a letter of inquiry, as follows :

" Have you ever heard of a man by the name of Jim Lane? Well, he wanted to be all of Kansas. He was elected to the United States Senate at the beginning of the war. Even his enemies gracefully acquiesced, and were willing to sustain him in his position. But he was not satisfied with that. He not only determined to have all his opponents under his feet, but to have full control of the State Government. Where his partisans were not in positions, he undertook to put them there, by means apparently regular, or by foul means, as the case demanded. Not only did he determine to be her senator, but Governor of the State also, and a department commander in the army, and to dictate all the army appointments of the State, rightfully belonging to the Governor; and he actually did usurp this power, by permission of the President and the Secretary of War—an outrage committed upon no other loyal State in the Union. This was not all : a system of terrorism was practiced upon loyal citizens who were not in the army, by means of deputy marshals, so-called detectives, and desperate, irresponsible men under other guises, to keep them in subjection to the wishes of Lane. And yet this was not all : gangs of reckless armed men infested every community in the State near the eastern border, who were known by the name of ' jay-hawkers,' every one a hot partisan of Lane, and who would resent an affront to him quicker than a disloyal act to the Government. These men, of course, were intensely loyal; but if the Rebel side had been on top, they (or the most of them) would have been just as intensely the other way. They were active, able-bodied, fine-looking men, as a rule, just such as would have been of valuable service in the army; but they were not in the army, but devoting themselves to pillage and robbing. They first despoiled men of known disloyal sentiments on the Missouri side of the river. When that field was worked out, they paid their respects to men on this side who were known to be sympathizers with the South. When that harvest was exhausted, they began to make disloyal men—that is, they would trump up charges of disloyalty against citizens, and proceed to steal their horses. Men who would not worship Lane, or men against whom local jay-hawkers had a grudge, were spotted as disloyal, and their horses were stolen. Many of the best citizens were opposed to this business from the start; but when it got down to this indiscriminate robbery of peaceable, loyal citizens by a gang of desperadoes who should have been in the army, they organized against them, and soon their graves began to dot the prairies of Kansas. Several of them were killed in Troy; one of the leaders at Geary City; and Cleveland, the chief of all, down

on the border below Kansas City. The survivors were finally driven
into the army.

"The foregoing state of affairs existed in the year 1862. In the Republican State Convention of that year commissions were almost openly
auctioned off to influence delegates. Lane had got the right to appoint
the officers of three regiments then being organized, and he used them
to run the State Convention. We saw one man in the Convention, the
most blatant Lane man, who less than two years before had had his
head broken in attempting to drive Republicans from the polls, and
who, at the beginning of the war, called a meeting in this county for
the purpose of taking action looking to uniting Kansas with the Southern Confederacy. He had a quartermaster's commission in his pocket.
Another noisy delegate had a similar commission. One of the Doniphan
County delegates, upon reaching Atchison, was feeling unwell. A
physician in the party told him he was taking typhoid fever, and ought
to get home as soon as possible. Thus frightened, he gave his proxy
to the doctor, who did Lane's work in the Convention, and came out
with a lieutenant-colonel's commission. One prominent anti-Lane man,
who suddenly flopped before the Convention assembled, got a revenue
appointment. It seemed as if fully one-half of the delegates in the
Convention went away with commissions in their pockets. A most excellent ticket was nominated, but it was by such scandalous means. It
was intended that they should be tools of Lane; but they disappointed
his expectations, and made good officers. But this was not the object
in their nomination, and was not foreseen at the time. The means employed to nominate them was what hurt, and it caused a big kick."

Captain James Christian, Lane's law partner, a man universally esteemed, has this to say :

"ARKANSAS CITY, KANSAS, January 21, 1889.
"*Governor Charles Robinson, Lawrence, Kansas:*

"DEAR SIR : I have read with much interest your paper read before
the Loyal Legion at Leavenworth, January 3, 1889, and from my standpoint—and few men in Kansas had a better opportunity of knowing
the true inwardness and the facts as they occurred during that period of
Kansas history, as I was intimately acquainted with all the leading
characters that figured in that period of Kansas and Missouri history,
including yourself—I must confess that you under rather than overstate
the character of that terrible period. Hell in its fury could not match
the malignity and depravity of the acts that were committed on the border of Kansas and Missouri during 1861, 1862 and 1863. I have a
personal knowledge of some of the facts you mention, and know them to
be strictly true, and from the source of knowledge I had at that time I

have no doubt of some of the facts that you state of a personal character being also true. I was stationed on the border at Paola some seven months as quartermaster, ordnance officer, and commissioner of subsistence, U. S. A., as brigade officer of the Twelfth Kansas, Colonel Charles W. Adams, and the First Colored, Colonel J. M. Williams, from the fall of 1862 to June, 1863. When I was first appointed I was ordered to report to General James H. Lane. This brought me in conflict with Major Easton at Fort Leavenworth, who would not recognize General Lane as an officer of the United States army, and refused to supply me with quartermaster stores. But when seeing my appointment from the War Department, he relented and filled my requisition. From that on I had no trouble. * * *

"In his brigadier-generalship he was notoriously aided by Stanton, Secretary of War, and poor President Lincoln was but a man, subject to like passions as the rest of us, subject to flattery and coercion. I was in Washington when Fred. P. Stanton appeared as senator in Lane's place, and there was terrible squirming and consulting at headquarters to smother the papers and expunge from the records certain papers and documents—but it was all fixed up by the whole-souled Christian statesman Edwin M. Stanton, Secretary of War. But the fact was, Governor, men of your way of thinking at that time were in a hopeless minority. Patriotism was not near so great an object as plunder and popularity. It was too much a political war—at least in Kansas. * * *

"Yours truly,

"JAMES CHRISTIAN."

The following, believed to be written by one of the best and most useful men Kansas ever had, who was promoted to a general in the army, is quoted, as it gives a correct picture of the times:

"BARNUM'S HOTEL, ST. LOUIS, MISSOURI, August 30, 1862.
"*Editor Missouri Republican:*

"I noticed in your paper three or four days ago, your Memphis correspondent quotes a letter from John Lockhart, Captain, etc., wherein John complains that 'General Curtis's army does not forage off the enemy, are guarding Rebel property, etc.,' and speaks of the infamous conduct of General Curtis and other generals, and says soldiers ought to desert unless his views are adopted. John is a Kansas man, and evidently don't like the way this war is being carried on. Some others of us don't like it either, but for quite different reasons from his. John was not with Curtis's army in its march through Arkansas, was not with it when it arrived at Helena; hence was too late to get his share and evidently feels mad about it, and must vent his spite on *somebody.*

Now, John, hold on a minute. You say, 'On every road leading from Helena, for ten miles, soldiers are at every house guarding Rebel property.' How indignant the whole country must feel on reading that.

" Now hear me. I was with Curtis on his march through Arkansas, was with the army when it arrived at Helena; and I now tell John Lockhart and the country that on the Arkansas side of the river, outside of Helena, *there is not a house for ten miles from Helena but what has been pillaged from cellar to garret* by our troops. Trunks broken open, bureaus opened and sacked—in fact, every drawer, cupboard, trunk, chest, sacked and pillaged; ladies' dresses, earrings, finger rings, breast-pins, in fact everything movable possessing value stolen. That is not all. On the road travelled by the army the same system of pillage has been carried on. If a dollar's worth of movable property has been left, it was because the soldier's knapsack would hold no more, or wagons could not be pressed to haul it. If guards are now placed at the houses, it is a laudable effort to try to repair the outrages of the past, or perchance to protect the ' colored ladies ' from exhibitions of love manifested by some of the followers of Jim Lane, in imitation of the chivalry of the South.

" John is opposed to *guarding Rebel property*, and would forage off the enemy. So am I, for any love I have for the enemy. I believe in so subsisting our army off of the enemy whenever it is possible; that their property should be taken by quartermasters, accounted for, and that much saved to the Government. But this is not what some mean by their great cry about ' guarding Rebel property ' and living off the enemy. They favor a promiscuous and indiscriminate system of stealing and plunder, where the best fellow gets the most, and which would never benefit the Government a dollar. I undertake to say it is the duty of a general to take care of his army, and, if necessary, to put out guards to keep soldiers from pilfering or plundering. He should do so, and stop it at once, and at all hazards. Unless this is done, the army is demoralized, and becomes worthless for fighting. I have heard it said at Helena that Curtis has regiments that could *steal* Vicksburg, or even Richmond, in a week, without a fight. John is a Kansas man, a disciple of Jim Lane, and, I suppose, would carry the war on on Lane's principles, or rather, Lane's want of principle. We all recollect Lane's marches in Missouri last year, when he was playing brigadier-general, and was so patriotic that he charged the Government ' nary a cent ' for it. We know that millions of dollars' worth of cattle, horses, and mules were driven off, but no one will pretend to say that one dollar went to Government. The Osceola bank lost $8000; scores of ladies lost silk dresses: Lane sent his wife, just afterwards, $1000 in gold, a lot of silk dresses, and other women fixings, with a letter cautioning her to be careful about using the money and articles, and not attract too much notice ; afterwards returned to Leavenworth, paid his debts, walked the streets with his hands full of gold, but Government *did not get a dollar.* How is it in Kansas now? You pay six cents per pound net for all the beef used in the Department, yet whoever heard of a Missouri or a Cherokee farmer getting pay for his cattle? A citizen of Kansas, slightly intoxicated, got into my room at midnight a few nights since, at Leavenworth, Kansas, and was boasting of clearing sixteen hundred and fifty dollars on beef ᵗhat day. * * *

" Lane's brigade, organized last year by authority of the President, without commissions from the Governor, became an irresponsible, unorganized mob, until the Governor reorganized them and brought system out of chaos. Six hundred thousand troops are again called for, yet the State of Kansas has not been called upon for a man. The Governor, whose loyalty no one will dispute, has offered time after time, in his official capacity, to raise troops, yet his letters are unanswered.

" But this same Jim Lane is commissioned to go to Kansas and take the exclusive charge of recruiting in that State. The people of Kansas are heartily sick of this. They have a State Government as loyal as any in the Union, and why it should be ignored by the President and Secretary of War is more than they can comprehend. But more anon.

" TRUTH TELLER."

The Kansas City *Star* gives this version :

"THE REVOLT AGAINST LANE IN 1862.

" What engendered the antagonism in the Republican party of Kansas?

" Mr. Willis J. Abbott, author of the ' Blue-jacket ' books, is preparing ' The Story of Kansas ' for Lothrop's ' Stories of the States ' series. A *Star* reporter asked him this morning the cause of the Republican revolt against Senator Lane in 1862, which brought Mr. Ingalls and others under the lash of the regular Republican newspapers.

" ' Briefly stated,' said Mr. Abbott, ' Senator Lane's quarrel with the authorities of Kansas was based upon his pretensions to the military control of the State. Robinson and Carney, who filled the gubernatorial chair of the State during the Civil War period, bitterly contested these pretensions, but Lane's influence with Lincoln and Stanton enabled him to maintain his supremacy until 1864, when Governor Carney went to Washington, and by personal interviews with the President and the Secretary of War secured for himself the recognition that was given the Governor of every other State. At the opening of the war the State authorities raised volunteer troops in the usual manner, and after this work was done Lane appeared, clothed with vague military powers, and taking command of the State forces began making predatory raids into Missouri. His course was deprecated by the Kansas authorities as well as by the officers of the regular army, on the ground that he was stirring up useless strife. While there was some secession sentiment in Missouri, there had been no overt acts of war, and it seems probable that much of the border warfare was due wholly to Lane's ill-advised zeal. When fully in control of the military forces of Kansas, Lane persuaded the War Department to authorize a military invasion of the southwest, representing that General Hunter joined with him in advising it. Hunter afterwards wrote the military authorities, disclaiming any knowledge of Lane's scheme, and refused to co-operate with him, thus breaking up the project.

" ' In 1862 Lane was appointed " commissioner for recruiting in the department of Kansas." He organized regiments and distributed military offices, but was checkmated by the refusal of Governor Robinson to issue the commissions. The first regiment of colored troops was formed by Lane.

" ' In 1864 Lane's pretensions became so unbearable to the Kansas authorities that Carney went to Washington to protest. After an interview with Lincoln he went to Secretary Stanton, bearing a letter from the President suggesting that the Governor of Kansas should be treated like other governors. Stanton tore the letter up, saying angrily :

" ' " Tell the President that I am Secretary of War."

" ' Carney turned away, but before he left the building the Secretary sent after him, and a long interview ended in the extinction of Lane's extraordinary powers.

" ' Lane's suicide was in no way due to his political quarrels. He had become reconciled to Carney, and his public position seemed secure, when certain dishonorable proceedings on his part in connection with Indian traders became known. After failing to exculpate himself, and trying in vain to secure a foreign appointment from the President, he put a pistol in his mouth, and discharged it. Though the wound would have killed an ordinary man immediately, he lived ten days, dying July 10, 1866.' "

A recent number of the Westport *Record* has this :

" Governor Charles Robinson, the ' War Governor ' of Kansas, has set the Kansas press on fire by speaking out on James H. Lane's methods during the war. We are glad there is one man in Kansas who dares to speak the truth in vindication of history. The Kansas-Missouri border war was a disgrace even to barbarism. Westport was a central point thereof. We have no excuses to offer, therefore, but retaliation. Could Governor Robinson have controlled his Kansas cutthroats and robbers, his policy would have saved bloodshed and fire at

least. Missouri law turned over to Kansas authorities the first company
of thieving excursionists, with their plunder, that visited Kansas. An
unwritten treaty existed between the State Government of Kansas and
western Missouri counties early in the war, which both sides endeavored
to sustain. Lane, Jennison, and their cut-throat followers, unrestricted
by patriotism, friends, or law, by murder, rapine, and plunder aroused
the western counties and drew over the line the worst and most lawless
elements of our citizenship. Quantrell and his bloodthirsty gang went
to Lawrence after Lane in vengeance for burning Sibley, plundered
Westport, and pillaged Jackson, Clay, Cass, and Bates counties. Bad
feeling is now over, and we only hail Governor Robinson's letter with
joy as being vindicatory of history and as being from the man whose
policy so thoroughly foiled all our well-laid plans for making Kansas a
pro-slavery State.''

Professor L. W. Spring, a writer on Kansas who dared to
tell the truth as he found it, has this to say, beginning on
page 273 of his '' Kansas '':

'' Lane's singular influence over Mr. Lincoln and the Secretary of
War, Mr. Stanton, is one of the most inexplicable and disastrous facts
that concerned Kansas in 1861–65. It was the source of the heaviest
calamities that visited the commonwealth during that period, because it
put him in a position to gratify mischievous ambitions, to pursue personal feuds, to assume duties that belonged to others, to popularize the
corruptest political methods, and to organize semi-predatory military
expeditions. His conduct not only embarrassed the State executive and
threw State affairs into confusion, but provoked sanguinary reprisals
from Missouri. In 1864 Mr. Lincoln, remarking upon Lane's extraordinary career in Washington to Governor Carney, offered no better explanation of it than this: ' He knocks at my door every morning.
You know he is a very persistent fellow, and hard to put off. I don't
see you very often, and have to pay attention to him.'

'' Lane's intrigues in Washington against the State administration
prospered. Though recruiting was energetically pushed by the local
authorities, and three regiments were already in the field—the first and
second obtaining honorable recognition for gallant conduct at the battle
of Wilson's Creek, Missouri—yet in August, Lane, technically a civil-
ian, appeared in Kansas clothed with vague but usurping military
powers. He reached Leavenworth on the 15th, and announced in a
public address the extinction of all his personal and political enmities—
a costly sacrifice laid on the altar of his country. Two days afterwards he set out for Fort Scott, where the Kansas Brigade, comprising

the Third and Fourth Infantry together with the Fifth and Sixth Cavalry regiments, was concentrating to repel attacks upon the southeast. He began his brief military career in this region by constructing several useless fortifications, among which the most considerable affair was Fort Lincoln, on the Little Osage River, twelve miles north of Fort Scott. September 2d there was a skirmish at Dry Wood Creek, Missouri, between a reconnoitering party and a force under the Confederate General Rains, which was not wholly favorable to the Kansans, and caused a panic at Fort Scott. Leaving a body of cavalry with orders to defend the town as long as possible, and then fire it, Lane retired to his earthworks on the Little Osage. ' I am compelled to make a stand here,' he reported September 2d, after getting inside Fort Lincoln, ' or give up Kansas to disgrace and destruction. If you do not hear from me again, you can understand that I am surrounded by a superior force.' The Confederates did not follow up their advantage, but retreated leisurely towards Independence, Missouri. Encouraged by their withdrawal, Lane took the field on the 10th ' with a smart little army of about fifteen hundred men,' reached Westport, Missouri, four days later, where he reported, ' Yesterday I cleaned out Butler and Parkville with my cavalry.' September 22d he sacked and burned Osceola, Missouri—an enterprise in which large amounts of property and a score of inhabitants were sacrificed. He broke camp on the 27th, and in two days reached Kansas City. The brigade converted the Missouri border through which the march lay into a wilderness, and reached its destination heavily encumbered with plunder. ' Everything disloyal,' said Lane, ' * * * must be cleaned out ; ' and never were orders more literally or cheerfully obeyed. Even the chaplain succumbed to the rampant spirit of thievery, and plundered Confederate altars in the interest of his unfinished church at home. Among the spoils that fell to Lane personally there was a fine carriage, which he brought to Lawrence for the use of his household.''

But enough of such wholesale crimes to gratify the cravings of a bloodthirsty maniac clothed with authority from Washington. Various reasons have been given for his final taking off, but it was a clear case of simple retribution for crimes that no human tribunal was adequate to punish. Retribution came in a most simple and natural way, as it always does under the immutable law of action and reaction. This man not only despoiled the inhabitants of Missouri and Kansas, but he joined a partnership concerned with Indian and army contracts. Not content with that, he is said to have formed a partnership with President Johnson to defeat a Republican measure in the Senate, the Civil-tenure-of-office Bill, in consideration of having a relative appointed Collector of New York. As he failed, however, to defeat the bill, he failed of the reward for his treachery to his party, but he secured the ill-will and contempt of his colleagues in the Senate. This opened the way for the exposure of his Indian partnership, which, if proven, would expel him from his senatorial seat. The man who possessed the proof of the partnership had been prepared for his part in the drama by Lane when first elected senator. This man's name was G. W. Deitzler, Colonel of the First Regiment of Kansas Volunteers, who by gallant conduct at Wilson's Creek and elsewhere had earned and received the appointment of brigadier-general. Before senators had been elected in 1861 in Kansas, Deitzler was appointed Indian agent, but his appointment had not been acted upon by the Senate when Lane took his seat in that body. Lane at once opposed Deitzler's confirmation, charging some improper conduct on his part, and his name was withdrawn by the President. Deitzler became permanently disabled from service in the army by sickness, and resigned as brigadier-general. He afterwards became a member of the firm of which Lane was private partner. By this means he acquired the information that would have been fatal to Lane had it been given to the Senate. Some of Lane's former friends who became enemies because of his course on the Civil-tenure Bill, or for some other reason, started the ball by damaging correspondence to leading newspapers. Lane referred to this in his place in the Senate, promising to give the reports due attention at another time. He started at once for Kansas to shut the mouth of Deitzler, but this was impossible. All manner of appliances were used without avail. General Deitzler refers to the efforts of Lane's friends in a letter to Robinson dated San Francisco, California, November 16, 1879, as follows:

"If it will answer your purpose, I will give you the solid facts respecting the Fuller and McDonald Indian and Army contracts, and Lane's interest therein, and his disgraceful conduct when he was exposed, and finally, of his death when he discovered that I could not be moved by blandishment nor threats to give up the testimony which a kind Providence had placed in my hands, and which, if submitted to the United States Senate, would certainly have resulted in his expulsion from that body, which facts you might place in the hands of General J. L. McDowell, to be incorporated in the letters which he proposes to write on such subjects. * * * If the facts which I have proposed to furnish for General McDowell should be called in question by the champions of Lane, I would be willing to swear to them and to produce such further evidence as would convince all of their truth. * * *

"Truly your friend,
"George W. Deitzler."

On January 31, 1884, Deitzler wrote from Oro Blanco, Arizona Territory, in part as follows:

"Now the cause which led to the grim chieftain's flirtation with his little pistol would form an interesting chapter in his infamous career, and I am perhaps better posted on that subject than any other person; and while the task is very distasteful to me, I am almost persuaded to regard it as a duty, and furnish the groundwork for you to dress it up when you shall have reached that point in your recollections of those times. I will do it, upon the following conditions: First, it must not go in as coming from me, and secondly, before it goes in you must get General McDowell's endorsement so far as he is cognizant of the facts in the case. General McDowell was postmaster at Leavenworth at the time, by the grace of Lane, and he came to my house and labored with me several days to let the old man down easily, as others had done. McDowell was my friend, and at heart despised Lane as much as I did; but he really worked hard to induce me to let up and to surrender certain official and partnership documents in my possession, which documents, supplemented by testimony, would have hoisted the old sinner disgracefully from his seat in the United States Senate. General McDowell's conduct was gentlemanly and proper in every sense, and he offered me no bribe, as Fuller, Dewolf, and others did. All he said was that Lane would secure me any appointment I might desire, while his more intimate friends and strikers offered appointments, money, land, etc., and finally threats. But Lane had not been good to me, and besides, I knew him to be a very bad man, and so on general principles I felt it my duty to do what I could to deprive him of his power. When he found that ' blandishments would not fascinate me nor threats of the halter intimidate me,' his courage failed him.   You know the rest."

Before General Deitzler had time to write out his facts he was accidentally killed, and they may never be given to the public.

Senator Lane, failing to get what he wanted from General Deitzler, started for Washington, but on reaching St. Louis, and hearing of new scandals at Washington, he concluded to return to Kansas, and soon after put a pistol in his mouth and sent a ball through his brain. Thus ended the career of a man without principles or convictions of any kind, who was comparatively weak and harmless when alone, but with the support of the Administration at Washington, with unlimited patronage and irresponsible power, was an instrument of untold evil.

At the time of the Wakarusa war, in the fall of 1855, Thomas Barber was wantonly murdered by the Governor's militia, and at his funeral this language was used: "Was Thomas Barber murdered? Then are the men who killed him, and the officials by whose authority they acted, his murderers. And if the laws are to be enforced, then will the Indian agent, the Governor, and the President be convicted of and punished for murder." Was this position right in that case? If so, here is another case, which was multiplied probably by hundreds, if not by thousands. At a meeting at Leavenworth, Lane is reported in *Lippincott's Magazine* as saying: "When I was marching through there [Missouri] the other day, I happened to inquire for the best Union man in the county. They told me Hook, and I went out of my way to visit him. I asked him in the presence of my men if he was for the Union. He said, ' Yes, for the Union as it was.' I then inquired if he harbored Rebels in his house. He answered, ' No, but he had heard them at his corn-crib sometimes at night.' I turned and rode away." A voice in the crowd: "Where's Hook now?" "In ——! I left him in the hands of the executioner."

Was this murder? If so, then are those who killed the man "and those by whose authority they acted his murderers," not excepting the men who gave Lane his roving commission. It is claimed that such conduct was in retaliation for the Quantrell raid, but unfortunately the Quantrell raid was itself a retaliation for similar raids into Missouri previously made by Lane.

Of this supplementary raid this writer in *Lippincott* truly says: "The victims of his [Quantrell's] massacre have been counted, but those whom Lane and Jennison left in the hands of their executioners, who will chronicle them? They are unnumbered as the murders of Attila."

Several lessons may be learned from the conflict in Kansas, and the conduct of the War of the Rebellion in the West, that may be of service to the oppressed, to philanthropists and statesmen.

It will be seen that the remedy for oppression in a Republican government is not the overthrow of that government, but resistance of oppression within it. If a people with votes in their hands, with power to replace every official, from President to constable, cannot exercise that power for their relief from oppression, a forcible overthrow of the government would leave them at the mercy of designing men who would as readily control the new government as the one destroyed. A Republican government is what the people make it, and if not what it should be, they only are to blame. The safety of such a government depends upon the education of the voters ; and the remedy for injustice in any direction is exposure of the wrong and agitation for the right. Defensive opposition to wrong and oppression with prudence will succeed, while offensive opposition to the government itself will fail. Amos A. Lawrence once said, "The Government may have many faults, but let it be assailed from any quarter and the whole people will rally for its defense." In resisting oppression no wrong or outrage must be committed by the oppressed. They depend for

relief upon the sympathy or sense of justice of the people
not directly interested; and so long as oppression only is
resisted, this sympathy will be with the oppressed, but so
soon as the oppressed or wronged turn oppressors and wrong
innocent parties, all sympathy ceases. The Free-State party
of Kansas retained the sympathy of the North because it did
nothing that could be called wrong in itself to any man, but
acted strictly on the defensive. And when Brown's massacre occurred, Redpath, knowing the effect of wrong-doing
upon the country at large, painted the men killed in the
blackest colors imaginable, making their taking off an act of
self-defense on the part of the Free-State men. Had the
facts been generally known at that time as they are known
now, that these men killed were no more guilty of crime than
were the men killed by Hamilton at the Marais des Cygnes,
a terrible revulsion would have occurred throughout the land.
But the Slave-State men knew the facts, and the retaliation
commenced immediately and lasted all summer. As fast as
Free-State men learned the facts and became undeceived,
apologies gave way to censure. So in the war of the rebellion: had Lane and his red-legs, regular or irregular, confined their operations to hostile armies protecting non-combatants of all parties from molestation, comparative peace
would have reigned on the borders of the two States, Missouri
and Kansas, and all parties would have remained at home
except such as chose to enlist in the regular service; but the
system of brigandage adopted by Lane and his partisans
drove nearly the entire State of Missouri into rebellion, and
all able-bodied men into the rebel army, besides causing
retaliatory raids upon Kansas like that of Quantrell upon
Lawrence in 1863.

Here was a most lamentable example of the abuse of
Federal patronage. The President, that he might insure his
re-election, or for other cause, placed the army at the disposal of a man so constituted that a little power over the
lives of other men would intoxicate him, and permitted him

to devastate, plunder, and kill at pleasure, restrained by no authority, human or divine.

But the lesson will not be forgotten by the ambitious. One of these men, not receiving the punishment due for his crimes in Kansas, sought to inaugurate a servile war, the most revolting of all wars, and suffered the penalty prescribed by law. Another was overtaken in his crimes, and executed himself; while the third, although glorified for his proclamation freeing the slaves of the South, has the luster of his fame and name terribly tarnished by his conduct of the war in the West, if not in the East.

[NOTE TO SECOND EDITION.—When Governor Robinson refused commissions to the men designated by Senator Lane for positions in the volunteer regiments, Secretary Stanton telegraphed to the Governor as follows: "If you do not issue the commissions, the War Department will."

To which Governor Robinson replied: "You have the power to override the constitution and the laws, but you have not the power to make the present Governor of Kansas dishonor his State."

This prompt and emphatic reply practically settled the controversy, and there was no further interference with the Governor's prerogatives.]

CHAPTER XIX.

THE GROWTH OF KANSAS.—HER INSTITUTIONS.—TEMPER-
ANCE.—PROHIBITION.—IMPORTANCE OF THE KANSAS
CONFLICT.

THE close of the war found Kansas with a population but little in excess of the population when admitted into the Union. In 1861 her population was 107,206, while in 1865 it was 140,179, the increase being chiefly after the close of the war in 1864.

After 1865 the prosperity of Kansas was unparalleled in population, wealth, production, internal improvements, educational facilities, charitable institutions, and religion.

The national census of 1890 shows a population for Kansas of 1,423,000; while the school population between the ages of five and twenty years, 1888, was 532,010. The total population for that year, 1888, estimated by Governor Martin, was 1,651,000.

The assessed valuation of all property in Kansas in 1860 was $22,518,232; while in 1888 it was $353,248,332. The number of school-houses in the State in 1888 was 8196, valued at $8,608,202; while the receipts from taxation and other sources for school purposes were $5,333,200.

Of the higher educational institutions, Governor John A. Martin, in his message, January, 1889, thus speaks:

"The State University now comprises six departments—Science, Literature and Arts, Law, Music, Pharmacy, Art and Medicine. The Preparatory Department has been recently discontinued, as the Normal Department was a few years ago, and advanced tests for admission have been established, so that the institution may be devoted to legitimate university work, leaving secondary education with the high-schools and academies of the State. These changes have largely reduced the number of students qualified for admission, but notwithstanding this fact the number in attendance shows a steady and gratifying increase. On the 1st of January, 1885, the students enrolled numbered four hundred and nineteen; and twenty-four professors, assistants, and instructors were employed. On the 1st of January last four hundred and eighty-three students were enrolled, and the corps of professors, assistants, and instructors numbered thirty. * * *

"The State Agricultural College has at present three hundred and fifty-nine students enrolled, an increase of twenty-one since the close of the fall term of 1884. Its instructors in all departments number twenty-five, an increase of four during the past four years. The improvements in buildings and fixtures since January 1, 1885, have aggregated in value $27,000, and the increase in the value of the farm, furniture, stock, and apparatus is over $70,000.

"The State Normal School has four hundred and forty students enrolled on the 1st of January, 1885, and six hundred and sixty are now enrolled. Fourteen instructors are now employed, an increase of three in four years. The expenditures during that period include $26,200 for buildings, $4800 for museum and apparatus, and $5000 for furniture and miscellaneous improvements.

"The buildings of all these institutions are commodious, handsome, substantially built, and admirably adapted for their purposes; and it can be fairly said that the reputation of the University, the College, and the Normal School, for thorough and exact work in their several departments, has more than kept pace with their improved facilities and attendance."

The subject of a college or university was considered early in the territorial period. Amos A. Lawrence, after whom the town of Lawrence was named, gave to S. C. Pomeroy and C. Robinson as trustees two notes, of $5000 each, with accruing interest, to endow a college or university at Lawrence in 1855. This endowment, amounting in 1863 to over $14,000, secured the location of the State University at that town.

The charitable institutions are on a most liberal scale.

The insane asylums in 1888 accommodated over sixteen hundred patients; the Institution for the Blind had eighty-six pupils; for Deaf and Dumb, three hundred and twenty-one pupils; State Reform School, two hundred and eight
30

pupils; Soldiers' Orphans' Home, one hundred and nine children; Asylum for Idiotic and Imbecile Youth, one hundred children. The churches of the various denominations were early in the field, Rev. S. Y. Lum, Congregationalist, and Rev. T. Ferrill, Methodist, arriving in Kansas in 1854, and Rev. E. Nute, Unitarian, in 1855. But as population increased denominations multiplied, furnishing every town and hamlet with as many religious societies as the people were able to support.

Internal improvements, especially transportation, have kept pace with the population. As Kansas is essentially an agricultural State, adapted to wheat, corn, and stock-raising, railroads were a necessity and, although expensive, no locality would part with them for twice their cost to the people. No new State has been so favored in this respect, the track laid reaching nearly nine thousand miles. While all power is apt to be arbitrary and oppressive, the vast corporations controlling the transportation lines in Kansas have been as reasonable in their charges and mindful of the interests of their patrons, the people, as could be hoped for under the circumstances. While some roads more than pay expenses, as through lines, their branches and feeders which accommodate sparsely settled communities fall behind. As business increases it can be done at lower rates, and with an ever-watchful Legislature justice will doubtless be done to all parties interested.

While some of the most reckless, unscrupulous, and abandoned men have found their way to Kansas, as a whole no State can show a better class of citizens. Nearly all the active Free-State men were strictly temperate in their habits, many of them never using intoxicants as a beverage. The Territorial Legislature passed stringent local option laws, and they were well enforced. The State Legislatures also have always kept abreast of the temperance movement in the country, and no State could show as few drinking-places in proportion to the population as Kansas. In 1880 there were less than a dozen towns in the State that did not have local option prohibition, and even where license prevailed the restrictions in most places were enforced and drunkenness was rarely seen upon the streets. So strong was the feeling against the liquor traffic that at that date an amendment to the constitution was adopted forbidding the sale of intoxicants for all purposes except medical, mechanical, and scientific. Should the amendment and laws passed under it be strictly enforced, no intoxicants could be procured for purposes of drink by purchase or manufacture within the State. The purpose of the amendment is thus set forth by the attorney-general in his report for the years 1889–1890.

"The prohibitory law of Kansas forbids the manufacture and sale of intoxicating liquor, except for medical, scientific, and mechanical purposes. Thus far in Kansas no attempt has been made to regulate by legislation the use of intoxicating liquors. Every person who can lawfully acquire and come into possession of any intoxicating liquor has been at perfect liberty to use the same in any manner he sees fit, and for any purpose, excepting that of sale to others. The only object of forbidding the manufacture and sale of intoxicating liquors, except for medical, scientific, and mechanical uses, must necessarily have been to diminish the use of said liquors except for such purposes. The object sought was the prevention of the use of intoxicating liquors as a beverage. The method employed was the indirect one of forbidding the manufacture or sale of intoxicating liquor except for these purposes. In order to justify the prohibitory law, it must be conceded that the use of intoxicating liquors for other than the excepted purposes is dangerous to the community, and is wrong to the people of the State. The admitted evils of intemperance are occasioned by the use of intoxicating liquors as a beverage.

"If it be true that a State by prohibiting the manufacture and sale of intoxicating liquors for other than the excepted purposes intends thereby to diminish the use of intoxicating liquors except for those purposes, why may not the State, as a police regulation in aid of accomplishing what the law seeks to accomplish, regulate the use of intoxicating liquor as well as its sale?"

According to this statement, the purpose is to deprive the citizen of the power of choice, or free agency, in regard to personal habits such as drinking, and place him under the

guardianship of the Legislature. One class of citizens takes
this view of the prerogative of the Legislature and laws,
while another class believes that the citizen should be left a
free moral agent in personal matters such as eating, drinking,
and believing. What will be the final result is unknown.
Good men differ as widely upon this question as th?y did
upon the questions of policy to be adopted in making a free
State of Kansas. The advocates of the different methods,
local option and constitutional prohibition, are very positive
they are right, and each school is thoroughly armed and
equipped with opinions, arguments, and facts to establish the
views they hold.

A few samples follow. Governor John A. Martin, one of
the best and most honored citizens Kansas ever had, in his
retiring message to the Legislature, January, 1889, said:

" There is no longer any issue or controversy in Kansas concerning
the results and benefits of our temperance laws. Except in a few of the
larger cities, all hostility to them has disappeared. For six years, at
four exciting general elections, the questions involved in the abolition
of the saloon were disturbing and prominent issues, but at the election
held November last this subject was rarely mentioned by partisan speakers or newspapers. Public opinion, it is plainly apparent, has under-
gone a marked change, and there are now very few citizens of Kansas
who would be willing to return to the old order of things.

" The change of sentiment on this question is well grounded and
natural. No observing and intelligent citizen has failed to note the
beneficent results already attained. Fully nine-tenths of the drinking
and drunkenness prevalent in Kansas eight years ago have been abolished; and I affirm, with earnestness and emphasis, that this State is
to-day the most temperate, orderly, sober community of people in the
civilized world. The abolition of the saloon has not only promoted the
personal happiness and general prosperity of our citizens, but it has
enormously diminished crime; has filled thousands of homes where vice
and want and wretchedness once prevailed with peace, plenty, and con-
tentment; and has materially increased the trade and business of those
engaged in the sale of useful and wholesome articles of merchandise.
Notwithstanding the fact that the population of the State is steadily increasing, the number of criminals confined in our penitentiary is steadily
decreasing. Many of our jails are empty, and all show a marked falling
off in the number of prisoners confined. The dockets of our courts are

no longer burdened with long lists of criminal cases. In the capital district, containing a population of nearly sixty thousand, not a single criminal case was on the docket when the present term began. The business of the police courts of our larger cities has dwindled to one-fourth of its former proportions, while in cities of the second and third class the occupation of police authorities is practically gone. These suggestive and convincing facts appeal alike to the reason and the conscience of the people. They have reconciled those who doubted the success and silenced those who opposed the policy of prohibiting the liquor traffic.

"The laws now on our statute books touching this question need few if any amendments. Fairly and honestly enforced, they make it practically impossible for any person to sell intoxicating liquors as a beverage in any Kansas town or city. What is needed, therefore, is not more rigorous laws, but a systematic and sincere enforcement of the laws we have."

The incoming Governor, Hon. L. U. Humphrey, on the same occasion delivered his message, and said, on page 28 of same volume, as follows:

"The growth of public sentiment in support of constitutional prohibition in Kansas is steady, healthy, and unmistakable. In the last campaign no political party had the temerity to demand a resubmission of the question to the people, in the face of a popular verdict that has been repeated and emphasized every time the popular sense has been taken. As an issue in Kansas politics, resubmission is as dead as slavery. The saloon as a factor in politics, as a moral iniquity, has been outlawed and made a 'fugitive and a vagabond on the face of the earth,' or that part of it within the territorial limits of Kansas."

The attorney-general reports the same year as follows:

"The administration of the law is growing more popular. The masses demand it, and scheming individuals are slow to oppose the will of the masses. Where there is a popular uprising against what the people have declared to be a common nuisance, dangerous to society, morals, and health, and conducive to crime and pauperism, the end is certain. The fight for supremacy has been tedious. The lawless elements of society are always arrayed against the law. Dens of infamy and hotbeds of crime are always found clustered around the saloon. Remove the saloon, and the threshold of the penitentiary is farther away from the rising generation. The saloon has been banished from Kansas soil, and already the result can be appreciated."

Ex-Senator Ingalls claims that the saloon-keeper and drunkard have joined the Troubadours and the Mound Builders, there being neither found in Kansas.

So much for one side.   A word from the other.   A committee of the lower house of the Legislature, appointed to investigate the workings of the metropolitan police, reported to the late session, 1891, in part as follows:

" Mr. Benning, a member of the board of police commissioners of the city of Atchison, testified that tippling-shops, gambling-dens, and the keepers of houses of prostitution were regularly fined.   His testimony was confirmed by a number of respectable citizens and the records of the board.   Evidence explanatory was given by Republicans, prohibitionists, and Democrats.   They all expressed their belief that the prohibitory law could not be enforced in Atchison, and that it was in the interest of society and the treasury of the city to have the laws executed to regulate and not to suppress the sale of intoxicating liquors. A joint-keeper testified that he and others were ordered by the police to close their doors during the visit of the Legislative committee.

" Major B. P. Waggener's letter:

" ' ATCHISON, KANSAS, February 19, 1890.
" '*Hon. Lyman U. Humphrey, Governor of Kansas, Topeka, Kansas ·*

" ' MY DEAR SIR : I am in receipt of your favor of the 7th, in which you advised me that you have had a conference with Mr. C. W. Benning, who stated that the board of police commissioners of Atchison were desirous that I should formulate and present to them any charges that I might desire to make touching the official conduct of the marshal or chief of police, and to submit the same with whatever testimony I desired in support thereof, and that the same should have prompt, fair, and vigorous attention on their part.

" ' I beg to advise you that on the 16th day of December, 1889, I addressed a communication to the Hon. W. L. Johnson, secretary of the board of police commissioners, a copy of which I herewith enclose, and up to the present time the receipt thereof has not been acknowledged, or any notice whatever taken of it.   I am therefore fully satisfied that any complaint that I might make to the board of police commissioners of this city would be treated in the same manner.

" ' During the month of December, 1889, I addressed you a letter, accompanied with affidavits which clearly established the following facts, namely :

" ' I. That since the appointment of the board of police commissioners in 1889, there has been in operation in this city an average of about forty ' joints,' or places where intoxicating liquors were sold in violation of the law.

" ' 2. That during all of that time the present chief of police had systematically collected money from the proprietors of these ' joints ' as a license for the privilege of selling liquors in violation of law, and to secure immunity from arrest.

" ' 3. That a large amount of money was collected by the chief of police without any arrests having been made, and which was paid for the express purpose, by parties who were selling liquors in violation of the law, to avoid arrest.   *   *   *'

" John L. Stewart, of Fort Scott, testifies that the metropolitan police force is detrimental to any city where they exist; that prohibition was not now nor never had been enforced since the appointment of said board; that there was a scare over the appointment of your committee, but he positively knew of three saloons, running wide open, selling intoxicants over the counter, and that there were probably fifty joints in the city, and numerous poker-rooms.

" W. A. Simpson, president of the metropolitan police board of Kansas City, Kansas, presented a statement showing the aggregate collections from April 1, 1889, to April 1, 1890, to have been $32,625.47, and from April 1, 1890, to January 1, 1891, from all sources, $26,925.20. When asked to explain the large increase over former years, he testified that it was partly owing to the increase in population and more complete set of ordinances and their more general application.   There were also exhibited papers, certified to by the clerk of Kansas City as being a p.rtial copy of the records of the police judge, which showed that the revenue from tippling-shops from April 1, 1890, to February 1, 1891, inclusive, had been from $1750 to $4500 per month, and gambling from $277 to $1158 per month, aggregating in ten months $28,977. He testified that there were a few places where intoxicating liquors had been sold by the same person for the past four years, and that the only convictions that had been made were by the sheriff of the county in the district court.

" Your committee believe there is collected under the ordinance fifty dollars as a cash forfeiture in most cases, and that there is no further punishment.

" The Leavenworth board is at present composed of three aged men; the president, William Fairchild, is over eighty years old.   They were said to have been selected because of their recognized belief in prohibition and prohibitory laws.   Prior to this appointment, there have been changes made in the board a number of times.   The president's testimony, which was confirmed by the secretary of the board, was to the effect that they had tried to enforce the law and ordinance governing

the city, but had failed to suppress the ' joints,' and were not now trying to abolish houses of prostitution; that there was little gambling
known to them or the force in said city. They testified further that
there were many places where intoxicants were sold, and that they were
now permitting forfeitures of cash bonds in the interests of a depleted
treasury. They stated their belief that corrupt methods had been resorted to by certain ones of their employees, who collected money from
jointists, and did not turn the same into the public treasury. * * *

"City Attorney S. B. Isenhart, being sworn, gave it as his opinion
that the metropolitan system had not been a success in the city of Topeka, and not independent of politics, as supposed they would be. They
do not feel under obligations to take advice of the city authorities, as
they owe allegiance only to the Governor. They do not care to econ-
omize when there is no money to pay, and operate in opposition to the
city government. They are inefficient in sanitary work and the collection of licenses imposed by the ordinances, which result in a loss to the
city of $5000 per annum, not considering the increased expense of the
system to the city. I think the system is against the best interests of
the community. I have not been in any joints myself, but I am just as
well satisfied that we have an unlimited number of them, and I think
there is just as much drunkenness here now as there was under the old
system. I am satisfied that the records of the district court show an
increase of crime. At one time, about two years ago, there was an
agitation about a decrease of crime by certain parties who seemed to
want it to appear that way, and it is a fact that, in some mysterious
way, one term of court there were no criminal cases on the docket; and
I know that the same belief is entertained by other attorneys, for the
next term of court was largely taken up in trying these criminal cases;
and when it used to take, some years ago, two weeks to finish the
criminal docket, it now takes one month to a month and a half to dispose of the docket each term of court.

"E. T. Allen, who was chairman of the police commission of
Wichita from July 24, 1889, until January 6, 1891, having been duly
sworn, said that the only time he had ever known the saloons to be
closed in that city was when he had been given authority of the board,
and had signed an order and given it to the marshal. He thought that
condition continued about two weeks, when the board was changed, by
the removal of the two men who had voted to close them. * * *

"The saloons are now open, and I believe with a cognizance of the
officials of the city. In fact, they are running every day, and money
put up for bonds of fifty dollars each, which are forfeited, and the jointists submitted to no other punishment.

"Your committee requested one of their own members (Mr. Kenton)
to go to Wichita and investigate the condition of the police government,

who visited numerous saloons having regular bars in the rear of the buildings, or upstairs, as a general rule; that in some of them there were a great number of boys from sixteen to twenty years of age. He visited one gambling-house that contained various gambling devices and a bar from which drinks were served, and which was thronged with men engaged in gambling.

"The mayor exhibited a report that showed that fines had been collected from some time in the autumn to the present, aggregating over $10,000.

"Your committee have heard no testimony that induces them to believe that the prohibitory law has been enforced in any city of the State through the agency of the metropolitan police or any other machinery of the law. In all of the six cities, fines, or forfeited recognizances called fines, are imposed. There is usually no further punishment inflicted. The statute, which imposes a fine of one hundred dollars and imprisonment for the offense of selling intoxicating liquors, is abrogated by ordinances that impose fifty or a hundred dollars only, without imprisonment, by recognizance being forfeited; the offense itself is thereby compromised in a manner which, if done by any other official action, would be a barbarous crime. The more vigorous the effort made to enforce prohibition in the cities, the more irresponsible and debased are the men who are engaged in the traffic, the more deceptive their devices and secluded their places of business.

"The authorities of Topeka have made a more determined effort to enforce prohibitory laws than any city of its class, as has been already shown. They are expending $15,000 per annum of the tax-payers' money in excess of all the revenue of the police department of the city, and yet the joints, drunkenness, and crime have not been banished. In the other five cities the system has been merely self-sustaining; but it is clearly made so through the encouragement it gives to crimes and misdemeanors; through fines imposed, which are given the semi-recognition of a license, and when the fines are not collected for the public treasury the temptation to bribe the police is increased, and the illegitimate joint remains through that influence.

"The system is so absolutely divorced from all responsibilities to the people that the officers exercise an independence in the interest of crime by not informing themselves of the character of the city ordinances, and when they do, neglect or refuse to enforce them. Your committee conclude that it is a mistake to establish dual governments in small cities, but as the Senate has refused to repeal the law authorizing the appointment of commissioners, we can only condemn the general administration of the metropolitan police law of the State, and petition the Governor. Your committee therefore recommends that the governor be memorialized, in the exercise of the discretion placed in him which is

474 THE KANSAS CONFLICT.

by the statutes, to withdraw the application of the metropolitan police law from the cities of Kansas and leave those cities to the enforcement of their own police regulations.

"All of which is respectfully submitted.

"LEVI DUMBAULD,
"S. F. NEELEY,
"B. F. FORTNEY,
"W. M. KENTON,
"E. D. YORK."

This legislative committee was composed of members of all political parties, and the report was unanimous.

The editor of the Lawrence *Record*, an ardent prohibitionist, has an editorial, July 7, 1891, as follows:

"PUT UP OR SHUT UP.

"Let us understand this matter fully. If the Republican party of Kansas is unwilling to uphold prohibition longer, let the statement be honestly made to that effect. This farce is played out. When Leavenworth alone sustains one hundred and seventy joints, when Atchison is full of liquor-houses, while Wichita has practically never closed its saloons, it is time for Prohibition (?) Kansas to take down the sign. The State is a by-word and a hissing everywhere. Countless thousands paid out yearly to Missouri and other States for liquor. If we are to have unrestrained sale in the large cities, why not in the small ones? If we must have beer and whiskey, why not make it at home, and save the money to the State, thus creating a home market also for the grains to be brewed and distilled?

"This is the devil's own logic. But it will be the rallying cry of the thousands of Republicans in the next election, unless some change is made in the present situation. We said some time ago that the purpose was rapidly forming to abandon prohibition by the Republican leaders. Every day makes more apparent the truthfulness of our information. We repeat the statement of that article, that prohibition was never in greater danger than now. There is not a Republican politician in the State who would not gladly trade all his stock in prohibition for an American-made tin pan. Protection to Eastern manufactories granted galore unasked, but protection to the home from the vile saloon is to be determined by its effects upon voters. And the purpose is resolved upon by these pirates who have scuttled the fair ship already, to abandon her to drift as a derelict over the political sea.

"It is time to know where we are and what we intend to do. It is time for prohibition Republicans to decide whether they endorse the damnable policy of this State administration in maintaining under the eyes of its special officials cities full of saloons. It has come to be the case that municipalities which desire to obtain money from the sale of liquors ask for the metropolitan police system, sure of their revenue if they obtain it.

" Away with the lying story that Kansas is a prohibition State! Let us tell the truth! The only party which advocated it is about to abandon it, and the organs of the party are silent witnesses of the crime. Unless public opinion is soon awake, the deed of treason will be done, and the best opportunities for a generation to clear Kansas from the curse of the saloon will be lost.

" There is more liquor sold and drunk to-day in Kansas than at any time since the passage of the amendment! Deny it, whoever dare!"

It may be proper to state that the Republican party was the only party that endorsed prohibition in its platform, and although having at the previous election over 80,000 plurality, at the last election it was put in the minority of 40,000, while the prohibition attorney-general who was so sanguine in his report in 1888 was defeated by a Democrat and People's-party man by about 40,000 votes. Here is a statement giving both sides of prohibition, and the reader can take his choice.

But whatever may be the present or future of Kansas, she has done a work for the cause of freedom that is her crowning glory. She had an opportunity denied every other Territory and State, and well did she improve it. The results of the territorial conflict are the inheritance of the State and the Union, and the handful of pioneers who turned back the dark waves of tyranny from Kansas and sent back slavery reeling in despair "to die amid its worshippers," can well afford to rest from their labors, trusting to the present generation to see that no harm shall come to the heritage purchased by their labor and sufferings.

The importance of these labors were briefly given in an address at the Quarter Centennial of Kansas, by the writer, which is here quoted as a fitting close to the foregoing reminiscences:

" *Mr. President and Fellow-Citizens:*

"We have assembled to celebrate the twenty-fifth birthday of the State of Kansas. On such an occasion, a review of her wonderful growth and achievements is eminently proper, and in these no State can excel our own; but I have been notified that I am expected to speak of Kansas in her antenatal days, and relate something of her struggles in embryo. While the territorial period was full of incident and worthy achievement, the field has been so often plowed and cross-plowed, harrowed and raked, as with a fine-tooth comb, for items to add to the fame or infamy of the contestants, that nothing fresh or interesting remains to be said appropriate to the occasion. Some of the results, however, of the territorial struggle have been inherited by the State, and constitute its chief glory. Of these I will briefly speak. To begin at the beginning, I will say that the difficulty which culminated in Kansas had its origin in the Garden of Eden. According to report, the first law ever given to the race was a prohibitory law, with death as the penalty for disobedience. This law, of course, was violated by the occupants of the Garden, and should the threatened penalty be inflicted, the Law-Giver would have no subjects, as the violators included the whole human family. Accordingly, the penalty was modified to suit the emergency—a precedent still followed by political parties when the enforcement of their laws will leave their party without a quorum in the Legislature, or in a minority at the polls. The amended penalty reads as follows : ' In the sweat of thy face shalt thou eat thy bread till thou return unto the ground.' The penalty attached not only to the law-breaker, but to all his posterity, and from that day to this the chief concern of mankind has been to escape this penalty. Every person seems desirous of making some one else do the sweating while he eats his bread. Every device has been resorted to. Sometimes a man escapes the penalty by withholding the earnings of his employees, in whole or in part; but a favorite method has been to capture, steal, or purchase a man, and to compel him to do the sweating both for himself and his master. This practice has been handed down from generation to generation, till the date of the opening of Kansas to settlement, and it was proposed to introduce it on Kansas soil. Hence the conflict. Many people had come to look upon this business not only as avoiding the penalty for eating the prohibited fruit, but as a great wrong to such as were compelled to suffer the double infliction. Some thought it was the ' sum of all villainies,' and others ' trembled when they remembered that God was just.' Many years of agitation had preceded the settlement of Kansas, both among the people and in Congress. Various compromises and provisos had been agreed to, but all such were as ropes of sand before the demands of the slave power. One of these barriers to the extension of slavery went down in the enactment of the

Kansas-Nebraska bill.   The opponents to the extension of slavery were beaten—hopelessly beaten—in Congress; the agitators of the North and East were powerless, and could anything be done to stay the progress of this institution?   A writer in the Charleston (S. C.) *Mercury* states the case as follows:

" ' First, by consent of parties the present contest in Kansas is made the turning-point in the destinies of slavery and abolitionism.   If the South triumphs, abolitionism will be defeated and shorn of its power for all time.   If she is defeated, abolitionism will grow more insolent and aggressive, until the utter ruin of the South is consummated.   Second, if the South secures Kansas, she will extend slavery into all territory south of the fortieth parallel of north latitude to the Rio Grande, and this, of course, will secure for her pent-up institution of slavery an ample outlet and restore her power in Congress.   If the North secure Kansas, the power of the South in Congress will gradually be diminished; the States of Missouri, Kentucky, Tennessee, Arkansas, and Texas, together with the adjacent Territories, will gradually become abolitionized, and the slave population, confined to the States east of the Mississippi, will become valueless.   All depends upon the action of the present moment.'

" This is an exact statement of the situation as it then appeared, and the prediction only failed of realization in consequence of the suicide of slavery by the Rebellion, which could not then be known.   Here, then, was the stake—not the extension of slavery to Kansas merely, but its extension indefinitely, or its final extinction.   Who could be found to enter the lists?   Slavery had all the advantages.   On its side were billions of dollars and the domestic relations of eight million people involved.   Congress was in favor of slavery extension, or it would not have removed the barriers from the west line of the State of Missouri.   The Judiciary was on the side of slavery extension, or it would never have made the Dred Scott decision.   The Executive Department of the Government favored slavery extension, or it could not have been elected, and would not have had Jefferson Davis for Secretary of War. Besides, Kansas had a slave State extending across its entire eastern border, whose inhabitants were alive to the situation, bold, reckless, and defiant, while the opponents of slavery were to be found chiefly at a distance of hundreds of miles from the field of conflict.   Congressmen from the North had been beaten and cowed; the old Anti-Slavery Society had no faith in success, or in the value of victory if achieved, and the Liberty and Free-soil parties had no machinery that could be useful in such an encounter.   Who, under these disadvantages, would enter the contest for this prize with the slave power of the nation that had never known defeat?   Individuals and individual effort could do something, as was shown in the person of him who will speak this evening for the pioneers of Kansas. But the whole North must be aroused and organization effected, to stimulate and aid emigration. A theretofore comparatively obscure man, a member of a State Legislature, was seized with inspiration, and he stepped forth in the winter of 1854, when it became evident that the Kansas-Nebraska bill would become a law, and organized emigration and preached the crusade till victory was secured. So obnoxious did this man become to the slave power that a price was set upon his head, dead or alive, even before the lands of Kansas were open to settlement. But emigration, while indispensable, was not all that was requisite. A State had to be organized, and this work must be done on the soil of Kansas. This was the work in hand, and the election of a Territorial Legislature was the first step to be taken. The party that should secure this would secure a great, if not decisive, victory. As is well known, this victory perched upon the banners of the South. Was there, then, hope left for a free State? All the machinery for making a State was now in possession of the enemy. This was in 1855, and there would be no new Legislature elected before 1857. In the meantime ' returning boards ' could be provided and a constitution inaugurated, which might settle the question in issue irrevocably. Could any power or any agency wrest victory from such a defeat, and under such circumstances? Every statesman, every politician, every student of history, and every person of ordinary information of affairs of government, would have answered, and did answer, this question in the negative, but the Free-State party of Kansas answered it in the affirmative, and made good their answer, as history has recorded. How this victory was achieved—by what measures or policy—belongs to the history of the territorial period, and not the State; but as its results must have been inherited by the State, some of them may properly be named here.

" First. The victory of the Free-State party made Kansas a free instead of a slave State.

" Second. According to the Charleston *Mercury*, it put an end to the extension of slavery in every direction, and secured freedom to all other Territories.

" Third. It made the Republican party of the nation. The ' Cyclopedia of Political Science ' says truly: ' The predominance of a moral question in politics, always a portentous phenomenon under a constitutional government, was made unmistakable by the Kansas struggle, and its first perceptible result was the disappearance, in effect, of all the old forms of opposition to the Democratic party, and the first national convention of the new Republican party, June 17, 1856.'

" Eli Thayer says that ' the Kansas fight made the Republican party.' Also he adds that it was ' a necessary training of the Northern States for subduing the Rebellion.'

"Fourth. This being conceded, Kansas made the election of Abraham Lincoln possible.

"Fifth. Securing a free State in Kansas and the election of Lincoln brought on the Rebellion, which—

"Sixth. Was the suicide and the end of slavery, in this nation and prospectively in all nations.

"All these results the State of Kansas inherits from the territorial struggle, as can be abundantly shown. I am aware that an attempt has been made to rob Kansas of some of these laurels, but the attempt will fail. One writer would make it appear that the raid at Harper's Ferry, to which he was a party, destroyed slavery, and not the work in Kansas. What are the facts? Were I to quote all the declarations of Southern politicians during the pending of the elections of 1856 and 1860, saying that should the Republican candidate for President be elected they would go out of the Union, my time and your patience would be exhausted. I will therefore refer to but two or three statements: Jefferson Davis, in his message to the Confederate Congress, does not mention Harper's Ferry, but gave this as a reason for withdrawing from the Union:

"'A great party was organized for the purpose of obtaining the administration of the Government, with the avowed object of using its power for the total exclusion of the slave States from all participation in the benefits of the public domain acquired by all the States in common, whether by conquest or purchase, surrounding them entirely by States in which slavery should be prohibited, thus rendering the property in slaves so insecure as to be comparatively worthless, and thereby annihilating, in effect, property worth thousands of millions of dollars. This party, thus organized, succeeded in the month of November last in the election of its candidate for the President of the United States.'

"I will next quote from a letter attributed to Judah P. Benjamin, senator from Louisiana, to the British Consul in New York, dated August 11, 1860, as follows:

"'The doctrines maintained by the great leaders of the Republican party are so unsuited to the whole South that the election of their candidate (which is almost certain) amounts to a total destruction of all plantation interests, which the South, as sure as there is a God in heaven, will not submit to. Sooner than yield to the arbitrary dictates of traitorous allies and false friends who have proven recreant to the solemn obligations of the old Constitution, we will either secede from the Union and form a separate government, or upon certain conditions at once return to the allegiance of Great Britain, our mother country.'

"Here again is no allusion to Harper's Ferry, but he proposes to secede because of the success of the Republican party, which was 'made' by the Kansas struggle.

"The 'Political Cyclopedia' says that 'Kansas, it might be said, cleared the stage for the last act of the drama, the Rebellion ; ' that the Kansas struggle was the ' prelude to the War of the Rebellion.' One more question remains to be considered : If the success of the Republican party, made by the Kansas struggle, was the immediate cause of secession, war, and consequent emancipation, did the Harper's Ferry raid contribute to that success? This question must be answered most decidedly in the negative. This same Cyclopedia says that 'the North almost unianmously condemned the whole insurrection,' while it is well known that from every stump during the Lincoln campaign it was most vehemently denounced. The Republican party, that there might be no mistaking its position, adopted this resolution in its national platform :

" ' *Resolved*, That the maintenance inviolate of the rights of the States, and especially the right of each State to order and control its own domestic institutions according to its judgment exclusively, is essential to the balance of power on which the perfection and endurance of our political fabric depends, and we denounce the lawless invasion by armed force of the soil of any State or Territory, no matter under what pretext, as among the gravest crimes.'

" After the election, President Lincoln, in his inaugural address, quoted this resolution, and added : ' I now reiterate these sentiments, and, in doing so, I only press upon the public attention the most conclusive evidence of which the case is susceptible, that the prosperity, peace, and security of no section are to be in anywise endangered by the new incoming Administration.'

" Can it be possible that the effect of such a raid as that at Harper's Ferry, almost ' unanimously denounced by the whole North,' especially denounced in the platform of the party, and the denunciations reiterated by its candidate, could be to aid in the election of Mr. Lincoln? To ask such a question is to answer it. Not only did the raid not help the Republicans, but as soon as the facts were developed it did not frighten the South. The pro-slavery members of the Senate Investigating Committee, Mason, Davis, Fitch, say that not a single slave could be induced to voluntarily join the raiders, and when arms were put in their hands they refused to use them, and escaped from their captors as soon as they could do so with safety.

" The Republican members of this committee, Collamer and Doolittle, said that ' the lessons which it teaches furnish many considerations of security against its repetition. The fatal termination of the enterprise in the death and execution of so large a part of the number engaged ; the dispersion of the small remainder as fugitives in the land ; the entire disinclination of the slaves to insurrection, or to receive aid for that purpose, which was there exhibited ; the very limited number and peculiar character of the conspirators—all combine to furnish assurance against the most distant probability of its repetition.' It is evident, from all the facts in the case, that this raid not only did not help, but hindered the Republican cause, and that it did not have a feather's weight in causing the Rebellion or the destruction of slavery in consequence of it.

"Let us reverse the picture for a moment. Suppose, instead of a free State, a slave State had been secured in Kansas, with the power to extend the institution at will, into all the Territories. Suppose, as a consequence, the Kansas struggle had not 'made' a victorious Republican party in 1860, but had secured the election of Breckenridge, the Southern candidate for President. Would the South have then seceded, and would slavery have been abolished? And would either event have transpired in consequence of the Harper's Ferry raid, or five hundred such raids? Cook had been at Harper's Ferry some twelve months, and Brown and his followers four or five months, and yet not a slave had been enlisted for the crusade by either. * How much effect would such a raid have to produce secession or the abolition of slavery, with Kansas and the Federal Government in the secure possession of the South?

"No, no; the flood-tide of slavery extension received its first permanent check in Kansas, and it was the refluent wave from her borders that carried Abraham Lincoln into the White House, drove the South into rebellion, and buried slavery so deep that for it there can be no resurrection. Not only is the State of Kansas thus indebted to the Territory, but the late slave States that contended so earnestly to extend their peculiar institution are doubly indebted. These States have not only been redeemed from a blighting curse, but have been prospered in every way as never before in their history. So general and widespread is their prosperity, that so far as known not a citizen can be found in the entire South who would re-establish slavery if he could. But the blessings resulting from the territorial struggle do not stop here, for the nation itself has been born again, with that birth which brings with it 'peace on earth, and good-will to men.' The old contentions, bitterness, and irrepressible conflict between the North and South have given place to mutual respect, love, and good-will. The United States now constitute a Union in reality as well as in name, with like institutions, like aspirations, and a common destiny. Our Union, thus cemented, has become the envy of all nations, and a terror to all enemies. The freest, happiest, and most prosperous people on the globe, we have become a place of refuge for the oppressed of all nations. Such being the result of the territorial conflict, well may the contestants embrace each other on the twenty-fifth birthday of this wonderful State, and henceforth dwell together in unity, under a Government that knows no North, no South, no East, no West, but that is 'one and inseparable, now and forever.' "

31

APPENDIX.

CORRESPONDENCE ABOUT JOHN BROWN.

SANBORN TO LAWRENCE.

CONCORD, MASSACHUSETTS, January 26, 1885.

Amos A. Lawrence, Esq., Brookline:

MY DEAR SIR: In your attack on John Brown at the Historical Society, May 8, 1884, you contrasted him very unfavorably with Charles Robinson, who, you said, "was in every respect worthy of the confidence reposed in him by the settlers (of Kansas), and by the Emigrant Society." If you still think so highly of him, you will doubtless take pleasure in submitting to the Historical Society the following letter from Robinson to Judge Hanway, of Lane, Kansas, which he wrote about six years ago, and before he found it expedient to disown all his former opinions concerning Brown. I copy from a copy sent me by a member of the Kansas Historical Society, on whose files the original letter of Robinson now stands:

(Copy.)

"LAWRENCE, February 5, 1878.

"Hon. James Hanway:

"DEAR SIR: Your favor of 30th ult. is received. I am also in receipt of a letter on the same subject from Mr. Adams. I never had much doubt that Captain Brown was the author of the blow at Potawatomie, for the reason that he was the only man who comprehended the situation and saw the absolute necessity of some such blow, and had the nerve to strike it. I will improve my first leisure to put on paper my views of the situation at that time, and forward them to Mr. Adams.

"Very truly,

(Signed) "C. ROBINSON."

The Mr. Adams here mentioned is F. G. Adams, the secretary of the State Historical Society, whom you perhaps know, as I do. On the 20th of August, 1878, Mr. Adams (who had doubtless heard from Charles Robinson in the six months since the date of his letter above cited) wrote to me as follows:

"Governor Robinson has expressed the opinion that it will be some time proven that Captain Brown was present at the affair (of Potawa tomie). He thinks the act was a justifiable and necessary one: that the act did in fact have the effect to check the career of wholesale murder, which the pro-slavery men had entered upon and intended to kill or to drive from Kansas every out-spoken Free-State man in the Territory." The original letter of Mr. Adams lies before me as I write. What he thus quotes as Robinson's opinion of Brown's act is the same to which Robinson gave utterance at Osawatomie in the summer of 1877, in a public speech, which has been reported to me by two Kansas gentlemen who heard it. It is also the same that Robinson expressed in a public speech at Lawrence in the winter of 1859–60, a printed report of which is also on file in the Kansas Historical rooms, Topeka. I printed in the *Transcript* of December 4, 1884 (which I sent you), Robinson's letter of September 14, 1856, commending Brown in the highest terms. These letters and speeches show that from 1856 to 1878 Charles Robinson took the same view of Brown's action on the Potawatomie that I now take, and by no means your views.

May I rely on your candor to state this to the Historical Society?

Yours truly,
F. B. SANBORN.

ROBINSON TO LAWRENCE.

LAWRENCE, February 6, 1885.
Hon. A. A. Lawrence:

DEAR SIR: Your favor enclosing a letter from F. B. Sanborn is received.

If Mr. Sanborn had read my letters published in the Boston *Transcript* of June 12 and August 15, 1884, he would have been saved the trouble of writing his letter of the 26th ult. In the *Transcript* of June 12 I say:

"Until the testimony of Mr. Townsley appeared, many Free-State men apologized for the massacre on the ground that the men killed were worthy of death for their crimes. With these apologies I sympathized, supposing what Redpath and others said was true. This was the testimony on which the case chiefly rested till Townsley's was given. Had Redpath's statements proved true as to the character and conduct of the men killed, I should have continued to apologize for the men who committed the deed, although it never could be justified. But I have now become satisfied that Redpath's account is all fiction, except the statement that the men were killed. I believe these men had committed no crime, and had threatened to commit none. Townsley's statement that Brown wanted him to go up the creek five or six miles and point out the cabins of all the pro-slavery men that they might make a clean sweep as they came down, shows conclusively that he was ready to kill any pro-slavery man, guilty or not guilty, and hence shows that his purpose was to inaugurate war, and not to make a free State."

Also in that paper of August 15 I wrote as follows:

"For Mr. Sanborn's information, I will say that I entertain no malice towards his hero, have apologized for him probably a thousand times, and never lifted a finger to oppose any honors to his memory by the State or nation. While I believed the men butchered were bad men, belligerents as described by Redpath and others, I excused the killing as best I could, and contemplated writing out a statement to be filed with our Historical Society, setting forth the outrages committed by these and similar men. But before I found the time to write this statement I became satisfied from new and conclusive evidence that these men were innocent of all crime or threatened crime, and that their taking off was not intended for the protection of Free-State men from their outrages and such as theirs, but was intended by Brown as an act of offensive war. When I became satisfied on these points, I abandoned the work and ceased apologies for Brown."

In your remarks before the Historical Society you say John Brown " deceived everybody," and also that when the truth with all the proofs should be published, as they soon would be, " there can be no such statements made as have deceived nearly a whole generation."

It is a sufficient answer to Sanborn that I with others was deceived until after the time referred to by him. When this massacre occurred I had been absent from the Territory and a prisoner some two weeks, and knew nothing whatever of the situation in the Potawatomie region. I was told that the pro-slavery men there had inaugurated a war of extermination of the Free-State settlers, and that this massacre had put a stop to it. This was uncontradicted, and I had every reason to suppose there was some foundation in fact for such statements as were made.

The quotation from Mr. Adams by Sanborn in his letter showed conclusively that when I wrote to Mr. Adams I had not been undeceived. He reports me as thinking " that the act (at Potawatomie) did in fact have the effect to check the career of wholesale murder which the pro-slavery men had entered upon, intending to kill or drive from Kansas every out-spoken Free-State man in the Territory."

In the Hanway letter I say, " I will improve my first leisure to put on paper my views of the situation at the time." What were my views of the situation? Adams's letter says that I thought a " career of wholesale murder had been entered upon, intending to kill or drive from Kansas every out-spoken man in the Territory."

Had that view proved correct, my apologies for Brown would have continued, but unfortunately it has no foundation in fact, and the conclusion is inevitable that John Brown by that act intended to " involve the sections in war " and not to protect Free-State men.

My view now is, after investigation, that not a man had been killed south of Douglas County up to that date; that the men killed by Brown had committed no crime, and threatened to commit none; and that Brown was ready to kill any pro-slavery man he could find simply because he was pro-slavery. It is unnecessary to say that this change of view of the situation has completely changed my view of Brown and the Potawatomie " affair."

Until after the date of the Hanway letter I had made no investigation into the matter, and apologized for the massacre as best I could. But as soon as an honest and impartial investigation was made the case was wholly changed. Instead of these men being criminals they had not even threatened to commit a crime, and as there was no war of extermination contemplated by them, no such war had been stopped by their massacre. These are the facts, as I have no doubt, and facts brought out by non-partisan and disinterested investigators, and I am obliged, if honest, to accept them, whatever may have been my previous opinion. The speech he refers to as made at Osawatomie was made at Paola the evening after the meeting at Osawatomie, and was simply an apology based upon a state of facts which I supposed existed, but which now I am satisfied did not. I made such apologies all through the Fremont campaign in answer to Democratic criticism, and made them honestly, as honestly as I now retract them. The letter of the 14th of September, 1856, if genuine, was called out by Brown's action in defending Osawatomie, as Sanborn has already stated, and could have had no reference to the Potawatomie massacre, as up to that time everybody denied Brown's connection with it. By the way, if Sanborn thinks it a disgrace to admit a mistake on discovery of new facts, what does he think of himself? Until long after Brown's death, Sanborn and all Brown's family and partisans denied that he was connected with or responsible for the Potawatomie massacre. Sanborn in his magazine article says, " that he was actually present, he (Brown) always denied to me, and I shall believe him until some eye-witness proves the contrary." R. J. Hinton, in the Boston *Traveller*, December 3, 1859, says: " Brown told me he was not a participator in the Potawatomie homicide. John Brown was incapable of uttering a falsehood."

John Brown's brother, J. R. Brown, in the Cleveland *Plaindealer* of November 22, 1859, says: " My brother, at the time William Doyle and others were killed, was not present, did not consent to the act, nor had any knowledge of it, and was eighteen miles distant at the time of the occurrence. I have this account from my brother and his two sons; also from a sister and brother-in-law, now living in Kansas, who had personal knowledge of this transaction."

John Brown, while in prison, awaiting execution, told M. B. Lowry that " G. W. Brown lies when he represents me as connected with those murders."

John Brown, while in prison, told the Valandingham party that called upon him : " I killed no man (in Kansas) except in fair fight. I fought at Black Jack Point and Osawatomie, and if I killed anybody it was at these places."

Thomas Drew, in his compilation of 1860, says : " His (Brown's) participation in the affair is denied, not only by himself, but by many witnesses who lived in the Territory at that time and had the best means of knowing who were the real perpetrators of the Potawatomie murders."

Redpath, in his " Life of John Brown," 1860, says, page 119 : " John Brown did not know that these men were killed until the following day ; for, with one of his sons, he was twenty-five miles distant at the time. He was at Middle Creek. This fact can be proved by living witnesses."

Also in his letter to the New York *Tribune*, November 5, 1859, he says : " I assert solemnly and with a knowledge of the fact, that old John Brown was more than sixteen miles distant when Doyle and his fellow-ruffians were justly killed. A man who participated in the killing of these murderers confessed the particulars of the transaction to me."

A correspondent in the New York *Tribune* of March 20, 1860, reports as follows : " John Brown, Jr., in a lecture at Gustavus, Trumbull County, Ohio, March 1, 1860, denied that his father was present at the killing of the Doyles, etc., or had any knowledge of it until the deed was done. He said that his father went down to the grave with the odium of the act because, as the old man said, for him to deny it publicly would seem to cast an imputation on the men who did kill the ruffians."

But enough ; I might add indefinitely statements of similar purport from Brown and his relatives and friends. That they all denied in the most direct and positive terms his participation in and responsibility for that massacre no person will question, yet Mr. Townsley, an eye-witness, whose testimony is unimpeached and unimpeachable, says : "After my team was fed and the party had taken supper, John Brown told me for the first time what he proposed to do. He said he wanted me to pilot the company up the forks of the creek, some five or six miles above, into the neighborhood where I lived, and show them where all the pro-slavery men resided ; that he proposed to sweep the creek as he came down of all the pro-slavery men living on it. I positively refused to do it. * * * The old man Doyle and two sons were called out and marched some distance from the house towards Dutch Henry's in the road, where a halt was made. Old John Brown drew his revolver and shot the old man Doyle in the forehead, and Brown's two youngest sons immediately fell upon the younger Doyles with their short, two-edged swords." After this testimony of Townsley's was published, and after consultation with John Brown, Jr., and Owen Brown, Mr. Sanborn wrote to John Hutchings, of Lawrence, as follows:

" PUT-IN-BAY, OHIO, August 29, 1882.
" *John Hutchings, Esq.:*
" I have talked with the Browns about Townsley's statement. In the main it is true.

" F. B. SANBORN."

If history furnishes a parallel to the cold-blooded, unblushing, persistent, and unscrupulous lying of John Brown, his family, and friends, I have not discovered it; yet it is of such men some people make heroes.

And why not? Sanborn himself belongs to the same school. In a letter to the Boston *Transcript* recently, he said Colonel Sam Walker told him that " shortly before the Potawatomie affair he was taken aside by Governor Robinson and General Lane, and it was proposed to him to go down in the Potawatomie country and secretly kill the border ruffians there."

Colonel Walker has written me that he " did not say so." Neither does he say that I ever had any such conversation with him. Really, if a person who can make a hero of a man who went to the gallows with a lie upon his lips, and glorify a family who persisted in lying for nearly thirty years, and who can himself manufacture lies to order out of whole cloth on occasion—if such a man is shocked at a person who changes his views only when a new discovery of facts warrants the change, he must be peculiarly sensitive. It is to be hoped that but few such characters are to be found outside of the Concord School of Philosophy.

It is announced that Mr. Sanborn is about to publish a book on John Brown, and he will doubtless publish these letters. Can we rely on his candor to publish this statement of mine with them? We shall see.

Very truly,
C. ROBINSON.